THE ENCYCLOPEDIA OF

CHILD ABUSE

Second Edition

THE ENCYCLOPEDIA OF

CHILD ABUSE

Second Edition

Robin E. Clark, Ph.D.
and
Judith Freeman Clark
with
Christine Adamec
Introduction by
Richard J. Gelles, Ph.D.

Facts On File, Inc.

The Encyclopedia of Child Abuse, Second Edition

Copyright © 2001, 1989 by Robin E. Clark and Judith Freeman Clark

Facts On File, Inc.
11 Penn Plaza
New York NY 10001

Library of Congress Cataloging-in-Publication Data
Clark, Robin E.
The encyclopedia of child abuse / Robin E. Clark and Judith Freeman Clark with Christine Adamec ;
introduction by Richard J. Gelles.—2nd ed.
p. cm.
Includes bibliographical references and index.
ISBN 0-8160-4060-5 (hardcover : alk. paper)
1. Child abuse—United States—Dictionaries. 2. Child abuse—Dictionaries. I. Clark, Judith Freeman. II.
Adamec, Christine A., 1949– III. Title.
HV6626.5.C57 2000
362.76'0973'03—dc21   00-035384

Facts On File books are available at special discounts when purchased in bulk quantities for businesses, associations, institutions or sales promotions. Please call our Special Sales Department in New York at (212) 967-8800 or (800) 322-8755.

You can find Facts On File on the World Wide Web at http://www.factsonfile.com

Text and cover design by Cathy Rincon

Printed in the United States of America

MP Hermitage 10 9 8 7 6 5 4 3 2 1

This book is printed on acid-free paper.

11/01
11/16

CONTENTS

PREFACE

Child abuse and neglect have many different dimensions. Though we often think of child abuse only in terms of physical violence, various forms of psychological threats, coercion, sexual exploitation and even folk medicine practices can also produce serious and long-lasting damage. The range of actions classified as child abuse or neglect is constantly changing as a result of social and economic conditions, political ideology, advances in medicine, improvements in communication and melding of cultures. Absence of a single, explicit and universally accepted definition of abuse makes studies of it difficult. Yet, child abuse and neglect are not simply cultural inventions. As international concern for the plight of children grows, those concerned with preventing abuse and neglect are beginning to find more and more common ground for collaboration.

The Encyclopedia of Child Abuse reflects the struggle to define, prevent and treat this problem. Entries reflect the range of disciplines (including law, medicine, psychology, sociology, economics, history, education and others) that contribute to our understanding of child maltreatment as well as the scope of debate within and among disciplines. Where there is disagreement on a particular point we have tried to identify the different arguments. Obviously, it is not possible to present an exhaustive discussion of each of the hundreds of topics included in this book. For those who wish to explore a topic in depth we make suggestions for further reading at the end of selected entries. An extensive bibliography is also included at the back of the book.

Space and time considerations forced us to be selective in choosing the topics we discussed. In attempting to present an overall view of child abuse and neglect we chose topics that we felt would give the reader a grasp of the central issues.

Information presented in this book comes from the most up-to-date sources available at the time of writing. We have attempted to present material in clear language that does not require specialized knowledge of medicine, law or other disciplines. Our use of "simple" language should not be construed as simplistic. We believe professionals and general readers alike will find the book contains a wealth of useful information.

Though we have attempted to present child abuse and neglect from an international perspective, readers will notice that most statistical information comes from the United States. This is a reflection of the availability of such information rather than a statement of relative importance.

In selecting entries, we chose not to include biographies of individuals who have contributed to the understanding and/or prevention of child abuse and neglect. The list of these individuals is long and new names are constantly being added. Such a listing, though important, is beyond the scope of this book. Biographical information is included only when it is relevant for the understanding of a particular case, concept or contribution.

Finally, we hope users of this book will be stimulated to learn more about child abuse and neglect. Only through a better understanding of the complex and often misunderstood phenomenon of child abuse can we hope to prevent it.

Robin E. Clark and Judith Freeman Clark

ACKNOWLEDGMENTS

Over the months that this book was researched and written, we contacted dozens of organizations to ask for information about child abuse and neglect. In particular, staff at the Clearinghouse on Child Abuse and Neglect Information; the House of Representatives Subcommittee on Children, Youth and Families; staff of the American Association for Protecting Children; and staff of the Incest Survivors Resource Network deserve special acknowledgment. Countless individuals at other public- and private-sector agencies answered our mail and telephone inquiries and sent us statistics and facts on hundreds of topics. Although it is impossible to mention each person by name, a sincere thank-you goes to these people for their cooperation and assistance.

The reference departments of libraries at Boston College School of Social Work, Brandeis University, Smith College, the University of Massachusetts at Amherst, as well as the Forbes Library, Northampton, Massachusetts, provided us with easy access to information. The graciousness and competence of staff at these libraries cannot be overemphasized; without the help of experts in the Government Documents Room at the University of Massachusetts, fact checking would have been tedious indeed.

Kate Kelly, our former editor, was unfailingly cheerful throughout all stages of the original project; her suggestions were thoughtful and her editorial comments helpful. Elizabeth Frost Knappmann of New England Publishing Associates deserves mention for her efforts on our behalf.

Friends and colleagues have been generous with support and encouragement during the time that we researched and wrote this book. Janet Logan and Susan Carter Sawyer are among those who were especially helpful to us.

Members of our family have been patient as we completed our work. We are grateful for their understanding and, in particular, would like to acknowledge the support of our mothers, Martha Clark and Elizabeth Bartlett. Finally, a very special thanks to Tim and Stephanie.

Thanks also to Suzan Cohen, Legal Research Associate for the National Clearinghouse on Child Abuse and Neglect Information, for her generous and knowledgeable assistance. Thanks to Pam Hobson, Reference Librarian; Marie Mercer, Reference Librarian; Mara Bailey, Library Assistant; and Chris Sullivan, Library Assistant of the DeGroodt Public Library in Palm Bay, Florida, for their help in locating journal articles and books.

INTRODUCTION
CHILD ABUSE—AN OVERVIEW

At the beginning of the new millennium, child abuse and neglect is widely recognized as a major social problem and policy issue in the United States and throughout much of the world. During the last 50 years, the United States and many of the world's nations have responded to child abuse and neglect with legislative efforts, a variety of programs and interventions, and organizational efforts to identify, respond to and prevent the abuse and neglect of dependent children. Today, there are innumerable local, national and international organizations, professional societies and advocacy groups devoted to preventing and treating child abuse and neglect.

The Social Transformation of Child Abuse and Neglect

While international concern about child maltreatment is relatively new, child abuse and neglect is not a recent phenomenon. The maltreatment of children has manifested itself in nearly every conceivable manner—physically, emotionally, sexually and by forced child labor (Ten Bensel, Rheinberger, and Radbill, 1997). Historians have been able to document the occurrence of various forms of the mistreatment of children back to the beginnings of recorded history. In some ancient cultures, children had no rights until the right to live was bestowed upon them by their fathers. The right to live was sometimes withheld by fathers, and newborns were abandoned or left to die. Although we do not know how commonplace abandonment or killing was, we do know that infanticide was widely accepted in ancient and prehistoric cultures. Newborns and infants could be put to death because they cried too much, because they were sickly or deformed, or

because of some perceived imperfection. Girls, twins and children of unmarried women were the special targets of infanticide (Robin, 1980).

Many societies subjected their offspring to survival tests. Some Native Americans threw their newborns into pools of water and rescued them only if they rose to the surface and cried. German parents also plunged children into icy waters as a test of fitness to live (Ten Bensel, Rheinberger, and Radbill, 1997). Greek parents exposed their children to natural elements as a survival test.

Survival tests and infanticide were not the only abuses inflicted by generations of parents. From prehistoric times to the present, children have been mutilated, beaten and maltreated. Such treatment was not only condoned but was often mandated as the most appropriate child-rearing method. Children were, and continue to be, hit with rods, canes and switches. Boys have been castrated to produce eunuchs. Girls have been, and continue to be, subjected to genital surgery or mutilation as part of culturally approved ritual. Colonial parents were implored to "beat the devil" out of their children (Greven, 1991; Straus, 1994).

Summing up the plight of children from prehistoric times until the present, David Bakan comments that "Child abuse thrives in the shadows of privacy and secrecy. It lives by inattention" (Bakan, 1971).

The Discovery of Childhood, Children, and Abuse and Neglect

Although abuse and neglect of children was sometimes condoned, and most of the time occurred within the intimacy and privacy of the home, social concern for children, their plight and their rights coexisted with the occurrence of maltreatment. Concern for the rights and welfare of children has waxed and waned over the centuries, but there has always been some attempt to protect children from mistreatment.

Six thousand years ago, children in Mesopotamia had a patron goddess to look after them. The Greeks and Romans had orphan homes. A variety of historical accounts mention some form of "fostering" for dependent children. The absolute rights of parents were limited by legislation. Samuel Radbill (1980) reports that child protection laws were enacted as long ago as 450 B.C.E. Attempts were made to modify and restrict fathers' complete control over their children. Anthropologists note that virtually all societies have had mores, laws or customs that regulate sexual access to children.

The Renaissance marked a new morality regarding children. Children were seen as a dependent class in need of the protection of society. At the same time, however, the family was expected to teach children the proper rules of behavior. Moreover, this was a historical period in which the power of the father increased dramatically. This dialectic—concern for children and increased demands and power of parents to control children—has been a consistent theme throughout history.

Defining childhood as a separate stage and children as in need of protection did not reduce the likelihood of maltreatment. In Colonial America, Puritan parents were instructed by leaders, such as Cotton Mather, that strict discipline of children could not begin too early (Greven, 1991).

The enlightenment of the 18th century brought children increased attention, services and protection. The London Foundling Hospital, established during the 18th century, not only provided medical care but also was a center of the moral reform movement on behalf of children (Robin, 1982).

In the United States, the case of Mary Ellen Wilson is usually considered the turning point in concern for children's welfare. In 1874, the then eight-year-old Mary Ellen lived in the home of Francis and Mary Connolly but was not the blood relative of either. Mary Ellen was the illegitimate daughter of Mary Connolly's first husband. A neighbor noticed the plight of Mary Ellen, who was beaten with a leather thong and allowed to go ill-clothed in bad weather. The neighbor reported the case to Etta Wheeler—a "friendly visitor" who worked for St. Luke's Methodist Mission. (In the mid-1800s, child welfare was church-based rather than government-based.) Wheeler turned to the police and the New York City Department of Charities for help for Mary Ellen Wilson and was turned down—first by the police, who said there was no proof of a crime, and second by the charity agency, which said they did not have custody of Mary Ellen. The legend goes on to note that Henry Bergh, founder of the Society for the Prevention of Cruelty to Animals, intervened on behalf of Mary Ellen and the courts accepted the case because Mary Ellen was a member of the animal kingdom. In reality, the court reviewed the case because the child needed protection. The case was argued, not by Henry Bergh, but by his colleague, Elbridge Gerry. Mary Ellen Wilson was removed from her foster home and initially placed in an orphanage. Her foster mother was imprisoned for a year, and the case received detailed press coverage for months. In December 1874, the New York Society for the Prevention of Cruelty to Children was founded (Nelson, 1984; Robin, 1982). This was the first organization that focused on child maltreatment in the United States.

Protective societies appeared and disappeared during the next 80 years. The political scientist Barbara Nelson (1984) notes that by the 1950s public interest in child maltreatment was practically nonexistent in the United States (and much of the world, for that matter). Technology paved the way for the rediscovery of physical child abuse. In 1946, the radiologist John Caffey reported on six cases of children who had multiple long bone fractures and subdural hematomas (Caffey, 1946). It would take nine more years before the medical profession would begin to accept that such injuries were the result of actions by children's caretakers. In 1955 P. V. Wooley and W. A. Evans not only concluded that the X rays revealed a pattern of injuries but that the injuries were committed willfully (Wooley and Evans, 1955). Wooley and Evans went on to criticize the medical profession for its reluctance to accept the accumulating evidence that long-bone fractures seen on X rays were indeed inflicted willfully.

In 1958, C. Henry Kempe and his colleagues formed the first hospital-based child protective team at Colorado General Hospital in Denver. Kempe and his colleagues would publish their landmark article, "The Battered Child Syndrome," in the *Journal of the American Medical Association* in July 1962. The article by Kempe and his colleagues, who represented several disciplines, was accompanied by a strong editorial on the battered child. The article and the editorial were the beginning of the modern concern for child abuse and neglect, a concern that has grown and expanded both nationally and internationally in the past four decades.

Prevention and Treatment Efforts

The United States Children's Bureau was founded in 1912 as an agency in the Department of Labor. (The bureau was later moved to the newly created Department of Health, Education, and Welfare, which was subsequently renamed the Department of Health and Human Services.) As far back as the 1950s, the Children's Bureau had begun to address the problem of child abuse and neglect. The Children's Bureau was founded by an act of Congress with a mandate to disseminate information on child development; it also acquired the budget and mandate to conduct research on issues concerning child development. The Children's Bureau has engaged in a variety of activities regarding child maltreatment and participated in the earliest national meetings on child abuse, sponsored by the Children's Division of the American Humane Association. After the publication of Kempe and his colleagues' article in 1962, the bureau convened a meeting in 1963 that drafted a model law for reporting child abuse. By 1967, all 50 states and the District of Columbia had enacted mandatory reporting laws based on the Bureau's model. In 1974, Congress enacted the Child Abuse Prevention and Treatment Act and created the National Center on Child Abuse and Neglect (Nelson, 1984). Today, the Office of Child Abuse and Neglect remains within the Children's Bureau and continues to coordinate the federal effort to prevent and treat the abuse and neglect of children in the United States.

The Definitional Dilemma

The most enduring problem in the field of child abuse and neglect has been the development of a useful, clear, acceptable and accepted definition of "abuse" and "neglect." Defining what is and is not abuse and neglect is at the core of research, intervention, prevention and social policy. Researchers must have a definition of abuse and neglect in order to engage in the most basic studies of extent, risk factors and causes. Those who are required to report child maltreatment need a benchmark or standard to determine what should be reported and what should not. And yet, there still is not a widely accepted definition of abuse and neglect. There is even variation across the 50 state definitions that are included in laws mandating reporting.

At the core of the definition problem is deciding what constitutes appropriate and inappropriate parent and caretaker behavior. Is a spanking an appropriate and even necessary method of disciplining children, or is it physical abuse? Most people agree that an adult having sexual intercourse with a minor child is sexual abuse. But what if the child is 13, 14 or even 17 years of age? Legally a 17-year-old is a child, but if the sex is consensual, is it abuse? Most people agree that appropriate parent behavior includes providing food and shelter for children. But what if poverty limits a parent's ability to provide—is this neglect? There is an infinite number of questions and dilemmas about where to draw the line between appropriate and acceptable behavior versus inappropriate and unacceptable behavior. There is general agreement at the extremes as to what is appropriate and inappropriate, but the middle area is subject to intense debate. The debate deepens when we consider cultural variations, both within our own society and across societies. In some cultures, female genital cutting (or what is called female circumcision or genital mutilation) is acceptable and even mandated. In the United States, cutting the genitals of females is considered abusive. Male circumcision is accepted in the United States and many other nations.

What is defined as abuse and neglect varies across societies, cultural groups and even across historical time. Kempe and his colleagues' first focus was restricted to physical abuse, or what they called "the battered child." In the subsequent 40 years, as concern for children's well-being expanded, so too did the definition of child abuse and neglect. The expansion of the definition can be seen in changes in how child abuse and neglect have been defined in the Federal Child Abuse Prevention and Treatment Act. In the 1974 version of the law, abuse and neglect were defined as:

The physical or mental injury, sexual abuse, negligent treatment, or maltreatment of a child under the age of eighteen by a person who is responsible for the child's welfare under circumstances which indicate that a child's health and welfare is harmed or threatened thereby (Public Law 93-237).

The Child Abuse Prevention and Treatment Act of 1984 defined child abuse and neglect as:

The physical or mental injury, sexual abuse or exploitation, negligent treatment, or maltreatment of a child under the age of eighteen or the age specified by the child protection law of the state in question, by a person (including an employee of a residential facility or any staff person providing out-of-home care) who is responsible for the child's welfare under circumstances which indicate that the child's health or welfare is harmed or threatened thereby, as determined in regulations prescribed by the Secretary.

The federal definition was expanded in 1988 to indicate that the behavior had to be avoidable and nonaccidental. This new clause attempted to address the issue of intent; however, it still provided no clear guidance as to how to classify or categorize cases based on intent.

That the federal government has a legal definition of child abuse and neglect still does not settle the matter. First, each state has its own legal definition of child maltreatment and those definitions do vary. Second, child welfare caseworkers and family and juvenile court judges vary in how they apply the state definitions during the course of child abuse and neglect investigations and court actions. Thirdly, researchers must "operationalize" the definitions; that is, they must determine how they will actually measure child abuse and neglect. Here too, there is considerable variation in how the concept "child abuse and neglect" is operationally defined. Finally, legal definitions and research operationalizations do not result in definitions that can be applied across cultures and subcultures.

All of the above problems actually arise out of the fact that there is no universal standard for what constitutes optimal child rearing. Thus, there is no universal standard for what constitutes child abuse and neglect (Korbin, 1981). David Finkelhor and Jill Korbin (1988) propose that a definition of child abuse and neglect that could be applied across subcultures and cultures should have two objectives: (1) it should distinguish child abuse clearly from other social, economic and health problems; and (2) it should be sufficiently flexible to apply to a range of situations in a variety of social and cultural contexts. The later recommendation is a caution that some of what is considered child abuse in Western societies has very little meaning in other societies and vice versa.

Finkelhor and Korbin (1988) propose the following definition of child abuse and neglect for cross-cultural research and study: "Child abuse is the portion of harm to children that results from human action that is proscribed (negatively valued), proximate (the action is close to the actual harm—thus deforesting land that results in child harm does not meet this definition), and preventable (the action could have been prevented)."

The Extent of Child Abuse and Neglect

As explained in the previous section, child abuse and neglect is a general term that covers a wide range of acts of commission and omission, either carried out by a child's caretaker or allowed to happen, that result in a range of injuries ranging from death, to serious disabling injury, to emotional distress, to malnutrition and illness.

Child abuse and neglect can take many and varied forms. The Office on Child Abuse and Neglect classifies the various forms of maltreatment into six major types (see National Center on Child Abuse and Neglect (NCCAN), 1988):

1. *Physical Abuse:* Acts of commission that result in physical harm, including death, to a child.
2. *Sexual Abuse:* Acts of commission including intrusion or penetration, molestation with genital contact or other forms of sexual acts in which children are used to provide sexual gratification for a perpetrator.
3. *Emotional Abuse:* Acts of commission that include confinement, verbal or emotional abuse or other

types of abuse such as withholding sleep, food or shelter.

4. *Physical Neglect:* Acts of omission that involve refusal to provide health care, delay in providing health care, abandonment, expulsion of a child from a home, inadequate supervision, failure to meet food and clothing needs, and conspicuous failure to protect a child from hazards or danger.

5. *Educational Neglect:* Acts of omission and commission that include permitting chronic truancy, failure to enroll a child in school and inattention to specific education needs.

6. *Emotional Neglect:* Acts of omission that involve failing to meet the nurturing and affection needs of a child, exposing a child to chronic or severe spouse abuse, allowing or permitting a child to use alcohol or controlled substances, encouraging the child to engage in maladaptive behavior, refusal to provide psychological care, delays in providing psychological care and other inattention to the child's developmental needs.

Prevalence

Various methods have been used in attempts to achieve an accurate estimate of child abuse and neglect in the United States, including tabulating official reports of child maltreatment received by state child welfare agencies, as well as self-report surveys.

The Office on Child Abuse and Neglect has conducted three surveys designed to measure the national incidence of reported and recognized child maltreatment (Burgdorf, 1980; NCCAN, 1988; NCCAN, 1996). The surveys assessed how many cases were known to investigatory agencies, professionals in schools, hospitals and other social service agencies. A total of 2.9 million children were known by the agencies surveyed in 1993 (see table).

A second source of data on the extent of child maltreatment comes from the National Child Abuse and Neglect Data System (NCANDS). NCANDS is a national data collection and analysis project carried out by the U.S. Department of Health and Human Services Office of Child Abuse and Neglect. In 1996, states received 2,025,956 reports of child maltreatment, representing just over 3 million individual child victims. Of the 970,000 child victims for whom maltreatment was indicated or substantiated and for whom there were data on type of maltreat-

---

ESTIMATES OF THE TOTAL NUMBER OF MALTREATED CHILDREN, 1993

Maltreatment Type	Total Number of Cases
Physical Abuse	614,000
Sexual Abuse	300,200
Emotional Abuse	532,200
Neglect	961,300
Physical Neglect	1,335,100
Emotional Neglect	584,100
Educational Neglect	397,300
Seriously Injured Children	565,000

Source: National Center on Child Abuse and Neglect, 1996.
Note: Children who experience more than one type of abuse or neglect are reflected in the estimates for each applicable type. As a result, the estimates for the different types of maltreatment sum to more than the total number of maltreated children.

---

ment, 229,332 experienced physical abuse, 500,032 experienced neglect, and 119,397 experienced sexual abuse (U.S. Department of Health and Human Services, 1998).

A source of data not based only on official reports or official awareness is The National Family Violence Survey, carried out in 1976 and again in

---

FREQUENCY OF PARENTAL VIOLENCE TOWARD CHILDREN

Percentage of Occurrences in Past Year

Violent Behavior	Once	Twice	More Than Twice	Total	Percentage of Occurrences Ever Reported
Threw something at child	1.5	.7	.9	3.1	4.5
Pushed, grabbed or shoved child	5.8	7.5	14.9	28.2	33.6
Slapped or spanked child	8.1	8.5	39.1	55.7	74.6
Kicked, bit or hit with fist	.7	.5	.3	1.5	2.1
Hit or tried to hit child with something	2.4	2.0	5.3	9.7	14.4
Beat up child	.3	.1	.2	.6	1.0
Burned or scalded child	.2	.1	.1	.4	.6
Threatened child with knife or gun	.1	.1	0	.2	.3
Used a knife or gun	.1	.1	0	.2	.2

Source: Second National Family Violence Survey, Richard J. Gelles and Murray A. Straus, 1989.

1985 by Murray Straus and Richard Gelles (Gelles and Straus, 1987; 1988). The National Family Violence Surveys interviewed two nationally representative samples of families: 2,146 family members in 1976 and 6,002 family members in 1985. (See table on page xv.)

Milder forms of violence, violence that many people think of as physical punishment, as represented by the first three items in this table, were of course, the most common. However, even with the severe forms of violence, the rates were surprisingly high. Abusive violence was defined as acts that had a high probability of injuring the child. These included kicking, biting, punching, hitting or trying to hit a child with an object, beating up a child, burning or scalding, and threatening or using a gun or a knife. Slightly more than two parents in 100 (2.3%) reported that they engaged in one act of abusive violence during the year prior to the survey. Seven children in 1,000 were hurt as a result of an act of violence directed at them by a parent in the previous year.

Among the most dramatic changes taking place over the last few decades has been the increased attention to child sexual abuse. In a comprehensive review of studies on the incidence and prevalence of child sexual abuse, Peters, Wyatt and Finkelhor (1986) report that estimates of the prevalence range from 6% to 62% for females and from 3% to 31% for males. They point out that this variation may be accounted for by a number of methodological factors, such as differences in definitions of abuse, sample characteristics, interview format (e.g., in person versus phone interview) and number of questions used to elicit information about abuse experiences. Whatever the number, it is clear that sexual abuse is a problem that affects large numbers of children.

The U.S. Advisory Board on Child Abuse and Neglect estimated (1995) that parents or caretakers kill 2,000 children under the age of 18 each year. The board suggests that this estimate is low. McLain and his colleagues (McLain, Sacks and Frohlke, 1993) report that abuse and neglect kill 5.4 out of every 100,000 children under 4 years of age, but this estimate is probably low as a result of misclassification of child deaths. A second estimate is that the rate of child death is 11.6 per 100,000 children

under 4 years of age (U.S. Advisory Board on Child Abuse and Neglect, 1995).

The National Committee to Prevent Child Abuse and Neglect estimates that 1,215 children were killed by parents or caretakers in 1995, for a rate of 1.81 children per 100,000 (Daro, 1996).

The varied estimates of the prevalence of child abuse and neglect most likely underestimate the true extent of child maltreatment. Given that caretakers carry out most maltreatment in the privacy of the home, much abuse and neglect goes undetected. Moreover, the lack of a cultural consensus about which acts constitute abuse and neglect and which acts are designated appropriate discipline techniques makes it difficult to assess the true level of child maltreatment. The above estimates of maltreatment, including the estimate of child homicide, should be considered a lower boundary of the full extent of abuse and neglect in the United States.

Risk and Protective Factors

The first research articles on child abuse and neglect characterized offenders as suffering from various forms of psychopathology (see for example, Bennie and Sclare, 1969; Galdston, 1965; Steele and Pollock, 1974). Thus, the initial approach to explaining, understanding and treating maltreatment was to identify the personality or character disorders that were thought to be associated with abuse and neglect. There were many methodological problems that limited studies that attempted to develop psychological profiles of caretakers who maltreated their children. Most early studies had small samples and no, or inappropriate, comparison groups. Collectively, the studies failed to develop a consistent profile of abusers.

Current theoretical approaches tend to recognize the multidimensional nature of abuse and neglect and locate the roots of child maltreatment in psychological, social, family, community and societal factors.

Researchers have identified both risk and protective factors for abuse and neglect. The following are the major risk and protective factors:

Age.   One of the most consistent risk factors is the age of the offender. As with violence between nonintimates, violence and abuse are most likely to be perpetrated by those between 18 and 30 years of age.

Sex. Men and women have somewhat similar rates of child homicide, although women appear more likely to be offenders when the child victim is young (under three years of age) and males are the more likely offenders when the child victim is older. Men are by far the most likely offenders in acts of sexual abuse of children, while women's rate of neglect and nonfatal forms of physical abuse is greater than that of men. Of course, women's higher rate of nonfatal abuse and neglect is not surprising given that women spend more time caring for children and are delegated far more responsibility for children than are men.

Income. Although most poor parents do not abuse or neglect their children, self-report surveys and official report data find that the rates of child maltreatment, with the exception of sexual abuse, are higher for those whose family incomes are below the poverty line than for those whose income is above the poverty line.

Race. Both official report data and self-report survey data often report that child abuse is overrepresented among minorities. However, both the second and the third study of the National Incidence and Prevalence of Child Abuse and Neglect (National Center on Child Abuse and Neglect, 1988; 1996) found no significant relationship between the incidence of maltreatment and the child's race/ethnicity. There was no significant relationship for any of the subcategories of maltreatment.

The two National Family Violence Surveys, however, found stronger relationships between race/ethnicity and violence toward children. Although in the first National Family Violence Survey, the difference in rates between blacks and whites disappeared when income was controlled, an analysis of the larger data set from the Second National Family Violence Survey found that the differences persisted even when income was controlled.

Situational and Environmental Factors

Stress. Unemployment, financial problems, single parenthood, teenage parenthood and sexual difficulties are all factors that are related to child maltreatment, as are a host of other stressor events (Gelles and Straus, 1988; Gelles, 1989; Parke and Collmer, 1975; Straus et al., 1980).

Social isolation and social support. The data on social isolation are somewhat less consistent than are the data for the previously listed correlates. First, because so much of the research on child abuse and neglect is cross-sectional, it is not clear whether social isolation precedes maltreatment or is a consequence of it. Second, social isolation has been crudely measured and the purported correlation may be more anecdotal than statistical. Nevertheless, researchers often agree that parents who are socially isolated from neighbors and relatives are more likely to maltreat their children.

Social support appears to be an important protective factor. One major source of social support is the availability of friends and family for help, aid and assistance. The more a family is integrated into the community and the more groups and associations they belong to, the less likely they are to be violent (Straus, et al., 1980).

The intergenerational transmission of violence. The notion that abused children grow up to be abusing parents and violent adults has been widely expressed in the child abuse and family violence literature (Gelles, 1980). Kaufman and Zigler (1987) reviewed the literature that tested the hypothesis of intergenerational transmission of violence toward children and concluded that the best estimate of the rate of intergenerational transmission appears to be 30% (plus or minus 5%). Although a rate of 30% is substantially less than the majority of abused children, the rate is considerably more than the 2–4% rate of abuse found in the general population (Straus and Gelles, 1986; Widom 1989). Egeland and his colleagues (Egeland, Jacobvitz and Papatola, 1987) examined continuity and discontinuity of abuse in a longitudinal study of high-risk mothers and their children. They found that mothers who had been abused as children were less likely to abuse their own children if they had emotionally supportive parents, partners or friends. In addition, the abused mothers who did not abuse their children were described as "middle class" and "upwardly mobile," suggesting that they were able to draw on economic resources that may not have been available to the abused mothers who did abuse their children.

Evidence from studies of parental violence indicates that although experiencing violence in one's family of origin is often correlated with later violent behavior, such experience is not the sole determining factor. When the intergenerational transmission of violence occurs, it is likely the result of a complex set of social and psychological process.

Although experiencing and witnessing violence is believed to be an important risk factor, the actual mechanism by which violence is transmitted from generation to generation is not well understood.

Presence of other violence.   A final general risk factor is that the presence of violence in one family relationship increases the risk that there will be violence in other relationships. Thus children in homes where there is domestic violence are more likely to experience violence than are children who grow up in homes where there is no violence between their parents. Moreover, children who witness and experience violence are more likely to use violence toward their parents and siblings than are children who do not experience or see violence in their homes (Straus et al., 1980).

Research on Victims

Compared to research on offenders, there has been somewhat less research on victims of child abuse and neglect that focuses on factors that increase or reduce the risk of victimization. Most research on victims examines the consequences of victimization (e.g., depression, psychological distress, suicide attempts, symptoms of post-traumatic stress syndrome, etc.) or the effectiveness of various intervention efforts.

The very youngest children appear to be at the greatest risk of being abused, especially the most dangerous and potentially lethal forms of violence (Fergusson et al., 1972; Gil, 1970; Johnson, 1974). Not only are young children physically more fragile and thus more susceptible to injury, but their vulnerability makes them more likely to be reported and diagnosed as abused when injured. Older children are underreported as victims of abuse. Adolescent victims may be considered delinquent or ungovernable and are thus thought of as contributing to their own victimization.

Younger boys are more likely to be abused than older boys are. The first National Family Violence Survey found that older girls were more likely to be victimized than younger girls (Straus et al., 1980).

Early research suggested that there were a number of factors that raise the risk of a child being abused. Low birth weight babies (Parke and Collmer, 1975), premature children (Elmer, 1967; Newberger et al., 1977; Parke and Collmer, 1975; Steele and Pollack, 1974) and handicapped, retarded or developmentally disabled children (Friedrich and Boriskin, 1976; Gil, 1970; Steinmetz, 1978) were all described as being at greater risk of being abused by their parents or caretakers. However, a review of studies that examines the child's role in abuse calls into question many of these findings (Starr, 1988). First, a major problem is that few investigators used matched comparison groups. Secondly, newer studies fail to find premature or handicapped children at higher risk for abuse (Egeland and Vaughan, 1981; Starr et al., 1984).

Factors Associated with Sexual Abuse of Children

There has been a great deal of research on the characteristics of sexual abusers, but current research has failed to isolate characteristics, especially demographic, social or psychological characteristics, that discriminate between sexual abusers and nonabusers (Quinsey, 1984).

One of the key questions raised in discussions about sexual abuse is whether all children are at risk for sexual abuse or whether some children, because of some specific characteristic (e.g., age or poverty status), are at greater risk than others are. In their review of studies on prevention, Finkelhor and Baron (1986) conclude that it is currently not clear what factors increase children's risk for sexual abuse. It appears that girls are at greater risk, although boys are also victimized. Girls are more likely to be victimized if they have sometime been separated from their mothers (e.g., ever lived away from mother, mother ill or disabled) or if they report poor relationships with their mothers. As the researchers note, these factors may be consequences of sexual abuse as much as risk factors. The data point to the importance of mothers in protecting children from sexually aggressive men.

Explaining the Abuse and Neglect of Children

Risk and protective factors do not, in and of themselves, explain why parents and caretakers abuse and neglect their children. The earliest explanatory theories and models focused on intra-individual factors (factors particular to the abusers) to explain maltreatment. These models included a psychopathological explanation that explained abuse and neglect as a function of individual psychopathology. Other models proposed that maltreatment arose out of mental illness or the use and abuse of alcohol and illicit drugs.

Later theories added social, cultural and environmental factors to the models. The major multidimensional models include:

Social learning theory. Social learning theory proposes that individuals who experienced abuse and neglect as children are more likely to maltreat their own children than individuals who experienced no abuse or neglect: Children who either experience abuse themselves or who witness violence between their parents are more likely to use violence when they grow up. This finding has been interpreted to support the idea that family violence and caretaking is learned. The family is the institution and social group where people learn the roles of husband and wife, parent and child. The home is the prime location where people learn how to deal with various stresses, crises and frustrations. In many instances, the home is also the site where a person first experiences violence and abuse. Not only do people learn violent behavior, but also they learn how to justify being violent. For example, hearing father say "this will hurt me more than it will hurt you," or mother say, "you have been bad, so you deserve to be spanked," contributes to how children learn to justify violent behavior.

Social situational/stress and coping theory. Social situational/stress and coping theory explains why maltreatment occurs in some situations and not others. The theory proposes that abuse and neglect occur because of two main factors. The first is structural stress and the lack of coping resources in a family. For instance, the association between low income and child abuse indicates that an important contributor to the risk of abuse is inadequate financial resources. The second factor is the cultural norm concerning the use of force and violence. In contemporary American society, as well as many societies, violence in general, and violence toward children in particular is normative (Straus, Gelles and Steinmetz, 1980). Thus, individuals learn to use violence both expressively and instrumentally as a means of coping with a pileup of stressor events.

Ecological theory. Garbarino (1977) and Belsky (1980; 1993) propose an ecological model to explain the complex nature of child maltreatment. The ecological model proposes that violence and abuse arise out of a mismatch of parent to child or family to neighborhood and community. For example, parents who are under a great deal of social stress and have poor coping skills may have a difficult time meeting the needs of a child who is hyperactive. The risk of abuse and violence increases when the functioning of the children and parents is limited and constrained by developmental problems such as children with learning disabilities and social or emotional handicaps, and when parents are under considerable stress or have personality problems, such as immaturity or impulsiveness. Finally, if there are few institutions and agencies in the community to support troubled families, then the risk of abuse is further increased.

Exchange theory. Exchange theory proposes that child rearing and child abuse is governed by the principle of costs and benefits. Abuse is used when the rewards are perceived as greater than the costs (Gelles, 1983). The private nature of the family, the reluctance of social institutions and agencies to intervene—in spite of mandatory child abuse reporting laws—and the low risk of other interventions reduce the costs of abuse and neglect. The cultural approval of violence as both expressive and instrumental behavior raises the potential rewards for violence. The most significant reward is social control, or power.

Sociobiology theory. A sociobiological, or evolutionary perspective of child maltreatment, suggests that the abuse and neglect of human or nonhuman primate offspring is the result of the reproductive success potential of children and parental investment. The theory's central assumption is that natural selection is the process of differential reproduction and reproductive success (Daly and Wilson, 1980). Males can be expected to invest in offspring when there is some degree of parental certainty (how confident the parent is that the child is his own genetic offspring), while females are also inclined to invest under conditions of parental certainty. Parents recognize their offspring and avoid squandering valuable reproductive effort on someone else's offspring. Thus, Daly and Wilson (1985) conclude that parental feelings are more readily and more profoundly established with one's own offspring than in cases where the parent-offspring relationship is artificial. Children not genetically related to the parent (e.g., stepchildren, adopted or foster children) or children with low reproductive potential (e.g., handicapped or retarded children) are at the highest risk for infanticide and abuse (Burgess and Garbarino, 1983; Daly and Wilson, 1980; Hardy, 1979). Large families can dilute parental energy and lower attachment to children, thus increasing the risk of child abuse and neglect (Burgess, 1979).

A model of sexual abuse.   Finkelhor (1984) reviewed research on the factors that have been proposed as contributing to sexual abuse of children and developed what he calls the "Four Precondition Model of Sexual Abuse." His review suggests that all the factors relating to sexual abuse can be grouped into one of four preconditions that must be met before sexual abuse can occur. The preconditions are:

1. A potential offender needs to have some motivation to abuse a child sexually.
2. The potential offender has to overcome internal inhibitions against acting on that motivation.
3. The potential offender has to overcome external impediments to committing sexual abuse.
4. The potential offender or some other factor has to undermine or overcome a child's possible resistance to sexual abuse.

Summary.   The intra-individual models of child abuse and neglect dominated the first decade of research, practice and policy. Although some professions still subscribe to psychopathological explanations for child maltreatment, such narrow models eventually gave way to more multidimensional approaches that included psychopathology, but also considered social, environmental and cultural factors. Current theoretical approaches tend to be based on the ecological model of child maltreatment (National Research Council, 1993).

The Consequences of Maltreatment

The consequences of child abuse and neglect differ by the age of the child. During childhood some of the major consequences of maltreatment include problematic school performance and lowered attention to social cues. Researchers have found that children whose parents are "psychologically unavailable" function poorly across a wide range of psychological, cognitive and developmental areas (Egeland and Sroufe, 1981). Physical aggression, antisocial behavior and juvenile delinquency are among the most consistently documented consequences of abuse in adolescence and adulthood (Aber et al., 1990; Dodge et al., 1990; Widom, 1989a; 1989b; 1991). Evidence is more suggestive that maltreatment increases the risk of alcohol and drug problems (National Research Council, 1993).

Research on the consequences of sexual abuse finds that inappropriate sexual behavior, such as frequent and overt sexual stimulation and inappropriate sexual overtures to other children, are commonly found among victims of sexual abuse (Kendall-Tackett et al., 1993). Widom (1995) has found that people who were sexually abused during childhood are at higher risk of arrest for committing crimes as adults, including sex crimes, compared to people who did not suffer sexual abuse. However, this risk is no greater than the risk of arrest for victims of other childhood maltreatment, with one exception: Victims of sexual abuse are more likely to be arrested for prostitution than other victims of maltreatment.

As severe and significant as the consequences of child abuse and neglect are, it is also important to point out that the majority of children who are abused and neglected do not show signs of extreme disturbance. Despite having been physically, psychologically or sexually abused, many children have effective coping abilities and thus are able to deal with their problems better than other maltreated children. There are a number of protective factors that insulate children from the effects of maltreatment. These include: high intelligence and good scholastic attainment; temperament; cognitive appraisal of events—how the child views the maltreatment; having a healthy relationship with a significant adult; and the type of interventions, including placement outside of the home (National Research Council, 1993).

Prevention and Treatment

As noted earlier, by the late 1960s, all 50 states had enacted mandatory reporting laws for child abuse and neglect. These laws require certain professionals (or in some states, all adults) to report cases of suspected abuse or neglect. When a report comes in, state or local protective service workers investigate to determine if the child is in need of protection and if the family is in need of help or assistance. Although a wide array of options are available to child protection workers, they typically have two basic ways to protect a victim of child abuse: (a) removing the child and placing him or her in a foster home or institution; or (b) providing the family with social support, such as counseling, food stamps, day care services, etc.

Neither solution is ideal, and there are risks in both. For instance, a child may not understand why he or she is being removed from the home. Children who are removed from abusive homes may be protected from physical damage, although some children are abused and killed in foster homes and residential placements. Abused children frequently require special medical and/or psychological care and it is difficult to find a suitable placement for them. They could well become a burden for foster parents or institutions that have to care for them. Therefore, the risk of abuse might even be greater in a foster home or institution than in the home of the natural parents. In addition, removal may cause emotional harm. The emotional harm arises from the fact that abused children still love and have strong feelings for their parents and do not understand why they have been removed from their parents and homes. Often, abused children feel that they are responsible for their own abuse.

Leaving children in an abusive home and providing social services involves another type of risk. Most protective service workers are overworked, undertrained and underpaid. Family services, such as crisis day care, financial assistance and suitable housing and transportation services, are often limited. This can lead to cases where children reported as abused who were investigated and supervised by state agencies are killed during the period when the family was supposedly being monitored. Half of all children who are killed by caretakers are killed after they have been reported to child welfare agencies (Gelles, 1996).

Only a handful of evaluations have been made of prevention and treatment programs for child maltreatment. In Elmira, New York, Olds and his colleagues (1986) evaluated the effectiveness of a family support program during pregnancy and for the first two years after birth for low-income, unmarried, teenage first-time mothers. Nineteen percent of a sample of poor unmarried teenage girls who received no services during their pregnancy period was reported for subsequent child maltreatment. Of those children of poor, unmarried, teenage mothers who were provided with the full compliment of nurse home visits during the mother's pregnancy and for the first two years after birth, 4% had confirmed cases of child abuse and neglect reported to the state child protection agency. Subsequent follow-ups by the home health visiting intervention worker demonstrated the long-term effectiveness of this intervention. However, the effectiveness varied depending on the populations receiving the service, the community context and who made the visits (nurses or others) (Olds et al., 1999).

Daro and Cohn (1988) reviewed evaluations of 88 child maltreatment programs that were funded by the federal government between 1974 and 1982. They found that there was no noticeable correlation between a given set of services and the likelihood of further maltreatment of children. In fact, the more services a family received, the worse the family got and the more likely children were to be maltreated. Lay counseling, group counseling and parent education classes resulted in more positive treatment outcomes. The optimal treatment period appeared to be between seven and 18 months. The projects that were successful in reducing abuse accomplished this by separating children from abusive parents, either by placing them in foster homes or requiring the maltreating adult to move out of the house.

The National Academy of Sciences panel on assessing family violence interventions identified 78 evaluations of child maltreatment intervention programs that met the panel's criteria for methodologically sound evaluation research. The one commonality of the 78 evaluations of child abuse and neglect prevention and treatment programs was, in scientific terms, a failure to reject the null hypothesis. While it may be too harsh a judgment to say these programs have not and do not work as intended, the National Research Council report did come to the following conclusion regarding social service interventions:

Social service interventions designed to improve parenting practices and provide family support have not yet demonstrated that they have the capacity to reduce or prevent abusive or neglectful behaviors significantly over time for the majority of families who have been reported for child maltreatment (National Research Council, 1998, p. 118).

Thus, while we have made great strides in identifying child abuse and neglect as a social problem, and we have developed numerous programs to attempt to treat and prevent abuse and neglect, we still have much to learn about what causes parents and caretakers to abuse their children and what steps society must take to prevent the maltreatment of children.

Richard J. Gelles, Ph.D.,
Joanne and Raymond Welsh Chair of
Child Welfare and Family Violence
Co-Director, Center for the Study of Youth Policy
Co-Director, Center for Children's Policy, Practice,
and Research School of Social Work
University of Pennsylvania, Philadelphia

References

Aber, J. L., J. P. Allen, V. Carlson, and D. Cicchetti. "The effects of maltreatment on development during early childhood: Recent studies and their theoretical, clinical, and policy implications." In D. Cicchetti and V. Carlson, eds. *Child Maltreatment: Theory and Research on Causes and Consequences.* New York: Cambridge University Press, 1990, pp. 579–619.

Bakan, D. *The Slaughter of the Innocents.* Boston: Beacon Press, 1971.

Belsky, J. "Child maltreatment: An ecological integration." *American Psychologist* 35 (1980): 320–335.

Belsky, J. "Etiology of child maltreatment: A developmental-ecological approach." *Psychological Bulletin* 114 (1993): 413–434.

Bennie, E. H., and A. B. Sclare. "The battered child syndrome." *American Journal of Psychiatry* 125 (1969): 975–978.

Burgdorf, K. *Recognition and Reporting of Child Maltreatment.* Rockville, Md.: Westat, 1980.

Burgess, R. L. "Family violence: Some implications from evolutionary biology." Paper presented at Annual Meeting of the American Society of Criminology, Philadelphia, Pa., 1979.

Burgess, R. L., and J. Garbarino. "Doing what comes naturally? An evolutionary perspective on child abuse." In D. Finkelhor, R. Gelles, M. Straus, and G. Hotaling, eds. *The Dark Side of the Families: Current Family Violence Research.* Beverly Hills, Calif.: Sage, 1983, pp. 88–101.

Caffey, J. "Multiple fractures in the long bones of infants suffering from chronic subdural hematoma." *American Journal of Roentgenology, Radium Therapy, and Nuclear Medicine* 58 (1946): 163–173.

Daly, M., and M. Wilson. "Discriminative parental solicitude: A biosocial perspective." *Journal of Marriage and the Family* 42 (1980): 277–288.

———. "Child abuse and other risks of not living with both parents." *Ethology and Sociobiology* 6 (1985): 197–210.

———. *Homicide.* New York: Aldine DeGruyter, 1988.

Daro, D. "Current trends in child abuse reporting and fatalities: NCPCA's 1995 annual fifty state survey." *The APSAC Advisor* 9 (1996): 21–24.

Dodge, K. A., J. E. Bates, and G. S. Pettit. "Mechanisms in the cycle of violence." *Science* 250 (1990): 1678–1683.

Egeland, B., and B. Vaughan. "Failure of 'bond formation' as a cause of abuse, neglect, and maltreatment." *American Journal of Orthopsychiatry* 51 (1981): 78–84.

Egeland, B., and L. A. Sroufe. "Attachment and early child maltreatment." *Child Development* 52 (1981): 44–52.

Egeland, B., D. Jacobvitz, and K. Papatola. "Intergenerational continuity of abuse." In R. J. Gelles and J. B. Lancaster, eds. *Child Abuse and Neglect: Biosocial Dimensions.* Hawthorne, N.Y.: Aldine de Gruyter, 1987, pp. 255–276.

Elmer, E. *Children in Jeopardy: A Study of Abused Minors and Their Families.* Pittsburgh: University of Pittsburgh Press, 1967.

Fergusson, D. M., J. Fleming, and D. O'Neil. *Child Abuse in New Zealand.* Wellington, New Zealand: Research Division, Department of Social Work, 1972.

Finkelhor, D. *Child Sexual Abuse: New Theory and Research.* New York: Free Press, 1984.

Finkelhor, D., and J. Korbin. "Child abuse as an international issue." *Child Abuse and Neglect: The International Journal* 12 (1988): 3–23.

Friederich, W. N., and J. A. Boriskin. "The role of the child in abuse: A review of literature." *American Journal of Orthopsychiatry* 46 (1976): 580–590.

Galdston, R. "Observations of children who have been physically abused by their parents." *American Journal of Psychiatry* 122 (1965): 440–443.

Garbarino, J. "The human ecology of child maltreatment." *Journal of Marriage and the Family* 39 (1977): 721–735.

Gelles, R. J. "Violence in the family: A review of research in the seventies." *Journal of Marriage and the Family* 42 (1980): 873–885.

———. "An exchange/social control theory." In D. Finkelhor, R. Gelles, M. Straus, and G. Hotaling, eds. *The Dark Side of Families: Current Family Violence Research* (pp. 151–165). Beverly Hills, Calif.: Sage, 1983.

———. "Child abuse and violence in single parent families: Parent-absence and economic deprivation." *American Journal of Orthopsychiatry* 59 (1989): 492–501.

Gelles, R. J., and M. A. Straus. "Is violence towards children increasing? A comparison of 1975 and 1985 national survey rates." *Journal of Interpersonal Violence* 2 (1987): 212–222.

———. *Intimate Violence.* New York: Simon and Schuster, 1988.

Gil, D. *Violence Against Children: Physical Child Abuse in the United States.* Cambridge, Mass.: Harvard University Press, 1970.

Greven, P. *Spare the Child: The Religious Roots of Punishment and the Psychological Impact of Physical Abuse.* New York: Knopf, 1990.

Hardy, S. B. "Infanticide among animals: A review classification, and examination of the implications for reproductive strategies of females." *Ethology and Sociobiology* 1 (1979): 13–40.

Johnson, C. *Child Abuse in the Southeast: An Analysis of 1172 Reported Cases.* Athens, Ga.: Welfare Research, 1974.

Kaufman, J., and E. Zigler. "Do abused children become abusive parents?" *American Journal of Orthopsychiatry* 57 (1987): 186–192.

Kempe, C. H., F. N. Silverman, B. F. Steele, W. Droegemueller, and H. K. Silver. "The battered child syndrome." *Journal of the American Medical Association* 181 (1962): 107–112.

Kendall-Tackett, K. A., L. Williams, and D. Finkelhor. "The impact of sexual abuse on children: A review and synthesis of recent empirical literature." *Psychological Bulletin* 113 (1993): 164–180.

Korbin, J., ed. *Child Abuse and Neglect: Cross-cultural Perspectives.* Berkeley: University of California Press, 1981.

National Center on Child Abuse and Neglect. *Study findings: Study of national incidence and prevalence of child abuse and neglect: 1988.* Washington, D.C.: U.S. Department of Health and Human Services, 1988.

———. *Study findings: Study of national incidence and prevalence of child abuse and neglect: 1993.* Washington, D.C.: U.S. Department of Health and Human Services, 1993.

National Research Council. *Understanding Child Abuse and Neglect.* Washington, D.C.: National Academy Press, 1993.

———. *Violence in families: Assessing prevention and treatment programs.* Washington, D.C.: National Academy Press, 1998.

Nelson, B. J. *Making an Issue of Child Abuse: Political Agenda Setting for Social Problems.* Chicago: University of Chicago Press, 1984.

Newberger, E., R. Reed, J. H. Daniel, J. Hyde, and M. Kotelchuck. "Pediatric social illness: Toward an etiologic classification." *Pediatrics* 60 (1977): 178–185.

Olds, D. L., C. R. Henderson Jr., R. Tatelbaum, and R. Chamberlin. "Preventing child abuse and neglect: A randomized trial of nurse home visitation." *Pediatrics* 77 (1986): 65–78.

Olds, D. L., C. R. Henderson, H. J. Kitzman, J. J. Eckenrode, R. E. Cole, and R. C. Tatelbaum. "Prenatal and infancy home visitation by nurses: Recent findings." *The Future of Children* 9 (1999): 44–65.

Parke, R. D., and C. W. Collmer. "Child abuse: An interdisciplinary analysis." In M. Hetherington, ed. *Review of Child Development Research.* Vol. 5. Chicago: University of Chicago Press, pp. 1–102.

Peters, S. D., G. E. Wyatt, and D. Finkelhor. "Prevalence." In D. Finkelhor, ed. *A Sourcebook on Child Sexual Abuse.* Beverly Hills, Calif.: Sage, 1986, pp. 15–59.

Quinsey, V. L. "Sexual aggression: Studies of offenders against women." In D. N. Weisstub, ed. *Law and Mental Health: International Perspectives.* Volume 1. New York: Pergamon Press, 1984, pp. 84–121.

Radbill, S. "Children in a world of violence: A history of child abuse." In C. H. Kempe and R. Helfer, eds. *The Battered Child.* 3rd ed. Chicago: University of Chicago Press, 1980, pp. 3–20.

Robin, M. "Historical introduction: Sheltering arms: The roots of child protection." In E. Newberger, ed. *Child Abuse.* Boston: Little, Brown, 1980, pp. 1–41.

Starr, R. H., Jr., K. N. Dietrich, J. Fischoff, B. Schumann, and M. Demorest. "The contribution of handicapping conditions to child abuse." *Topics in Early Childhood Special Education* 4 (1984): 55–69.

Starr, R. H., Jr. "Physical abuse of children." In V. B. Van Hasselt, R. L. Morrison, A. S. Bellack, and M. Hersen, eds. *Handbook of Family Violence.* New York: Plenum, 1988, pp. 119–155.

Steele, B. F., and C. Pollock. "A psychiatric study of parents who abuse infants and small children." In R. Helfer and C. H. Kempe, eds. *The Battered Child.* Chicago: University of Chicago Press, 1968, pp. 103–137.

Steele, B. F., and C. Pollock. "A psychiatric study of parents who abuse infants and small children." In R.

Helfer and C. Kempe, eds. *The Battered Child.* 2nd ed. Chicago: University of Chicago Press, pp. 89–134.

Steinmetz, S. K. "Violence between family members." *Marriage and Family Review* 1 (1978): 1–16.

Straus, M. A. *Beating the Devil Out of Them: Corporal Punishment in American Families.* New York: Lexington Books, 1994.

Straus, M. A., and R. J. Gelles. "Societal change and change in family violence from 1975 to 1985 as revealed in two national surveys." *Journal of Marriage and the Family* 48 (1986): 465–479.

Straus, M. A., R. J. Gelles, and S. K. Steinmetz. *Behind Closed Doors: Violence in the American Family.* New York: Doubleday/Anchor, 1980.

Ten Bensel, R. L., M. Rheinberger, and S. X. Radbill. "Children in a world of violence: The roots of child maltreatment." In M. E. Helfer, R. S. Kempe, and R. D. Krugman, eds. *The Battered Child.* 4th ed. Chicago: University of Chicago Press, 1997, pp. 3–28.

U.S. Advisory Board on Child Abuse and Neglect. *A Nation's Shame: Fatal Child Abuse and Neglect in the United States.* Washington, D.C.: U.S. Department of Health and Human Services, 1995.

U.S. Department of Health and Human Services, Administration on Children, Youth and Families. *Child Maltreatment 1996: Reports from the States to the National Child Abuse and Neglect Data System.* Washington, D.C.: U.S. Government Printing Office, 1998.

Widom, C. S. *The Cycle of Violence.* Science 244 (1989a): 160–166.

———. "Child abuse, neglect, and violent criminal behavior." *Criminology* 27 (1989b): 251–271.

———. *Victims of Childhood Sexual Abuse—Later Criminal Consequences.* National Institute of Justice research in brief. Washington, D.C.: U.S. Department of Justice, Office of Justice Programs, 1995.

Wooley, P., and W. Evans. "Significance of skeletal lesions resembling those of traumatic origin." *Journal of the American Medical Association* 158 (1955): 539–543.

AAPC *See* AMERICAN ASSOCIATION FOR PROTECTING CHILDREN

ABA Center on Children and the Law Founded in 1978, this organization is sponsored by the Young Lawyers Division of the American Bar Association. Its staff provides services relating to issues about child abuse and neglect, missing and exploited children, adoption, learning disabilities, child support and foster care. It maintains a training and technical assistance program, the Resource Center for Child Welfare Programs, dealing with child advocacy and protection. It offers publications and a detailed web site. For more information, contact: ABA Center on Children and the Law, 740 15th St. NW, Washington, DC 20005. Tel. (800) 285-2221. Web site: www.abanet.org/child

abandonment Leaving a minor child alone for an extended period, depending on the definitions of the laws of the state or area. Criminal abandonment generally means that the caregiver, usually a parent, made no provisions for another adult to care for the child during an absence, particularly an infant or young child. Infants may be abandoned in hospitals or, much worse, in dumpsters or deserted areas where they are likely to die.

In the United States and other Western countries, parents who abandon the child can, in some cases, be charged with neglect. Each state has its own, different statute with regard to the legal definition of abandonment; these statutes apply not only to infants and small children but to adolescents as well. There are legal precedents for abandonment charges to be brought against parents who lock their teenage children out of the house.

Most states have statutes regarding criminal neglect and abandonment, although the laws and the penalties for violating such laws vary greatly.

Abandonment is a felony offense in some states and a misdemeanor in others. The age of the child who was abandoned is also addressed in some statutes; for example, it being a crime to abandon a child under 10, 12, or some other age. The federal ADOPTION AND SAFE FAMILIES ACT allows states to terminate the parental rights of parents of abandoned children after a hearing is held.

In non-Western countries, parents sometimes abandon their children (usually infants) at orphanages or in hospitals or churches because they are unable to care for them. They may hope that another family will adopt the child.

As of this writing, this practice is relatively common in China, where there is a state-imposed limit of one child per family. Most families want male children, and as a result, if a female child is born, she may be abandoned. Children are also abandoned in other countries, such as in Latin America, because the biological mother cannot care for her child but is too ashamed, in large part because of social stigma against unmarried mothers, to come forth and express her desire for the child to have another family. It may also be illegal or extremely difficult for her to openly arrange an adoption, depending on the laws of the country. Thus, abandonment may be seen as the only option.

abdominal injuries Abdominal trauma is a common but often overlooked result of physical abuse. Such trauma includes damage to kidneys, blood vessels, stomach, duodenum, small bowel, colon, pancreas, liver or spleen. Frequently more than one organ is affected. Because there are few outward signs of abdominal injuries, they may go untreated for extended periods of time, subjecting the child to a great deal of pain and sometimes resulting in death.

Injuries to the abdomen are usually caused by one of three forces: compression, crushing or acceleration. A blow to the midsection can compress organs filled with fluid or gas, causing them to rupture. Compression injuries most often affect the stomach and colon. Crushing of internal organs can occur when a blow to the front of the abdomen presses the organ against a hard structure such as the spinal column or rib cage. Rupture of the kidneys, pancreas, spleen or liver may result from such crushing. Rapid acceleration, such as when a child is thrown or struck so forcefully that he or she is knocked down, can tear connective tissue, resulting in hemorrhage or perforation of the small intestines.

A thorough screening for abdominal trauma is recommended when children show evidence of having been physically abused or when abuse is suspected. (*See also* GASTROINTESTINAL INJURIES.)

Norman S. Ellerstein, *Child Abuse and Neglect: A Medical Reference* (New York: John Wiley and Sons, 1981).

Alejandro Rodriguez, *Handbook of Child Abuse and Neglect* (Flushing, N.Y.: Medical Examination Publishing Co., 1977).

abduction   *See* CHILD STEALING.

abuse, adolescent   *See* ADOLESCENT ABUSE.

abuse, cycle of   *See* INTERGENERATIONAL CYCLE OF ABUSE.

abuse, drug   *See* SUBSTANCE ABUSE.

abuse, emotional   *See* PSYCHOLOGICAL MALTREATMENT.

abuse, incidence of   *See* INCIDENCE OF CHILD ABUSE.

abuse, indicators   *See* INDICATORS OF CHILD ABUSE AND NEGLECT.

abuse, institutional   *See* INSTITUTIONAL ABUSE AND NEGLECT.

abuse, neurological manifestations   *See* NEUROLOGICAL MANIFESTATIONS OF ABUSE AND NEGLECT.

abuse, passive   *See* PASSIVE ABUSER.

abuse, physical   *See* PHYSICAL ABUSE.

abuse, prediction of   *See* PREDICTION OF ABUSE AND NEGLECT.

abuse, psychological   *See* PSYCHOLOGICAL MALTREATMENT.

abuse, psychopathological   *See* PSYCHOPATHOLOGY.

abuse, sexual   *See* SEXUAL ABUSE.

abuse, sibling   *See* SIBLING ABUSE.

abuse, situational   *See* SITUATIONAL ABUSE AND NEGLECT.

abuse, social   *See* SOCIAL ABUSE.

abuse, spouse   *See* SPOUSE ABUSE.

abuse, substance   *See* SUBSTANCE ABUSE.

abuse, verbal   *See* VERBAL ABUSE.

abused children, placement   *See* PLACEMENT OF ABUSED CHILDREN.

abusive parents   *See* CHARACTERISTICS OF ABUSING AND NEGLECTFUL PARENTS.

acting out   The term *acting out* is often used to refer to aggressive or socially undesirable behavior displayed by children or adults. Some mental health professionals see such behavior as an outward manifestation of internal (intrapsychic) conflict. According to psychodynamic theory, individuals may act out feelings that, because of their highly sensitive emotional content, are difficult to discuss directly. In some cases these feelings may be unconscious.

Psychodynamic theorists and practitioners often attribute abusive behavior of parents to the expression of repressed or unconscious feelings. Abusive behavior directed toward a child may be traced to internal conflicts that have little direct connection with the child. Based on this theoretical model, treatment of abusers focuses on helping the patient to become aware of internal conflicts and to address these problems in a more effective and socially acceptable manner.

Acting out may partially explain the behavior of abusers. When displayed by a child, however, it may help to identify him or her as a possible victim of abuse. Though antisocial behavior is a feature of normal child development some behaviors are associated with maltreatment.

Sexually abused children may display sexual knowledge and aggressiveness beyond that expected for their age. Conversely, some child victims may display fear and/or aggression toward all males. Behaviors that have no apparent rational basis may lead the trained child protection worker to question the child further.

In adolescents, running away from home and sexual promiscuity are often connected to abuse. Studies of runaways show a high incidence of incest and other forms of abuse.

Physically abused children sometimes display extreme aggression toward other children. This behavior may be seen as an attempt by the child to gain control over his or her life. A child, defenseless against physical attacks by an adult, may become abusive toward other children as a way of acting out aggressive feelings that cannot be expressed safely in the presence of the abuser.

Most child development experts agree that a certain amount of acting out is to be expected of children. These experts caution, however, that such behavior should be examined closely when it is persistent and extreme.

addiction, infantile Infants born to drug-addicted mothers are at great risk of being addicted at birth. Withdrawal symptoms usually appear during the first 24 hours following birth. Severity of symptoms is proportional to the quantity of any drug used on a daily or frequent basis by the mother. Symptoms frequently observed in infants experiencing narcotic withdrawal are listed in the following table.

While most acute symptoms of infantile addiction disappear within 10 days of birth, follow-up studies have shown that these infants continue to appear irritable, restless and unresponsive for up to a year. They need frequent feeding, tend to regurgitate often and require almost constant attention. These characteristics would challenge even a non-addicted mother and increase the likelihood that the infant will be physically abused by the primary caretaker if or when she continues to use drugs. (*See* "AT RISK" CHILDREN.)

In a study reported in a 1998 issue of the *Journal of Perinatology,* researchers studied the impact of fetal crack cocaine exposure on infants. The babies who were born addicted to cocaine had more medical and neurological problems than the control group. Their head circumferences, heights and weights were less than those of the control group and they were also more likely to have been born prematurely. Cocaine-exposed infants usually stay in the hospital longer (by at least one day) than nonaddicted infants.

According to a study of drug-exposed children in Jacksonville, Florida, reported in a 1997 issue of *Pediatrics,* the cocaine-exposed infants were in the hospital for an average of three days versus the two days the nonexposed infants spent in the hospital.

NEONATAL WITHDRAWAL SYMPTOMS

Tremors
Irritability
Tachypnea (unusually rapid respiration)
Muscular rigidity
Diarrhea
Watery stools
Vomiting
Shrill crying
Excessive perspiration
Sneezing
Yawning
Fever
Myoclonic jerks (erratic muscular spasms)
Convulsions

Hospital expenses were $7,054 for the addicted infants and $3,058 for the nonaddicted infants.

Some studies of children born addicted to cocaine have revealed outcomes far better than the severe outcomes that had been predicted in the mid- to early 1980s; however, the children appear more likely to experience learning disabilities and other problems, such as attention deficit hyperactivity disorder (ADHD). On the other hand, the children may be more prone to ADHD because they inherited the predisposition from their impulsive biological parents, who themselves may have had ADHD.

Laws on Protection of Drug-Exposed Infants

A small number of states have enacted laws that require physicians to report drugs in a newborn infant. Laws may also require the state social services department or another organization to monitor a drug-addicted infant and his or her mother shortly after birth. Some states take into account the mother's use of illegal drugs during the pregnancy.

A Minnesota law passed in 1999 can require the addicted mother to enter drug rehabilitation. The Minnesota statute says, "If the report alleges a pregnant woman's use of a controlled substance for a nonmedical purpose, the local welfare agency shall immediately conduct an appropriate assessment and offer service indicated under the circumstances. Services offered may include, but are not limited to, a referral for chemical dependency assessment, a referral for chemical dependency treatment if recommended, and a referral for prenatal care. The local welfare agency may also take any appropriate action, including seeking an emergency admission pursuant to the law. The local welfare agency shall seek an emergency admission if the pregnant woman refuses recommended voluntary services or fails recommended treatment." (MINN. STAT. ANN § 626.5561 [1999])

Such laws are controversial because some legal experts challenge whether a pregnant woman's drug-taking behavior can legally be used against her because of its effect on the fetus. Others are concerned about laws that affect both a mother and her newborn baby, requiring social services to become involved if the baby tests positive for drugs.

They feel that the mother may not seek medical treatment if she fears legal or punitive action will be taken against her. Several states have included in their laws that the new mother who is an illicit drug user will not be referred to police but rather to social services personnel.

As of this writing in 1999, the following states have statutes related to drug-exposed infants: Arizona, California, Illinois, Iowa, Michigan, Minnesota, Missouri, Oklahoma, Utah and Virginia. (*See* "AT RISK" CHILDREN.)

addiction, maternal   *See* MATERNAL DRUG DEPENDENCE.

adjudicatory hearing   Once charges of abuse or neglect have been filed, a court hearing is held to determine the extent to which these charges are supported by admissible evidence. If insufficient evidence is presented, a judge may decide not to proceed with a trial. A trial may be scheduled if, in the judge's opinion, there is sufficient evidence to warrant further consideration of the charges. An adjudicatory hearing may also be called a "fact-finding" hearing. (*See also* EVIDENCE.)

adolescent abuse   Abuse of adolescents has attracted less public attention than maltreatment of children. Many assume that the age of the child is relatively unimportant or that adolescents are better able to defend themselves and thus adolescent abuse is less serious. Yet, the abuse of adolescents can have profound and lifelong impacts on the adolescents, their peers and others with whom they interact.

Available data indicate that adolescent abuse is, in many ways, significantly different from abuse of children under the age of 12. Psychological and sexual abuse levels are higher among adolescents. Adolescents receive less serious injuries as a result of abuse, reflecting both fewer physical assaults and a greater ability to protect themselves.

Boys are at greatest risk of abuse during early childhood, becoming less susceptible as they grow older. Conversely, girls are more likely to be abused as they grow older, particularly in the case of SEXUAL ABUSE.

Some abuse of adolescents is a continuation of an abusive pattern that began in early childhood. In other cases abuse of adolescents is a new phenomenon brought on by a complex set of factors. Children may outgrow methods of parental control that relied heavily on use of physical force, indulgence or intrusion. Abusive families may be less able to adapt to these changes, thereby increasing the level of conflict.

Adolescents at high risk of abuse often have more poorly developed social skills and display more negative behavior than their peers. The combination of an aggressive or defiant adolescent with a parent who uses a harsh or inappropriate parenting style greatly increases the likelihood of abuse.

Abuse and Runaways

A disproportionate number of adolescents who run away from home are victims of abuse. Studies show that abused adolescents tend to run farther from home and stay away longer than those with no history of maltreatment. Further, the act of running away greatly increases the likelihood of sexual abuse for both boys and girls. Runaways, particularly those who have been sexually abused, often fall into prostitution as a means of supporting themselves. One study found that 60% of runaways involved in prostitution had been sexually abused at home. Another study of adolescents housed in a Canadian runaway shelter found that 38% of boys and 73% of girls had been sexually molested.

Not all adolescent runaways leave home by choice. Statistics show that 10% to 25% of adolescents housed in runaway programs had been put out of their homes by their parents. These adolescents are considered victims of parental neglect, just as infants are abandoned by their parents. (*See also* ABANDONMENT.)

Sexual Abuse and Psychological Maltreatment and Consequences

A Canadian study reported in a 1997 issue of *Development and Psychopathology* looked at the impact of perceived and actual abuse among adolescents and the victims' subsequent adjustment. Researchers studied 160 children (70 boys and 90 girls) ages 11–17, with a mean age of about 14 years. Most (96%) were white, with a small percentage of blacks and Native Canadians. Most of the children (68%) came from families receiving public assistance and most (about 69%) had been in child services custody more than once.

All the children had experienced abuse, as documented by child protective services. About one-third had been sexually abused and about two-thirds had experienced physical abuse. Most (87%) had also experienced neglect or psychological maltreatment (92%). The researchers interviewed and tested the children, reviewed the child protective service records and also interviewed and tested caretakers.

The researchers found that PSYCHOLOGICAL MALTREATMENT had the most significant impact on the negative behavior of the adolescents studied, and it also seemed to make the effects of physical or sexual abuse worse.

One interesting finding was that when there was a discrepancy between the adolescent's perception of sexual abuse and documented abuse in social service records, greater maladjustment then occurred. For example, the best adjustment occurred when both the adolescent and the record reflected no sexual abuse. However, the next best level of adjustment occurred when the adolescent and the record reflected that sexual abuse *did* occur. In contrast, the poorest levels of adjustment occurred when sexual abuse was documented in the record but it was denied by the adolescent OR when abuse was not documented in the record but it was reported by the adolescent.

Interestingly, these findings for sexual abuse did not also hold in the case of psychological maltreatment. Instead, as the perception of actual psychological maltreatment increased, so did the stress and maladjustment of the adolescent. Thus, learning about and accepting psychological maltreatment caused greater maladjustment than learning about and accepting sexual abuse.

Said the researchers, "One might speculate that as youths' 'eyes are opened' to a harsh emotional family climate, their attachment system comes under new strain—the resulting conflict produces acute inner pain. If this finding is borne out in future research, one implication is that clinicians must tread carefully when helping youth recognize ongoing psychological maltreatment."

Why did stress and acting-out behavior decrease with the acceptance of previous sexual abuse but increase with acceptance of psychological abuse? The researchers said, "One might speculate that a psychical experience such as sexual abuse is more difficult to deny or minimize, and that such denial would result in more serious affective and behavioral distortion."

The researchers also found gender differences, in that females were more likely to exhibit behavior problems than were males in response to psychological maltreatment, and they speculated that females might have a "developmentally greater vulnerability to parental criticism and hostility."

Abuse and Antisocial Behavior

In another study of abuse and adolescents, researchers used questionnaires on 4,790 public school children in grades 8, 10 and 12 in the state of Washington. The goal was to determine if abuse was linked to antisocial and suicidal behavior.

Students were asked "Have you ever been abused or mistreated by an adult?" (which researchers considered "abuse") and "Has anyone ever touched you in a sexual place, or made you touch them, when you did not want them to?" (which researchers considered "molestation").

Antisocial behavior among students was determined by responses to questions on whether the student had ever carried a handgun, sold illegal drugs, stolen a motor vehicle, been arrested or taken a handgun to school. Questions about suicidal behavior ranged from questions about having suicidal thoughts to making a suicide plan through making an actual suicide attempt.

Most students (about 74%) did not report abuse. With regard to antisocial behavior, about 18% reported one or more such acts. About 7% reported a suicide attempt.

The researchers found a positive correlation between mild and severe antisocial behavior and abuse and molestation. They also found a significant correlation between abuse or molestation and suicidal thoughts and behavior. They noted that "[t]he associations were especially strong for the more severe forms of the behaviors (such as injurious suicide attempts) and for the combination of antisocial and suicidal behaviors."

Although not all children who exhibit antisocial or suicidal behavior are abuse victims, it is possible that abuse could be an underlying factor for some children.

Sometimes It Is Their Own Peers Who Torment Adolescents

In a Canadian study of abused adolescents, researchers found a significant correlation between sexual harassment of female adolescents and their subsequent attempts at suicide. Females who experienced more sexual harassment by their male peers were more likely to be emotionally disturbed and more likely to make suicide attempts.

Abuse Affects Relationships

Abuse also can have a profound impact on the way the adolescent interacts with peers in friendship and dating relationships. In a study reported in a 1998 issue of *Development and Psychopathology,* researchers studied 132 abused teenagers and compared them to 227 nonabused teens. The average age of the teens was about 15 years. Researchers found significant differences between the maltreated adolescents and the nonabused teens.

For example, the abused adolescents had more hostility and problems related to closeness and trust in intimate relationships. Abused adolescents were significantly more negative and hostile toward dates or friends of the opposite sex than were nonabused teens. The authors said, "Adolescents who were abused as children appear to choose partners who continue to act abusively toward them (and to whom they can act abusively as well)." (*See also* ADOLESCENT PERPETRATORS, SUICIDE.)

Lillian Southwick Bensley, et al., "Self-Reported Abuse History and Adolescent Problem Behaviors. I. Antisocial and Suicidal Behaviors," *Journal of Adolescent Health* 24 (1999): pp. 163–172.

Robin A. McGee, et al., "Multiple Maltreatment Experiences and Adolescent Behavior Problems: Adolescents' Perspectives," *Development and Psychopathology* 9 (1977): 131–149.

David A. Wolfe, et al., "Factors Associated with Abusive Relationships Among Maltreated and Nonmaltreated Youth," *Development and Psychopathology* 10 (1998): 61–85.

adolescent perpetrator network This multidisciplinary group, based at the Kempe National Center at the University of Colorado School of Medicine (*see* APPENDIX 1 for complete listing), was conceived as a way of providing support for professionals working with adolescent offenders. Currently, the Network serves over 300 individuals who work specifically with adolescent perpetrators of SEXUAL ABUSE. Information about Network services can be found in a newsletter, *Interchange*. An annotated bibliography prepared by the Network contains material on adolescent sex offenders and their treatment. (*See also* ADOLESCENT PERPETRATORS OF SEXUAL ABUSE.)

adolescent perpetrators of sexual abuse The extent of SEXUAL ABUSE perpetrated by adolescents is unknown; however, many who work with adult sex offenders believe it to be a serious problem. Adolescent perpetrators may engage in sexually abusive or exploitative behavior toward dates or friends or while employed as babysitters. Like adult child molesters, adolescent offenders are predominantly male and usually known to their victims.

The amount of sibling-to-sibling abuse is thought to be greatly underreported. Parents may view it as harmless sexual play or may be embarrassed to talk about it with others outside the family. In some cases, sexual abuse by a sibling can have more harmful effects on the victim than an incident involving an extrafamilial offender, especially if allowed to continue over an extended period of time. Sexual abuse by a sibling often involves a high degree of coercion. As with other forms of INCEST this type of exploitation may make it difficult for the victim to form trusting relationships and may result in marital difficulty and a sexual dysfunction later in life.

Sexual abuse by adolescents is often passed off as experimentation or diagnosed as an adolescent adjustment reaction. Many professionals who work with adolescents are reluctant to label them as sex offenders. Adolescents who sexually molest children or other adolescents are seldom brought to court.

Recent evidence indicates that many incarcerated adult sex offenders began their sexually abusive behavior as adolescents. Some professionals who work with sex offenders believe that the seriousness of adolescent sexual assault has been minimized. Some argue that the failure of court- and youth-serving institutions to intervene effectively in such behavior has prevented young offenders from receiving treatment at a critical period. Repeat adult offenders have proven to be especially resistant to treatment. Treatment providers believe that these adult offenders may have been more amenable to intervention at an earlier age.

Another problem associated with the failure to recognize the seriousness of sexual abuse perpetrated by adolescents is that offenses often go undocumented. In the absence of a record of past assaults each offense may be treated as an isolated incident. Young offenders can sometimes engage in a number of assaults before being charged with a criminal offense.

A large number of adolescent sexual offenders are themselves victims of sexual abuse. This fact suggests that, like PHYSICAL ABUSE, there may be a cyclical pattern to sexual abuse. Most psychotherapists believe early intervention with victims as well as offenders is an effective way to break the CYCLE OF ABUSE.

Though relatively little research has been done on the problem of adolescent sex offenders, most treatment providers agree that it is important for them to be held accountable for their behavior. Further, most providers believe treatment should be specific to the problem and should combine individual treatment with peer group and family counseling. Court involvement can be helpful in making sure offenders follow through with treatment recommendations.

adopting abused or neglected children Many of the abused or neglected children adopted by North Americans are adopted from the foster care system; however, many others are adopted from foreign orphanages where they may have experienced abuse and neglect at the hands of caregivers and/or other children. Experts say there are many similarities between foster children in the West and children in orphanages from other countries, including health problems, emotional disorders and adjustment difficulties. In both cases, children adopted at earlier ages generally tend to adapt the most successfully to new families; however, infants and young children may still be at risk from FETAL ALCO-HOL SYNDROME, malnutrition and other problems.

In the U.S.

From October 1, 1996 to September 30, 1997 (the latest data as of this writing), 15,548 foster children were adopted in the U.S. Numbers for subsequent years are likely to be somewhat higher because of the enactment of new legislation promoting adoption and providing states with additional funds and incentives for children who are adopted.

With the passage of the ADOPTION AND SAFE FAMI-LIES ACT OF 1997, the federal government in the U.S. changed the emphasis from family reunification of foster children with their biological families to an emphasis on the safety of the child. Reunification was still a goal; however, if the child continued to be at risk for abuse, then termination of parental rights was made a stated goal for children so that they could be adopted. If the children could be cared for by relatives, this was another goal, also known as KINSHIP CARE. However, one problem with kinship care is that the abusive parent may still have access to the child. In addition, the grandparent or other relative of the abusive parent might also be an abuser.

Children from Non-Western Countries

In 1998, nearly 16,000 children were adopted from other countries by Americans and about 2,000 were adopted by Canadians, doubling the number of intercountry adoptions that had occurred a decade before. The children who were adopted in the late 1990s from other countries were very different from the children adopted in past years; for example, until the late 1980s most children adopted from other countries came from Korea. Few Korean children had been abused and both health care and child care in Korea were adequate. In stark contrast, health care and child care for children in Romania and the countries that comprised the former Soviet Union were much less favorable, exposing many of the children to bad conditions. Many people who took pity on images of children in orphanages and who later adopted the children were shocked by the children's physical and emotional states. Many of the children have made astonishing progress since their adoptions, but some continue to have serious

difficulties because of the severe neglect they suffered in the orphanages.

Adaptations Abused Children Must Make to Adoptive Families

Experts say that children who were abused or neglected often developed specific behavior patterns that enabled them to survive. Although these behaviors were effective in an abusive family, they are maladaptive in a healthy family. Adoptive parents who do not realize that the child needs time to adapt to his or her new family can have difficulties in parenting the child.

In her article "Resilience in Maltreated Children: Implications for Special Needs Adoption" (in *Child Welfare*), author Darla L. Henry describes five overall themes of abused children who were resilient in coping with their abusive families. She explains that these themes encompass coping skills that worked well in an abusive family but do not work well at all in a normal family. However, the children need time to adjust to their new, nonabusive family before changing their coping strategies and behavior.

The first theme was "loyalty to parents." Although the biological parents were abusive, the resilient adolescents remained convinced that their parents loved them and they also expressed love for the parents. Despite their loyalty, however, the children were able to separate the parents' abusive behaviors from themselves, i.e., the children did not internalize the abuse in their own minds—they did not think that the abuse was their fault nor did they think that they deserved it.

This loyalty, however, can be very difficult for adoptive parents and others to accept. They may wish to challenge the loyalty, seeing it as maladaptive. Some adoptive parents may try to prevent the child from talking about the past and his or her parents, which can be very difficult for the child because he or she is trying to integrate the past with the new life. Experts say that the belief in the parents' love may be needed by the child. In addition, the child may also need to talk about the past and try to make sense of what has happened to him or her.

The second theme, "normalizing the abusive environment," was an acceptance of their lives with the abusive parents. Although the resilient children did not see abuse as acceptable, they did view it as routine for their former abusive family. In this way, they avoided the feeling of being trapped and helpless. The author said, "Normalizing the environment results in predictability for the children who, expecting possible abuse, can plan ways to avoid situations when their parents may be more included to be abusive."

The child who normalized the abusive world may seem aloof and overly independent to adoptive parents, who often perceive children as dependent or weak. The adoptive parents may also feel that it is important for the child to see that in the past, he or she was victimized; however, Henry notes that pressing the child to perceive himself or herself as a victim can be confusing to the child's self-image.

The third theme was "invisibility to the abuser." It reflects the children's ability to maintain a very low profile and especially to avoid the abusive parent when indications were that he or she was upset and likely to abuse the child. If they were unable to be physically absent, the children fantasized or daydreamed. The children may also have used lying and manipulation to avoid abuse.

In their new adoptive family, dishonesty, avoiding family members and other coping strategies that worked in the abusive home are not effective at all; however, experts say the child needs to develop a sense of safety before truly joining the family in his or her own mind. This does not mean such behaviors are acceptable: it is an explanation rather than an excuse.

The fourth theme, "Self-Value," reflected the adolescents' abilities to see themselves as persons of worth. Said the author, "Professionals saw a 'toughness' in children who succeed after experiencing an abusive home. By not showing weaknesses, children actually reinforce strengths within themselves and enhance their self-value. Knowing that they can be strong and withstand the abuse enhances the value they place on themselves."

Such children have also learned self-confidence and may be risk takers, traits adoptive parents need to understand and deal with.

Lastly, the fifth theme was "Future Vision," meaning that the abused children had developed the ability to imagine a future for themselves and think beyond the immediate moment. They also had positive expectations for the future and planned to graduate from high school, obtain employment and lead successful lives.

A positive future vision is generally not a problem for adoptive parents; however, again, they need to understand that part of the child's life was the life he or she led before joining the adoptive family. By accepting the "whole child," the new parents can enable the child to succeed at future goals.

Children Who Were Sexually Abused

Children with behavioral or emotional problems are usually difficult for adoptive parents to deal with. Beyond this group, experts report that sexually abused children are the most difficult children for adoptive parents to cope with. First, the idea of sexual abuse of a child is extremely troubling and offensive to most people. Second, the child may exhibit overly sexual behaviors or even make overtures toward a parent or other family member because this is how he or she was reared. These behaviors may be very distressing to the adoptive parent.

In an article entitled "The Impact of Previous Sexual Abuse on Children's Adjustment in Adoptive Placement" in *Social Work,* researchers Susan Livingston-Smith and Jeanne A. Howard compared the adoptive placements of 35 children who had been sexually abused with 113 children who, as far as was known, had not been sexually abused. They found six behaviors that were significantly more problematic among the sexually abused children, before and also after the adoptive placement. These behaviors were sexual acting out, tantrums, lying, defiance, profanity and vandalism. For example, about 37% of the sexually abused children threw tantrums before the adoption. This did not change after the adoption: 37% still had tantrums. In contrast, before the adoption about 17% of the non–sexually abused children had tantrums. After the adoption, the percentage dropped somewhat, to 15%.

In looking at problems with lying, it was found that 40% of the sexually abused children lied before the adoption and the lying actually increased to nearly 46% after the adoption. However, in the non–sexually abused group of children, about 23% lied before the adoption and that number fell to about 16% after the adoption.

Sexually abused children also had much more difficulty in attaching to their new family. About 34% of this group had trouble attaching to their new mother, while this was a problem for only about 14% of the non–sexually abused children.

These factors do not mean that it is impossible to have a successful relationship with an adopted child who had been sexually abused. Rather, it means that parents should be fully prepared and aware of potential problems ahead of time. Study after study has revealed that adoptive parents who were told ahead of time, before the adoption, about problems that children experienced in the past are much more likely to establish successful parental relationships. This is true no matter what type of problem the child experienced or what type of abuse he or she has encountered.

Christine Adamec and William L. Pierce, Ph.D., *The Encyclopedia of Adoption.* Revised ed. (New York: Facts On File, Inc., 2000).

Darla L. Henry, "Resilience in Maltreated Children: Implications for Special Needs Adoption," *Child Welfare* 78, no. 5 (1999): 519–540.

Susan Livingston Smith and Jeanne A. Howard, "The Impact of Previous Sexual Abuse on Children's Adjustment in Adoptive Placement," *Social Work* 39, no. 5 (1994): pp. 491–501.

Adoption and Safe Families Act of 1997   Refers to the federal law that directed U.S. states on actions to take regarding children in foster care and mandated states to consider the child's safety as paramount. The new law, commonly known as ASFA, was primarily an effort to correct problems which stemmed in part from the ADOPTION AND CHILD WELFARE ACT OF 1980, the most recent child welfare law prior to ASFA.

Attempt to Decrease the Number of Children in Foster Care: The 1980 Law Failed

Although the primary goal of the Adoption Assistance and Child Welfare Act of 1980 was to decrease the number of children in foster care, the law itself, along with other societal factors (for example, the increased use of illegal drugs such as cocaine), ultimately had the opposite effect: The number of children in foster care increased to as many as 500,000 by 1996, nearly double the number in care in 1982. By the time states were initiat-ing action to terminate parental rights so that the children could be adopted, many had been in care for years (or in and out of care) and were adoles-cents. Many children "aged out" in the system and were never adopted, including children who entered foster care as infants or toddlers.

Some of the key problems underlying the foster care system, the old law and ASFA solutions are described below.

"Reasonable Efforts" Undefined

The 1980 act had caused confusion in its require-ment for states to make "reasonable efforts" to reunite children with their biological families. Since states had to follow the law in order to obtain federal funds, the law was very important to states and in many cases, it was interpreted to mean that children should *always* be returned to parents. In some states, social workers placed children with parents who had tortured, sexually abused or chronically abused their children. In effect, children were forcibly sent back to situations which adults would never agree to go to—nor would they have to. For example, a battered woman can leave an abusive husband, as difficult as it may be. But state "protective services" staff were compelling children to return to abusive parents.

In addition, common sense often seemed to take a back seat to reunifying all families. In some cases, children were placed back (or simply not removed from the home) even when parents had murdered or tortured other children. Some experts termed children who had been returned to their parents and then killed "reunification murders."

In effect, the old law equalized all abusive par-ents by the underlying assumption that with suffi-cient effort by social services personnel, all families could be reunited.

In a 1999 article for the *University of Illinois Law Review,* Cristine Kim said,

> In some cases, no amount of effort could help reha-bilitate a parent, but state agencies assumed that they must try anyway. When children were returned to abusive parents, they were often reabused and came back to foster care. Worse yet, some were killed by their abusive parents. Sadly, abuse and neglect is the number one killer of children age four and under. Of those killed, almost half had been previously investi-gated by state child welfare agencies.

In contrast, ASFA does not require that efforts be made to reunite children with their families in cases where the child was abandoned or would be in danger of sexual abuse, chronic physical abuse or torture or when another sibling was murdered or tortured. In those cases, a permanency hearing would be held within 30 days. Said Kim,

> The rationale behind the reasonable efforts requirement under AACWA was that children are always better off with their natural parents. This has been shown to be untrue, for adoptive or other substitute parents can be just as loving, if not more so, than a child's natural parents. Under ASFA, the message is clear: the "rights" of parents to their children are not so great as to justify jeopardizing children's health and safety.

ASFA provided guidance on what constituted "reasonable efforts" and also in what cases mandatory reasonable efforts need not be made, such as in the case of a child who had been tortured or a sibling who had been severely abused or murdered, among other circumstances.

The Old Law Allowed Children to Remain in Foster Care for Years

ASFA requires that a permanency plan be made within 12 months of a child's entry into foster care and also sets rules on the termination of parental rights. For example, it requires a plan for TERMINATION OF PARENTAL RIGHTS if the child has been in foster care for 15 of the past 22 months.

There are several exceptions to the 15-month requirement, such as when the child is in KINSHIP CARE (living with a relative) or when there is a "compelling reason" that termination of parental rights would not be in the child's best interest.

The law requires a formal permanency plan, which must be created at the one-year point; however, a problem in the past, and one which continues, is that it is often difficult to successfully treat people with drug or alcohol abuse problems within one year. Experts say that such individuals make up as much as two-thirds of all biological parents of foster children. On the other hand, they are also more likely to reabuse and neglect their children and they are a key reason why so many children are in care, as social workers seek to resolve family problems.

Congress decided that the child's safety and the child's "timeline" were paramount, which is another reason for the time limitations in ASFA. To a child, a month or a year is much longer than to an adult. For example, a year to a five-year-old is almost unfathomably long. For this reason, it is important to make permanency plans in a timely manner.

Financial Incentives Worked to Keep Children in Foster Care

Under the old law, states received funds for family preservation and for children in foster care. Thus, in effect, the 1980 act provided financial incentives for states with children remaining in foster care, incentives that would be lost if a child were adopted. ASFA instituted financial incentives for adoption, while at the same time funds were to be provided to assist families to recover from the problems that had led to children being placed in foster care. Under the old law, if a child was adopted, the family did not receive funds. Thus, there was a financial disincentive for states and for social service offices to move foster children into adoption.

In contrast, in addition to continuing family preservation funds, ASFA provided for "adoption incentive payments" to states, providing $4,000 per child who is adopted out of foster care and $6,000 for a child with special needs (considered hard to place) who is adopted. Bonuses were also included that would pay states that increased their number of adoptions. (These programs will end in 2002, unless they are reauthorized.)

On September 24, 1999, President Bill Clinton announced bonus awards of $20 million to 35 states that had increased the number of children who were adopted from foster care. In addition, President Clinton announced $5.5 million in grants to programs that would remove barriers to adoption. One step to that end began in 1999: two organizations, the National Center for Adoption and Children Awaiting Placement (CAP) in partnership launched a web site on the Internet to promote the adoption of children with special needs: Faces of Adoption: America's Waiting Children (www.adopt.org).

Switching from Foster Care to an Adoption Plan Took Time

Another reason why foster children remained in care for so many years was that once the decision was made to terminate parental rights, the adoption unit of social services would need to make an adoption plan. This involved a paradigm shift from family reunification to adoption and it also caused practical problems. The foster care worker had to turn the case over to the adoption worker. The foster care worker might not have provided the documentation needed to terminate parental rights, so that documentation had to be gathered. It also took time to decide what kind of family the child needed and to locate such a family.

To address this problem, ASFA allowed for "concurrent planning," which means that states can work toward reunifying a family but can also make a plan to find an adoptive family for the child in care should the reunification not work out.

Many States Changed Their Laws to Comply with ASFA

As a result of the enactment of ASFA, most states changed their laws to be in compliance with ASFA. (See the charts "State Legislation in Response to ASFA" and "Mandatory Cases in Which Reasonable Efforts Shall Not Be Required.")

Another key provision of ASFA was that it listed specific circumstances under which states could require the termination of parental rights. Because termination of parental rights is such a serious step, forever severing the parental rights of a parent to a child, states do not take this provision lightly. However, many states have enacted laws incorporating key provisions of ASFA into their laws. (See the chart at the end of this essay, "Required Initiation of Termination of Parental Rights Proceedings.")

Will ASFA Be Effective?

Many experts have lauded ASFA. Others, although supportive, note that the Adoption Assistance and Child Welfare Act of 1980 was equally well-meaning but did not play out as Congress had intended. Such people worry that the loopholes in the law will enable states to keep children in foster care indefinitely.

Attorney and author Elizabeth Bartholet has made positive statements about ASFA, but she is also among those who remain unsure if its intention will be carried forth. In her book *Nobody's Children: Abuse and Neglect, Foster Drift, and the Adoption Alternative* (Beacon Press, 1999) Bartholet says,

STATE LEGISLATION IN RESPONSE TO ASFA

State	Enactment
Alabama	Acts 98-370; 98-372 (1998)
Alaska	Chap. 99 (1998)
Arizona	Chap. 276 (1998)
Arkansas	Act 401, 328 (1999)
California	Chap. 1056 (1998)
Colorado	Chap. 311 (1998); H.B. 99-1299 (1999)
Connecticut	P.A. 98-241 (1998); P.A. 99-166 (1999)
Delaware	Chap. 71-317 (1998)
Florida	Chap. 403 (1998)
Georgia	Act 872 (1998)
Hawaii	S.B. 2987 (1998); H.B. 1117 (1999)
Idaho	Chap. 257; S.C.R. 124 (1998)
Illinois	P.A. 90-608 (1998)
Indiana	Act 425 (1998); P.L. 197-1999 (1999)
Iowa	Chap. 1190 (1998)
Kansas	Chap. 139
Kentucky	Chap. 57 (1998)
Louisiana	H.B. 827 (1999); H.B. 1067 (1999); H.B. 544 (1999)
Maine	Chap. 715 (1998)
Maryland	Chap. 539 (1998)
Massachusetts	Chap. 3 (1999)
Michigan	P.A. 383 (1998)
Minnesota	Chap. 406 (1998)
Mississippi	Chap. 516 (1998); Chap. 569 (1999)
Missouri	H.B. 1822; S.B. 674 (1998)
Montana	Chap. 566 (1999)
Nebraska	L.B. 1041; 1041A (1998)
Nevada	Chap. 435 (1999)
New Hampshire	Chap. 133 (1999)
New Jersey	Chap. 22, 53 (1999)
New Mexico	Chap. 77 (1999)
New York	Chap. 7 (1999)
North Carolina	Chap. 98-229 (1998)
North Dakota	S.B. 2171 (1999)
Ohio	H.B. 484 (1998)
Oklahoma	Chaps. 421, 415, 414 (1998)
Oregon	Chap. 859 (1999)
Pennsylvania	Act 126 (1998)
Rhode Island	Chap. 87 (1998)
South Carolina	Act 391 (1998)
South Dakota	H.B. 1306 (1998)
Tennessee	Chap. 1097 (1998)
Texas	H.B. 1622 (1999)
Utah	Chap. 274 (1998); H.B. 156 (1999)
Vermont	Act 139 (1998)
Virginia	Chap. 550 (1998)
Washington	Chap. 314 (1998)

State	Enactment
West Virginia	S.B. 773 (1998)
Wisconsin	Act 237 (1998)
Wyoming	Chap. 111, 44 (1998); Chap. 156 (1999)
District of Columbia	Act 13-117 (1999)

Source: National Conference of State Legislatures, 1999.

"ASFA is filled with loopholes and exceptions which could potentially undermine Congress's apparent intent. It's understandable that Congress would have wanted to leave the states plenty of room to decide how to administer their child protection systems. This has traditionally been an area for state and not federal regulation. But ASFA may have left too much room for those in the child welfare system who are committed to family preservation to resist and evade ASFA's apparent purpose."

For example, the law allows for KINSHIP CARE and if a child is living with a relative, the provisions for termination of parental rights are not required. Another loophole in the law is that if the state fails to provide family services that are needed before the child can return home, then they do not have to terminate parental rights. Bureaucracies are notoriously slow and underfunded, so this provision might undercut the intentions of ASFA.

REQUIRED INITIATION OF TERMINATION OF PARENTAL RIGHTS PROCEEDINGS

Child in foster care for 15 of most recent 22 months	AL, AK, CA, CT, GA, ID, IL, IN, IA, KS, ME, MD, MA, MN (for children in placement on day after enactment), MO, MT, NE, NH (12/22), NC, ND, NY, OH (12/22), OK, PA, RI, SC, TN, WV, WI
Child is abandoned	AL, AK, CT, GA, IN, IA, IL, KS, ME, MD, MA, MI, MN, MO, MT, NE, NC, ND, NJ, NY, OH, OK, PA, RI, SC, TN, TX, UT, WV, WI
Parent has committed murder of another child of parent	AL, CT, GA, IL (any child), IN, IA, KS, ME, MD (crime of violence), MA, MI, MN (crimes under "egregious harm"), MO, MT, NE, NC, ND, NJ, NY, OH, OK, PA, RI, SC, TN, UT, WV, WI
Parent has committed voluntary manslaughter of another child of parent	AL, CT, GA, IN, IL (2nd deg. murder), IA, KS, ME, MD (crime of violence), MA, MN (crimes under "egregious harm"), MO, MT, NE, NC, ND, NJ, NY, OH, OK, PA, RI, SC, TN, UT, WV, WI
Parent has aided, abetted, attempted or conspired to commit murder or manslaughter of another child of parent	AL, CT, GA, IL (murder of any child), IN, IA, KS, ME, MD (crime of violence), MI (murder), MO, NE, NC, OH, OK, PA, RI, SC, TN, UT, WV, WI
Parent has committed felony assault resulting in serious bodily injury to child or another child of parent	AL, CT, GA, IA, IL, IN, KS, ME, MD (crime of violence), MA, MI, MN (crimes under "egregious harm"), MO, MT, ND, NE, NJ, NY, OK, PA, RI, SC, TN, UT, WV, WI
Failure to remedy conduct or conditions	AK, NJ
Child's best interest	AK, AZ, NJ
If child is not returned home within 12 months and case plan is not extended	CA, FL, MI, NJ, RI
Court has determined the existence of aggravated circumstances and/or that reasonable efforts are not required	AK, AR (filing req'd if perm. goal is TPR), CA (court shall determine whether to hold TPR hearing), IA, IN, KS (when adoption or guardianship in child's best interest), ME, MT, OH, PA, WA (if in child's best interest)
Other	IL (aggravated sexual assault), MI (certain criminal sexual conduct; sibling TPR; torture), MS (child placed in custody of relative), MN (other crimes under "egregious harm"), RI (cruel and abusive conduct), WV (sibling TPR)

Source: National Conference of State Legislatures.

AGGRAVATED CIRCUMSTANCES

1. Abandonment of child	AL, AK, AR, CA, CO, CT, DE, GA, ID, IN, IA, KS, LA, ME, MS, MT, NE, NJ, NV, ND, NC, OH, OK, RI, SC, TN, TX, UT, WA, WV, WI
2. "Torture" of child	AL, AK, GA, ID, KS, LA, ME, MD, MS, MT, NE, NV, NM, NY, ND, NC, OK, RI, SC, WV, WI
3. "Chronic abuse" of child	AL, AK, AR, FL, GA, ID, KS, LA, MD, ME, MA (repetitive conduct), MS, MT, NE, NC, ND, NM, NY (repeated abuse), OK, RI, SC, WV, WI
4. Physical abuse, assault or battery of child	AZ, CA, CO, CT, DE, FL, IA, IN, LA, ME, MD, MS, MT, NJ, MO, OH (child endangerment), SC, TN, TX, UT, WA
5. Rape, sexual assault or other sexual abuse of child	AL, AK, AR, CO, CT, FL, GA, ID, IN, IA, KS, LA, ME, MD, MA, MS, MO, MT, ND, NJ, NE, NM, NY, NC, OH, OK, PA, RI, SC, SD, TN, TX, UT, VA, WA, WV, WI
6. Parental substance abuse	AL, CA, ND, OH, OK, WA
7. Failure to comply with or make progress under treatment plan (includes extended foster care stays)	AK, FL, HI, KS, LA, ME, OK
8. Parent cannot be located after diligent search	AK, AZ, CA, CO, LA, PA, UT
9. Mental illness or deficiency precluding parent from caring for child, even with services	AK, AZ, CA, CO, ND, UT
10. Child previously removed due to physical or sexual abuse, was returned and has now been removed again because of physical or sexual abuse	AK, AZ, CA, LA, OK, NV, UT
11. Serious or chronic neglect	AK, IA, KS, LA, MD, MN, MT, NV, NJ, OH (withholding food or treatment), OK, PA (aggravated physical neglect), SC, SD
12. Child removed on at least 2 prior occasions, services offered, and parent still unable to protect child	AK, AZ, UT
13. Parental incarceration or institutionalization	AK, CA, CO, LA, ND
14. Mental or emotional abuse (specific reference)	AK, AZ, MA, MO, OK
15. Child conceived during sex offense	CA, OK
16. Kidnapping or abduction of child	CA, ME, TN
17. Parent declines services	CA
18. Crimes generally (victims unspecified)	CA (violent felony), CT (sexual assault), ID (murder, voluntary manslaughter), OK (certain sexual offenses), SD (various crimes), TN (various crimes), TX (possession of child pornography)
19. Another child physically or sexually abused or assaulted (without reference to serious bodily injury)	CA, CO, DE, FL, IN, LA, MD, OH, OK, PA, SC, SD, TN
20. General descriptors of conduct or harm	FL (egregious), LA (egregious), ME (heinous or abhorrent), MN (egregious harm), NJ (cruelty), RI (cruel or abusive)
21. Violent crimes against parent of child	AK, IN, LA, MD, MA (murder in presence of child), VA, WA
22. Other crimes or status	DE (dealing in children), IN (causing suicide, criminal recklessness), ME (promotion of prostitution), MN (promotion of prostitution, felony restraint), WA (parent is sexually violent predator)
23. Court discretion	AL, AZ, GA, ID, IL, LA, ME, MN, MS, NE, NC, SC, UT, WI

Source: National Conference of State Legislatures.

MANDATORY CASES IN WHICH REASONABLE EFFORTS SHALL NOT BE REQUIRED	
Murder of another child of parent	AL, AK (homicide), AZ, AR, CA (death of another child through abuse, neglect), CO (serious bodily injury or death), CT (deliberately killed sibling), DE (felony offense against the person), FL, GA, HI, ID, IL (1st or 2nd degree murder), IN, IA, KS, LA, ME, MD (crime of violence), MA, MN, MS, MO, MT, NC, ND, NE, NV, NJ, NM (death of child), NY, OH, OK, PA, RI, SC, SD, TN, TX, UT, VA, WA, WV, WI
Voluntary manslaughter of another child of parent	AL, AK (homicide), AZ, AR, CA (see above), CO (serious bodily injury or death), CT (deliberately killed sibling), DE (felony offense against the person), FL, GA, HI, ID, IN, IA, KS, LA, ME, MD (crime of violence), MN, MS, MO, MT, NC, ND, NE, NV, NJ, NM (death of child), NY, OH, OK, PA, RI, SC, SD, TN, TX, UT, VA, WA, WV, WI
Aiding, abetting, attempting, conspiring or soliciting to commit such murder or manslaughter	AL, AK, AZ, AR, CT (attempted or solicited to kill child or sibling), DE (felony offense against the person), FL, GA, HI, ID, IL (attempt, conspiracy or solicitation to commit 1st or 2nd degree murder), IN, IA, KS, LA, ME, MD (crime of violence), MA, MN, MS, MO, MT, NE, NV, NC, ND, NJ, NM (attempt, conspire), NY, OH, OK, PA, RI, SC, TN, UT, VA (attempt, conspiracy or solicitation), WA (attempt, solicit or conspire), WV (attempt, conspiracy, accessory), WI
Felony assault resulting in serious bodily injury to child or another child of parent	AL, AK, AZ (serious physical injury to child), AR, CA (child under 5 suffered severe physical abuse, parent convicted of violent felony), CO (serious bodily injury or death), CT, DE (felony offense against the person), FL, GA, HI, ID, IL, IN, IA, KS, LA, ME, MD (crime of violence), MA, MN, MS, MO, MT, NE, NV, NC, ND, NJ, NM (great bodily harm), NY, OH, OK, PA, RI, SC, SD, TN, TX, UT (severe abuse), VA, WA, WV, WI
Parental rights to sibling terminated involuntarily	AL, AK (when parent fails to remedy conduct), AZ (parent fails to remedy), AR, CA (parent failed to remedy), CT (within 3 years and state has made r.e. to reunify for 90 days), DE, FL, GA, HI, ID, IL, IN, IA (services not likely to correct conditions), KS, LA, ME, MD, MA, MN, MS, MO, MT, NE, NV, NC, ND, NJ, NM, NY, OH, OK (parent failed to remedy), PA, RI, SC, SD, TN, TX, UT, VA, WA, WV, WI

Source: National Conference of State Legislatures.

Despite possible shortcomings, most experts agree that ASFA was a breath of fresh air in a system that seemed out of control.

Christine Adamec and William Pierce, Ph.D., *The Encyclopedia of Adoption* (New York: Facts On File, Inc., 2000).
Cristine H. Kim, "Putting Reason Back into the Reasonable Efforts Requirement in Child Abuse and Neglect Cases," *University of Illinois Law Review,* 1999, no. 1 (1999).
Amy Printz Winterfeld, J.D., "An Overview of the Major Provisions of the Adoption and Safe Families Act of 1997," *Protecting Children* 14, no. 3 (1998): 4–8.

Adoption Assistance and Child Welfare Reform Act of 1980 (P.L. 96–272) Concerned about large

numbers of children living in foster care, the United States Congress amended the Social Security Act in 1980 to include specific guidelines for out-of-home placements and to remove barriers to adoption. Congress hoped to encourage adoption of those children in foster care who, due to physical or mental disability or other factors, were the least likely to be adopted. The act made special provisions for medical assistance and other payments to families who adopted such children.

The law defined conditions under which a child could be removed from a family and prescribed certain periodic reviews of foster care cases. It also discussed preventive services such as HOMEMAKER SERVICES, CRISIS INTERVENTION, counseling, day care and other supports that states could make available to families before a child was voluntarily or involuntarily removed from home. Except for EMERGENCIES, a child could not be involuntarily removed from home unless a judge determined that: (1) the child was in substantial and immediate danger, which could not be addressed by preventive services; (2) preventive services were available and had either been refused or had failed to improve the situation; or (3) the child was guilty of a delinquent offense.

When children were to be placed in foster care, the law required that they be placed in the "least restrictive setting," which, taking their special needs into consideration, approximated a family setting as closely as possible. Children were to be placed with a relative when appropriate. Placements were to be made within reasonable proximity to the original home. States were also required to offer family reunification services designed to "ensure the swiftest possible return of the child to his home."

The act allowed any party to a foster placement to request and receive a review of the placement decision by an impartial hearing officer. Each child was to have a case plan outlining services to be provided to the child and family, a description of the foster placement, how the state planned to facilitate the child's return home or permanent placement and other relevant information. Case plans were to be reviewed at least once every six months.

Adults Molested As Children United (AMACU)
Self-help group for adults who were sexually abused as children. Affiliated with PARENTS UNITED. For more information, *see* APPENDIX 1.

advisement After arguments of both sides are presented in a court of law the judge or jury takes evidence under advisement. Advisement takes place before rendering of an opinion and includes consideration of evidence presented and consultation among jurors.

advocacy For most children, a parent acts as an advocate. Various needs, including physical, psychological, educational and emotional, are met by the parent or parents so that children are nurtured and protected until they are able to care for them-

selves. For children who are the victims of neglect or abuse, however, advocacy extends to institutions, groups and individuals in society who are best able to provide for children whose needs are not met by their parent(s).

In the United States at different times a variety of efforts have constituted child advocacy. Among these, the report in 1969 from the Joint Commission on the Mental Health of Children recommended that a child advocacy system be put in place in order to guarantee that children be represented adequately no matter what their family situations. Some decades earlier, in 1909, as a result of the first WHITE HOUSE CONFERENCE ON CHILDREN, the CHILDREN'S BUREAU was established by the federal government to meet this goal of advocacy for children.

According to some experts, there are certain factors that characterize effective child advocacy. These include: (1) the making of connections among the different units (family, society etc.) of a child's life; (2) addressing child development; (3) conflict resolution; (4) fact-finding; (5) interdisciplinary teamwork; and (6) legal protection for CHILDREN'S RIGHTS. Ideally, combinations of all these factors exist when a group or individual works on behalf of the needs of children.

In legal proceedings where a child's welfare is concerned, an advocate is often appointed by the court. Recognizing that the child's interests may differ from those of the parents and the state, the court seeks to have the child represented by a competent adult who functions independently of other parties to the case. This advocate may represent the child in other proceedings as well (i.e., case conferences, administrative hearings etc.). (*See also* GUARDIAN AD LITEM, COURT APPOINTED SPECIAL ADVOCATE [CASA].)

affidavit In legal proceedings, a written, sworn statement known as an affidavit is sometimes introduced as evidence. The document must bear the seal of a notary public who has administered a legal oath to the signer. False statements contained in an affidavit are subject to penalties for perjury. Affidavits are frequently used in juvenile court hearings.

Africa Experts generally agree that various forms of child abuse, neglect and maltreatment are widespread in many African nations. However, researchers, cognizant of the cross-cultural aspect of their work, use carefully defined criteria when gathering data on these subjects. The size of the African continent (the world's second-largest land area) and the diversity of the African population (more than 800 groups divided according to custom and language) make most observations general at best. There have been very few studies of child care practices among African peoples so that definitions of abuse, neglect or maltreatment may be limited to data available on small groups or individual countries or cultures.

Most experts concur that internationally applicable standards used to define child abuse, neglect or maltreatment should include indictments of practices that result in serious physical harm, whether or not the practices are part of locally accepted norms. Actions leading to developmental impairment or death are often included in discussions of African child abuse, neglect or maltreatment. Such culturally acceptable practices as, for example, scarification or genital mutilation, would fall under the heading of abusive treatment in Western nations and so are included in studies of its incidence in Africa. In 26 African countries, CLITORIDECTOMY is a common practice involving girls who are generally between ages three and eight years but it sometimes involves infants only several days old.

Some African nations and some tribal groups identify certain behaviors as abuse, neglect or maltreatment according to the standards of their culture. These behaviors might include excessive disciplinary actions taken by an angry parent toward a child or a child-slavery incident that results in government intervention. However, other practices, such as child marriage, are considered part of the socialization process and are culturally acceptable.

Jill E. Korbin, *Child Abuse and Neglect: Cross-Cultural Perspectives* (Berkeley: University of California Press, 1981).

Defense for Children International–USA Collective, *The Children's Clarion, Database on the Rights of the Child, 1987* (Brooklyn, N.Y.: DCI–USA, 1987), Record No. 736.

aggressor, identification with *See* IDENTIFICATION WITH THE AGGRESSOR.

aid, categorical *See* CATEGORICAL AID.

AIDS Children who have been sexually abused may be at risk for contracting human immunodeficiency virus (HIV) which leads to acquired immune deficiency disease. In addition, a positive test for HIV in a preadolescent child is strong proof of sexual abuse. (It is also true that newborn infants may test positive for HIV if their mothers had the virus. Later, it may be determined the child is not HIV positive.)

If there is any suspicion of sexual abuse, blood testing for the HIV virus should occur.

alcoholism *See* SUBSTANCE ABUSE.

allegation Legal proceedings related to child abuse or neglect are initiated by statements, called allegations, of what a particular party seeks to prove. These allegations are usually contained in a petition that outlines specific charges of maltreatment against the defendant. Both parties may introduce evidence to support or disprove allegations.

alopecia, traumatic Alopecia refers to hair loss in both children and adults, usually as a result of disease. Traumatic alopecia is a term used to describe hair lost as a result of pulling. While traumatic alopecia may occur by accident as well as by deliberate abuse, it is a symptom that generally calls for further investigation. Close examination by a trained physician can generally determine the cause of hair loss.

American Humane Association This group was founded in 1877 as the first national organization of locally based societies for the prevention of cruelty to children. Today, the society maintains two divisions: one promotes humane treatment of animals; the other is known as the American Humane Association Children's Division. This division provides training, evaluation and assistance to community and state agencies in the area of child maltreatment. It publishes materials detailing various aspects of child protection, including *Protecting Children*, a quarterly newsletter, and acts as an advocate for child protection legislation and maintains a database of reports on abuse and neglect. For more information, *see* APPENDIX 1 or contact the organization at 63 Inverness Drive East, Englewood, CO 80112-5117. Tel: (800) 227-4645 or (303) 792-9900.

American Indians   According to reports from the U.S. Department of Justice, American Indian children were at greater risk for child abuse and neglect than any other racial group in 1995. In addition, although abuse rates dropped for other groups over the period 1992–95, with an average 8% rate decrease for all ethnic groups, the rate for American Indians actually increased over that period by 18%. The only other ethnic category to show an increase was Asians, who experienced a child abuse rate increase of 6%; however, compared to all the other ethnic groups, the rate of child abuse for Asians was extremely low.

Another problem was that the rate of child abuse was already high for American Indians in 1992, before the increase occurred. As the chart below reveals, the rate for all children in 1992 was 1,866; however, the rate for American Indian children who were abused was 2,830. By 1995, the rate of child abuse for American Indians was nearly double that for all other children, at 3,343 per 100,000 children. The only other ethnic group that was at about this level was blacks, with a rate of 3,323 in 1995. However, blacks had previously had a higher rate and their rate of child abuse had decreased.

American Indians still represent only a tiny portion of all abused children in the U.S. because they constitute a small minority of the population. In 1992, American Indian children represented 1.5% of all abused children. By 1995, they represented 1.9% of all abused children.

anatomically correct dolls   *See* NATURAL DOLLS.

animal abuse in relation to child abuse   The purposeful abuse or murder of a family pet or the family pet of someone known to the abuser may be a precursor of maltreatment of a family member. It may also be an indicator of ongoing abuse to both humans and animals in the household; for example, an adult who abuses family pets may be abusive to other adults and/or children in the household.

Sometimes children exhibit abusive behavior toward animals. When the cruel and abusive actions of a child result in the torture or death of an animal, this is a clear sign that the child has a serious problem. Experts advise that the child should receive psychological assistance so that the pattern of violence can be interrupted before it escalates.

Sometimes abuse of an animal can occur in a group setting outside the family, in which one or more children slowly torture or kill an animal to impress or shock other children. Such behavior is abnormal and the children involved should receive psychological treatment, again, to halt the cycle of violence before it advances further. Experts may also find a pattern of violence and abuse within the families of those children who severely abuse animals. It may be necessary for state or county social workers to intervene.

When animal abuse or murder is perpetrated by an adult family member, the offender is usually a male. In some cases, the abusing adult uses torture or murder of a pet—or the threat of torturing and murdering a pet—as a means of punishment or a way to control or harm children. Experts have found that if a child genuinely fears the death of a pet, that child may actually murder the pet himself, to provide a more merciful death than the one the child fears would be inflicted by the adult abuser. However, that act in itself causes psychological trauma and can perpetuate the cycle of abuse into adulthood.

In an essay in *Child Abuse, Domestic Violence, and Animal Abuse: Linking the Circles of Compassion for Prevention and Intervention*, Barbara Boat says,

NUMBER OF CHILD ABUSE AND NEGLECT VICTIMS PER 100,000 CHILDREN AGE 14 OR YOUNGER, BY RACE

	1992	1995	Percent Change
All Children	1,866	1,724	−8%
American Indian	2,830	3,343	18%
White	1,628	1,520	−7%
Black	3,560	3,323	−7%
Asian	454	479	6%
Hispanic	1,486	1,254	−16%

Source: "Measuring Criminal Victimization Among American Indians," Bureau of Justice Statistics, Department of Justice, 1999.

The evidence continues to mount that where animals are abused people are abused and vice versa. . . . Higher rates of animal abuse by parental figures have been found in substantial cases of child physical abuse than in the general population. . . . Abused animals were found in 88 percent of the homes of 57 families with pets where child physical abuse had been substantiated. Two-thirds of the pets were abused by fathers; a disconcerting one-third of pet abuse was perpetrated by the children.

Frank R. Ascione and Phil Arkov, eds. *Child Abuse, Domestic Violence, and Animal Abuse: Linking the Circles of Compassion for Prevention and Intervention* (West Lafayette, Indiana: Purdue University Press, 1999).

apathy-futility syndrome Based on studies of families in southern Appalachia and Philadelphia, Norman Polansky, a professor of social work at the University of Georgia, developed a diagnostic description of mothers who tended to be most neglectful. These mothers appeared passive, withdrawn and lacking in expression. In his description of the apathy-futility syndrome, Polansky de-emphasizes the role of poverty, pointing to the majority of poor families in which there is no abuse or neglect. Extreme apathy exhibited by some mothers is compared to the sense of futility displayed by individuals suffering from characterological disorders or schizophrenia.

Major features of the apathy-futility syndrome include the following traits:

- a feeling that nothing is worth doing (futility)
- emotional numbness similar to deep psychological depression
- development of superficial, clinging interpersonal relationships, often accompanied by intense loneliness
- unreasonable fear of failure resulting in an unwillingness to attempt new tasks and leading to a lack of competence in many tasks of daily living
- passive-aggressive expression of anger
- stubborn negativism
- limited verbal communication, making it difficult to engage in meaningful dialogue and limiting problem-solving capability

- an uncanny skill in bringing to consciousness the same feelings of futility in others—a trait interpreted as a defense against change, which appears very threatening to the parent

Though mothers suffering from the apathy-futility syndrome are severely and chronically neglectful of their children, they are unlikely to abandon them outright. Little information is available concerning the father/husband's role in the family. They are described as typically "the first or second man who showed interest in [the mother] and . . . ill equipped in education and in vocational skills."

Often limited in intellectual ability, these mothers tend to be lacking in basic knowledge of child rearing. Polansky cites the mother's own deprived childhood as evidence for an INTERGENERATIONAL CYCLE OF ABUSE.

Norman A. Polansky, Mary Ann Chalmers, Elizabeth Buttenwieser and David P. Williams, *Damaged Parents* (Chicago: University of Chicago Press, 1981).

appeal Any party to a child abuse or neglect case has the right to request that the procedures followed and decision reached be reviewed by a higher court. In cases where accurate records are not available (e.g., some juvenile courts) the appeal may involve a rehearing of all evidence, including testimony. At the second hearing a record is kept from which an appeal can be filed.

Upon reviewing court transcripts, the court to which the appeal was made may: (1) uphold the lower court's decision; (2) reverse the decision and return the case to the lower court; or (3) in the event of a procedural or DUE PROCESS violation, order a new trial.

asphyxia *See* CENTRAL NERVOUS SYSTEM INJURIES.

assault Any violent act, physical or verbal, may be called assault. The term assault is sometimes used as a euphemism for sexual molestation or rape.

Legally, assault is defined as "an intentional or reckless threat of physical injury." Aggravated assault implies an intent to carry out the threat. Simple assault refers to a threat without intent actually to commit the act. If an act is not attempted the threat is considered a simple assault.

Assault and BATTERY often appear together in legal charges related to PHYSICAL ABUSE or SEXUAL ABUSE OF CHILDREN.

assessment Following an initial INVESTIGATION to verify that a child has been abused or neglected, an assessment is conducted. The primary function of this process is to determine why abuse occurred and identify specific areas where intervention is needed. Assessment is the basis for development of a SERVICE PLAN. While assessment serves a purpose separate from investigation the two terms are sometimes used interchangeably. In practice, gathering of information for assessment often begins during an initial investigation to determine the validity of a report of suspected abuse. The investigatory process includes an assessment of immediate risk to the child. This initial evaluation serves as the basis for emergency intervention on behalf of the child and is followed by a more thorough social assessment.

The social assessment is based on the child protection worker's direct observation of the child's home environment and family interaction patterns. Important information is also obtained from interviews with the family, teachers, physicians, neighbors and others who have special knowledge of the child's living situation. Under certain circumstances a psychological, psychiatric or medical examination may be required for a thorough assessment.

The United States' National Center on Child Abuse and Neglect (Part of HHS, formerly HEW) recommends the following information be included in a social assessment:

- factual information on the family—names, ages occupations of members of the immediate family, and existence of extended family
- a brief summary of the family's contact with other agencies, as part of the investigation
- the family's perceptions of the incidence of abuse and neglect, the worker's perceptions and notations of any discrepancies between the two
- strengths and weaknesses in the family
- ways in which the family interacts
- significant historical data about the parents' upbringing that describe events that formed their

ideas of child rearing, parent-child relations, appropriate behavior for children etc.

- a listing of the family's needs that should be met to assure the health and safety of the child

The result will be a report summarizing family problems related to abuse and neglect, family strengths and the type of help families will need. Information is usually gathered by a single social worker; however, a MULTIDISCIPLINARY TEAM often assists in reviewing and interpreting data gathered.

U.S. Department of Health, Education and Welfare, Office of Human Development Services, Administration for Children, Youth and Families, Children's Bureau, National Center on Child Abuse and Neglect, *Child Protective Services: A Guide for Workers* (Washington, D.C.: 1979; (OHDS) 79-30203).

"at risk" children A variety of personal, familial and environmental factors serve to place some children at greater risk of abuse or neglect than others. Even prenatal occurrences such as parental substance abuse or an unwanted pregnancy can predispose a child to maltreatment.

Usually the presence or absence of a particular trait is less important than the perception that it exists. Perpetrators of abuse may attempt to explain their behavior as a response to a characteristic of the child. Such characteristics, in some instances, may be seen as contributing factors. They are never considered as justification for abuse.

Infants born prematurely have been shown to have a significantly greater chance of subsequent abuse than those carried to full term. Studies of abused children have identified from 12% to 33% as prematurely born. These children tend to have a low birth weight and may be more restless, distractible, unresponsive and demanding than the average child. Child-specific factors when combined with a parent who is inexperienced or easily frustrated greatly increase the risk of abuse.

Age is also an important characteristic in determining the likelihood and type of maltreatment. A nationwide study conducted by the Children's Division of the American Humane Association noted that, in general, younger children are at greater risk than their older peers. Young children are especially likely to experience neglect. Reports of sexual and emotional maltreatment, however, increase as children get older. And, while abused children of all ages show high rates of physical injury, older children are the most frequently reported victims.

Mentally retarded, physically handicapped, mentally ill and emotionally impaired children all have an increased chance of being singled out for abuse. Developmentally delayed children require more attention from caregivers and often do not respond to parental direction and affection as quickly as others. Parents may become frustrated or embarrassed by these behaviors. In such cases the risk of abuse is increased, especially if the parent is inadequately prepared or under a great deal of stress.

A child or adolescent's gender is also a contributing factor. Girls are over five times more likely to be sexually abused than boys.

Characteristics of parents play an important role in determining the likelihood of abuse. A child whose primary caregiver is under 18 years old, e.g., a teenaged parent, is more likely to be abused or neglected. Children of parents who were themselves abused are at risk. Parental substance abuse, mental retardation, social isolation, marital discord, mental illness and rigidity are all associated with child abuse and neglect.

Divorce increases the likelihood that girls will be abused. This phenomenon is attributed to increased contact with unrelated adult males as a result of the mother's dating. Statistics also show that stepfathers are more likely than natural fathers to assault the daughter sexually.

Inexperienced parents may have unrealistically high expectations of their children. Children are often punished for not meeting these expectations. When the child has a disability, unrealistic expectations can be intensely frustrating to the caregiver and damaging to the child.

Other environmental stresses can increase the risk of abuse or neglect. Over 40% of all reported abuse and neglect cases involve families receiving public assistance. Many researchers and clinicians have noted the role of POVERTY in child maltreatment. In some cases poverty may prevent a parent from providing for basic needs of food, shelter, clothing, medical and educational care. More often poverty is seen as a source of family stress that combines with other factors to create a climate conducive to maltreatment.

Many students of family violence point to cultural norms that condone and even promote violence as a tool for child rearing. They argue that culturally sanctioned familial violence places all children at risk and is an underlying factor in most child abuse.

Any child may be at risk of abuse from time to time. No one factor or combination of factors make abuse or neglect inevitable. Most low-income families are free of abuse; many disabled children receive adequate and loving care. The majority of stepfathers are not child molesters. Nevertheless, the presence of these and other factors does place children at greater risk of maltreatment.

In evaluating the potential for abuse it is important to consider the number of risk factors present, the severity of each factor and the length of time the child is at risk. To date, there is no foolproof method for evaluating the level of risk.

Australia The Australian Institute of Health and Welfare (AIHW) collects and reports on child abuse and neglect statistics. As of June 30, 1997, 14,078 children were in "out of home care" (known as FOSTER CARE in the U.S.) and most (89%) were in home-based care with another family. Most children were in out-of-home care because of abuse or neglect, although a small number awaited adoption or were in care for "respite" reasons. A "respite" is a brief time away from the child when the caregiver is unable to provide care because of physical or emotional illness. It could be days or weeks or a month or two but generally is no longer.

The rate of children in out-of-home care was 3.0 per 1,000, with a low range of 1.9 in the Northern Territory to a high of 3.7 in Tasmania. Child abuse and neglect in Australia has a history dating back, at least, to the years when the British established the nation as a penal colony. The First Fleet arrived in Australia in 1788, carrying among its passengers 36 children who were subsequently abandoned. According to one historian, there were 1,832 children in Australia in 1806. At least 1,000 of these children were illegitimate and abandoned.

Child welfare groups became active in Australia during the 19th century and worked to save some of the most desperate cases, like five-year-olds who were often forced into prostitution or other crimes. In 1864, the Neglected and Criminal Childrens Act set up industrial schools to take care of poor children who were either abandoned or neglected, in many instances as a result of the gold rushes of the period. Children were sometimes removed from their homes by the state and sent to institutions, where overcrowding and unsanitary conditions provided little in the way of relief from the neglect to which they were previously subject under their parents' care. By the 1930s, children had been recognized by the government as an important national resource, and funding was provided to establish research centers that focused on child development issues, although these centers did relatively little to alleviate social problems identified as causes of abuse and neglect.

During the 1970s, the Commonwealth Royal Commission into Human Relationships detailed child abuse as a topic in need of further investigation. Too, in recent years, various groups in Australia have met and held conferences to discuss child abuse and neglect, its prevention and treatment as well as its parameters. At present, there are slightly different definitions of child abuse and neglect in each of the Australian states. Each has its own Department for Community Welfare, which is responsible for child protection services; currently, mandatory reporting of child abuse exists only in New South Wales.

Since the 1960s, some attention has been focused on the incidence of INCEST in Australia. Results of some surveys show that incest is a problem that is reported more frequently now than in the past. In the state of Western Australia, the Department for Community Welfare Survey in 1978 revealed that 127 cases of incest came before the courts or to professional attention during a five-month period. Of these cases, 86% were against female children. South Australia showed similar findings.

These are a range of services and programs, both government run and private, that address issues of child abuse and neglect. In 1974, the first shelter for battered women and their children was founded in New South Wales, others have followed in neighboring states. Parents Anonymous is one self-help group that was established in Australia in 1973 by concerned mothers who sought professional guidance but who found that peer counseling and support was helpful to them as well. Some voluntary parent aide programs have been established also, modeled after similar programs in the U.S., which were based on work done by C. Henry Kempe. These parent aides act as peer support for abusing parents, generally in cases of physical or emotional abuse. In addition, public opposition to the use of corporal punishment in Australian schools prompted establishment of Parents and Teachers Against Violence in Education (PTAVE) in 1978. As a result of its lobbying actions, guided by PTAVE founder Jordan Riak, an American who was living in Sydney during the 1970s, corporal punishment by educators is now illegal in some parts of Australia.

Carol O'Donnell and Jan Craney, eds., *Family Violence in Australia* (Melbourne: Longman Cheshire Pty. Ltd., 1982).

autoptic evidence   *See* EVIDENCE.

autopsy   Postmortem examination by a forensic pathologist is recommended whenever abuse or neglect is the suspected cause of a child's death. The forensic medical specialist often works with a team of law enforcement and social work personnel in investigating circumstances surrounding the death.

A careful autopsy includes information gained from an examination of the child's environment. Assessment of the cleanliness and adequacy of the child's physical surroundings and interviews with family members, neighbors and others to learn more about family relationships, discipline patterns etc. often provide useful information.

The autopsy begins with a thorough external medical examination. Items such as the child's clothing, cleanliness, height, weight and apparent nutritional state are noted. A careful inspection of the skin for evidence of trauma or neglect includes a search for bruises, cuts, scars, swelling, untreated or infected lesions, parasitic infestation and severe diaper rash. Physical evidence that might lead to identification of the assailant is carefully labeled and preserved.

The medical examiner is also alert to attempts to conceal abuse. Appearance of severe diaper rash on a freshly washed, carefully scrubbed body may suggest an attempt to conceal previous neglect. Close inspection of the soles of the child's feet sometimes yields evidence of abuse, such as cigarette burns or bruises, at the hands of a caretaker attempting to avoid detection.

Internal examination includes thorough examination and description of all organ systems, with careful photographic documentation of pathology. When neglect is the suspected cause of death the examiner is alert for evidence of chronic disease that might provide an alternative explanation of starvation or nutritional deficiency. Careful attention is given to determining when the trauma occurred. Dating of injuries may be helpful in establishing evidence of long-standing abuse and may help identify the perpetrator. Toxicological screens are also used to identify any poisons or medication that might have contributed to death. A thorough SKELETAL SURVEY is always conducted to detect fractures and separations of the bones.

An autopsy may reveal evidence of serious internal injury such as liver or spleen damage when there is scant external evidence of trauma. Examination of the galea (area between the scalp and the cranium) sometimes shows well-defined hemorrhages that reflect the outline of the weapon used to strike the child.

Comparison of evidence obtained from an autopsy with the caretaker's explanation often serves as the basis for criminal charges. By carefully establishing and documenting the probable cause of death an autopsy can support or call into question such an explanation. In combination with other evidence, medical evidence can help convict a child abuser and possibly protect other children from abuse or neglect by the same perpetrator.

James T. Weston, "The Pathology of Child Abuse and Neglect," in C. Henry Kempe and Ray E. Helfer, eds, *The Battered Child,* 3d ed. (Chicago: University of Chicago Press, 1980).

aversive conditioning   Painful measures such as spanking or electric shock have been used in the treatment of certain psychiatric disorders as a way of controlling behavior considered dangerous or socially undesirable. This mode of treatment has often been abused and is the subject of continuing debate among advocates, practitioners and lawyers. Nevertheless, aversive conditioning continues to be used, especially in the treatment of autism.

In 1975, the National Society for Autistic Children detailed guidelines for the use of aversive measures in treatment. The society stated that use of painful stimuli was permissible as a way of controlling behavior that "threatens the child's safety or survival in an optimal environment."

Sharon R. Morgan, *Abuse and Neglect of Handicapped Children* (Boston: College-Hill Press, 1987).

avitaminosis   A condition caused by a deficiency of one or more essential vitamins. This condition may occur in children suffering from nutritional neglect. Also called hypovitaminosis.

Some examples include children whose diets contain insufficient levels of vitamin C. These children are at risk of developing SCURVY, a disease that is characterized by multiple hemorrhages. Also, children with vitamin D-deficient diets may develop RICKETS, in which stunted growth and skeletal deformities are common. Vitamin A deficiency often denotes a general malnourished state. Children who lack sufficient intake of vitamin A are at risk for a range of eye problems, including, in cases of severe vitamin A deficiency, blindness.

John Marks, *The Vitamins, Their Role in Medical Practice* (Lancaster, England: MTP Press Limited, 1985).

Baby Doe A controversial court case in the United States illustrates the difficulty in defining child abuse. In October of 1983 a baby, known simply as Baby Jane Doe, was born in a New York hospital. In addition to an exposed spine (spina bifida), Baby Doe suffered from excess fluid on the brain and an abnormally small head. Corrective surgery could add several years to her life but could not correct her severe mental and physical retardation. After consulting with several physicians, the parents decided not to give permission for an operation to enclose the spine. Baby Doe was treated with nonsurgical techniques, including antibiotics and measures to encourage natural enclosure of the spine.

The U.S. Department of Health and Human Services, reeling from public criticism for failure to intervene in a similar case in Indiana, filed a child abuse complaint with the New York Child Protection Services. When NYCPS did not substantiate the complaint, a private citizen from Vermont filed suit to force the parents to give permission for surgery. Again the parents' decision was upheld. HHS then attempted to enforce newly developed regulations that forbade withholding medical treatment or nutrition on the basis of an infant's impairment. The Department appealed the case to the U.S. Supreme Court, arguing that disabled infants were entitled to protection from discrimination under the Rehabilitation Act of 1973. In 1986, the Supreme Court ruled the new regulations unconstitutional. Baby Doe continued to receive nonsurgical medical treatment.

Concern over this and similar cases led the U.S. Congress to amend the CHILD ABUSE PREVENTION AND TREATMENT ACT to include withholding of medically indicated treatment as a form of abuse. Subsequent regulations allowed parents to deny permission for treatment if it is judged ineffective in improving or correcting a life-threatening condition, if it only prolongs dying, or if the infant is irreversibly comatose. This expanded definition of child abuse is similar in content to the regulations struck down by the U.S. Supreme Court.

In no case have parents in the United States been convicted for withholding extraordinary medical care.

baby farms The practice of nursing or rearing children in exchange for money was widespread in 19th-century England. Working mothers often entrusted infants to a caretaker for a lump sum payment. Unscrupulous "nurses" were known to accept large numbers of infants at prices far lower than what was necessary to provide adequate care. Needless to say, these "baby farms" provided substandard care and were often filthy.

In 1868, Ernest Hart, editor of the *British Medical Journal* decried the practice of professional adoption, saying ". . . many of these women carried on the business with a deliberate knowledge that the children would die very quickly and evidently with a deliberate intention that they should die." Hart's attempts to regulate baby farms were largely unsuccessful until a celebrated case known as the "Brixton Horrors" was brought to light in 1870.

While investigating a large number of abandoned infant corpses found in various parts of the city, police discovered a baby farm run by a Margaret Waters and her sister, Sarah Ellis. Evidence found at the Waters home showed that infants were fed only limewater and that many had been drugged, poisoned or starved to death.

Subsequent investigations of other baby farms uncovered additional horror stories. It was estimated that 80% to 90% of the infants entrusted to the care of "professional nurses" perished.

Public outrage stimulated the passage of the INFANT LIFE PROTECTION ACT in 1872. Though it was an important first step, the act was largely ineffectual in curbing the abuses found in baby farms. Twenty-five years later the act was amended to increase protections for adopted children.

Baker v. Owen, 1975 The issue of schools' use of CORPORAL PUNISHMENT has been the subject of a great deal of litigation and public debate in recent years. United States courts have consistently ruled in favor of a school's right to use physical punishment as a means of discipline as long as certain safety precautions are followed.

In the case of *Baker v. Owen*, the United States Supreme Court upheld a teacher's right to punish a child physically in spite of a parent's wishes to the contrary. The case involved a sixth-grade student in a North Carolina school. A school official punished the child after his mother had submitted a note forbidding the official to do so.

BAPSCAN *See* BRITISH ASSOCIATION FOR THE PREVENTION AND STUDY OF CHILD ABUSE AND NEGLECT.

battered child syndrome The late C. Henry Kempe, a professor of pediatrics at the University of Colorado School of Medicine, is credited with coining the term "battered child syndrome." Concerned by the number of abused infants and children receiving medical care who were misdiagnosed or improperly treated, Dr. Kempe sought to bring the problem of child abuse to the attention of physicians. Using his position as president of the American Academy of Pediatrics, he organized a symposium on the subject in 1961. The name battered child syndrome was chosen, in part to create public interest in a phenomenon many people considered repugnant. The symposium generated a great deal of interest and was followed a year later by a much-quoted article of the same name published in *The Journal of the American Medical Association*. In the article, Kempe and others outlined the basic features of the syndrome. Though many of the symptoms had been outlined previously by John Caffey, Frederick Silverman and other pediatric radiologists, the Kempe article was the first to bring together information on clinical/radiologic manifestations, psychiatric factors, evaluation and incidence.

The battered child syndrome as originally described included a range of physical abuse suffered by children primarily under age three. Later definitions have expanded the age to five years and even older. Specific symptoms may include: general poor health, evidence of neglect, poor skin hygiene, multiple soft tissue injuries, malnutrition, a history suggesting parental neglect or abuse, marked discrepancy between clinical evidence and information supplied by the caretaker, subdural hematoma and multiple fractures in various stages of healing. Symptoms can be present in different combinations but the last two were particularly important to physicians. Due to advances in pediatric radiology, physicians were able to verify the presence of subdural hematomas and, more importantly, to distinguish between bone fractures caused by accidental injury and those typical of inflicted abuse. Kempe wrote: "To the informed physician, the bones tell a story the child is too young or too frightened to tell."

Linking verifiable clinical/radiological phenomena to child abuse was a particularly important step in encouraging physicians to pursue adequate measures for protecting children from further abuse. Indeed the general reluctance on the part of physicians, social workers and others to acknowledge child abuse is still a cause for concern. However, willingness to identify and report child abuse has increased somewhat as a result of mandatory reporting laws in many areas.

Though not widely used today, the term battered child syndrome played an important role in refocusing public attention on child abuse. By making child abuse a medical phenomenon, the considerable influence of physicians was brought to bear on a problem that many had chosen to ignore. Increasing concern over abuse has shifted the focus from protection of parents and caretakers to an emphasis on the rights and welfare of the child. This approach attributes most child abuse to a poorly functioning family system or to individual pathology on the part of parents or caretakers.

C. Henry Kempe, N. Frederick Silverman, Brandt F. Steele, William Droegemueller, and Henry K. Silver. "The Battered-Child Syndrome," *Journal of the American Medical Association* 181 (1962): 17–24.

battering child Attacks from other children represent a small percentage of reported child abuse. These attacks may range from relatively harmless sibling rivalry (*see* SIBLING ABUSE) to attempted murder.

Abuse by a child outside the family is more likely to be reported to authorities than sibling abuse. Parents are often reluctant to report abuse that occurs at the hands of an older brother or sister. In such cases, parents may be afraid to acknowledge that a child's behavior is beyond their control. Rather than taking steps to protect the victimized sibling, parents attempt to placate the aggressor and downplay the extent of the abuse. Some psychotherapists have suggested that child batterers are acting out the parents' unconscious wish to be rid of a younger child.

A parent or caretaker's failure to protect children from harmful assaults by another child constitutes, at a minimum, neglect. In particularly serious cases, caretakers may be considered coconspirators in the abuse.

Ironically, mental health professionals, like parents, have tended to focus more attention on the treatment needs of the abuser than on those of the abused child. Victims of sibling attacks, lacking parental support or fearing further abuse, are reluctant to participate in psychotherapy. This being the case, they frequently require extended treatment before improvement is seen.

Battering children attack others for a variety of reasons. These include jealousy, emotional disturbance or a history of being abused themselves. As mentioned earlier, abusive children are sometimes acting out a parent's wishes. Older children are sometimes given too much responsibility in caring for younger brothers and sisters. Children may misunderstand a parent's idle threats to strangle a crying child and actually attempt to carry out such a punishment.

battery Illegal contact, especially physical violence, with a person is known as battery. The term is most often used in reference to beating.

For contact to be considered illegal it must take place without the consent of the victim. Since a minor cannot give legal consent, any offensive or violent contact with a child can be considered battery. Acts of battery may be classified as either aggravated or simple. Aggravated battery refers to intentional acts of violence. Unintentional acts or acts that do not cause severe harm may be called simple battery. (*See also* ASSAULT.)

bed-wetting *See* ENURESIS.

behavior *See* SEDUCTIVE BEHAVIOR, SELF-DESTRUCTIVE BEHAVIOR.

best interests of the child It has long been held that parents usually act in the best interests of children. In cases of child abuse or neglect, however, this benevolent parental action is found lacking and judicial intervention on behalf of the children is necessary.

The legal standard of a child's best interest was developed in response to a need to establish guidelines in safeguarding children's rights. The standard of best interest of the child takes into consideration the many variables of a child's life, including the fitness of parent(s) or legal guardian. Aside from abuse and neglect cases, it is a standard invoked most frequently in cases of custody or placement, when a court is obliged to determine with whom a child should make his or her home.

In recent years, the best interest standard has been challenged on the grounds that it places too much emphasis on an unattainable ideal. A suggested substitute, the "least detrimental alternative," holds that a court's determination should be based on careful weighing of many alternatives open to discussion. According to proponents of the least detrimental alternative standard, placement made on the basis of best interest generally seeks to find a solution without negative ramifications for the child. It is against this ideal of "best" interest that critics argue.

Joseph Goldstein, *The Best Interests of the Child: The Least Detrimental Alternative.* (New York: The Free Press, 1996).

beyond a reasonable doubt This is a legal standard of proof required in criminal trials and, frequently, for termination of parental rights. *See* EVIDENTIARY STANDARDS.

biting Human bites leave distinctive, crescent-shaped bruises containing tooth marks. In some cases the bruise marks may join to form a ring. Bite marks on children may be self-inflicted or the result of an attack by a playmate or caretaker. Careful measurements of the space between the canine teeth can determine whether the perpetrator has permanent teeth (greater than 3 cm) or not (fewer than 3 cm). Location of bite marks in areas that would be difficult for the child to reach is also an indicator of suspicious origin. Since bite marks usually leave a distinct impression, they can sometimes be traced to the abusers by comparing them to wax dental impressions taken from suspected perpetrators. The attacker's blood type can sometimes be identified from small amounts of saliva surrounding the wound.

blaming the victim   A common rationalization of child maltreatment is that the victim of the abuse is in some way responsible for the abuse. Abusive parents often have unrealistic expectations of their children and punish them for behavior that may be natural for children of a given age. Punishing children for behavior over which they have little control is not only ineffective but may cause further negative behavior. Thinking the child has not learned his or her lesson, immature parents may increase punishment to the point of physical or emotional injury. Frustrated caretakers often label the child sick or bad and use these judgments as excuses for further abuse.

Blaming the child for the parent's abusive behavior is a form of denial that prevents parents from accepting responsibility for their own actions. Sometimes abusers are able to convince others that a child's extreme behavior justifies severe punishment. Family members and friends may engage in a conspiracy of denial to avoid acknowledging abuse. In such instances perceptions of the child as the initiator of abuse are reinforced, increasing the likelihood of further abuse.

Often parents choose particular traits of the child as justification for abuse. Low birth weight infants may cry incessantly, developmentally disabled children may not respond to parents' demands or children may simply be defiant. These and other characteristics of children may make parenting more difficult. They do not, however, justify abuse. Responsibility for abuse rests with the abuser's own inability to manage his or her actions.

Children often come to believe that they are indeed responsible for their own abuse. Even when abuse is unprovoked a child may feel that he or she must have done something to deserve punishment. Internalized feelings of guilt and negative self-worth become deeply ingrained in the child's psyche and respond slowly to treatment. Often, long-term psychotherapy is recommended to help abuse victims overcome self-blame.

Abusers must learn to accept responsibility for their own actions before they can make full use of treatment services. Repeat sexual offenders can be particularly persistent in blaming children for being seductive or for initiating sexual contact. Their inability to acknowledge the child's vulnerability and to accept their own responsibility as adults makes them particularly slow to respond to treatment.

bonding   *See* BONDING FAILURE.

bonding failure   Several studies have demonstrated a link between failure to develop a strong parent-infant attachment or emotional bond and subsequent FAILURE TO THRIVE SYNDROME and battering. Research indicates that the type and amount of parent-child interaction during the first two to three days following birth can be important in determining the strength of the parent-child bond although it is certainly possible for parents who are ill, adoptive parents and others to bond with an infant in the first year or two of life.

Newborns who suffer from developmental disabilities may not respond to parents' attempts to communicate. Parents sometimes reject infants who, for these and other reasons, fail to meet expectations. Very young parents are more likely to have unrealistic expectations of an infant and fail to establish a strong bond.

Research has shown that newborns have more advanced sensory capabilities than previously thought. Newborns can focus on close objects and can follow movement with their eyes. Infants respond to human speech and as early as 36 hours after birth can imitate facial expressions. By six days of age newborns can recognize their mother's scent.

Not only do babies respond to adults' communications, but they also seem to evoke speech. Observations in hospital nurseries indicate that adults begin speaking to newborns (not just making sounds) from the first day of life. The newborn's ability to evoke and respond to human communication is an important part of the bonding process. During such early communication parents usually develop a strong emotional attachment and come to view the infant as a separate, yet very dependent, person. Abusive or neglectful parents may have unrealistic expectations of the parent-child relationship and fail to develop such an attachment. In addition, if a child suffers from FETAL ALCOHOL SYNDROME or is born addicted to drugs, it is very difficult for the substance-abusing mother to provide the enormous attention the new baby needs. In a vicious cycle, because the baby does not receive what he or she needs, the mother may become frustrated and ignore the baby, exacerbating the problem yet further.

Recognition of the bonding period's importance has led many professionals to focus prevention efforts on the perinatal period (the time surrounding birth). Many hospitals have changed policies to allow fathers to be present during birth and to increase both the amount and quality of parent-infant contact during the first hours of life.

Some experts have stated that an overemphasis on bonding has led some parents to believe that all hope is lost if, for some reason, they are unable to be with their infants in the first hours or days after birth. Such experts argue that most bonding studies are based on animal studies of ducks and other species and that humans are very different from these animals. Other frequently cited bonding studies are based on institutionalized children separated from their parents, a situation very different from that of the average family.

Other experts believe that bonding and attachment are important (with bonding the response and attachment the result) but they say that infants can bond when they are months old or older.

In studies of children adopted from other countries, experts have found that children adopted before the age of about 18 months to two years do well with their adoptive parents and compare favorably to children adopted at birth or even non-adopted children. Older institutionalized children, however, who have never had an opportunity to have a one-on-one relationship with a caregiver,

may find it difficult or sometimes impossible to bond with their new parents. As a result, they will exhibit undue friendliness to strangers and will not show concern when their parents leave, as most children around the ages of two or three do.

Christine Adamec, *Is Adoption For You? The Information You Need to Make the Right Choice.* (New York: John Wiley and Sons, 1998).

brain damage   *See* CENTRAL NERVOUS SYSTEM INJURIES.

Britain   The government of England and Wales has a clearly defined position on child abuse and neglect—it administers and provides referral, treatment and prevention services via the National Health Service and a network of voluntary, charitable and self-help organizations. A concrete response to child welfare needs occurred in Britain during the 19th century, although awareness of the needs of neglected, abused or maltreated children had developed as early as the 17th century in England. Services that parallel British offerings are found in Scotland and are administered there under the auspices of the Scottish Development Department and the Scottish Home and Health Department.

Parliament has passed a variety of legislation dealing with three separate categories: juvenile offenders, children in need of care and protection and children beyond parental control. Issues of abuse, neglect or maltreatment generally fall into one of these three categories and are addressed by appropriate laws. Generally speaking, all local health and social service authorities make prevention of child abuse a priority, with the result that cases are dealt with in reasonably effective fashion. Recent studies indicate that sexual abuse victims now benefit from specially designed programs and therapeutic strategies via hospital-based services and mental health units. In 1986, a national campaign in Britain entitled "Forgotten Children" targeted child neglect. It was sponsored by the National Society for the Prevention of Cruelty to Children.

The National Health Service runs a number of programs for detection and treatment of child abuse and neglect, as well as prevention and education projects. Although provisions of legislation regarding child maltreatment are complex, it is useful to note some Acts of Parliament, pertaining most specifically to child abuse and neglect: the Children's Acts, Children and Young Persons Acts, Adoption Acts, and the Child Care Act of 1980.

The British established a National Society for the Prevention of Cruelty to Children in the late 1800s. Currently, voluntary services doing work in the area of child abuse and neglect, and in general child welfare, receive some government financial support as well as referrals from state agencies. There are also a number of charitable and self-help groups for parents and families, organizations that often aid directly in prevention of abusive treatment or in support and respite services for situations in which abuse or neglect has been an issue in the past. These nonstatutory, voluntary organizations include: Church of England Children's Society; Dr. Barnardo's; Family Service Units; Family Welfare Association; National Society for the Prevention of Cruelty to Children; the Rainer Foundation; Save the Children Fund; Organization for Parents Under Stress; National Association for Young People in Care.

Juvenile courts hear cases dealing with care or delinquency involving children aged 14 years or less and young persons between the ages of 14 and 17 years. Cases of family violence, which comprise physical abuse or sexual abuse, are under the jurisdiction of several different courts.

Shelters for mothers and children are operated by the Women's Aid Federation (England) and the Welsh Women's Aid (Wales). These organizations both have affiliated groups that receive some government support as well as private donations.

George K. Behlmer, *Child Abuse and Moral Reform in England, 1870–1908* (Stanford, Calif.: Stanford University Press, 1982).

J. P. Gallagher, *The Price of Charity* (London: Robert Hale, 1975).

Emmeline W. Cohen, *English Social Services* (London: Robert Hale, 1975).

Family Welfare Association, *Guide to the Social Services 1988*, 76th ed. (London: The Family Welfare Association, 1988).

———, *Guide to the Social Services 1987*, 75th ed. (London: The Family Welfare Association, 1987).

Benedict Nightingale, *Charities* (London: Allen Lane/Penguin, 1973).

Nigel Parton, *The Politics of Child Abuse* (New York: St. Martin's Press, 1985).

boyfriend as perpetrator Although no national statistics are currently available, experts report that violence against children may be committed by the live-in boyfriend or girlfriend of the parent, although it may be officially recorded as "neglect" by the biological parent. In one study in North Carolina of 220 child abuse homicides, 28% of the perpetrators were the mothers' boyfriends. Mothers' boyfriends were the third most likely perpetrators, after the fathers and then mothers themselves. In 1999, the state of Illinois social services department launched an advertising campaign to warn single mothers about the perils of using their boyfriends as babysitters. (It is also possible for girlfriends to be abusive but they appear to be much less likely to abuse the children of their paramours than males are.)

According to child abuse expert and researcher Murray Straus, Ph.D., codirector of the Family Research Laboratory and a sociology professor at the University of New Hampshire, the boyfriend perpetrator is a real problem today, not only in the physical abuse of children but particularly with their sexual abuse.

Stepfather/Boyfriend Abuse

Canadian and psychology professors Martin Daly and Margo Wilson, authors of *The Truth About Cinderella* (Yale University Press, 1999) and numerous journal articles, have performed unique research on abuse perpetrated by "stepfathers," a term they use to include men who are married to or not married to but living with the mother. (These men are not the children's biological fathers.) They found a much higher rate of abuse from these men: the homicide risk to the children was about 70 times greater. They also found a difference in the methods of murder: stepfathers were 120 times more likely to beat a child to death than genetic fathers.

Wilson and Daly used research from Canada and the U.S.; for example, they studied police department homicide records in Chicago for 1965–90 and found that 115 children under age 5 were killed by their fathers "while 63 were killed by stepfathers or (more or less co-resident) mothers' boyfriends. Most of these children were less than 2 years old, and because very few babies reside with substitute fathers, the numbers imply greatly elevated risk to such children."

These researchers studied homicide; however, it seems likely that if boyfriends and/or stepfathers are more likely to kill children, then it is probably also true that they are more likely to physically or sexually assault them than are their biological parents, supporting the theories of Dr. Straus.

Dr. Straus, telephone discussion with the author, November 30, 1999.

Martin Daly and Margo I. Wilson, "Some Differential Attributes of Lethal Assaults on Small Children by Stepfathers versus Genetic Fathers," *Ethnology and Sociobiology* 15 (1994): 207–216.

———, "Violence Against Stepchildren," *Current Directions in Psychological Science* 5 (1996): 77–81.

British Association for the Prevention and Study of Child Abuse and Neglect (BAPSCAN)   Due to the increased frequency of child abuse and neglect cases, concerned individuals formed BAPSCAN to urge that professionals pay strict attention to all aspects of abuse. In one instance, BAPSCAN's actions worked to bring the issue of child sexual abuse into discussion when it had been omitted from government documents dealing with child abuse and neglect. By monitoring policies and procedures of government agencies, BAPSCAN tries to ensure that important issues not be overlooked and that both the public and the professional workers are kept abreast of new developments that may affect delivery of services to children.

bruises   Easily recognizable as discolored patches of skin, bruises are caused by bleeding beneath the skin. They are perhaps the most common observable indicator of child battering. For purposes of easier description bruises are divided into three categories.

Petechiae: very small bruises caused by broken capillaries. These lesions may be caused by trauma such as bumps or blows or may be the result of a clotting disorder. Clotting factor tests are sometimes conducted to determine the origin of bruises.

Purpura: the term purpura may refer to a group of petechiae or a small bruise up to one centimeter in diameter.

Ecchymosis: refers to any bruise larger than one centimeter in diameter.

burden of proof   In a court of law the petitioner or plaintiff is responsible for producing evidence establishing the truth of allegations made against the defendant. This duty is referred to as the burden of proof or, in Latin, *onus probandi*. The burden of proof in child abuse and neglect cases rests with the governmental unit charged with enforcing such laws, usually the state. Depending on the nature of the charges different standards of proof may be required (*see* EVIDENTIARY STANDARDS).

Burden of proof can also refer to the "burden of going forward with the evidence," which may shift back and forth between the two parties. Under this meaning of the term either party may be required to raise a reasonable doubt concerning the existence or nonexistence of a particular fact.

burnout   Staff burnout is a frequent problem among child protection services (CPS) workers. The work is demanding and the benefits of staff efforts often cannot immediately be seen by the staff. Typically, CPS workers carry caseloads that are too large to permit satisfactory attention to each case. Time pressures, hostile reactions of parents and children and inadequate support from supervisors also take their toll on workers.

Frustration with working conditions has led to a high rate of turnover among CPS staff. Some workers who do not leave their jobs may become apathetic or angry. In addition to the obviously negative consequences of burnout for workers, frequent turnover and worker apathy also diminish the effectiveness of the child protection system.

Apathy and frustration associated with burnout can be reduced and in some cases prevented. Thorough, ongoing training plays an important role in reducing burnout. Well-trained workers feel more confident and are better prepared to handle the inevitable stresses they encounter in their work.

Competent and accessible supervision is essential. Regular feedback and emotional support from the supervisor is especially important for CPS workers. Peer support and consultation from specialists may also help reduce stress when workers must make difficult decisions concerning a child's well-being. Many child protection agencies have found that regularly scheduled meetings of workers are important ways of encouraging peer support and exchanging professional information.

Finally, the CPS worker must be careful to set limits between his or her personal and professional activities. The intense nature of child abuse investigation and the dedication of many workers often cause them to bring job-related problems home. Workers who have a variety of interests outside of work are often better able to avoid burnout than those who have few outside supports.

burns One of the leading causes of accidental death to children, burns are also a frequent method of abuse. Treatment of burns is painful and permanent scarring may result from third-degree burns.

Records show that 10% of all physically abused children suffer from burns. One researcher has estimated that more than 90% of abused children exhibit skin findings such as bruises and burns. Children who are burned abusively are most likely to be victims of scalds, the most common type of burn injury in children. Contact burns are the second most common type of burn and may result from cigarettes or heated objects being placed against the skin. Contact burns also occur when a child is held against a heated surface, such as a stove burner or heater. Chemical burns occur when acid, lye or other caustic substances are thrown on the child's skin. In some cases, children have been forced to drink such substances, causing internal lesions. Friction burns are sometimes observed on the wrists and ankles of children who have been bound with rope or cord.

Abuse by burning is often detected when the nature of the burn is suspicious or when caretakers offer implausible stories for a burn's occurrence. Intentional cigarette burns are easily distinguished from accidental burns. Location of burns in areas that are usually clothed is also an indicator of possible abuse.

Burns are usually inflicted in conjunction with other forms of PHYSICAL ABUSE. When burns arouse suspicion of child abuse, medical personnel seek to obtain independent accounts of the incident from all caretakers. A SKELETAL SURVEY may be obtained to determine evidence of fractures or separations, which also may be indicative of abuse.

Caffey-Kempe Syndrome   *See* PARENT-INFANT TRAUMATIC SYNDROME (PITS).

Caffey's Disease   *See* INFANTILE CORTICAL HYPEROSTOSIS.

caida de mollera   *See* FALLEN FONTANEL.

callus   A meshwork of new bone tissue develops (usually beneath the periosteum) as a result of a fracture. The new tissue, called callus, forms along the pattern of the original clot caused by the injury. Callus shows up as a hazy, undifferentiated mass on X rays. Presence of callus sometimes provides confirmation of battering injuries not immediately observable at the time of occurrence. Later in the healing process, the new bone tissue thickens and is incorporated into the cortex or shaft of the damaged bone.

Canada   As in the United States, widespread interest in child protection had its origins in 19th-century concern over the plight of urban poor children. In Toronto, Ontario, the first Children's Aid Society was founded in July 1891, and its establishment was followed two years later by protective legislation, the first of the early provincial laws passed to address child welfare issues.

According to Karen J. Swift in *Combatting Child Abuse: International Perspectives and Trends* (edited by Neil Gilbert, published by Oxford University Press in 1997), the 10 provinces and two territories of Canada have each developed their own system of child protection; however, she contends that generalities can be made. Swift writes:

> It is a system premised on the belief that parents bear the primary responsibility for the welfare of

their children and have a concomitant right to raise their children in accordance with their own wishes. It is a residual system, one that deals with the most serious problems of care and generally intervenes with the most vulnerable of families. It is a system that provides more investigation than preventive or treatment service, and it is an underfunded system, one that requires service providers to respond to the greatest crises while overlooking or postponing attention to their serious, high-risk situations.

According to Swift, most areas of Canada have moved toward mandated reporting to the police when certain types of offenses occur, such as sexual abuse, serious physical abuse and in some cases, serious neglect. In addition, most areas require reporting of abuse committed by someone outside the family.

She also noted that children most at risk for entering the foster care system in Canada are Native children. Some areas place children with families while others place them in institutional care.

In 1997, a report in *JAMA*, published by the American Medical Association, described a study of nearly 10,000 Ontario residents ages 15 and older who participated in a study on child maltreatment. Researchers found that males reported more physical abuse during childhood than did females (31.2% for males versus 21.1% for females). Severe physical abuse was reported about equally in males and females: 10.7% of male victims and 9.2% of female victims. Severe physical abuse was defined as an "often" answer to specific acts an adult performed on respondents as a child, either "often," "sometimes," "rarely" or "never." Such acts of severe physical abuse included "kicked, bit, or punched you," or "hit you with something." In some cases, if specific acts were performed at all, either "often," "sometimes" or "rarely," they were considered severe physical abuse. Such acts included "choked, burned, or scalded you," and "physically attacked you in some other way."

Acts of "non-severe" physical abuse include either "often" or "sometimes" the adult "pushed, grabbed or shoved you," or "threw something at you."

Sexual abuse was more common among female victims (12.8%) than male victims (4.3%). Non-severe sexual abuse was considered a "yes" answer to whether when they were children an adult "exposed themselves to you more than once."

Severe sexual abuse included "yes" responses to questions on whether adults did such things against the child's will as "threatened to have sex with you," "touched the sex parts of your body," or "tried to have sex with you or sexually attacked you."

Each province's statute separately distinguishes the parameters of abuse or neglect and these definitions vary in complexity and scope. Some provincial statutes include requirements for maintaining a registry of reported cases; again, these vary depending on the area. There is no overall reporting law encompassing all of Canada.

Perpetrators of the Abuse

In the Canadian study reported in *JAMA*, the most common perpetrator of physical abuse was the biological father, followed by the biological mother. In the case of sexual abuse, "some other persons" were most often identified as the perpetrator, followed by other relatives.

Other Patterns

According to the study reported in *JAMA*, physical abuse against females was found more frequently in rural areas (25.4%) than urban areas (19.5%). This pattern did not hold for males who were physically abused. Nor were there patterns of size of community and sexually abused children.

For boys, physical abuse rates were more commonly found when the supporting parent had not completed secondary school. (35% for noncompletion of secondary school versus 26.2% for completion of secondary school.)

Few studies have been done concerning child abuse and neglect nationwide in Canada. Most

available discussions comprise data taken from a single province or territorial region.

Harriet L. MacMillan, M.D., et al., "Prevalence of Child Physical and Sexual Abuse in the Community," *JAMA* 278, no. 2 (July 9, 1997): 131–135.

caning   Until recently, as part of an established disciplinary tradition, teachers have, for centuries, caned students. To implement this CORPORAL PUNISHMENT, adults most generally use a flexible rod made of rattan or bamboo, which is usually about 3 feet long and 0.5 inches in diameter.

Caning in British public schools (the equivalent of U.S. private, independent schools) has long been an accepted practice; masters and students alike proclaim its efficacy both as a deterrent and as a disciplinary technique. In 18th- and 19th-century America, teachers widely employed caning as a means of maintaining classroom order.

Numerous accounts by educators and pupils attest to the fear and injury resulting from caning. Currently, caning is merely one of the many legal forms of corporal punishment that continue to be carried out in the 21st century. (*See also* PADDLING; *ingraham v. wright*.)

Irwin A. Hyman and James D. Wise, eds., *Corporal Punishment in American Education* (Philadelphia: Temple University Press, 1979).

Cao Gio   Often, practices considered therapeutic in one culture are considered abusive in another. *Cao Gio*—a Vietnamese folk medicine practice believed to cure fever, chills and headaches—is an example of this phenomenon. Meaning literally, "scratch the wind," *Cao Gio* is thought to rid the body of "bad winds." The procedure involves rubbing hot oil on the skin of the afflicted child, then stroking the area with a heated metal object, usually a coin. BRUISES may result from this procedure and cause it to be reported as suspected child abuse.

It is not clear how painful this practice is or whether it presents a significant health risk to the child. The cultural origins and practices of the family generally must be taken into consideration in evaluating suspected abuse and neglect.

CASA   *See* COURT-APPOINTED SPECIAL ADVOCATE.

case plan   *See* SERVICE PLAN.

castration   Though often condemned, the castration of young boys was widely practiced in earlier times. In the Middle and Far East castration produced eunuchs to serve in harems, in the military and as servants. Trade in castrated boys continued into the 20th century in some countries. In western culture, boys were routinely castrated as a way of preserving high-pitched singing voices until Pope Clement XIV (pontificate: 1769–1774) effectively ended the practice by forbidding these castrati from singing in church.

categorical aid   Government financial aid provided to individuals in different categories, e.g., children in low-income families or disabled individuals, is known as categorical aid. Categorical aid is one response to societal child abuse and neglect.

In the United States, most categorical aid available to children and their families is authorized under the Social Security Act. Title IV of the act provides for payments to low-income families with children. This program, known as Temporary Aid to Needy Families (TANF), is designed to allow single parents to care adequately for children in their own homes. During 1984 the federal government paid over $14 billion to AFDC recipients. Payments averaged $110 per person or $322 per family.

celiac syndrome   A condition in which gluten, a protein found in grains, is incompletely absorbed by the intestines. Symptoms of celiac syndrome can include diarrhea, GROWTH FAILURE, anorexia, irritability and a distended abdomen. Celiac disease is one of several malabsorption problems that can cause organic FAILURE TO THRIVE SYNDROME in infants.

central nervous system injuries   Damage to the central nervous system (CNS) is the leading cause of child abuse-related death. Injury to the brain and spinal cord can be caused by shaking as well as by a direct blow. CNS injuries include hemorrhaging, skull fracture, cerebral contusion, subdural hematoma and spinal cord injury.

The rapid acceleration and deceleration of the head that occurs when a child or infant is shaken can tear blood vessels inside the cranial cavity and can cause contusion of the brain. Severe brain swelling resulting from contusion is difficult to treat and can be fatal. Brain injury not resulting in death may cause atrophy or scarring and produce seizures and/or permanent neurologic deficits.

The thin, soft skull of the infant, with its open fontanel, is particularly susceptible to trauma. A blunt blow directly to the skull can cause immediate trauma to the brain or result in intracranial swelling that may not be noticeable for a period of weeks. Skull fractures are sometimes indicated by bleeding from the nose or ears. In some cases, ecchymosis (*see* BRUISES) behind the ear indicate fracture; in others, bone trauma can be detected only by X ray.

Spinal cord injuries may result from twisting or shaking of a child or infant. Because the vertebral column of the infant is cartilaginous it can withstand a good deal of trauma without permanent damage; however, the spinal cord, located inside the vertebral column, is easily damaged. X rays often do not reveal spinal cord damage; therefore, this type of injury may be overlooked in infants and young children. Indications of possible spinal cord damage include development of kyphosis (abnormal curvature of the spine) without adequate explanation of trauma, tenderness in the area of the spine, pain in the extremities when moved, difficulty walking, sudden development of quadriplegia or paraplegia, urinary retention and progressive neurologic deficits.

Asphyxia, a combination of too little oxygen and too much carbon dioxide in the bloodstream, is also a cause of CNS damage in children. Lack of oxygen in the brain can result in seizures, neurologic deficit, increased pressure within the cranium, coma and death. Unless the victim is forcibly strangled it may be difficult to establish child abuse as the cause of asphyxia. Physicians and investigators often must rely on implausible or inconsistent explanations by the caretaker, or indicators of past maltreatment, as aids in detecting abuse.

Norman S. Ellerstein, ed., *Child Abuse and Neglect: A Medical Reference* (New York: John Wiley and Sons, 1981).
Alejandro Rodriguez, *Handbook of Child Abuse and Neglect* (Flushing, N.Y.: Medical Examination Publishing Co., 1977).

central registry   Child protection agencies and law enforcement authorities in many countries maintain a central register of reported abuse and neglect. In the United States registers are kept by the state agencies charged with investigation of child abuse.

Information contained in a registry usually includes the names of children who have been the subject of child protection reports, names of suspected or verified perpetrators of maltreatment and the results of past investigations and interventions.

Central registries serve several different purposes. One of the most important of these is the documentation of past allegations of abuse and the results of previous investigations. Parents or other persons responsible for the care of children often seek to avoid detection by moving frequently, bringing the child to different hospitals or physicians for treatment of injuries (*see* HOSPITAL HOPPING) and giving inaccurate or misleading information to investigators. By checking a central registry a child protection worker can identify patterns of maltreatment that may otherwise have gone undetected.

Other uses of a central registry include improving coordination of treatment and prevention efforts, monitoring the performance of child protection agencies and providing data for research and planning.

Some critics have opposed central registries because of their potential for misuse. Many fear that the reputations of persons who are wrongly accused of child abuse may be damaged if such information is carelessly or maliciously revealed.

central reporting agency   Most areas designate one agency to receive all reports of suspected abuse or neglect. A central reporting agency is responsible for conducting an investigation of alleged abuse or assigning that duty to another appropriate agency.

In the United States each state and territory has designated an agency to receive reports of child abuse. Most jurisdictions designate a social service department; however, some have designated juvenile courts or law enforcement agencies.

See APPENDIX 3 for a list of central reporting agencies in the United States.

cerebral palsy   A number of brain syndromes that interfere with motor function are grouped under the inclusive name cerebral palsy. These syndromes may be the result of genetic traits or may be acquired through trauma, illness or nutritional

deficiency. Conditions that give rise to cerebral palsy can occur before or during birth or in infancy. Low birth weight and premature birth are often contributing factors.

In addition, cerebral palsy may be induced through head injuries caused by battering or shaking. Extreme nutritional deficiency caused by neglect can also damage brain tissue, causing cerebral palsy. Victims of cerebral palsy frequently become targets for abuse by caretakers because of adults' reactions to symptomatic muscular control problems, feeding difficulty and need for additional care.

characteristics of abusing and neglectful parents
Although each case of child abuse is unique and there is no specific type of parent who abuses or neglects a child, it is also true that factors such as psychological stress, poverty, illness or substance abuse often contribute to child abuse.

Some generalizations can also be made about perpetrators, based on research done in the field of child abuse, and this information follows. It is primarily based on data provided by the states to the federal government and is included in the report *Child Maltreatment 1997: Reports from States to the National Child Abuse and Neglect Data System* published in 1999 by the U.S. Department of Health and Human Services.

Note: observation of one or more of these indicators described in the sections or on the list at the end of this essay does not prove that a parent is abusive.

Perpetrators Are Usually Relatives

Most perpetrators (75%) of child abuse are parents and about 10% are relatives of the victim. Thus, in only 15% of the cases are children victimized by a nonrelative.

Age of Perpetrators

The majority of perpetrators (about 80%) are under the age of 40 and the largest single group of perpetrators (about 42%) are 30–39 years old. Individuals who are age 19 and under represent about 6% of the abuse perpetrators. About 6% of the perpetrators are aged 50 or older.

Gender of Perpetrator

The sex of the perpetrator varies depending on the type of abuse. For example, in the case of sexual abuse, the majority (74%) of perpetrators are male. However, in the category of child neglect, the majority (74%) are female. Physical abuse is perpetrated at about an equal rate for both males and females. Medical neglect is heavily perpetrated by females, who represent 82% of the cases of medical neglect. Women also lead slightly in incidents of psychological abuse, representing about 52% of the perpetrators.

When it comes to the category of "multiple maltreatments"—which means the child suffers from more than one form of abuse and may, for example, be both physically and psychologically abused—women form a higher percentage than men: about 57%.

At about 63%, women also predominate as the perpetrators in the category of child fatalities. In looking at both the age and sex of the perpetrator of a child death, there are some variations, as seen below. For example, women and men are almost equal at the age of 30 to 39 years. But in the age group of 40 to 49 years, it is men who are more often the perpetrator: about 56% are men and about 44% are women. It is unclear why these changes within age groups occur.

Type of Household

An earlier federal report on child abuse, *The Third National Incidence Study of Child Abuse and Neglect,* published in 1996, looked at types of households, including households with both parents, mother only, father only and other arrangements. A striking difference was noted: in households with fathers only, children were twice as likely to experience physical abuse than if they lived in a household with both parents. Children were also about 1.7 times more likely to be abused when living with their father only than if they lived with their mother only.

Children are also at much greater risk for maltreatment in single-parent households. In some cases, children are better off living with a nonrelative than they are living with a single mother or father, except in cases of sexual abuse. In that form of maltreatment, the risk for sexual abuse is nearly tripled when the child lives with a nonrelative (see chart below). In the category of neglect, single fathers are at greater risk of perpetrating neglect, with a rate of 21.9 versus the next highest for a single mother, which is 16.7. In this case, a nonparent would be better than the single parents: the rate for nonparents is 10.3. Married parents were the least neglectful, at 7.9 per 1,000. In the category of emotional abuse, single mothers showed a lower rate than married parents: the single mothers' rate was only 2.1 versus 2.6 for married parents and 5.7 for single fathers. For more information, review the chart below.

Family Size

Another impact on maltreatment appears to be family size, and families with four or more children are at greatest risk. Interestingly, families with two or three children are at lower risk in some categories of abuse than families with one child only. Perhaps when there are two or three children, there is some protective factor. If so, this factor disappears when there are four or more children in the household. The chart below illustrates the differences.

PERPETRATORS OF CHILD FATALITIES, BY SEX AND AGE

Fatality Perpetrator Age	Perpetrator Sex	
	Male	Female
19 years or younger	33.3%	66.7%
20 to 29 years old	33.2%	66.8%
30 to 39 years old	46.4%	53.6%
40 to 49 years old	55.6%	44.4%
50 years or older	25%	75%
Total	37.2%	62.8%

Adapted from: *Child Maltreatment 1997: Reports from the States to the National Child Abuse and Neglect Data System,* Children's Bureau, Administration on Children, Youth and Families, 1999.

INCIDENCE RATES PER 1,000 CHILDREN FOR MALTREATMENT

	Both Parents	Mother Only	Father Only	Neither Parent
ALL MALTREATMENT	15.5	26.1	36.6	22.9
Physical Abuse	3.9	6.4	10.5	7.0
Sexual Abuse	2.6	2.5	2.6	6.3
Emotional Abuse	2.6	2.1	5.7	5.4
Neglect	7.9	16.7	21.9	10.3

Adapted from: *The Third National Incidence Study of Child Abuse and Neglect, (NIS-3)* Administration on Children, Youth and Families, 1996.

Childhood Abuse Experienced by Parents

Most experts agree that if a person is abused as a child, that person is more likely to be abusive when he or she becomes a parent. (Note that this is not a certainty; it is only a higher probability than if the person had not been abused.)

A study of 25 mothers known to child protective services as abusive in the year 1987 (CPS mothers) and a control group of 25 nonabusive mothers was studied by researchers in 1994–95 and reported on in a 1999 issue of the *Journal of Interpersonal Violence*. The goal was to look for predictive patterns and also to determine if women who were abused as children were more likely to become abusive parents than were nonabused individuals.

Case files revealed that most of the children (61%) had been neglected rather than physically abused and about a third of the CPS mothers had abused and neglected their children. The researchers found that the key predictor of abuse was whether or not the mothers' social problems continued. Having been abusive in the past was an indicator of future abuse but it was not as significant as the continuing existence of substance abuse, mental illness and/or criminal behavior.

The CPS mothers also scored significantly higher on having experienced psychological abuse during their childhoods, but they did not differ significantly from the nonabused group in experiencing other forms of abuse. According to the researchers, the CPS mothers experienced more rejection in their childhoods (40%) than the non-CPS mothers (4%). They were also the brunt of more accusations during childhood (28%) than the non-CPS mothers (4%). About half the CPS mothers reported being terrorized during childhood versus 20% of the non-CPS mothers. This finding underlines the potential long-term impact of psychological abuse on children who, as adults, may be abusive or neglectful to the children that they later bear.

Patterns of Family Violence and Child Abuse

In their landmark studies of FAMILY VIOLENCE in 1975 and 1985, Murray Straus and Richard Gelles found patterns between family violence and child abuse. For example, they found that blue-collar workers were about one-third more likely to abuse their children than were white-collar workers. In addition, wives of blue-collar workers were also more likely to abuse their children than were wives of white-collar workers.

Parents who were verbally aggressive to their children were more likely to be physically abusive than nonverbally aggressive parents: verbally aggressive parents had a six times greater probability of abusing their children. If it was the mother who was verbally abusive, she was almost 10 times more likely to be physically abusive as well. In addition, parents who were verbally aggressive to each other were more likely to abuse their children than parents who did not exhibit verbal aggression.

There are some general characteristics that may indicate that a parent is abusive. The lists that follow were developed from information obtained from a large number of cases. Observation of one or more indicators does not prove that a parent is abusive. The presence of such characteristics simply suggests that further investigation by a trained child protection worker should be considered. In general, we can state that in many cases the following characteristics apply to abusive or neglectful parents.

Abusive parents:

- seem unconcerned about the child

- see the child as "bad," "evil," a "monster" or "witch"

- offer illogical, unconvincing, contradictory explanations or have no explanation of the child's injury

- attempt to conceal the child's injury or protect the identity of person(s) responsible

MALTREATMENT INCIDENCE RATES PER 1,000 CHILDREN FOR DIFFERENT FAMILY SIZES

	1 child	2 or 3 children	4+ children
ALL MALTREATMENT	22.0	17.7	34.5
Physical Abuse	5.1	5.2	6.4
Sexual Abuse	3.2	2.5	5.8
Emotional Abuse	3.2	2.8	3.4
Neglect (All Forms)	12.6	8.8	21.5

Adapted from: *The Third National Incidence Study of Child Abuse and Neglect, (NIS-3)* Administration on Children, Youth and Families, 1996.

- routinely employ harsh, unreasonable discipline that is inappropriate to the child's age, transgressions and condition
- were often abused as children
- were expected to meet high demands of their parents
- were unable to depend on their parents for love and nurturance
- cannot provide emotionally for themselves as adults
- expect their children to fill their emotional void
- have poor impulse control
- expect rejection
- have low self-esteem
- are emotionally immature
- are isolated; have no support system
- marry a non-emotionally supporting spouse, and the spouse passively supports the abuse

Neglectful parents:
- may have a chaotic home life
- may live in unsafe conditions (no food; garbage and excrement in living areas; exposed wiring; drugs and poisons kept within the reach of children)
- may abuse drugs or alcohol
- may be mentally retarded, have low IQ or have a flat personality
- may be impulsive individuals who seek immediate gratification without regard to long-term consequences
- may be motivated and employed but unable to find or afford child care
- generally have not experienced success
- had emotional needs that were not met by their parents
- have little motivation or skill to effect changes in their lives
- tend to be passive

(*See also* FAMILY VIOLENCE, INCEST, PRISONS, CHILD VICTIMIZERS.)

Jaana Haapasalo and Terhi Aaltonen, "Child Abuse Potential: How Persistent?" *Journal of Interpersonal Violence* 14, no. 6 (June 1999): 571–585.
Murray A. Straus and Richard J. Gelles, *Physical Violence in American Families: Risk Factors and Adaptations to Violence in 8,145 Families* (New Brunswick, N.J.: Transaction Publishers, 1995).

chickenhawk A slang expression for men who seek young boys as sexual partners. The boys on whom these pederasts prey are known as "chickens."

Chickenhawks represent a broad cross section of society, including both professional and working-class men. Their boy victims often come from poor families and are lured by money or gifts; some work for prostitution rings.

Organizations such as the North American Man/Boy Love Association (NAMBLA) and Great Britain's Pedofile Information Exchange have sought to legalize sex between men and boys, claiming children have a civil right to such activities.

Several newsletters with names such as *Hermes* and *Straight to Hell* help match chickenhawks with groups through which they can meet boys. In some Asian and Middle Eastern countries boys as well as girls are openly sold into white slavery. Boys are commonplace in the brothels of these countries. Prepubic boys who are feminine in appearance are usually preferred; however, many adolescent boys also serve as prostitutes. (*See also* CHILD PROSTITUTION, PEDERASTY.)

chickens A slang name for boys used by pederasts. The term usually refers to boys who have not yet reached puberty. (*See also* CHICKENHAWK.)

child The term child is used generally to refer to a person, from birth to the legal age of maturity. Age of legal maturity varies from state to state and from country to country. Some states consider anyone who has a developmental disability—regardless of age—as a child. In the United States, the CHILD ABUSE PREVENTION AND TREATMENT ACT OF 1974 defines a child as anyone under age 18.

child, removal of *See* DISPOSITION, PLACEMENT OF ABUSED CHILDREN.

child abuse   Refers to maltreatment of a child and can include, physical, sexual or emotional abuse or neglect and often includes a combination of different forms of maltreatment. According to an article in the April 1999 issue of *The Lancet,* the World Health Organization (WHO) estimates that 40 million children from infancy to age 14 are abused and neglected worldwide.

In the United States, under the Child Prevention and Treatment Act (CAPTA), an encompassing definition of both abuse and neglect was used subsequent to 1998: "Any recent act or failure to act on the part of a parent or caretaker, which results in death, serious physical or emotional harm, sexual abuse, or exploitation, or an act or failure to act which presents an imminent risk of serious harm."

Each state in the U.S. has its own definitions of what constitutes abuse and all must, in order to receive federal grants, have a plan for reporting abuse to state authorities. According to statistics for 1997 (reported in 1999), there were about 984,000 substantiated or indicated (probable) cases of children who were maltreated (abused) in 1997 in the U.S., the District of Columbia, Puerto Rico, the Virgin Islands and Guam. This figure is down slightly from 1 million child victims in 1996.

Worldwide, there is no universally agreed upon definition of child abuse (or "maltreatment"), although each country has its own definitions for what constitutes abuse. In its broadest sense the term refers to any harm, physical or emotional, done intentionally to a child. Abuse may include physical assault, sexual exploitation, verbal or emotional assault. (See "Definitions of Child Abuse and Neglect" table on page 42.)

Traditionally, child abuse has been limited to actions of a parent/guardian or other person responsible for a child's welfare. Crimes committed against children by strangers or by other children were not, strictly speaking, known as child abuse. More recently statutes have expanded to include teachers, day care workers and others responsible for out-of-home care of children.

Age of the Child

Children of all ages, including adolescents, are abused; however, according to U.S. statistics on child maltreatment in 1997, infants comprised the largest single age group of victims, at 7%. Children under age four represented more than 75% of all fatal child abuse cases.

Gender of Abused Children

Slightly more girls are abused than boys, although in some categories, such as SEXUAL ABUSE, there are many more girls than boys. According to 1997 overall statistics on child abuse in the U.S., 47.4% were male victims and 52.3% were female victims.

Race of Abused Children

According to national statistics for the U.S. in 1997, most child victims (67%) were white. African-American children represented the next largest racial grouping of abused children, at 29.5%. Hispanic children represented 13% of victims. American Indian/Alaska Native children represented about 2.5% of all victims. Asian/Pacific Islander children were 1% of victims.

African-American and American Indian/Alaska Native children were overrepresented in terms of their population: there were twice as many abused children in these groups than seen for proportions of children in the general population; thus, if the victims were in proportion to their numbers in the population, then there would have only been about 15% of African-American children (versus 29.5% of actual victims) and about 1% of American Indian/Alaskan Native (versus the actual of 2.5%.)

How Children Are Abused

The means to abuse the child can vary greatly, from physical force using the hands (which can cause death or permanent injury in an infant or small child) to use of belts, irons, paddles and many other items. Even a substance as innocuous as water can cause death; a June 1999 article in *Pediatrics* reports on the deaths of three children who were forced to drink more than six liters of water as punishment, causing water intoxication and then death. Because the forced water intoxication was not revealed to emergency room staff, nurses or physicians, the children were not treated for the actual problem and they subsequently died.

Politics of Child Abuse

Many experts say that political issues inevitably enter into what (if anything) is done about the problem of child abuse. Creating a program for abused children uses up money and assets that a country may wish to use to resolve other problems. In *The Politics of Child Abuse,* the authors write that child abuse laws are often vague and child protective services workers are inexperienced. In addition, it may take weeks or months for a case to be heard by a judge. They conclude, "Caught in this crossfire are the innocent victims of child abuse, who find themselves enmeshed in a complex web of money, power, politics and ideology that they neither understand nor care about. These children are the ones who never make it into show trials, television news shows, or tabloids; their deaths often rate only one column in the back page of a metropolitan newspaper."

For additional information *see* ADOLESCENT ABUSE, BATTERED CHILD SYNDROME, CHARACTERISTICS OF ABUSING AND NEGLECTFUL PARENTS, CULTURAL FACTORS, INCEST, PHYSICAL ABUSE, PSYCHOLOGICAL MALTREATMENT, MUNCHAUSEN SYNDROME BY PROXY, SEXUAL ABUSE, SIBLING ABUSE and VERBAL ABUSE.

Douglas J. Besharov, *Recognizing Child Abuse: A Guide for the Concerned* (New York: Free Press, 1990).

Lela B. Costin, et al., *The Politics of Child Abuse in America* (New York: Oxford University Press, 1996).

Neil Gilbert, ed., *Combatting Child Abuse: International Perspectives and Trends* (New York: Oxford University Press, 1997).

C. Henry Kempe and Ray E. Helfer, eds., *The Battered Child,* 3rd ed. (Chicago: University of Chicago Press, 1980).

"WHO Recognises Child Abuse as a Major Problem," *The Lancet* 353 (April 17, 1999): 1,340.

child abuse, continuum model of   *See* CONTINUUM MODEL OF CHILD ABUSE.

child abuse, media coverage   *See* MEDIA COVERAGE OF CHILD ABUSE.

Child Abuse Prevention and Treatment Act of 1974 (P.L. 93-246)   This act, originally introduced into Congress by Sen. Walter F. Mondale, was signed into law on January 31, 1974. Its purpose was to establish the NATIONAL CENTER ON CHILD ABUSE AND NEGLECT (NCCAN) as part of the federal CHILDREN'S BUREAU and to appropriate annual funding for NCCAN.

The act was amended in 1996 (P.L. 235) by the Child Abuse Prevention and Treatment Act Amendments of 1996. As part of the amendments, the National Center on Child Abuse and Neglect ceased to be a separate agency. Instead, child abuse and neglect functions were consolidated under the Children's Bureau, which was divided into five divisions, including the Office on Child Abuse and Neglect, the Division of Policy, the Division of Program Implementation, the Division of Data, Research and Innovation and the Division of Child Welfare Capacity Building.

The federal monies provided by this act support research into causes and consequences of child abuse and neglect, and also provide a clearinghouse for information on the incidence of child abuse in the United States. Training materials are used in prevention programs, and various technical assistance, as well as some direct support, is given to state programs.

child, battering   *See* BATTERING CHILD.

child, best interest of   *See* BEST INTERESTS OF THE CHILD.

Child Find   Established in 1980 in the United States, Child Find is a private nonprofit organization that serves as a link between missing children and their parents. Child Find's services include a toll-free telephone number (1-800-1-AM-LOST) for use by missing children and others who may have information leading to the location or recovery of a missing child. The organization also seeks to publicize the problem of missing children and maintains a directory, the *Child Find of America Directory of Missing and Abducted Children,* which contains photographs and physical descriptions of children who have been reported as missing. If the abduction is a parental one, Child Find requires certified custody papers.

A mediation program administered by Child Find maintains a toll free number, 1-800-A-WAY-OUT, to help those concerned with child abduction and works to establish communication between parents and to reconcile disputes. Affiliate groups, known collectively as Friends of Child Find (FOCF), work to raise public awareness about missing children at state and local levels. Among the activities sponsored by FOCF are fingerprinting sessions and programs aimed at educating the public about parental and stranger abduction. Child

Definitions of Child Abuse and Neglect

STATE/STATUTE	Standard	Exemption(s)	Physical Abuse	Neglect	Sexual Abuse	Sexual Exploita- tion	Emotional/ Mental Injury
ALABAMA §§ 26-14-1(1)-(2) 26-14-7.2(a)	• Harm or threatened harm	• Religious exemption	✓	✓	✓	✓	✓
ALASKA §§ 47.17.290 47.17.020(d)	• Health or welfare harmed or threatened	• Religious exemption	✓	✓	✓	✓	✓
ARIZONA §§ 8-201(1),(2),(6), (8),(12),(13),(21)	• Inflicting or allowing	• Christian Science treatment • Unavailability of reasonable services	✓	✓	✓	✓	✓
ARKANSAS § 12-12-503	• Intentionally, • Knowingly, or • Negligently and without cause	• Corporal punishment • Poverty	✓	✓	✓	✓	✓
CALIFORNIA Penal Code §§ 11165.1 11165.2 11165.3 11165.4 11165.5 11165.6	• Inflicted by non-accidental means	• Informed medical decision • Reasonable force • Religious exemption	✓	✓	✓	✓	
COLORADO § 19-1-103(1), (27),(32a),(35), (66),(67),(94), (97),(108),(111) 19-3-102 19-3-103	• Threatens child's health or welfare	• Corporal punishment • Cultural practices • Reasonable force • Religious exemption	✓	✓	✓	✓	✓
CONNECTICUT § 46b-120(1)-(3), (8)-(9) 17a-104	• Inflicted injuries by non-accidental means	• Christian Science treatment	✓	✓	✓	✓	✓
DELAWARE tit. 16, §§ 902 913	• Injury by other than accidental means	• Religious exemption	✓	✓	✓	✓	✓
DISTRICT OF COLUMBIA §§ 16-2301(9),(23)- (25) 6-2101(1), (4)-(6),(16)(18),(20)	• Inflicts or fails to make reasonable efforts to prevent the infliction of	• Religious exemption • Poverty	✓	✓	✓	✓	✓
FLORIDA §§ 39.01(1),(2),(10), (12),(14),(27), (30),(32),(44), (46),(48),(53), (64),(72)	• Willful or threatened act that harms or is likely to cause harm	• Religious exemption • Corporal punishment • Poverty	✓	✓	✓	✓	✓

Find publishes a newsletter and an annual report. For more information, contact Child Find of America, 7 Innis Ave., P.O. Box 277, New Paltz, NY 12561-9277.

child labor laws   The incidence of child labor in the United States had always been high when, in the 19th century, vigorous reform efforts were aimed at passage and enforcement of legislation

Definitions of Child Abuse and Neglect

STATE/STATUTE	Standard	Exemption(s)	Physical Abuse	Neglect	Sexual Abuse	Sexual Exploitation	Emotional/ Mental Injury
GEORGIA § 19-7-5(b)	▪ Inflicted by non-accidental means	▪ Religious exemption	✓	✓	✓	✓	
HAWAII § 350-1	▪ Acts or omissions resulting in the child being harmed or subject to any reasonably foreseeable, substantial risk of being harmed		✓	✓	✓	✓	✓
IDAHO § 16-1602(a),(b), (k),(q),(s),(t)	▪ Conduct or omission	▪ Religious exemption	✓	✓	✓	✓	✓
ILLINOIS 325 ILCS 5/3	▪ Inflicts, causes to be inflicted, or allows to be inflicted ▪ Creates a substantial risk ▪ Commits or allows to be committed	▪ Plan of care ▪ Religious exemption ▪ School attendance	✓	✓	✓		✓
INDIANA §§ 31-34-1(1)-(11), (12)-(15) 35-42-4 35-46-1(3)	▪ Acts or omissions	▪ Corporal punishment ▪ Prescription drugs ▪ Religious exemption	✓	✓	✓	✓	✓
IOWA § 232.68(2),(7)	▪ Acts or omissions	▪ Religious exemption	✓	✓	✓	✓	✓
KANSAS § 38-1502(a),(b),(c)	▪ Infliction of injury or causing deterioration	▪ Religious exemption	✓	✓	✓	✓	✓
KENTUCKY § 600.020(1),(15), (16),(20),(35), (38)(40),(49)-(51)	▪ Harmed or threatened with harm	▪ Religious exemption	✓	✓	✓	✓	✓
LOUISIANA Children's Code art.603(1),(3),(5), (7),(9),(10),(14)-(17)	▪ Seriously endangers	▪ Poverty ▪ Religious exemption	✓	✓	✓	✓	✓
MAINE tit. 22, § 4002 (1),(1-A),(1-B), (6),(9),(9-B), (9-C),(10),(11) § 4010(1)	▪ Threat to child's health or welfare ▪ Deprivation of essential needs ▪ Lack of protection	▪ Religious exemption	✓	✓	✓	✓	✓
MARYLAND § 5-701	▪ Harmed or substantial risk of being harmed		✓	✓	✓	✓	✓

against such practice. Available statistics from 1880 indicate that over one million children ages 10 to 15 years worked—fully one-sixth of all American children in that age bracket. It was not until the early 20th century that any effective legislation against child labor was passed. In general, these laws were proposed to eliminate exploitation of children and to make possible their education, as well as to protect young people from hazardous workplace conditions. Particularly in

Definitions of Child Abuse and Neglect

STATE/STATUTE	Standard	Exemption(s)	Physical Abuse	Neglect	Sexual Abuse	Sexual Exploita-tion	Emotional/ Mental Injury
MASSACHUSETTS Ch. 119, § 51A Ch. 209, § 38	▪ Inflicted harm ▪ Substantial risk of harm		✓	✓	✓		✓
MICHIGAN §§ 722.622(b)-(f), (h)-(j),(m),(o), (q),(r),(u),(v) 722.628(3)(c) 722.634	▪ Harm or threatened harm	▪ Religious exemption	✓	✓	✓	✓	✓
MINNESOTA §§ 260C.007 Subd.3,4,8,12, 14,15,18,21-26 626.556 Subd. 2(a)-(e), (k), (l)	▪ Infliction of harm ▪ Inadequate ability to provide adequate parental care	▪ Corporal punishment ▪ Religious exemption	✓	✓	✓	✓	✓
MISSISSIPPI § 43-21-105(d)-(g), (l)-(n),(v)	▪ Caused or allowed to be caused	▪ Corporal punishment ▪ Religious exemption	✓	✓	✓	✓	✓
MISSOURI §§ 210.110 210.115(3)	▪ Inflicted by non-accidental means	▪ Corporal punishment ▪ Religious exemption	✓	✓	✓		✓
MONTANA § 41-3-102(1)-(9), (11)-(15),(17)- (18),(21)-(23)	▪ Actual harm ▪ Substantial risk of harm	▪ Religious exemption ▪ Reasonable medical judgment	✓	✓	✓	✓	✓
NEBRASKA § 28-710	▪ Knowingly, ▪ Intentionally, or ▪ Negligently causing or permitting		✓	✓	✓	✓	✓
NEVADA §§ 432B.020(1)-(2) 432B.070 432B.090 432B.100 432B.110 432.130 432.140 432.150	▪ Caused or allowed ▪ Harmed or threatened with harm	▪ Religious exemption	✓	✓	✓	✓	✓
NEW HAMPSHIRE § 169-C:3	▪ Immediate peril or risk	▪ Religious exemption	✓	✓	✓	✓	✓
NEW JERSEY § 9:6-8.9	▪ Inflicts or allows to be inflicted ▪ Creates or allows to be created a substantial or ongoing risk		✓	✓	✓		✓

the earlier part of the 20th century, the number of children who benefited from child labor laws remained low.

Historically in the U.S. the experience of children with regard to work was affected by a number of factors that helped determine expectations about a child's function within the family unit. Children in urban areas had vastly different labor experiences when compared to those living in rural locations. The latter group, part of an agrarian economy

Definitions of Child Abuse and Neglect

STATE/STATUTE	Standard	Exemption(s)	Physical Abuse	Neglect	Sexual Abuse	Sexual Exploitation	Emotional/ Mental Injury
NEW MEXICO § 32A-4-2	▪ Knowingly, ▪ Intentionally, or ▪ Negligently	▪ Religious exemption	✓	✓	✓	✓	✓
NEW YORK Soc. Serv. §§ 412(1)-(12), 384b(8) Fam. Crt. § 1012(e),(f),(h)	▪ Inflicts or allows to be inflicted ▪ Creates or allows to be created ▪ Commits or allows to be committed		✓	✓	✓	✓	✓
NORTH CAROLINA § 7B-101(1)-(3), (6),(7),(12),(13), (16),(17)	▪ Inflicts or allows to be inflicted ▪ Creates or allows to be created ▪ Uses or allows to be used ▪ Commits, permits, or encourages ▪ Encourages, directs, or approves		✓	✓	✓	✓	✓
NORTH DAKOTA §§ 50-25.1-02 27-20-02(1)- (3),(8)	▪ Serious harm caused by non-accidental means		✓	✓	✓	✓	✓
OHIO §§ 2151.011(B)(1), (19),(23)-(25), (29),(43),(C) 2151.03(A)-(B) 2151.031 2151.04 2151.05 2907.01	▪ Harms or threatens to harm	▪ Corporal punishment ▪ Religious exemption	✓	✓	✓	✓	✓
OKLAHOMA Tit. 10, §§ 7102(B) 7103(E) 7106(A)(3)	▪ Harms or threatens to harm	▪ Religious exemption ▪ Corporal punishment	✓	✓	✓	✓	✓
OREGON § 419B.005(1)-(4)	▪ Inflicted harm by non-accidental means ▪ Threatened harm; substantial risk of harm	▪ Corporal punishment	✓	✓	✓	✓	✓
PENNSYLVANIA tit. 23, § 6303(a)- (b)	▪ Recent act or failure to act	▪ Poverty ▪ Religious exemption	✓	✓	✓	✓	✓

that required youthful participation in various farm tasks, was expected to perform work that would today be considered far beyond the physical capacities of a child.

City children, generally the offspring of laboring-class parents who in many cases were foreign immigrants, were expected to contribute to the family economy either by working or by caring for younger siblings while their parents worked. In virtually all cases, 19th century child labor was a function of economic class, ethnicity, race or a combination of these.

Only in relatively recent times have activities by state and federal officials focused on elimination of

Definitions of Child Abuse and Neglect

STATE/STATUTE	Standard	Exemption(s)	Physical Abuse	Neglect	Sexual Abuse	Sexual Exploitation	Emotional/ Mental Injury
RHODE ISLAND § 40-11-2	• Harmed or threatened with harm • Inflicts or allows to be inflicted • Creates or allows to be created • Commits or allows to be committed		✓	✓	✓	✓	✓
SOUTH CAROLINA §§ 20-7-490(2)- (21)	• Harmed or threatened with harm • Inflicts or allows to be inflicted • Commits or allows to be inflicted	• Corporal punishment	✓	✓	✓	✓	✓
SOUTH DAKOTA § 26-8A-2	• Threatens with substantial harm		✓	✓	✓	✓	✓
TENNESSEE § 37-1-401 37-1-602(a) 37-1-408(a)(2)(B)	• Commits or allows to be committed		✓	✓	✓	✓	✓
TEXAS Fam. Code § 261.001 Penal Code § 43.01	• Substantial harm or the genuine threat of substantial harm • Failure to make a reasonable effort to prevent		✓	✓	✓	✓	✓
UTAH § 62A-4a-402	• Causing harm or threatened harm		✓	✓	✓	✓	✓
VERMONT tit. 33, §§ 4912(1)-(10)	• Harmed or substantial risk of harm	• Religious exemption	✓	✓	✓	✓	✓
VIRGINIA § 63.1-248.2	• Creates or inflicts, threatens to create or inflict, or allows to be created or inflicted • Commits or allows to be committed	• Religious exemption	✓	✓	✓	✓	✓
WASHINGTON §§ 26.44.020(2)- (6), (12)- (16),(19) 26.44.030 (1)(c) 26.44.015(1)- (3)	• Health, welfare, and safety is harmed	• Corporal punishment • Physical disability • Christian Science treatment	✓	✓	✓	✓	

child labor. During the early to mid-1800s, efforts to control or eliminate child labor stemmed largely from concerns over children's educational needs. In fact, the growth of opposition to child labor coincided with state and federal efforts to establish compulsory public education.

On the eve of the Civil War, a handful of states required several months of school annually for children working in factories. In 1913, a Connecticut law established regulations concerning education for children who worked in specific manufacturing concerns. By 1930, fully 38 states had passed laws

Definitions of Child Abuse and Neglect

STATE/STATUTE	Standard	Exemption(s)	Physical Abuse	Neglect	Sexual Abuse	Sexual Exploitation	Emotional/ Mental Injury
WEST VIRGINIA § 49-1-3(a)-(c),(e), (h),(j)-(n),(q)	• Harm or threat • Knowingly or intentionally inflicts, attempts to inflict, or allows to be inflicted	• Poverty • Exemption to state compulsory education	✓	✓	✓	✓	✓
WISCONSIN §§ 48.981(1) 48.02(1),(2), (2c),(4),(5j), (14g)	• Injury by non-accidental means	• Poverty	✓	✓	✓	✓	✓
WYOMING § 14-3-202(a)	• Inflicting or causing physical or mental injury, harm, or imminent danger	• Religious exemption	✓	✓	✓		✓

Source: National Clearinghouse on Child Abuse and Neglect Information, 1999.

requiring a minimum of education for working children under age 15. By this time also most states limited the number of hours children could work each day and specified as well a minimum age for employed children.

Efforts to control child labor were spearheaded by a number of individuals and organizations at the federal level as well as in individual states. As early as 1902, New York State had established a Child Labor Committee that attempted to control various street trades primarily employing children (newspaper selling, flower selling etc.). And in 1904, the federal government had established a National Child Labor Committee to report on child labor conditions and to sponsor legislation on behalf of child workers.

The federal CHILDREN'S BUREAU was founded in 1912 in part to lobby against child labor. By 1916, with support from the Children's Bureau, the National Child Labor Committee had successfully pushed for passage of the KEATING-OWEN BILL (the Child Labor Act of 1916), which abolished factory and mine work for children under the age of 16. Despite its initial passage, however, the bill was short-lived and was struck down two years later as unconstitutional when the Supreme Court ruled on *Hammer v. Dagenhart.*

The same year that Keating-Owen was abolished, another attempt was made on behalf of limiting child labor. The Child Labor Tax Act of 1918 was designed to impose a 10% tax on items manufactured by children, but this, too, was repealed soon after passage. Reformers then attempted to gain support for an amendment to the U.S. Constitution that would protect children—the Child Labor Amendment, which was approved by Congress and sent to the states for ratification in 1924. By 1938 the amendment had garnered only minimal support in the form of ratification by six states. Opposition to this unpopular amendment was great—38 states had rejected it by 1931. Later attempts to resurrect this child labor amendment were consistently unsuccessful as well.

During the New Deal administration of President Franklin D. Roosevelt, however, several laws with provision for child labor protection were passed, including the Fair Labor Standards Act. Others were the National Recovery Act (1933), which established minimal codes to protect child workers; the Federal Sugar Act; and the Fair Labor Standards Act, which barred interstate commerce in goods produced by individuals under age 16 in jobs considered hazardous to health or general welfare. Despite the intentions of the latter, however, this legislation was worded so broadly that estimates indicate that only 50,000 of working children under age 16 were covered by its provisions, although in 1938 there were an estimated 850,000 such youth employed in the United States.

Currently, each state has legislation that controls child labor, although regulations vary widely. In general, these laws affect commercial activities, although some in the nonprofit sector are also governed by child labor legislation.

Limits on the number of hours worked, age minimums and restrictions with regard to hazardous or unhealthy working conditions figure prominently in each state's child labor laws. In a large number of states, work permits are required as well. Too, parents are prohibited from arranging work contracts for their children if those contractual agreements conflict with the protection given to the child under the law. (*See also* LATIN AMERICA; ISRAEL; SLAVERY, CHILD.)

child molester   A child molester is any adult who engages in sexual activity with a child. Most molesters are male. The molester may be a stranger or may be known to the victim, as in the case of intrafamilial SEXUAL ABUSE.

The term *child molester* encompasses a wide spectrum of offenders and types of sexual exploitation. Molestation can range from verbal sexual stimulation or exhibitionism to forced rape. Contrary to the popular image of the child molester as a "dirty old man" obsessed with PEDOPHILIA, the term applies equally to customers of child prostitutes, single and repeat offenders, male and female perpetrators. Though many child molesters are pedophiles a significant number are not. Some child molesters actually prefer sex with adults and prey on children only because they are more readily available or more vulnerable.

Mental health professionals may differ from law enforcement officials in their application of this term. The former sometimes make a distinction between the child molester who attempts to coax or lure the child into sexual activity and rapists who use violence or physical force. Law enforcement officials are more likely to refer to a child molester as anyone who engages in legally prohibited sexual activity with children. In the case of convicted child sex offenders, federal law requires the registration of sex offenders with state officials. (*See* WETTERLING ACT.) In addition, in most states (45 as of this writing) a community must be notified if a previously convicted child sex offender is moving to their community. (*See* MEGAN'S LAW.) The purpose of such laws is to enable parents to be more protective of their children in residential areas and to refuse contact between them and the molester. Since many molesters are repeat offenders, this seems like a logical step. Others have argued that it is a violation of the rights of the individual (the offender) in that once he has served his term, he has met his debt to society and should be allowed the life of a private citizen. (*See also* PRISONS, CHILD VICTIMIZERS IN.)

child pornography   The issue of where art ends and pornography begins has been, and continues to be, widely debated. Generally, pornography is taken to be the presentation of sexually related subject matter that is purveyed solely for the stimulation of the viewer. Child pornography may include written material, photographs, drawings, film video and computer graphics of children engaged in sexual acts or posed provocatively.

In 1978 Congress enacted the PROTECTION OF CHILDREN AGAINST SEXUAL EXPLOITATION ACT, an effort to aid in prosecuting those who produce and sell child pornography. The problem continues to be the subject of congressional hearings and investigations.

Law enforcement experts consider child pornography to be directly linked to sexual molestation and CHILD PROSTITUTION. Since pedophiles are the largest producers and buyers of such material investigators often identify and track potential sexual offenders through various pedophile information exchange publications or Internet web sites. Increased efforts by postal inspectors to monitor the exchange of child pornography caused consumers to look for other means of making contact. They found such means in the INTERNET.

With the explosion of the Internet, producers of child pornography have rapidly expanded their markets. The key reasons for this rapid expansion are that those interested in child pornography can gain easy access and in most cases, cannot be easily identified or prosecuted, although efforts by police officers posing as children have successfully targeted some on-line pedophiles. The international police agency Interpol has estimated that more than 30,000 pedophiles use the Internet in Europe to create child pornography rings.

Pornography serves a number of functions for the pedophile. It may be used as a fantasy aid in masturbation. Exchange of material with other pedophiles serves as reassurance that the pedophile is not alone in his preoccupation. Photographs of children engaged in sexual acts are often employed as a means of convincing a child to pose and/or engage in a sexual act with the adult. The molester hopes to convince the child that it is all right to engage in these acts because other children do it too. Later, photographs taken by the molester may be used as blackmail to prevent the child from telling others about the exploitation. As the child grows older and is no longer attractive to the pedophile, photographs may be exchanged with other pedophiles as a means of gaining access to other children.

Arguments for legalization of child pornography put forth by organizations promoting pedophilia assert that pornographic material in itself is harmless when used privately. One group argues that depictions of adult-child and child-child relations are not harmful as long as prophylactics are used. Most law enforcement officers and mental health professionals strongly disagree with this assertion. Almost all pornographic material requires that children engage in or simulate an illegal act. Even artistic renderings that do not use real children as models are considered dangerous by experts opposed to child pornography, because such drawings can be used to seduce children. Many studies have documented the harmful effects, both immediate and long-term, of SEXUAL ABUSE. Finally, sexual exploitation is, by definition, an abuse of power on the part of the adult. Though some children may appear to participate willingly they are usually not in a position to evaluate the possible future consequences of their actions nor are they in a position of power in which they can say "no" with ease.

Many experts argue that child pornography is not only a product of exploitation but that it encourages future sexual abuse as well. Potential child molesters may be stimulated by such material and led to believe that sexual relations with children are desirable. Pornographic material may also be used to convince children that sexual relations with adults are harmless or even pleasurable.

Child pornography is becoming an increasingly important international concern. Several European countries have enacted tougher antipornography laws and are engaging in cooperative efforts with other countries to stop international trade in child pornography.

According to Lesli Esposito, author of an article on battling child pornography by regulating the Internet, the U.N. Convention of the Rights of the Child, a treaty among United Nations countries that was adopted by the United Nations in 1990, is the best vehicle for controlling child pornography. However, countries will have to come to an agreement on what constitutes child pornography, an area where countries clearly did not agree in 1999. Some countries such as Spain and Sweden do not allow the ownership of child pornography.

Esposito says, "The Convention lays sold ground work for a united, international movement, but it falls short in many areas. A successful effort to regulate child pornography on the Internet must do three things: 1) establish universal standards which are adopted into law by every country, 2) mandate enforcement of those standards on a national level, and 3) create a mechanism for global monitoring of national enforcement and a means of global enforcement."

In the United States, federal law has addressed child pornography specifically in 18 U.S.C.A. § 2252 (West Supp 1999).

Lesli C. Esposito, "Regulating the Internet: The New Battle Against Child Pornography," *Case Western Reserve Journal of International Law* 30, no. 2 (April 1, 1998): 541–565.

child prostitution Refers to children receiving money or other items of value in exchange for performing sexual acts on an adult or for the entertainment of an adult or allowing sexual acts to be performed on them.

In the United States, federal legislation as of 1999 stipulates that child prostitution is a federal offense and states in 18 U.S.C.A § 2423 (West Supp. 1999):

> A person who knowingly transports any individual under the age of 18 years in interstate or foreign commerce, or in any commonwealth, territory or possession of the United States, with intent that the individual engage in prostitution, or in any sexual activity for which any person can be charged with a criminal offense, or attempts to do so, shall be

fined under this title or imprisoned not more than fifteen years, or both.

A person who travels in interstate commerce, or conspires to do so, or a United States citizen or an alien admitted for permanent residence in the United States who travels in foreign commerce, or conspires to do so, for the purpose of engaging in any sexual act (as defined in section 2246) with a person under 18 years of age that would be a violation of section 2241 et. seq., if the sexual act occurred in the special maritime and territorial jurisdiction of the United States, shall be fined under this title, imprisoned not more than 15 years, or both.

In Central America

Child prostitution is also common in Central America, despite efforts to halt the problem. One study of sexual exploitation in Costa Rica, conducted by UNICEF in 1998, looked at 121 child prostitutes. All came from poor families and the majority, about 68%, had alcoholic parents. Thirty-seven percent had parents who were drug addicts. About 61% had seen physical abuse directed against their siblings. The study also found a child prostitution ring that was comprised of a network of hotel owners, taxi drivers and other adults.

Throughout history children have been sought out as prostitutes. In ancient Rome and Greece prepubescent boys were especially popular in brothels. Captain Cook, the British explorer, forbade sexual relations between members of his crew and young Polynesian women when the trading of iron nails for sexual favors threatened to destroy his ship. A sensational scandal involving child prostitution in England during the late 19th century caused Parliament to raise the legal age of sexual consent. In the early 20th century citizens of the United States became very disturbed over reports of unscrupulous traders who kidnapped young girls and shipped them to foreign countries where they were in great demand as prostitutes. Newspaper accounts estimated 60,000 girls were lost to white slavery each year. Today youthful prostitutes are still in the greatest demand. Most prostitutes begin their careers as adolescents and by age 30 are in greatly reduced demand.

Almost as long as there have been prostitutes there have been laws against prostitution. Legal penalties have usually been imposed on those who operate prostitution rings and the prostitutes themselves. Antiprostitution laws are often enforced halfheartedly or not at all. It is only recently that penalties have been imposed on customers. Some countries prohibit prostitution in any form while others attempt to regulate it by imposing minimum age limits on prostitutes and requiring their registration. Both practices have resulted in various attempts to circumvent laws, including creating false identification for young prostitutes to make them appear to be of legal age and transportation of children across governmental boundaries for purposes of exploitation.

Customers of child prostitutes are most often adult men between the ages of 40 and 65. Many, but not all, are pedophiles (*see* PEDOPHILIA) who have an exclusive desire for sex with children. These men may go to great lengths and take significant risks to engage in sex with children.

Though sexual traffickers in some locations may demand higher prices for sex with a young child, children in many parts of the world may be sold into prostitution for less than $50. Many children who are not part of organized sex rings may prostitute themselves in exchange for small amounts of money, gifts, drugs, alcohol or simply companionship. Contrary to the popular image of prostitutes as exclusively female, child prostitution claims approximately equal numbers of boys and girls.

Runaways are particularly at risk of involvement in prostitution. Unable to obtain legal employment and often lonely, runaways are easy targets for recruitment by pimps and sexual traffickers. Studies of runaways show a high percentage have been sexually victimized at home. Ironically, these children may actually be running from one sexually exploitative situation to another.

There appears to be a close connection between CHILD PORNOGRAPHY and prostitution. Some underground publications advertise tours expressly designed to take pedophiles to cities and countries where child prostitutes are easily obtainable. One guide listed 378 places in 59 U.S. cities where child victims could be located. Other publications list guides who match customers with prostitutes in cities such as Bangkok, Manila and Seoul.

There is little evidence to support the popular myth of the happy prostitute. Child prostitutes often see the selling of sexual favors as the only way they can survive in the adult world. In developing countries, impoverished children may be lured into prostitution by promises of marriage to a wealthy foreigner. In some cases children are sold for a small fee by parents.

Though some may be lured into the practice by promises of money and an exciting lifestyle, most young prostitutes suffer a great deal of abuse, unhappiness and poor health. Drug addiction, violence and suicide claim the lives of many prostitutes. Those who manage to avoid serious physical harm are likely to bear significant psychological scars, including depression, extreme feelings of worthlessness and difficulty forming close relationships. *See also* CHILD SLAVERY.

child protection team   *See* MULTIDISCIPLINARY TEAM.

child slavery   In the New World, child slavery existed among African slaves as early as the 17th century, although this was clearly a practice imposed by slave owners and not endemic to the African culture from which the slaves came. These children did not represent a significant percentage of the slave population in the U.S. until the 1800s (slavery was abolished in Caribbean colonial holdings in 1832), when slave families had grown in number and stability. Most of these children lived in Maryland, Virginia and other Southern Colonies. Contrary to some beliefs, the majority of these slave children were not segregated from their families but lived with their parents until about age 10.

While child slavery is now uncommon (and illegal) in almost all countries, there have been isolated incidents in which some forms of enslavement have surfaced in various parts of the world. In the 1960s, Kenyan government officials put a stop to the practice of fathers in the Kisii District selling their young sons into forestry work in Tanzania. There are reports that in Bolivia and Colombia today, very young Indian girls are adopted by white families so that they will perform domestic tasks without pay. In China, according to a United Nations report in the mid-1980s, schoolchildren had been forced to work while in school, earning money to supplement the school's budget. In India, there are reports of children being kidnapped, maimed, then forced to work as beggars, collecting money for those who

seized them. Another report from India, in 1986, described a case in which several children between the ages of seven and 14 had been bonded to work for a carpet shed owner and forced to work over 12 hours a day for no wages.

In countries such as Malaysia, Jamaica, Morocco, the Philippines, Thailand and Mexico, weakly enforced or nonexistent child labor legislation results in exceptionally negative working conditions for children, who often receive only a few pennies per day in wages. These children work on sugar plantations, in factories, sweatshops, rug factories, as domestic workers and as dump pickers. The International Labor Organization, the United Nations, and various antislavery and anti–child labor organizations view many of these situations as forms of child slavery.

Publicity concerning the current sex trade in countries such as Thailand, Peru, the Philippines, Sri Lanka, Brazil and Bangladesh has revealed that young girls (and sometimes young boys) are reportedly being sold into prostitution by parents or other relatives. In India, this form of child slavery involves girls who are sold as Devadasis—females forbidden to marry for religious reasons but dedicated to sacred prostitution.

Another well-publicized form of child slavery involves prostitution rings, many of which are involved in international sex tourism schemes. These involve both boys and girls, some reportedly as young as six years old, who are either kidnapped or sold as prostitutes. (*See also* TRAFFICKING, SEXUAL.)

Defense for Children International-USA Collective, *The Children's Clarion, Database on the Rights of the Child, 1987* (Brooklyn, New York: DCI-USA, 1987).

child stealing   Primarily as a result of child custody disputes, large numbers of children are victims each year of parental abduction. This phenomenon is known as child stealing or, less accurately, child snatching, to differentiate it from third-party abduction or kidnapping. The International Parental Kidnapping Crime Act of 1993, as well as similar state laws, make it a crime for a noncustodial parent to abduct a child. The Federal Bureau of Investigation is the primary agency that pursues parents who have abducted their children.

In addition to U.S. laws, the 1980 HAGUE CONVENTION ON THE CIVIL ASPECTS OF INTERNATIONAL CHILD

ABDUCTION is an agreement between 48 countries, including the U.S. It established the procedures in locating or returning abducted children. About half of the abductions of children from the U.S. are to member countries. The State Department is the central authority for the United States.

In 1983, Richard J. Gelles, a sociologist who specializes in family violence, published survey results indicating the probability that between 459,000 and 751,000 such abductions per year occurred among American families. Further, Gelles's research suggested that large numbers of child stealing cases involve more than one child per family. He also indicated that households other than that of the child and the parent are often involved. These other households typically include grandparents, uncles, aunts and other relatives and may include professionals such as lawyers, teachers, police officers and private detectives.

As a result, separate states adopted the UNIFORM CHILD CUSTODY JURISDICTION ACT, and the U.S. Congress worked to support individual states' efforts at cutting down on parental child stealing by passing the Federal Parental Kidnapping Prevention Act and the International Parental Kidnapping Crime Act of 1993. This law makes parental abduction a federal felony.

In 1994, the Justice Department created a Missing and Exploited Children's Task Force to help state and local authorities with difficult cases. In 1997, the task force established the Subcommittee on International Child Abduction. In 1998, the U.S. Attorney General created the Policy Group on International Parental Kidnapping.

Experts have identified some problems with the statutes. In a statement before the Committee on International Relations of the U.S. House of Representatives on October 14, 1999, Jess T. Ford, associate director of international relations and trade issues, national security and international affairs, pointed out several major problems including:

- gaps in federal services to the left-behind parents, thus making it difficult for them to recover their abducted children. One parent told the General Accounting Office he spent more than $200,000 pursuing the return of his abducted child while the foreign government where his child was taken to paid the abducting parent's full legal expenses

- weaknesses within the State Department's case-tracking process which impair case coordination

- lack of aggressive diplomatic efforts to improve international responses to parental child abductions

- limited use of the International Parental Kidnapping Crime Act of 1993 in pursuing abducting parents. State attorneys general may be reluctant to use the federal law. Only 62 abducting parents were indicted as of 1999 and of these, 13 parents were convicted of felony parental kidnapping

The disruption in a child's life that results from abduction by a parent or other family member is considered by most experts to be quite serious and to have a long-term, negative effect. Besides a child's home life, his or her school life and general social development are seriously affected by the abrupt and invariably confusing incidents surrounding parental abduction. Some children who are taken from, but subsequently retrieved by, the custodial parent are described as hostile, frightened and physically unhealthy following their return to the custodial home.

Michael W. Agopian, *Parental Child Stealing* (Lexington, Massachusetts: Lexington Books, D.C. Heath, 1981).

Phyllis Chesler, *Mothers on Trial, the Battle for Custody and Children* (New York: McGraw-Hill, 1986).

Richard J. Gelles, "Parental Child Snatching: A Preliminary Estimate of the National Incidence," *Journal of Marriage and the Family* (August 1984): 735–739.

Sanford N. Katz, *Child Snatching: The Legal Response to the Abduction of the Children* (Chicago: ABA Press, 1981).

Bobbi Lawrence and Olivia Taylor-Young, *The Child Snatchers* (Boston: Charles River Books, 1983).

Child Welfare League of America (CWLA)   A privately supported, not-for-profit organization incorporated in 1920. The CWLA provides information, conducts research and develops standards for children's services. It publishes a bibliography of its numerous publications, including articles from *Child Welfare,* a bimonthly journal of the CWLA. For more information, *see* APPENDIX 1.

Childhelp USA   Childhelp USA is a nonprofit organization that serves the needs of neglected and abused children. It operates the National Child

Abuse Hotline (1-800-4-A-CHILD), disseminates literature, posters and other materials related to prevention of child abuse, provides treatment and evaluation services, operates two residential treatment centers for children and funds research related to child abuse and neglect. For contact information, see APPENDIX 1.

Childhood Level of Living Scale Unlike some forms of PHYSICAL ABUSE that are easily recognized, child neglect is difficult to define. Though various statutes have attempted to define neglect, such legal definitions are often vague and too broadly defined to be of use to the average person. One reason for the difficulty in defining neglect is the absence of agreed-upon standards for child rearing. In an attempt to measure the quality of child care more accurately Norman Polansky, a professor of social work at the University of Georgia, and others have developed a scale for assessing child care.

The Childhood Level of Living Scale (CLL) was adopted for use in urban areas. It is divided into two parts, which focus on physical care and emotional/cognitive care. Part A, physical care, consists of 47 items broken down into five subcategories: general positive child care, state of repair of house, negligence, quality of household maintenance and quality of health care and grooming. Emotional/cognitive questions, part B, focus on: encouraging competence, inconsistency of discipline and coldness, encouraging superego development and material giving (to the child). Part B contains 52 items.

Families are evaluated on each item by an independent scorer. Maximum possible score on the CLL is 99. A score of 62 or less is considered indicative of neglect. Acceptable child care begins at 77. A score of 88 or higher is judged as good.

In addition to its use as a research tool, the CLL has been used by protective service workers in several areas to assess the quality of child care in a family where neglect is suspected.

For the full text of the CLL see: Carolyn Hally, Nancy F. Polansky, and Norman A. Polansky, *Child Neglect: Mobilizing Services* (Washington, D.C.: Government Printing Office, 1980; DHHS, OHDS 80-30257).

Norman A. Polansky, Mary Ann Chalmers, Elizabeth Buttenwieser, and David P. Williams, *Damaged Parents* (Chicago: University of Chicago Press, 1981).

childhood, loss of   *See* PARENTIFIED CHILD.

children as property   Traditionally, the law has treated children not as individuals with legal standing equal to that of adults but as the property of their parents or the state. When viewed as property, children have no rights to self-determination.

In earlier times, children were viewed as an economic asset. Families often depended upon their children's labor for survival. In 19th-century England and in North America children were treated in much the same way as farm animals. They could be placed in servitude, beaten and, if they consistently disobeyed, even killed by their parents. Though communities did occasionally condemn parents for cruel treatment of their children, the children themselves had no legal standing to complain about maltreatment. Indeed, some of the first child protection cases in both England and America were brought by societies organized to prevent cruelty to animals. No child protection societies existed in the U.S. or in Britain before the latter half of the 19th century.

Abused and neglected children still cannot directly petition the court for protection. Child protection agencies and the courts typically make decisions in what they believe to be the BEST INTERESTS OF THE CHILD. The child is often consulted but has little recourse if he or she disagrees with a decision.

Recent decisions by the United States Supreme Court have established that children do have some legal standing under the Constitution. *tinker v. des moines,* for example, held that children have a right to free speech under the First Amendment. Still, the relationship between children under the age of legal majority and their parents is heavily tilted in favor of parents.

Some child advocates favor treating children and adults equally under the law. Others believe parents need legal power in order to protect children adequately from their own immature judgments. In the United States, courts and lawmakers have attempted to give children a status above that of property but below that of parents. (*See also* CHILDREN'S RIGHTS, PARENTS' RIGHTS, PARENS PATRIAE.)

Children's Aid Society   This organization was founded in BRITAIN in 1856, one of numerous voluntary societies that addressed the welfare of disadvantaged, underrepresented and powerless groups. Children's Aid Societies also were established in CANADA during the 19th century.

Children's Bureau Until the late 19th century, children in the United States were afforded little legal protection from abuse and neglect. A variety of factors contributed to the formation of federal government policies concerning child welfare in the United States, factors that converged during the Progressive Era. Increased legislative reform during this period resulted in federal involvement in social welfare issues.

Chief among these progressive reforms was formation of the United States Children's Bureau in 1912. The bureau was founded in the wake of activities at the first WHITE HOUSE CONFERENCE ON CHILDREN in 1909 and was part of the Department of Commerce and Labor. The Children's Bureau, with only a small staff, investigated and reported on issues concerning children. By 1938, the Children's Bureau had been instrumental in passage of federal legislation prohibiting child labor. Concerns over infant mortality rates in the United States led the bureau, shortly after its formation, to formalize registration of infant births and deaths nationwide. The bureau also published a variety of pamphlets aimed at educating parents about the care of young children.

Strong supporters of and contributors to establishment of the Federal Children's Bureau included Florence Kelley and Lilian Wald, both social workers. Along with Julia Lathrop (the first chief of the Children's Bureau, from 1913 to 1921) and Grace Abbott (chief from 1921 to 1934), these and many other Children's Bureau workers promoted systematic, broad support of child welfare in the United States. (*See also* CHILD LABOR LAWS, KEATING-OWEN BILL, SHEPPARD-TOWNER INFANCY AND MATERNITY ACT.)

Joseph M. Hawes and N. Ray Hiner, *American Childhood, A Research Guide and Historical Handbook* (Westport, Conn.: Greenwood Press, 1985).

Barbara J. Nelson, *Making an Issue of Child Abuse* (Chicago: University of Chicago Press, 1984).

Children's Charter *See* PREVENTION OF CRUELTY TO AND PROTECTION OF CHILDREN ACT OF 1889 (BRITAIN).

Children's Defense Fund A privately supported, nonprofit organization founded in the United States in 1969. It gathers data and provides information about programs and policies affecting children and provides "long-range and systematic advocacy on behalf of the nation's children."

Among its major interests are: adolescent pregnancy prevention, early screening and diagnosis to prevent medical problems, support for federal projects such as Headstart and other health care, job training, foster care and child support programs. The CDF annually publishes a variety of books and reports, including several volumes concerning the civil rights of children, the public schools, children in jail and handbooks addressing handicapped children's rights, education of minority children, children's health care, homeless children and availability of services to children provided under Title XX of the Social Security Act.

The CDF lobbies for legislation and views children's welfare as a prime responsibility of public agencies. The CDF encourages support for local child advocacy groups and programs. The fund works as well toward establishment of efficient fund-raising sources for its many projects and activities.

The CDF has a board of directors made up of child advocates who represent a variety of national public interest groups. Marian Wright Edelman is founder and director of the Children's Defense Fund. For more information, contact Children's Defense Fund, 25 E St. NW, Washington, DC 20001 (202) 628-8787.

Children's Division of the American Humane Association *See* AMERICAN ASSOCIATION FOR PROTECTING CHILDREN.

Children's Petition of 1669 (Britain) This appeal to the British Parliament was the first formal attempt in Britain to place legal limitations on CORPORAL PUNISHMENT of children in schools. A sequel to the petition came in 1698–1699, and it contains the passage, "There is nothing but an Act of Parliament about the education of children can deliver the nation from this evil."

children's rights When speaking of children's rights, advocates often combine the concepts of legal and moral rights. Claims for children's moral rights are usually broad statements of principle such as "All children have a right to develop to their full potential." Moral rights often are not enforceable under existing laws. Rather, they are principles whose existence is often debated. Legal rights are entitlements under existing law. The right to vote is an example of a legal right.

Children's legal rights vary from state to state and from country to country. In the United States the ages at which children may marry, obtain a driver's license, purchase alcohol or quit school differ according to locale.

In Scotland legal rights and responsibilities of children are spelled out very specifically, including such items as when the child may go to the cinema (age seven), when he or she may be given alcohol at home (age five) and when the child is considered capable of committing a criminal offense (age eight). A legal distinction is made between prepubescent children, called "pupils," and adolescents, who are known as minors. Girls obtain minority at age 12 while boys must wait until they are 14 to be termed minors. Different treatment of girls and boys is apparently based on differences in physical maturation, although both males and females attain legal adulthood at 18 years of age.

In many countries children are treated as the property of their parents and, as such, have no legal rights. Not until the 1960s did courts in the United States begin to consider children as individuals having constitutional rights of their own.

The first Supreme Court case to clearly establish constitutional protections for children was in *in re gault.*

In this 1967 ruling involving a delinquency hearing for an Arizona youth, the high court ruled that children are entitled to procedural due process under the 14th Amendment. Specific due process protections include proper notice of charges, the right to counsel, the right to confront and cross-examine witnesses, privilege against self-incrimination, the right to a transcript of the proceedings and the right to an appellate review of the case.

The right to political expression was affirmed two years later in TINKER V. DES MOINES. Subsequent rulings in some states have invoked due process protections for dependent children who are committed to a mental institution against their wishes.

Some states now allow children to sue parents for willful acts of physical violence that go beyond the limits of reasonable discipline.

Despite these protections, children are far from having legal status equal to that of adults. In *Ginsberg v. New York* the Supreme Court affirmed that children's rights can be restricted in some instances.

Internationally, the United Nations issued a DECLARATION ON THE RIGHTS OF THE CHILD in 1959. This document spells out 10 basic rights and freedoms of children throughout the world. Among the rights claimed for children by the United Nations declaration are the right to grow and develop in a healthy manner and freedom from abuse and neglect. Though the declaration as well as the U.N. CONVENTION ON THE RIGHTS OF THE CHILD, which was proposed in 1978, represent important philosophical and political statements, neither document affords children specific legal status or protection. (*See also* CHILDREN AS PROPERTY, PARENTS' RIGHTS.)

Bob Franklin, *The Rights of Children* (Oxford: Basil Blackwell, 1986).

C. A. Wringe, *Children's Rights* (London: Routledge & Kegan Paul, 1981).

Children's Trust Funds   Beginning in 1980 the NATIONAL COMMITTEE FOR PREVENTION OF CHILD ABUSE spearheaded an effort to establish trust or prevention funds in each state. The United States Congress authorized a challenge grant program in 1985 to encourage states to establish and maintain trust funds. By 1988, 44 states had established such trusts.

The goal of the effort is to make available to community-based child abuse services a dependable source of funding. Money placed in the trust fund is usually earmarked specifically for child abuse prevention and cannot be used for other purposes. Though sources of revenue for trust funds vary, many states generate income for these projects by increasing fees for marriage licenses or divorce decrees. Since funds are held in trust, they are less susceptible to changes in government funding policy.

Children and Young Persons Acts (Britain)
Between 1908 and 1969, the passage of several parliamentary acts evolved a range of policies, procedures and agencies to meet the needs of children and

youth. The first, the Children and Young Persons Act of 1908, set up a juvenile court system. The Children and Young Persons Act of 1933 brought closer together the provisions for care and treatment of delinquent as well as deprived, abused or neglected children, since delinquent children and youth had previously been viewed as a separate group with entirely separate problems. The 1933 act also established a system of alternative living arrangements for children in need of care and protection.

In 1948, the Children and Young Persons Act made it possible for the court to order specific placement for children, i.e., send a child to an approved school, place a child with a local authority or other fit person, place a child in the care of a probation officer or order a child's parent or guardian to promise proper care. The act also empowered local authorities to set up Children's Departments, which now are part of the local Social Services Department. These Children's Departments were made responsible for homes, hostels, remand homes, reception centers and special schools into which children in need of different categories of care were placed. The act shifted the courts' focus away from the punishment of abusive parents and toward enhancing the welfare of the child. It allowed voluntary placement of children by parents and guardians as a preventative measure for "at risk" children. This eliminated the need to convict parents of a criminal act in order for children to be placed out of the home. Social workers became more active in working with families of abused children as a result of expanded roles granted them under this act.

In recognition of the importance of family in a child's life, the Children and Young Persons Act of 1963 enabled local authorities to take steps to prevent the breakdown of families, such as providing financial assistance when needed. Several years later, the Children and Young Persons Act of 1969 eliminated the approved school orders and fit person orders laid down by the 1948 act. By so doing, it placed care orders in the hands of the local authorities, leaving the court with the power to remove a child from the home but relinquishing the power to determine under whose care the child should be placed. This act also helped develop a system of community homes and facilities to replace the schools and homes designated under the 1948 act.

The Children and Young Persons Act of 1975 was an outgrowth of the much publicized inquiry into the death of Maria Colwell, a seven-year-old Brighton girl who, despite protective intervention, was beaten to death by her stepfather. It made sweeping changes in the way children under the care of the government were treated. Parliament placed increased emphasis on the use of community (foster) care and gave greater control to local authorities. By emphasizing the needs of the child over those of the parent, the act made it easier to sever parental ties and also made it less difficult for abused children to be adopted. As a result of this act, children received separate representation in court proceedings for the first time.

China, People's Republic of   *See* PEOPLE'S REPUBLIC OF CHINA.

chylous ascites   When chyle, a milky substance normally absorbed during the process of digestion, accumulates in the peritoneal cavity, the resulting condition is known as chylous ascites. This condition can occur as a result of physical anomalies, obstruction of the thoracic duct or injury. It is sometimes observed in children who have experienced abdominal trauma as a result of battering.

circumstantial evidence   *See* EVIDENCE.

civil commitment laws   In some states, laws provide for violent sexual predators to be involuntarily civilly committed to an institution subsequent to serving their jail sentences. This is because they are deemed to be a serious threat to society although they do not fit the definition of a person with a mental illness. Such individuals are committed to high-security psychiatric facilities.

According to the journal *State Legislatures,* the first sex offender civil commitment law was passed in the state of Washington in 1990. However, it was the state of Kansas whose law was challenged and subsequently upheld by the U.S. Supreme Court in 1997. The U.S. Supreme Court held in *Kansas v. Hendricks,* 117 S. Ct. 2072 (1997) that the Kansas law did not violate the double jeopardy provisions of the

Involuntary Civil Commitment of Sexually Violent Predators

STATE/CODE	Commitment Eligibility	Standard Of Future Dangerousness	Jury Trial	Burden Of Proof
ARIZONA 36-3701 et seq.	Convicted or found incompetent to stand trial of a sexually violent offense Must be at least 18 years old	Mental disorder that makes the person *likely* to engage in acts of sexual violence	Yes	Beyond a reasonable doubt
CALIFORNIA 6600 et seq.	Convicted of a sexually violent offense against two or more victims for which he or she received a determinate sentence	Mental disorder that makes the person a danger to the health and safety of others in that the person *will* engage in sexually violent criminal behavior	Yes, unanimous	Beyond a reasonable doubt
FLORIDA 916.32 et seq.	Convicted, adjudicated delinquent, or found not guilty by reason of insanity of a sexually violent offense Must be 18 years of age	Mental abnormality or personality disorder that makes the person *likely* to engage in acts of sexual violence if not confined	Yes, unanimous	Clear and convincing
ILLINOIS 207/1 et seq.	Convicted, adjudicated delinquent, or found not guilty by reason of insanity of a sexually violent offense	Dangerous because the person suffers from a disorder that makes it *substantially probable* that the person will engage in acts of sexual violence	Yes, unanimous	Beyond a reasonable doubt
IOWA 229A.1 et seq.	Convicted, found incompetent to stand trial, or not guilty by reason of insanity of a sexually violent offense	Mental abnormality which makes the person *likely* to engage in predatory acts constituting sexually violent offenses.	Yes, unanimous	Beyond a reasonable doubt
KANSAS 59-29a02 et seq.	Convicted, or found incompetent to stand trial, or not guilty by reason of insanity of a sexually violent offense	Mental abnormality or personality disorder which makes the person *likely* to engage in predatory acts of sexual violence	Yes, unanimous	Beyond a reasonable doubt
MINNESOTA 253B.02 et seq.	Engaged in a course of harmful sexual conduct	Person has a sexual personality or other mental disorder or dysfunction; and as a result, is *likely* to engage in acts of harmful sexual conduct	No	Clear and convincing
MISSOURI 632.480 et seq.	Pled guilty, found guilty, or found not guilty by reason of mental disease of a sexually violent offense or has been committed as a sexual psychopath	Mental abnormality which makes the person *more likely than not* to engage in predatory acts of sexual violence	Yes, unanimous	Beyond a reasonable doubt
NEW JERSEY 30:4-27.24 et seq.	Convicted, or adjudicated delinquent, or found incompetent to stand trial, or found not guilty by reason of insanity of a sexually violent offense Must be 18 years old	Mental abnormality or personality disorder that makes the person *likely* to engage in acts of sexual violence	No	Clear and convincing
NORTH DAKOTA 25-03.3-0 et seq.	Shown to have engaged in sexually predatory conduct	Sexual disorder, personality disorder, or other mental disorder or dysfunction that makes the individual *likely* to engage in further acts of sexually predatory conduct	No	Clear and convincing

Constitution nor did it violate the provisions of substantive due process or equal protection. Other states worked to ensure that their laws were in line with the Kansas law so that they could not be overturned.

States with laws on involuntary civil commitment of sexually violent predators include: Arizona, California, Florida, Illinois, Iowa, Kansas, Minnesota, Missouri, New Jersey, North Dakota, South Carolina, Washington and Wisconsin.

Proponents of such laws say that they are needed to protect children from repeat violent offenders, some of whom are quite open about stating that they will "do it again." They believe that such individuals are a danger to society. Opponents

Involuntary Civil Commitment of Sexually Violent Predators

STATE/CODE	Commitment Eligibility	Standard Of Future Dangerousness	Jury Trial	Burden Of Proof
SOUTH CAROLINA 44-48-20 et seq.	Convicted, or adjudicated delinquent, or found incompetent to stand trial, or found not guilty by reason of insanity of a sexually violent offense Includes children under 17 years of age	Mental abnormality or personality disorder that makes the person *likely* to engage in acts of sexual violence	Yes, unanimous	Beyond a reasonable doubt
WASHINGTON 71.09.020 et seq.	Convicted, or adjudicated delinquent, or determined incompetent to stand trial, or found not guilty by reason of insanity of a crime of sexual violence	Mental abnormality or personality disorder which makes the person *likely* to engage in predatory acts of sexual violence	Yes, unanimous	Beyond a reasonable doubt
WISCONSIN 980.01 et seq.	Convicted, or adjudicated delinquent, or found not responsible by reason of insanity of a sexually violent offense	Dangerous because person suffers from a mental disorder that makes it *substantially probable* that the person will engage in acts of sexual violence	Yes, unanimous	Beyond a reasonable doubt

Source: National Center for Prosecution of Child Abuse, 1999

of such laws believe they exemplify double jeopardy, or being punished for a crime twice. They also state their fear that such involuntary civil commitment laws might be expanded to other crimes in the future. For an exhaustive discussion of these laws and criticisms of them, see Adam J. Falk's article on sex offenders in the spring 1999 issue of *American Journal of Law & Medicine*. (*See also* MEGAN'S LAW, PEDOPHILIA.)

Adam J. Falk, "Sex Offenders, Mental Illness and Criminal Responsibility: The Constitutional Boundaries of Civil Commitment," *American Journal of Law & Medicine* 25 (Spring 1999): 117–147.
"Involuntary Civil Commitment of Sexually Violent Predators," Child Abuse and Neglect State Statutes Series, Investigations, U.S. Department of Health and Human Services, National Center for Prosecution of Child Abuse (1999).
"What Are States Doing to Confine Dangerous Sex Offenders?" *State Legislatures* 25, no. 3 (March 1999): 52.

civil court   *See* COURT.

civil proceeding   Sometimes referred to as a civil action, this term describes any lawsuit that is not a criminal prosecution. Juvenile court cases and family court (or domestic relations court) cases fall under the general description of civil proceedings, as do probate court cases. Child abuse and neglect cases can be civil or criminal proceedings. Criminal proceedings concern punishment of abusers while civil proceedings usually focus on matters pertaining to the child's well-being. Each state handles abuse and neglect cases differently, assigning a case to a court depending on a variety of judicial factors or criteria. (*See also* COURT.)

clear and convincing evidence   *See* EVIDENTIARY STANDARDS.

clitoridectomy   Sexual mutilation of females is practiced in many countries throughout the world. Clitoridectomy is one form of painful mutilation widely practiced in African countries. Specifically, this ritual involves removal of the clitoris and accompanying labia minora. Among the Gusii, an African tribe, young girls have their clitoris removed in a brutal ceremony, which also includes other extremely painful and humiliating rituals. Originally performed in late adolescence, victims now average eight to 10 years of age. Young girls who wish may postpone participation in the ritual. However, due to the great cultural significance attached to it, virtually all females eventually submit to the practice. To refuse is to be denied status as an adult member of the tribe.

The procedure is typically performed by older women on children, beginning as early as age three. In some areas, removal of the clitoris is performed, ostensibly as a medical procedure, in hospitals. Wherever it takes place, it is an extremely painful and dangerous procedure. Children often die from shock, excessive bleeding or infection following such operations. Survivors may experience a number of painful complications later.

Origins of this practice are unclear. Though some explain it as a religious rite there is little evidence that any religion specifically requires such a procedure. All major religions are represented in groups that practice clitoridectomy. Other explanations include custom, prevention of female promiscuity and a host of "health" reasons. As recently as the 1940s clitoridectomy was practiced in the United States and Great Britain as a cure for child masturbation, insomnia and other ills.

Although approved of within many subcultures the practice of clitoridectomy is widely condemned around the world as a cruel and abusive practice. Many groups that formerly engaged in this painful ritual have now abandoned it. (*See also* CULTURAL FACTORS, FEMALE GENITAL MUTILATION, INITIATION RITES, INFIBULATION.)

clotting factor   When child battering is expected, one of the laboratory tests sometimes used by physicians is a test for clotting factor. Clotting factor refers to the length of time it takes for the blood to clot. Children with the hereditary condition known as hemophilia have a very low clotting factor. These children tend to bruise easily and may appear to have been subjected to battering when in fact their bruises are the result of normal daily activities.

Colwell, Maria   The unfortunate death of Maria Colwell and the resulting inquiry into the handling of her case had far-reaching effects on the protective service system in Great Britain. Maria, born on March 25, 1965, was one of nine children. Authorities placed her in foster care with an aunt for more than five years. Shortly before her seventh birthday, Maria was returned home to live with her mother and her stepfather, Mr. Kepple, in Brighton, England. Despite concerns expressed by a schoolteacher and neighbors over the ill-treatment she received, Maria was allowed to remain at home until she was beaten to death by her stepfather early in January of 1973. Maria had achieved only

about 75% of the expected normal height and weight for a child her age.

Maria Colwell's stepfather, Mr. Kepple, was sentenced to eight years in prison on manslaughter charges and the case sparked a public inquiry that ultimately revealed numerous faults in Britain's existing child protection system. This inquiry eventually resulted in parliament's passage of the Children Act of 1975.

Nigel Parton, *The Politics of Child Abuse* (New York: St. Martin's Press, 1985).

Commission on Children's Rights 1978 (Sweden)
As early as 1920, Swedish legislation made provision for the rights of parents to punish their children. By 1949, the Parenthood and Guardianship Code used the term "reprimand" as a substitute for the previous word "punish" in reference to parental behavior toward children. Until 1957, the Swedish Penal Code exempted a parent from liability in the event that offspring sustained minor injury as a result of disciplinary action. By 1966, the Parenthood and Guardianship Code had removed the right of parents to beat their children, and the handling of parents who continued to beat their children was placed under the jurisdiction of the Criminal Code. In this situation, parents who beat their children would receive the same consideration as if they had acted violently toward another adult or a child who was not a member of the family.

In 1978, the Swedish Commission on Children's Rights proposed that parents be further prohibited from spanking their children as a means of discipline. The commission suggested that this prohibition be incorporated as part of the Parenthood and Guardianship Code, with jurisdiction of cases to fall to civil, rather than criminal courts. On July 1, 1979, when this recommendation became law, spanking children became illegal in Sweden.

Community Council for Child Abuse and Neglect
The concept of a multidisciplinary council was developed in the United States for the purpose of maximizing efforts to prevent child abuse. Composed of community members from a variety of disciplines, the central role of the community council is to coordinate community education, protective services and treatment providers.

Depending upon the specific needs of the community the council may: coordinate case consultation, present or assist in the development of educational programs, identify gaps in services and encourage the development of new services, stimulate research, assess the overall effectiveness of programs serving abused and neglected children and/ or advocate for legislative and procedural reforms to improve services to victims of abuse.

The term community council is sometimes used in reference to the program coordination component of a COMMUNITY TEAM.

community education   Education is an important tool in the prevention of child abuse. Efforts to educate citizens about child abuse often focus on identification and reporting of abuse. However, parent education programs also play an important role in preventing abuse.

Community education efforts that heighten public awareness of the nature and extent of child abuse lay the groundwork for future efforts to treat and prevent maltreatment. Recent surveys indicate that, in the United States, public knowledge about child abuse has risen dramatically over the past two decades. Heightened awareness of child abuse has contributed to increased reporting of suspected abuse and to expansion of services to families. (*See also* MEDIA COVERAGE OF CHILD ABUSE.)

community neglect   The term community neglect assumes that members of a community, and the government that represents them, have a collective responsibility to provide an environment that promotes healthy growth and development for the community's children. Communities that fail to provide adequate support for families and children are considered neglectful of their responsibility to children. Examples of community neglect include: condoning or failing to control activities that are illegal or discriminatory, failure to provide adequate social services for the support of children and families and failure to provide adequate educational opportunities for all children. Unlike individuals, communities cannot be legally prosecuted for neglect. The absence of widely accepted standards for social support services hampers efforts to eliminate community neglect.

community team   A community team consists of three components. The first is a multidisciplinary team of professionals responsible for diagnosis, crisis intervention and initial treatment planning for all child abuse and neglect cases. The second or long-term treatment component is made up of representatives of all programs involved in treatment of children or their families, of child advocacy groups and supportive services. This group reviews the treatment progress of cases on a regular basis. A third component, also known as the COMMUNITY COUNCIL, is responsible for education, training and public relations.

complaint   This is a legal term that is used, variously, in reference to a written or oral assertion. It can describe a statement made orally when charging criminal, abusive or neglectful conduct toward a child. The term may be used in describing a document employed by a district attorney to begin a criminal prosecution. Further, it is employed when referring to a document that begins a civil proceeding, although it is generally referred to as a PETITION in either juvenile or family court. Less often, the term complaint is used in some jurisdictions instead of the term report, in cases of suspected abuse or neglect.

compliance   When state legislation conforms to the requirements detailed in the CHILD ABUSE PREVENTION AND TREATMENT ACT OF 1974, as well as certain Department of Health and Human Services regulations, it is said to be in compliance. This compliance therefore allows for federal funding of state-sponsored child abuse and neglect activities.

The term is also used to describe the behavior of children who are anxious to please an abusive or neglectful parent. Compliant children are more than ordinarily yielding and biddable in the face of demands made by the abusing or neglectful adult.

comprehensive emergency services (CES)   In order to respond effectively to a variety of child protection emergencies some communities have developed a comprehensive system of services. Such services are usually available around the clock and can be reached by telephone. Components of these systems may include availability of a child protection worker at all times, homemaker services, crisis nurseries, family shelters and emergency foster care. (*See also* EMERGENCIES.)

conciliation, court of   *See* COURT.

conditioning, aversive   *See* AVERSIVE CONDITIONING.

confidentiality   Reports of suspected child abuse or neglect as well as the results of investigations are usually considered confidential and specifically protected by law. In the United States the confidentiality of child protection records is required under the CHILD ABUSE PREVENTION AND TREATMENT ACT. In most states unauthorized disclosure of such information is a misdemeanor.

Many areas specifically restrict access to child protection records to the agency legally mandated to investigate cases of suspected maltreatment. Some states allow all MANDATED REPORTERS access to the CENTRAL REGISTER, a practice that has been criticized by some as compromising the right to privacy.

The confidentiality of communications between certain professionals and religious leaders is specifically protected by law. A breach of confidentiality by a professional can result in legal action on behalf of the client, patient or communicant. Laws requiring these parties to report suspected child abuse and neglect supersede laws that provide for privileged communication. Not only are mandated reporters allowed to share with child protection workers information that is normally considered confidential, they are also subject to legal action if they fail to do so.

continuum model of child abuse   Some experts suggest there is no fundamental difference between abusive and nonabusive parents. In contrast to others who view abuse as evidence of psychopathology, proponents of this model see parental behavior on a continuum from affectionate, loving interactions at one end to extreme abuse or murder at the other. The specific point at which behavior becomes abusive is hard to determine and is often interpreted differently. All parents are seen as potential abusers. Whether or not a parent actually batters or otherwise abuses a child depends on environmental and familial factors.

Based on this model, treatment of abusive parents focuses on management of stress and development of a sense of which behaviors are appropriate and which are not. Behavioral therapy and educational techniques are sometimes used. The continuum model eliminates some of the stigma that attaches to abusers under a psychopathological approach.

contusion   *See* BRUISES.

Convention on the Rights of the Child (U.N.)   In order to address more completely the rights of all children under international law, in 1978 the government of Poland submitted a draft Convention on the Rights of the Child to the United Nations General Assembly. This draft was one of many contributions made by various national governments in conjunction with observances of the International Year of the Child.

Previously, children's rights had been encompassed most principally by adoption in 1959 of the U.N. DECLARATION ON THE RIGHTS OF THE CHILD. The 1978 draft is different from other U.N. conventions because it specifies not only social and economic rights of children but their political and civil rights as well. It has yet to be determined which of the many children's rights detailed in the convention are mandatory on the part of states/parties affected by the convention when it is made part of international law.

In 1979, the draft Convention on the Rights of the Child was referred for consideration by a group that is part of the U.N. Center on Human Rights. This group has been meeting annually to work on the provisions included in the convention. The group has also been discussing means of implementing the convention. Currently, most members of the working group favor establishment of a formal committee on the rights of the child to review the convention on a periodic basis and to report to the General Assembly on compliance etc., once the convention is made law.

The General Assembly adopted the convention in 1990. The U.S. is not a signatory as of 1999.

cord injuries   The use of electric cords as instruments for punishing children is particularly dangerous due to the high potential for severe laceration and permanent scarring. In one study, 95% of all children who had been struck with electric cords had visible lacerations or scarring. In the remaining 5% the skin was marked but unbroken. Particularly distressing is the finding, in the same study, that

96% of the parents who used electric cords to strike their children saw nothing wrong with the practice.

Electric cords leave easily recognizable linear or hook-shaped lacerations, bruises and scars. Children between the ages of six and 13 consistently appear most likely to be victims of this method of abuse.

corporal punishment Broadly defined as the inflicting of bodily pain as a response to an offense, corporal punishment of children has been commonplace for centuries. Some examples of corporal punishment are spanking, slapping, paddling and flogging. The purpose of such punishment is to cause pain and shame. In 1998, the American Academy of Pediatrics stated their strong opposition to corporal punishment. In an article in the April 1998 issue of *Pediatrics,* the authors stated that "aversive techniques or disciplines" were found to be used more frequently when parents were upset and irritable. Among 44% of a sample surveyed, corporal punishment was used more than half the time because of the parent's anger. Many other arguments against corporal punishment were cited.

Parents are allowed to use corporal punishment in all states except Minnesota, although if the punishment is considered to be extreme and abusive, it is not allowed.

The issue is most generally discussed in connection with children in public institutions, namely schools. When children are the subjects of corporal punishment in the home, there is less public controversy surrounding the issue. According to sociologist Richard J. Gelles, "the normal kind of violence such as spanking . . . is typically dismissed by clinicians as being part of family relations." It is true, however, that extreme forms of corporal punishment administered by parents are often labeled a form of child abuse. Another researcher, Ralph S. Welsh, has defined Severe Parental Punishment (SPP) as "any type of physical discipline utilizing an object capable of inflicting physical injury. Included are belts, boards, extension cords, fists or the equivalent. Excluded are open hands, switches and minor forms of corporal punishment." Even supporters of corporal punishment agree that problems can occur. For example, the age and physical and emotional condition of the child must be considered. It is never appropriate to spank a two-month-old baby for crying, nor it is acceptable to strike an ill or disabled child. Another problem is that some-

times the mere act of hitting a child can cause the parent to become even more angry and to cause harm much greater than intended. Many experts also agree that corporal punishment is ineffectual at changing behavior and other techniques are far better, such as sending a child to his or her room, depriving the child of special outings and so forth. (Of course, these methods can also be carried to extremes, such as locking a child in a room for days, depriving him or her of food and so forth.)

History of Corporal Punishment

In ancient Greece and Rome, as well as in Egypt, students were regularly beaten for a variety of infractions. Medieval Europe saw a continuation of this practice, which also has biblical precedents. The books of Proverbs, Chronicles, Joshua and Kings in the Old Testament positively sanction violence against children and have provided moral defenses for those accused of being too harsh with children.

One of the more significant references to corporal punishment in modern times came in 1669 with the CHILDREN'S PETITION, in Britain. This appeal to the British Parliament was the first formal attempt to place legal limitations on corporal punishment of children in schools. A sequel to the petition came in 1698–1699, although neither effected any change in the practice of corporal punishment.

Corporal punishment was not limited to European schools. As a means of keeping order in the classroom, corporal punishment was widely employed in Colonial America. There exist specific references to various types of corporal punishment used by parents and community officials as well as by educators, in the interest of maintaining social order. In fact, obedience was so prized by the Puritans that laws governing corporal punishment made provision for capital punishment as well. According to the 1642 records of the Massachusetts Bay Colony,

> If a man have a stubborn or rebellious son, of sufficient years and understanding, viz, 16, who will not obey . . . then shall his father and mother . . . bring him to the magistrate assembled in Court, and testify unto them . . . that this son is stubborn and rebellious, and will not obey their voice and chastisement, but lives in sundry notorious crimes, such a son shall be put to death.

Thus, from its inception American law viewed corporal punishment as an effective and acceptable means of maintaining order, in and out of the classroom.

Corporal punishment has been the subject of criticism as well as being an accepted practice. Educators, parents and civil authorities in the United States and elsewhere have long debated the ultimate effectiveness of corporal punishment. As well, its inherent morality (or immorality) and long-term effects on the child victim have been the focus of discussion. But not until the mid-19th century was any legal action taken against perpetrators of corporal punishment in American schools.

In 1867, New Jersey banned corporal punishment in public school classrooms. More than 100 years passed before another state, Massachusetts, made corporal punishment illegal in schools, although many cities and towns, including New York and Chicago, prohibit corporal punishment of students.

In 1977, legal challenges to policies of corporal punishment resulted in a clear message to children and adults alike. That year, the United States Supreme Court upheld the constitutionality of corporal punishment in *ingraham v. wright,* a case involving a student whose physical injuries resulted from paddling by school authorities and who required hospitalization for treatment of these injuries. The court determined in this ruling that corporal punishment remains an acceptable means of maintaining discipline in the schools. In a related case, *baker v. owen,* the United States Supreme Court ruled that the school has authority over parents in issues involving discipline. This case upheld the constitutional authority of schools over parents, despite a parent's objection to the corporal punishment of a child. These two cases, as well as some others, clearly establish acceptability of legal violence toward children in institutional settings in the United States.

Some groups—notably the National Education Association in the United States—have repeatedly called for elimination of corporal punishment in schools. Despite this objection, however, children continue to be subjected to various corporal punishments.

Despite the severity of damage that can result from corporal punishment (CNS hemorrhage, spinal and whiplash injuries, sciatic nerve damage), such practices remain legal, albeit hotly debated, public school procedures in about half of the 50 states in the United States. State laws vary on whether individuals at day care centers, group homes and other institutions may use corporal punishment.

Some states have banned corporal punishment against schoolchildren by school officials, including the following states: Alaska, California, Connecticut, Hawaii, Illinois, Iowa, Maine, Maryland, Massachusetts, Michigan, Minnesota, Montana, Nebraska, Nevada, New Hampshire, New Jersey, New York, North Dakota, Oregon, South Dakota, Utah, Vermont, Virginia, Washington, West Virginia and Wisconsin.

Organizations that actively seek to abolish corporal punishment in schools include the National Coalition to Abolish Corporal Punishment in Schools, (155 W. Main St., Ste. 100B, Columbus, OH 43215. Tel. (614) 221-8829) and the National Center for the Study of Corporal Punishments and Alternatives at Temple University, 255 Ritter South, Philadelphia, PA 19122. Tel. (215) 204-6091.

Many professional organizations also oppose the use of corporal punishment by any person.

Other nations widely and routinely prohibit corporal punishment in schools. Among those countries that have outlawed these practices are: Austria, portions of Australia, Belgium, Cyprus, Denmark, Ecuador, England, France, Finland, Holland, Iceland, Italy, Israel, Japan, Jordan, Luxembourg, Mauritius, Norway, Poland, Russia, Qatar, Sweden, Portugal and the Philippines. In 1979, Sweden passed a law prohibiting all corporal punishment of children, by teachers or parents, in any setting, home or school. (*See also* CANING, CORD INJURIES.)

Irwin A. Hyman and James D. Wise, eds., *Corporal Punishment in American Education* (Philadelphia: Temple University Press, 1979).

Sureshrani Paintal, "Banning Corporal Punishment of Children," *Childhood Education* 76, no. 1 (October 1999): 36–40.

Mark L. Wolraich et al., "Guidance for Effective Discipline," *Pediatrics* 101, no. 4 (April 1998).

cot death   *See* SUDDEN INFANT DEATH SYNDROME.

court   Most child abuse and neglect cases are handled outside the court system. When legal action is necessary child abuse cases may appear in different types of courts depending on the purpose of the hearing. Alleged perpetrators of child abuse or neglect may be tried in a *criminal court.* The purpose of criminal courts is to determine guilt or innocence and, if guilty, assign appropriate punishment. *Civil court* proceedings focus primarily on the child's welfare.

Criminal Proceedings

Perpetrators of abuse or neglect are often prosecuted under criminal codes that apply to a wide range of behavior such as ASSAULT, BATTERY and homicide. Some states have separate laws dealing with criminal aspects of child maltreatment. Criminal courts typically operate in a more formal manner than civil courts and require a higher standard of proof (i.e., BEYOND A REASONABLE DOUBT).

The defendant in a criminal hearing is entitled to: trial by jury, strict adherence to EVIDENTIARY STANDARDS, cross-examination of WITNESSES, appointed legal representation if necessary and a speedy and public trial. Evidence that may be admissible in a civil court proceeding may not meet stricter evidentiary standards imposed in criminal courts. Criminal courts can sentence those convicted of child abuse or neglect to penalties ranging from probation and counseling to incarceration or, in some areas, death.

Child victims are often called on to testify in criminal court, but such courts deal only with punishment and rehabilitation of the offender. Issues related to the child's welfare are handled through a variety of noncriminal courts.

Civil Proceedings

Legal questions related directly to a child's welfare are decided through a civil court process. States vary in the names they assign to civil courts as well as the jurisdiction assigned to each court. Cases related to child abuse may be tried in any of the following courts:

Domestic Relations—hears divorce and custody cases.

Court of Conciliation—a division of domestic relations court that seeks to promote reconciliation in divorce and custody disputes.

Juvenile Court—often handles issues such as protective custody, adjudicatory hearings to establish that a child has been abused and is therefore "dependent" (i.e., in need of state care of protection), dispositional hearings related to the family's ability to care for the child and recommendations for treatment and/or placement, periodic review of dependency cases and termination of parental rights for the purpose of freeing the child for adoption. Juvenile courts also hear cases involving alleged delinquent behavior of minors and children

or families in need of court-supervised services for reasons other than child abuse and neglect.

Family Court—may combine domestic relations, juvenile and probate functions into one court. In some areas family courts hear criminal cases involving family relations.

Probate Court—processes adoption and guardianship cases and handles matters related to the estates of deceased persons.

The largest number of child abuse-related cases are heard in family or juvenile courts. Civil courts are usually more informal than criminal courts and require less stringent standards of proof (evidentiary standards). In some situations a case may be the subject of both criminal proceedings against the alleged abuser and civil proceedings related to the child's welfare. Recently the number of child abuse cases heard in United States criminal courts has increased substantially.

U.S. Department of Health and Human Services, Office of Human Development Services, Administration for Children, Youth and Families, Children's Bureau, National Center on Child Abuse and Neglect, *Child Protection: The Role of the Courts* (Washington, D.C.: Government Printing Office, 1980; [OHDS] 80—30256).

court, civil　*See* COURT.

court, criminal　*See* COURT.

court, family　*See* COURT.

court, juvenile　*See* COURT.

court, probate　*See* COURT.

court-appointed special advocate (CASA)
Judges often appoint an adult to represent a child's interests. The advocate should be someone who has no personal stake (i.e., is independent of parents and state), knows the legal and child welfare systems, is sympathetic to the child and has the time necessary to research and present the child's interests. CASAs are usually volunteers with special training. Court-appointed advocates need not be lawyers but should have access to independent legal counsel. (*See also* GUARDIAN AD LITEM.)

court of conciliation　*See* COURT.

crib death   *See* SUDDEN INFANT DEATH SYNDROME.

criminal court   *See* COURT.

criminal prosecution   Persons who abuse or neglect children may be subject to criminal as well as civil charges. Alleged child abusers are often prosecuted under statues that deal with contributing to the delinquency of a minor, ASSAULT, BATTERY, homicide or RAPE. Some jurisdictions have separate criminal laws written specifically for child abuse.

Criminal proceedings are conducted for the sole purpose of determining the guilt or innocence of the alleged perpetrator. Convicted abusers are subject to a range of penalties including probation and incarceration. Legal questions concerning the victim of child abuse or neglect are decided in civil court.

Typically, criminal proceedings afford defendants far greater legal protection than civil trials. In the United States defendants have rights to trial by jury, to cross-examine witnesses, to free legal counsel and to a speedy public trial. Criminal courts adhere more closely to rules of evidence than civil courts. The highest standard of evidence, proof beyond a reasonable doubt, is required to convict someone of a criminal offense.

Prosecution of child abusers is often made more difficult by the absence of credible evidence. Young children may not be allowed to testify or may have their credibility challenged by the defendant. Testifying in court can be a traumatic experience for a child, particularly when the defendant is a family member.

Despite the difficulty of successfully prosecuting child abusers, the number of criminal cases brought to trial in the United States has risen substantially over the past 10 years. Many states have enacted laws that permit children to testify in the judge's chambers, on videotape or closed circuit television. Use of NATURAL DOLLS as an aid to testimony for young victims of sexual abuse is also widely accepted in courts. (*See also* EVIDENTIARY STANDARDS, COURT, TESTIMONY.)

crisis intervention   A speedy response may be necessary to protect a child who is being abused. In other cases prompt intervention may prevent abuse or neglect. For further discussion of crisis intervention, see EMERGENCIES.

crisis nursery   In some areas specialized nurseries are available to relieve parental stress that might lead to abuse. Crisis nurseries provide short-term child care for parents temporarily unable or unwilling to care for their children. A child may attend a crisis nursery for periods ranging from a few hours to several days. Parents who have requested the service or who have been identified as likely to abuse their children are encouraged to seek child care relief as a preventative measure. Such services are particularly important for parents who are isolated from friends and relatives.

cruelty, mental   *See* MENTAL CRUELTY.

cultural factors   Patterns of child rearing vary widely from culture to culture. Parental practices considered normal and necessary in some societies may be looked on with horror by members of another society.

The Western practice of allowing infants and children to sleep alone in their own beds, often in separate rooms, is seen as cruel and neglectful by parents in other parts of the world. Likewise, Westerners are frequently shocked by various disciplinary and folk medicine practices of other cultures. The traditional Vietnamese remedy for chills and fever, known as CAO GIO, sometimes leaves multiple bruises on a child's body. In the United States concerned teachers and neighbors have reported Vietnamese children to child protection agencies as suspected victims of physical abuse. Child protection workers are placed in the difficult position of having to decide whether the parents' actions, which were actually intended to relieve the child's suffering, constitute abuse. Such folk practices are generally not defined as abuse unless they severely endanger the health or well-being of the child.

Cultural values and practices must be taken into consideration when determining whether a specific act constitutes child abuse. This does not mean, however, that any action that stems from a specific cultural belief should be condoned. Experts generally agree that some forms of child maltreatment are so damaging and so abhorrent that they should be prohibited anywhere in the world. CLITORIDECTOMY and INFIBULATION of young girls are frequently cited as examples of practices that are abusive in spite of cultural justifications. Torture, murder and the use of young children to clear minefields are examples of wartime activities that, despite alleged approval by some political regimes, are widely held to be cruel and abusive.

Increasingly, experts are turning their attention to international issues in child abuse and neglect. One of the most difficult tasks in studying and in combating child abuse on a global level is arriving at an acceptable definition of abuse. To achieve acceptance a definition must be sensitive to cultural differences yet must not condone practices that are clearly harmful to children. In a 1988 article in *Child Abuse and Neglect: The International Journal* David Finkelhor and Jill Korbin offer a cross-cultural definition of child abuse that attempts to address this problem.

According to Finkelhor and Korbin, "child abuse is the portion of harm to children that results from human action that is proscribed, proximate, and preventable." By focusing on human action, such a definition distinguishes child abuse from such unfortunate events as disease, flood or drought. Accidental harm to children is eliminated by confining the definition to "proscribed" (negatively valued) behavior. This part of the definition takes cultural norms into account and allows for some variation from society to society in the specific acts that constitute abuse. Practices that are condoned in one culture but thought by a consensus of other countries to be abusive should be clearly defined. "Demonstrable serious physical harm" is considered a primary criterion for distinguishing such acts. The term "proximate" limits the definition to behaviors that directly cause injury. Various acts such as war or inadequate nutrition resulting from government policy may indirectly result in harm to children but are eliminated from this definition of abuse. Finally, only acts that could reasonably have been prevented are considered abusive.

Until recently, many observers considered child abuse to be a "culturally relative" term. Recent work, such as that by Finkelhor and Korbin, is changing this attitude and may lead to a worldwide campaign against child abuse. Still, some experts fear such efforts will result in powerful countries imposing their cultural beliefs on weaker nations. (*See also* FALLEN FONTANEL, TOE TOURNIQUET SYNDROME.)

David Finkelhor and J. Korbin, "Child Abuse as an International Issue," *Child Abuse and Neglect: The International Journal* 12, no. 1(1988): 3–23.

cunnilingus   Oral stimulation of the female genitals. In the case of SEXUAL ABUSE, the child may be the subject of the stimulation or may be forced to perform the act on an adult or another child.

custody   Primary responsibility for the care of a child usually rests with the biological parents. If both parents die, become incapacitated or otherwise unable to discharge adequately their parental responsibility the court may award custody to another person or persons. In cases of abuse and neglect a state protective services agency or juvenile probation department usually assumes custody. Court-awarded custody may be temporary, for example, while the parent seeks psychological treatment, or permanent, upon formal TERMINATION OF PARENTAL RIGHTS. Temporary custody places control of the child in the hands of the state but does not relieve parents of the duty to provide financial support.

The state's right to assume custody of an abused or neglected child stems from the doctrine of PARENS PATRIAE. During the late 19th and early 20th centuries, removal of maltreated children from parents was the primary intervention used by child protection workers. More recently, concern over inadequate treatment of children in institutions and by foster families has caused child advocates to be more cautious. Many experts now believe even temporary removal of children from the home may have long-term psychological consequences that must be weighed carefully against the risk to the child of staying at home. (*See also* BEST INTERESTS OF THE CHILD, DETENTION, EMERGENCIES, EMERGENCY CUSTODY, PROTECTIVE CUSTODY.)

Phyllis Chesler, *Mothers on Trial, The Battle for Custody and Children* (New York: McGraw-Hill, 1986).

custody, emergency   *See* EMERGENCY CUSTODY.

custody, protective   *See* PROTECTIVE CUSTODY.

cycle of abuse   *See* INTERGENERATIONAL CYCLE OF ABUSE.

Daughters and Sons United (DSU) Daughters and Sons United is a self-help group for victims of intrafamilial child SEXUAL ABUSE. DSU is affiliated with PARENTS UNITED, a similar self-help organization for families of sexually abused children. At weekly meetings, children are given emotional support and helped to cope with the initial crisis. Group meetings are designed to help victims understand their feelings about the abuse, improve communication skills and learn how to prevent future sexual assaults. Children between the ages of five and 18 years are accepted as members. For more information, *see* APPENDIX 1.

de homine replegando This legal proceeding is an English writ invoked in the 1874 case in the United States involving Mary Ellen Wilson, an eight-year-old New York girl abused by her stepparents (*see* WILSON, MARY ELLEN). The proceeding was unique for this type of case at that time. It provided a means by which a child could be removed from the custody of the home without prior parental consent. Initially, an injury into Mary Ellen Wilson's situation was brought to the attention of Henry Bergh, founder of the American Society for the Prevention of Cruelty to Animals. Later, in the courtroom, Mary Ellen Wilson's lawyer, Elbridge Gerry, successfully argued that a child deserved protection in the same way that animals required protection from cruel owners. The landmark case eventually led to Gerry's helping to establish the New York Society for the Prevention of Cruelty to Children. This New York group was the first charitable group of its kind in the United States and was a forerunner of the American Humane Association.

De homine replegando, a judicial order delivering a person out of prison or out of the custody of another person, has been superseded by a writ of habeas corpus but is still used in an amended or altered form in some areas of the United States. *See* EMERGENCY CUSTODY.

defect model of child abuse A great number of treatment, prevention and research efforts are guided by the belief that child abuse is the result of a defect inside the perpetrator. This approach has also influenced thinking about differences in educational achievement, mental illness and poverty. The tendency to abuse children may be seen as genetic or biological inferiority, a malformed personality structure or moral weakness. Repeated efforts to identify a particular trait or defect that makes an individual more likely to abuse children have been unsuccessful.

The defect model leads practitioners and policymakers to focus on individual problems, often at the cost of ignoring larger societal factors that may be related to abuse and neglect. This approach represents one extreme in a long-standing debate over the origins of child abuse and other forms of deviance. An opposing view seeks to explain social problems wholly in terms of societal forces. Most experts now agree that abuse and neglect are the result of many different factors, some individually based, others not.

demonstrative evidence *See* EVIDENCE.

denial Failure to acknowledge reality plays an important role in the psychodynamics of abuse and neglect. Parents who neglect their children may unconsciously deny their existence. Such parents cut themselves off from their children emotionally and sometimes physically. Denial of children is often seen in parents who have a great deal of difficulty naming a child.

The psychological process of PROJECTION may contribute to denial. The parent, seeing the child as the personification of his or her own negative self-image, wishes to avoid or deny existence of the child. When confronted with their own neglect, parents may blame the child for rejecting them. In this case, denial represents a defense mechanism protecting parents against their own unconscious desires.

Abusive families also practice denial. Incest is often referred to as "the family secret." Frequently, several nonparticipating family members are aware of sexual abuse but deny its existence to outsiders. Denial may reflect embarrassment or a feeling that "things like this should not be discussed outside the family." Also, other family members may derive secondary benefits from the abuse and therefore wish it to continue. Mothers are sometimes accused of being silent partners to father-daughter incest in order to avoid sexual relations with their own husbands or to protect themselves from abandonment or abuse.

Finally, BLAMING THE VICTIM is a form of denial in which abusers try to avoid responsibility for their actions by accusing the child of provoking the abuse. Children may be portrayed as seductive or evil. By investing the child with negative intentions, abusers hope to convince others that maltreatment is excusable or even necessary. Many self-help and treatment groups place a great deal of emphasis on cutting through denial and getting abusers to accept responsibility for their own actions.

Denmark Historically, Denmark's record of physically abusive behavior toward children bears similarities to many other Western nations. In particular, corporal punishment as a means of maintaining control within the family was long an accepted practice. In 1683, King Christian V declared that parents had the right to strike their children or their servants with a stick, as long as the beatings did not affect the victims' health. However, parents were forbidden to use weapons to beat children and servants.

Since the 17th century, Denmark has passed a variety of legislation concerning behavior toward children. Under the supervision of the ministry of Family Services, local child and youth welfare committees serve municipalities with populations of up to 130,000 people, overseeing care and protection of children and ensuring compliance with the law, which includes mandatory reporting of abuse.

In 1934, a law prohibited parents from punishing children for bed-wetting and also forbid them to cut a child's hair as a means of punishment or discipline. Three years later, in 1937, physical punishment in child care institutions was permitted only as a procedure of last resort. By 1967, physical punishment of children in schools and child care institutions was totally banned.

Following the model of a ban on spanking passed in SWEDEN in 1979, Denmark amended its parental code in 1985, dictating that parents should protect their children from physical and emotional violence or other forms of abuse and neglect.

In large part, contemporary professional concern over child abuse and neglect in Denmark focuses on diagnosis and treatment issues. According to some observers, sexual abuse of children in Denmark is not a topic that receives a great deal of attention. Compared to other developed nations, there appears to be less consensus in Denmark over definitions of child abuse. Some experts feel that this may result from the lack of a perceived problem with child abuse in Danish society.

Denver model A multidisciplinary approach to identification and treatment of child abuse and neglect developed in Denver, Colorado served as a model for many other programs. The model is based on close cooperation between hospital and community-based programs.

depression Clinical depression is marked by deep feelings of hopelessness in combination with physical symptoms such as changes in appetite and sleeping too much or too little. It is often cited both as a factor contributing to maltreatment and as the result of abuse and neglect. Deep depression may immobilize a parent, rendering him or her unable to meet parental responsibilities and so contribute to neglect. Poor IMPULSE CONTROL is sometimes linked to depression. The depressed parent often lacks sufficient ego strength to cope with the inevitable stresses of childrearing and may impulsively lash out at the child in frustration.

THE DENVER MODEL

Time	Task	Performed By
Within first 24 hours	Identification of the child as a suspected victim of child abuse or neglect	Community
	Admission of child to hospital	Hospital
	Telephone report to protective services agency	Hospital
	Home evaluation	Community (Protective Services)
Within first 72 hours	Dispositional conference	Hospital and Community
	Court becomes involved (if necessary)	Community
Within first two weeks	Dispositional plan is implemented	Hospital and Community
Six to nine months	Case management	Community
	Long-term treatment is provided	Hospital and Community
	Child goes home after it is safe	Hospital and Community

Adapted from: U.S. Department of Health and Human Services, *Interdisciplinary Glossary on Child Abuse and Neglect;* and C.H. Kempe and R. Helfer, *Helping the Battered Child and His Family* (Philadelphia: Lippincott, 1972).

Psychological depression of child abuse and neglect victims is well documented. Depression in later life is sometimes attributed to a sense of "learned helplessness" acquired by the child who feels trapped in a painful situation with no hope of escape. Indeed the sense of being unable to control one's situation is a pervasive characteristic of psychologically depressed people. Abuse-related depression may last well into adulthood. Studies of adults who were sexually abused as children often reveal unusually high levels of clinical depression.

Treatment for depression often employs a combination of drug therapy and psychotherapy. Given adequate treatment over a period of time, most people can recover from the debilitating effects of psychological depression.

deprivation   *See* EMOTIONAL NEGLECT, SLEEP DEPRIVATION.

deprivation/failure to thrive syndrome   *See* FAILURE TO THRIVE SYNDROME.

detention   A public authority may take a child into temporary custody pending a hearing to determine whether it is safe for him or her to return home. Children may be detained in an emergency shelter, foster home or hospital. (*See also* EMERGENCY CUSTODY.)

diagnostic team   *See* MULTIDISCIPLINARY TEAM.

diphenylhydantoin   Diphenylhydantoin, also known as Dilantin, is a seizure-suppressing drug that has been used with limited success in the treatment of extremely abusive parents.

disabilities, children with   A disability is a physical or mental impairment that significantly impairs an individual in one or more major life activities. Studies indicate that children with disabilities compared to nondisabled children are about 1.7 times more likely to be abused, 1.8 times more likely to be neglected and 2.2 times more likely to be sexually abused. In addition, some disabled children are disabled as a direct result of abuse; as many as 16% of disabled children are estimated to have a physical disability or a learning disability stemming from previous abuse.

"Abuse and Neglect of Children with Disabilities: Report and Recommendations," The National Symposium on Abuse and Neglect of Children with Disabilities, November 1994.
Helen L. Westcott and David P. H. Jones, "Annotation: The Abuse of Disabled Children," *Journal of Child Psychology and Psychiatry and Allied Disciplines* 40, no. 4 (May 1999): 497–506.

direct evidence   *See* EVIDENCE.

discipline   Methods of child discipline have varied widely over the centuries and across cultures, but their purposes have generally aimed at proper socialization. Effective discipline will result in the child's being able to fill his or her role in the culture.

Nevertheless, the means by which this goal of socialization is achieved is fraught with controversy. U.S. history alone is filled with examples of adult behavior that appears, to contemporary eyes at least, to have overstepped the bounds of disciplinary punishment and emerged as abuse—physical, emotional or psychological. In other countries, even in the mid-20th century, disciplinary practices sometimes appear either useless or dangerous or both.

There are also benign examples of discipline used by adults whose sole intent seemed to be to educate and to instill a sense of reason in a child. Most child advocates have been encouraged by the growing international trend to condemn violent forms of discipline in favor of methods that teach children to identify inappropriate behavior and to prevent it from happening in the first place. Perhaps the culmination of this attitude can be seen in a 1979 law passed in Sweden that forbids parents to use corporal punishment when disciplining their children. Most international child welfare specialists applauded the actions of the Swedish government in legislating against what its own society viewed as an ineffective disciplinary measure.

There are supporters of harsh disciplinary measures, as well as educators, parents and others who draw correlations between aberrant behavior in later life and excessive discipline in childhood. Most experts agree that parents who resort to disciplinary measures such as spanking, yelling, humiliation or restricting a child's freedom or action, do so as a way of asserting their own power over the child. Power-assertive parents who vigorously act out through punishment differ from non-power-assertive parents, who use withholding of affection and turning away as a means of disciplining children. The latter group may refuse to speak to a disobedient child as a way of punishment. Experts tend to agree that neither method is in the best interests of the child's health development. Further, no matter which disciplinary approach is used, it is clear that an adult who disciplines a child as soon as possible after an infraction is more successful in preventing recurrent disobedient behavior. A child disciplined some time after an infraction is less able to associate the punishment with the disobedience. Because of this, discipline is less effective, since it fails to achieve the desired goal—to imbue a child with a sense of appropriate behavior.

The most effective means of discipline has proven to be inductive in nature. That is, parents who explain negative effects of unwanted behavior immediately after the behavior occurs are thought to have a better chance at success in disciplining children than parents who either assert their power through physical means or who withhold and turn away from the disobedient child.

In other cultures, there are differing standards by which disciplinary measures are viewed. For example, based on norms in the sub-Saharan African Chaga tribe, a parent is considered overwrought if he punishes a child for disobedience by beating him, rubbing salt in his wounds and placing him in a bag of stinging weeds. In Taiwan, a child in need of discipline is often forced to kneel as an exercise in psychological humiliation that is, if carried out for a long period of time, physically painful as well. In some rural Indian villages, hanging a disobedient child by the hands is considered an effective, if severe, form of discipline. Research indicates that this punitive measure is sometimes augmented by a simultaneous beating.

In New Guinea, discipline of children under age seven is unusual because of the general concept of a young child being unable to understand the difference between "good" and "bad" behavior. According to one researcher, adults in New Guinea value individualism and tolerance of varying views and actions and extend this attitude to children as well as to other adults. In Turkey, discipline of children is shared among all adults. Corporal punishment as a means of discipline is common since most families are fairly authoritarian in structure, although studies show that it is not administered harshly, especially to very young children. Traditional Turkish society has been described as providing a warm emotional atmosphere for child rearing, within which corporal punishment (mostly spanking) occurs naturally. Researchers have termed this atmosphere as restrictive-permissive.

dismissal   *See* DISPOSITION.

disposition   In addition to questions of fact surrounding alleged child abuse or neglect, civil courts must decide what actions should be taken on behalf of the child. This type of decision, known as a disposition, is equivalent to sentencing in a criminal case.

Dispositional choices available to judges are different in different jurisdictions. Most dispositions related to child abuse or neglect fall into one of the following categories: dismissal, adjournment in contemplation of dismissal, suspended judgment, issuing an order of protection, removal of the child from the caretaker or termination of parental rights.

Dismissal. When evidence is not sufficient to prove child abuse or the child is no longer in danger a judge may terminate or dismiss the case. No further action may be taken following dismissal.

Adjournment in contemplation of dismissal. Parties to a case may agree to a specific court order (e.g., a family treatment program) before the court makes a decision concerning the facts. Compliance with the agreement is monitored for a specified period of time after which the court may decide that the child is no longer in danger and dismiss the case. If, after a hearing, the court determines that all parties have not complied with the agreement it may then proceed to a DISPOSITIONAL HEARING without completing a full fact-finding hearing.

Suspended judgment. In some areas a court may issue specific orders to the parties and delay its decision for a specified period of time. During this time (usually six months to a year) the court monitors compliance. At the end of the time period the court may decide to dismiss the case, extend the monitoring period or, in the case of noncompliance, issue an order based on the evidence presented at the original adjudicatory hearing.

An order of suspended judgment is issued after all evidence has been heard. Adjournment in contemplation of dismissal may take place before fact-finding.

Order of protection. The order of protection allows a child to remain at home under the supervision of a designated agency. Conditions that must be met by the caretakers are carefully spelled out in the order. Failure to comply with provisions of the order may result in caretakers being held in contempt of court. The order of protection may be used in conjunction with other dispositions.

Removal of the child. When less drastic measures fail, the abused child may be removed from home and placed in the custody of a public or private agency. Placement orders usually specify time limits and the conditions necessary for the child to return home. In the United States the ADOPTION ASSISTANCE AND CHILD WELFARE REFORM ACT requires regular review of out-of-home placements.

Termination of parental rights. In extreme cases where it appears that parents will never be able to care adequately for the child the court may permanently sever the parents' rights to serve as legal guardians of the child. Many states require that separate hearings be held when termination of parental rights is at issue. (*See also* DISPOSITIONAL HEARING.)

dispositional hearing The dispositional hearing is held to determine what actions should be taken on behalf of the child. In most areas the dispositional hearing is a separate proceeding that follows the ADJUDICATORY HEARING or fact-finding hearing.

Information taken into consideration at the hearing may include medical and mental health evaluations, social assessments and similar materials as well as specific recommendations of the probation officer or child protection worker. (*See also* DISPOSITION, ASSESSMENT, COURT.)

doctrine of sovereign immunity A professional child protection worker in the United States often works for a state or for a state-sponsored agency. As a MANDATED REPORTER of suspected child abuse or neglect, a professional so employed cannot always expect legal immunity from lawsuits stemming from such reports or cases. Although the agency (or the state itself) may be free of legal liability under the doctrine of sovereign immunity, the individual employee is not. In more than a few situations, however, all professionals who work for the state or state agency receive unqualified immunity. Some individual state provisions for modification in the immunity laws exist as well. (*See also* APPENDIX I.)

Doe, Baby Jane *See* BABY DOE.

dolls, anatomically correct *See* NATURAL DOLLS.

domestic relations *See* COURT.

drug dependence, maternal   *See* MATERNAL DRUG DEPENDENCE.

due process   Due process refers to the fundamental fairness of the law and the procedures by which it is administered. There are two types of due process. *Substantive due process* requires that a law be reasonable, not arbitrary or capricious. *Procedural due process,* more often an issue in child abuse cases, deals with the right of each person to a fair trial. Fairness is often defined in terms of three basic rights: privacy, proper notice of the hearing and an impartial hearing.

Investigations of suspected abuse or neglect often give rise to concerns that the alleged abuser's right to privacy has been violated. The line between a reasonable investigation and invasion of personal privacy is often unclear. Some actions that would normally be construed as privacy violations are permissible if they are clearly in the interest of the child's welfare. For example, it may be necessary for a protective service worker to enter a private home without permission in order to prevent further harm to a child. In general, invasions of privacy are permissible only if an overriding public interest is at stake.

Parties to a child abuse hearing are entitled to timely notice of the hearing. The notice should inform them of the charges, names of the parties involved, where and when the hearing is to be held.

Several rights are subsumed under the general right to a fair hearing. These include the right to be represented by counsel, to confront and cross-examine witnesses, the right to a jury trial and family integrity. Actual application of these rights may vary depending upon the type of proceeding (i.e., civil or criminal), the court in which the case is tried (criminal, juvenile, etc.) and the specific charges made. Criminal proceedings usually adhere closely to due process procedures; juvenile courts are often less strict in adherence.

In keeping with the right to counsel, most states specifically provide for the appointment of a GUARDIAN AD LITEM to represent the interests of the child. The guardian ad litem must act independently of attorneys for both the prosecution and defense.

The right to confront one's accusers and to cross-examine witnesses is often problematic in child abuse trials, particularly when the victim is very young. Normal court procedures may be intimidating to the child; testimony and cross-examination can subject the child to additional trauma. Many courts now allow videotaped or closed-circuit television testimony. Others allow testimony IN CAMERA. Whatever methods are used, provisions for cross-examination must be made.

Some states do not permit trial by jury in juvenile court proceedings. In others a judge may, at the request of one or both parties, make a jury trial available.

United States law requires that reasonable attempts be made by the state to maintain family integrity by offering rehabilitative services. Before PARENTS' RIGHTS can be terminated, the state must prove that attempts have been made to keep a child at home or that the child is in immediate danger. (*See also* IN RE GAULT, CHILDREN'S RIGHTS, ADVOCACY, TERMINATION OF PARENTAL RIGHTS.)

due process, procedural   *See* DUE PROCESS.

due process, substantive   *See* DUE PROCESS.

dwarfism   Prolonged abuse or neglect can inhibit the body's secretion of the growth-producing hormone somatotropin, which causes significant physical, emotional and intellectual retardation. This syndrome is known by several names, including: psychosocial dwarfism, abuse dwarfism, deprivation dwarfism, reversible hyposomatotropism, reversible growth failure, and post-traumatic hypopituitarism.

Diagnosis is based on the observation of a significant slowdown in physical growth after infancy. Skeletal growth is severely retarded, and height is below the third percentile as compared to children of the same chronological age.

Endocrinological tests demonstrate a lack of somatotropin (growth hormone) production before the child is removed from the unhealthy environment. The factor that distinguishes these symptoms from other organically induced growth failure is the rapid reversal seen when children are hospitalized. Significant increases in pituitary secretion have been observed as rapidly as two weeks following removal of the child from the abusive situation. Other symptoms may take much longer to improve. SUBDURAL HEMATOMA, often a result of shaking or battering, has also been identified as a cause of hypopituitarism.

Psychosocial dwarfism is in some ways similar to the FAILURE TO THRIVE syndrome seen in infants. The major distinction between the two is the age of the child at onset. A generally, but not universally, accepted demarcation point is age three. Growth failure occurring prior to that point is known as failure to thrive, afterward as psychosocial dwarfism.

In addition to a background of especially cruel or neglectful treatment at home, children suffering from psychosocial dwarfism may present a history of unusual behavioral symptoms. They may exhibit an exaggerated desire for food or drink, sometimes eating from trash cans or drinking from toilet bowls. Bouts of excessive eating may be followed by self-starvation or vomiting. These children often lack age-appropriate control of urination and bowel movements and may throw aggressive tantrums or appear socially withdrawn.

Sleep appears to play an important part in producing the growth failure seen in psychosocial dwarfs. Unusual patterns of sleep and wakefulness are frequently observed. Research has shown a direct correspondence between the normalization of sleep patterns and the growth spurt experienced by children when they are removed from the abusive situation.

Retarded motor and intellectual development is frequently present in the psychosocial dwarf. Like skeletal growth, these symptoms usually show remarkable improvement when the child is moved to a healthy living environment. Improvements in IQ scores up to as much as 55 points have been recorded. When deprivation continues into adolescence, a delay in the onset of puberty is usually observed. The exact cause, or causes, of somatotropin deficiency in the psychosocial dwarfism syndrome is not clear. As mentioned earlier, sleep patterns seem to be related to production of the growth hormone, however there is no consistent explanation for the sleeping difficulties. Significant increase in somatotropin production is usually observed when the child is removed from the home in which the initial symptoms occurred. The relative rarity of psychosocial dwarfism coupled with the difficulty of collecting accurate information about the child's treatment prior to intervention has left many questions about this syndrome unanswered.

John, Money, *The Kaspar Hauser Syndrome of "Psychosocial Dwarfism": Deficient Statural, Intellectual, and Social Growth Induced by Child Abuse* (Buffalo, N.Y.: Prometheus Books, 1992).

Early and Periodic Screening, Diagnosis and Treatment (EPSDT) The Early and Periodic Screening, Diagnosis and Treatment (EPSDT) program was enacted in 1967 by the Congress of the United States as part of the MEDICAID program. The required services were defined specifically in the Omnibus Budget Reconciliation Act of 1989. EPSDT now requires periodic screening, vision, dental and hearing services. Medicaid is jointly funded by the states and the federal government to provide medical care to low-income families and individuals.

EPSDT was specifically designed to detect potentially disabling physical or mental conditions in poor children. Screening begins in infancy and may continue up to age 21. In addition to screening, the program provides treatment of any medical problems and transportation to and from the medical facility.

All states are required to provide this service to Medicaid-eligible children. Welfare departments are responsible for administration of EPSDT in most areas.

Regular monitoring can help identify cases of maltreatment that might otherwise have gone undetected. Screening programs such as EPSDT can also help reduce the incidence of SITUATIONAL ABUSE AND NEGLECT. (*See also* POVERTY.)

ecchymosis *See* BRUISES.

edema Bumps or BRUISES can result in edema, a swelling of body tissue caused by an excessive collecting of fluid in the body tissue. Such swelling is a possible indicator of battering but may also be the result of various diseases, malnutrition or allergies.

education, community *See* COMMUNITY EDUCATION.

education, parent *See* PARENT EDUCATION.

educational neglect The National Center on Child Abuse and Neglect offers the following definition of educational neglect:

> Failure to provide for a child's cognitive development. This may include failure to conform to state legal requirements regarding school attendance.

Little information is available on the incidence of this problem. Most child protection agencies do not keep separate statistics on this form of neglect. Because educational neglect is not considered life threatening, it may receive less attention from child abuse experts than other forms of abuse and neglect.

In recent years several proposals have been made that would penalize parents of children who are chronically truant from school. Proposed penalties range from fines and imprisonment to reductions in welfare assistance. These proposals illustrate a growing tendency to deal with the problem of school attendance outside of the child protection system.

emergencies Abused or neglected children may need immediate intervention to protect them from further severe maltreatment or to ensure proper treatment of injuries. All areas of the United States are covered by HOTLINES that provide around-the-clock telephone screening of potential child abuse emergencies. These phone services are usually operated by, or have a direct link with, local child protection agencies and law enforcement authorities.

Assessment of danger to the child is the first and perhaps the most important step in the screening and investigatory process (*see* INVESTIGATION). The

United States' National Center on Child Abuse and Neglect defines potential emergencies as:

- all complaints of severe physical abuse
- all complaints of sexual abuse
- complaints alleging that children under the age of eight have been left alone
- complaints alleging that children and their parents are in need of food or housing
- complaints alleging that parents of young children are psychotic, behave in a bizarre manner or act under the influence of drugs or alcohol
- complaints alleging bizarre punishment (e.g., locking a child in a closet)
- complaints alleging that children or adolescents are suicidal
- complaints involving abandonment
- complaints from hospital emergency rooms concerning children under their care
- self-referrals from parents who state they are unable to cope, feel that they will hurt or kill their children or desire their children's removal and placement away from home
- cases in which protective custody is authorized

U.S. Department of Health, Education and Welfare, Office of Human Development Services, Administration for Children, Youth and Families, Children's Bureau, National Center on Child Abuse and Neglect. *Child Protective Services: A Guide for Workers* (Washington, D.C.: 1979; [OHDS] 79-30203).

If the child is determined to be in immediate physical or emotional danger several alternatives are available. PARENT AIDES or HOMEMAKER SERVICES may be called to assist the family and ensure proper treatment of the child. The abusing adult may be voluntarily or involuntarily removed from home. When abuse is discovered in a hospital emergency room, the child may be placed on HOSPITAL HOLD for his or her protection.

Removing a child from home is usually the least preferable of emergency interventions. Emergency removal may place additional strain on a child who has already suffered severe emotional trauma. Children often find it difficult to adjust to abrupt changes brought on by out-of-home placement.

Emergency placement further disrupts families and may reduce parents' willingness to cooperate with subsequent efforts to protect the child. When emergency removal of a child is necessary, trauma to the child and family may be reduced by placing the child with a friend or relative. Placement in an emergency shelter or foster home is considered only if no suitable alternatives are available.

Most developed countries make legal provisions for placing children in protective custody. In the United States, children may be removed from parents' custody by court order or, in an emergency, by state authority. Many states allow police to take a child into protective custody without prior court approval. When children are removed without a court order, a HEARING must be held to review the decision. Court supervision of protective custody focuses on rights of the child, parents and the state.

emergency custody   Virtually all states have legal provisions for an authorized person to remove a child from a dangerous or abusive situation. This immediate removal into emergency custody can occur either with or without a court order, although states have varying requirements governing this action; some states require that a court order be obtained before emergency custody without parental consent is effected. In addition, each state has different definitions of who is authorized to take emergency custody action.

Despite the clear necessity of emergency custody in some cases, most experts currently agree that, in general, every effort should be made to avoid unnecessary removal of a child from the home. The entire concept of interfering with what has been termed the "sanctity of the home and family" is one that has received increasing judicial scrutiny in recent years.

emergency room   Most severely abused children and many with less serious physical injuries are brought to hospital emergency rooms for treatment. Specialized training both in detection of child abuse and in crisis intervention is considered essential for emergency room personnel.

Emergency room physicians and nurses must often work without benefit of adequate social or medical histories of the child who receives treatment. In urban areas, emergency room personnel must be alert to HOSPITAL HOPPING, a practice employed by some chronic abusers.

Metropolitan hospitals may see 50% to 65% of reported cases of abuse as opposed to the 2% to 5% treated by private physicians. Figures such as these have led some observers to speculate that private physicians tend to underreport abuse.

According to a 1997 report on violence-related injuries treated in hospital emergency departments published by the Bureau of Justice Statistics, about 26% of the violence-related injuries were experienced by children aged 18 and under. Of these, 5.3% were children under age 12 and 6.1% were children ages 12–14.

Although data were not generally broken down into categories of younger children, researchers did note that preschool children were at great risk for injuries. Of children under age 12 who were examined or treated for sexual abuse, approximately half were age four or younger. Of children treated for physical abuse, about half were age five or younger.

The perpetrator of the injury varied according to the age of the individual and is reflected in the chart below. As can be seen from the chart, children age 12 and under who are treated in emergency departments of hospitals are most at risk for abuse from relatives (56.3%), followed by acquaintances (34.1%). In contrast, those who are age 10–12 are most at risk from acquaintances (58.2%), followed by strangers (29.9%). (Adults age 20 and over are also most at risk from acquaintances [43.9%] and strangers [35.2%])

emotional abuse   *See* PSYCHOLOGICAL MALTREATMENT.

emotional neglect   The NATIONAL CENTER ON CHILD ABUSE AND NEGLECT defines emotional neglect as

RELATIONSHIP TO THE PATIENT OF THE PERSON WHO INFLICTED THE INJURY

Age of ED Patient	Total	Relative	Acquaintance	Stranger
Child under age 12	100%	56.3%	34.1%	9.7%
Age 12–19	100%	11.9%	58.2%	29.9%
Adult 20+	100%	20.9%	43.9%	35.2%

Source: Michael R. Rand, "Violence-Related Injuries Treated in Hospital Emergency Departments," Bureau of Justice Statistics Special Report, 1997.

"failure to provide the psychological nurturance necessary for a child's psychological growth and development."

Numerous studies have documented the crucial importance of a warm, safe and loving relationship with an adult for the healthy physical and emotional development of children. Early studies of HOSPITALISM in infants separated from their mothers at birth documented physical and cognitive impairment. These deficits appeared to result from a lack of physical contact and emotional interaction. Institutionalized infants in the studies received adequate food, shelter and medical care yet appeared undernourished, listless and withdrawn. In many cases the condition of these infants continued to worsen and eventually resulted in their death. Their FAILURE TO THRIVE was attributed to impersonal care received in the hospital. Overburdened nurses had little time to hold or interact with the infants. The sterile hospital environment offered little sensory stimulation. Conversely, infants in another ward who received a good deal of loving attention in a sensory-rich environment appeared happier and followed normal developmental patterns. Similar characteristics have been observed in children who receive insufficient parental attention at home.

Tactile stimulation (touching) appears to be especially important for both cognitive and emotional development of infants and children. Infants whose parents are physically undemonstrative may reach out indiscriminately to strangers at a time when others their age normally exhibit a fear of strangers.

Emotionally neglected children often show signs of psychopathology in later life. As children they may appear depressed and withdrawn or may engage in frantic ACTING OUT in the hopes of attracting some type of attention from caretakers. Norman Polansky, a professor of social work at the University of Georgia, has described a phenomenon that he calls the APATHY-FUTILITY SYNDROME, in which neglected children develop a form of emotional numbness and immaturity that may later result in their becoming neglectful parents.

Despite the potentially devastating effects of emotional neglect, many areas do not specifically identify it as a condition to be reported to child protection agencies. Legal definitions of emotional neglect, when they exist, are often so vague as to be useless in a court of law. Further, while the results of emotional neglect can be observed, it is often difficult to prove that parental neglect, rather than other factors, was the cause.

encopresis   Repeated involuntary defecation (soiling) occurring in children over the age of four years is termed encopresis. Boys are over three times more likely than girls to suffer from this condition. Encopresis is usually accompanied by chronic constipation. Physical causes of encopresis include neurogenic megacolon, a nerve deficiency that inhibits peristalsis in the bowel, and anatomic megacolon, the obstruction of the bowel by a tumor or lesion. When no physiological cause is found encopresis is sometimes interpreted as the child's attempt to express hostility or resolve conflict. Many encopretic children live in families where open conflict is avoided at all costs.

Some psychotherapists have observed similarities between a parent's somatic concerns and those of the child. For example, the encopretic child may have a parent who suffers from irritable bowel syndrome or from chronic constipation.

Fecal soiling may be seen as both a precipitant and a consequence of abuse. Caretakers find an encopretic child extremely frustrating and enraged parents may resort to harsh punishment in an effort to stop the behavior. Harsh treatment can actually prolong the problem and is almost never helpful.

In a child who has been toilet trained for over one year encopresis sometimes is seen as indicative of internal conflicts that the child cannot address directly. These conflicts may be related to abuse.

A careful assessment, beginning with a thorough medical examination, is recommended as the first step in treating encopresis.

Charles E. Schaefer, *Childhood Encopresis and Enuresis: Causes and Therapy* (New York: Van Nostrand Reinhold Company, 1979).

England   *See* BRITAIN.

enuresis   Repeated involuntary discharge of urine in a child over three years of age. Enuresis is derived from the Greek word meaning "I make

water." Approximately 10% of children between the ages of six and 10 in the United States are enuretic.

A number of myths have grown up around the problem of enuresis. Many caregivers believe that bed-wetting is done out of spite, although psychotherapists strongly oppose this interpretation. Most believe enuresis is related to anxiety, usually due to situational stress.

Another myth is that enuretic children are emotionally disturbed. Though the incidence of emotional problems is slightly higher among this group, many of these problems vanish as the enuresis is controlled.

Many cruel and inhumane remedies have been tried in an effort to cure enuresis. Seventh-century parents forced bed wetters to drink a pint of their own urine. Other "cures" included beating, tying a string around the penis, placing the child's buttocks on a hot stove, making the child wear wet garments, shaming or ridiculing the child. All of these methods are ineffective and abusive. There is no evidence that punishment is an effective treatment for enuresis.

Physicians and psychologists generally attribute nonphysiologically based enuresis to situational stress. Punishment usually exacerbates the problem in these cases.

As with ENCOPRESIS, treatment of enuresis should begin with a thorough medical examination.

Charles E. Schaefer, *Childhood Encopresis and Enuresis: Causes and Therapy* (New York: Van Nostrand Reinhold, 1979).

EPSDT   *See* EARLY AND PERIODIC SCREENING, DIAGNOSIS AND TREATMENT.

evidence   Statements by various parties, written documents, material objects and the opinions of experts may all serve as evidence in an investigation of suspected child abuse or neglect. Not all such evidence is allowed in court hearings. Courts have rules that govern the kinds of evidence that may be considered. Types of evidence allowed may differ according to the type of hearing. Preliminary or pretrial hearings are held for the purpose of issuing temporary orders. Evidence allowed at a preliminary hearing may not meet the rules of evidence applicable to a later court proceeding.

Adjudicatory or "fact-finding" hearings usually require that evidence conform to the legal rules of evidence and have a direct bearing on the issue before the court. In general four kinds of evidence are allowed.

Direct evidence is based on the witness's own observations and perceptions and does not depend on proof of any other facts. A neighbor's account of having watched the accused beating the child is direct evidence.

Real, demonstrative or autoptic evidence is concrete physical evidence. A child's injuries, X rays showing broken bones, instruments used to harm a child and photographs are examples of real evidence.

Circumstantial evidence includes observations that allow the court to reach a specific conclusion, for example, testimony that a parent was shouting, threatening and visibly enraged at a child shortly before the alleged abuse occurred.

Expert or opinion evidence is usually given by someone who has special skills or expertise beyond that of the court. Opinions of expert witnesses are admissible only if they are related to an expert's area of expertise. Physicians are often called upon to give expert testimony concerning the nature and extent of a child's physical injuries.

Evidence that is not based on a witness's direct observations or experience is called "hearsay" and is generally not admissible in a fact-finding hearing. (*See* TESTIMONY for special cases where hearsay evidence may be allowed.)

In most court proceedings certain conversations such as those between a physician and patient or between psychotherapist and client are considered "privileged" and therefore may be excluded from testimony. Many states have laws specifically abrogating these privileges where child abuse or neglect is involved. Such communications can serve as important evidence in court.

evidence, autoptic   *See* EVIDENCE.

evidence, circumstantial   *See* EVIDENCE.

evidence, clear and convincing   *See* EVIDENTIARY STANDARDS.

evidence, demonstrative   *See* EVIDENCE.

evidence, direct   *See* EVIDENCE.

evidence, expert   *See* EVIDENCE.

evidence, opinion   *See* EVIDENCE.

evidence, preponderance of   *See* PREPONDERANCE OF EVIDENCE.

evidence, real   *See* EVIDENCE.

evidentiary standards   Different types of court cases require different levels or standards of proof. The three most common standards are: a fair preponderance of the evidence; clear and convincing evidence; and proof beyond a reasonable doubt.

Jurisdictions differ in the particular evidentiary standard applied to specific types of cases. If a standard is not specified by law, the preponderance of evidence standard is usually applied.

Preponderance of evidence is the least restrictive, or easiest, standard. To meet this standard a party must simply give a greater amount of credible evidence than that provided by the opposing party. Evidence presented may leave some degree of doubt in the minds of the judge or jury. When all evidence presented in court is considered a jury must decide if one side has presented more credible evidence in support of its case than has its opponent. The preponderance of evidence standard is used most often in civil court proceedings.

Clear and convincing evidence requires more confidence on the part of the decision maker than a simple preponderance of evidence. This standard is usually applied to removal of a child from home due to child abuse or neglect. By requiring a somewhat higher standard of proof courts seek to strike a balance between parents' interests in maintaining their children at home and the child's need for protection.

Beyond a reasonable doubt, the highest standard, is applied in criminal court proceedings. Evidence must support a party's contentions to a moral certainty. There must be no "reasonable" doubt in jurors' minds. The word reasonable implies a comparison of the jurors' standards for absolute certainty to those of the average person. This standard is particularly challenging to prosecutors of child sexual abuse cases who often must rely on circumstantial evidence and/or testimony from very young children to prove a case.

Proof beyond a reasonable doubt is also required for TERMINATION OF PARENTAL RIGHTS.

ex parte Crouse   In Pennsylvania in 1838, a court ruling upheld the right of the state to determine whether a young girl, Mary Ann Crouse, should remain in the Philadelphia House of Refuge, outside the custody of her parents. Crouse had been remanded to the House of Refuge at her mother's request, although without her father's knowledge or approval. In an attempt to obtain custody of his daughter, the father demanded Mary Ann's release on the grounds of the Sixth Amendment, which provides for due process of law. The institution countered that the young girl was ineligible for such protection since she was a minor and the Pennsylvania Supreme Court subsequently ruled against the father. Mary Ann Crouse was the first juvenile in the United States whose custody was determined by a court that successfully invoked the doctrine of PARENS PATRIAE as a way of removing her from parental jurisdiction.

excited utterance   Courts usually do not accept hearsay testimony (observations concerning statements made by someone other than the witness) as evidence. An exception to this rule may be made when a person under great stress (usually the victim of a crime) makes a statement. In such instances a person who heard the statement may be allowed to testify concerning the victim's original exclamation.

The excited-utterance exception to the hearsay rule is frequently applied in trials involving child abuse. Because the credibility of a young child's testimony is often questioned, corroborating testimony from an adult is considered important evidence. Some states require that testimony of a young child be supported by testimony from an adult. A child's statements made shortly after an incident of alleged abuse and in the presence of a child protection worker, teacher or other adult are allowed under the ancient rule of *res gestae.* This rule may be interpreted literally as "things done." It extends to things said, gestures made and thoughts expressed that are so closely related to the occurrence of an event as to be considered a part of the event.

Excited utterances are justified by the theory that a victim's statements immediately following a crime are likely to be truthful because the victim is under stress and unable to construct a false account of events. The victim's mental state (i.e., excitement and the length of time that elapses between the event in question and the victim's statement) are of crucial importance.

Acceptance of excited utterance testimony from children is controversial. Courts are sometimes criticized for allowing this type of testimony when several hours, even days, have passed between the incident and the excited utterence. Another problem associated with reliance on excited utterance testimony is that children often delay reporting abuse out of fear or shame. Very young children may fail to understand an event and therefore do not become upset immediately following abuse. In such cases the child's statements would fail to meet the criterion of being under stress. (*See also* TESTIMONY.)

exhibitionism   Exposure of the sex organs as a means of sexual gratification. Some experts also refer to flaunting of past abuse as exhibitionism.

Sexual Exhibitionism

One-third of all reported sex offenses involve exhibitionism. Research indicates that only 17% of all exhibitionistic episodes are referred to the police.

Victims of exhibitionism include both children and adults but are almost always female. Girls at or near the age of puberty are the most frequent victims. The majority of victims show no long-term effects though a small proportion may be significantly traumatized.

Perpetrators of sexual exhibitionism are most likely to be young adult males with interpersonal difficulties but without serious psychopathology. Exhibitionists usually do *not* progress to more serious sex crimes.

Almost three-fourths of all exhibitionism takes place outdoors. Most incidents occur in streets, alleys and parking lots. Only 5% take place in public parks or school playgrounds. About 14% of exhibitionist incidents occur at home.

Many states have statutes that impose harsher penalties against offenders when the victim is a child.

Children who have been subjected to repeated sexual abuse sometimes engage in seductive or exhibitionistic behavior toward adults. Incest victims may behave seductively as a means of getting love or attention when their emotional needs cannot be met in more conventional ways. These children come to view themselves as dehumanized sexual objects in much the same way that they have been treated by their abusers. Such behavior has contributed to the damaging myths that children enjoy sexual relations with adults and that children are the seducers.

Other Forms of Exhibitionism

A second and rather rare form of exhibitionism has been observed in abused children following their removal from the abusive situation. Displaying an eagerness to describe their abuse to others these children have developed an identity centered around their history of abuse. Self-labeling is used as justification for current negative behavior or as a means of gaining special consideration from others. For example, a child may blame all failures to comply with the wishes of teachers or foster parents on his or her status as an abused child, e.g., "I can't do it because I was abused by my parents." This form of exhibitionism should not be confused with a normal, healthy desire to understand past abuse by talking about it with others.

Daniel J. Cox and Reid J. Daitzman, *Exhibitionism: Description, Assessment and Treatment* (New York: Garland Press, 1980).

exhibitionism, sexual   *See* EXHIBITIONISM.

expert evidence   *See* EVIDENCE.

expert witness   In any court situation, a witness is called upon to testify according to firsthand knowledge of an event or series of events. Some witnesses may have special education, experience or skills that are valuable in a child abuse or neglect case.

These witnesses contribute either to the defense or to the prosecution or are important in terms of general edification of the court. This type of witness may be asked to comment upon details of the case and to give an opinion based on the specialized training or background he or she has in a specific area. In this situation, the witness is called upon to do more than simply state facts as seen or heard. Some expert witnesses in child abuse or neglect cases are physicians, psychiatrists, psychologists and social workers.

Expert Witnesses in Child Abuse Cases: What Can and Should be Said in Court (American Psychological Association, 1998) is a book that describes the many problems and pitfalls surrounding therapists who act as expert witnesses. For example, a therapist who has been counseling a child may see him or herself as the child's advocate and thus objectivity may be problematic.

Another problem may be that the therapist is unfamiliar with the current research on the subject. Richard Lawlor, an author in *Expert Witnesses in Child Abuse Cases* is particularly condemning of psychologists acting as expert witnesses and said,

> A significant portion of what passes for expert testimony in child sexual abuse cases is poorly grounded in the psychological research literature, reflects a lack of the knowledge of this constantly expanding literature, and often demonstrates a significant role confusion on the part of many experts who testify in court. Even psychologists, who presumably have both a research and clinical underpinning to their testimony, seem to be prey to the same difficulties as most other expert witnesses in these cases. Of even more concern is the fact that much of the investigation done in cases of child sexual abuse appears to be done by the least trained professionals and paraprofessionals, without adequate knowledge, skills, experience, training, and sometimes even motivation to apply the knowledge and skills that they have been taught.

Lawlor also said some techniques used to determine whether child sexual abuse had occurred could actually result in an iatrogenic effect—meaning that a child who was not abused could begin to believe in imagined abuse and could also exhibit clinical symptoms of distress that were not present in the recent past. Lawlor stated that children who may have been abused but who do not display emotional distress should not be referred to a therapist for investigative purposes.

Another concern has been with the techniques of investigative experts; for example, with using anatomically correct dolls, children's drawings and so forth. Lawlor and others contend that these techniques have not been scientifically validated as indicative of child abuse. In fact, in one of the few controlled studies of the drawings of children who were known to be sexually abused, only 10% (five of 52) drew genitalia in their pictures of people. This 10% was more than the 2% of nonabused children who drew genitalia but it was not statistically significant enough to draw conclusions of evidence of abuse.

In some cases, individuals have been convicted of child abuse primarily on the basis of an expert witness. For example, in a 1986 New Jersey case, Margaret Kelly Michaels was convicted of 155 counts of child sexual abuse on children who had attended the Wee Care Nursery School. The chief prosecution witness was a psychologist who testified that the children exhibited "child sexual abuse syndrome" based on her interviews with them and their behavior. This conviction was reversed in 1993 by the New Jersey Superior Court Appellate Division, which found that the expert testimony was inadequate and stated, "Unquestionably, this erroneously admitted evidence was capable of producing an unjust result and thus requires the reversal of defendant's convictions."

This does not mean that expert witnesses are never useful nor does it mean they are always wrong. Experts report that expert witnesses can be very helpful in explaining facts about child abuse that the jury may not understand; for example, that not all child abuse victims will sob on the stand and in fact, some may act very stoically. Depending on the state and the jurisdiction, they may also be able to talk about common behaviors of children who have been sexually abused.

Some therapists who have served as witnesses have been accused of overzealously leading children toward the finding that the therapist wants— for or against child abuse. One problem is that the therapist may have uncovered real child abuse, but if a videotape appears to be leading to a judge or jury, they may be unable to find that child abuse occurred.

The main criteria for a good expert witness are knowledge of the topic, an ability to be objective and neutral during the interview(s) with the child and also the capability of reporting any factual data about the child which has been learned and which indicates abuse, particularly data that can be corroborated. (*See also* SEXUAL ABUSE, WITNESS.)

Stephen J. Ceci and Helene Hembrooke, eds., *Expert Witnesses in Child Abuse Cases: What Can and Should Be Said in Court.* (Washington, D.C.: American Psychological Association, 1998).

exploitation, physical   *See* CHILD LABOR LAWS, CHILD SLAVERY.

exploitation, sexual   *See* SEXUAL EXPLOITATION.

exposure   This procedure is a form of INFANTICIDE in which a newborn is abandoned to die from such indirect causes as hypothermia or starvation. Some ancient cultures positively sanctioned or encouraged exposure of weak, premature or deformed infants. Believing that such children would pass their deformities along to their offspring, Aristotle recommended that rearing of disabled or deformed children be forbidden by law.

Roman law allowed exposure of infants born in cases where marital infidelity was suspected, a practice that continued until outlawed by the Emperor Valentinian III in A.D. 434. Exposure was practiced by many other cultures as well. In 19th-century China, female infants were routinely cast into a river or left to die.

expungement   Judges may order the destruction or expungement of court records. In many states records of juvenile court proceedings are expunged after a predetermined number of years. Some jurisdictions allow either party to a child abuse case to apply for expungement. When requesting expungement a convicted defendant must satisfy the court that he or she has been rehabilitated, i.e., no longer engages in the conduct that lead to conviction.

Expungement of unverified reports of abuse has been a hotly debated issue among proponents and critics of child abuse reporting laws. Those in favor of expungement argue that an individual's reputation can be severely harmed by such information, even though an investigation has determined the report to be unfounded. Some child advocates believe it is important to maintain such information for use in future investigations. State policies differ regarding expungement of unverified reports.

eye injuries Vision problems and eye injuries are important and usually easily recognizable indicators of abuse. Close examination of the eyes by a trained physician using an ophthalmoscope can sometimes reveal evidence of trauma and internal injuries that would otherwise have gone unnoticed.

Abuse-related eye injuries can be caused by a number of different kinds of trauma. Sharp objects can lacerate eyelids, cornea and sclera. Subsequent scarring from these cuts can permanently impair vision. Harsh chemicals introduced into the eye can cause burns and scarring. A direct blow from a fist or other blunt object can cause retinal damage as well as external damage to the cornea. Force transferred through the vitreous (jellylike substance inside the eye) to all parts of the eye applies sudden and extreme pressure to delicate internal structures and may damage the optic nerve. Collection of blood and damaged tissue inside the eye following trauma can also impair vision.

Blows to the front of the head may injure the visual cortex, causing blindness or other visual problems. Damage to the optic nerve can occur when head trauma causes cranial bones to splinter or when swelling applies pressure. Gouging can separate the optic nerve from the eye, resulting in permanent vision loss.

A sudden blow to the chest may produce a rapid increase in pressure within the blood vessels, causing retinal hemorrhaging. This condition, known as PURTSCHER RETINOPATHY, is common among young children who have been battered. Though retinal hemorrhages are often found in abused children they can also occur as a result of other childhood activities, such as participation in contact sports or gymnastics.

An ophthalmoscopic examination is an important part of a thorough medical assessment of PHYSICAL ABUSE.

Norman S. Ellerstein, *Child Abuse and Neglect: A Medical Reference* (New York: John Wiley, 1981).

Alejandro Rodriguez, *Handbook of Child Abuse and Neglect* (Flushing, N.Y.: Medical Examination Publishing Co., 1977).

failure to bond *See* BONDING FAILURE.

failure to grow *See* GROWTH FAILURE.

failure to thrive syndrome (FTT) A child who, during the first three years of life, experiences a marked retardation or cessation of growth is said to suffer from the failure to thrive syndrome. The most frequently used technical criterion for diagnosing FTT is when the child's weight falls below the third percentile on a standard growth chart. At this level of physical retardation, the child has a serious and often life-threatening condition.

Cases of FTT are divided into two major categories: organic and nonorganic. Organic FTT may be the result of genetic predisposition, constitutional factors, chronic illness or diseases that affect the intake, absorption or utilization of food.

Nonorganic FTT—a lack of adequate nurturing also known as deprivation DWARFISM and the maternal rejection syndrome—may stem from any one of a long list of environmental conditions, including: the parents' lack of knowledge about child rearing, inadequate technical advice or support for mothers who breast-feed their babies, nutritional deficiencies caused by extended breast-feeding as the sole source of nourishment, rigidity in feeding practices, maternal depression and anxiety over the ability to care for the infant. In some cases the primary caretaker feels that the child is in some way damaged, retarded or intractable and uses this as a basis for rejection. BONDING FAILURE resulting from maternal illness or a difficult birth may also contribute to a lack of proper nurturance or to rejection.

Though some researchers attribute nonorganic FTT solely to insufficient nutritional intake, others believe it may also be due to a neuroendocrine dis-turbance that occurs when an infant or child is deprived of emotional nurturance.

Mothers of nonthriving infants have been characterized as cold, rejecting, aggressive, anxious and inadequate. They are frequently undernourished themselves and live a life of social isolation with little or no help from friends, family or neighbors. In addition, fathers of these nonthriving children are often absent from the home.

Children suffering from FTT usually appear emaciated, weak, irritable, listless or apathetic. At the same time, infants may display a kind of HYPERVIGI-LANCE—looking to anyone who approaches for nurturance, devoid of the customary wariness of strangers exhibited by other children of their age. Infants suffering from the sensory deprivation associated with FTT often maintain a posture in which the arms are held out, flexed at the elbow with the hands up and legs drawn in. This position of apparent surrender is held for long periods of time.

Some children may not appear to be malnourished at first glance, but upon careful examination may have poor muscular development, dull or pale skin, sparse, dry hair or similar evidence of poor nourishment. Young victims of FTT often show a remarkable growth spurt upon hospitalization, with rapid gains in both weight and head circumference. Behavioral manifestations are slower to improve and may linger for some time after the child has regained an adequate rate of physical growth.

Unfortunately the rapid improvement experienced during hospitalization is often reversed when the child is returned home. Unless significant changes are made in the quality of care provided at home the child may continue to suffer from retarded physical, psychological and intellectual development.

Follow-up studies of children hospitalized for FTT show that about half of them remain below the third percentile in height and weight. Additionally, many of these children are intellectually retarded and experience a higher-than-average number of educational and emotional problems.

Ernesto Pollitt and Rudolph Leibel, "Biological and Social Correlates of Failure to Thrive," in *Social and Biological Predictors of Nutritional Status, Physical Growth and Neurological Development,* Lawrence Green and Francis Johnston, eds. (New York: Academic Press, 1980).

fallen fontanel (caida de mollera) Traditional medicine in many Latin American countries, as well as among Mexican-Americans, holds that fallen fontanel (the soft cranial bones) in infants can result in listlessness, diarrhea and vomiting. There is no evidence, however, that these symptoms are attributable to displacement of the cranial bones.

The traditional cure for this condition is to turn the baby upside down, place the top of the head in water and shake the infant to return the fontanel to its proper position. Though this practice can produce RETINAL HEMORRHAGE, or even SUBDURAL HEMATOMA if applied too forcefully, it is not considered abusive since it is a widely held, culturally based belief.

Families Anonymous *The National Center for the Prevention and Treatment of Child Abuse and Neglect* often refers to self-help groups for abusive parents as Families Anonymous. These groups are similar to PARENTS ANONYMOUS but, unlike P.A., are not affiliated with a nationwide network of similar organizations. Families Anonymous is also a name used in the substance abuse treatment field for self-help groups that focus on the members of a drug or alcohol abuser's family

family court *See* COURT.

family preservation The concept that it is extremely important to help abusive or neglectful families, despite the nature of their problems, so that they may continue to parent their children or that they may later be able to parent them again. This concept was embodied in the ADOPTION ASSISTANCE AND CHILD WELFARE ACT OF 1980 and was followed by state social services agencies until the mid-1990s.

Some experts criticized the concept of family preservation and said that it forced children to stay in foster care for too long or caused them to be reabused by parents who could not or would not resolve the problems that led to the abuse, such as substance abuse or mental illness. Others said family preservation was a workable idea but the available funds were insufficient to accomplish the therapeutic aims of family preservation. Generally, both sides agreed that children were remaining in the foster care system for too long.

A review of the table on the next page on child victims whose families received family preservation services in a five-year period reveals that in many cases, the children were victimized again despite the services their parents had received. For example, of the 1,649 children in Colorado whose families received services, nearly 30% of the children were victimized again in 1997. The numbers were even higher in Oklahoma: of the children whose families received services, 41.2% were victimized again.

Reunification of children with their families (return of children to their family home) is another major goal of the family preservation advocates. The second chart shows the percentage of child victims in 1997 who were reunited with their families over the previous five years. Although information is provided for only eight states and the District of Columbia, it is clear that the success of reunification policies is very spotty; for example, 32% of the child victims in Oklahoma were children who had been reunited with their families and were then reabused. (As seen in the first table, Oklahoma was a state whose family preservation policies were apparently the least effective of the states listed, since 41.2% of the children who were victimized again came from biological families who received family preservation services.)

In the case of children reunified with their families, two states had apparent successes in that less than 1% reentered the foster care system: Florida and Utah.

With the passage of the ADOPTION AND SAFE FAMILIES ACT OF 1997, the timetable for achieving family preservation goals was shortened, and if a child had

FAMILY PRESERVATION, 1997

State	Victims	Child Victims Whose Families Received Family Preservation Services in the Previous 5 Years	Percent of Victims
Colorado	5,532	1,649	29.8%
Florida	79,785	22,331	28.0%
Kansas	18,592	1,491	8.0%
Oklahoma	13,800	5,680	41.2%
Oregon	9,742	1,642	16.9%
Utah	9,356	363	3.9%
Vermont	1,041	182	17.5%
Total/Percent	137,848	33,338	24.2%
Number Reporting	7	7	7

been in foster care for 15 of the past 22 months, then the new law said the child should either be returned to his or her family or actions to terminate parental rights should begin so that the child could be adopted. States that increased their adoption rates were rewarded with financial grants from the federal government. Family preservation funds were also provided, but the timetable was limited, a change from the past when many children grew up in foster care or moved in and out of care throughout their childhoods.

REUNIFICATION, 1997

State	Child Victims	Child Victims Who Were Reunited With Their Families in the Previous 5 Years	Percent of Victims
District of Columbia	5,341	341	6.4%
Florida	79,785	731	0.9%
Kansas	18,592	91	0.5%
Missouri	15,845	1,103	7.0%
Oklahoma	13,800	4,415	32.0%
Oregon	9,742	602	6.2%
Utah	9,356	81	0.9%
Vermont	1,041	41	3.9%
Washington	21,806	1,819	8.3%
Total/Percent	175,308	9,224	5.3%
Number Reporting	9	9	9

Source (both charts): *Child Maltreatment 1997: Reports from the States to the National Child Abuse and Neglect Data System.* (U.S. Department of Health and Human Services, 1999.)

family violence The term family violence includes physical attacks on a child, spouse or sibling by another member of the family unit. Attacks by or on an unmarried live-in partner may also be referred to as family violence.

Research suggests that inappropriate or excessive use of force frequently occurs in more than one form in a family. Child abuse and sibling abuse are often present in families where there is spousal abuse and vice versa. Countries also differ in the characteristics and levels of familial violence. Though Western industrialized countries appear to have higher levels of family violence it is a problem in all countries.

National surveys conducted in the United States in 1975 and 1985 indicate that the level of severe violence (kicking, hitting with a fist, biting, beating, use of a gun or knife) may be decreasing. The 1985 survey estimated that 19 of every 1,000 children were victims of severe violence, a 47% decrease from 1975 estimates. The study did not include children under the age of three years.

In contrast to physical child abuse, which may be declining, spousal abuse remained relatively stable. Estimates in 1985 of husband-to-wife abuse were 30 couples out of every thousand. Wife-to-husband levels of severe violence were 44 per thousand. Overall, at least one severe assault occurred among 58 of every thousand couples during 1985.

Though wives may attack husbands more frequently, many of these attacks are in self-defense. Because their average size and strength is greater, men are more likely to inflict serious injury.

Violence between siblings may be the most frequent form of family violence. Unfortunately, little information is available on the incidence or effects of sibling-to-sibling attacks. SIBLING ABUSE is thought to represent a significant proportion of child abuse; however, it is the type of family violence least likely to be reported to authorities.

Richard J. Gelles, a sociologist specializing in child abuse and family violence, identifies four factors that are related to family violence. The first is the intergenerational nature of abuse. An abused child is more likely to become an abusive adult than a child who has not been abused.

Poverty is also related to violence in families. Though the majority of families with incomes below poverty guidelines are not violent, rates of child abuse and spouse abuse in poor families are higher than in families with substantially higher incomes.

A third characteristic of violent as well as neglectful families is social isolation. These families are observed to have infrequent contacts with friends and relatives, participate in few community activities and move often.

A final factor, social stress, may combine some of the three previous factors with other stressful circumstances. Unemployment, low levels of education, high-stress jobs, marital conflict, poor living conditions and many other factors can increase the level of family stress.

Eli Newberger and Richard Bourne, eds, *Unhappy Families* (New York: PSG Publishing Co., 1985).

David Finkelhor, Richard J. Gelles, Gerald Hotaling, Murray Straus, eds, *The Dark Side of Families* (Beverly Hills, Calif.: Sage Publications, 1983).

James Garbarino and G. Gilliam, *Understanding Abusive Families* (Lexington, Mass.: D.C. Heath, 1980).

Richard J. Gelles and Claire Pedrick Cornell, eds, *International Perspectives on Family Violence* (Lexington, Mass.: Lexington Books, 1983).

Richard J. Gelles and Murray Straus, *Intimate Violence* (New York: Simon and Schuster, 1988).

fatalities, child abuse   In at least 1,000 cases per year (some experts say the true number is at least double), children are killed by their parents and other caretakers. According to the U.S. Department of Health and Human Services, there were 1,196 fatalities in 1997 that resulted from child maltreatment.

Sometimes such deaths generate intense media attention and sometimes they warrant only a paragraph in the newspaper. The death may be a homicide or may be caused by long-term and severe abuse or neglect.

Babies and Small Children Are At Greatest Risk

Babies and children under age five are most at risk for fatalities. According to the National Clearinghouse on Child Abuse and Neglect Information, infants and small children are most likely to die from chronic abuse over time (battered child syndrome) or by an impulsive act, such as choking, drowning or suffocating the child.

Indications of Underreporting of Fatalities

In a study reported in *JAMA,* in 1999, researchers found a serious underestimation of child homicide caused by child abuse, in part because of methods of coding child deaths and in part because of the lack of child fatality teams to evaluate the cause of a child's homicide. Other reasons for underreporting were inaccurate death certificates, lack of information on the perpetrator and differing case definitions. The researchers studied all child homicides in North Carolina from 1985 to 1996. They found that about 85% of all child homicides resulted from child abuse, although almost 60% of the homicides were not defined as caused by child abuse. Based on their findings, the researchers stated, "For the United States, we estimated that 6,494 more children were killed by fatal child abuse from 1985 through 1996 than reflected by vital records coding." The researchers also looked at the perpetrators of the incidents and said, "Although the public may believe that biological parents are less likely to kill their own offspring, we found they accounted for 63% of the perpetrators of fatal child abuse. The findings from this study indicate that caregiving males, biological parents, and caregivers of children younger than 1 year are the most common perpetrators of fatal abuse and, therefore, need to be especially targeted in prevention efforts."

Perpetrators

Perpetrators of child fatalities due to child abuse vary in characteristics, but researchers have found some patterns. Usually the person causing the death is a high school dropout at the poverty level who is depressed and in the age group of the mid-20s.

Infant Deaths in the Military

In a study of family maltreatment conducted by the U.S. Air Force that was reported in *Child Abuse and Neglect* in 1998, cases of infanticide from 1989 to 1995 were analyzed. The mean age of the victim was 4.9 months old. About half (55%) of the infant victims suffered physical abuse before the fatal accident. The perpetrators were primarily male (84%) and the majority were the biological father of the baby (77%). About half (54%) of the perpetrators were first-time parents.

Other significant factors were the infant crying before the fatal abuse (58%) and the child being alone with the perpetrator in 86% of the cases. In about half the cases (47%) the abuse occurred on the weekend.

Punishment of Passive Parents Who Allow Children to Be Abused to Death

One controversy surrounding child abuse fatalities is that some groups believe that mothers who do nothing to prevent child abuse may be abuse victims themselves who thus feel helpless and unable to take any action to protect their children. Another group believes that passive parents should be actively prosecuted and rejects that such parents could not protect their children.

In their article, "Murder By Omission: Child Abuse and the Passive Parent," in the *Harvard Journal on Legislation,* authors Bryan A. Liang and Wendy L. MacFarlane make a strong case for taking action against parents who do nothing about children who are abused to the point of death. They discuss numerous cases throughout the U.S. but conclude,

> In most cases of death by child abuse, only the person who actually inflicts the injuries is charged with murder; the parent who fails to protect the child is rarely charged as an aider and abettor unless she too has inflicted injuries. Rather, that parent is generally charged with child endangerment, felony child abuse, or a similar, though lesser, crime. (These authors also renounce the "Battered Woman Syndrome" defense.)

Marcia E. Herman-Giddens, et al., "Underascertainment of Child Abuse Mortality in the United States," *JAMA* 282, no. 5 (August 4, 1999): 463–467.

Bryan A. Liang and Wendy L. MacFarlane, "Murder by Omission: Child Abuse and the Passive Parent," *Harvard Journal on Legislation* 36, no. 2 (Summer 1999): 397–450.

Federal Republic of Germany   *See* GERMANY, FEDERAL REPUBLIC OF.

fellatio   This term refers to oral contact with the male genitals. Fellatio is a form of sexual abuse when a child is forced or encouraged to perform, submit to or observe the activity. Children are sometimes forced to engage in fellatio with another child for the sexual stimulation of a pedophile. In such cases the adult is responsible for the behavior even though he or she is not physically engaged in the act itself. (*See also* SEXUAL ABUSE.)

felony   Crimes punishable by death or by imprisonment for longer than one year are called felonies. In common law, murder, mayhem, arson, rape, robbery, burglary, larceny, escape from prison and rescue of a convicted felon were considered felonies.

Criminal acts of abuse or neglect may be classed as either a felony or a MISDEMEANOR, depending on the severity of the act. Jurisdictions may vary in the specific acts they consider felonies; however, a felony is always a more serious crime than a misdemeanor.

female genital mutilation   Although illegal in the U.S. and in many other countries, female genital mutilation (FGM) is still practiced today in some parts of the world. The term refers to purposeful, unnecessary surgical procedures performed on female infants, girls and women, usually as a cultural ritual.

The practice is most commonly found in parts of Africa as well as in some areas in Asia and the Middle East. However, it is known that some immigrants to the U.S. and other countries may practice FGM. Most pediatricians do not believe that such procedures are an acceptable form of "cultural diversity," seeing them instead as child abuse, and nearly all Western pediatricians condemn such procedures.

FGM may be seen as a means to protect a female's virtue or to make her more marriageable. As many as 4 to 5 million such procedures occur each year, often with no anesthesia and by nonmedical personnel using razor blades, broken glass or other sharp objects.

According to a 1998 issue of *Pediatrics,* all forms of FGM are condemned by the American Academy of Pediatrics, which actively discourages physicians from participating in any way in such a procedure. The authors describe several key forms of FGM: Type I FGM, or CLITORIDECTOMY; Type II, or excising of all of the clitoris as well as some or all of the labia minora (similar to infibulation); and Type III, which is the most radical and includes excision of the clitoris and all or part of the labia minora, followed by cuts that are made in the labia majora.

The authors write, "The labial raw surfaces are stitched together to cover the urethra and vaginal introitus, leaving a small posterior opening for urinary and menstrual flow. In Type III FGM, the patient will have a firm band of tissue replacing the labia and obliteration of the urethra and vaginal openings.

Another type of FGM includes a variety of practices, such as cutting or stretching the clitoris and labia, cauterizing the clitoris and introducing corrosive substances into the vagina.

The physical effects of various forms of FGM, particularly Type III, are very severe. Females who have just undergone such a procedure may experience severe bleeding, pain, infection, tetanus and other complications. Adult women may later experience painful intercourse, recurrent urinary tract infections, pelvic infections and other complications. An episiotomy is required for a vaginal childbirth.

The psychological effects have not been studied but individuals who have experienced FGM report feeling great terror and anxiety.

Joel E. Frader, et al., "Female Genital Mutilation," *Pediatrics* 102 (July 1998): 153–157.

fetal alcohol syndrome (FAS)

Brain damage and other severe birth defects are found in some children whose mothers abused alcohol during pregnancy. The damage may be mild or severe. Alcohol exposure during pregnancy is the number one cause of preventable mental retardation and such serious problems including fetal alcohol syndrome (FAS).

Substance abuse is a common problem among mothers who abuse or neglect their children; as many as two-thirds of children in foster care are born to mothers who have an alcohol or drug problem. There are estimates of anywhere from 2,000 to 12,000 children born each year in the U.S. with FAS.

Features of FAS

Often children with fetal alcohol syndrome are born prematurely and underweight with small heads and are likely to remain unusually small and thin. They may also experience seizures and a host of other medical problems they will not outgrow.

Only an experienced physician should diagnose a child with FAS because diagnosis can be very difficult; however, there are some identifiable facial features: folds in the eyelids, short noses, thin upper lips, small chins and an overall "flattened" appearance.

Other characteristics of FAS are growth deficiency and central nervous system dysfunctions that lead to impulsivity, memory problems, learning disabilities and other problems.

P. Minugh, et al., "Drinking of Alcoholic Beverages—Health Aspects, Health Behavior—Surveys," *American Journal of Drug and Alcohol Abuse* 24, no. 3 (August 1998): 483–498.

Ann Streissguth, *Fetal Alcohol Syndrome: A Guide for Families and Communities* (Baltimore, MD: Paul Brookes Publishing Company, 1997.)

Naimah Z. Weinburg, "The Adverse Effects that Parental Alcohol Use May Have on Children are Numerous, Pervasive, Costly and Often Enduring," *Journal of the American Academy of Child & Adolescent Psychiatry* 36, no. 9 (September 1997): 1177–1187.

William R. Yates, et al., "Effect of Fetal Alcohol Exposure on Adult Symptoms of Nicotine, Alcohol, and Drug Dependence," *Alcoholism: Clinical and Experimental Research* 22, 4 (1998): 914–920.

filicide

Murder of a child by the parent is termed filicide. Statistics from 1985 show that 3% of all homicides reported in the United States during that year were filicides. This figure may underestimate true incidence, however, because many child abuse-related deaths are reported as accidents. Over twice as many children are killed by their parents than parents killed by their children.

fixated offender

This type of male sexual offender presents a pattern, beginning in adolescence, of being sexually attracted to children. Though he may occasionally engage in sexual activity with adults, such an offender rarely initiates the activity. The fixated offender actively seeks the company of children and fantasizes about sexual contact with them.

PEDOPHILIA is deeply ingrained in the psyche of the fixated offender. Unlike regression, fixation is not the result of a frustrated desire for sex with an adult or similar situational cause, and the offender rarely shows any remorse for his sexual attacks on children. Often compared to an addiction, this pattern of abusive behavior is particularly resistant to treatment.

Though the terms fixated and regressed have been widely used to differentiate perpetrators of child sexual abuse, it has been suggested recently that the motivation of the offender can be better understood as a continuum ranging from appropriate display of affection to brutal rape. David Finkelhor, a noted researcher of child sexual abuse, has suggested that the two major factors that differentiate pedophiles are: (1) the exclusivity of their attraction to children, and (2) the strength of that attraction. This idea is known as a CONTINUUM MODEL OF CHILD ABUSE.

fondling   In the context of child SEXUAL ABUSE, fondling refers to touching of the genitals, breasts or buttocks. Fondling may be a prelude to more extensive sexual activity or an end in itself. Adults are most frequently the fondlers; however, some sexual abuse involves encouraging or coercing children to fondle adults.

As is the case with other forms of sexual abuse, men are more likely to be reported for fondling. While men are the most frequent sexual aggressors, some writers speculate that women's role of primary caretaker of children permits inappropriate fondling to go unnoticed. Reports of nurses and child care workers who routinely use fondling as a way of quieting upset infants appear with reasonable frequency but are often difficult to document.

fontanel, fallen   *See* FALLEN FONTANEL.

forensic medicine   In cases of suspected child abuse or neglect specialized medical knowledge is often necessary to answer questions of law. A physician may be asked to examine a child and to testify in court whether, in his or her professional opinion, the child has been abused. When a child dies under suspicious circumstances a medical examiner, usually a pathologist, is called upon to conduct an autopsy to determine the probable cause of death. Both of these physicians are practicing forensic medicine.

Forensic medicine requires special training in gathering medical evidence and providing expert court testimony. With respect to child abuse, forensic specialists must have thorough knowledge of various methods of abuse and must be able to dis-

tinguish between accidental injuries and those likely to be intentionally inflicted. In such cases the physician is often asked to determine the validity of a caretaker's explanation of the injury. Through careful examination and application of specialized knowledge the physician is often able to find evidence to support or refute the caretaker's claim.

The ability to date injuries is particularly important in determining who was responsible for the child at the time of injury and also in establishing evidence of a pattern of abuse. Physicians frequently rely on microscopic examination of damaged tissue and use of X rays to determine the approximate date of the abuse. By applying knowledge of the normal healing process, the examiner is able to determine the amount of time that has elapsed since the injury. Multiple injuries, fractures for example, in various stages of healing are usually indicative of abuse over an extended period of time. Such evidence belies explanations of a "freak accident" or a single episode of abuse.

When neglect is a suspected cause of death the forensic examiner's task is somewhat different. In addition to looking for evidence of abuse and neglect, the physician must also rule out other medical explanations for the death. Some chronic diseases can inhibit the normal absorption of nutrients, causing a child to die of starvation despite being fed a healthy diet. In some cases, such as SUDDEN INFANT DEATH SYNDROME, no satisfactory explanation of death can be determined.

Evidence presented by the forensic medical examiner is usually presented in combination with other evidence concerning the child's psychosocial history, the parent's history, the current family situation, reports from teachers, neighbors etc. (*See also* RADIOLOGY, PEDIATRIC.)

foster care   If abused and neglected children are believed to be in danger, they are placed in the foster care system. This may mean they are placed with a family; or it could mean children are placed in a group home. Foster placement was intended to provide short-term substitute care until a child could return home; however, in the late 1980s and the 1990s, many children remained in foster care for most of their lives as social workers attempted to assist the parents with whatever problem (drugs, alcohol, emotional disorders, etc.) led them to abuse or neglect the child. In many cases, children entered the system, were "reunited" with their families, were reabused and entered the system again, in a "revolving door" fashion.

Alarmed at the large numbers of children in foster care (as many as 500,000 nationwide), Congress passed the ADOPTION AND FAMILY SAFETY ACT in 1997. This act enabled states to terminate parental rights if parents were unable or unwilling to resolve their severe family problems. It also enabled TERMINATION OF PARENTAL RIGHTS if the parents had murdered another child in the family and provided for termination in other circumstances as well. AFSA did not preclude efforts to continue to provide assistance to families; however, it did put time limits on them.

Most foster care is provided by families licensed by a state agency, although in some cases, foster care is contracted out to private agencies. Typically, state agencies license foster parents, who receive a small stipend to defray the cost of food and clothing for their foster child or children. Many children are also placed in KINSHIP CARE, which means they live with a relative. In the United States children in foster care are eligible for MEDICAID coverage.

Long periods of out-of-home placement are difficult for the child, the biological parents and the foster family. Children in placement are sometimes reluctant to form a close bond with their foster families because they expect (realistically or not) to be returning home soon. As time passes they may find themselves cut off emotionally from both their biological parents and foster family. In other cases the child may form an immediate bond with the foster parents and may be reluctant to return home to his or her biological family.

Due to changes in the foster family's status, incompatible matches and agency practices, children who remain in foster care for any length of time are often subject to frequent moves. The potentially negative effects of foster placement have led to attempts to limit its use. In 1980, the United States Congress passed the ADOPTION ASSISTANCE AND CHILD WELFARE REFORM ACT in an attempt to address the problem of extended foster placements. The act required that extensive efforts be devoted to maintaining the child at home if at all possible. When foster placement was considered necessary, a judge reviewed the decision. This act was superseded by AFSA which continued many of the previous provisions but stressed the need for a child's safety over the need for the child's return to a biological family, particularly when that family was severely abusive.

Many foster children are considered to have "special needs," which means they are developmentally delayed, have a learning disability or another problem which could make it difficult to find an adoptive family if parental rights were terminated. However, many experts believe that there are sufficient numbers of families to adopt the children if recruitment were performed in a positive way. All foster children must have a CASE PLAN. Plans are subject to an independent administrative review at least once every six months.

Health Problems

Studies have indicated that foster children have many medical problems. For example, one study showed that nearly 23% of children ages 0–6 had developmental delays. Among adolescents who were foster children, there was an alarmingly high rate of tuberculosis, with a rate of about 12% versus 6% for prisoners and about 3% for new recruits to the U.S. Navy.

According to an article by Moira Szilagyi, medical director of Foster Care Pediatrics in Rochester, New York, about 80% of foster children have one or more chronic medical problems. Chief among them are respiratory problems, with about 18% experiencing asthma. Blood disorders such as anemia are found in about 20% of foster children. Other common problems cited by Szilagyi were: hearing impairments, visual impairments, neurological disorders from mild to serious, sexually transmitted diseases and other infectious ailments. In many cases, children have not received their recommended childhood immunizations.

Foster children may also have developmental delays, language disorders, learning disabilities and behavioral problems. The children may also experience emotional problems such as oppositional defiant disorder, attention deficit hyperactivity disorder or anxiety disorders. Experts say that despite the severe problems many foster children have experienced, as well as existing emotional disorders they often struggle with, they often do not receive appropriate psychiatric or psychological services.

Long-Term Impacts

Studies have revealed that children who remain in foster care for years often experience many problems as adults. For example, according to the 1996 book *Assessing the Long-Term Effects of Foster Care,* only half of all foster children graduate from high school, compared to 78% in the general population. As many as 40% will receive welfare benefits as adults or will be incarcerated. In addition, adults who were former foster children have a homeless rate that is at least four times that of the general population.

Despite its problems, foster care is an important resource for abused children. The majority of foster families offer competent, warm and loving care. Under good conditions, foster families receive adequate support from caseworkers and in turn provide a stable environment for the child. To be effective, foster care must be part of a comprehensive system of treatment involving the child, biological family and foster family.

Thomas P. McDonald, et al., *Assessing the Long-Term Effects of Foster Care: A Research Synthesis,* (Washington, D.C.: CWLA Press, 1996).

Moira Szilagyi, "The Pediatrician and the Child in Foster Care," *Pediatrics in Review* 19, no. 2 (February 1998): 39–50.

John I. Takayama, M.D., et al., "Relationship Between Reason for Placement and Medical Findings Among Children in Foster Care," *Pediatrics* 101, no. 2 (February 1998): 201–207.

founded report Reports of suspected child abuse or neglect are considered founded if verified by an investigation. The process of verifying reports is called SUBSTANTIATION.

Statistics from several states indicate a wide variation in the percentage of reports that are founded. Differences in rates of substantiation may reflect legal definitions of abuse and neglect or variations in protective service agencies policies.

foundling hospital The first known foundling hospital for unwanted children was established in A.D. 787 by Datheus, Archpriest of Milan. During the late 19th century, a large foundling hospital in St. Petersburg, Russia, handled an average of 25,000 babies annually.

Although they were established to care for large numbers of unwanted babies who were being killed or abandoned by their parents, the foundling hospitals themselves often provided inadequate care or engaged in exploitation. About one in every four babies placed in early foundling hospitals died there. Early studies of the FAILURE TO THRIVE SYNDROME by Rene A. Spitz, John Bowlby and others were conducted in foundling hospitals. These studies concluded that even when infants were provided with excellent physical and medical care they often became listless, failed to grow at the normal rate and sometimes died—apparently as a result of inadequate emotional nurturance.

New methods of birth control, legalized abortion, the availability of public financial support for the poor and an expanded interest in adoption have combined to reduce the need for foundling hospitals in most Western nations since World War II.

fractures The ability of physicians to identify and date fractures was greatly enhanced by advances in the use and interpretation of X rays. By employing X-ray technology, pediatric radiologists are able to tell approximately when a fracture occurred and often what type of force caused the fracture. By comparing this information with the caretaker's explanation of an injury the physician can often identify cases of suspected abuse.

While certain types of fractures are indicative of abuse, a diagnosis of abuse requires information about the child's environment, how the injury occurred, the child's caretakers and medical history. Some childhood diseases can render the bones brittle and thus more susceptible to injury. Conditions such as OSTEOGENESIS IMPERFECTA and congenital insensitivity to pain must be ruled out in the process of diagnosing child abuse. It is not uncommon for infants, particularly breech deliveries, to sustain fractures during childbirth. As a general rule, fractures incidental to childbirth will be visible on X rays by the 11th day of life. Bone trauma appearing after this time is assumed to have occurred following birth.

In evaluating the possibility of child battering, consideration of the child's age is important. While it is quite possible for a child to sustain certain types of fractures while learning to walk, the presence of a transverse (crosswise) or spiral fracture in a child who is not yet able to walk may arouse suspicion.

Bone fractures related to child abuse are caused by a direct blow, twisting (usually of a limb), shaking or squeezing. The particular kind of force used may produce a characteristic type of fracture. A direct blow often produces a transverse or spiral fracture to the shaft of a long bone. Blows to the head often produce internal injuries in addition to fractures of the cranium, mandible and maxillary bones. Swelling due to increased pressure inside the cranium can cause the sutures of the skull to separate.

Twisting forces may produce spiral fractures in the long bone shaft. This type of fracture, like those resulting from direct blows, occurs frequently from accidental causes. A spiral fracture of the tibia (one of two bones in the forearm) is somewhat more likely to be the result of abuse than similar fractures of other bones.

Fractures at the epiphyseal-metaphyseal junction are also produced by twisting and are more frequently related to abuse. The epiphysis, the cartilaginous end of a child's long bones, can be detached from the relatively stronger metaphysis by twisting or vigorous jiggling of a child's limbs. This type of injury is difficult to identify in the early stages of healing. In some cases a fragment of bone or cartilage may be visible on an X ray, in others the only visible sign is swelling of tissues around the joint. Epiphyseal-metaphyseal injuries to the hip and shoulder sometimes cause the joint space to fill with blood. Widening of the hip or shoulder joint space usually indicates this type of injury. As healing progresses formation of CALLUS becomes visible in X rays, allowing easier identification of the injury.

Violent shaking of a child can cause spinal damage as well as epiphyseal-metaphyseal fractures. Spinal fractures usually follow hyperflexion (exaggerated twisting or bending) of the vertebral column. Typical injuries are compression, notching and/or dislocation of the vertebrae.

Squeezing injuries usually involve rib fractures. According to Dr. Sills et al., "Rib fractures are seen in 5–26% of abused children with 90% of abuse-related fractures occurring in children under 2 years of age." Fractures resulting from squeezing are usually bilateral, caused by an adult grasping both sides of the chest and applying pressure. They may also

FRACTURES ASSOCIATED WITH BATTERING

Transverse —Long Bones	often accidental in children who are old enough to walk, rarely accidental in nonambulatory children; may result from a direct blow
Spiral —Long Bones	can be caused by twisting or a direct blow; often accidental in older children
Fractures of the Cranium	young children and infants are especially susceptible to these injuries; may result in macrocephaly, separation of the cranial sutures, CNS damage
Vertebral Fractures —Compression, Notching	often caused by shaking; may also be associated with CNS injury, subdural hematoma, internal organ damage
Epiphyseal-Metaphyseal Injury—Long Bones	caused by twisting forces; most frequently associated with battering; may not be immediately detectable on X rays
Rib Fractures	may result from squeezing of the chest; sometimes associated with shaking injuries; frequently concomitant with internal organ injury
Humerus Fractures	may result from twisting or rotating the child's arm, commonly results from abuse when child is 3 years or younger

be caused by shaking the child. When rib fractures are detected internal injuries may also be present.

Determining When Fractures Are Present
Dating of fractures is especially important in detecting child abuse. By comparing physical evidence of the fracture's age with the caretaker's explanation of the accident the physician can detect discrepancies that might lead to a suspicion of battering. Presence of multiple fractures in various stages of healing is a hallmark of the BATTERED CHILD SYNDROME.

Determination of the age of a particular fracture usually depends on observation of soft tissue changes, observation of a visible fracture line, formation of CALLUS around the fracture and ossification of the periosteum (membrane covering the bone, which is usually damaged by trauma and the resulting bleeding). Immediate soft tissue manifestations of a fracture are EDEMA and swelling. Four to five days after the injury the first stages of new bone growth begin. Actual calcification is not visible on X rays until 10 to 14 days following the injury.

While a fracture line may be immediately visible following the injury some fractures are difficult to detect and are identifiable only after calcification begins to occur. Bone resorption along the line of the fracture during the first few days following the injury usually makes the fracture easier to detect. Most long bone fracture lines remain visible on X rays for four to eight weeks.

Detection of child battering involves the use of information obtained from several sources. When bone fractures are detected information from visual and X-ray examination can help determine the type of force that caused the injury and the approximate date of its occurrence. A SKELETAL SURVEY can also detect the presence of other fractures that may not have been reported. Medical information is then compared to accounts of the injury provided by the caretaker, other witnesses and the child (if old enough). Use of clinical data increases the accuracy with which a diagnosis of child battering can be made. Increased accuracy of diagnosis can help prevent further abuse as well as false accusations of caretakers.

Robert M. Sills, DO, FAAP, et al., "Bones Breaks, and the Battered Child: Is It Intentional or Is It Abuse?" *Pediatric Emergency Medicine Reports Archives* (Jan. 1998).

France Currently, child abuse and neglect in France receives a great deal of attention and is the subject of a wide array of preventive efforts. Both private and government agencies cooperate in providing services for abused children and their families, with the government making policy determinations. General child protective services form a basis on which specialized programs dealing with child maltreatment are built, although specific delin-

eation of child abuse has received less attention than programs that serve all maltreated children. This is due in part to some reluctance to separate abuse from the larger issue of child maltreatment.

French welfare policies and services are established with the intention of serving the broad interests of families; a maternal and child health program is an important component of government-sponsored child welfare offerings in France. This maternal and child health service includes periodic physical examinations. Ninety-five percent of children aged three to five or six years are enrolled in preschool programs that include physical health exams. Court intervention in family situations where neglect or abuse occurs is permitted in France, although parents are not automatically held guilty as a result of a necessary emergency intervention.

Certain diagnostic methods help detect child abuse or child battering, procedures that have been employed in France since the late 1960s. Sexual abuse of children and sexual violence in French institutions are areas in which some research attention has recently been focused. Also, recent French studies have focused on the possible negative effects of institutional care on child development. According to the 1999 Country Reports on Human Rights Practices, released on February 25, 2000, by the Bureau of Democracy, Human Rights, and Labor in the U.S. Department of State, there were about 19,000 reported cases of child maltreatment in France in 1998, including physical abuse, sexual abuse, mental cruelty and severe negligence. About 5,000 of these cases were incidents of sexual abuse.

Special sections of the police and of the judiciary deal with cases of child abuse in France. The French government provides counseling, financial aid and out of home care such as foster homes or orphanages. The Ministry for Family Affairs is in charge of government programs for children.

Immigrants primarily from Gambia, Mali, Mauritania and Senegal have been prosecuted for FEMALE GENITAL MUTILATION of children in France. In one case, a Paris jury convicted a Malian women for inflicting female genital mutilation upon 48 girls, ages one month to 10 years. She received a sentence of eight years in jail. The parents of the girls were also prosecuted and they received suspended sentences. French authorities have sought to educate immigrants since 1993 that this practice is not allowed in France, as it is not allowed in many other countries.

frustration-aggression theory One explanation of physically abusive behavior focuses on the link between biological factors, characteristics of the particular situation and learned response patterns. Seymour Feshbach, a leading proponent of the frustration-aggression approach, focuses primarily on situational factors and learned responses in his explanation of abuse. Aggressive biological impulses are mentioned only as innate impulses to strike out when provoked.

Situational factors that contribute to abusive behavior are broken down into three subgroups: intent, responsibility and perceived justification. Immature or inexperienced parents often have unrealistic expectations of children. A parent may believe an infant intentionally soils a clean diaper or purposely refuses to go to sleep at the appointed time. The parent believes the child is responsible for these actions in the same way an older child or adult would be accountable. Finally, instead of seeing the situation as a normal part of child-rearing the abusive parent feels treated unfairly by the child. These three perceptions combine to intensify the parent's frustration.

Feshbach credits social learning for increasing the likelihood of an aggressive response. Abusive parents learn, through various means, aggressive ways of dealing with frustration. While frustration does not automatically trigger aggression, parents who have learned aggressive responses are more likely to be abusive.

Following the frustration-aggression approach, treatment of the abusing parent would focus on changing unrealistic perceptions and expectations of the child's behavior and on learning new ways of responding to frustration. Many treatment programs incorporate these elements.

gastrointestinal injuries The stomach and intestines are frequently damaged by forceful blows to the child's abdomen. Hollow organs, particularly the stomach and colon, are most susceptible to injury when they are filled with gas or partially digested food. Rapid compression of these viscera resulting from a blow to the abdomen can rupture organ walls. Such damage to the stomach causes its contents to spill into the peritoneal cavity. Hydrochloric acid from the stomach is highly irritating to other body tissues and can cause a child to go into shock. If the peritoneal cavity is not cleansed, spillage of stomach contents may cause abscesses to develop. Surgical repair of stomach and intestinal ruptures is necessary to prevent further contamination of the peritoneal cavity.

Rapid acceleration when a child is thrown or pushed is likely to tear connective tissue attaching the small intestine to the abdominal wall. Such injuries may cause hemorrhaging of damaged blood vessels.

HEMATOMA (buildup of blood) of the duodenum may result from a blunt blow to the abdomen. This type of injury occurs when the duodenum, with a rich blood supply, is crushed against the vertebral column. The resulting buildup of blood in the walls of the bowel obstructs normal flow of material through the gastrointestinal tract. Indicators of duodenal hematoma include vomiting of greenish material and complaints of tenderness in the upper abdomen. Laboratory tests and X rays are required to confirm the diagnosis.

This type of injury can usually be treated without surgery. With proper medical treatment the hematoma usually dissipates in 10 to 14 days. (*See also* ABDOMINAL INJURIES.)

gatekeepers Professionals, agencies and institutions in frequent contact with children are the "gatekeepers" of child protection services. Gatekeepers are often mandated by state or federal law to report cases of suspected child abuse or neglect. Doctors, teachers, child care workers, social workers, counselors, psychologists, dentists and others are often the first to identify and report abuse. Unfortunately, many individuals in these positions lack adequate training in detection and reporting of suspected abuse and neglect. Widespread efforts are underway in many areas to provide training to those who work with children on a regular basis.

Gault *See* IN RE GAULT.

genital mutilation *See* CASTRATION, CLITORIDECTOMY and INFIBULATION.

Germany In addressing concerns over abuse and neglect of children, Germany puts a primary emphasis on PHYSICAL ABUSE, although there is no clear-cut definition of what constitutes abuse. Neglect of children is more specifically detailed in laws concerning the overall maltreatment of children and the responsibility of parents. While parents' rights in Germany are treated with a great deal of consideration, in the mid-1970s the government nevertheless enacted legislation depriving parents of custody of their children if convicted of child abuse or neglect and sentenced to six months or more in prison. One researcher notes that, as a result, few parents are sentenced for more than five months in these cases.

Education programs aimed at reducing the incidence of child abuse and neglect were set up by the Senate in Bonn after a series of abuse cases resulted in the death of a number of children. Also, national health insurance provides a limited number of voluntary, no-cost medical exams for children between birth and four years of age. About 75% of preschool-age German children (three to six years old) are examined by health care professionals as part of public education programs, enabling officials to detect cases of abuse and neglect that might otherwise go unnoticed or unreported.

There is no mandatory reporting legislation for child abuse or neglect in Germany. As a matter of historical note, while corporal punishment of children is illegal in Germany today, in the 1930s the Nazi government in Germany reinstated legally permissible CORPORAL PUNISHMENT in schools and institutions, although it had earlier been banned as inappropriate behavior.

According to the 1999 Country Reports on Human Rights Practices, released in February 2000, German police reported 16,596 cases of sexual abuse against children in 1998.

Researchers on child abuse in Germany estimate that about half of all child abuse cases are cases of sexual abuse. Cases of neglect are generally regarded as a social problem rather than as prosecutable offenses.

Author Reinhard Wolff says Germany refrains from a punitive child abuse model, concentrating instead on providing childcare, health services, counseling and an array of other services.

This liberal attitude does not extend to pornography: the German Criminal Code was amended in 1993 and yet again in 1997 to cover child pornography and the sexual abuse of children. The 1993 code also included a provision that criminalized sexual abuse committed by German citizens abroad even if it is not illegal in the child's country.

Reinhart Wolff, "Germany: A Nonpunitive Model," in *Combatting Child Abuse: International Perspectives and Trends.* (New York: Oxford University Press, 1997).

gonorrhea The most common venereal disease, gonorrhea, is caused by a bacterium commonly known as gonococcus. It infects the mucous membranes causing them to become inflamed. A discharge of pus is also common to cases of gonorrhea.

Gonococcus bacteria are spread through direct contact, predominantly during sexual intercourse. In addition, infants may contract gonorrhea at birth when passing through the vagina of an infected mother. If so infected and left untreated, infants

can be blinded by the disease. As a part of a complete physical examination for child SEXUAL ABUSE, cultures are obtained from the genitals, rectum and throat of victim children—regardless of reported method of sexual contact. These cultures are then examined for gonococcus bacteria, which, if present, may indicate sexual abuse.

Great Britain   *See* BRITAIN.

Greece   In the late 1970s, work related to prevention and treatment of child abuse and neglect first became the subject of concerted professional effort in Greece. Currently, at the Institute of Child Health in Athens, as well as at various child welfare agencies throughout Greece, abuse and neglect of children is generally examined in the light of cultural pressures.

Traditionally, Greek society has placed greater expectations on sons, rather than daughters, leading child abuse experts to surmise, for example, that harsh or abusive disciplinary practices directed toward boys can often be attributed to the higher value that boys and men represent. Similarly, the closely knit family structure in traditional Greek society obligates the child and parent in ways that can produce tensions leading to abusive behavior.

CORPORAL PUNISHMENT within the home appears to be standard practice in Greece; one recent study of maternal attitudes toward discipline revealed that 10% of mothers surveyed spanked their children and 40% either shout at their children, isolate them in a darkened room, or subject them to some other form of verbal discipline. Further, there has been some concern over the treatment of Greek schoolchildren. Investigations into behavior of children in their school environment has suggested to researchers that some level of emotional abuse may occur regularly in Greek schools.

As one means of addressing growing concern about child abuse and neglect, the first European Congress on Child Abuse and Neglect was held in early 1987 in Greece. It was organized by the Greek Institute of Child Health working together with the INTERNATIONAL SOCIETY FOR THE PREVENTION OF CHILD ABUSE AND NEGLECT (ISPCAN) and several other Greek organizations, including the Greek Ministries of Culture and Health and Welfare.

growth failure Failure to meet age-appropriate milestones for physical development is primarily caused by inadequate nutrition. A number of organic problems, such as malabsorption of vital nutrients, genetically linked characteristics, disease or infection can interfere with a child or infant's maturation. In some cases, inadequate nutrition is linked to nonorganic factors, such as lack of knowledge by parents, rigid feeding practices or parental neglect and rejection.

Between birth and age three, significant growth failure is most often referred to as FAILURE TO THRIVE SYNDROME. After age three, growth retardation is known as DWARFISM.

Though Rene A. Spitz, John Bowlby and other researchers hypothesized that growth failure could result directly from a lack of emotional nurturance, it is now believed that this phenomenon is primarily related to poor nutrition. However, emotional factors frequently contribute to inadequate nutrition. Clinical evidence shows that when children suffering from psychosocial dwarfism are removed from the abusive situation, they experience a rapid growth spurt. This is also true of infants suffering from nonorganic failure to thrive syndrome.

growth failure, reversible *See* DWARFISM.

guardian An adult other than the biological parent may be appointed by a court of law to serve as a child's guardian. A guardian has virtually the same legal powers and responsibilities as a parent; however, guardianship is subject to change or termination by the court. In some cases the guardian may not have actual CUSTODY of the child. (*See also* GUARDIAN AD LITEM.)

guardian ad litem In a child protection case involving suspected abuse or neglect, a child is granted an adult advocate, usually but not always an attorney. This individual represents the child for the duration of the litigation, with primary responsibility to ensure that procedural aspects of the case are legally correct. A guardian ad litem is appointed by the court when circumstances dictate that the best interests of the child would be served by so doing.

State laws differ concerning the right to counsel in juvenile proceedings. However, some state courts have found that in cases of child abuse or neglect, the right to counsel is required by the United States Constitution, which calls for due process and equal protection. The guardian ad litem—literally, guardian at law—is charged with protecting only legal rights. This differs from a guardian of the person, whose responsibility is to safeguard the physical and emotional well-being of a child in abuse or neglect proceedings.

H

Hague Convention on the Civil Aspects of International Child Abduction In order to address issues of concern relative to return of abducted children and international visiting rights, on October 6, 1980, delegates and representatives of 36 nations convened in the 14th session of the Hague Conference on Private International Law. Their intent was to submit to their governments a comprehensive statement concerning the protection of children in matters relating to custody. On October 24, the assembly adopted the Hague Convention, which was subsequently signed by the United States on December 23, 1981.

The stated desire of the convention was to "protect children internationally from the harmful effects of their wrongful removal or retention." Among other things, the convention establishes a central authority in each country to help individuals who seek return of children abducted from or retained outside the nation in which they are legal residents. In 1986, the United States Senate gave "advice and consent" to the Hague Convention and in 1987 legislation was introduced to implement policies and procedures outlined in the international document.

According to the U.S. Department of State, the following countries are parties to the Hague Convention of 1980 on the Civil Aspects of International Child Abduction as of March 2000:

Country	Effective Date
Argentina	June 1, 1991
Australia	July 1, 1988
Austria	October 1, 1988
Bahamas	January 1, 1994
Belgium	May 1, 1999
Belize	November 1, 1989
Bosnia and Herzogovina	December 1, 1991
Burkina Faso	November 1, 1992
Canada	July 1, 1988
Chile	July 1, 1994

China:	
Hong Kong Special Administrative Region	September 1, 1997
Macau	March 1, 1999
Colombia	June 1, 1996
Croatia	December 1, 1991
Czech Republic	March 1, 1998
Cyprus	March 1, 1995
Denmark	July 1, 1991
Ecuador	April 1, 1992
Finland	August 1, 1994
France	July 1, 1988
Germany	December 1, 1990
Greece	June 1, 1993
Honduras	June 1, 1994
Hungary	July 1, 1988
Iceland	December 1, 1996
Ireland	October 1, 1991
Israel	December 1, 1991
Italy	May 1, 1995
Luxembourg	July 1, 1988
Former Yugoslav Republic of Macedonia	December 1, 1991
Mauritius	October 1, 1993
Mexico	October 1, 1991
Monaco	June 1, 1993
Netherlands	September 1, 1990
New Zealand	October 1, 1991
Norway	April 1, 1989
Panama	June 1, 1994
Poland	November 1, 1992
Portugal	July 1, 1988
Romania	June 1, 1993
St. Kitts and Nevis	June 1, 1995
Slovenia	April 1, 1995
South Africa	November 1, 1997
Spain	July 1, 1988
Sweden	June 1, 1989

Switzerland	July 1, 1988
United Kingdom	July 1, 1988
Bermuda	March 1, 1999
Cayman Islands	August 1, 1998
Falkland Islands	June 1, 1998
Isle of Man	September 1, 1991
Montserrat	March 1, 1999
Venezuela	January 1, 1997
Zimbabwe	August 1, 1995

For further information, contact:

United States Central Authority
U.S. Department of State
The Office of Children's Issues
2401 E St. NW, Room L127
Washington, DC 20037
Tel.: 202-736-7000
FAX: 202-663-2674

hair pulling   Hair pulling may result in traumatic ALOPECIA (hair loss) and SUBGALEAL HEMATOMA.

Head Start   A nationwide, comprehensive educational program for disadvantaged preschool children that is funded by the United States government, Head Start provides a range of educational enrichment services to young children. Recent studies have shown it to be an effective tool in countering the effects of poverty on children's educational readiness.

As a matter of federal policy, all Head Start staff are MANDATED REPORTERS of child abuse and neglect.

health visitor   In BRITAIN, National Health Service provisions include education and prevention programs and general promotion of good health through the services of a health visitor. Most generally, a health visitor's primary concern is with preschool children and their families. In this capacity, the health visitor may be involved in surveillance of child health and welfare, making regular and routine exams of children. British law requires that newborns be seen by a health visitor at least once during the first 12 months of life; high-risk cases are visited more often.

In the United States, there is no permanently established health visitor system, although a short-term experimental lay health visitor program was established at the Department of Pediatrics of Col-

orado General Hospital in the late 1970s. Specifically designed to offer routine support and after-care in pediatric cases, this program provided services to families in which parenting problems were considered either to exist or to be at risk of developing. (*See also* PARENT AIDES.)

hearing   Any proceeding where evidence is considered for the purposes of determining an issue of fact is known as a hearing. Usually a hearing takes the form of a formal trial; however, administrative hearings may take place outside of the court process.

Judicial hearings may be held for the purpose of issuing temporary orders (preliminary hearing), fact-finding (adjudicatory hearing) and to determine what action should be taken (dispositional hearing). Emergency removal of a child from home and changes in custody also require hearings. In emergencies a hearing must take place within a specified period of time following removal of the child. (*See also* ADJUDICATORY HEARING, DISPOSITIONAL HEARING, EMERGENCY CUSTODY, CUSTODY.)

hearing, adjudicatory   *See* ADJUDICATORY HEARING.

hearing, dispositional   *See* DISPOSITIONAL HEARING.

hebephelia   Sexual desire and responses directed exclusively toward pubescent children by an adult are termed hebephelia. Hebephiles are often mislabeled as pedophiles, adults who are sexually attracted to prepubescent children (*see* PEDOPHILIA). The hebephile usually shows little interest in young children and will engage in sexual activity with adults or children only when adolescents are unavailable. (*See also* ADOLESCENT ABUSE, CHILD MOLESTER and SEXUAL ABUSE.)

helpline   Telephone counseling services are often called helplines. Usually staffed by trained volunteers, helplines offer information, referral and paraprofessional counseling. Unlike HOTLINES, which are frequently connected to protective service agencies, helplines usually do not directly report suspected abuse or neglect. Calls to these services are often anonymous. If abuse or neglect is suspected the callers are encouraged to seek help on their own.

Helplines can serve an important early intervention function. By helping families cope with stress and relieving the social isolation many parents feel, these services can prevent abuse and neglect.

hematemesis   The vomiting of blood, usually as a result of abdominal trauma. Hematemesis can be indicative of internal battering injuries when no external signs are observable.

hematoma, jejunal   *See* JEJUNAL HEMATOMA.

hematoma, subdural   *See* SUBDURAL HEMATOMA.

hematoma, subgaleal   *See* SUBGALEAL HEMATOMA.

hematuria   Trauma to the kidneys or bladder can frequently be detected by the presence of hematuria—blood in the urine. Hematuria is a sign of serious internal injury. Children who present this symptom should be examined by a knowledgeable physician for other evidence of abuse when battering is suspected.

hemoptysis   Spitting or coughing of blood, usually caused by damage to the lungs. Hemoptysis is sometimes observed in battered children.

hemorrhage, intradermal   *See* INTRADERMAL HEMORRHAGE.

hemorrhage, retinal   *See* RETINAL HEMORRHAGE.

herpes, genital   Herpes simplex is an inflammatory disease that causes clusters of small vesicles to form on the skin. Genital herpes or herpes simplex of the genitals is characterized by blisters or sores on the penis or vagina. Herpes simplex is not curable but alternates between periods of inflammation and remission. During periods of remission when there are no skin lesions the disease is not considered transmissible.

Observation of genital herpes, or any venereal disease, in a prepubertal child is likely to be the result of SEXUAL ABUSE. Children with this disease should be screened by a physician for other evidence of sexual abuse.

homelessness   Lack of adequate, stable shelter is a significant problem for children in industrialized as well as developing countries. In the United States families comprise over 25% of the homeless population. Most of these families are headed by a young single mother with two to three young children. The typical child in a homeless family is subject to a great deal of poverty, stress and disruption.

One study of children in Massachusetts temporary shelters for the homeless found that many had been abused. Almost half of children five years of age and younger were developmentally delayed in some way. Results of psychological tests indicated that approximately 50% of all homeless children studied were in need of psychiatric care. Only 9% were actually receiving such care.

Fathers were absent in 90% of the families studied. Of the mothers, one-third reported having been abused as children, two-thirds came from families in which there was a major disruption during their childhood. In the year prior to being housed in the shelter the families had moved an average of four times.

Homeless children suffer from poverty, abuse and neglect in addition to instability and lack of adequate housing. In some developing countries homeless children, abandoned by their families, must live on their own, supporting themselves by whatever means are available. Because of its connection to POVERTY, homelessness may be seen as a form of SOCIETAL or SOCIAL ABUSE. Responsibility for such abuse is often seen as resting with the society, which denies children the basic requirements for healthy development. (*See also* LATIN AMERICA, INDIA.)

Ellen Bassuk and Leonore Rubin, "Homeless Children: A Neglected Population," *American Journal of Orthopsychiatry* 57, no. 2 (April 1987): 279–286.

Jean I. Layzer, Barbara D. Goodson and Christine deLange, "Children in Shelters," *Children Today* (March–April 1986): 6–11.

homemaker services—home health aide services
The origin of homemaker-home health aide programs in the United States can be traced at least as far back as the 1920s. There are also some reports detailing groups in the late 19th century that provided in-home care to children and families. These were often affiliated with a religious organization, e.g., the Little Sisters of the Poor, a Roman Catholic order, or the Jewish Welfare Society in Philadelphia. In general, these early services were available to new mothers who needed help with infants or to

mothers too ill to convalesce and care for their families simultaneously.

Not until the 1960s was there any large-scale federal funding for regular in-home care to children and families. In 1965, Title XVIII of the Social Security Act included benefits for homemakers-home health aides under Medicare.

The range of services that homemaker–home health aides provide includes help for families in which situational neglect has been identified. This neglect is often the result of an overburdened caretaker. Respite care is another role assumed by the homemaker-home health aide. In families where a child is disabled, terminally ill, retarded or mentally disturbed, such respite care can alleviate parental stress. The homemaker–home health aide can both teach and assist, in order to alleviate the parental stress and the neglect to children. Also, in cases of suspected or known abuse, homemaker-home health aides play multiple roles. These may include observation and reporting, as well as the above-mentioned assistance and education. In cases of suspected child abuse and neglect, the homemaker-home health aide may be asked to provide TESTIMONY in court.

Many professionals recognize the value of homemaker-home health aide services as an alternative to less costly forms of care. Foster care or other out-of-home care for children is also less desirable, since it is disruptive to family life. Homemaker-home health aides can play an important part in diminishing potential disruption in family settings, particularly those in which real or suspected abuse and neglect may already have caused disruption.

Guidelines and accreditation for training and employing homemaker-home health aides are advocated by the National Home-Caring Council, an organization that had its inception in the early 1960s. The council's standards, for example, require that if any homemaker-home health aide program does not have a social worker or a nurse "on staff, the expertise of that professional must be available through a written contract or agreement." The council's address is: 519 C Street NE, Washington, DC 20002.

Hong Kong (Special Administrative Region of the People's Republic of China)   According to the 1999 Country Reports on Human Rights Practices, released in February 2000, by the Bureau of Democracy, Human Rights, and Labor in the U.S.

Department of State, in the Special Administrative Region (SAR) of the People's Republic of China (formerly known as Hong Kong), and in the first eight months of 1999, there were reports of 193 cases of physical abuse and 134 cases of sexual abuse.

Since 1996, children with anxiety about testifying against their abusers may receive a child information witness kit in Chinese that includes books explaining court and legal actions. The government provides shelters and foster care for children. The age of criminal responsibility for children in the SAR is age 7, although it must be proved that a child under age 14 understood the consequences of his or her criminal act. As of this writing in 2000, the SAR is considering laws against child pornography. (*See also* DISCIPLINE, TAIWAN, PEOPLE'S REPUBLIC OF CHINA.)

hospital hold   In many areas hospitals are granted broad powers to hold children in custody for up to 24 hours when, in the opinion of the administrator, a child's safety is in danger or the parents may leave before a protective service worker can make a home visit. A hospital hold is used as an interim measure to protect abused children who are brought to hospital EMERGENCY ROOMS for treatment. The procedure allows child protection agencies sufficient time to act on cases when a child is in immediate danger.

hospital hopping   Abusive parents and caretakers often go to great lengths to avoid detection. Chronic child abusers sometimes engage in an evasive practice called hospital hopping. While fearing detection, the abuser will avoid using the same hospital or doctor twice when seeking medical care for the abused child. Medical personnel have greater difficulty recognizing a pattern of abuse when they are unfamiliar with the child's medical and social history.

hospitalism   High mortality rates among infants in European and American hospitals became a cause for concern during the early part of the 20th century. The FAILURE TO THRIVE SYNDROME observed in institutionalized infants, known as hospitalism, was initially attributed to poor nutrition and infection. Later, physicians began to suspect that lack of social and sensory stimulation might be related to this plight of institutionalized infants.

A well-known study conducted by Rene Spitz during the 1940s compared four groups of infants—three raised by their mothers in different settings and a fourth group raised in a FOUNDLING HOSPITAL. Infants who were cared for by their mothers all received similar types of attention. The foundling hospital provided a much different kind of care. Infants in this setting spent their days in cribs located in separate cubicles. Human contact was limited to brief visits from custodial and medical staff. After the first year of life infants reared by their mothers were within normal developmental limits. Foundling infants were retarded in their physical development, withdrawn, apathetic, less active and scored poorly on infant intelligence tests (these characteristics are sometimes referred to as MARASMUS).

Later studies of maternal deprivation showed that infants raised at home by severely neglectful mothers exhibited characteristics similar to those of the foundling infants. Subsequent research showed that retardation of physical growth was more likely related to inadequate feeding habits rather than lack of physical and emotional stimulation. Intellectual, developmental and emotional impairment associated with the deprived infants appeared to be more closely related to the lack of social and sensory stimulation.

Rene A. Spitz, "Hospitalism," *The Psychoanalytic Study of the Child* 1 (1945): 53.

———, "Hospitalism: A Follow-up Report," *The Psychoanalytic Study of the Child* 2 (1946): 113.

hotlines   Hotlines play an important role in child protection. These telephone services provide around-the-clock information and referral for victims and reporters of suspected child abuse or neglect.

Telephone crisis services were originally designed to facilitate a quick response to emergencies that required a child to be removed immediately from an abusive situation. Many hotlines now provide non-emergency information and referrals as well.

Hotlines are an important part of a comprehensive child protection system. Most government-sponsored child protection programs around the world maintain some form of 24-hour availability, usually in the form of a telephone hotline. Hotlines are usually staffed by professional child protection workers or trained volunteers backed up by an on-call professional. Workers are trained to screen reports and to respond appropriately to emergency situations. By necessity, hotline workers are called upon to provide counseling to callers in crisis. However, unlike HELPLINES, which are intended to provide telephone counseling, the role of the hotline worker is to match the caller to the appropriate service. This requires workers to be skilled in assessing calls quickly and knowledgeable concerning the range of resources available.

In the United States, most state-affiliated child protection agencies operate hotlines with 24-hour availability. In addition, there are two national hotlines that provide toll-free services to callers from anywhere in the country. (*See also* NATIONAL CHILD ABUSE HOTLINE and PARENTS ANONYMOUS.)

hydrocephaly   Enlargement of the head caused by a buildup of cerebrospinal fluid. Increased pressure within the cranial cavity can result in permanent CENTRAL NERVOUS SYSTEM INJURY and death.

Hydrocephaly can develop as a result of disease or trauma. Child abuse should be considered as a possible cause in cases where explanation of the head trauma seems implausible and where no evidence of disease is present.

hypervigilance   Severely abused children may become hypervigilant as a result of the random nature of past abuse. These children are watchful and withdrawn, constantly on guard, lacking an ability to trust others yet seeking emotional nurturance. Lengthy treatment and much patience on the part of the therapist and caretaker are usually required to overcome this manifestation of abuse.

A form of hypervigilance is also observed in infants suffering from FAILURE TO THRIVE SYNDROME. These infants sometimes lack the wariness of older children, seeking affection indiscriminately from anyone who approaches. (*See also* WITHDRAWAL.)

hyphema   Hemorrhage in the front portion of the eye is known as hyphema. Observable as a "bloodshot" eye, hyphema may be the result of a blow directly to the eye or other head trauma.

hypopituitarism, post-traumatic   *See* DWARFISM.

hyposomatotropism, reversible   *See* DWARFISM.

hypovitaminosis   *See* AVITAMINOSIS.

identification with the aggressor Psychoanalytic theory explains aggressive behavior of abused children as an ego defense mechanism. In an attempt to cope with feelings of powerlessness the abused child often adopts a violent mode of relating to others. Rage that cannot be expressed toward the abuser for fear of retaliation is redirected at other, less powerful individuals. Identification with the aggressor may explain the high degree of SIBLING ABUSE in families where one or both parents are abusive.

Though adopting an aggressive self identity may give the child a temporary sense of control over a situation that is largely beyond control, it ultimately causes the child to feel even worse. In becoming the aggressor the child may also internalize negative feelings toward the abuser. When others condemn the child for violent acts the child, remembering anger at the abuser, feels that he or she is also hopelessly bad. The child becomes trapped in a cycle in which feelings of low self-worth lead to acts of aggression that, in turn, bring confirmation of the child's badness from others.

identification with the victim Passive, dependent behavior of abused children may result from identification with a parent who is also the victim of abuse. Though this form of ego defense appears to be less common than IDENTIFICATION WITH THE AGGRESSOR it can be observed in many children who are withdrawn and who appear to be perpetual victims.

Psychoanalytic theorists believe identification with the victim is likely to occur when the child forms a strong early attachment to a passive-dependent parent. Identity as a victim offers a clearly defined, though maladaptive, role. Unlike the child who identifies with the aggressor, the child who copes with abuse in this way may be less burdened by feelings of guilt. Both types of ego defense are likely to lead to deep, long-lasting feelings of low self-esteem.

immunity, legal Most jurisdictions that have laws specifically requiring individuals to report suspected abuse and neglect also protect reporters from legal liability for such reports. MANDATED REPORTERS are typically granted immunity from criminal and civil charges arising from a report made in good faith. In many areas all reports are presumed to be in good faith unless it can be proven that the reporter knowingly filed a false report. Immunity from criminal and civil prosecution removes a significant legal barrier to reporting suspected abuse and neglect.

Critics of immunity for reporters argue that it leads to overreporting and abuse of reporting laws. In particular, opponents argue that the difficulty of proving a report was filed in bad faith encourages divorced parents to use false reports as a tactic in custody disputes. Some states have attempted to address this problem by increasing penalties for false reports. (*See also* APPENDIX 7, DOCTRINE OF SOVEREIGN IMMUNITY.)

Douglas J. Besharov, "Child Welfare Liability: The Need for Immunity Legislation," *Children Today* (September–October 1986).

impetigo A highly contagious skin disease occurring primarily in young children and infants, impetigo produces rapidly spreading red blisters. Severe cases of impetigo are often indicators of neglect and unsanitary living conditions.

impulse control Poor impulse control may be both a precipitant and a result of abuse. Parental immaturity, reflected in an inability to separate emotions from actions, is often blamed for abuse. Impulse control is lacking when the parent's frustrations and emotional needs are translated directly into action. In psychoanalytic terms, impulsive behavior reflects a weak superego (internal control mechanism).

When parents become frustrated or angry they may lash out at the first convenient target—usually the child. Though they may later regret their actions, abusive parents often lack sufficient control to avoid impulsive maltreatment of their children. Pedophiles and repeat sexual offenders are also cited as having poor control over sexual impulses. Development of internal controls is an important goal in psychoanalytic treatment of abusers. Until sufficient internal controls are developed, protection of the child may depend on external controls exercised by another adult or a child protection agency.

Learning to control aggressive impulses is a normal task in child development. Children of abusive parents usually lack adequate role models for controlling or sublimating anger. Though a child may develop a kind of pseudo-impulse control founded on fear of punishment, this mechanism quickly breaks down under stress. The resulting behavior often takes the form of unpredictable temper tantrums. Failure to master aggressive impulses leads the child to feelings of hopelessness and negative self-worth. If the abused child does not later develop adequate internal controls, he or she may grow up to be an abusive parent.

in camera In some cases of suspected child abuse or neglect, a legal hearing is held in the judge's chambers. This closed hearing is described by "in camera," the Latin term meaning, literally, in secret.

in loco parentis Literally, in place of the parents—this term is applied when either the state or a court-appointed individual acts on behalf of a child in cases of suspected abuse or neglect.

in re Gault Due to the lack of a clearly defined body of legal rights for children, the United States Supreme Court in 1967 established basic principles

governing those rights. *In re Gault,* the legal case that prompted the court's decision, concerned itself with the rights of juveniles charged with delinquency. Specifically, the case involved a 15-year-old Arizona boy, Gerald Francis Gault, who was accused of making an obscene telephone call to a neighbor. After an informal hearing in juvenile court, he was committed to a state institution for juvenile delinquents until age 21. Had he been an adult he would have received DUE PROCESS protections and a maximum incarceration of two months. The Supreme Court overturned the juvenile court's decision and found that juveniles—who could possibly be jailed if found guilty—had the right to notice, counsel, confrontation and cross-examination. They were protected as well against self-incrimination.

Establishing this precedent in the Gault case meant that the traditional PARENS PATRIAE view taken by juvenile court was no longer viable. Gault provided judicial guarantees that children's rights would be protected in the same way that adults' rights were preserved under the Constitution. This ruling bears directly on child abuse and neglect cases, since legal rights of children in such court proceedings can be considered independent of those of their parents.

Robert H. Mnookin, *Child, Family and State: Problems and Materials on Children and the Law* (Boston: Little, Brown, 1978).

incest Contrary to the popular image of the child molester as a stranger lurking in a park or dark alley, most perpetrators of SEXUAL ABUSE are known to the child. A great deal of sexual abuse involves incest, the sexual assault of family members by other family members. Stepfathers and fathers are, by a substantial margin, the most frequent molesters. Despite almost universal cultural, religious and legal prohibitions against father-daughter incest, studies show that it accounts for three-quarters of all intrafamily sexual assault. Girls who have stepfathers are five times more likely to be sexually assaulted than those who do not. While stepfathers themselves account for a significant portion of this increased risk, stepdaughters are also more likely to be assaulted by other men as well. One explanation for this phenomenon is that the mother's dating often brings the daughter into close contact with a number of adult men to whom she is not related. These men may have fewer inhibitions concerning sexual relations with the daughter than her male relatives may have. Obviously, increased divorce and remarriage rates during the past decades have placed girls at greater risk for this type of abuse. On the other hand, the increased viability of divorce as an option may have made it possible for some mothers and their daughters to escape abusive situations more easily than in previous times.

Father-son incest ranks a distant second to father-daughter incest in the number of cases reported. Mother-son incest accounts for an even smaller proportion of incest, while cases of reported mother-daughter incest are the least frequently documented. Incest involving siblings as both perpetrators and victims is less likely to be reported than incidents involving parent-child exploitation. This may reflect an attitude that such occurrences are less serious or a parental preference for handling such matters within the family.

Many experts believe, however, that such factors as decreased family stability, increased economic stress and changing sex roles and sexual norms have contributed to a real increase in the number of sexual assaults within the family.

Sibling Offenders

When the offender is a sibling, in the majority of cases, it is a male and often a brother who instigates or forces the incest. According to John V. Caffaro and Allison Conn-Caffaro, authors of *Sibling Abuse Trauma: Assessment and Intervention Strategies for Children, Families, and Adults* (Haworth Maltreatment and Trauma Press, 1998), the following are characteristics of sibling incest:

- Sexual contact is forced on a child by an older brother or sister.
- Attempts at intercourse, oral/genital contact or other compulsive sexual activity.
- May extend over long periods.
- May include unwanted sexual references in conversation, indecent exposure, forcing a sibling to observe sex, forcing a sibling to view pornography or taking pornographic pictures of a sibling.

- Behavior is not limited to age-appropriate developmental curiosity. It may not appear to be forced but nonetheless is based on manipulation, fear, threats and/or coercion or may occur while the victim is unconscious.
- Sexual contact occurs when both participants are engaging in the behavior as an attempt to cope with unmet needs for affection.

Other characteristics found among families of sibling incest were a lack of parental warmth, a lack of supervision and a confusion of normal boundaries between individuals. In many cases, the children have observed their parents openly having sex with each other.

It is also true that occasionally females are the perpetrators in incest cases. This problem has been studied very little by clinicians but is known to exist. When a boy is sexually pursued by his sister, evidence indicates that he is much less likely to reveal the incest than is a sister who is abused by a brother.

Brother-brother incest also occurs, particularly when there is little supervision and in large families. Older brothers may rape or allow others to rape the child. Sister-sister incest is known to happen but is considered very rare. Indications are that in such cases, the sisters have been sexually abused by their father or older brothers before the onset of the sister-sister incest.

Treatment of Sibling Incest Is Important

In an article in a 1998 issue of *Child Welfare*, Janet DiGiorgio-Miller describes how the family and offender should be treated by therapists. She points out the necessity of involving child protective services workers. If the parents refuse to contact protective services, then the therapist must contact them. She also points out the necessity of ensuring that the offender never be left alone with the victim. This may mean that the offending sibling must go live with a relative or other family during treatment. Trial visits may be arranged at a later date.

It is also important to make sure that the offender considers factors that led to the abuse (such as low self-esteem, excessive preoccupation with sex and other factors) and that he (or she) acknowledge the negative effect his (or her) actions had on the sibling.

Incest Through History

The phenomenon of incest has a long and complex history. The story of Oedipus, who unknowingly married his own mother, is often cited as an example of early attitudes toward incest. When finally faced with the knowledge that he had married his mother, Oedipus gouged out his eyes. His mother committed suicide. Both acts illustrate the extreme shame and disgrace felt as a result of a strong cultural prohibition against incestual relations.

Biblical references to incest range from sympathetic, in the case of Lot—who engaged in sexual relations with his daughters after the death of his wife—to a strong injunction against incest in the book of Leviticus. Among ancient Egyptian royalty, marriage between brothers and sisters was expected as a way of maintaining the purity of blood lines. Generally, however, sexual relations between close relatives have been looked upon with disgust and have been subject to strong negative sanctions throughout history.

Reasons for Incest

Explanations for the incest taboo have ranged from the now-refuted idea that biological barriers to incest are inherited to sociological, psychological, moral, legal and economic reasons. One theory states that the incest taboo serves the function of promoting interdependence between families through marriage, encouraging important economic and social exchange.

A great deal of debate has taken place concerning the genetic consequences of incest; however, the actual supporting evidence for predicting substantially increased risk of genetic defects is unclear. Perhaps the most compelling argument is found in more recent clinical evidence that points to the lasting psychological damage suffered by many child incest victims. While such damage is not inevitable, the fact that many prostitutes, drug addicts and convicted sexual offenders were incest victims strongly supports the idea that intrafamily sexual abuse can be very damaging.

Incest that begins during, or continues into, adolescence appears to be more likely to have severe and lasting effects than incest that ceases prior to the onset of puberty. Though sons are much less likely to be victimized than daughters, some researchers believe sons are both more likely to be seriously affected and less likely to overcome the psychological effects of incest.

Victim Is Often Not Believed

A serious problem faced by victims of incest, particularly adolescent girls, is that often when they *do* tell someone in authority about the incest, they are not believed. This may be partly because it is hard for many people to believe that a family member would sexually abuse another family member. But other factors come into play as well.

For example, when the incest has occurred for years before it is reported, the victim may not exhibit much emotion during the telling; rather, she may exhibit a very "flat," unemotional appearance. Many individuals, including those with knowledge of abuse, expect to see crying and distress, and when such behavior is not apparent, they may assume that the individual is lying about the abuse. Leslie Feiner explained this problem in her 1997 article for the *Journal of Criminal Law and Criminology.*

The incest dynamic itself can also affect the credibility of the traumatized teenage storyteller, because such victims do not tend to testify in ways that jurors would typically expect. Just as victims of long-term abuse tend to become more passive over time with their abusers, so too can they withdraw from others; they are plagued by low self-esteem, and their communication and social skills are often weak. Jurors who expect an incest survivor to relate a narrative in an expressive, direct and tearful way are likely to be disappointed. On the contrary, it is entirely likely to see such a witness testify flatly, without emotion, tears or even eye contact.

Feiner further states,

Teenage girls are particularly vulnerable to negative judgments regarding their credibility. In simulated sexual abuse trials where only the age of the victim was manipulated, researchers found that jurors tended to find girls over twelve years of age to be significantly less credible than adolescent girls under the age of twelve. As researchers polled their jurors, they found that as victims entered adolescence, jurors perceived them as partly responsible for the abuse they were subjected to, and that belief correlated with a decrease in their perceived credibility. . . .

In this respect the skepticism people demonstrate toward teenage sexual abuse victims is similar to the skepticism that greets adult victims of acquaintance rape. However, even if adult women face serious obstacles in pressing claims of rape, teenage incest victims face even more.

The following list of characteristics compiled by the NATIONAL CENTER ON CHILD ABUSE AND NEGLECT (NCCAN) suggests some commonalities of parents who sexually abuse their children. The presence of one or more of these characteristics does not prove that a parent is sexually abusive; it merely suggests that further investigation may be useful.

Characteristics of Sexually Abusive Parents
Both parents:
- have low self-esteem
- had emotional needs that were not met by their parents
- have inadequate coping skills
- may have experienced the loss of their spouse through death or divorce
- may be experiencing overcrowding in their home
- may have marital problems causing one spouse to seek physical affection from a child rather than the other spouse (a situation the "denying" husband or wife might find acceptable)
- may abuse alcohol
- lack social and emotional contacts outside the family
- are geographically isolated
- have [different] cultural standards that determine the degree of acceptable body contact

Adult male:
- is often a rigid disciplinarian
- is passive outside the home
- does not usually have a police record nor is he known to be involved in any public disturbance
- does not engage in social activities outside the home
- is jealous and protective of the child
- often initiates sexual contact with the child by hugging and kissing, which tends to develop over time into more caressing, genital-genital and oral-genital contacts

Adult female:
- is frequently cognizant of the sexual abuse but subconsciously denies it
- may hesitate reporting for fear of destroying the marriage and being left on her own
- may see sexual activity within the family as preferable to extramarital affairs
- may feel that the sexual activity between the husband and daughter is a relief from her wifely sexual responsibilities and will make certain that time is available for the two to be alone
- often feels a mixture of guilt and jealousy toward her daughter

(*See also* SEXUAL ABUSE; SIBLING ABUSE.)

John V. Caffaro and Allison Conn-Caffaro, *Sibling Abuse Trauma: Assessment and Intervention Strategies for Children, Families, and Adults.* (New York: The Haworth Maltreatment and Trauma Press, 1998).
Janet DiGiorgio-Miller, "Sibling Incest: Treatment of the Family and the Offender," *Child Welfare* 77, no. 3 (May 1998): 335–338.
Leslie Feiner, "The Whole Trust: Restoring Reality to Children's Narrative in Long-Term Incest Cases," *Journal of Criminal Law and Criminology* 87, no. 4 (Summer 1997): 1385–1429.
Wendy Maltz and Beverly Holman, *Incest and Sexuality* (Lexington, Mass.: Lexington Books, 1987).

Incest Survivors Resource Network International An educational resource service of the Task Group on Family Trauma, New York Yearly Meeting of the Religious Society of Friends (Quakers). Members help promote education, professional therapeutic intervention and self-help to help incest survivors resolve trauma. For more information, *see* APPENDIX 1. P.O. Box 7345 Las Cruces, NM 88006-7325 (505) 521-4260.

incidence of child abuse   No one knows exactly how many children are abused or neglected. Attempts to determine the incidence of child abuse have been hampered by use of retrospective data, varying definitions of abuse and other research problems. Casual observers often confuse reported abuse with incidence. Most experts believe the actual number of children who suffer from these problems is much greater than reported. Some estimate that only one-half of all physical abuse is reported. Reports of child sexual abuse are thought to represent less than one-third of all victims. In the U.S., child maltreatment is reported by the states to the U.S. Department of Health and Human Services, which provides an annual report and analysis.

Actual estimates of the incidence of abuse vary widely. Different studies have estimated the incidence of SEXUAL ABUSE to range from 6% to 62% for females and from 3% to 31% for males in the United States. In a survey of family violence conducted in 1975 and again in 1985, family violence researchers Murray Straus and Richard J. Gelles estimated that the rate of very severe violence (kicking, biting, hitting with a fist, beating, using a gun or knife) toward children declined from 3.6% to 1.9%. Their study did not include children under the age of three and thus underestimates the true incidence of PHYSICAL VIOLENCE. Still, this study is one of the few that manages to overcome definitional problems in studying the incidence of abuse.

Outside the United States even less information is available on incidence. Many observers believe violence toward children is more common in Western, developed countries. Scandinavian countries are thought to have a lower rate of violence, as are China, Russia, Poland, Japan and Italy. Unfortunately, few data exist to confirm or refute these beliefs. For detailed charts on the incidences of abuse in the U.S., see Appendix 5 Child Maltreatment Charts.

Murray A. Straus and Richard J. Gelles, "Societal Change and Change in Family Violence From 1975 to 1985 As Revealed by Two National Surveys," *Journal of Marriage and the Family* 48 (August 1986), 465–479.

Indecency with Children Act 1960 (Britain) Provisions of this act of Parliament specifically dictate the criminal nature of sexual behavior toward children. The acts states that, "Any person who commits an act of gross indecency with or towards a child under the age of 14, or who incites a child under that age to such an act with him or another, shall be liable on conviction."

indenture In previous centuries, those in Europe and colonists in America devised a way to handle neglected children. This was to place them in the care of a family who provided food and shelter in exchange for a legal promise that the children would act as servants until a certain age or, in the case of girls, until marriage. Many children placed in indenture were either orphans or from poor families who could not afford to provide food and shelter.

The indenture system was originally formalized in the 17th century to permit adults without money a means of immigrating to the North American colonies. These individuals would enter an agreement, similar in some ways to an apprenticeship, in which they contracted with an employer for a specific period. This system soon accommodated children, many but not all of whom were orphans, who had no other means of support.

Indentured servants were under the absolute control of a master or mistress, who was bound by law to provide for the indentured servant's basic needs. In 17th-century North America, the usual term of labor for an indentured servant was about five years, after which the servant received his or her freedom. Terms of indenture and conditions under which servants were bound varied widely from colony to colony. In some areas, indentured servants were treated quite harshly, in others they received fair and reasonable treatment.

In 19th- and early 20th-century Canada, nearly 100,000 poor children under the age of 14 were sent from Britain to serve terms of indenture on farms and as household servants. This trend reflected concerns of philanthropic reformers who wanted to save children from working in mines and factories under conditions considered unsafe and unhealthy. Eventually, other reformers agitated for changes in these programs, which essentially deprived school-age children of their education and placed many of them in situations devoid of comfort, where they performed menial and arduous agricultural or domestic tasks. By 1925, indenture arrangements effectively ended when British policies were changed to prohibit emigration of children under age 14 not accompanied by parents.

India The constitution of the Republic of India addresses children's needs as well as the responsibility of society in meeting those needs. Nevertheless, there is widespread neglect of children in

India, particularly with respect to nutritional needs, and many cases of infant mortality and childhood morbidity, as well as serious instances of exploitation of children. The India Council of Child Welfare and the Department of Social Welfare have established community programs to provide for physical, emotional and social care of children. Likewise, begging has been prohibited in some Indian states, child labor is regulated by law and health care services in both rural and urban areas are designed to promote child well-being.

These protective measures aside, India appears to present a clear example of the connection between poverty and illiteracy and Western concepts of child abuse and neglect. Estimates indicate that about 40% of Indian children live under the poverty level and that the illiteracy rate in the urban population is near 60%.

Research also indicates that nutritionally deprived children are commonplace in India. Poor economic conditions account for this, in both rural and urban settings. The high rate of disease-related deaths among children in India is a social problem, due also in large part to economic conditions and the lack of sufficient health services for children and families. Inadequate public health safeguards are a significant contributor to child mortality and morbidity.

A facet of traditional Indian society, the different social value ascribed to males and females, has often been cited as a contributing factor in the abuse of female children, especially in cases of INFANTICIDE. The latter was historically practiced with some regularity in almost all areas of India; it was outlawed by the British during the early 19th century although some researchers believe infanticide persisted into the 20th century. (*See also* CHILD SLAVERY.)

Female children have very low status in India. Although a 1994 law banned pregnant women from obtaining amniocentesis and sonograms for the sole purpose of sex determination—for the reason that so many women who learned they were bearing female children chose abortion—this practice continues. The government has prosecuted one physician for using sex determination tests and he was acquitted.

In addition, female infanticide continues to be a major problem in India. Experts estimate at least 10,000 cases of live baby girls who are killed occur throughout India each year. In one district, 1,260 female infants were killed but police did not investigate these cases.

Male children are given high priority and receive food and medical care before female children. Many girls, in some areas the majority of female children, are married on or before age 16, despite the fact that the age of consent is 18.

Jill E. Korbin, *Child Abuse and Neglect: Cross-Cultural Perspectives* (Berkeley: University of California Press, 1981).

Indian Child Welfare Act of 1978 (P.L. 95-608)

The Indian Child Welfare Act was designed to prevent the breakup of Native American families in the United States by: (1) shifting authority for out-of-home placement from the state to the tribe; (2) establishing minimum standards for the removal of Native American children from their families; and (3) encouraging the development of programs to assist families and children in distress.

According to a 1976 study 25% of all such children were in foster homes, adoptive homes or boarding schools. Native American children were found to be from five to 25 times more likely to be placed outside their home than other children. Reasons cited for the large number of Native American children removed from their homes included a tendency of welfare agencies to confuse poverty with neglect, blatant discrimination and lack of understanding of Native American culture by public and private child protection workers. In hearings on the act, Senator James Abourezk, chairman of the Select Committee on Indian Affairs stated, "Because of poverty and discrimination Indian families face many difficulties, but there is no reason or justification for believing that these problems make Indian parents unfit to raise their children, nor is there any reason to believe that the Indian community itself cannot, within its own confines, deal with problems of child neglect when they do arise."

Legislators were also concerned about adoption practices that seemed to favor non–Native American families. As a result of what were termed abusive child removal practices tribal councils were given jurisdiction over child custody proceedings involving tribal members.

The act also provided grants to tribes for establishing and operating child and family service

INDICATORS OF CHILD ABUSE AND NEGLECT

Category	Child's Appearance	Child's Behavior
Physical Abuse	Bruises and welts (on the face, lips or mouth; in various stages of healing; on large areas of the torso, back, buttocks or thighs; in unusual patterns, clustered or reflective of the instrument used to inflict them; on several different surface areas) Burns (cigar or cigarette burns; glove or socklike burns or doughnut-shaped burns on the buttocks or genitalia indicative of immersion in hot liquid; rope burns on the arms, legs, neck or torso; patterned burns that show the shape of the item [iron, grill etc.] used to inflict them) Fractures (skull, jaw or nasal fractures; spiral fractures of the long [arm and leg] bones; fractures in various states of healing; multiple fractures; any fracture in a child under the age of two) Lacerations and abrasions (to the mouth, lip, gums or eye; to the external genitalia) Human bite marks	Wary of physical contact with adults Apprehensive when other children cry Demonstrates extremes in behavior (e.g., extreme aggressiveness or withdrawal) Seems frightened of parents Reports injury by parents
Neglect	Consistently dirty, unwashed, hungry or inappropriately dressed Without supervision for extended periods of time or when engaged in dangerous activities Constantly tired or listless Has unattended physical problems or lacks routine medical care Is exploited, overworked or kept from attending school Has been abandoned	Is engaging in delinquent acts (e.g., vandalism, drinking, prostitution, drug use etc.) Is begging or stealing food Rarely attends school
Sexual Abuse	Has torn, stained or bloody underclothing Experiences pain or itching in the genital area Has bruises or bleeding in external genitalia, vagina or anal regions Has venereal disease Has swollen or red cervix, vulva or perineum Has semen around mouth or genitalia or on clothing Is pregnant	Appears withdrawn or engages in fantasy or infantile behavior Has poor peer relationships Is unwilling to participate in physical activities Is engaging in delinquent acts or runs away States he/she has been sexually assaulted by parent/caretaker
Emotional Maltreatment	Emotional maltreatment, often less tangible than other forms of child abuse and neglect, can be indicated by behaviors of the child and the caretaker	Appears overly compliant, passive undemanding Is extremely aggressive, demanding or rageful Shows overly adaptive behaviors, either inappropriately adult (e.g., parents other children) or inappropriately infantile (e.g., rocks constantly, sucks thumb, is enuretic). Lags in physical, emotional and intellectual development Attempts suicide

Source: U.S. Department of Health and Human Services, Office of Human Development Services, Administration for Children, Youth and Families, Children's Bureau, National Center on Child Abuse and Neglect, *Interdisciplinary Glossary on Child Abuse and Neglect* (Washington, D.C.: Government Printing Office, 1980; [OHDS] 80-30137, p. 22).

programs. These programs were funded for the purpose of helping Native American children remain either at home or with families of their own tribe. According to the 1999 Country Reports on Human Rights Practices, released in February 2000, by the Bureau of Democracy, Human Rights, and Labor in the U.S. Department of State, there are an estimated 500,000 homeless children living in poverty in India. There are also about 575,000 child prostitutes nationwide, and children represent about 15% of all prostitutes in the country.

Children who have run away to large cities are at high risk for sexual victimization and for contracting HIV and other sexually transmitted diseases. Many runaway children work 18–20 hour days.

The Union Ministry of Social Justice and Empowerment has 24-hour phone hotlines and receives as many as 25,000 calls in six months.

Indian Child Welfare Act of 1977, hearing before the U.S. Senate Select Committee on Indian Affairs, 95th Congress, 1st Session on S. 1214 ("To Establish Standards for the Placement of Indian Children in Foster or Adoptive Homes, To Prevent the Breakup of Indian Families, and for Other Purposes"), (Washington, D.C.: Government Printing Office, August 4, 1977).

indicators of child abuse and neglect   Various signs and symptoms, alone or in combination, may be helpful in identifying an abused or neglected child. The chart lists several such indicators of abuse. The presence of one or more indicators suggests that a child *may* be a victim of abuse or neglect. Further assessment is usually necessary to determine whether or not the specific sign or symptom was related to maltreatment or to some other cause.

Indicators such as those listed are useful in identifying possible abuse and neglect. Actual determination (substantiation) of whether a child is suffering from abuse requires more extensive evaluation by someone with special training in assessment techniques.

indictment   Criminal prosecution for child abuse begins with a written accusation known as an indictment. The document is prepared by a public

CARETAKER'S BEHAVIOR

Has history of abuse as a child

Uses harsh discipline inappropriate to child's age, transgression and condition

Offers illogical, unconvincing, contradictory or no explanation of child's injury

Seems unconcerned about child

Significantly misperceives
    child (e.g., sees him as bad, evil, a monster etc.)

Psychotic or psychopathic

Misuses alcohol or other drugs

Attempts to conceal child's injury or to protect identity of
    person responsible

Misuses alcohol or other drugs

Maintains chaotic home life

Shows evidence of apathy or futility

Is mentally ill or of diminished intelligence

Has long-term chronic illnesses

Has history of neglect as a child

Extremely protective or jealous of child

Encourages child to engage in prostitution or sexual acts in
    the presence of caretaker

Has been sexually abused as a child

Is experiencing marital difficulties

Misuses alcohol or other drugs

Is frequently absent from the home

Blames or belittles child

Is cold and rejecting

Withholds love

Treats siblings unequally

Seems unconcerned about child's problem

prosecuting attorney and submitted, under oath, to a grand jury for review. Members of the grand jury must determine whether the accusations, if proven true, would be sufficient to convict the accused of a crime. An indictment approved by a grand jury is known as a true bill.

Indictments serve as formal notices to parties accused of crimes. Charges must be spelled out clearly enough to allow the defendant to prepare an adequate defense. (*See also* PETITION.)

Infant Life Protection Act, 1872 (Britain)   The 19th-century practice of "baby farming" gave rise to the Infant Life Protection Act. Mothers unable or unwilling to care for their children often entrusted their care to women who ran BABY FARMS. These infants were frequently subjected to cruel treatment and were even sold by women who ran these farms. In two cases of such maltreatment, involving Margaret Walters and Sarah Ellis, such a public outcry was raised that Parliament passed the act.

Although by itself a somewhat ineffective statute, it received a great deal of publicity and set the precedent for a series of reforms affecting the care and well-being of infants. Among them were registration of homes in which infants were cared for, compulsory registration of births and deaths and more stringent regulations governing burial of stillborn infants.

infanticide   Murder of infants has been practiced throughout history and in virtually every society. Infanticide may take the form of violent trauma, such as strangulation or battering; exposure, wherein the child is left to die of starvation or hypothermia; or ritual sacrifice for religious purposes.

History is rife with accounts of infanticide. Biblical accounts of mass murder of infants include the pharaoh's order that all male children be drowned and Herod's attempt to slaughter all Jewish males under the age of two. Ancient Roman law permitted the destruction of unwanted infants. Aristotle advocated infanticide as a way of dealing with disabled or deformed infants.

Until the 19th century the Indian practice of casting female infants into the Ganges River was widespread. Polynesians expected mothers of lower social status to destroy all newborns immediately following birth. Babies born to upper-class mothers were protected from slaughter. In ancient Norway, Viking brothers were obligated to kill their sister's infant if she died during childbirth. A particularly brutal form of infanticide is said to have been practiced in rural Ireland in the 20th century. Changeling babies, infants who were born with congenital anomalies or who were simply unattractive (because these children were thought to be bewitched) were roasted alive over an open fire.

Though prevalent, infanticide was by no means condoned. In 18th-century Prussia, infant murderers were punished by sacking. Sewn into a cloth sack and weighted with heavy rocks, perpetrators were thrown into a river to drown. Sacking was forbidden by Frederick the Great, who thought

decapitation more appropriate. Other punishments included burning at the stake and impaling.

In 1871, the infant death toll in BABY FARMS had reached such proportions that the British House of Commons appointed a special committee to investigate the problem. As a result of the inquiry the INFANT LIFE PROTECTION ACT was passed. For the first time, minimum standards for child care were established.

Some societies did not consider an infant a person until ritually confirmed. In ancient Rome, a newborn was placed on the floor in front of the mother's husband. If he picked the child up, it was considered his offspring, if not, the child was often killed. The Romans viewed this as a way of protecting the purity of their race. Vikings presented the male infant with a spear. If the infant grasped the spear, he was allowed to live. Medieval English society protected the child's right to live only after it had consumed earthly nourishment. Many early Christians did not consider a child fully human until baptized and children who died before baptism were not allowed to be buried in sanctified ground. Excluded from church cemeteries, these children were given the same burial afforded a domestic animal.

In some civilizations, infants were placed in building foundations or in dikes to ensure the structure's strength. Brazilian tribes have been reported, as recently as 1977, as casting children from a high ledge into the ocean. The stated purpose of this ritual slaying was to ensure a bountiful harvest.

Infanticide has long been practiced as a means of population control. Native Hawaiian tribes were known routinely to kill infants born to a mother after her third or fourth child. Australian aboriginal mothers have been reported to kill a child when there was insufficient food or water to sustain the family. This phenomenon is not limited to historical or primitive cultures. Numerous infanticides committed by unwed mothers have been documented in Japan, the United States and other industrialized countries. The United States Federal Bureau of Investigation statistics listed 190 infanticides in 1985.

Statistical studies have indicated an inverse relationship between a country's positive sanction of abortion and the incidence of infanticide. Opponents of legalized abortion argue, however, that the procedure is simply another form of infanticide. Though the ethics of abortion are hotly debated, many countries use access to abortion as one means of controlling population growth. (*See also* NEONATICIDE.)

S. Radbill, "A History of Child Abuse and Infanticide," in Ray Helfer and C. Henry Kempe, eds., *The Battered Child,* 3rd ed. (Chicago: University of Chicago Press, 1980), 3–20.

infantile addiction   *See* ADDICTION, INFANTILE.

infantile cortical hyperostosis   A condition, also known as Caffey's disease, in which new bone forms beneath the periosteum of infants. A healed lesion of infantile cortical hyperostosis is similar in appearance to a fracture suffered during battering. In 95% of cases of this condition, the mandible (jaw bone) is affected—a bone unlikely to be fractured as a result of battering.

infibulation   This brutal ritual is practiced on young females in many cultures but is particularly prevalent on the African continent. It involves the complete removal of the clitoris and labia. The sides of the vulva are then sewn together leaving only a small opening for discharge of fluids. At marriage, infibulated females have their vaginas reopened to permit intercourse and childbirth. The main function of this procedure is to ensure that the female will be a virgin at the time of marriage.

Some have linked CLITORIDECTOMY and infibulation to the widely practiced custom of male circumcision; however, both infibulation and clitoridectomy are more extensive and more dangerous. Removal of the clitoris effectively eliminates the female's capacity for sexual stimulation. Many young girls die or suffer painful, chronic problems as a result of these operations. Though the practice is defended by some as an important cultural, religious or social ritual, it is widely condemned around the world. Elimination of sexual mutilation has been the topic of several international health conferences. (*See also* CULTURAL FACTORS, INITIATION RITES.)

Ingraham v. Wright   An important United States Supreme Court decision in 1977 held that CORPORAL PUNISHMENT in schools was not inherently cruel or abusive. This ruling was based on common-law precedents establishing disciplinary corporal punishment in public schools. The case, *Ingraham v. Wright,* was one that received a great deal of public attention, as it was argued and decided on the basis of the Eighth Amendment, which provides for protection against cruel and unusual punishment.

The plaintiff in the case, James Ingraham—a 14-year-old junior high school student—received hospital treatment for bruises received after being "struck repeatedly by a wooden instrument." The school principal responsible for Ingraham's corporal punishment was absolved of legal responsibility by the court ruling. The court held that "the administration of corporal punishment in public schools, whether or not excessively administered, does not come within the scope of Eighth Amendment protection."

Many child abuse and neglect experts denounced this finding as one that further validates violence against children—and legalizes child abuse—in one of the nation's most influential social institutions, its public schools.

Robert H. Mnookin, *Child, Family and State: Problems and Materials on Children and the Law* (Boston: Little, Brown and Company, 1978).

initiation rites   Virtually all cultures have rituals to mark the transition to adulthood. These events are sometimes referred to as puberty rites or rites of passage. Though initiation rites are often harmless ceremonies, rituals practiced by some primitive societies have been widely denounced as forms of institutionalized child abuse.

In New Guinea for example, boys are subjected to a series of increasingly painful rites before they can be officially recognized as adults. Bloodletting plays an important role both as a cleansing ritual and as a symbol of the male's ability to withstand pain. Passage to manhood may also include ritual scarification of the back, face or chest, sleep deprivation, burning, forced vomiting and verbal harassment. Some New Guinea tribes, the Sambia and the Keraki for example, force boys to serve as sexual partners for older initiates. These practices are attributed to a cultural belief that ingestion of semen is necessary for boys to acquire strength. By contrast initiation of girls into womanhood appears much less abusive. The traditional ritual of defloration, once practiced by tribal elders, appears to have ended in New Guinea.

Conversely, some African tribal groups engage in brutal mutilation of females. CLITORIDECTOMY and INFIBULATION are still practiced as initiation rites among remote tribes like the Gusii. Both males and females are expected to endure mutilation and other extremely painful acts unflinchingly.

Though Western child abuse experts classify many initiation rites as abusive, these practices may be seen as normal, even essential, in the societies where they are practiced. Practices such as clitoridectomy and infibulation, and sexual exploitation, are almost universally condemned. However, experts are less likely to agree that practices such as scarification and psychological humiliation constitute abuse. Some even speculate that these institutionalized forms of abuse are responsible for a lower incidence of idiosyncratic (deviating from cultural norms) abuse in non-Western societies. (*See also* CULTURAL FACTORS.)

injuries, abdominal   *See* ABDOMINAL INJURIES.

injuries, central nervous system   *See* CENTRAL NERVOUS SYSTEM INJURIES.

injuries, cord   *See* CORD INJURIES.

injuries, eye   *See* EYE INJURIES.

injuries, gastrointestinal   *See* GASTROINTESTINAL INJURIES.

injuries, mental   *See* MENTAL INJURY.

injuries, mouth   *See* MOUTH INJURIES.

innoculation   Since the development of modern vaccines, the innoculation of children against life-threatening and debilitating disease has become standard practice. Innoculation against disease has significantly reduced child mortality and increased the average life span. Many pediatricians now recommend that children be innoculated by 18 months to two years of age. Some consider failure to innoculate by age two to be MEDICAL NEGLECT.

This form of prevention has proven so effective that a majority of states and countries have laws requiring that all children be vaccinated against certain diseases. Legally required innoculation has not, however, been without controversy. Some parents dispute such requirements on the basis of religious beliefs. Others believe such vaccinations are dangerous or an infringement on their right to do what they think is best for their children.

In the United States, laws requiring innoculation vary from state to state. Most states tie innoculation to school attendance. Children are denied entry into the school system until they can produce evidence that they have received the required vaccinations. Parents who refuse to allow their children to be innoculated may be charged with MEDICAL and/or EDUCATIONAL NEGLECT. In some cases physicians, educators or child welfare workers can petition the court to order the parents to have their child innoculated.

Though widely practiced, mandatory innoculation continues to be a controversial subject in many areas.

institutional abuse and neglect   Sometimes social policies and institutions designed to help children do more harm than good. As the number of children enrolled in day care, treatment facilities, correctional institutions and foster care increases so does concern with institutional maltreatment.

Some child advocates argue that any institutionalization of children is abusive. Placement of children with adults in jails, correctional facilities or treatment centers puts children at significant risk of abuse and is prohibited in many areas.

Children placed in treatment and correctional facilities must be given a label. Designation as retarded, delinquent, emotionally disturbed or mentally ill can enable a child to receive special services that may benefit him or her. Such a label also places a child at significant risk of subsequent maltreatment. Some advocates say that institutional labeling is itself a form of abuse. Others point to the deprivation of freedom and denial of legal protection that often goes with institutional care.

Abuse within institutions may take several forms. Residents of full-time, 24-hour residential institutions may suffer physical neglect associated with poor nutrition, lack of exercise and idleness due to a lack of programmed activities. Medical abuse and neglect may also occur when health problems go untreated or when medication is dispensed without adequate monitoring or controls.

Many institutions, due to their age or lack of adequate funding, do not meet minimal standards for safety. Children living in these institutions may suffer burns from unprotected radiators, lacerations or fractures from poorly designed or defective buildings and furnishings and numerous other environmentally induced injuries.

Children in institutional settings may suffer physical abuse at the hands of staff, other residents or outsiders. Some children suffering developmental disabilities or mental illness must be protected from self-inflicted injuries.

In recent years a number of child sexual abuse cases in residential facilities and day care centers have received media attention. Historical accounts indicate that sexual exploitation of children in institutions has long been a problem. Recent publicity has caused institutions and lawmakers to consider new ways of protecting children from sexual abuse outside the family.

Problems associated with institutional abuse stem from many different sources. Treatment and correctional facilities are often inadequately funded. Lack of funds may lead to neglect of physical facilities and inadequate supervision of children. Poor recruitment procedures for child care workers and foster families also share blame for the increased risk of maltreatment. Finally, many institutions have simply failed to realize or acknowledge real or potential abuse.

Residential facilities have a responsibility to protect children from abuse. Most governmental, licensing and accreditation authorities require specific procedures for investigation of alleged maltreatment of children. Institutions are typically required to involve a neutral third party, in most cases a child protection or licensing agency, in the investigation of all such complaints. Recent civil suits have forced child care facilities to screen applicants for employment more carefully and to develop more thorough procedures for ensuring safety of children.

interdisciplinary team   *See* MULTIDISCIPLINARY TEAM.

intergenerational cycle of abuse   Numerous studies have documented the increased risk that abused children will become abusive parents when they reach adulthood. Though estimates vary, roughly one-third of parents with a history of childhood abuse also abuse their children. Children of such parents are six times more likely to be abused than their peers.

Despite these sobering figures, the connection between childhood victimization and later abusive behavior is far from inevitable. While there is no doubt that the experience of abuse increases the likelihood of becoming abusive this experience is but one of many factors contributing to child abuse. Other contributing factors include poverty, stress, social isolation and characteristics of the child.

Abused children are not condemned to become abusive parents. However, under stress the parent with a history of abuse appears to be more likely to lash out at a child than to find other ways of expressing frustration and anger.

Many parents who were abused as children find ways of breaking the cycle of abuse. The approximately two-thirds of parents who do not repeat the abuse they received as children appear to have more extensive social supports (friends, family etc.), have fewer negative feelings about pregnancy, give birth to healthier babies and are better able to express anger over their past abuse. These parents are also more likely to have suffered abuse from only one parent and have frequently reported a satisfactory relationship with the non-abusive parent.

Many mental health professionals agree that early intervention with abused children is an effective way to break the cycle of abuse. In the absence of such intervention it is still possible for parents with a history of abuse to avoid maltreating their children by developing a network of friends and family to call on in time of crisis, by developing appropriate ways of expressing anger and frustration and by learning new child-rearing techniques.

Many self-help organizations such as PARENTS ANONYMOUS (PA) seek to help parents break the cycle of abuse by providing social support on a 24-hour basis. Groups such as PA have proven to be particularly effective in preventing further child abuse.

International Society for Prevention of Child Abuse and Neglect   Based at the KEMPE NATIONAL CENTER FOR THE PREVENTION OF CHILD ABUSE AND NEGLECT, the International Society provides a worldwide forum for disseminating information on child abuse and neglect. The society holds international congresses on a biennial basis and publishes *Child Abuse and Neglect: The International Journal.* For more information, *see* APPENDIX 1.

Internet   In the latter part of the 20th century, the Internet became a popular vehicle for individuals throughout the world to obtain information, buy and sell items and communicate with each other. Unfortunately, it also appeared to be an ideal vehicle for the purveyors and buyers of CHILD PORNOGRAPHY.

Until the Internet became popular, child pornography was thought to be disappearing, primarily because of the active crackdown of postal authorities and police. However, individuals using their computers to gain access to child pornography are usually invisible to law enforcement authorities, and the child pornography business can be highly profitable. As a result, child pornography has become a serious global problem.

In addition to the problem of child pornography, some individuals have used the Internet as well as chat rooms on individual online services such as America Online and others to identify and communicate with minor children and to induce them to engage in sexual relations. In some cases, police officers posing as minors have engaged pedophiles in such talk and made arrangements to meet in a public place. Sometimes, expecting to meet the "child," the pedophile actually flies to the appointed place from a remote site, only to be met and arrested by a police officer.

A major problem with controlling child pornography on the Internet is that adults have protested that they have the right to view pornographic materials (although in the U.S., they do not have the right to view child pornography). They allege that constraints and active policing of web traffic (were it possible) would infringe upon their rights of free speech. This premise was upheld when the Communications Decency Act, signed in 1996 by U.S. President Bill Clinton, was found unconstitutional by the U.S. Supreme Court in 1997 because it was deemed to be an intrusion on the rights of adults to view pornography. (Child pornography is still illegal in the U.S., and laws against child pornography are enforceable and enforced.)

Another complicating problem is that the Internet is global. Thus, if one country creates strict rules restricting access to child pornography and controlling who may use the Internet, users may transfer their access to other countries which allow them more freedom.

Some states in the U.S. have passed "computer crime" statutes regarding children and computers, primarily centering around the purveyance of child pornography. The following states have passed laws regarding computer crimes and child abuse as of 1999: Alabama, Arizona, Arkansas, California, Colorado, Delaware, Florida, Georgia, Idaho, Illinois, Indiana, Kansas, Maryland, Massachusetts, Michigan, Mississippi, Montana, Nevada, New Hampshire, New Jersey, New Mexico, Pennsylvania, Texas and Virginia. In addition, some states have passed laws that specifically address the solicitation of a child via computer: Alabama, Florida, Illinois, New Hampshire, North Carolina and Oklahoma. For example, the Alabama statute (Ala. Code § 13A-6-110 (Supp. 1997)) states, in part,

> A person is guilty of solicitation of a child by a computer if the person is 19 years of age or older and the person knowingly, with the intent to commit an unlawful sex act, entices, induces, persuades, seduces, prevails advises, coerces, or orders, by means of a computer, a child who is less than 16 years of age and at least three years younger than the defendant, to meet with the defendant or any other person for the purpose of engaging in sexual intercourse, sodomy, or to engage in a sexual performance, obscene sexual performance, or sexual conduct for his or her benefit.

Federal law also bans adults from producing or selling child pornography created or transported by mail, by computer or by any other means (18 U.S.C.A. § 2252 [West Supp. 1999]).

intervention, voluntary   *See* VOLUNTARY INTERVENTION.

intradermal hemorrhage   Bleeding within the skin. (*See also* BRUISES.)

intraocular bleeding Bleeding inside the eye can be caused by a blow directly to the eye or head. In the case of PURTSCHER RETINOPATHY, sudden compression of a child's chest due to hitting, shaking or squeezing can cause a hemorrhage of the retina. The most common cause of intraocular bleeding is head trauma. Retinal hemorrhage is frequently a symptom of child battering, although it may be caused by accidental injury or participation in sports such as football and gymnastics. Studies of battered children have shown that the presence of bleeding inside the eye—especially the retina—is an indicator that a SUBDURAL HEMATOMA may also be present. Small clots that appear in the retina as a result of trauma generally last approximately two weeks. Other forms of intraocular bleeding may indicate serious damage to the eye, possibly resulting in blindness.

investigation Once a report of suspected child abuse or neglect has been made, an investigation is necessary to determine: (1) if the report is accurate and (2) if the child is in danger. Investigations of suspected abuse and neglect are typically conducted by child protection workers; however, in some areas law enforcement officers are responsible for investigation of such reports.

The first responsibility of the investigator is to assess the level of danger to the child and, if necessary, take immediate steps to ensure the child's safety. Situations such as those listed below suggest a child is in immediate danger:

- The maltreatment in the home, present or potential, is such that a child could suffer permanent damage to body or mind if left there.
- Although a child is in immediate need of medical or psychiatric care, the parents refuse to obtain it.
- A child's physical and/or emotional damage is such that the child needs an extremely supportive environment in which to recuperate.
- A child's sex, age, physical or mental condition renders the child incapable of self-protection—or for some reason constitutes a characteristic the parents find completely intolerable.
- Evidence suggests that the parents are torturing the child or systematically resorting to physical force, which bears no relation to reasonable discipline.
- The physical environment of the home poses an immediate threat to the child.
- Evidence suggests that parental anger and discomfort with the investigation will be directed toward the child in the form of severe retaliation against him or her.
- Evidence suggests that the parent or parents are so out of touch with reality that they cannot provide for the child's basic needs.
- Evidence suggests that the parent's physical condition poses a threat to the child.
- The family has a history of hiding the child from outsiders.
- The family has a history of prior incidents or allegations of abuse or neglect.
- The parents are completely unwilling to cooperate in the investigation or to maintain contact with any social agency and may flee the jurisdiction.
- Parent or parents abandon the child.

The investigation centers on allegations specified in the report of suspected abuse. While evidence of other maltreatment may be collected in the course of an investigation it is important to determine the accuracy of each allegation contained in the original report.

A typical investigation begins with a check of available records to see if the child or family has been the subject of other investigations. The child protection worker may then interview the child, family, the alleged abuser (if not a family member) and others who may have special knowledge of the child or family.

Interviewing the Child

It is usually best that a child be interviewed alone to minimize embarrassment or intimidation; however, in some cases a parent or other trusted adult may facilitate questioning. Though parental permission is not required to interview a child concerning suspected abuse or neglect, a parent should be notified that the child will be interviewed. When sexual abuse is suspected it is recommended that the interviewer and child be of the same gender.

Children are frequently reluctant to discuss alleged abuse with a stranger. Interviewers should make every attempt to put the child at ease. A child may need to be reassured that he or she has done nothing wrong and will not be punished. Criticism of the parent(s) may cause the child to become defensive and uncooperative with the interviewer. As much as possible, children should be allowed to tell their own story in their own words, without leading questions, prompts or undue pressure. Some child protection workers have found anatomically correct dolls useful in interviewing young children who are thought to have been sexually abused.

Reliving abuse through an interview can be traumatic for a child. Often child protection workers, law enforcement officers, lawyers and judges can combine questioning into one interview, thereby reducing trauma to the child. In some cases videotaped interviews may be used as evidence in court.

Direct observation of any injuries is an essential part of an interview. If it is necessary for the child to remove his or her clothing care should be taken to explain the reasons for disrobing in a nonthreatening, careful manner. In some cases it may be necessary to have the child examined by a physician to determine the existence and extent of injury.

Care must be given to explain to the child both the purpose of the interview and what to expect next. The child's questions should be answered truthfully and in language appropriate to his or her age.

Interviewing Adults

Adults should be informed of the reason for the interview and their legal rights with regard to the investigation. When possible, family members should be interviewed both separately and as a group. Separate interviews allow the child protection worker to compare accounts of an incident and may encourage the interviewee to share information more freely. Observing the family together often supplies important data on family interaction patterns.

Parents accused of abuse and neglect are often hostile and uncooperative. Interviewers who convey a neutral attitude toward the alleged abuse and who avoid direct confrontation are often successful in securing a reasonable level of cooperation. Keeping the focus on the child's welfare and asking open-ended questions are also useful strategies for soliciting necessary information. The child protection worker must be supportive of parents without appearing to condone inappropriate behavior.

Other Methods of Obtaining Information

Direct observation of a child's environment can supply useful information. Cleanliness of the home, presence of nutritious food, cooking and sanitary facilities, adequate sleeping arrangements, lighting, heat and water are all important.

Behavior of the child and family members should also be observed. An angry outburst or emotional coldness toward a child may belie a parent's description of a close relationship with the child.

Secondary information may be obtained from medical, school and police records. These kinds of data can help verify information obtained from interviews and observation.

A medical or mental health evaluation of a child may help identify or confirm evidence of abuse or neglect.

Observable physical evidence of injury should be documented with carefully taken photographs. Photographs should be identified accurately (name of subject, time, location, age etc.) and should include distinguishing features that allow identification of the child as well as a clear view of the injury itself. Color film is preferred to black and white. Infrared film may increase visibility of injuries where dark skin coloring inhibits clear observation of trauma. Production of photographs that are acceptable as evidence in court requires the careful attention of a skilled photographer.

Outcome of the Investigation

After all relevant information has been collected the investigator must make a decision concerning the accuracy of the alleged abuse or neglect and the need for further intervention.

The investigator may conclude that abuse or neglect exists, does not exist or that further information is necessary to make a determination. When abuse or neglect is substantiated interventions vary depending on the level of risk to the child, the child's needs and the family's willingness to cooperate. If the family refuses to cooperate a court order may be necessary to ensure treatment. In some cases the investigator may conclude that abuse or neglect does not exist but that services should be offered to the family.

U.S. Department of Health, Education and Welfare, Office of Human Development Services, Administration for Children, Youth and Families, Children's Bureau, National Center on Child Abuse and Neglect. *Child Protective Services: A Guide for Workers* (Washington, D.C.: 1979; [OHDS] 79-30203).

isolation   *See* SOCIAL ISOLATION.

Israel   There are currently no laws dealing specifically with child abuse in Israel. Rather, the prevailing opinion is that abused or neglected children should receive the same concern afforded maltreated children under conventional child protection legislation.

Israel provides free or low-cost child health services that act as a screen for possible child abuse and neglect. Children are seen at clinics virtually from birth.

Child labor laws in Israel specifically prohibit children under age 16 from working unless they have special permission. In 1986, the chief of Israel's Labor Ministry commented on the prevalence of child labor despite prohibitive legislation and noted the difficulty in finding and prosecuting those who break child labor laws.

In Jerusalem, according to a recent *Jerusalem Post* article, a children's ombudsman has worked to protect the rights of children who, statistics show, make up 40% of the city's population. The ombudsman's role is to hear complaints, oversee weaknesses in the legal system and raise public awareness about children's rights. According to the 1999 Country Reports on Human Rights Practices, released on February 25, 2000, by the Bureau of Democracy, Human Rights, and Labor in the U.S. Department of State, Israel has comprehensive mandatory reporting requirements for child abuse.

Five shelters provide assistance for children at risk for abuse.

Some children's rights advocates have estimated that there are several hundred child prostitutes in Israel. As of this writing, the Ministry of Justice, working with police and other experts, are attempting to determine the extent of child prostitution.

Italy   There is an Association for the Prevention of Child Abuse and Neglect in Italy and a Family Crisis Center in the city of Milan. However, many experts who specialize in international perspectives on child abuse concur on the lower level of awareness of child abuse and neglect in Italian society compared to some other European nations. In one Italian study, however, physical abuse was targeted as a major problem. Information gathered during research into child maltreatment in Italy suggested there was a need for better definitions of child abuse and neglect and recommended both legislative reform and upgrading of Italian social services as ways of dealing more effectively with child abuse. As in many other countries, cultural perceptions of children in Italy influence the way abusive behavior is seen, understood and acted upon. According to the 1999 Country Reports on Human Rights Practices, released on February 25, 2000, by the Bureau of Democracy, Human Rights, and Labor in the U.S. Department of State, research contracted for by the Italian government indicated that there were about 11,000 children involved in some form of violence in Italy, including up to 2,500 child prostitutes. The majority of the child prostitutes were illegal immigrants, primarily from Albania, and who had been sold into prostitution.

In 1998, the Italian Parliament passed a law against pedophilia, child pornography, the possession of pornographic material involving children, sex tourism that involved minors and trafficking in children.

Japan Most research reports dealing with Japan indicate that there is virtually no perception of child abuse as a social problem. Statistics indicate that Japanese culture is less violent than, for example, that of the United States. One researcher indicates that low child abuse reporting rates in Japan are a fairly accurate reflection of reality. Physical punishment of, or violence toward, children in Japan is rare, although occasional newspaper accounts of abuse or neglect do appear. Japanese schoolchildren are subject to biannual physical examinations, during which signs of physical abuse would most likely be detected. The apparent lack of child maltreatment in Japan may be due in part to different cultural definitions of abuse, a common issue when discussing international aspects of abuse and neglect.

According to available research, more common or apparent forms of child abuse or neglect involve young children and infants. Infanticide would appear to be more prevalent, for example, than severe physical abuse of a child. The assumption is that a parent (and Japanese statistics show it is more often the child's mother) resorts to killing her infant rather than letting the child live and abusing or neglecting the child later. In the mid-1970s, a Japanese government survey on child abuse, abandonment and murder revealed that abuse or neglect represented slightly over 6% of all cases reported during one year. Abandonment made up nearly 33% of reports. The combined categories of murder (including infanticide) or murder-abandonment (when an abandoned child died before being discovered) represented 45.2% of cases. Joint suicide, where a parent kills the child before committing suicide, made up nearly 16% of reports in the government study. The June 1999 issue of *Pediatrics* included an article about a two-

year study by the Japanese Ministry of Health and Welfare, released in 1998, which reported that 500 babies die of SUDDEN INFANT DEATH SYNDROME (SIDS) in Japan every year and about 19% die because they are sleeping in the prone position rather than on their backs. The article took the Japanese to task for waiting for the results of their own study rather than using the results of studies performed by other countries earlier.

"Japan's Study of Cot Deaths," *Pediatrics* 103 (June 1999): A64.

Jill E. Korbin, ed., *Child Abuse and Neglect: Cross-Cultural Perspectives* (Berkeley: University of California Press, 1981).

jejunal hematoma The collection of blood in the jejunum or middle part of the small intestine. Usually the result of a blow to the abdominal area. (*See also* ABDOMINAL INJURIES and GASTROINTESTINAL INJURIES.)

Johnson and Wife v. State of Tennessee In the 1830s, a Mr. and Mrs. Johnson were convicted of excessively punishing their daughter. This case was one of the earliest recorded occasions where parents in the United States were tried for child maltreatment. The conviction was later overturned because an overzealous judge issued an improper charge to the jury.

juvenile court *See* COURT.

juvenile court movement The origins of the juvenile court in the United States date to the early 19th century. At that time, children over age 14 were treated as adults by the court systems, arrested, brought to trial, sentenced and punished

125

according to criminal laws framed with adult offenders in mind. Even children between the ages of seven and 14 years were not always guaranteed immunity from criminal prosecution. It was the state's prerogative to hold a child legally accountable in criminal court if it preferred to do so, and judicial mechanisms for this purpose existed prior to establishment of a juvenile court.

Juvenile court system supporters worked to make judicial law more responsive to the needs of children. In recognition of these needs, by 1875 New York state prohibited placement of children with adults in almshouses for more than 60 days. Proponents of separate and special judicial treatment for children urged use of psychology, social work and medical science when sentencing, treating and rehabilitating youth. As a result, the first juvenile court in the United States was established in 1899 in Chicago, Illinois.

By the early 1900s, the juvenile court movement had been successful in permanently establishing this separate arena where the child's unique needs were taken into account. Wanting to guard the child against societal dangers, the juvenile court movement emphasized rehabilitation rather than retribution. Establishment of a juvenile court system was also to keep children separate from adult offenders. Much earlier, New York City had founded the House of Refuge in 1825, a correctional facility that segregated children from older, more hardened criminals. The juvenile court movement supported this and also sought more informal court procedures, as compared to the legalistic formality of a criminal court. The juvenile court movement desired also that the court consider each child's needs separately. More specifically, the juvenile court movement recognized that children must be protected if they are unable to seek and find their own protection. The juvenile court, therefore, was charged with acting as a substitute parent.

Juvenile Justice Standards Project   This project, completed in 1979, was sponsored by the American Bar Association and the Institute of Judicial Administration. The final report was a 21-volume set of recommendations to each state. Basically, these recommendations would eliminate juvenile court jurisdiction over most status offenses (an action that is an offense because it is committed by a minor, not because of the act itself) in cases of noncriminal misbehavior. This change is intended to encourage more extensive use of voluntary services and especially to make more room in juvenile courts for cases involving abused and neglected children.

Keating-Owen Bill As a general result of Progressive Era protective legislation, in 1916 this child labor law was passed as a response to pressure from various groups opposing child labor in the United States. In particular, the Keating-Owen Bill was designed to protect children under the age of 16 from long hours and dangerous working conditions in factories and mines. Despite widespread acknowledgment of abusive child labor practice, the Keating-Owen Bill was declared unconstitutional two years after its passage.

Kempe Children's Center The center was named for one of the foremost U.S. experts on child abuse and neglect, C. Henry Kempe. Affiliated with the Department of Pediatrics of the University of Colorado Medical School since its establishment in 1972, the center provides training, consultation, program development and evaluation and research in all forms of child abuse and neglect. Affiliated organizations include Hope for the Children, a diagnostic and treatment center; the KEEPSAFE project; the National Association of Counsel for Children; the International Society for Prevention of Child Abuse and Neglect; and the Colorado Child Protection Council. For more information, *see* APPENDIX 1.

key masters *See* UNDERGROUND NETWORKS.

kidnapping Any unlawful seizure of a person and detention against that person's will is generally described as kidnapping. In modern times and in most nations of the world, kidnapping is a crime punished by death or lengthy imprisonment. In the United States, federal laws governing kidnapping were amended following the 1932 abduction and subsequent murder of aviator Charles A. Lindbergh's infant son. The Lindbergh baby kidnapping

was the most famous among numerous early 20th-century abductions, many of which involved wealthy or well-known families and a large number of which had extortion as a key factor. The notoriety surrounding the Lindbergh case led directly to federal legislation that imposed the death penalty for anyone convicted of transporting a kidnap victim across state lines. When a noncustodial parent resorts to this type of action in order to secure unlawful custody of a child or children, it is termed CHILD STEALING.

Historically, abducting female children or young women for the purpose of selling them into prostitution was considered in many cultures a form of kidnapping. (*See also* CHILD STEALING, MANN ACT, PARENTAL KIDNAPPING PREVENTION ACT OF 1980, CHILD SLAVERY.)

kinky hair syndrome *See* MENKES' KINKY HAIR SYNDROME.

kinship care When children are abused and neglected and removed from their primary caretakers, sometimes they are placed with extended-family members: this is referred to as *kinship care.*

In some states, caregiver relatives may receive the same foster care payment as would an unrelated foster parent. The advantage of kinship care is that it provides continuity for the child, who may be able to stay with people he or she already knows and who care about him or her. There is an advantage to society itself because it is difficult to recruit sufficient numbers of nonrelative foster parents.

The disadvantages are that kinship care providers are usually women living alone, such as grandmothers or aunts, who have few financial resources. Often they are less closely monitored than are nonrelative foster parents and thus the potential for abuse may be greater, either by the visiting biological relative who abused the child in the first place or by the kin caregiver herself, in a case of intergenerational abuse. In addition, kinship care providers are less likely to obtain medical treatment for foster children, including immunizations, well-child visits and appointments when the child is ill. Thus the child may be at risk for medical neglect.

laboratory tests   Several routine tests are used by doctors to aid in the diagnosis of child abuse. Included are:

Partial thromboplastin time and *prothrombin time* tests measure blood-clotting factors. Knowledge of clotting time helps distinguish between bruising and bleeding associated with hemophilia and trauma-induced injuries.

Urinalysis helps detect sugar, protein, blood or other substances in the urine. Blood in the urine is evidence of internal injury that may not be immediately apparent to the casual observer.

A complete *blood count* yields information about the level of red and white blood cells. This test may give evidence of poor nutrition or infection.

The *Rumpel-Leede* or *tourniquet* test is used to measure the plasticity of capillaries. Fragile capillaries may cause a child to bruise more easily than other children. Abusive parents frequently claim "the child bruises easily." This test helps verify claims of bruisability.

Landeros v. Flood   This 1976 ruling by the California Supreme Court established the liability of physicians and hospitals when they negligently fail to diagnose and report child abuse.

Gita Landeros, the plaintiff, was severely and repeatedly beaten by her mother and her mother's common-law husband. When brought to the San Jose Hospital for treatment the infant showed clear evidence of suffering from BATTERED CHILD SYNDROME, including a fractured tibia and fibula (apparently from severe twisting) and multiple bruises and abrasions. The physician, A. J. Flood, failed to perform a full SKELETAL SURVEY and therefore did not discover a skull fracture. In failing to properly diagnose the child's condition the physician also did not report the case to the proper law enforcement and child protection authorities.

The child was returned to the mother and her partner who continued to abuse her until she was brought to another hospital for treatment of blows to her eyes and back, puncture wounds, bites on her face and burns on a hand. At the second hospital a physician properly diagnosed the child's condition and reported the case to local authorities who took her into protective custody.

The court reversed a dismissal by a lower court and held the physician and the hospital responsible for failing to diagnose and report child abuse. This ruling opened the door for future malpractice suits against physicians and medical institutions who fail to report suspected child abuse.

Robert H. Mnookin, *Child, Family and State: Problems and Materials on Children and the Law* (Boston: Little, Brown, 1978).
Irving Sloan, *Child Abuse: Governing Law and Legislation* (New York: Oceana Publications, 1983).

Latin America   The diverse cultural groups that make up the countries of Central and South America show similar diversity in terms of abuse and neglect of children. In general, however, it can be said that among indigenous peoples, many of whom are isolated from Western culture, many child-rearing practices exist that would be considered abusive by Western standards. This is particularly true of tribes that inhabit the Amazon region, where primitive lifestyles embrace a generally harsh, subsistence-level existence. Some of these practices persist in nonaggressive tribal cultures where deliberate maltreatment of children is not intentional. Bathing infants in scalding water to drive out anger, scraping a child's skin during puberty rites to ensure stamina against pain or dipping a baby in a river to force it to stop crying are carried out by generally nonviolent tribes, which apparently seek to strengthen children, physically and psychologically, for a life of relative hardship.

Other native groups characterized as aggressive and violent in their general behavior are known to give hallucinogenic drugs to children, spank disobedient children with nettles and leave very young children (of one year or less) alone and unattended for hours at a time. Researchers explain that these tribal practices toward children are representative of general social patterns among adults rather than manifestations of abuse or neglect aimed specifically at their children.

While observers can sometimes dismiss abusive practices among primitive societies as exotic aberrations, it is also true that most countries in Central and South America show high rates of abuse and neglect in their modern communities. In urban areas of Latin America child abuse, neglect and maltreatment is common. This is due not only to the huge number of people living below the poverty level but also to social attitudes, economic circumstances and political environments that accept or encourage abusive practices, i.e., child disappearance, torture, child prostitution and child labor.

Reports from international groups, like the United Nations and Amnesty International, as well as domestic human rights organizations, describe a range of situations that embody extreme abuse and neglect of children. In Argentina between 1976 and 1979 many thousands of people, including infants and children, were abducted by the military. Large numbers were never heard from again although in some cases the "disappeared," as they are called, were given to other families and have been raised as their own children. In Chile, Colombia, Guatemala and Peru, similar cases of disappeared children have been reported.

A Study of Abusive Mexican Mothers

In a study of "harsh parenting" among Mexican mothers, including mothers referred to child abuse agencies as well as abusive mothers identified from the community, researchers (understandably) found a higher level of abuse among the mothers who had been referred to child welfare authorities. For example, about 13% of the "maltreating mothers" had burned their children, compared to about 2% of the mothers from the community. Fifteen percent of the maltreating mothers reported kicking, biting or hit-

ting their children, versus none of the community mothers. All of the maltreating mothers used corporal punishment (spanking and slapping), versus about 75% of the community mothers.

The researchers found maltreating mothers to be more likely to have experienced abuse themselves as children. Mothers with less education were also more likely to be abusive. The researchers found that the most significant factor affecting the use of physical punishment was an authoritarian parenting style.

In Bolivia, *los polillas* (street children) of Cochabamba is the name given to several thousand abandoned children between the ages of eight and 15. They steal, sell drugs and are often addicted to drugs themselves. Brazil has upward of 10,000,000 street children out of a total of 50,000,000 aged 15 or under, according to a UNICEF worker. Similar numbers have been reported for El Salvador, Guatemala and Peru.

In Mexico City, many children die each year from working in a dump called Basurero de Santa Fe. Here, they sort trash, contracting parasites and skin and intestinal diseases.

In Honduras in 1987, there were allegations that trafficking in children existed for the purpose of selling body parts.

In Recife, Brazil, where brothels abound, there are numerous cases of younger teenage girls working as prostitutes.

Torture of children is known to be common in Chile, Guatemala and Honduras, where violence resulting from clashes between left-wing and right-wing forces is the result of political turmoil. Electric shocks, beatings, kickings, slashings, psychological torture and sexual abuse are among the practices used against children as young as 10 years of age. It is not uncommon also for children to be forced to witness the torture of parents and other adults.

In Brazil, children as young as seven work on sugar plantations; in Chile, many children work as street vendors after being forced out of their homes for economic reasons; Mexican children between eight and 14 work on sugar plantations cutting sugar cane.

Martha Frias-Armenta and Laura Ann McCloskey, "Determinants of Harsh Parenting in Mexico," *Journal of Abnormal Child Psychology* 26, no. 2 (April 1998): 129–139.

least detrimental alternative   *See* BEST INTERESTS OF THE CHILD.

legal immunity   *See* IMMUNITY, LEGAL.

legal rights of persons identified in reports   In the United States persons criminally accused of child abuse have a right to be represented by a lawyer. In juvenile or family court proceedings the right to counsel varies from state to state. Approximately one-half of all states grant the right to counsel in civil as well as criminal proceedings.

Some critics of present child abuse laws argue that persons accused of child abuse should be entitled to counsel in all proceedings. Civil proceedings can establish the basis for removal of a child from the home and for further criminal charges. Even when a civil proceeding does not result in criminal charges or removal of the child, some believe that the investigation itself and subsequent supervision by a child protection agency is likely to infringe on the parent's legal rights.

lesion   A term frequently used to describe injuries resulting from abuse, lesion can refer to an injury of any type to any part of the body.

liability of reporters   The fear of being sued could prevent some people from reporting suspected abuse or neglect to child protection authorities. This is especially true when abuse is suspected but cannot be proven without further investigation. In an effort to remove this barrier to reporting, all MANDATED REPORTERS in the United States are granted immunity from civil and criminal prosecution when reports are made in good faith. Further, in at least 40 states voluntary (nonmandatory) reporters are exempt.

Communications between doctor and patient, psychologist or social worker and client, and clergy and parishioner often receive special legal protection under the law. Although some jurisdictions require these professionals to report confessions of dangerous crimes, most states classify information passed between these parties as privileged communication. However, reports of suspected abuse or neglect are not afforded this protection. In fact, these professionals are usually classified as man-

dated reporters and are therefore required to report all cases of suspected maltreatment. A majority of states in the United States impose criminal and/or civil penalties on mandated reporters for failure to report such cases. In at least one case (*LANDEROS V. FLOOD*) a physician has been found legally liable for failing to report suspected abuse.

lice   Head lice are not uncommon in children. These small parasitic insects attach themselves to the scalp and survive by sucking blood through the skin. Children frequently acquire them from casual contact while playing or at school.

Treatment of an infested child involves repeated application of medicated shampoo and careful inspection of the hair for the insects or their eggs. This process requires persistence and usually takes place at home under a physician's instructions. If untreated, lice can cause significant discomfort to the child and may result in infection. Neglected children are sometimes found to have severe infestations of head or body lice that have gone untreated for a lengthy period of time.

Pubic lice are found in the groin area and sometimes produce bluish spots on the skin that disappear when the lice are treated. The presence of pubic lice on a child who has not reached sexual maturity is a strong indicator of possible SEXUAL ABUSE. When pubic lice are discovered on a child of any age, a careful examination should be conducted to determine how the insects were transmitted and whether there is other evidence of sexual abuse.

Liverpool Society for the Prevention of Cruelty to Children   Founded in Britain in 1883, this society was a project of a Liverpool banker, Thomas Agnew. After visiting the United States in 1881 and learning of the New York Society for the Prevention of Cruelty to Children, Agnew took steps to establish a similar welfare organization in his home city. He was subsequently involved in helping to found the London Society in July 1884. This organization merged in 1889 with many other child welfare groups and was then renamed the National Society for the Prevention of Cruelty to Children. (*See also* NATIONAL SOCIETY FOR THE PREVENTION OF CRUELTY TO CHILDREN.)

local authorities   In the United States the child protection agency designated by the mandated state agency to serve a particular area is known as the local authority. A local authority may be a branch of the state agency, a private agency under government contract or a county department of social services. The term may also be applied to a COMMUNITY COUNCIL FOR CHILD ABUSE AND NEGLECT.

Local authorities have primary responsibility for child protection in BRITAIN. Specifically, local authorities include councils of nonmetropolitan counties and metropolitan districts, the London boroughs and the common council of the City of London. Local social service authorities are under the general supervision of the secretary of state for social services or the secretary of state for Wales. Policy making for management of child abuse cases is the responsibility of an Area Review Committee appointed by the local authority. In addition to child protection, local authorities have responsibility for child care, delinquency prevention, foster care, legal advocacy for children and adoption. (*See also* PROTECTIVE SERVICES.)

loss of childhood   *See* PARENTIFIED CHILD.

low birth weight   Premature birth, inadequate prenatal care or SUBSTANCE ABUSE by the mother during pregnancy can cause infants to be significantly below normal weight at birth. Low birth weight may require an extended hospital stay until infants are healthy enough to be cared for at home. Premature infants often spend the first days of their lives in an incubator.

Many experts believe treatment for low birth weight and other medical problems can interfere with the natural mother-infant bonding process, placing the child at increased risk of abuse (BONDING FAILURE). Many hospitals are now taking steps to increase contact between mothers and infants who require intensive medical attention.

malabsorption syndrome   Any of a number of specific conditions, often inherited, that interfere with the absorption of nutrients in the intestines. Malabsorption can be caused by a number of childhood diseases, many of them fatal. It is a frequent cause of organically based FAILURE TO THRIVE SYNDROME.

malpractice   Failure to diagnose and report child abuse or neglect may leave physicians and other professionals open to malpractice suits. In LANDEROS V. FLOOD the California Supreme Court held a physician and hospital liable for failure to diagnose abuse in an infant who showed clear signs of BATTERED CHILD SYNDROME.

mandated agency   Under the CHILD ABUSE TREATMENT AND PREVENTION ACT OF 1974 each state is required to designate an agency responsible for receiving and investigating reports of child abuse and neglect. Most states designate their social services departments. *See* APPENDIX 2 for a list of each state's mandated agency and its address.

mandated reporter   Many people, by virtue of their professional or occupational status, are specifically required by state or federal law to report all cases of suspected child abuse or neglect to the mandated agency. Legal penalties are imposed for failure to report, and some mandated reporters have been sued successfully for failing to report cases.

The occupational and professional categories whose practitioners are mandated reporters vary slightly according to different state laws but usually include: health care worker, social worker, counselor, teacher, law enforcement officer and child care personnel.

In the following states, all citizens are considered mandated reporters: Delaware, Florida, Idaho, Indiana, Kentucky, Maryland, Mississippi, Nebraska, New Hampshire, New Jersey, New Mexico, North Carolina, Oklahoma, Rhode Island, Tennessee, Texas, Utah and Wyoming.

Penalties for failure to report vary from state to state. (See the essay on MANDATED REPORTING for more information.) There are also gray areas that concern experts, for example, if abuse may have occurred but the reporter is unsure. Generally, if abuse is likely, it must be reported and then others will determine if the abuse actually occurred or not. However, the investigation process is traumatic for guilty and innocent parent alike and his or her children. As a result, some experts have recommended eliminating or limiting who should be mandatory reporters; this action seems unlikely to occur at this time.

The mandate to report abuse overrules husband-wife privilege as well as physician-patient privilege. Only attorney-client privilege or clergy-penitent privilege is upheld in most states. For state-by-state information on mandatory reporters, the chart on the next page provides more details.

mandated reporting   Most countries now require reporting of suspected child abuse and neglect to law enforcement authorities or a child protection agency. In the United States, the CHILD ABUSE PREVENTION AND TREATMENT ACT, a federal law enacted in 1974, encouraged states to strengthen laws specifically requiring reporting of child abuse and neglect.

Every state has a listing of individuals who must report child maltreatment when they observe it. According to the NATIONAL CLEARINGHOUSE ON CHILD ABUSE AND NEGLECT INFORMATION, most reporting laws

Mandatory Reporters of Child Abuse and Neglect

STATE	PROFESSIONS THAT MUST REPORT					OTHERS WHO MUST REPORT		STANDARD FOR REPORTING	PRIVILEGED COMMUNICATIONS
	Health Care	Mental Health	Social Work	Education/ Child Care	Law Enforcement	All Persons	Other[2]		
ALABAMA §§ 26-14-3(a) 26-14-10	✓	✓	✓	✓	✓		▪ Any other person called upon to give aid or assistance to any child	▪ Known or suspected	▪ Attorney/client
ALASKA §§ 47.17.020(a) 47.17.023 47.17.060	✓	✓	✓	✓	✓		▪ Paid employees of domestic violence and sexual assault programs and drug and alcohol treatment facilities ▪ Members of a child fatality review team or multidisciplinary child protection team ▪ Commercial or private film or photograph processors	▪ Have reasonable cause to suspect	
ARIZONA §§ 13-3620(A) 8-805(B)-(C)	✓	✓	✓	✓	✓		▪ Parents ▪ Anyone responsible for care or treatment of children ▪ Clergy	▪ Have reasonable grounds to believe	▪ Clergy/penitent ▪ Attorney/client
ARKANSAS § 12-12-507(b)-(c)	✓	✓	✓	✓	✓		▪ Prosecutors ▪ Judges	▪ Have reasonable cause to suspect ▪ Have observed conditions which would reasonably result	
CALIFORNIA §§ 11166(a), (c), (e) 11165.7(a) 11165.8	✓	✓	✓	✓	✓		▪ Firefighters ▪ Animal control officers ▪ Commercial film and photographic print processors ▪ Clergy	▪ Have knowledge of or observe ▪ Know or reasonably suspect	▪ Clergy/penitent

Mandatory Reporters of Child Abuse and Neglect

STATE	PROFESSIONS THAT MUST REPORT					OTHERS WHO MUST REPORT		STANDARD FOR REPORTING	PRIVILEGED COMMUNICATIONS
	Health Care	Mental Health	Social Work	Education/ Child Care	Law Enforcement	All Persons	Other		
COLORADO §§ 19-3-304(1), (2), (2.5) 19-3-311	✓	✓	✓	✓	✓		• Christian Science practitioners • Veterinarians • Firefighters • Victim advocates • Commercial film and photographic print processors	• Have reasonable cause to know or suspect • Have observed conditions which would reasonably result	
CONNECTICUT §§ 17a-101(b) 17a-103(a)	✓	✓	✓	✓	✓		• Substance abuse counselors • Sexual assault counselors • Battered women's counselors • Clergy	• Have reasonable cause to suspect or believe	
DELAWARE tit. 16, § 903 tit. 16, § 909	✓	✓	✓	✓	✓	✓		• Know or in good faith suspect	• Attorney/client • Clergy/penitent
DISTRICT OF COLUMBIA §§ 2-1352(a), (b), (d) 2-1355	✓	✓	✓	✓	✓			• Know or have reasonable cause to suspect	
FLORIDA §§ 39.201(1) 39.204	✓	✓	✓	✓	✓	✓		• Know or have reasonable cause to suspect	• Attorney/client
GEORGIA §§ 19-7-5(c)(1), (g) 16-12-100(c)	✓	✓	✓	✓	✓		• Persons who produce visual or printed matter	• Have reasonable cause to believe	
HAWAII §§ 350-1.1(a) 350-5	✓	✓	✓	✓	✓		• Employees of recreational or sports activities	• Have reason to believe	
IDAHO §§ 16-1619(a), (c) 16-1620	✓	✓	✓	✓	✓	✓		• Have reason to believe • Have observed conditions which would reasonably result	• Clergy/penitent • Attorney/client

Mandatory Reporters of Child Abuse and Neglect

STATE	PROFESSIONS THAT MUST REPORT					OTHERS WHO MUST REPORT		STANDARD FOR REPORTING	PRIVILEGED COMMUNICATIONS
	Health Care	Mental Health	Social Work	Education/ Child Care	Law Enforcement	All Persons	Other		
ILLINOIS 325 ILCS 5/4 720 ILCS 5/11-20.2	✓	✓	✓	✓	✓		▪ Homemakers, substance abuse treatment personnel ▪ Christian Science practitioners ▪ Funeral home directors ▪ Commercial film and photographic print processors	▪ Have reasonable cause to believe	
INDIANA §§ 31-33-5-1 31-33-5-2 31-32-11-1	✓	✓	✓	✓	✓	✓	▪ Staff member of any public or private institution, school, facility, or agency	▪ Have reason to believe	
IOWA §§ 232.69(1)(a)-(b) 728.14(1)	✓	✓	✓	✓	✓		▪ Commercial film and photographic print processors ▪ Employees of substance abuse programs	▪ Reasonably believe	
KANSAS § 38-1522(a), (b)	✓	✓	✓	✓	✓		▪ Firefighters ▪ Juvenile intake and assessment workers	▪ Have reason to suspect	
KENTUCKY §§ 620.030(1), (2) 620.050(2)	✓	✓	✓	✓	✓	✓		▪ Know or have reasonable cause to believe	▪ Attorney/client ▪ Clergy/penitent
LOUISIANA Ch. Code art. 603(13) Ch. Code art. 609(A)(1) Ch. Code art. 610(F)	✓	✓	✓	✓	✓		▪ Commercial film or photographic print processors	▪ Have cause to believe	▪ Clergy/penitent ▪ Christian Science practitioner
MAINE tit. 22, §§ 4011(1) 4015	✓	✓	✓	✓	✓		▪ Guardian *ad litems* and CASA ▪ Fire inspectors	▪ Know or have reasonable cause to suspect	▪ Clergy/penitent

Mandatory Reporters of Child Abuse and Neglect

STATE	PROFESSIONS THAT MUST REPORT					OTHERS WHO MUST REPORT		STANDARD FOR REPORTING	PRIVILEGED COMMUNICATIONS
	Health Care	Mental Health	Social Work	Education/Child Care	Law Enforcement	All Persons	Other		
MARYLAND §§ 5-704(a) 5-705(a)(2), (a)(3)	✓	✓	✓	✓	✓	✓		▪ Have reason to believe	▪ Attorney/client ▪ Clergy/penitent
MASSACHUSETTS ch. 119, § 51A ch. 119, § 51B	✓	✓	✓	✓	✓		▪ Drug and alcoholism counselors ▪ Probation and parole officers ▪ Clerks/magistrates of district courts ▪ Firefighters	▪ Have reasonable cause to believe	
MICHIGAN § 722.623 Sec. 3(1), (8), 722.631	✓	✓	✓	✓	✓			▪ Have reasonable cause to suspect	▪ Attorney/client
MINNESOTA §§ 626.556 Subd. (3)(a) 626.556 Subd. 8	✓	✓	✓	✓	✓			▪ Know or have reason to believe	▪ Clergy/penitent
MISSISSIPPI § 43-21-353(1)	✓	✓	✓	✓	✓	✓	▪ Attorneys ▪ Ministers	▪ Have reasonable cause to suspect	
MISSOURI §§ 210.115(1) 568.110 210.140	✓	✓	✓	✓	✓		▪ Persons with responsibility for care of children ▪ Christian Science practitioners ▪ Probation/parole officers ▪ Commercial film processors	▪ Have reasonable cause to suspect ▪ Have observed conditions which would reasonably result	▪ Attorney/client
MONTANA § 41-3-201(1)-(2), (4)	✓	✓	✓	✓	✓		▪ Guardian *ad litems* ▪ Clergy ▪ Religious healers ▪ Christian Science practitioners	▪ Know or have reasonable cause to suspect	▪ Clergy/penitent

Mandatory Reporters of Child Abuse and Neglect

| STATE | PROFESSIONS THAT MUST REPORT | | | | | OTHERS WHO MUST REPORT | | STANDARD FOR REPORTING | PRIVILEGED COMMUNICATIONS |
	Health Care	Mental Health	Social Work	Education/ Child Care	Law Enforcement	All Persons	Other		
NEBRASKA §§ 28-711(1) 28-714	✓	✓	✓	✓	✓	✓		▪ Have reasonable cause to believe ▪ Have observed conditions which would reasonably result	
NEVADA §§ 432B.220(3), (5). 432B.250	✓	✓	✓	✓	✓		▪ Clergy ▪ Religious healers ▪ Alcohol/drug abuse counselors ▪ Christian Science practitioners ▪ Probation officers ▪ Attorneys	▪ Know or have reason to believe	▪ Clergy/penitent ▪ Attorney/client
NEW HAMPSHIRE §§ 169-C:29 169-C:32	✓	✓	✓	✓	✓	✓	▪ Christian Science practitioners	▪ Have reason to suspect	▪ Attorney/client
NEW JERSEY § 9:6-8.10	✓	✓	✓	✓	✓	✓		▪ Have reasonable cause to believe	
NEW MEXICO §§ 32A-4-3(A) 32A-4-5(A)	✓	✓	✓	✓	✓	✓	▪ Judges	▪ Know or have reasonable suspicion	
NEW YORK Soc. Serv. § 413(1)	✓	✓	✓	✓	✓		▪ Alcoholism/substance abuse counselors ▪ District Attorneys	▪ Have reasonable cause to suspect	
NORTH CAROLINA §§ 7B-301 7B-310	✓	✓	✓	✓	✓	✓		▪ Have cause to suspect	▪ Attorney/client
NORTH DAKOTA §§ 50-25.1-03 50-25.1-10	✓	✓	✓	✓	✓		▪ Clergy ▪ Religious healers ▪ Addiction counselors	▪ Have knowledge of or reasonable cause to suspect	▪ Clergy/penitent ▪ Attorney/client

Mandatory Reporters of Child Abuse and Neglect

STATE	PROFESSIONS THAT MUST REPORT					OTHERS WHO MUST REPORT		STANDARD FOR REPORTING	PRIVILEGED COMMUNI-CATIONS
	Health Care	Mental Health	Social Work	Education/ Child Care	Law Enforcement	All Persons	Other		
OHIO § 2151.421(A)(1)(a) (b), (G)(1)(b), (A)(2)	✓	✓	✓	✓	✓		▪ Attorney	▪ Know or suspect	▪ Attorney/client
OKLAHOMA Tit. 10 §§ 7103(A)(1) 7104 7113 Tit. 21 § 1021.4	✓	✓	✓	✓	✓	✓	▪ Commercial film and photographic print processors	▪ Have reason to believe	
OREGON §§ 419B.005(3) 419B.010(1)	✓	✓	✓	✓	✓		▪ Attorney ▪ Clergy ▪ Firefighter ▪ Court appointed special advocates	▪ Have reasonable cause to believe	▪ Mental health/ patient ▪ Clergy/penitent ▪ Attorney/client
PENNSYLVANIA § 23-6311(a),(b)	✓	✓	✓	✓	✓		▪ Funeral directors ▪ Christian Science practitioners ▪ Clergy	▪ Have reasonable cause to suspect	▪ Clergy/penitent
RHODE ISLAND §§ 40-11-3(a)-(c) 40-11-6(a) 40-11-11	✓	✓	✓	✓	✓	✓		▪ Have reasonable cause to know or suspect	▪ Attorney/client
SOUTH CAROLINA §§ 20-7-510(A) 20-7-550	✓	✓	✓	✓	✓		▪ Judges ▪ Funeral home directors and employees ▪ Christian Science practitioners ▪ Film processors	▪ Have reason to believe	▪ Attorney/client ▪ Priest/penitent
SOUTH DAKOTA §§ 26-8A-3 26-8A-15	✓	✓	✓	✓	✓		▪ Chemical dependency counselors ▪ Religious healers ▪ Parole or court services officers	▪ Have reasonable cause to suspect	

Mandatory Reporters of Child Abuse and Neglect

STATE	PROFESSIONS THAT MUST REPORT					OTHERS WHO MUST REPORT		STANDARD FOR REPORTING	PRIVILEGED COMMUNICATIONS
	Health Care	Mental Health	Social Work	Education/ Child Care	Law Enforcement	All Persons	Other		
TENNESSEE §§ 37-1-403(a) 37-1-605(a) 37-1-411	✓	✓	✓	✓	✓	✓	▪ Judges ▪ Neighbors ▪ Relatives ▪ Friends ▪ Religious healers	▪ Knowledge of/reasonably ▪ Know or have reasonable cause to suspect	
TEXAS §§ 261.101(a)-(c) 261.102	✓	✓	✓	✓	✓	✓	▪ Juvenile probation or detention officers ▪ Employees or clinics that provide reproductive services	▪ Have cause to believe	
UTAH §§ 62A-4a-403(1)-(3) 62A-4a-412(5)	✓	✓	✓	✓	✓	✓		▪ Have reason to believe ▪ Have observed conditions which would reasonably result	▪ Clergy/penitent
VERMONT Tit. 33 § 4913(a)	✓	✓	✓	✓	✓		▪ Camp administrators and counselors	▪ Have reasonable cause to believe	
VIRGINIA § 63.1-248.3(A)	✓	✓	✓	✓	✓		▪ Mediators ▪ Christian Science practitioners	▪ Have reason to suspect	
WASHINGTON §§ 26.44.030 (1), (2), (3) 26.44.060(3)	✓	✓	✓	✓	✓		▪ Any adult with whom a child resides ▪ Responsible living skills program staff	▪ Have reasonable cause to believe	
WEST VIRGINIA §§ 49-6A-2 49-6A-7	✓	✓	✓	✓	✓		▪ Clergy ▪ Religious healers ▪ Judges, family law masters or magistrates ▪ Christian Science practitioners	▪ Reasonable cause to suspect ▪ When believe ▪ Have observed	▪ Attorney/client

Mandatory Reporters of Child Abuse and Neglect

STATE	PROFESSIONS THAT MUST REPORT					OTHERS WHO MUST REPORT		STANDARD FOR REPORTING	PRIVILEGED COMMUNICATIONS
	Health Care	Mental Health	Social Work	Education/ Child Care	Law Enforcement	All Persons	Other		
WISCONSIN § 48.981(2), (2m)(c), (2m)(d)	✓	✓	✓	✓	✓		▪ Alcohol or drug abuse counselors ▪ Mediators ▪ Financial and employment planners	▪ Have reasonable cause to suspect ▪ Have reason to believe	
WYOMING §§ 14-3-205(a) 14-3-210	✓	✓	✓	✓	✓	✓		▪ Know or have reasonable cause to believe or suspect ▪ Have observed conditions which would reasonably result	▪ Attorney/client ▪ Physician/patient ▪ Clergy/penitent
TOTALS, ALL STATES	51	51	51	51	51	18	N/A	N/A	26

Source: National Clearinghouse on Child Abuse and Neglect Information, 1999.

Reporting Penalties

STATE/STATUTE	FAILURE TO REPORT		FALSE REPORTING	
	Standard	Penalty	Standard	Penalty
ALABAMA §§ 26-14-13 13A-10-9(a)-(b)	Knowingly	Misdemeanor: • imprisonment not exceeding 6 months; or • a fine not exceeding $500	Knowingly	Class A misdemeanor
ALASKA § 47.17.068	Knew or should have known	Class B misdemeanor	*	*
ARIZONA §§ 13-3620(K) 13-3620.01(A)-(B)	Not specified	Class 1 misdemeanor	Knowingly and intentionally; with malice	Class 1 misdemeanor
ARKANSAS § 12-12-504(a), (b), (d)	Willfully; Negligently	Class C misdemeanor Civilly liable for damages proximately caused	Willfully	Class A misdemeanor Class D felony, when there is a prior conviction
CALIFORNIA § 11172(a), (e)	Knows or reasonably should know	Misdemeanor: • confinement in county jail not exceeding 6 months; and/or • a fine not exceeding $1,000	Reckless disregard of truth; knowingly	Liable for damages proximately caused
COLORADO § 19-3-304(3.5), (4)	Willfully	Class 3 misdemeanor Liable for damages	Knowingly	Class 3 misdemeanor Liable for damages
CONNECTICUT §§ 17a-101a 17a-101e(c)	Not specified	A fine not exceeding $500	Knowingly	A fine not exceeding $2,000 and/or Imprisonment for not more than one year
DELAWARE Tit. 16, § 914	Knowingly or willfully	A fine not exceeding $1000; and/or Imprisonment not exceeding 15 days	Knowingly and willfully	A fine not exceeding $1000; and/or Imprisonment not exceeding 15 days
DISTRICT OF COLUMBIA § 2-1357	Willfully	A fine not exceeding $100; and/or Imprisonment not exceeding 30 days	*	*
FLORIDA §§ 39.205(1)-(2), (6) 39.206(1)	Knowingly or willfully	Misdemeanor of second degree	Knowingly and willfully	Felony of third degree Possible fine not exceeding $10,000
GEORGIA § 19-7-5(h)	Knowingly or willfully	Misdemeanor	*	*
HAWAII § 350-1.2	Knowingly	Petty misdemeanor	*	*

* Not addressed in statutes reviewed

Reporting Penalties

STATE/STATUTE	FAILURE TO REPORT		FALSE REPORTING	
	Standard	Penalty	Standard	Penalty
IDAHO §§ 16-1619(d) 16-1620A	Not specified	Misdemeanor	Knowingly; in bad faith or with malice	Liable for damages sustained or statutory damages of $500, whichever is greater, plus attorney's fees and costs
ILLINOIS ch. 325, para. 5/4 ch. 325, para. 5/4.02	Knowingly and willfully Willfully	Class A misdemeanor Physician: referred to Illinois State Medical Disciplinary Board[2]	Knowingly	Class 4 felony
INDIANA §§ 31-33-22-1 31-33-22-3(a)-(b)	Knowingly Knowingly	Class B misdemeanor Staff member of a medical or other institution, school, facility, or agency: Class B misdemeanor penalty imposed in addition to above	Intentionally	Class A misdemeanor Liable for actual damages and possibly punitive damages Class D felony, if there is a prior conviction
IOWA § 232.75	Knowingly and willfully Knowingly	Simple misdemeanor Civilly liable for damages proximately caused	Knowingly	Simple misdemeanor
KANSAS § 38-1522(f),(g)	Knowingly and willfully	Class B misdemeanor	*	*
KENTUCKY § 620.050(1)	*	*	Knowingly, with malice	Class A misdemeanor
LOUISIANA La. Children's Code Ann. art. 609(A)(2),(C)	Not specified	Subject to criminal prosecution	Knowingly	Subject to criminal prosecution
MAINE Tit. 22, § 4014(1)	*	*	Knowingly	Subject to criminal or civil action
MASSACHUSETTS ch. 119, § 51A	Not specified	A fine not exceeding $1,000	Knowingly	A fine not exceeding $1,000
MICHIGAN § 722.633(1),(2),(5)	Knowingly	Misdemeanor Imprisonment not exceeding 93 days and/or fine not exceeding $100 Civilly liable for damages proximately caused	Knowingly, Intentionally	Misdemeanor, punishable by imprisonment of not more than 93 days for a fine of not more than $100, if the abuse reported would be a misdemeanor if true. Felony, if the abuse reported would be a felony if true, punishable by imprisonment of not more than 4 years and/or a fine of not more than $2,000

Reporting Penalties

STATE/STATUTE	FAILURE TO REPORT		FALSE REPORTING	
	Standard	Penalty	Standard	Penalty
MINNESOTA § 626.556 Subd. 5, 6	Knows or has reason to believe Knows or reasonably should know	Mandatory reporter: ▪ misdemeanor Parent, guardian, or caretaker: ▪ gross misdemeanor if child's health is in serious danger and child suffers great bodily harm due to lack of medical care; ▪ felony if child dies Imprisonment not exceeding 2 years and/or fine not exceeding $4,000	Knowingly or recklessly	Civilly liable for actual and punitive damages Responsible for costs and reasonable attorney fees
MISSISSIPPI § 43-21-353(7)	Willfully	Imprisonment not exceeding 1 year and/or a fine not exceeding $5,000	*	*
MISSOURI § 210.165(1)-(4)	Not specified	Class A misdemeanor	Intentionally	Class A misdemeanor Class D felony if previously convicted
MONTANA § 41-3-207	Purposely or knowingly	Misdemeanor Civilly liable for damages proximately caused	*	*
NEBRASKA § 28-717	Willfully	Class 3 misdemeanor	*	*
NEVADA § 432B.240	Knowingly or willfully	Misdemeanor	*	*
NEW HAMPSHIRE § 169-C:39	Knowingly	Misdemeanor	*	*
NEW JERSEY § 9:6-8.14	Knowingly	Imprisonment not exceeding 6 months	*	*
NEW MEXICO § 32A-4-3(F)	Not specified	Misdemeanor	*	*
NEW YORK Soc. Serv. § 420(1),(2) Penal § 240.55(3)	Willfully Knowingly and willfully	Class A misdemeanor Civilly liable for damages proximately caused	Knowingly	Class A misdemeanor

Reporting Penalties

| STATE/STATUTE | FAILURE TO REPORT | | FALSE REPORTING | |
	Standard	Penalty	Standard	Penalty
NORTH DAKOTA § 50-25.1-13	Willfully	Class B misdemeanor	Willfully	Class B misdemeanor If made to a law enforcement official: Class A misdemeanor Civilly liable for damages
OHIO § 2921.14	*	*	Knowingly	Misdemeanor of first degree
OKLAHOMA tit. 10, § 7103(C), (D)	Knowingly or willfully	Misdemeanor	Knowingly and willfully	Misdemeanor A fine not to exceed $5,000 if made during a child custody proceeding.
OREGON § 419B.010(2)	Not specified	Class A violation	*	*
PENNSYLVANIA Tit. 23, § 6319	Willfully	Summary offense for first violation Misdemeanor of third degree for second or subsequent violation	*	*
RHODE ISLAND §§ 40-11-6.1 40-11-3.2	Knowingly	Misdemeanor: • a fine not exceeding $500; and/or • imprisonment not exceeding 1 year Civilly liable for damages proximately caused	Knowingly and willingly	Misdemeanor: • A fine not exceeding $1000; and/or • Imprisonment not exceeding one year.
SOUTH CAROLINA §§ 20-7-560 20-7-567	Knowingly	Misdemeanor: • a fine not exceeding $500; and/or • imprisonment not exceeding 6 months	Knowingly	Misdemeanor: • A fine not exceeding $5000; and/or • Imprisonment not exceeding 90 days
SOUTH DAKOTA §§ 26-8A-3 26-8A-4 26-8A-6 26-8A-7	Intentionally Knowingly and intentionally	Class 1 misdemeanor If child dies: Class 1 misdemeanor	*	*
TENNESSEE §§ 37-1-412(a) 37-1-413	Knowingly	Class A misdemeanor	Knowingly and maliciously	Class E felony (only applies to sexual abuse reporting)

Reporting Penalties

STATE/STATUTE	FAILURE TO REPORT		FALSE REPORTING	
	Standard	Penalty	Standard	Penalty
TEXAS Fam. §§ 261.107 261.109	Knowingly	Class B misdemeanor	Knowingly or intentionally	Class A misdemeanor State jail felony, if there is a prior conviction
UTAH § 62A-4a-411	Willfully	Class B misdemeanor	*	*
VERMONT tit. 33, § 4913(e)	Not specified	A fine not exceeding $500	*	*
VIRGINIA §§ 63.1-248.3(B) 63.1-248.5:1.01(A)	Not specified	A fine not exceeding $500 for first violation A fine of no less than $100 nor exceeding $1,000 for subsequent violations	Knowingly	Class 1 misdemeanor Class 6 felony, if there is a prior conviction
WASHINGTON §§ 26.44.060(4) 26.44.080	Knowingly	Gross misdemeanor	Intentionally and in bad faith or maliciously; knowingly	Misdemeanor
WEST VIRGINIA § 49-6A-8	Knowingly	Misdemeanor: • imprisonment in county jail not exceeding 10 days; and/or • a fine not exceeding $100	*	*
WISCONSIN § 48.981(6)	Intentionally	A fine not exceeding $1,000; and/or imprisonment not exceeding 6 months	*	*

Source: National Clearinghouse for Child Abuse and Neglect Information, 1999.

stipulate that the following categories of individuals must report the abuse of a child:

- physicians, nurses, hospital personnel and dentists
- medical examiners
- coroners
- mental health professionals and social workers
- school personnel
- law enforcement officials
- child care providers

In addition, some states have other categories of individuals who must report. Some states mandate that any person who knows of abuse to report. (*See* MANDATED REPORTER.) Most states also specify when

communication is privileged. Generally, the only privilege that is recognized is attorney-client or clergy-penitent. Husband-wife privilege is not recognized, nor is physician-patient.

Reporters of suspected abuse or neglect are usually asked to supply the name and address of the child, the parents' names and addresses, the type and extent of injuries suffered, any evidence of previous abuse and information that may lead to the identification of the perpetrator. In some areas reports can be filed anonymously. Others require that the reporter identify him/herself to the agency receiving the report but withhold the reporter's name from the accused perpetrator.

To facilitate prompt investigation of life-threatening situations most laws allow initial reports to be made verbally. Reporters are usually required to file a full written report within a certain period of time. Many jurisdictions have established toll-free 24-hour HOTLINES to facilitate reporting.

Mandated reporters are usually granted immunity from civil or criminal prosecution for reports made in good faith. Penalties, ranging from a small fine to imprisonment, are often imposed on mandated reporters who fail to report suspected abuse or neglect. In about half the states, there are penalties that may be imposed on people who purposely submit false reports to the authorities. (See the state-by-state chart at the end of this essay for laws on penalties for those who fail to report suspected abuse and penalties for knowingly reporting abuse that did not occur.)

While reporting laws are usually clear about who is required to report suspected maltreatment, the are often vague about exactly what kinds of injuries or behavior should be reported. Many local statutes define abuse and neglect in broad terms or not at all. Conditions specifically mentioned range from serious physical injuries to vaguely defined MENTAL INJURIES and NEGLECT.

In Canada, Britain and the United States, lack of specificity in the types of injuries that should be reported has led to charges of frivolous reporting. Some critics believe that the failure to clearly define abuse and neglect overburdens child protection agencies and causes some families to be subjected to needless invasions of privacy. Proponents of present laws argue that a broad definition of abuse and neglect is necessary to cover all situations that might seriously harm a child. This view holds that it is better to tolerate some overreporting than to run the risk of failing to identify children in need of help.

Attorneys who are acting on behalf of children who are clients may be exempted from the mandatory reporting requirement, although state laws vary on this issue. For a complete discussion on the responsibility of attorneys in mandatory reporting, read the article by Ellen Marrus, "Please Keep My Secret: Child Abuse Reporting Statutes, Confidentiality, and Juvenile Delinquency" in the spring 1998 issue of *The Georgetown Journal of Legal Ethics.*

Mann Act   In response to concern over what was termed white slavery, in 1910 the U.S. Congress passed the Mann Act. This legislation made inter-state transportation of females for prostitution or enticement for immoral purposes a federal offense. If found guilty under the terms of the Mann Act an individual can be fined up to $5,000, receive five years in prison, or both. In some circumstances, cases involving SEXUAL ABUSE of children can incur judicial action under the terms of the Mann Act. (*See also* CHILD SLAVERY.)

marasmus, nutritional   A lack of sufficient protein in the diet causes a condition known as nutritional marasmus. Characterized by emaciation, an apparently enlarged head, wide, staring eyes, shrunken buttocks and loose skin folds, it is the product of prolonged and severe dietary inadequacy. Nutritional marasmus may occur when breast feeding is reduced or ended and not replaced by an adequate source of nutrition. Repeated severe infection can also cause symptoms similar to those of marasmus.

masked deprivation   *See* EMOTIONAL NEGLECT.

masturbation   Masturbation refers to the manipulation of one's own or another's genitals for sexual gratification. Exhibitionists may seek to obtain sexual gratification by masturbating in the presence of a child. Other CHILD MOLESTERS may force or encourage children to masturbate in their presence or may participate in the masturbation. Nurses, baby-sitters and parents have been reported, on occasion, to masturbate infants and young children as a way of quieting them.

Though self-masturbation by children is not considered a damaging behavior, frequent or open masturbation may be an indicator that the child is a victim of sexual abuse. This is especially true in the case of young children.

Masturbation also plays an important role in the practice of PEDOPHILIA. Pedophiles are strongly aroused by children and often maintain large collections of CHILD PORNOGRAPHY as a fantasy aid to masturbation.

maternal drug dependence   Use of drugs, including alcohol, during pregnancy can cause severe and lasting damage to the fetus. Facial malformation, growth retardation and damage to the central nervous system are all present in children suffering from FETAL ALCOHOL SYNDROME. Infants born to mothers addicted to opiates may also become addicted, and they experience painful withdrawal symptoms at birth.

Many states now require that pregnant women who are drug or alcohol dependent be reported to a mandated agency for investigation of child abuse or neglect. Instances in which an infant is removed from the mother's care at birth are, however, rare. (*See also* SUBSTANCE ABUSE and ADDICTION, INFANTILE.)

maternal rejection syndrome   *See* FAILURE TO THRIVE SYNDROME.

matricide   This term refers to the murder of one's mother. Matricide is relatively rare; Federal Bureau of Investigation crime statistics list 152 matricides out of a total of 18,996 murders in the United States during 1985. Statistics show that most matricides are committed by sons. Though little is known about the motivation of children who kill their mothers, information from case studies suggests a strong link between matricide and child abuse. Most such murders occur during or shortly after an episode of child abuse.

Psychiatric profiles of mothers murdered by a son show a pattern of overly restrictive and harsh treatment of the son. Close examination of these profiles often indicates a strong sadistic component of the relationship. Also, mothers in these studies often behaved seductively toward the son yet quickly followed such behavior with brutal treatment. Despite the strong erotic component of these relationships INCEST was rarely consummated. Further, in most of these cases fathers were typically absent or extremely passive. (*See also* PARRICIDE, REACTIVE and PATRICIDE.)

media coverage of child abuse   It has long been true in the United States that there is widespread public response to media coverage of child abuse and neglect. Newspapers and magazines in the 19th century and, more recently, radio and television coverage of child maltreatment issues have been useful and effective means of publicizing needs in this area.

As early as the 1870s, when the now-famous MARY ELLEN WILSON case was written about in the *New York Times,* reporters and editors recognized the public's interest in child abuse. Some observers have drawn a correlation between the increase in media coverage of abuse and neglect and the response via private organizations and public agencies that seek to protect children and prevent child maltreatment. Whether or not there is a cause-and-effect relationship and despite some critics' charges that sensational reporting often does little more than titillate its audience, it is clear that, beginning in the late 19th century, the media in all its forms has promoted greater public awareness of child abuse and neglect.

Following C. Henry Kempe's report, "The Battered-Child Syndrome," in the July 7, 1962 issue of the *Journal of the American Medical Association,* many professional journals, popular magazines and newspapers increased their coverage of a wide range of child maltreatment issues. Numerous articles detailed the problem, focusing particularly on the psychopathology of abusing parents and varieties of physical abuse cases but also reported on other facets such as sexual abuse and corporal punishment.

According to one source, over the last three decades there have been over 1,700 articles published in professional journals alone, pieces that focus on child abuse and attendant issues. Likewise, newspaper coverage of the topic has grown enormously. In the 30-year period between 1950 and 1980, the *New York Times Index* lists 652 articles on child abuse. And popular magazine coverage of abuse and neglect increased as well. For the 10 years following publication of Kempe's article in the AMA journal, 28 articles about child abuse were printed in magazines read by the general public, a figure contrasting sharply with the previous decade during which only three stories on abuse were published.

It is apparent to many experts that, in the 1970s and 1980s, changes in public policy regarding child abuse and neglect were precipitated to some degree by greater coverage of the subject. In this respect, the 20th century is similar to the previous century, when public and private agencies were established in apparent response to news coverage of child protection issues. In this sense, the media has positively influenced the heightened public awareness of and interest in child abuse and neglect.

George Gerbner, Catherine J. Ross, and Edward Zigler, eds., *Child Abuse: An Agenda for Action* (New York: Oxford University Press, 1980).

Medicaid   Title XIX of the Social Security Act—known as Medicaid—was signed into law by President Lyndon B. Johnson on July 30, 1965. Medicaid is jointly funded by the federal government and the states. It provides a range of medical services to low income individuals who meet state criteria for that category. Of particular relevance to child abuse is the inclusion of families who participate in the Temporary Aid to Needy Families Program (TANF). Children in those eligible families receive a number of medical services under Medicaid. Among those services are early and periodic screening, diagnosis and treatment (EPSDT). EPSDT provides medical screening to children on a regular basis, beginning in infancy. Medicaid and TANF are credited with making a strong contribution toward eliminating or reducing SITUATIONAL ABUSE AND NEGLECT associated with POVERTY and poor health care. (*See also* SOCIAL SECURITY ACT.)

medical evaluation   A thorough medical evaluation is important in the identification of abuse or neglect as well as the treatment of injuries resulting from maltreatment. The physician conducting the evaluation should be trained in recognition of medical conditions associated with abuse. Serious injury may be overlooked due to a lack of visual evidence or because the examiner fails to recognize subtle signs of trauma.

Thorough assessment requires the involvement of several different disciplines, including psychiatry, pediatrics, social work and nursing. In many cases a specialist in pediatric neurology, radiology, ophthalmology, dentistry or other area is necessary to evaluate the existence and the extent of injury fully. When abuse or neglect is suspected as the cause of death, an AUTOPSY by a pathologist trained in FORENSIC MEDICINE is appropriate.

In many cases evidence of trauma is easily recognizable. Since one purpose of the medical evaluation is to gather evidence for the existence of nonaccidental injury, the physician must be skilled in determining the possible causes of a particular injury as well as the approximate time it was inflicted. While it is not often possible to say with absolute assurance precisely how a child was injured, it is often possible to rule out certain causes. Suspicion of abuse is often aroused when a caretaker's account of how a child was injured does not coincide with medical evidence.

More often a physician is called upon by parents to treat a sick or injured child when no suggestion of maltreatment is made. A physician must constantly be aware of suspicious explanations or behavior by caretakers as well as physical evidence of abuse.

A complete medical evaluation may involve a SKELETAL SURVEY to detect the FRACTURES and evidence of other internal injury. When SEXUAL ABUSE is a possibility a thorough examination of the genitalia, mouth and anus, with appropriate tests for VENEREAL DISEASE and, in adolescents, pregnancy, is conducted. Other tests may reveal inadequate nutrition or other evidence of NEGLECT.

Frequently, more than one form of maltreatment is observed in a child. Presence of PHYSICAL ABUSE will alert the medical specialist to look for other evidence of maltreatment such as neglect or PSYCHOLOGICAL MALTREATMENT.

The medical specialist must be skilled in differentiating abuse-related trauma from disease-related symptoms that mimic abuse. Various diseases, congenital conditions and even birthmarks can be confused with sequelae of abuse or neglect. Certain folk medicine remedies (*see* CAO GIO) also produce lesions that are frequently interpreted as evidence of abuse by examining physicians.

Despite the difficulty of confronting a parent with the information that the child could not have injured him or herself, the physician's first responsibility is to protect the child. This involves notifying the proper child protection authorities and, in some cases, arranging for the child to be hospitalized for treatment, observation and/or protection. Honest and sensitive discussion of the problem with caretakers immediately following diagnosis may improve the likelihood that they will cooperate in efforts to prevent further maltreatment. The primary purpose of the medical evaluation is to identify evidence of abuse or neglect, not specifically to identify the abuser. Evidence obtained by the physician should be presented to the proper law enforcement or child protection authorities charged with the INVESTIGATION of child abuse.

medical model　Since World War II, the medical model has greatly influenced public perceptions of child abuse and neglect. By presenting abuse as a form of psychopathological illness, the medical model held out hope that it, like other sicknesses, could be isolated and cured. Dominance of the medical approach to child abuse may stem in part from developments in pediatric radiology (*see* RADIOLOGY, PEDIATRIC) that allowed physicians to diagnose unusual patterns of bone trauma that appeared to be the result of battering.

Popularization of the term BATTERED CHILD SYNDROME by C. Henry Kempe and his associates further strengthened the perception of child abuse as illness. Subsequent attention by the popular media created the perception of all abused children as victims of sadistic PHYSICAL ABUSE. This vision of child abuse played an important role in mobilizing political action on behalf of abused children. Within five years of publication of an article entitled "The Battered Child Syndrome" in the *Journal of the American Medical Association,* each of the 50 states had adopted a law that required reporting of suspected child abuse and neglect. The medical image of child abuse continues to heavily influence approaches to treatment and prevention.

In spite of its usefulness in generating public action the medical model is frequently criticized for ignoring societal causes of abuse and neglect. Focusing attention on individual pathology, while useful and appropriate in many situations, may not be sufficient to eliminate underlying causes of child maltreatment. Some critics of the medical model argue that it amounts to BLAMING THE VICTIM and call for a more balanced approach to the problem. (*See also* DEFECT MODEL OF CHILD ABUSE, PSYCHOPATHOLOGY.)

medical neglect　The issue of medical care neglect has been the subject of much heated debate and many legal battles. Failure of parents to provide for or permit necessary medical treatment may be based on religious belief, fear, ignorance, misunderstanding or lack of concern.

In the United States, there are 24 states that provide some grounds for religious exemption from state criminal child abuse and neglect laws that relate to failing to provide medical assistance to a child. The following states have such provisions in their laws: Alabama, Alaska, Arkansas, California, Colorado, Delaware, Idaho, Indiana, Iowa, Kansas, Louisiana, Minnesota, New Hampshire, New York, Ohio, Oklahoma, Oregon, Rhode Island, Tennessee, Texas, Utah, Virginia, West Virginia and Wisconsin.

In cases of serious acute illness and life-threatening or disabling chronic disease it may be necessary to obtain a court order to allow treatment. When ongoing treatment is required, supervision of the court or foster placement may be necessary to ensure proper medical care. A distinction is usually made between situations in which medical intervention has a reasonable possibility of succeeding and fatal diseases such as cancer in which medical procedures are mostly palliative.

Parents are also expected to provide preventive or "well-child" care. While standards may vary, most states and countries have laws requiring immunization against life-threatening communicable disease. In the United States many states will not allow unimmunized children to enroll in school. Most pediatricians recommend that children be fully immunized before age two.

It is also recommended that the nutritional status of an infant be monitored by a physician. An absolute minimum of two visits during the first year of life, with the first visit taking place before two months of age, is considered the least amount of care necessary for healthy development. Pediatricians differ in their minimum standards of well-child care. Many believe that two visits during the first 12 months is insufficient. Other examples of inadequate preventive care are failure to treat recognized visual impairment and allowing a child to suffer painful tooth decay without dental treatment.

Barton Schmitt, a professor of pediatrics at the University of Colorado School of Medicine, has recommended that physicians take a five-step approach when faced with a medically neglected child:

First, care should be taken to determine the existence of financial, transportation or similar barriers. Parents or caretakers should be helped to eliminate such barriers.

Second, the parents' questions about their child's condition should be answered as completely as possible. The risks associated with treatment and the expected outcome should be explained as should the risks of forgoing treatment.

Third, the physician should attempt to work through a third party such as a relative, friend or member of the clergy.

Fourth, if the family continues to refuse treatment the physician should inform them and the third party that he or she is obligated to refer the case to the courts.

Fifth, if the family fails to respond to the warning the physician should seek a court order.

Norman S. Ellerstein, ed., *Child Abuse and Neglect: A Medical Reference* (New York: John Wiley, 1981).
Alejandro Rodriguez, *Handbook of Child Abuse and Neglect* (Flushing, N.Y.: Medical Examination Publishing Co., 1977).

medicine, forensic   *See* FORENSIC MEDICINE.

Megan's Law   This term was first used to describe a law requiring community notification of released sex offenders, which was passed in 1994 in New Jersey (New Jersey State Sex Offender Registration Act) subsequent to the abduction and murder of a child, Megan Kanka, by a twice-convicted sex offender who had completed his prison term and had moved in with two other sex offenders to a house across the street from the Kankas' house. He asked Megan to come over and see his puppy. She was subsequently kidnapped, raped and murdered.

In 1996, the federal government passed its own version of Megan's Law as an amendment to the Violent Crime Control and Law Enforcement Act of 1996. This law ordered all states to establish a form of community notification of child sex offenders. This information must be released to the public when necessary for public safety. (Each state's interpretation of the federal law varies.) Opponents of the law believed it was tantamount to double jeopardy for the offender, that it gave neighborhood residents a false sense of security and that it simply did not work—even with this law, repeat sex offenders have been released and victimized more children. They also point out that most abuse (80% or more) is perpetrated by individuals known

to the child, such as family members, and that "stranger danger" is not the main problem. Supporters of Megan's Law, however, counter that Megan Kanka knew her abuser, as he was a neighbor. (See the summary of state statutes on community notification on the next page.)

Another act, the WETTERLING ACT, requires released child sex offenders to register their addresses with the state and to report any changes of address. (*See also* CIVIL COMMITMENT, PAM LYNCHNER SEXUAL OFFENDER TRACKING AND IDENTIFICATION ACT OF 1996, RAPE.)

"National Conference on Sex Offender Registries: Proceedings of a BJS/SEARCH Conference," Bureau of Justice Statistics, April 1998, NCJ-168965.

Menkes' kinky hair syndrome   This rare inherited disease inhibits the absorption of copper into the system, resulting in brittle bones and possibly death. Due to the multiple fractures present in infants suffering from this disease it is often confused with the BATTERED CHILD SYNDROME. The name derives from characteristic changes in the hair of those with this disease. Hair is stubby, coarse and ivory in color.

mental cruelty   Often used as grounds for divorce, mental cruelty may also form the basis for intervention in a family by child protection agencies. As a legal term, mental cruelty refers to a pattern of behavior by an individual that threatens the mental and physical health of another. Courts differ in the type and severity of actions they consider to be mental cruelty. In recent years the definition has generally expanded to include behavior that was not previously considered abusive. A child who is the target of mental cruelty by a parent or caretaker is a victim of PSYCHOLOGICAL MALTREATMENT.

mental injury   A term used in some child abuse laws, mental injury refers to intellectual or psychological damage. Determination of the existence and extent of mental injury is usually based on a comparison of a child's performance and behavior with that of other children of the same age and cultural background.

Public Notification of the Release of Sex Offenders

STATE/STATUTE	Available only to law enforcement OR released only to specified organizations (not the public)	Available to general public upon request	Police notify community upon release
ALABAMA 15-20-21 et. seq.			Law enforcement shall notify all persons, schools, and child-care facilities within a specified proximity of offender
ALASKA 18.65.087		Confidential and "not subject to public disclosure except as to the sex offender's name, address," and other information	
ARIZONA 13-3825		Registration information may be posted on the Internet	Law enforcement shall notify the community upon an offender's release (pursuant to guidelines)
ARKANSAS 12-12-913			Law enforcement may release information based on risk level of offender
CALIFORNIA Penal Code 290 (m) et. seq.		Public may call "900" number to inquire if a person is listed	Information may be disclosed to the public under several enumerated conditions
COLORADO 18-3-412.5(6.5)			Law enforcement may release information when necessary for public protection
CONNECTICUT 54-258		Available on the Internet, registration information available to the public during normal business hours	Law enforcement may notify public when necessary to protect the public or any individual
DELAWARE tit. 11, § 4336			Law enforcement may release information to community organizations or the public, depending on the risk level of the offender
FLORIDA 775.21		Law enforcement shall notify the public of all designated sexual predators through the Internet	Law enforcement must release information about sexual predators in the interest of public safety
GEORGIA 42-9-44.1(e) 42-1-12(b)(B)	List of registered sex offenders made available to schools in the county	Registry open to public inspection, law enforcement may post list in a prominent location in the sheriff's office or city hall	
HAWAII 846E-3		The public shall have access to a file containing relevant information that is necessary to protect the public	Law enforcement shall release relevant information to protect the public
IDAHO 18-8323		Registrant's name and offense shall be provided to any person upon written request	

Public Notification of the Release of Sex Offenders

STATE/STATUTE	Available only to law enforcement OR released only to specified organizations (not the public)	Available to general public upon request	Police notify community upon release
ILLINOIS ch. 730, § 152/125	Law enforcement shall disclose sex offender registration information to schools and child care facilities in the county where the sex offender resides	Names, addresses, and offenses open to public inspection	Information may be related to persons likely to encounter an offender
INDIANA 5-2-12-11	Copy of sex offender registry sent to schools and other agencies that hire people to work with children; not specifically classified as confidential		
IOWA 692.A.13		The sheriff shall release information to a member of the public who requests the information in writing	
KANSAS 22-4909		Information shall be open to inspection in the sheriff's office by the public and specifically is subject to the provisions of the Kansas Open Records Act	
KENTUCKY 17.572			Law enforcement must release information to the public, the level of notification is based on the risk of reoffense
LOUISIANA tit. 15, § 546 et. seq.			Release of information to the public authorized when necessary for public protection
MAINE tit. 34-A § 11004; tit. 16 § 612		Governed by laws allowing access to criminal justice records; allows dissemination of conviction data upon request	
MARYLAND tit. 27 § 792 (d)(5) & (6)		Upon written request to a local law enforcement agency, the agency shall send a copy of a registration statement to the person who submitted the request	
MASSACHUSETTS ch. 6, § 178I et. seq.		Any person who is 18 years of age or older shall receive at no cost a report indicating whether an individual is a sex offender	Law enforcement shall release information based on the risk level of the offender
MICHIGAN 4.475 (10)		Law enforcement shall make registration information available to public during normal business hours	
MINNESOTA 244.052			Law enforcement shall disclose information to the public if relevant and necessary to protect the public

Public Notification of the Release of Sex Offenders

STATE/STATUTE	Available only to law enforcement OR released only to specified organizations (not the public)	Available to general public upon request	Police notify community upon release
MISSISSIPPI 45-33-17			Law enforcement may release information to the public when necessary for public protection
MISSOURI 584.417		Law enforcement shall maintain a list of the names, addresses and crimes for all offenders registered in the county, any person may request a copy of the list	
MONTANA 46-23-508			Law enforcement may release information to community organizations or the public, depending on the risk level of the offender
NEBRASKA 29-4009			Law enforcement shall release information that is relevant to protect the public
NEVADA 179D.700 et. seq.			Law enforcement shall release information to the public, depending on the risk level of the offender
NEW HAMPSHIRE 651-B:7	Law enforcement may notify organizations that work with children in the community where the person intends to reside		
NEW JERSEY 2C: 7-6 et. seq.			Law enforcement agencies shall be authorized to release relevant and necessary information regarding sex offenders to the public when the release of the information is necessary for public protection
NEW MEXICO 29-11A-5.1		Public may request information contained on the sex offender registration	
NEW YORK Correct. Law 168-1 et. seq.		Public may call "900" number to inquire whether an individual is registered; list of Level III sexual offenders available for public inspection at local law enforcement sites	Information may be released on most violent sexual predators to any entity with vulnerable populations related to the nature of the offense committed by such predator; information about the predator may be further disclosed by these entities
NORTH CAROLINA 14-208.10		Registration information is a public record and shall be available for public inspection; sheriff may disclose information to persons who request it	

Public Notification of the Release of Sex Offenders

STATE/STATUTE	Available only to law enforcement OR released only to specified organizations (not the public)	Available to general public upon request	Police notify community upon release
NORTH DAKOTA § 12.1-32-15(11)			Information may be disclosed to the public if necessary for public protection
OHIO § 2950.08			Law enforcement shall provide notice to the public regarding sexual predators
OKLAHOMA tit. 57 § 584(D) & (E)	Available to law enforcement and child care employers	Each local law enforcement office shall make sex offender registration available on request	
OREGON § 181.589			Police may notify community of the release of a predatory sex offender
PENNSYLVANIA 42 Pa. Cons. Stat. § 9798		All information available to general public upon written request	Information about a sexually violent predator may be released to members of the community and community organizations as specified under this chapter
RHODE ISLAND § 11-37.1-12			Law enforcement may release information to community organizations or the public, depending on the risk level of the offender
SOUTH CAROLINA § 32-3-490		Open to public inspection upon request to the sheriff	Sheriff may disseminate information if facts give rise to a reasonable suspicion of criminal activity and sheriff has reason to believe release will deter the criminal activity
SOUTH DAKOTA § 22-22-40		Registration records are public records	
TENNESSEE § 40-39-106(c)		For all sex offenses committed on or after July 1, 1997, the information shall be public; information shall be placed on the State of Tennessee Internet home-page; the information shall also be available on a toll-free number	For all sex offenses committed prior to July 1, 1997, information is confidential, except law enforcement may release "relevant information deemed necessary to protect the public concerning a specific sexual offender"
TEXAS art. 6252-13c.1(5)-(5A)		Information available to any person upon written request	Information published in newspaper upon person's release; schools notified
UTAH § 77-27-21.5		Department of Corrections may release information to a petitioner upon request	

Public Notification of the Release of Sex Offenders

STATE/STATUTE	Available only to law enforcement OR released only to specified organizations (not the public)	Available to general public upon request	Police notify community upon release
VERMONT tit. 13 § 5402	Available only to law enforcement, government agency responsible for background checks, and employers already authorized to request information from the criminal information center		
VIRGINIA § 19.2-390.1	Available only to law enforcement and organizations that hire people to work with children: further dissemination prohibited	Information disclosed upon request; information on certain violent offenders shall be available on the Internet	
WASHINGTON			Information released to public when necessary for public protection
WEST VIRGINIA § 61-8F-5		Information may be provided to any person upon application to the circuit court when the court finds it relevant to public safety	Law enforcement shall disseminate information about sexually violent offenders
WISCONSIN § 301.46(5)		Police chief or sheriff may release information to a person who submits a written request	
WYOMING § 7-19-303			Law enforcement may release information based on the risk level of the offender

Source: National Center for Prosecution of Child Abuse, 1999.

Legal definitions of mental injury usually depend upon evaluation by a qualified psychiatrist, psychologist or pediatrician. Further, the impairment must be attributable to an act or acts of omission or commission by an adult responsible for the child. Pennsylvania law (Act 124, 1975) defines mental injury as "a psychological condition . . . which: (1) renders the child chronically and severely anxious, agitated, depressed, socially withdrawn, psychotic, or in reasonable fear that his/her life and/or safety is threatened; (2) makes it extremely likely that the child will become chronically and severely anxious, agitated, depressed, socially withdrawn, psychotic, or be in reasonable fear that his/her life is threatened; or (3) seriously interferes with the child's ability to accomplish age-appropriate developmental milestones, or school, peer, and community tasks."

Mental injury may result from PSYCHOLOGICAL MALTREATMENT as well as PHYSICAL ABUSE, SEXUAL ABUSE and NEGLECT.

mental retardation   Ironically, mental retardation is seen as both a cause and a result of child abuse.

Mental retardation can result from child battering, nutritional and medical neglect, drug or alcohol use during pregnancy and other forms of maltreatment. SUBDURAL HEMATOMA due to battering is perhaps the major cause of traumatically induced mental retardation among children. Battered infants are especially susceptible to brain damage because the infant cranium is soft and does not afford the same protection provided by the fully developed adult bone structure.

Mentally retarded or develomentally delayed children are often singled out as targets for abuse by their caretakers. Parents may feel angry, frustrated and/or guilty as a result of having a retarded child. These feelings are sometimes directed toward the child in the form of abusive behavior. The child is also more likely to be the recipient of abuse connected with family stress, alcohol and drug abuse and mental illness on the part of the parent or primary caretaker. Mentally retarded children and adults are more vulnerable to physical and sexual assaults from outside as well.

Because many children suffering from mental retardation are cared for in institutions or community-based programs, they are often the victims of INSTITUTIONAL ABUSE AND NEGLECT. For centuries these children and adults were subjected to imprisonment, beating, sexual misuse and starvation and were sometimes put to death. Even now, vast differences exist in the quality of care provided for mentally retarded individuals in different communities and countries around the world.

Sharon R. Morgan, *Abuse and Neglect of Handicapped Children* (Boston: College-Hill Press, 1987).

A. Sandgrund, R. Gaines, and A. Green, "Child Abuse and Mental Retardation: A Problem of Cause and Effect," *American Journal of Mental Deficiency,* 79, no. 3 (1975): 327–330

microcephaly A condition in which the cranial capacity is abnormally small, microcephaly may develop following a blow to the head. Damage caused by microcephaly is usually irreversable. (*See also* CENTRAL NERVOUS SYSTEM INJURIES.)

Minnesota Multiphasic Personality Inventory (MMPI) Psychometric tests are sometimes used to detect emotional disturbance in children who have been abused. Most such tests can be administered and interpreted only by trained psychologists. The Minnesota Multiphasic Personality Inventory (MMPI) is one of the most popular tests used in the assessment of older children.

The MMPI consists of over 500 items that must be answered true, false, or "cannot say." Originally developed as a means of classifying patients in mental hospitals, the test is divided into 10 basic scales that measure characteristics such as hypochondria, depression, hysteria, paranoia, hypomania and schizophrenia.

minor *See* CHILD.

Miranda warnings In cases of alleged child abuse and neglect, as in other alleged crimes, an accused person is protected against self-incrimination by the so-called Miranda warnings, based on the 1966 U.S. Supreme Court decision in *Miranda v. Arizona.* In that ruling, the court held that statements made by an individual who has been taken into custody cannot be used by the prosecution *against that individual* unless procedural safeguards against self-incrimination have been exercised. Briefly stated, the Miranda warnings cover the following points:

1. An individual has the right to remain silent.
2. Anything said by an individual can and will be used against that individual in a court of law.
3. An individual has the right to talk with a lawyer and to have the lawyer present during questioning.
4. If an individual cannot afford to hire a lawyer, one will be appointed to represent that individual prior to any questioning, if the individual so desires.

misdemeanor In criminal court proceedings offenses are distinguished according to how serious they are perceived to be. FELONIES are considered most serious and are punishable by more severe penalties. Misdemeanors are treated less severely, traditionally receiving prison sentences no longer than one year. In some cases misdemeanors and felonies are tried in different courts, with alleged felons receiving greater procedural safeguards. (*See also* COURT, DUE PROCESS.)

Model Protection Act The NATIONAL CENTER ON CHILD ABUSE AND NEGLECT in Washington, D.C. has prepared a guide for states wishing to develop their own child abuse legislation. Known as the Model Protection Act, this document served as the basis of new child abuse laws in virtually all of the 50 states.

molestation *See* CHILD MOLESTER.

Mongolian spots Birthmarks are sometimes mistaken for bruises on young children and infants, arousing suspicion of child abuse. Mongolian spots appear on some children at birth. These are grayish blue in color and last from two to three years. These spots can appear on any part of the body, but are most commonly found on the back and buttocks.

Though Mongolian spots are found on children of all races, they appear more frequently on dark-skinned infants.

moral neglect   Failure of parents to instill positive social values in their children is sometimes referred to as moral neglect. Early child protection efforts leaned heavily on inadequate moral training as justification for intervening in a family. Delinquency by children and family poverty were seen as evidence of parents' moral weakness, and early societies for the protection of children often removed children from their homes for these reasons.

Today, moral neglect alone is usually not considered grounds for removing a child from home. Poverty is largely seen as a societal rather than a moral problem. Illegal acts of children are handled through the juvenile court system. Removal of a child from home due to delinquency takes place in the context of treatment or, in some cases, punishment. Parents who allow or encourage their children to engage in illegal activity may be subject to criminal charges for contributing to the delinquency of a minor.

Mothers Anonymous   Self-help groups for mothers who abuse their children are sometimes called Mothers Anonymous. Although these groups operate similarly to PARENTS ANONYMOUS (PA) they are not affiliated with a national organization such as PA.

mouth injuries   Injuries to the mouth and surrounding area are relatively common in children. Determination of whether trauma is due to accident or abuse often depends on the plausibility of the caretaker's explanation of the accident and on the age of the child. While some types of oral injuries are common in children learning to walk, such injuries are less likely to be accidental in pre-toddlers or children who have been walking for some time.

Mouth injuries include tearing of the frenum (the small, V-shaped muscle joining the lip to the gum at the front of the mouth); cuts, abrasions and contusions of the lips; loosening, intrusion (forcing back into the gum), avulsion (total removal) and fractures of the teeth; and laceration of the tongue

or gums. Fracture of the mandible (lower jaw), and less frequently the maxillary bone (upper bone structure), may also result from a forceful blow to the mouth area.

Prompt attention to oral injuries by a physician or dentist is important. Avulsed teeth have a 90% chance of being saved if replaced in the socket within 15 minutes of removal. The success rate of reimplantation drops 15% after one hour. Tooth fractures should also receive prompt attention from a dentist to avoid loss of the tooth.

Neglect of proper oral hygiene can cause unnecessary pain and discomfort as well as permanent damage to a child's mouth. Though it is often difficult to determine whether neglect of dental needs is intentional, poor oral hygiene is often indicative of more general MEDICAL NEGLECT.

Dentists can be especially helpful in early identification of possible abuse or neglect involving oral damage and hygiene. Many areas require that dentists report suspected child maltreatment to local child protection or law enforcement authorities.

multidisciplinary team   Identification and treatment of child abuse and neglect often requires a variety of different skills and perspectives. Multidisciplinary teams have been found to be an effective way of helping professionals work together in diagnosing and treating child abuse. Such teams are used widely in many different countries. In the United States some states specifically require the use of multidisciplinary teams.

Composition of teams may vary but most teams include representatives from the fields of social service and medicine. Members of the mental health, nursing, education, legal and law enforcement professions are frequently included. Inclusion of a representative of the agency legally charged with investigation of reported abuse is recommended as a means of improving coordination of services and reducing conflict.

In addition to identification and treatment planning, multidisciplinary teams may also provide consultation, community education and prevention services. Many teams are based in hospitals. Other models include interagency programs and teams directly connected to a government agency.

Though some teams experience relatively high levels of disagreement between members and occasional disputes over turf, most experts agree that the advantages of the multidisciplinary approach outweigh the disadvantages. Use of multidisciplinary teams has been credited with improving the quality and coordination of treatment, lessening the need for out-of-home placement, strengthening families, reducing the chance of reinjury and lowering the overall cost of treatment.

multiple maltreatment   Child abuse is rarely confined to a single incident or mode of abuse. Investigation of suspected abuse often reveals forms of maltreatment other than that reported. Physically abused children are often neglected. Victims of sexual abuse may also be subjected to psychological or physical abuse.

The combination of several forms of maltreatment often presents special problems for treatment of abused and neglected children. Failure to identify all forms of maltreatment may lead to inappropriate intervention. Unrecognized or untreated abuse may have lasting effects. Careful ASSESSMENT of each child's situation is essential to ensure proper treatment and protection.

Munchausen Syndrome by Proxy   Baron K. F. H. von Munchausen was an 18th-century German mercenary with a penchant for telling tall tales. Accounts of his adventures were further embellished in a pamphlet entitled "Baron Munchausen's Narrative of His Marvellous Travels and Campaigns in Russia." In the early 1950s Richard Asher, an English physician, used the term "Munchausen Syndrome" to describe a psychiatric disorder characterized by dramatic and untruthful medical histories and feigned symptoms.

The first paper on Munchausen Syndrome by Proxy (MBP) was described in a paper by British pediatrician Roy S. Meadow, who had a patient with frequent and puzzling illnesses and whose urine was apparently infected by one bacteria in the morning and another in the evening. Some urinalyses would be normal. The mystery was solved when it was discovered that the bacteria were present only when the mother helped to collect the urine specimen.

MBP is a form of abuse in which a child's medical disorder is fabricated by another person, in most cases, the biological mother. The perpetrator may present false medical histories, inflict physical symptoms, alter lab specimens and directly induce disorders in the child. As a result of these fabrications, the child may be subjected to frequent unnecessary hospitalizations, painful tests, potentially harmful treatment and even death.

A Florida child was hospitalized more than 200 times and had suffered 40 operations before her mother's abuse was discovered. Other children have suffered equally harrowing experiences. In an article in a 1997 issue of *Pediatrics,* a discussion of MBP is followed by a distressing account of an adult who had as a child experienced repeated and purposeful abuse at the hands of her mother, whose usual modus operandi was to break or injure bones with a hammer.

MBP is referred to in the *Diagnostic and Statistical Manual of Disorders* (DSM-IV) as "factitious disorder by proxy." The four criteria are that an illness in another person is either caused or faked, the motivation of the perpetrator is to obtain sympathy from others, the motivation is not a desire for economic gain, and the behavior cannot be explained by another psychiatric diagnosis.

It can be difficult to diagnose MBP because the mother usually appears to be a loving and caring person, and experts say that if and when MBP is suspected, hospital staff can become very polarized between accusers and defenders. The underlying reason for the abuse is the attention the mother receives. Often she may be a person with medical training or even a nursing degree.

A very thorough description of this disorder is provided in a 1999 issue of *Critical Care Nursing Quarterly.* The authors report that children under five are at greatest risk. They provide clinical profiles of both the victim and the perpetrator. According to the authors, the typical child victim profile is as follows:

1. Persistent or recurrent illness cannot be explained readily by the consulting physician despite a thorough medical workup. The illness presents as an atypical pattern, even to experienced clinicians. Usually, the symptoms are associated

with only one system; for example, gastrointestinal problems of vomiting, diarrhea and bloody stool; and neurological problems of seizures, apnea and lethargy. On occasion, a presentation will consist of many different symptoms representing a multisystem disorder.

2. A diagnosis is merely descriptive of the symptoms or a diagnosis of an extremely rare disorder.

3. Symptoms do not respond to the usual treatment regime. Incidents may occur that interfere with treatment effectiveness, such as intravenous lines coming out, repeated line infections or persistent vomiting of medications.

4. Physical or lab findings are not consistent with the reported history. Lab findings may be unusual or physiologically impossible.

5. Physical findings and reported symptoms conflict with the child's generally healthy appearance.

6. A temporal relationship exists between the child's symptoms and the mother's presence. The reported symptoms fail to occur in the parent's absence and may not have been observed by anyone other than the parent.

7. Pertinent medical history cannot be substantiated. The parent may be unable to provide sufficient information about previous medical care or the records conflict with the parent's report.

8. Presenting complaints include bleeding, seizures, unconsciousness, apnea, diarrhea, vomiting, fever and lethargy. These most commonly reported symptoms should serve as warning signs.

The clinical profile of the abusive perpetrator is as follows, according to the authors:

1. The MBPS parent is reluctant to leave the child while hospitalized. The parents may refuse to leave the child's beside for even a few minutes or to take care of his or her own personal needs. He or she often will attend to the child-victim to the exclusion of his or her other children to a degree that it is detrimental to them.

2. The parent develops close personal relationships with hospital staff. The parent may spend the little time he or she does leave his or her child's side socializing with the health care staff and parents of other ill children. Nurses and physicians may find themselves becoming emotionally involved with the parent, blurring practitioner/patient boundaries.

3. The parent's educational or employment background is in the medical field or he or she aspires to be a health care provider. Often the parent is medically knowledgeable and well versed in medical terminology and procedures.

4. The parent displays an unusual calm when facing child care problems. Although the parent expresses concern for the child, when an emergency occurs, he or she remains unaffected. The parent actually may be highly supportive and encouraging of the medical/nursing practitioner, even when the practitioner expresses confusion about the child's problems. A minority of MBPS parents goes to the opposite extreme and becomes angry, degrading the staff and demanding additional procedures that are not medically indicated.

5. The medical problems of the parent are similar to those of the child. A substantial number of MBPS parents exhibit some or all of the features of Munchausen Syndrome.

6. Information fabrication may not be confined to the child's symptoms or history but may include aspects of the parent's family, education, previous employment, illness and other historical data.

7. In some cases, prominent religious beliefs, superstitions or cultural beliefs are integral parts of the parent's presentation and personality.

Mary Bryk and Patricia T. Siegel. "My Mother Caused My Illness: The Story of a Survivor of Munchausen by Proxy Syndrome," *Pediatrics* 100, no. 1 (July 1997): 1–7.
Georgia A. Pasqualone and Susan M. Fitzgerald, "Munchausen by Proxy Syndrome. The Forensic Challenge," *Critical Care Nursing Quarterly* 22 (May 1999): 52–64.

mutilation, genital   *See* CASTRATION, FEMALE GENITAL MUTILATION, CLITORIDECTOMY and INFIBULATION.

mysopedic offender   This type of pedophile (*see* PEDOPHILIA) is the most sadistic of all sexual offenders. Mysopeds are sometimes referred to as "child haters" and are responsible for most brutal rapes and murders of children. Though quite uncommon, mysopeds have often been the focus of a great deal of media attention. Some of the more widely publicized cases involve mentally disordered men with long histories of molesting children, who commit a number of rape/murders before being apprehended.

One well-known case involved an Illinois man, John Wayne Gacy, who worked as a clown entertaining children in hospitals and at home. When finally arrested for a sexual offense, he confessed to sexually assaulting and strangling 32 teenage boys and young men.

National Advisory Centre on the Battered Child

Located in London, the National Advisory Centre on the Battered Child was formed from the National Society for the Prevention of Cruelty to Children's battered child research department. The National Centre later became the NSPCC Haringey Special Unit, an interdisciplinary team providing treatment and consultation services.

National Center for Missing and Exploited Children

The National Center for Missing and Exploited Children began operations in 1984, a result of growing public concern over the problem of missing and sexually exploited children in the United States. A nonprofit organization, the center was created by an act of Congress and funded initially by the Office of Juvenile Justice and Delinquency Prevention, United States Department of Justice.

In addition to operating a toll-free hotline for reporting information leading to the location or recovery of a missing child (1-800-843-5678), the center serves as a clearinghouse for information concerning the problem of missing and exploited children. Technical assistance is available to individuals, groups, state and local agencies on the prevention of the exploitation and victimization of children. Training is also provided to law enforcement and child protection agencies on procedures to be followed in the investigation and prosecution of cases involving missing or exploited children. For more information, *see* APPENDIX 1.

National Center for the Study of Corporal Punishment and Alternatives in the Schools (NCSCPAS)

Founded in 1976, as part of the Department of School Psychology at Temple University, this center provides information and opportunity to study the psychological and educational aspects of school discipline. As one of several such organizations devoted to eliminating corporal punishment from the schools, the NCSCPAS established the Delaware Valley Discipline Clinic to provide diagnoses and counseling as well as consultation to schools.

The NCSCPAS runs workshops, nationally and internationally, arranges legal advocacy for protesting corporal punishment in schools and has an extensive collection of articles and news clippings that focus on discipline. The center publishes *Discipline Helpline*, a journal, several times annually as well as a bibliography of publications related to corporal punishment. It holds semiannual executive committee meetings and maintains a free telephone consultation service.

National Center on Child Abuse and Neglect (NCCAN)

NCCAN is a government office administered by the Children's Bureau, Administration for Youth and Families, Office of Human Development Services, United States Department of Health and Human Services. The center was established in 1974 by the National Child Abuse Prevention and Treatment Act. The purpose of the center is to:

1. generate new knowledge and improve child protection, prevention and treatment programs;
2. collect, analyze and disseminate information related to child abuse and neglect;
3. help states and local communities implement programs; and
4. coordinate all federal initiatives related to child abuse and neglect.

In 1998, NCCAN was reorganized and merged with the Children's Bureau.

National Child Abuse and Neglect Data System (NCANDS) Technical Assistance Program   This program compiles and analyzes annual abuse and neglect statistics from the states in the U.S. and produces an annual report on child maltreatment. It also helps states to improve child protective services information systems and the analytic capability of their agencies. For more information, contact NCANDS, Social Science Statistician, Children's Bureau, 330 C St. SW, Washington, DC 20447. Tel. (202) 205-8625

National Clearinghouse on Child Abuse and Neglect Information   Originally established in 1975 as a central resource for abuse and neglect information and today a service of the Children's Bureau, the National Clearinghouse on Child Abuse and Neglect Information provides a searchable database, publications, state laws, fact sheets, statistical data, training manuals and other helpful and important materials related to child abuse and neglect. For more information, contact: National Clearinghouse on Child Abuse and Neglect Information, 330 C St. SW, Washington, DC 20447. Tel: (800) 394-3366 or (703) 385-7565. Web site: www.calib.com/nccanch

national register   The idea of a nationwide repository of child abuse reports has often been advanced as a way to monitor trends, conduct research and track offenders who move from place to place to avoid apprehension. It has not been possible to establish such a register in the United States because differences in state laws, definitions of abuse and rules regarding confidentiality have made this information difficult to collect and compare. Similar impediments to a national register of child abuse reports exist in Canada and in Great Britain, which consist of separate territories, provinces and/or countries.

National Society for the Prevention of Cruelty to Children   This British organization was originally named the London Society for the Prevention of Cruelty to Children and was founded by clergyman Benjamin Waugh in 1884. In 1889 it merged with 31 other child welfare groups that had been established throughout Britain, taking the name by which it is known today. Queen Victoria was a patron of the NSPCC, which received a royal charter in May 1895. Its official mission is "to prevent the public and private wrongs of children."

The NSPCC was instrumental in securing passage of the landmark Prevention of Cruelty to and Protection of Children Act of 1889. The society operated branches in Dublin, Belfast and Cork until 1956, when the Irish Society assumed jurisdiction. The Scottish National Society, formed in 1899, received a royal charter as the Royal Scottish Society for the Prevention of Cruelty to Children.

Today, NSPCC inspectors make home visits and rely also on a network of community playgroups to help prevent abuse of children. In some areas of Britain, the NSPCC provides 24-hour support.

Native Americans   *See* AMERICAN INDIANS, INDIAN CHILD WELFARE ACT OF 1978.

natural dolls   These are also known as "anatomically correct" dolls. A young victim of SEXUAL ABUSE may not have developed verbal skills to communicate accurately her/his experience or may simply find it very difficult or threatening to tell anyone about the episode. Hence, gathering information from the child is a difficult and sensitive task and dolls are sometimes used.

In past years, some therapists felt that such dolls were a useful tool in the diagnosis and treatment of young victims of sexual abuse because they believed that children found it less difficult to act out the abuse using the dolls or to point to the doll's sexual organs when discussing the abuse. Many therapists still use the dolls, although they have come under criticism. For example, in their chapter on the validity of child sexual abuse allegations in the book, *Expert Witnesses in Child Abuse Cases: What Can and Should be Said in Court* (American Psychological Association, 1998), Celia B. Fisher and Katherine A. Whiting question the validity of findings from the use of such dolls. The authors write that the "rapid, widespread use of the dolls evokes popular concern over the appropriateness of presenting explicitly sexual material to children, professional concern over their potentially coercive and suggestive nature, and judicial concern regarding their ability as assessment tools for the validation of child sexual abuse. . . ."

They add that although sexually abused children are more explicit in their play with the dolls, sex play has also been found with children who had not been sexually abused. There is also some concern that the use of the dolls could be regarded as a form of entrapment. The authors said that research has revealed that asking nonabused children detailed questions about sexual behavior increases the incidences of such behavior in doll play. But they said that leading questions are common in sexual abuse cases. In other words, if the interviewer asks many questions related to genitalia, the questions themselves can increase the child's attention to the doll's oversized genitalia. This behavior then "proves" to the interviewer that the child was abused, but in fact the child's interest and behavior was piqued by the questioning of the interviewer. The authors said "psychologists using these dolls as a diagnostic instrument risk operating in an ethically indefensible manner."

neglect Repeated failure to meet the minimal standards for a child's nutritional, clothing, medical, educational, safety and/or emotional needs constitutes neglect. Neglect is the most frequent form of maltreatment; according to statistics for 1997 (reported in 1999), neglect represented 55.9% of all child maltreatment cases in the U.S. This figure represented an increase from the 1990 statistic of 48.4%.

Although other forms of child maltreatment, especially SEXUAL ABUSE, receive more media attention, the fact is that deaths and serious injury of children are more likely to result from neglect than abuse. It is true that children are harmed by beatings and sometimes, if the beatings are severe enough, they die. But they will also certainly die without food or water, and sometimes children are deprived of these basic necessities of life, both accidentally and by design.

Neglect may also be considered criminal if it endangers the life of a child. Each state has a statute on what constitutes neglect.

ABANDONMENT is also a form of neglect and may be criminal, depending on state laws and the circumstances of the case. Often children as young as two or three years old (or younger) are left in charge of their younger siblings with no food, no instructions and no idea where their parents are. Children this young cannot read and do not know how to ask for emergency help.

Sometimes they are discovered wandering around their neighborhoods, often clothed inappropriately; for example, a child might have a T-shirt, shorts and no shoes on in the middle of a cold winter. In extreme cases, children have actually consumed their own fecal matter to stay alive. These are conditions unimaginable to most Americans, who would be far more likely to attribute such treatment to children in poverty-stricken countries. Yet it happens in Western nations too, every day. Children in the U.S. and other Western countries need not die of malnutrition, rickets and other diseases that can be easily treated by physicians—but if no one intervenes, they can and do suffer from such ailments and worse. Some longitudinal research indicates that neglected children may suffer more lasting emotional damage than physically abused children. In addition, studies have revealed that neglected children, along with children who have been abandoned or are in failed placements, suffer from more health problems and worse health overall than children who were sexually or physically abused.

Neglect may be willful, as when a parent refuses to send a child to school, or unintended, as in the case of a caretaker suffering from severe mental illness who is incapable of providing adequate care. Some parents may refuse to obtain appropriate medical care for their child, which could be deemed as MEDICAL NEGLECT. (However, religious exemptions are sometimes made if the religion prohibits medical intervention and if state law allows for such an exemption.)

Parents who neglect a child's needs because they lack adequate knowledge of parenting usually respond to teaching when it is given sensitively. Ignorance of proper child care can often be corrected by arranging for instruction from a visiting nurse or PARENT AIDE.

Poor judgment may be exercised by caretakers who are immature or who were themselves neglected. Safety neglect is a significant cause of death among young children. Children under the age of three years have not developed a safety consciousness and are especially susceptible to accidents. While all children are likely to suffer preventable accidents on occasion, repeated serious accidents indicate that a child's caretaker is unable or unwilling to take the necessary steps to protect him or her.

Parents who repeatedly refuse to change behaviors that are grossly neglectful pose a serious threat to a child's welfare. In such cases, court intervention and possible removal from the home may be necessary to protect the child's safety and even life.

POVERTY may affect parents' ability to provide the physical necessities for their children. By itself poverty does not provide a sufficient reason for labeling parents as neglectful. Studies show that the majority of children living in poor families are not neglected. Often conditions that are unhealthy for children can be corrected by the provision of adequate support for food, clothing and housing. Failure by a society to provide an adequate minimum level of support for all children is sometimes called SOCIAL ABUSE.

Various forms of mental illness or emotional disturbances can play a role in parental neglect. Psychotic parents are unable to care for children and may become neglectful or abusive. More often, depression contributes to parents' inability to provide for their children. Norman Polansky, author of several studies on child neglect, has described a condition known as APATHY-FUTILITY SYNDROME, similar to psychological depression, which may be observed in severely and chronically neglectful mothers. This syndrome is characterized by emotional numbness, limited intellectual ability and other factors that are often related to the mother's own deprivation during childhood. SUBSTANCE ABUSE is another major cause of child neglect because addicts are often more centered on obtaining their next injection or pill than on feeding or clothing their children. Experts say as many as 75% of the children in foster care have been removed from their families because of problems with substance abuse, primarily alcohol and/or cocaine as well as other illegal drugs.

Parents who are developmentally delayed may be very well-intentioned but may be unable to provide for the needs of their children. They may be able to manage parenting with the assistance of others.

Gross neglect resulting in serious physical harm to a child is not difficult to identify. In other situations the identification of neglect may depend on the awareness of day care, school or medical professionals and their own individual standards of child care. Statutory definitions of neglect are often vague and may differ according to geographical location and cultural values.

In an effort to standardize the concept of neglect Polansky and others developed the CHILDHOOD LEVEL OF LIVING SCALE. This checklist is completed by a protective service worker or other child care professional and yields a numerical rating of the quality of the child's care. Scores are then compared to predetermined standards to determine the adequacy of care.

Investigation of suspected neglect must take into account each child's unique situation as well as the cultural and familial context in which he or she lives. A thorough evaluation includes a medical examination; a review of medical records for evidence of immunization status, number of accidental injuries and frequency of medical checkups; a report from day care or school officials concerning attendance, academic performance, behavior and diet; and a family assessment conducted by a trained social worker, including a home visit to assess the child's environment.

Behavioral indicators of neglect in the child include: development delays, begging or stealing food, frequent absences or chronic lateness from school and destructive behavior.

neglect, community   *See* COMMUNITY NEGLECT.

neglect, emotional   *See* EMOTIONAL NEGLECT.

neglect, indicators   *See* INDICATORS OF CHILD ABUSE AND NEGLECT.

neglect, institutional   *See* INSTITUTIONAL ABUSE AND NEGLECT.

neglect, medical   *See* MEDICAL NEGLECT.

neglect, moral   *See* MORAL NEGLECT.

neglect, neurological manifestations   *See* NEUROLOGIC MANIFESTATIONS OF ABUSE AND NEGLECT.

neglect, prediction of   *See* PREDICTION OF ABUSE AND NEGLECT.

neglect, situational   *See* SITUATIONAL ABUSE AND NEGLECT.

C. Henry Kempe and Ray E. Helfer, eds., *The Battered Child*, 3rd ed. (Chicago: University of Chicago Press, 1980).

Norman A. Polansky, Mary Ann Chalmers, Elizabeth Buttenwieser, and David P. Williams, *Damaged Parents* (Chicago: University of Chicago Press, 1981).

neglectful parents   *See* CHARACTERISTICS OF ABUSING AND NEGLECTFUL PARENTS.

neonaticide   The killing of an infant immediately following birth is known as neonaticide. In some cultures neonaticide has been considered an acceptable form of limiting family size or eliminating malformed infants. Historically, some societies drew a sharp distinction between neonaticide and INFANTICIDE. These groups often developed rituals by which a child was accepted or rejected by the mother's husband. Until ritually accepted, an infant was not considered human and could therefore be murdered or abandoned with impunity.

Today neonaticide is relatively rare; however, reports of murdered or abandoned newborns are still heard from time to time in most countries.

Netherlands   In 1970, the Society for the Prevention of Child Abuse and Neglect was founded in the Netherlands. Through this agency and via the Child Welfare Counselling Centres, cases of child abuse and neglect are reported. There is an emphasis on supportive programs and treatment for victims of child abuse and neglect, in particular toward victims of sexual abuse and incest. The Dutch government is actively involved in prevention and education programs to combat child abuse and neglect, and the Health and Welfare Ministry has sole responsibility for administering these services.

As a result of international pressure, the Dutch government curtailed the sale of child pornography after the Netherlands was identified as a center of its production and distribution.

neurologic manifestations of abuse and neglect   Over half of all abused or neglected children show signs of impaired cognitive, language, learning, motor or psychological development. Physical abuse of children is a significant cause of mental retardation and cerebral palsy. Studies have shown that even in the absence of retardation, abused children tend to score lower than nonabused children on intelligence tests.

Neurologic impairment may be caused by obvious damage to the CENTRAL NERVOUS SYSTEM, such as MICROCEPHALY or spinal cord injury; however, neurologic injury is often the result of more subtle trauma. Nerve damage caused by shaking may not be readily apparent to an examining physician but may be reflected later in developmental delays.

Neglect also plays an important role in the production of neurological and developmental impairment. Poor nutrition and lack of social and sensory stimulation is associated with retarded intellectual, motor and emotional development. These forms of neglect are typical in battered children but are also found when no evidence of physical abuse is apparent. Infants who do not receive adequate TACTILE STIMULATION may exhibit signs of motor and intellectual impairment and later may have difficulty forming emotional attachments. Failure to provide adequate medical treatment for illness or injury may also cause neurological damage.

Because of the high rate of neurological problems associated with abuse and neglect, all child victims should be screened for neurodevelopmental deficits. A careful neurologic examination includes assessment of cranial nerve and cerebellar functioning, reflexes and focal damage, as well as evaluation of gross and fine motor skills, sensory-motor abilities, activity level and attention span.

Developmental screening can involve compiling a careful history of the child's development from a caretaker, observation by a medical practitioner trained in the identification of neurologic impairment, use of developmental checklists, and formal developmental screening tests. Using screening tests, such as the Denver Developmental Screening Test (DDST), is the preferred method of assessment.

Neurologic impairment can be both the cause and the result of abuse. Developmentally delayed children require additional time and patience from parents. Frustrated parents especially those with unrealistically high expectations for their child's behavior, are more likely to abuse their children. Abuse increases the likelihood of neurological impairment which, in turn, increases the probability of abuse.

Norman S. Ellerstein, *Child and Neglect: A Medical Reference* (New York: John Wiley and Sons, 1981).

Alejandro Rodriguez, *Handbook of Child Abuse and Neglect* (Flushing, N.Y.: Medical Examination Publishing Co., 1977).

New York House of Refuge   The New York House of Refuge, the first reform school in the United States, was opened by the Society for the Reformation of Juvenile Delinquents in 1825. As its name suggests, the facility also housed children who had been abused or neglected along with children who had committed delinquent acts.

Norway   As in other Scandinavian nations, Norway has a highly refined social welfare system that seems to preclude perception of widespread violence against children. Extensive child care provisions for all workers, maternity leave and education classes for new parents, as well as readily available contraception and abortion foster an atmosphere that appears to alleviate some tensions and preconditions associated with abuse or neglect.

Although some incidents of child abuse do occur and family violence is recognized as a problem, the focus in Norway is weighted heavily toward diagnosis and treatment rather than prevention, since abuse appears to take place relatively seldom. Some programs have been established in Norway to find ways of assisting violence-prone families. In 1972, Norway passed legislation that prohibited use of violent disciplinary actions against children. According to the 1999 Country Reports on Human Rights Practices, released on February 25, 2000, by the Bureau of Democracy, Human Rights, and Labor in the U.S. Department of State, 23,500 children in Norway (2% of all children under age 17 years) received welfare services in 1998 due to abuse and neglect. Forms of assistance in Norway include protective custody, financial help and/or guidance and support for their families.

nutritional deficiency   *See* MARASMUS, NUTRITIONAL; RICKETS; SCURVY.

nutritional marasmus   *See* MARASMUS, NUTRITIONAL.

offender, fixated   *See* FIXATED OFFENDER.

opinion evidence   *See* EVIDENCE.

***opu hule* (turned stomach)**   Originating among Native Hawaiian islanders, this culturally based belief stipulates that tossing or jiggling a young child up and down will result in *opu hule,* or a "turned stomach." This term means that the stomach has been twisted or displaced. Children who suffer from symptoms of indigestion, fussiness or general discomfort are often thought to be suffering from *opu hule.* Tossing or bouncing a child is considered to be a form of child abuse and is frowned upon in the Native Hawaiian culture.

order of protection   In the United States, the legal basis for court intervention in the family of an abused or neglected child is an order of protection. The order is typically issued by a juvenile court and places the child under the supervision of an authority, usually the designated child protection agency. Typically, children are allowed to remain at home while under an order of protection, provided the family meets specific conditions spelled out in the order. Failure to comply with these terms may result in the parents being held in contempt of court, fined and/or imprisoned. Violation of such orders is also likely to prompt the court to take custody of the child.

The NATIONAL CENTER ON CHILD ABUSE AND NEGLECT lists the following conditions that are usually included in an order of protection:

- Refrain from any conduct that is detrimental to the child.
- Refrain from any conduct that would make the home an improper place for the child.

- Give adequate attention to the care of the home.
- Comply with visitation terms if the child has been removed from the home.
- Comply with the treatment plan.

ossification   Formation of new bone, known as ossification, is visible on X rays and can be an important clue in the detection of child battering. A trained physician can determine if there is a history of multiple fractures by examining a series of X rays for evidence of ossification, which indicates the healing of old fractures, as well as searching the X rays for more recent trauma. (*See also* FRACTURES.)

osteogenesis imperfecta   Sometimes, mistaken for BATTERED CHILD SYNDROME, osteogenesis imperfecta is an inherited condition that causes bones to be very brittle and easily fractured.

overlaying   Overlaying refers to the suffocation of an infant by an adult lying on top of it. Prior to the 20th century many infants were thought to have died as a result of overlaying (also known as stifling). Deaths that are now attributed to SUDDEN INFANT DEATH SYNDROME were frequently thought to be the result of the mother intentionally or accidentally overlaying the infant during the night. Overlaying was considered a negligent act by a mother and was punished in the Roman Catholic and Anglican churches. Fear of accidental suffocation led to the custom of mothers and infants sleeping in separate beds, an uncommon practice in earlier times.

A special device was developed in 17th-century Europe to prevent accidental overlaying. This device, called an *arcuccio,* consisted of a metal and wood arch. The infant, protected underneath the *arcuccio,* could sleep in the same bed with the mother without the possibility of accidental suffocation. Some countries made failure to use the *arcuccio* a punishable offense. References to the use of the *arcuccio* can be found as late as 1890. (*See also* CULTURAL FACTORS, SUDDEN INFANT DEATH SYNDROME.)

PA buddy   PARENTS ANONYMOUS groups, much like Alcoholics Anonymous, assign sponsors, or buddies, to members. The buddy, usually a more experienced member of the group, serves a function similar to a PARENT AIDE. A PA member may contact her/his buddy for advice and support at any time. Use of the buddy system serves an important function in preventing child abuse by providing a nonthreatening source of support in a crisis. The buddy receives the benefit of an increased sense of confidence and self-control by helping another person improve his/her parenting skills.

paddling   One of many forms of CORPORAL PUNISHMENT, paddling is a variation of CANING in which school officials (teachers or administrators) sometimes strike students with the flat side of a wooden paddle to promote discipline. Although the practice is a time-honored one, it has numerous detractors and several international children's rights organizations work to prohibit paddling and other forms of corporal punishment.

In the United States, the practice of paddling was challenged in a case brought before the United States Supreme Court by three junior high school students in Dade City, Florida. The case, INGRAHAM V. WRIGHT, exposed the potential and real injuries accruing from the practice of paddling. Ultimately, the Supreme Court found that public schools had the constitutional right to exercise paddling or any other form of "reasonable" corporal punishment. To date, there are only nine states in the United States in which paddling or any other means of corporal punishment is prohibited. In many other countries of the world corporal punishment in any form is illegal.

pancreatitis   This term refers to damage to the pancreatic ducts, usually caused by abdominal trauma. Laceration of the pancreas causes the enzymes amylase and lipase to be released into the peritoneal cavity causing a large buildup of fluid and inflammation of the peritoneum (the membrane enclosing the abdominal cavity).

Occasionally pancreatitis is contained within a smaller area, causing an abscess or a fibrous capsule called a pseudocyst to develop. These developments result in the appearance of a painful lump in the upper abdomen two to three weeks after the injury. Surgical intervention is required to correct such lesions.

Pancreatitis is rare is childhood. When it is present child abuse is strongly suspected. A radiographic study of long bones to detect other evidence of battering can be helpful in confirming this suspicion.

parens patriae   This legal doctrine provides the foundation for a court's entry into the realm of the family. When parents are determined to be unable or unfit to provide adequate and proper care for a child, the court can step in to safeguard the BEST INTERESTS OF THE CHILD. Parens patriae literally means "guardian of the community" and rests on the principle that the state is the ultimate and absolute protector of all citizens, especially children.

This doctrine was first established in the United States in 1838 in the case of Mary Ann Crouse. At that time, the court ruled that a child's parents, "when unequal to the task of education or unworthy of it, be supplanted by the parens patriae." The ruling was widely upheld in the courts throughout the 1800s. By the early 20th century it had become the legal basis on which the juvenile court was established. Its acceptance as a fundamental prerogative of a court means that in cases of suspected child abuse or neglect, the court is the best judge of a child's home environment and that environment's effect on a child's welfare.

In 1968, passage of the UNIFORM CHILD CUSTODY JURISDICTION ACT limited use of parents patriae in cases of CHILD STEALING. The exception occurs in cases where a child requires emergency protection. Under the UCCJA, an emergency condition can result in the court's instituting immediate measures to protect the child. In custody dispute cases that involved child stealing, the doctrine of parens patriae was found to contribute directly to multiple child custody adjudications. (*See* EX PARTE CROUSE.)

parent, surrogate *See* SURROGATE PARENT.

parent aides Many child abuse treatment programs provide special assistance to families in the form of paraprofessionals who serve as role models to parents. These parent aides may be paid or may volunteer their time. Aides perform many different services, such as modeling appropriate parenting techniques, helping to identify problems, teaching specific skills, serving as advocates and giving emotional support and nurturance. Most of all, parent aides serve as friends of the family.

Parent aides are sometimes described as SURROGATE PARENTS. They provide emotional support for both parents and children. Some experts believe it is necessary for parents to go through a REPARENTING process in which they experience the warmth, acceptance and positive learning they did not receive from their parents. Parent aides are usually older adults or couples who, in addition to having been parents themselves, have had special training in working with abusive or neglectful parents.

This type of family support works best in combination with a comprehensive treatment program. Parent aides are often members of a MULTIDISCIPLINARY TEAM. Some hospitals in the United States use parent aides to perform a role similar to that of the HEALTH VISITOR in Britain. Aides are assigned to parents within a few days of the child's birth and continue assisting the parents as long as necessary, usually six to 18 months.

parent education Special programs designed to teach parenting skills are used to treat and prevent child abuse and neglect. Specific parenting skills taught in these programs vary. Many courses for young or neglectful parents focus on basic skills such as proper hygiene and feeding. Abusive parents often expect children to perform beyond their developmental capabilities. Learning about normal developmental patterns helps create more realistic expectations and may help reduce frustration. Programs for parents of older children often focus on improving communication skills. Parent Effectiveness Training, developed by Thomas Gordon, PhD, is an example of such a program.

During the past decade many public schools have begun to offer family life education classes as part of the regular school curriculum. These programs are designed to help adolescents make informed choices about marriage and child rearing.

Many child protection experts believe parent education programs are ineffective for unmotivated parents. Further, some abusive parents have sufficient knowledge but need assistance of other kinds. However, when used as part of a comprehensive treatment and prevention effort, parent education is an important resource for many families.

Thomas Gordon, *Parent Effectiveness Training: The Proven Program for Raising Responsible Children* (New York: Three Rivers Press, 2000).

Parental Kidnapping Prevention Act of 1980 (P.L. 96-611) In order to address more effectively issues related to child stealing in custody disputes, this federal law requires that each state honor other states' custody determinations.

parenthood, psychological *See* PSYCHOLOGICAL PARENTHOOD.

parentified child Children inappropriately placed in the role of parent are said to be parentified. A parentified child may be expected to behave as an adult or be given primary responsibility for care of younger siblings. In some cases children are expected to take care of a parent's emotional or physical needs. Forcing children into adult roles too soon may lead to impaired emotional development sometimes referred to as loss of childhood. (*See also* PSEUDOMATURITY and ROLE REVERSAL.)

parent-infant traumatic syndrome (PITS) The combination of subdural hematomas and specific types of bone lesions was labeled the parent-infant traumatic syndrome by radiologist John Caffey in 1946. By using improved X-ray techniques, Caffey and his associates were able to detect a pattern of trauma that they believed to be of suspicious origin.

Specifically the PITS, also called the battered baby syndrome, involves multiple fractures and other lesions of bone and cartilage in various states of healing. Bone damage typically occurs at joints and often appears to be the result of twisting or vigorous shaking. The combination of bone lesions and head trauma suggests a specific type of injury that is unlikely to be accidental.

The ability to detect unusual patterns of bone injury was an important advance in recognition and treatment of physical child abuse. Physicians who suspected nonaccidental injury could examine full skeletal X rays for additional evidence of abuse. Radiologic evidence is still an important tool in the diagnosis of battered children and is often presented in court as physical evidence of abuse. (*See also* BATTERED CHILD SYNDROME, RADIOLOGY, PEDIATRIC.)

parents, abusive   *See* CHARACTERISTICS OF ABUSING AND NEGLECTFUL PARENTS.

parents, neglectful   *See* CHARACTERISTICS OF ABUSING AND NEGLECTFUL PARENTS.

Parents Anonymous   Begun as a parent group in Redondo Beach, California, Parents Anonymous is now the largest child abuse treatment program in the United States. Parent groups have also been formed in Canada, Australia, West Germany and England. In addition to these groups for parents, PA offers groups for abused children.

Membership includes parents who have abused their children and others interested in preventing child abuse. Members are not required to admit to parenting problems though many find it helpful to share such problems. First names are used at weekly meetings to protect the anonymity of group members.

Informal support provided by members serves an important purpose in preventing future abuse. Members share telephone numbers and are encouraged to call one another when a crisis arises.

Seventy-five percent of PA members are self-referred; 25% are ordered by courts to attend Parents Anonymous meetings.

Though sometimes described as a self-help program, Parents Anonymous is actually a blend of peer support and professional treatment. Parent groups are led by a parent and facilitated by a mental health professional. All professional facilitators volunteer their time to help the group function effectively. Leadership responsibility rests with a member selected by the group to serve as chapter chairperson.

Evaluations have demonstrated the success of Parents Anonymous in reducing both frequency and severity of physical, verbal and emotional abuse. The longer parents participate in the program the more lasting the improvement.

Because it relies heavily on volunteers PA is considered to be one of the most cost-effective means of preventing child abuse. Costs of operating national and regional offices, the hotline and other services are funded through grants and donations.

Parents Anonymous was founded in 1971 as a private, not-for-profit corporation "dedicated to the identification, treatment and prevention of child abuse." The group works with families through "peer led professionally facilitated self help groups" in the interest of preventing child abuse and avoiding placement of children. PA also operates toll-free crisis hotlines and referral telephones, offering telephone counseling and referral to adults and children. For more information, contact: Parents Anonymous, 675 West Foothill Blvd., Suite 220, Claremont, CA 91711. Tel. (909) 621-6184. Web site: www.parentsanonymous-natl.org

Parents Anonymous buddy   *See* PA BUDDY.

parents' rights   Legal rights of parents often come into conflict with those of children and the state during the course of INVESTIGATION or treatment of child abuse or neglect. Parents have the right to custody and supervision of children and to make decisions on behalf of a child under the legally established age of majority.

In the United States, the balance between rights of parents and those of the state has been defined in several court cases. *PRINCE V. MASSACHUSETTS* limited a parent's discretion in requiring or allowing a child to work. *Wisconsin v. Yoder* confirmed the right of Amish parents to educate children at home rather than send them to secondary school. Other decisions have allowed parents to withhold permission for nonessential medical treatment for religious reasons, established parents' right to use reasonable physical force in disciplining children and have denied parents the right to prevent school officials from using CORPORAL PUNISHMENT on their child.

Parents' rights are frequently at issue when a government agency seeks to remove a child from parental custody. Most states require an agency to provide clear and convincing evidence that a child is at risk before parental custody can be terminated. Concern over the legal rights of parents has led many child protection agencies to seek alternatives to removal of children from parental custody.

In the United States a group of parents and professionals calling themselves Victims of Child Abuse Laws (VOCAL) has formed to promote parents' rights and to combat what they believe are overzealous attempts to protect children.

While some countries do not operate according to a concept of individual rights, most have laws pertaining to a parent's role. In SWEDEN, for example, parents are not allowed to use physical force in disciplining their children. (*See also* TERMINATION OF PARENTAL RIGHTS.)

parents' rights, termination of   *See* TERMINATION OF PARENTAL RIGHTS.

Parents United   A self-help group for families of sexually abused children, Parents United began in Santa Clara, California in 1972. The organization now has many chapters in the United States and Canada. Parents United also promotes Daughters and Sons United (DSU), a self-help group for sexually abused children, and Adults Molested As Children (AMACU), a self-help organization for men and women who were victims of child sexual abuse.

Parents United groups meet weekly but members may contact their sponsor, an experienced group member assigned to them, at any time. The groups were designed to function as a part of a Child Sexual Abuse Treatment Program (CSATP). The CSATP model, developed by Henry and Anna

Giarretto, combines professional counseling with crisis intervention and long-term support provided by PU members.

Parents United also sponsors educational conferences for members and professionals and publishes a bimonthly newsletter, the *PUN*.

For more information on Parents United, Daughters and Sons United, and Adults Molested as Children, *see* APPENDIX 1.

parricide, reactive   A rare and extreme reaction to child abuse is murder of the abusive parent by the victim. Parricide accounts for approximately 1% of all murders.

Most children maintain a strong, albeit conflicted, attachment to the parent even in the face of repeated abuse. Profiles of children who murder an abusive parent or parents generally show that these children have no significant history of violent behavior. In most cases there is a long history of abuse. Murders usually occur shortly after, or during, an abusive episode. Handguns or rifles are the most frequent murder weapons.

Little is known about the reasons for reactive parricide. Theorists disagree as to the motivation of children who kill their parents. Some attribute the phenomenon to a preference for violent behavior learned from the parents themselves. Others believe these murders to be the desperate reaction of extreme rage committed by a child who feels powerless.

Eli Newberger and Richard Bourne, eds., *Unhappy Families* (Flushing, N.Y.: PSG Publishing Co., 1985).

passive abuser   Child abuse can include other perpetrators, in addition to the person who actually beats or otherwise abuses the victim. It also includes the parent or caretaker who stands by and fails to take action to protect the child from abuse. Termed a passive abuser, this person is also responsible for the abuse and may face legal charges.

patria potestas   According to the terms of this early Roman law, a father had full and absolute power over his children. Historically, this legal power originally included INFANTICIDE, but that was gradually eliminated from the law.

patricide The murder of one's father is termed patricide. In 1985, 209 fathers in the United States were murdered by one of their children. Patricide accounted for about three-fourths of 1% of all homicides. Case studies suggest a strong connection between child abuse and patricide.

Fathers who are murdered by a son tend to be cruel, dominant, critical and competitive with them. Mothers are often passive, sometimes dependent, sometimes overprotective of the son. Fathers frequently display jealousy of the son's attachment to the mother. In many cases the father is physically abusive to the mother in the presence of the son. The son, unable to gain the father's approval, becomes the mother's protector. Patricide usually occurs during or shortly following an episode in which the father abused a family member. Murder of a parent by a daughter is rare.

pederasty Anal intercourse between an adult male and a boy (usually between the ages of 12 and 16 years) is known as pederasty. Men who engage in this practice are known pederasts. Though others may label the pederast as homosexual this may be a misnomer. Many pederasts also have sexual relations with women and are often repelled by the thought of intercourse with other adult males. Likewise it is improper to assume that homosexuals are pederasts. Most homosexuals are not pederasts and strongly disavow the practice.

The term pederasty is derived from the Greek roots *ped*, meaning boy, and *erastes*, meaning lover. Originally the word had much the same meaning as pedophile and the two words are sometimes used interchangeably. (*See also* PEDOPHILIA.)

pedophilia Pedophilia refers to a sexual preference for children. Specifically, the pedophile is an adult who is sexually attracted to children who have not yet reached the age of puberty. Sexual attraction of an adult for an adolescent is known as HEBEPHILIA. Definitions notwithstanding, the term pedophile is often used to refer to any adult who is sexually attracted to someone below the legal age of consent.

True pedophiles are exclusively attracted to sexually immature children and have little to do with adolescents who are more sexually developed.

Most pedophiles are not violent toward children and may go to great lengths to gain the child's confidence before attempting a sexual act. In some cases a pedophile's desires may be confined to fantasy and not manifested in overt sexual molestation of children.

Not all sexual molestation of children is perpetrated by pedophiles. Children are often victims of sexual assaults simply because they are less able to defend themselves.

Pedophiles frequently develop a great deal of skill in meeting children and developing their trust. Formal and informal networks of child molesters are often used to share information on individual children or sites where it is easy to meet children. Some organizations such as the North American Man/Boy Love Association in the United States and the British Pedofile Information Exchange claim large memberships and actively support the practice of pedophilia. Some pedophiles choose a job such as teaching or managing a video arcade that will bring them into contact with children. Others may volunteer to coach a children's team, serve as a scout leader, baby-sitter or in a similar capacity. The pedophile is often known to the parents and may seek to gain their trust as well as the child's.

Pornography and prostitution also play an important role in pedophilia. Pedophiles are, of course, the primary purchasers of child pornography. They are also frequently the suppliers of such material, often exchanging material among themselves. Children are in great demand as prostitutes. Though many countries impose strict penalties for engaging in sex with a minor, some travel agencies have organized sex tours to countries where laws are less stringent and child prostitutes more plentiful. (*See also* FIXATED OFFENDERS.)

People's Republic of China Although there has been little, if any, formal investigation into child abuse and neglect in China, existing evidence suggests that there is little abusive behavior toward children there. Western observers have remarked on child-rearing practices that follow a much different pattern than in most other nations of the world. Some of these practices reflect prevailing beliefs about the state's responsibility toward providing for children's needs. Other behaviors and attitudes are tied closely to the notion that the individual is less important than society as a group.

Physical punishment of children in China is not condoned, although it does occur; it is not permitted in schools. Because of extensive government-sponsored health care that begins during the preschool years (before age seven), it is considered unlikely that a child could be physically abused and have it go undetected.

Chinese children do, however, experience ABANDONMENT, primarily because of China's one-child per family policy, which is usually strictly enforced, particularly in urban areas. Most Chinese families want sons, and if they bear a female child, they may abandon the child to a hospital or orphanage so that they can attempt to have a male child. Abandonment is illegal, but in most cases, officials take no action against parents.

In the 1990s, the Chinese government began to allow individuals from other countries to adopt Chinese infants and children. China subsequently became a very popular source for children for Americans, Canadians and other prospective adoptive parents.

Researchers studied the birth parents of the abandoned children and found that, in contrast to American birth parents (individuals whose children are adopted), the overwhelming majority of the Chinese birth parents were married: only 3 of 237 were not married. Most of the birth parents were also in their mid to late 20s or 30s and had an education equivalent to other people in the area.

According to an article in *Population and Development Review* on abandoned Chinese infants, in about 50% of cases, the biological father of the child decided that the child would be abandoned. Both birth parents made the decision together in about 40% of the cases. Nearly all of the abandoned children were healthy, although the few abandoned male infants were disabled or sick.

Kay Johnson, et al., "Infant Adoption and Abandonment in China," *Population and Development Review* 24, no. 3 (Sept. 1998).

periostitis   Inflammation of the periosteum (the fibrous membrane covering bones) is periostitis. Presence of periostitis in a child is evidence of physical trauma. Twisting of a limb or a blow directly to the bone can tear the periosteum away from the bone, causing blood to collect in the newly created cavity. Periostitis is not immediately detectable on an X ray but begins to appear as new bone forms in the affected area. (*See also* RADIOLOGY, PEDIATRIC and BATTERED CHILD SYNDROME.)

perjury   False testimony under oath, given with the knowledge that it is untrue, constitutes the crime of perjury. In child abuse trials perjury is most often a concern with the testimony given by adults. Groups representing divorced parents express concern that false accusations of SEXUAL ABUSE are increasingly used as a tactic in bitter custody disputes. Proving sexual abuse of young children often depends on the testimony of adults close to the alleged victim. Even when no corroborating evidence is found, it is often difficult to prove that a witness intended to deceive the court.

Young children may become confused and may be more susceptible to coercion than adult witnesses. However, many experts believe that perjury is rarely an issue when children testify concerning their own abuse. Controversy over the reliability of young children's testimony continues to build as more and more courts allow children to testify. (*See also* TESTIMONY.)

petechiae   Very small bruises, caused by broken capillaries, are called petechiae. (*See also* BRUISES.)

petition   A petition filed in juvenile or family court serves a purpose similar to that of an INDICTMENT in a criminal court. Sometimes referred to as a COMPLAINT, the petition spells out specific conditions that give rise to charges of abuse or neglect as well as the time, date and place where each event was observed. Filing a written petition is the first step in initiating court action. The petition serves as a formal notice of charges to the alleged abuser.

In most jurisdictions the petitioner is the child protection worker; however, law enforcement officers and physicians may file a petition. A few states allow anyone to file child abuse or neglect petition.

Child protection workers usually do not file a petition until after an initial INVESTIGATION has been conducted and the report is considered to be founded. FOUNDED REPORTS do not necessarily result in a petition. If the child protection worker believes parents will comply voluntarily with recommendations, or that the conditions that precipitated maltreatment no longer exist, it is unlikely that a petition will be filed. Civil court intervention is usually initiated for the purpose of ensuring compliance with recommendations and/or removing a child from home.

Before filing a petition the child protection agency, usually in consultation with an attorney, may attempt to determine whether: (1) there is sufficient admissible evidence to obtain a favorable judgment; (2) whether the complainants, witnesses and victim are available for trial; (3) whether the witnesses are credible; and (4) whether there is physical evidence to support the charges. Child protection workers must also consider the probable effects of a trial on the victim and his or her family.

physical abuse   This is an act of commission by a parent or caretaker which is not accidental and which results in physical injury, including fractures, burns, bruises, welts, cuts and/or internal injuries. States in the U.S. vary in how they define abuse and in whether abuse is covered in a separate child abuse statute. In many states, the degree of harm that has been inflicted is a factor in the level of abuse. In addition, in some states, even if a parent does not abuse a child, the law addresses the failure of the parent to protect the child from known maltreatment. Sometimes the age of the child also is a factor in determining the category of felony that the perpetrator will be charged with.

According to statistics for 1997 (reported in 1999), physical abuse represented 24.6% of all types of abuse cases. (See CHARACTERISTICS OF ABUSERS for more information on the perpetrators of physical abuse.)

It is hard to convey the agony of physical abuse in an essay, but perhaps the following excerpt from *Nobody's Children*, a book by attorney and author Elizabeth Bartholet, can put a human face on this issue.

Loving foster parents, relatives, Cook County's Public Guardian, and the mother's own psychiatrist had testified to the dangers of returning Joseph Wallace to the mother who had been institutionalized for mental problems repeatedly since her own childhood, had threatened to kill Joseph, his infant brother and herself, had beaten her children in the past, and had repeatedly mutilated herself and tried to burn herself. The State Division of Child Protection had warned that she might maim or kill him. But Joseph was returned by a judge who believed in family preservation and said he felt governed by state and federal law requirements after a court hearing in which lawyers and social workers argued for the mother's parental rights. Two months after Joseph's return his mother tied an electric cord around the three-year-old boy's neck and to a door transom, gagged him, watched him wave good-bye, and then pulled the chair out from under his feet.

This above example is not provided to imply in any way that mentally ill people are murderous or that they are more prone to be abusive to their children than others. The reality is quite the contrary: most severely mentally ill people are more likely to be victims than victimizers. Instead, the anecdote is provided to show that, even in egregious and extreme situations, sometimes agencies that should protect children will completely fail them. Many others have written movingly about child abuse victims, including child welfare advocate Richard Gelles, a former proponent of FAMILY PRESERVATION who became disillusioned with the concept and subsequently wrote *The Book of David: How Preserving Families Can Cost Children's Lives.*

Do Social Workers Sometimes Overreact?

Occasionally child welfare workers err by removing children from families that are not abusive, based on little or no evidence. This may happen in the wake of community furor over the death of a child who should have been removed from the family; workers subsequently decide not to make such an error and instead err on the other end of the scale.

The furor of unproven physical and sexual abuse charges against day care centers in the mid-1980s was later seen as a witch-hunt by many in the legal and medical community. Sometimes workers err in the eyes of their own court system: in 1999, a Massachusetts minister and father had been charged with child abuse for admittedly spanking his son with a strap. The Massachusetts Supreme Judicial Court held that it was his right to discipline his child. The court added, "Today, we conclude only that, on the totality of the record presented in this case, the effects of the plaintiff's physical discipline on his minor child did not satisfy the department's own regulatory definitions of physical injury and abuse. However, a method of corporal punishment similar to the plaintiff's could, in different circumstances, rise to a level of severity that would result in the actual infliction of impermissible injuries."

Generally, however, physical abuse can be identified and documented by trained physicians. Sometimes medical expertise is not even necessary, however. When a parent punishes a toddler by sitting her bare buttocks on a hot oven and holding her there, to the extent that she has permanent burn marks on her buttocks, it is evident to virtually everyone that this is physical abuse. (This is a true case.) When a child is cut or wounded in some other way, it is clearly physical abuse.

Reasons for Physical Abuse

Experts endlessly debate reasons why parents abuse their children. Some believe that abusive parents feel caught in a negative spiral of poverty and hopelessness. Parents may be frustrated and angry about their own life's situations and allow the anger to boil over onto their children. Another possibility is ignorance; for example, some young parents may have little knowledge about child development. It may seem reasonable to a 14-year-old girl to spank a one-year-old child for wetting her pants if she does not realize most children are not toilet trained until they are two or three years old.

Sometimes the violence escalates beyond what the perpetrator intended and the act of hitting seems to make the abuser more violent and angry. Many abusers have said that they "lost it" and did not mean to harm the child as severely as they did.

Substance abuse is another major problem. If the parent is intoxicated on drugs or alcohol, the normal inhibitions are gone and negative impulses may take over. Mental illness can also be a causal factor. One woman was repeatedly abused as a child by her mother, who thought she was the "spawn of Satan."

The problem could stem from physical abuse that was experienced by the adult when he or she was a child. The adult may see such abuse as acceptable behavior, despite information conveyed in the culture that it is not acceptable.

Although most people do not like to think about it, there are also some parents who exhibit sadistic tendencies and who will expose their children to severe and unspeakable injuries.

Throughout history children have been subject to all types of physical abuse, from beatings to INFANTICIDE. The maxim "spare the rod and spoil the child" continues to serve as a guide to child rearing for many parents. With the exception of some Scandinavian countries physical punishment is a legal and accepted form of parental discipline around the world. However, if the punishment is severe enough to cause lasting marks, such punishment crosses the line into abuse.

Despite its widespread acceptance, most countries attempt to place limits on physical punishment. Some experts think of abuse as a continuum beginning with mild forms of physical discipline such as light spanking and ranging all the way to severe beating and murder. The definition above implies physical punishment is permissible as long as no permanent or observable injury results. In Denmark all forms of corporal punishment are outlawed.

Recognition of physical abuse has increased substantially since the early 1960s. C. Henry Kempe's efforts called the attention of physicians and others to the BATTERED CHILD SYNDROME. Advances in pediatric radiology made it possible to detect patterns of bone trauma that tended to conflict with caretakers' explanations of accidental injury. Child abuse reporting laws now require a wide range of professionals to report all forms of suspected abuse. In at least one case, LANDEROS V. FLOOD, physicians have been held liable for civil penalties for failure to report abuse. Still, cases of physical abuse are sometimes overlooked.

When a child is brought for medical treatment, the caretaker's account of the injury can alert the examining physician to the possibility of abuse. An unexplained injury, e.g., "I just found him this way," is sometimes an attempt to deny abuse. Explanations that do not seem plausible also merit further investigation. Allegedly self-inflicted injuries of young children may be suspicious in origin. Often children will readily state that an adult caused the injury. Experts believe children rarely lie about such matters.

Most parents bring their children to a physician or hospital immediately after an injury. Abusive parents often delay seeking medical attention for their child, hoping the child will not need treatment. Often the person who brings the child for treatment is not the person who was with the child at the time of injury. If the abusive parent does bring in the child, the story he or she relates about the cause of the injury is often not credible to a doctor or sometimes even to nonmedical personnel.

Pediatrician Barton Schmitt recommends the following steps be followed by physicians in evaluating possible child abuse.

1. Take a complete history of the injury.
2. Perform a complete physical examination, including mouth, eardrums and genitals, noting signs of physical trauma and the approximate age of bruises and other injuries.
3. Order a SKELETAL SURVEY.
4. Order LABORATORY TESTS to determine clotting time.
5. Take color photographs of injuries for later documentation.
6. Examine siblings for signs of possible abuse.
7. Write a complete medical report.
8. Observe and record the child's behavior.
9 Conduct a developmental screening.

Physical abuse can take many different forms and can result in a number of different injuries. Internal trauma such as SUBDURAL HEMATOMA or ABDOMINAL INJURIES, though serious, are not immediately apparent. For a more detailed description of injuries resulting from physical abuse, *see* ALOPECIA, TRAUMATIC; BATTERED CHILD SYNDROME; BITING; BRUISES; BURNS; CENTRAL NERVOUS SYSTEM INJURIES; CORD INJURIES; EYE INJURIES; FRACTURES; MOUTH INJURIES; MUNCHAUSEN SYNDROME BY PROXY; POISONING; and SHAKEN INFANT SYNDROME.

Elizabeth Bartholet, *Nobody's Children: Abuse and Neglect, Foster Drift, and the Adoption Alternative* (New York: Beacon Press, 1999.)
Richard Gelles, *The Book of David: How Preserving Families Can Cost Children's Lives.* (New York: HarperCollins, 1997).
Barton D. Schmitt, in C. Henry Kempe and Ray E. Helfer, eds., *The Battered Child,* 3rd ed. (Chicago: University of Chicago Press, 1980).
David G. Gil, *Violence Against Children* (Cambridge, Mass.: Harvard University Press, 1973).
C. Henry Kempe and Ray E. Helfer, eds., *The Battered Child,* 3rd ed. (Chicago: University of Chicago Press, 1980).

place of safety order Under provisions of the Children and Young Persons Act of 1969, anyone in BRITAIN can apply for an order to remove a child from a dangerous place. The emergency order, known as a place of safety order, may be issued by a magistrate at any time. Magistrates can authorize applicants to take custody of the child for a period not to exceed 28 days.

Applicants for such an order do not have to prove abuse or neglect; however, the magistrate must have reasonable cause to believe that: (1) the child's proper development is being avoidably prevented or neglected; (2) his or her health is being avoidably impaired or neglected; or (3) the child is being ill-treated.

A place of safety order may also be used to prevent removal of a child from a safe place. Siblings of the identified child are also covered by the order. Children may be taken without parents' knowledge, but applicants are expected to inform them as soon as possible after removal. Parents have little opportunity to appeal a place of safety order.

Place of safety orders are typically used in emergencies where a child is in immediate danger. Concern has been expressed by some experts that these orders are too easy to obtain, increasing the possibility of unnecessary removal.

placement of abused children Removal of maltreated children from their parents may be necessary to ensure proper treatment and to prevent further abuse. Governments base their authority to assume custody of a child on the doctrine of PARENS PATRIAE. Under this doctrine the state assumes a vital interest in ensuring the safety and welfare of children. However, many critics charge that the governments have overstepped this responsibility by removing children unnecessarily.

When a child is in immediate danger, law enforcement officials and, in most states, protective service agencies have authority to take EMERGENCY CUSTODY of the child. Prior approval of a court is not necessary in most areas; however, emergency placement decisions must be reviewed by a judge within 48 to 72 hours after the child is removed.

In BRITAIN, children can be removed from home for up to 28 days under a PLACE OF SAFETY ORDER. The order can be obtained by anyone but must be approved by a magistrate.

Placement decisions are difficult. Child protection authorities must balance possible benefits of removal against the inevitable trauma that will be experienced by both children and parents. *See also* ADOPTING ABUSED OR NEGLECTED CHILDREN; KINSHIP CARE.

poisoning   Abuse-related poisoning of children is relatively rare; however, a significant number of accidental poisonings are a result of parental NEGLECT of normal safety precautions.

Deliberate poisoning of children may be due to a disturbed parent's impulsive act or desire to get revenge. More frequently, intentional poisoning involves a drug overdose, ostensibly for the purpose of quieting an upset child.

Failure of caretakers to exercise adequate safety precautions is more often a cause of child poisoning than deliberate acts. Specifically, improper storage of chemicals and medications significantly increases the likelihood of accidental poisoning. Multiple accidental poisonings occur most often in households characterized by high levels of stress, including illness, recent death of a family member, marital discord and parental drug or alcohol abuse. Children whose caretakers abuse alcohol or drugs are particularly at risk. The easy accessibility of these substances increases the risk of accidental ingestion. Substance abusers also have a diminished capacity to provide adequate care and are frequently neglectful.

Poison centers offer immediate telephone consultation in the event of poisoning. There are over 650 such centers in the United States. Telephone numbers of nearby centers are usually listed under emergency numbers at the front of most telephone directories. In addition to providing lifesaving emergency advice these centers can be especially helpful in identifying victims of repetitive poisoning (approximately one-fourth of all poisonings).

polymorphic perverse offender   Sexual offenders are sometimes classified according to the type of victim and/or sexual acts they prefer. PEDOPHILES, for example, direct their sexual feelings and actions primarily (in many cases exclusively) toward children. Most rapists attack only female victims. However, some sexual offenders appear to be indiscriminate in their choice of victims or sexual acts. They may be described as polymorphic perverse offenders.

This description follows a classification used by Sigmund Freud to describe indiscriminate sexuality. Freud coined the term polymorphous perversity to describe the behavior of individuals who had been seduced as children.

As currently used, the term refers to sex offenders who engage in many different forms of sexual assault (i.e., vaginal rape, sodomy, exhibitionism) and who may attack people of any age. This type of offender accounts for a very small percentage of all child SEXUAL ABUSE.

Polynesia   As a cultural area, Polynesia comprises numerous islands scattered throughout a portion of the Pacific Ocean. Although their urban areas and most towns are now considered in large part Western in culture and practice, Hawaii, Samoa and New Zealand are among those islands that were traditionally included in Polynesian culture.

Over the last five decades, research conducted into child-rearing practices in both traditional and transitional Polynesian society has enabled observers to make some assessments concerning the incidence of child abuse. Insofar as it has been possible to judge, traditional Polynesian culture does not support abusive behavior toward children; in fact, Polynesian kinship structure, with its concept of collective family, promotes a degree of affection and warmth among all adults for all children seldom found elsewhere. According to informed observers, it is fairly clear that there has never been the tendency toward aggressive or neglectful child-rearing behaviors on any level of the traditional Polynesian culture. Although INFANTICIDE had been acceptable (and encouraged) during earlier times, studies indicate that it was practiced only as a way of maintaining optimum population levels and preserving existing life.

All adults in Polynesian villages are viewed as parents by all children. Living arrangements encourage a casual, relaxed attitude toward small children, who are not expected to maintain any particular standards of behavior until they are about two years old. At that time they are considered ready to join the circle of children somewhat older than they are, to learn appropriate social behavior from peers and siblings, as well as from adults. At this time, children begin to be disciplined, to learn independence (which is a highly valued trait) and to mature to the point that they will be able to join the circle of adults when they reach maturity. The latter occurs when girls begin menstruation and when boys are ritually circumcised, usually at about age 15.

Studies show that when individuals from traditional Polynesian villages move to urban and suburban settings, the strong cultural patterns that have served to prevent child abuse are no longer maintained in the same way.

pornography, child   *See* CHILD PORNOGRAPHY.

post-traumatic hypopituitarism   *See* DWARFISM.

poverty   Although child abuse and neglect has been described as a classless phenomenon by numerous writers, researchers and clinicians, the problem of child abuse is most evident among the poor, particularly when there is a problem of substance or drug abuse. While it is true that abuse and neglect can be found in every socioeconomic stratum, statistics show that a disproportionate number of reported cases of abuse and neglect involve low-income families. Studies have shown that poverty status is strongly related to neglect. Poor children are also highly represented among victims of more serious forms of abuse.

It has been argued that low-income families are more likely to be investigated and reported on than middle- and upper-income families. Suggestions have been made that if higher income families were subjected to the same scrutiny, an equal amount of abuse would be found. To date no significant evidence has been presented to support this position. In fact, a comprehensive analysis of possible bias was provided in a 1998 issue of the *American Journal of Orthopsychiatry,* and the researchers found no grounds for such bias. Indeed, they stated their concern that the "myth of classlessness" in child abuse maltreatment acts or could act to prevent poor families and their children from receiving assistance from social service authorities. The authors wrote:

> We can no longer afford to cling to untenable positions regarding the equitable distribution of risk to children across class boundaries. We must concentrate our efforts in those areas in which the problems are most severe, and we must devise tools for working with poor families that address the special concerns, problems, and stresses they face. Ultimately, the close association between poverty and child maltreatment suggests that the most effective way to prevent child abuse will be to reduce the number of families in poverty. If child maltreatment is born largely of the stresses and wants associated with being poor, then primary prevention efforts might best target the underlying political, social, and economic structure that perpetuate poverty.

A Global Look at Poverty and Abuse

Cross-cultural evidence from Western and Eastern societies also supports the assertion that poverty and child abuse are related. Anthropological studies from New Guinea, Africa, Turkey and South America all have documented the increased risks to children raised in poverty.

The mere existence of poverty has been labeled as a form of societal abuse. Poor children who are denied the basic elements necessary for healthy development suffer many of the same consequences as those from whom these elements are intentionally withheld. Social policy researchers David Gil, Leroy Pelton and others have argued that attributing abuse and neglect to individual or family pathology masks true societal causes of the phenomenon. Further, the individual, as opposed to societal, view of child abuse is seen as a means of promoting certain professional and political interests at the expense of a more lasting solution.

High Stress Levels Contribute to Problem

Increased stress is often given as the reason for the association between poverty and abuse. Families with severely restricted incomes are constantly faced with difficult choices and may suffer from inadequate housing, poor health care and malnourishment. Such conditions are seen as neglectful and may contribute to physical, emotional or sexual abuse.

Not All Poor People Are Abusers

Despite its obvious contributions to increased stress and poor living conditions, poverty is by no means synonymous with abuse or neglect as statutorily defined. Only a relatively small proportion of children living in impoverished families are reported to child protection agencies. Parents of such children, through skill, determination and luck, are frequently able to overcome the burdens of poverty. It is clear, however, that poverty places children at significant risk.

Brett Drake and Susan Zuravin, "Bias in Child Maltreatment Reporting: Revisiting the Myth of Classlessness," *American Journal of Orthopsychiatry* 68, no. 2 (April 1998): 295–304.
Michael B. Katz, *Poverty and Policy in American History* (New York: Academic Press, 1983).
——, *In the Shadow of the Poorhouse* (New York: Basic Books, 1986).
Leroy H. Pelton, *The Social Context of Child Abuse and Neglect* (New York: Human Sciences Press, 1981).
——, "Child Abuse and Neglect: The Myth of Classlessness," *American Journal of Orthopsychiatry* 48 (October 1978): 607–617.

prediction of abuse and neglect Several researchers have attempted to develop screening tests that will predict the likelihood of abuse. Various methods used include pencil and paper questionnaires, standardized interviews and direct observation of parent-child interaction. Presently, all screening is voluntary. High-risk groups such as teenaged parents are most often targeted for screening; however, some hospital programs have attempted to screen all parents of newborns.

Many tests focus on parental characteristics such as emotional deprivation, history of abuse as a child and intelligence. Others examine characteristics of the child. Studies indicate that developmental disabilities, irritability and other traits increase the likelihood that a child will be abused. Several screening devices attempt to measure stress factors, such as POVERTY and SOCIAL ISOLATION. Some researchers attempt to measure the quality of interaction between parent and child. Finally, various attempts have been made to combine these approaches.

To date no completely accurate screening method has been developed. Experts caution that although screening may be useful in targeting prevention efforts, it should not be considered a diagnostic tool. Identification of people as potentially abusive does not mean they are in fact abusing a child. Parents cannot be forced to submit to screening tests nor can potentially abusive parents be required to accept help. Concern over PARENTS' RIGHTS has caused many practitioners to be very cautious in use and interpretation of various screening methods.

preponderance of the evidence *See* EVIDENTIARY STANDARDS.

presentment In some situations, usually an emergency, a grand jury may issue a written accusation of a crime without having received a COMPLAINT from a prosecutor. This document is the equivalent of an INDICTMENT.

Prevent Child Abuse Founded in 1972, this volunteer-based organization is concerned with preventing all forms of child abuse and provides public awareness campaigns, advocacy and research as well as statistics on child abuse. For more information, contact: Prevent Child Abuse, 200 S. Michigan Ave., Suite 170, Chicago, IL. 66064. Tel. (312) 663-5520. Web site: www.childabuse.org

prevention Efforts to prevent child abuse and neglect are often classified as either primary or secondary. Primary prevention seeks to protect children from maltreatment before it occurs. This approach may be directed at the general public or at specially targeted high-risk families. Secondary prevention attempts to prevent the recurrence of maltreatment or to keep a potentially abusive situation from getting worse. Subjects of secondary prevention are usually identified through reports of suspected abuse or neglect.

Prevention can take many different forms. Methods frequently used in *primary prevention* include hospital-based neonatal programs that promote mother-infant bonding, home visitors (also called home HEALTH VISITORS or PARENT AIDES), parent education and counseling programs. Most such programs are directed at parents and operate from the premise that by learning more about child rearing they will be less likely to abuse or neglect their children. SEXUAL ABUSE prevention usually directed at children often takes the form of school-based programs that use books, films, plays and puppetry to inform children about the dangers of sexual abuse and ways in which they might protect themselves.

Secondary prevention often involves the entire family in some form of counseling, behavior modification or treatment. Intervention is usually targeted to specific family problems, such as a parent's ways of disciplining children or stress management, that are thought to underly the abuse.

Michael Wald and Sophia Cohen, in a review of prevention efforts published in the *Family Law Quarterly,* identified four problems that must be addressed in developing successful prevention programs. First, abuse must be clearly defined. There is much disagreement as to what sorts of situations constitute abuse or neglect. Programs must have a clear definitions of the type(s) of behavior they wish to prevent if they are to be successful. Second, some understanding of the causes of abuse and neglect is necessary. Causes are often complex and poorly understood. Third, prevention strategies should be directed where they will do the most good. Most primary prevention efforts are too costly to allow inefficient use. Fourth, there is little accurate information about the effectiveness of various prevention techniques. Prevention of child abuse and neglect is a relatively new field. Adequate evaluation of programs would require large, carefully designed studies.

Treatment after confirmation of child abuse or neglect is sometimes referred to as *tertiary prevention.*

Michael S. Wald and Sophia Cohen, "Preventing Child Abuse—What Will It Take," *Family Law Quarterly* 20, no. 2 (Summer 1986): 281–302.

prevention, primary   *See* PREVENTION.

prevention, secondary   *See* PREVENTION.

prevention, tertiary   *See* PREVENTION.

Prevention of Cruelty to and Protection of Children Act of 1889 (Britain)   As a direct result of actions taken by the National Society for the Prevention of Cruelty to Children (NSPCC), in 1889 the British Parliament enacted a law that established penalties for the ill-treatment and neglect of children. The act was amended in 1894 and again in 1904. In cases where neglect or abuse of a child

meant the parent or guardian could benefit financially from a child's life insurance policy, legal penalties were increased.

prima facie   Literally, this means "at first sight." Prima facie evidence is that which is sufficiently strong to prove the allegations in a case of suspected child abuse or neglect. It is considered proof of the suspected charges; however, this evidence is only considered proof in the absence of contradictory or rebutting evidence.

In virtually all states, admissible evidence in a child abuse or neglect case must fall within one of the two following standards of proof. Either clear and convincing evidence must be presented or a preponderance of the evidence must fall in favor of either the plaintiff or the defendant. Prima facie evidence could come under either of these two standards. (*See also* EVIDENTIARY STANDARDS.)

primary prevention   *See* PREVENTION.

Prince v. Massachusetts   In 1944, a landmark United States Supreme Court case determined that "the custody, care, and nurture of the child resides first in the parents, whose primary function and freedom include preparation for obligations that the state can neither supply nor hinder." However, the court went on to say that, in some cases, the state has an overriding interest in protecting children.

This decision involved a child whose aunt permitted her to sell religious literature on the streetcorner. At legal issue in the case was the charge that parents, guardians or custodians are not free to make martyrs of their children. Sarah Prince, a Jehovah's Witness, was charged with violating Massachusetts's child labor laws by having her nine-year-old niece, of whom she had custody, sell copies of *Watchtower* and *Consolation* on the street. The court affirmed Prince's conviction by a lower court. Its assertion that "the power of the state to control the conduct of children reaches beyond the scope of its authority over adults" affirmed the state's right to intervene against the wishes of parents and children when necessary for a child's protection.

The findings in *Prince v. Massachusetts* provided the basis for subsequent judicial rulings in which the rights of other individuals (i.e., parents) or groups (i.e., schools) take precedence over those of children. (*See also* WISCONSIN V. YODER; TINKER V. DES MOINES.)

Robert H. Mnookin, *Child, Family and State: Problems and Materials on Children and the Law* (Boston: Little, Brown and Company, 1978).

prisons, child victimizers in A 1996 report from the Office of Juvenile Justice and Delinquency Prevention provided a wealth of information about prison inmates who were imprisoned as violent child victimizers. Prisoners had committed such crimes as homicide, kidnapping, rape and sexual assault and other abuses. Researchers surveyed inmates in state prisons who had been convicted of violent crimes and found that 61,000, or about 19% of all state prisoners, had been convicted of a crime against a victim under the age of 18. More than half of the violent crimes were perpetrated against a child under the age of 12. About 70% of the child victimizers in prison were in jail for a rape or sexual assault against a child.

General Characteristics of Imprisoned Child Victimizers

Researchers found that 97% of the offenders were male. Nearly a third had never been arrested before. About 19% of the offenders had been convicted of prior acts such as statutory rape, child abuse or lewd acts with a child. Most did not carry a weapon; only 14% were armed. About a third had committed their crimes against their own child and approximately half had some other relationship with the child such as a friend, relative or acquaintance. Most of the violent victimizations (75%) occurred in either the victim's home or the victimizer's home.

Demographic Characteristics

The majority of the violent child offenders, about 70%, were white. Most, or 78%, had been employed in the month before they were arrested. Their marital status varied: about 37% had never married, 33% were divorced and 23% were married. The others were widowed or separated. The mean age for child victimizers was 33 years.

The educational status of the child victimizers varied. The majority of offenders, about 55%, had less than a high school education; however, about 27% were high school graduates and about 18% were college graduates.

Background as a Child

The majority of the offenders (54%) grew up with both parents and only about 17% had ever spent time in a foster home or institution. Most (69%) said their parents or guardians did not abuse drugs or alcohol. Most (64%) said their immediate family members had never served any jail time.

Most of the offenders (69%) said they had never been physically or sexually abused. Of the ones who reported abuse as a child, most knew their abuser, who was usually a parent or guardian or other relative or acquaintance.

Drug Use

Most of the violent child offenders (57%) said they were not abusing drugs or alcohol at the time of the crime. About 24% were using alcohol and about 5% were using drugs only. About 14% were using both alcohol and drugs. Of those who were drinking at the time of the offense about 79% had been drinking for three or more hours.

Special Sentencing

Judges ordered special sentencing conditions in a greater percentage of cases of child victimizers than of adult victimizers. About 13% of the child victimizers were ordered to participate in a sex offender treatment program or to receive psychological or psychiatric counseling. Only about 2% of those who victimized an adult received such a special sentence. (*See also* CHARACTERISTICS OF ABUSING AND NEGLECTFUL PARENTS, CHILD MOLESTERS.)

Laurence A. Greenfeld, "Child Victimizers: Violent Offenders and Their Victims," U.S. Department of Justice, Office of Justice Programs, Bureau of Justice Statistics, 1996.

private zone Private zone is a term used in teaching young children how to identify and avoid sexual advances. Breasts, buttocks and genitalia (areas covered by a bathing suit) are all considered to be part of the private zone, which should not be touched by anyone other than the child. Obvious exceptions are made for situations such as examination by a physician or bathing by a parent or appropriate caretaker. In such instances, the quality of the touching is emphasized and the child is encouraged to use various means to avoid contact that makes them feel uncomfortable. Among other options, children are taught to call for help loudly and to run to a safe place nearby, such as a neighbor's house or a police station, for help. *Private Zone* is also the title of a read-aloud book for children written by Frances S. Dayee (New York: Warner Books, 1984).

privileged communications In many countries the patient or client may refuse to allow information revealed in a personal conference with his or her physician, pyschotherapist or lawyer to be presented in court. This legal protection is sometimes called the doctor-patient privilege. Child abuse reporting laws often override privileged communications in situations where the reporting of abuse or prosecution of an abuser might be inhibited. Most jurisdictions, however, continue to protect communications between lawyer and client. (*See also* CONFIDENTIALITY.)

probate court *See* COURT.

procedural due process *See* DUE PROCESS.

proceeding, civil *See* CIVIL PROCEEDING.

projection Psychodynamic explanations of abuse emphasize the abusing parent's reliance on projection as a mechanism for coping with stress. Projection can be described as a process whereby an individual ascribes his or her own feelings to another person. A parent may project feelings of self-hatred onto a child. The child then becomes a scapegoat for the parent's anger and low self-esteem.

Often a particular child becomes unconsciously associated with painful earlier events in the parent's life. The TARGET CHILD may be described as a monster or a demon, suggesting a symbolic association between the child and the parent's own uncontrollable rage. Externalizing feelings of self-hatred is a form of denial that prevents the parent from acknowledging and confronting these feelings. The parent's unconscious need to avoid confronting internal rage may be so strong that when the target child is removed from home another child becomes the object of projection.

Psychodynamic treatment of abusers often centers on helping them acknowledge and understand

their own feelings. If treatment is successful the abuser learns to differentiate between his or her own feelings and the child's behavior.

proof, burden *See* BURDEN OF PROOF.

proof, standards of *See* EVIDENTIARY STANDARDS.

property, children as *See* CHILDREN AS PROPERTY.

prosecution, criminal *See* CRIMINAL PROSECUTION.

prostitution, child *See* CHILD PROSTITUTION.

protection, order of *See* ORDER OF PROTECTION.

Protection of Children Against Sexual Exploitation Act of 1977 (P.L. 95-225) Enacted into law in February of 1978, this was the first piece of federal legislation in the United States to deal directly with CHILD PORNOGRAPHY. Prosecutors found it difficult to obtain convictions due to a provision that limited the law's application to pornographic material produced for commercial purposes. Most child pornographers were able to avoid prosecution by trading material rather than selling it.

In 1984 Congress deleted the commerciality requirement as well as a provision that required the material to be legally obscene. This amendment, known as the Child Protection Act of 1984, greatly increased the number of convictions for production and distribution of child pornography. In the two years following enactment of the Child Protection Act, 164 child pornographers were convicted compared to 64 convictions in the five-plus years preceding the amendment.

protective custody Physicians, social workers and certain other professionals often have the power to detain a child until a DETENTION request can be filed with the court. In some cases oral permission of a judge must be obtained before a child is held in protective custody. (*See also* EMERGENCIES, EMERGENCY CUSTODY.)

protective services This refers to assistance provided by the organization designated to help abused and neglected children. Vincent DeFrancis, a prominent figure in the United States' child protection movement and former director of the Children's Division of the American Humane Association (now the American Association for Protecting Children), defines protective services as:

> A specialized casework service to neglected, abused or exploited children. The focus of the services is preventive and non-punitive and is geared toward a rehabilitation of the home and a treatment of the motivating factors.

In the United States every state has a legally designated child protection agency. Each Canadian province provides for child protection services. In Britain child protection is the responsibility of LOCAL AUTHORITIES.

Child protective services are distinguished from other social services by their involuntary nature. Abused and neglected children are often too young or do not know how to ask for help. Few abusive parents request intervention from a protective services agency. Typically, clients are resistant and hostile toward protective service workers.

Protective service workers have legal authority to intervene against parents' wishes in order to determine whether a child is being abused or neglected. If evidence of abuse or neglect is found, the protective service agency may petition a court for additional powers to act on behalf of the child. When a child is in immediate danger of serious injury the child protective worker may be granted EMERGENCY CUSTODY powers.

Despite their legal authority, child protection services focus on rehabilitation rather than punishment. Though most parents initially resist help, protective service workers attempt to engage them in a cooperative effort to eliminate conditions that contributed to maltreatment of their children. If at all possible, protective service agencies try to keep children at home with their families.

Tasks of protective service workers can be divided into five categories: INVESTIGATION of complaints, diagnosis or ASSESSMENT of service needs, case planning, TREATMENT and case monitoring. Agencies often have separate units that perform investigatory and treatment-related functions respectively. In practice, the investigation phase often comprises a large proportion of protective services. Increased reporting of suspected abuse and neglect in the United States coupled with relatively stable funding has forced protective service agencies to shift resources away from treatment and prevention to investigation.

Experts believe that if the punitive arm of protective services were transferred to law enforcement, then families would be more likely to see child welfare workers as family advocates. They also believe this is a more logical choice and point out that a stranger would be arrested for the same kinds of abuse that a parent inflicts upon a child. If that same parent assaulted another child outside the family, then he or she would likely be arrested. In effect, the value of children within the family appears somehow diminished.

Part of the reason for this is that for many years, child welfare officials and social service agencies have believed that their therapeutic intervention could work, if only they had the right mix: enough money, caseworkers, or other resources. Yet clinical studies have revealed that even intensive efforts with groups that perform massive interventions with families, helping them shop, advising them on financial affairs, providing parenting tips, etc., fail to provide any better results.

Some individuals and organizations believe protective services should be privatized while others believe the function should remain state run and be expanded. Despite the difference in opinion, one point seems clear: few people are satisfied with the protective services system as it stands.

With the passage of the ADOPTION AND SAFE FAMILIES ACT in 1997, protective services workers were still encouraged to preserve families whenever possible, but the law also required states to consider terminating parental rights within a quicker time frame than before, if families could not be reunited. The child would then be adopted or remain in long-term foster care. In 1999, President Bill Clinton awarded $20 million in grants to states that increased the adoptions of children in foster care the most.

For a better understanding of the process whereby a child is reported as abused and enters

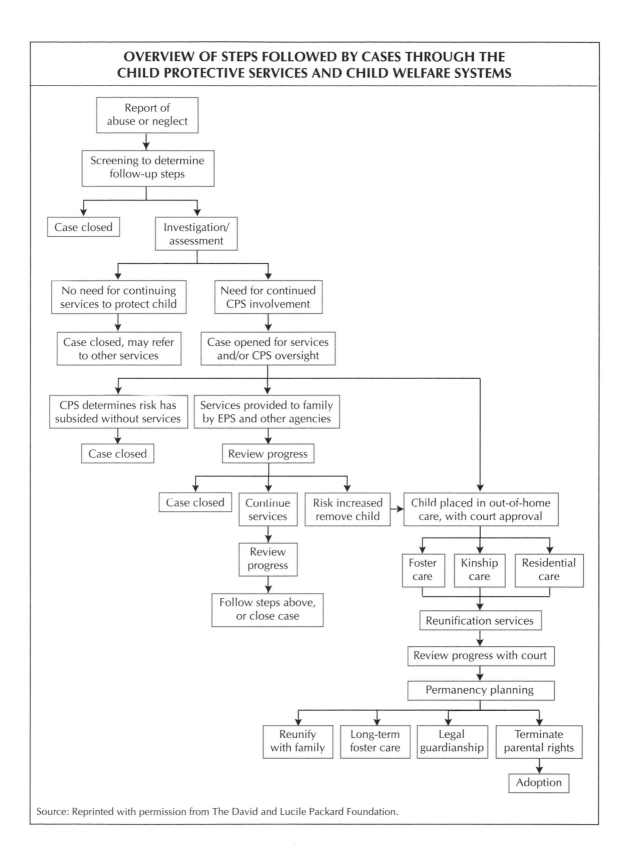

OVERVIEW OF STEPS FOLLOWED BY CASES THROUGH THE CHILD PROTECTIVE SERVICES AND CHILD WELFARE SYSTEMS

Report of abuse or neglect

Screening to determine follow-up steps

Case closed

Investigation/ assessment

No need for continuing services to protect child

Need for continued CPS involvement

Case closed, may refer to other services

Case opened for services and/or CPS oversight

CPS determines risk has subsided without services

Services provided to family by EPS and other agencies

Case closed

Review progress

Case closed

Continue services

Risk increased remove child

Child placed in out-of-home care, with court approval

Review progress

Foster care

Kinship care

Residential care

Follow steps above, or close case

Reunification services

Review progress with court

Permanency planning

Reunify with family

Long-term foster care

Legal guardianship

Terminate parental rights

Adoption

Source: Reprinted with permission from The David and Lucile Packard Foundation.

the system to the final outcome (return to parent, adoption, etc.), see the flowchart.

Problems Faced by Protective Services Units

Protective services units are plagued with high turnovers of staff and poor or no computer equipment, as well as low morale and low pay. A 1997 General Accounting Office (GAO) report studied protective services units in four states: California, Florida, Missouri and New York. They found significant problems with a lack of automated case management and heavy reliance on paper files. According to the report, New York City caseworkers and supervisors relied on "hand-written case information on 5"-by-8" cards for the current status of cases and their history. Retrieving data recorded from agency archives or transferring the files from one field office to another can take weeks and files can become lost, according to New York City caseworkers."

A 1999 GAO report on juvenile courts indicated that computers were seriously underused in the child welfare environment. It is therefore likely the record-keeping problem persists in many areas. The inability to find a file may seem trivial until it is revealed that such inability can cause a child to be returned to an abusive home because a social worker or judge does not have access to needed information.

Guilty Until Proven Innocent

Another problem with protective services units in general is that if a charge is made, it is up to the accused person to prove his or her innocence. Issues of due process and individual rights can be disregarded. In many cases, children who are severely abused are removed from their homes and thus, they are protected. In a few cases, the system is abused by overly zealous therapists and protective services workers. In one noted case in Wenatchee, Washington, a police detective, who was also a foster parent, arrested his foster child's biological parents after she had been with his family for six months. The allegations did not end there, however. The girl and her sister subsequently accused many others in the town of abuse.

According to Susan Orr, Ph.D., author of a study on child protection, current director of the Center for Social Policy at the Reason Public Policy Insti-

tute and former child welfare program specialist for the National Center on Child Abuse and Neglect (for which she oversaw the Third National Incidence Study on Child Abuse and Neglect),

> Many more children were taken from their families, interviewed, and after repeated questioning, spun elaborate, but similar, tales of satanic worship and sexual abuse eventually involving a minister, his wife, and their entire Pentecostal church. The children—sometimes members of the same family—who refused to corroborate the stories were diagnosed with post-traumatic stress disorder and placed in therapy, sometimes in out-of-state institutions. Anytime a member of the community (including the pastor) protested that the charges were fabricated, they found themselves charged in the conspiracy and had their children removed as well.

Orr also said, "Many of the children later recanted. But not before 43 adults—most of whom were desperately poor, unable to read, write, or afford good attorneys—were charged with 30,000 counts of rape involving 60 children. Not understanding what they were doing, some even signed confessions, fearing that unless they cooperated, they would never see their children again. Over a two-year period, ten were convicted while 18 pled to lesser felony charges."

According to Orr, a social worker was fired because she challenged the manner of the investigation. She later filed a civil suit against the Washington Department of Social and Health Services for wrongful termination and was awarded $1.57 million in damages.

"Child Protective Services: Complex Challenges Require New Strategies," U.S. General Accounting Office, Report to the Honorable Nydia Velázquez, House of Representatives, July 1997. (GAO-HEHS-97-115)

Susan Orr, "Child Protection at the Crossroads: Child Abuse, Child Protection, and Recommendations for Reform," Policy Study No. 262, Reason Public Policy Institute, 1999.

Patricia A. Schene, "Past, Present, and Future Roles of Child Protective Services," in the special issue, "Protecting Children from Abuse and Neglect," *The Future of Children* 8, no. 1 (Spring 1998): 23–38.

pseudocyst of the pancreas A fibrous capsule indicative of acute pancreatitis. Development of a pseudocyst may become apparent as a painful mass in the upper abdomen two to three weeks following injury of the pancreas. Surgical intervention is required. (*See also* PANCREATITIS.)

pseudomaturity Neglected children sometimes appear to be much more mature than other children of their age. This pseudomaturity is usually the result of ROLE REVERSAL in which an immature parent looks to the child for care and nurturance. Immature parents may have unrealistic expectations of their children, which place them in the role of caretaker to younger siblings, protector of the parent or even the parent's romantic partner.

Pseudomaturity exacts a high price from children. Forced to forgo their own emotional development in order to care for parents, they typically grow into adults lacking the emotional resources to form healthy, close relationships. They may be extremely dependent on others for emotional support and as parents may follow a pattern similar to that of their own upbringing.

psychological maltreatment Psychological, or emotional, maltreatment encompasses acts of abuse as well as acts of neglect. Often the terms *psychological maltreatment* and *emotional abuse* are used interchangeably. The NATIONAL CENTER ON CHILD ABUSE AND NEGLECT defines emotional abuse as "acts or omissions by the parents or other caregivers that have caused, or could cause, serious behavioral, cognitive emotional or mental disorders." An example would be locking a child in a dark closet for hours or all day. Emotional neglect includes lack of adequate nurturing, withholding affection, knowingly allowing a child to engage in maladaptive behavior and/or refusal to provide other essential care. An example would be allowing a minor child to consume alcoholic beverages or use illegal drugs. In the U.S., psychological abuse represented 6.1% of all types of child maltreatment in 1997, according to the report "Child Maltreatment 1997: Reports from the States to the National Child Abuse and Neglect Data System," released in 1999 by the Children's Bureau of the U.S. Department of Health and Human Services.

Psychological maltreatment/emotional abuse is difficult to prove and state laws vary on this issue.

Some statutes designate psychological maltreatment as a criminal offense because it causes mental or emotional damage or endangers the child's emotional or mental state. Psychological maltreatment may be separately addressed in a state law or included within all abuse statutes.

For an overview of state laws on psychological maltreatment, read "Emotional Abuse, Child Abuse and Neglect State Statutes Series," published by the U.S. Department of Health and Human Services and the National Center for Prosecution of Child Abuse. This information is available from the NATIONAL CLEARINGHOUSE ON CHILD ABUSE AND NEGLECT INFORMATION. Outside Washington, D.C., call them at (800) FYI-3366, or in Washington call (703) 385–7565. Address: 330 C St. SW, Washington, DC 20447.

About half the states address psychological maltreatment in their laws. For example, the Missouri statute says,

> A person commits the crime of abuse of a child if such person knowingly inflicts cruel and inhuman punishment upon a child less than 17 years old, or photographs or films a child less than 18 years old engaging in a prohibited sexual act or in the simulation of such an act or who causes or knowingly permits a child to engage in a prohibited sexual act or in the simulation of such an act for the purpose of photographing or filming the act.
>
> Abuse of a child is a class C felony, unless in the course thereof the person inflicts serious emotional injury on the child, or the offense is committed as part of a ritual or ceremony in which case the crime is a class B felony. Mo. Rev. Stat. § 568.060 (Supp 1999).

Nevada, in contrast, specifically alludes to mental injury. Their law states, "Mental injury means an injury to the intellectual or psychological capacity or the emotional condition of a child as evidenced by an observable and substantial impairment of his ability to function within his normal range of performance or behavior." (Nev. Rev. Stat. § 432B.070 [1997].)

Cultural norms for child rearing play an important role in determining what kinds of behavior are viewed as injurious to a child's psychological well-being. In practice, definitions of psychological maltreatment may vary widely within a particular culture. However, cultural norms are not relevant if, for example, the behavior is considered a criminal act in the state or country where it is performed. For example, CLITORIDECTOMY is a cultural norm in some other countries but it is considered an act of child abuse in the U.S.

Despite the ambiguity of child protection laws on psychological maltreatment, some children have been removed from their parents due to the parents' emotional instability or after being allowed to witness acts of cruelty inflicted on another family member.

Most experts agree that psychological maltreatment involves a pattern of destructive behavior on the part of an adult—not a single incident. Though virtually all children will be exposed to some form of emotional abuse or neglect at times, those who are repeatedly subjected to such treatment may suffer permanent psychological or intellectual damage.

In an attempt to create a better understanding of the types of behavior that constitute psychological maltreatment, Dr. James Garbarino, president of the Erikson Institute for Advanced Study in Child Development, Chicago, Illinois, and his colleagues have identified five categories of abuse/neglect: rejecting, isolating, terrorizing, ignoring and corrupting.

Rejecting refers to an attitude of hostility toward the child or a total indifference to the child's needs. Cross-cultural studies have shown that this type of behavior exists in many different cultures and is frequently associated with high levels of social and economic stress.

Preventing a child from normal social experiences, i.e., SOCIAL ISOLATION, may also constitute abuse. An example of isolation is the parent who consistently denies a child the opportunity to associate with his or her peers.

Terrorizing involves repeated verbal assaults on a child, causing the child to live in constant fear. Threats of abandonment, severe punishment or death fall into this category.

Ignoring a child can inhibit normal emotional and intellectual development. This type of maltreatment may be especially damaging to infants who need emotional, tactile and intellectual stimulation for healthy development.

Finally, corrupting refers to the parent or caregiver who encourages a child to engage in behavior that is destructive, antisocial or damaging. Two obvious examples of corrupting are encouraging a child to engage in prostitution or stealing. Both activities place the child at significant risk of harm and deny him or her a normal social experience.

James Garbarino, Edna Guttmann, and Janis Wilson Seeley, *The Psychologically Battered Child* (San Francisco: Jossey-Bass, 1986).

James Garbarino, "Psychological Maltreatment Is Not an Ancillary Issue," *The Brown University Child and Adolescent Behavior Letter* 14, no. 8 (August 1998): 2–4

psychological parenthood   Psychological parenthood plays an important role in decisions concerning removal of an abused child from the home. The concept is based upon the idea that a child may establish close psychological bonds with an adult other than a biological parent. An adult becomes a psychological parent through daily interaction and sharing with a child. A parent who is absent, rejecting or inactive is unlikely to fulfill a child's need for a psychological parent.

In their influential book, *Beyond the Best Interests of the Child,* Joseph Goldstein, Anna Freud and Albert Solnit argue that such a close relationship is crucial for healthy development of a child. They advocate restraint in removing children from psychological parents. Since the book's publication, many courts have given greater consideration to the quality of the relationship between a child and his or her primary caretaker.

Separation from a psychological parent is usually painful and upsetting to a child. Child protection workers and courts usually avoid interrupting ties between a child and his or her psychological parent unless separation is absolutely necessary for the protection of the child.

Joseph Goldstein, Anna Freud and Albert Solnit, *The Best Interests of the Child: The Least Detrimental Alternative* (New York: The Free Press, 1996).

psychological tests   A variety of psychological tests are used to evaluate emotional and adjustment problems in children who have been abused. The four most commonly used tests are the Minnesota Multiphasic Personality Test (MMPI), Rorschach, Thematic Apperception Test (TAT) and Draw a Person Test (DAP).

The MMPI presents a number of statements to the subject, who is asked to respond "true," "false" or "cannot say." In the Rorschach children are asked to interpret a series of inkblots. These interpretations are used as an aid in understanding the child's perceptions of reality and social interaction patterns. The TAT consists of a series of pictures suggesting some type of social interaction. Respondents are required to describe what they think is happening in the picture. Children taking the DAP are directed to draw a picture of themselves, a family member, friend or group of people. Interpretation of the drawings is based on the details included (or excluded), the relationships among the figures and the story the child tells about the drawing. All of these tests may be used in the assessment of a variety of emotional problems and are designed to be administered by persons specifically trained in psychometry.

In addition to these tests, several tests have been designed especially for the assessment of PSYCHO-LOGICAL MALTREATMENT or related problems. Many of these tests were originally developed as research instruments. While most focus on maltreatment in the home some were specifically designed for out-of-home settings.

psychopathological abuse   *See* PSYCHOPATHOLOGY.

psychopathology   The importance of mental illness and emotional disturbance as factors contributing to child abuse and neglect is the subject of an ongoing debate among experts. While virtually all scholars and practitioners admit that mental illness may cause parents to neglect or abuse their children there is widespread disagreement as to the prevalence of psychopathological abuse.

A rather extreme view holds that all child abuse is, by definition, psychopathological. Labeling child abuse as a specific form of illness ignores the complex interplay between intrapsychic factors and external forces that may lead to abuse in some situations but not in others. Further, traditional ways of treating mental illness, such as psychotherapy or drug therapy, are not always effective in changing abusive behavior.

Several psychologists and psychiatrists have attempted to isolate a diagnostic category similar to the medical classification, BATTERED CHILD SYNDROME.

Though some have been successful in identifying relationships between various diagnostic categories, for example depression (or schizophrenia) and child abuse, the specific role of psychopathology continues to be elusive. Though it is relatively easy to understand how severe depression may lead to parental neglect, it is more difficult to explain why many parents who suffer from this and other forms of mental illness do not neglect or abuse their children.

Many researchers argue that psychopathology is secondary to cultural and environmental factors as a contributor to child maltreatment. Indeed, a great number of abusers do not appear to suffer from any serious mental disorder as defined by currently accepted diagnostic categories. Some experts have argued that preoccupation with the notion that abuse reflects psychopathology has diverted attention from underlying problems of poverty and family stress. Critics charge that by identifying the individual rather than society as the root of child maltreatment, efforts to combat abuse and neglect have been misdirected. Current approaches to treatment and prevention seem to take a middle ground in this debate, combining psychotherapeutic approaches with education, public awareness programs and support services.

In individual cases, severe mental illness of a caretaker may form the basis for temporary removal of a child from home. Parents who are prone to frequent psychotic breaks or deep depression may be unable to care for their children during these episodes. However, most forms of mental illness are cyclical, and parents are usually quite capable during periods of remission.

psychosocial deprivation   *See* EMOTIONAL NEGLECT.

psychosocial dwarfism   *See* DWARFISM.

puberty rites   *See* INITIATION RITES.

punishment, corporal   *See* CORPORAL PUNISHMENT.

purpura   A purplish collection of petechiae less than one centimeter in diameter. (*See also* BRUISES.)

Purtscher retinopathy This term refers to retinal hemorrhaging as a result of sudden compression of a child's chest. Pressure applied to the chest by hitting, grasping or shaking can produce Purtscher retinopathy without the additional intracranial bleeding that normally occurs in conjunction with ocular hemorrhaging. (*See also* EYE INJURIES.)

radiology, pediatric Documentation and development of the BATTERED CHILD SYNDROME owes a great deal to advances in pediatric radiology. As early as 1906 physicians began to study X rays of infants. The first X-ray department in a children's hospital was established in 1926. Twenty years later John Caffey, a pediatric radiologist, published an article describing the joint occurrence of SUBDURAL HEMATOMAS and FRACTURES of the long bones in infants. Though he lacked confirming evidence, Caffey suggested that the injuries might have been the result of unreported child abuse. Subsequent findings by Caffey, Frederick Silverman (Stanford University) and others established a strong link between certain types of infant fracture and abuse. This phenomenon of multiple fractures in various stages of healing, accompanied by subdural hematomas, was subsequently called the PARENT-INFANT TRAUMATIC SYNDROME, the battered baby syndrome and the CAFFEY-KEMPE SYNDROME.

In 1979, several papers were written on the use of the computed tomography (CT) scan in identifying injuries stemming from child abuse. Experts say that CT scans are especially effective in diagnosing abdominal injuries. CT scans can also detect liver, spleen, kidney, pancreatic and adrenal injuries caused by child abuse. Thoracic injuries caused by abuse may also be found using the CT scan.

Other diagnostic radiologic tools for child abuse are ultrasound and magnetic resonance imaging (MRI).

According to the authors of *Diagnostic Imaging and Child Abuse: Technologies, Practices and Guidelines*, some types of fractures are particularly likely to be caused by abuse. "These include metaphyseal 'chip' or 'bucket handle' fractures of the long bones, posterior and lateral rib fractures in infants, fractures of the acromion process and scapula, sternal frac-

tures and spinous process fractures. Fractures moderately specific for child abuse include compression fractures of the vertebrae, multiples fractures, fractures of different ages in the same child, epiphyseal separations, digital fractures, and complex skull fractures."

X rays may be used as evidence in a courtroom trial and it is up to the judge to determine whether they are admissible or not. Experts say that in general, photographs, X rays and the results of CT and MRI scans are admissible.

Telemedicine in Child Abuse Diagnosis

Some experts believe that remote assistance from physicians expert in diagnosing child abuse may play a part in assisting physicians in diagnosing children who may have been abused. For example, in Florida, Dr. J. M. Whitworth, professor of pediatrics at the University of Florida, assists physicians in detecting child abuse through a teleconferencing system which allows for microscopic examinations. Qualified physicians at participating sites in Florida conduct and send data to the University of Florida site. Experts hope that the system will be expanded to all counties in Florida.

"Diagnostic Imaging and Child Abuse: Technologies, Practices, and Guidelines," Medical Technology and Practice Patterns Institute, Washington, D.C. (1996)

rape Though some writers refer to any unwanted sexual contact as rape, the term is most often understood to mean sexual attack involving penile penetration. Laws often distinguish two different types of rape: forcible and statutory. Forcible rape is defined by the combination of penetration, use of force or threat and nonconsent of the victim. Statutory rape involves sexual assault on a child under the age of consent. Since a child is not considered capable of giving informed consent to sexual relations prior to a specific, legally defined age, the use of force and the child's agreement are irrelevant in cases of statutory rape. The actual age at which a child may legally consent to sexual relations varies. In most locations children may give legal consent at age 14 or 16.

Emergency assessment and treatment of child rape victims focuses on three separate areas: (1) treatment of physical and psychological trauma; (2) collection of evidence for legal prosecution; and (3) prevention of pregnancy and venereal disease. A thorough medical examination is standard procedure for rape victims. It is preferable that the physician be of the same sex as the victim. A trained counselor and/or supportive relative may also help put the child at ease. Virtually all rape victims can benefit from counseling or psychiatric services.

For subsequent legal prosecution it is important that physical evidence be collected by a trained examiner as soon after the assault as possible. Many hospital emergency rooms have rape kits available for gathering legal evidence. Specimens are collected, labeled and sealed in the kit, usually a manila envelope or box. The sealed container is then given to the investigating police officer.

Specimens are taken from the vagina, mouth and anus and tested for evidence of sperm and/or gonorrhea. Serological tests for syphilis and HIV are also ordered. When the victim is of child-bearing age a pregnancy test is also performed.

Rape is a criminal act and, as such, should be reported to law enforcement officials immediately. Reports to a child protection agency are necessary if the perpetrator is a family member or when there is reason to believe the child will not receive adequate treatment or protection.

Because of differing legal definitions of rape it is difficult to determine the number of children who are victimized. Reports of child sexual abuse often involve acts other than penetration. Further, some jurisdictions do not include male victims in their statistics. Incestuous rapes often go unreported.

Though some laws make a distinction between penetration and other acts of sexual assault, the psychological effects of such abuse may not be that different. Studies show that factors such as the level of violence involved, the relationship of the perpe-trator to the victim and the period of time over which the abuse took place are more significant than the specific type of sexual act. (*See also* INCEST, SEXUAL ABUSE.)

Statistics on Child Rape

According to data provided by the Bureau of Justice Statistics (BJS) in 1998, a self-report study of 14,000 state prisoners revealed that two-thirds of all sex offenders (for rape or sexual assault crimes) had victimized a child under the age of 18. In the majority of cases, the victims were age 12 and under.

The BJS also reported on a study of rapists and their victims based on FBI data for Alabama, North Dakota and South Carolina. Children under age 12 represented 15% of all rape victims of all ages. (Adults were included in the population of rape victims.) Twenty-nine percent of all rape victims of all ages were ages 12–17. In the cases of the youngest victims, the victim and offender knew each other in 90% of the cases. No racial differences were found; and blacks and whites were equally victimized.

A pattern of when rapes occurred was also revealed. In looking at specific times, a rape was most likely to occur between 8 P.M. on Friday and 8 A.M. on Saturday. As for the method of force, 5% of the rapists used a gun, 7% used a knife and 80% relied on their own physical force.

"National Conference on Sex Offender Registries: Proceedings of a BJS/SEARCH Conference," Bureau of Justice Statistics, April 1998, NCJ-168965.

reactive parricide   *See* PARRICIDE, REACTIVE.

real evidence   *See* EVIDENCE.

reasonable doubt   *See* BEYOND A REASONABLE DOUBT.

receiving home   When temporary PLACEMENT OF ABUSED CHILDREN is needed, a receiving home may be used. The home may be a family, a group home or shelter. Receiving homes are intended to provide temporary housing while more permanent plans are being made.

records, sealing of   *See* SEALING OF RECORDS.

regional resource centers Under the CHILD ABUSE PREVENTION AND TREATMENT ACT OF 1974, 10 regional centers were established. These centers serve as extensions of the NATIONAL CENTER ON CHILD ABUSE AND NEGLECT, providing information and technical assistance to local residents. Regional centers have since been replaced by 10 National Child Welfare Resource Centers, which focus on specific topics related to abuse and neglect.

See APPENDIX 2 for a listing of National Child Welfare Resource Centers.

regressed offender The regressed offender represents one of two categories commonly used to describe male perpetrators of child SEXUAL ABUSE. Unlike the FIXATED OFFENDER, who has a long-standing preference for children, the regressed offender is primarily attracted to adults as sexual partners. And he may continue to have relations with adults after he becomes sexually involved with children.

The psychosexual development of the regressed offender usually gives few indications of later sexual deviance. However, it appears that he may harbor strong doubts about his sexual adequacy. A particularly stressful situation or series of events, such as marital difficulty, a physical ailment or financial strain, may cause these doubts to resurface. As a way of coping with what he experiences as an overwhelming situation, the regressed offender engages in sexual activity with children, hoping to regain control. Sexual assault on children may be temporary or it may become a permanent regression to deviant behavior.

Though they usually express regret for their actions later, regressed offenders are often deeply depressed and may not think or care about the consequences of their behavior during the actual molestation.

religious aspects From time to time questions arise as to whether certain religious practices constitute child abuse. Religious beliefs concerning punishment, child labor, medicine and sexuality may conflict with social norms of child rearing and, sometimes, with the law. Such conflicts usually pit parents' rights to raise their children according to their own beliefs against the state's duty to protect children.

The question of when to intervene in religiously motivated child-rearing practices is often decided on a case-by-case basis. In the United States, where freedom of religion is guaranteed by the First Amendment, the Supreme Court has traditionally been reluctant to interfere with parents' religious practices. *WISCONSIN V. YODER* established the right of Amish parents to remove their children from school after the eighth grade. In *PRINCE V. MASSACHUSETTS* the high court affirmed parents' right to require their children to engage in certain religious practices. Several medical neglect cases have affirmed the right of parents to withhold medical treatment on religious grounds in all but life-threatening circumstances.

Religious practices involving punishment or deprivation of children may constitute abuse. In such cases the actual and potential harm done to the child must be weighed against parents' rights and any possible benefits the child might derive from this type of religious training. Public agencies are most likely to intervene in situations where children are severely abused or neglected. Child protection workers are sometimes placed in the position of having to distinguish legitimate religiously based child-rearing practices from idiosyncratic abuse. Situations in which parents are responding to religious delusions or are not members of any recognized religious group are not considered to constitute grounds for special consideration. For example, Texas penal code in 1999 on this issue stated, "It is an affirmative defense to criminal injury to a child that an act or omission was based on treatment in accordance with the tenets and practices of a religious method of healing with a generally accepted record of efficacy."

In the U.S., there are 24 states that provide some grounds for religious exemption from state criminal child abuse and neglect laws that relate to failing to provide medical assistance to a child. The following states have such provisions in their laws: Alabama, Alaska, Arkansas, California, Colorado, Delaware, Idaho, Indiana, Iowa, Kansas, Louisiana, Minnesota, New Hampshire, New York, Ohio, Oklahoma, Oregon, Rhode Island, Tennessee, Texas, Utah, Virginia, West Virginia and Wisconsin.

Internationally, differing religious and cultural beliefs pose a significant problem for comparing child-rearing practices of different nations. Attempts to launch an international campaign against child abuse have been hampered by disagreement over certain practices that have religious significance yet are considered abusive by most standards. Nevertheless, some practices such as genital mutilation have been widely condemned.

removal of child   *See* DISPOSITION.

reparenting   Many parents who abuse or neglect their children did not receive adequate parenting during their own childhood. Reparenting is an attempt to intervene in the intergenerational cycle of abuse by providing parents with the nurturance and structure they missed in their early years. Parents are provided with a SURROGATE PARENT such as a PARENT AIDE who can provide the necessary emotional support while serving as a positive parenting role model. Through identification with surrogate parents, the abusive parents are able to become more effective in raising their own children.

reporting   Most countries now require reporting of suspected child abuse and neglect to law enforcement authorities or a child protection agency. In the United States, the CHILD ABUSE PREVENTION AND TREATMENT ACT, a federal law enacted in 1974, encouraged states to strengthen laws specifically requiring reporting of child abuse and neglect.

Reporters of suspected abuse or neglect are usually asked to supply the name and address of the child, the parents' names and addresses, the type and extent of injuries suffered, any evidence of previous abuse and information that may lead to the identification of the perpetrator. In some areas reports can be filed anonymously. Others require that the reporter identify him/herself to the agency receiving the report but withhold the reporter's name from the accused perpetrator.

To facilitate prompt investigation of life-threatening situations most laws allow initial reports to be made verbally. Reporters are usually required to file a full written report within a certain period of time. Many jurisdictions have established toll-free 24-hour HOTLINES to facilitate reporting. In addition to these local services there are two hotlines that serve the entire United States.

BASIC ELEMENTS OF REPORTING LAWS

- Who is required to report
- What should be reported
- Where or to whom it should be reported
- How much evidence is necessary to trigger a report
- Penalties for failure to report
- Immunity from prosecution for "good faith" reports
- Suspension of privileged communication laws

Reporting laws usually require or specifically permit certain professionals to report cases of suspected maltreatment to the agency charged with investigation. In some jurisdictions anyone who has reason to suspect that a child is being abused or neglected is legally obligated to report. About 50% of all reports of child abuse and neglect are made by friends, relatives or neighbors. MANDATED REPORTERS are usually granted immunity from civil or criminal prosecution for reports made in good faith. Penalties, ranging from a small fine to imprisonment, are often imposed on mandated reporters who fail to report suspected abuse or neglect.

While reporting laws are usually clear about who is required to report suspected maltreatment, they are often vague about exactly what kinds of injuries/behavior should be reported. Many local statutes define abuse and neglect in broad terms or not at all. Conditions specifically mentioned range from serious physical injuries to vaguely defined MENTAL INJURIES and NEGLECT.

In Canada, Britain and the United States lack of specificity in the types of injuries that should be reported has led to charges of frivolous reporting. Some critics believe that failure to define clearly abuse and neglect overburdens child protection agencies and causes some families to be subjected to needless invasions of privacy. Proponents of present laws argue that a broad definition of abuse and neglect is necessary to cover all situations that might seriously harm a child. This view holds that it is better to tolerate some overreporting than to run the risk of failing to identify children in need of help.

American Association for Protecting Children, *Highlights of Official Child Neglect and Abuse Reporting, 1985* (Denver: American Humane Association, 1987).

res gestae   *See* EXCITED UTTERANCE.

resilience of abused children   Experts say that some children are more resilient in the face of abuse than others, including children who have been severely abused. Factors affecting resilience appear to be:

- temperament of child (easygoing children are more resilient)
- the ability to avoid abusive parents and "make themselves invisible"
- children who have another adult or adults who they can rely upon
- an ability to separate the abuse from themselves and not blame themselves for the abuse

Interestingly, the factors that enable a child to adapt to an abusive environment can also make it difficult in some cases for the child to adapt to an adoptive family or to a nonabusive environment. Tactics that worked well in the abusive home, such as avoidance of a parent, lying when necessary to avoid abuse, emotional detachment and other reactions, may be seen as maladaptive in the adoptive home. Experts say that new adoptive parents should realize that the child needs to learn that the survival strategies that worked well for him or her in the past are not necessary and are a hindrance in a healthy family.

res ipsa loquitur   This legal doctrine is borrowed from the evidentiary law of negligence. It is invoked in child abuse or neglect cases and permits use of circumstantial evidence. This admissible evidence only infers that abuse or neglect has occurred, but as the term implies, "the thing speaks for itself." Evidence of this sort presented to the court includes, for example, medical reports or X rays detailing the condition of a suspected victim of abuse or neglect. (*See also* EVIDENTIARY STANDARDS.)

retardation   *See* MENTAL RETARDATION.

retinal hemorrhage   A blow to the body causes blood to rush out of the impacted area into surrounding vessels. This rapid increase in pressure

causes capillaries to rupture. A blow to the head or chest causes small clots to form inside of or in front of the retina. Evidence of these hemorrhages remains present for up to two weeks.

Since retinal hemorrhages are often caused by head trauma, the child should also be examined for the presence of SUBDURAL HEMATOMA.

reversible growth failure   *See* DWARFISM.

reversible hyposomatotropic dwarfism   *See* DWARFISM.

rickets   Lack of sufficient quantities of vitamin D causes rickets, a condition that disturbs the normal development of bones. Rickets may occur as a result of nutritional neglect (*see* NEGLECT).

role reversal   Parents who abuse or neglect their children often have unrealistically high expectations for their behavior. Sometimes these parents engage in a reversal of roles in which the child becomes the comforter and caretaker of the parent while the parent largely ignores his or her parental responsibilities. Evidence of role reversal may be seen in young children who demonstrate a kind of PSEUDOMATURITY, shouldering responsibilities normally assumed by much older children or adults. Parents, on the other hand, may be unable to give emotional support and direction.

Role reversal may also be seen in cases of INCEST. The child assumes the role of sexual partner to the parent and, frequently, takes on other responsibilities normally performed by the spouse. Being forced prematurely to act as an adult, the child is denied the opportunity to follow the normal pattern of maturation. The child's own developmental needs are suppressed, leading to what is often referred to as the loss of childhood (*see* PARENTIFIED CHILD).

Some mental health experts speculate that parents may be repeating their own childhood in which they assumed a parental role. An alternate explanation is that parents who, as children, were not required to accept responsibility and were protected from the consequences of their actions are, as adults, unable to function maturely. It is likely that both types of childhood experience can contribute to role reversal; however, different treatment approaches might be taken depending upon the parent's specific developmental deficit.

runaways   Studies of children and adolescents who run away from home show that many are running away from abuse. One study of runaway youths found that 73% of females and 38% of males reported having been abused. A 1998 study of 26 teenage runaways living in a New England shelter revealed that most reported that they left their homes only as a last resort and after having been physically, sexually or emotionally abused.

Ironically, some teenagers may actually increase their chances of abuse by leaving home. Runaways are often easy prey for adults seeking to lure them into prostitution. Unable to secure a job that pays enough to support them, both males and females are enticed by the promise of large sums of money in exchange for engaging in illicit activities. In addition to sexual exploitation, youths living on the streets are often robbed or assaulted. Most runaways do not live far from home, and several studies have revealed that the wide majority reside less than 100 miles from their families. (*See also* ADOLESCENT ABUSE, SEXUAL ABUSE, THROWAWAY CHILDREN.)

Arlene McCormack, Mark-David Janus, and Ann Wolbert Burgess, "Runaway Youths and Sexual Victimization: Gender Differences in an Adolescent Runaway Population," *Child Abuse and Neglect* 10 (1986): 387–395.

Laurie Schaffner, "Searching for Connection: A New Look at Teenaged Runaways," *Adolescence* 33 (Fall 1998): 619–627.

sadism Sadism is a relatively rare form of sexual perversion in which sexual gratification is derived by hurting or humiliating another person. Though assaults involving sadism comprise a very small proportion of all child SEXUAL ABUSE, highly publicized accounts of MYSOPEDIC OFFENDERS have led to a public misconception concerning their prevalence.

The overwhelming majority of sadistic sexual offenses are committed by men. When sadistic assaults occur they are likely to result in physical injury or, in extreme cases, death. Sexual pleasure is derived from the victim's visible suffering. The sadist usually exerts much greater force than would be necessary to overpower the child. Though usually described as a sexual offense, sadism actually combines physical, psychological and sexual abuse.

Some psychodynamically oriented therapists have explained sadism as a PROJECTION of the attacker's own self-hatred. By punishing the child the perpetrator symbolically punishes himself.

scalds The most frequent type of abusive burns of children is a wet burn, or scald. Over one-fourth of all reported scalds can be likened to abuse. Most nonaccidental scalds are caused by overheated tap water. At 130 degrees Fahrenheit, a full thickness scald can occur on an adult in 30 seconds; at 150 degrees in two seconds. A child's thin skin burns even more quickly.

Abusive scalds often have different patterns than accidental scalds. Forcing a child to sit in a bath tub of hot water may result in a "donut burn," where the center of the buttocks is protected by the relative coolness of the tub while the surrounding area is burned. Glove or stocking burns are most likely to result from the hand or foot being forcibly held in hot water. When scalds are caused by splashing careful observation of burn marks can reveal the direction from which the hot liquid came. This evidence should be compared to the caretaker's account for inconsistencies.

A study of scald victims revealed that 71% of the cases in which the child was brought to treatment by someone other than the primary caretaker were the result of abuse. Of children whose treatment was delayed two hours or more, 70% were found to be victims of abusive burns. (*See also* BURNS.)

SCAN team SCAN stands for suspected child abuse and neglect. Usually attached to a hospital or outpatient mental health facility, the SCAN team is charged with assessing children and their families to determine whether abuse has occurred. If it is determined that the child has, in fact, been abused the team makes specific recommendations for treatment.

Teams are composed of professionals from different disciplines, all of whom have special training in diagnosis of child abuse and neglect. Typically, SCAN teams review only the most difficult cases, such as those involving SEXUAL ABUSE of a young child. More clear-cut decisions are handled by protective service staff. (*See also* ASSESSMENT and MULTIDISCIPLINARY TEAM.)

scapegoating Often one child in a family is singled out as the recipient of the most abuse. Reasons for this type of selection are complex and varied. Usually scapegoating begins at a very early age, sometimes at birth. Infants who are irritable, colicky and who do not respond well to parental nurturing may become targets for abuse. Premature infants are more likely to become scapegoats than those carried to full term.

Scapegoating is frequently described as an interactive process in which the child's physical, social or psychological characteristics combine with those of the parent to increase the likelihood of abuse. Children perceived as difficult, unresponsive or hyperactive are at risk. Other traits can include psychological impairment, learning disabilities, physical defects or chronic illness.

Caretakers of scapegoated children range from normally capable persons under stress to those with severe PSYCHOPATHOLOGY. Parents may perceive a particular child as reflecting their own defects or inadequacies. In such situations the parent's self-hatred is misdirected toward the child. The child has become a symbol of all the parent dislikes in him or herself.

Maltreatment by caretakers is quickly internalized by children. Scapegoated children come to have low self-esteem and see themselves as bad and deserving of punishment. As they grow older many of these children actually seek punishment by acting out at home or in school. They may also invite abuse from peers by taunting and provoking them. Because the children see themselves as deserving of abuse they offer only token self-defense when they are subsequently attacked.

As they grow older, victims of severe scapegoating continue to have difficulty in establishing close relationships with peers, teachers and others. Prolonged treatment is often required to help these children develop a capacity for displaying warmth toward themselves and others.

Scotland In Scotland, child protective services fall under the general jurisdiction of the Scottish Development Department and the Scottish Home and Health Department. In 1968, the Social Work Act in Scotland reorganized the various services provided to children and families, and replaced juvenile courts with a system thought to be more responsive to the needs of children.

The judicial services change was made in 1971 from a court system dealing with juveniles to one that brings a youthful offender before a panel of individuals (generally three people) plus the reporter of the offense, a social worker and one or both of the child's parents. Children who fall within the confines of this hearing system are under 16 years of age and there are a variety of statutory grounds under which a child may be required to

appear. Options after a hearing are discharge of a case, placement on supervision and residential supervision.

scurvy Scurvy, a result of vitamin C deficiency, increases susceptibility to bruising and is often mistaken for BATTERED CHILD SYNDROME. Conversely, many cases of child battering were misdiagnosed as scurvy during the late 19th and early 20th centuries by physicians who failed to consider the possibility of abuse or who wished to protect the parents.

sealing of records Many jurisdictions require a court order to examine criminal records of youthful offenders. Such records are considered "sealed."

Sealing of records is a controversial issue. Many youth advocates believe that by restricting access to court records adolescents will be protected from negative labeling and discrimination in school or in later employment. Others believe sealing makes it difficult to identify serious offenders who pose a threat to society. When the youthful offender has a history of abusing other children, sealing of criminal records may prevent parents, school officials and law enforcement officers from taking steps to protect younger children adequately.

Under certain circumstances records of adult offenders may be sealed or expunged. While sealing of adult records is less common, many of the same arguments, for and against, apply.

secondary prevention *See* PREVENTION.

secrecy SEXUAL ABUSE that continues for an extended period of time usually involves an element of secrecy. The abuser may bribe or coerce the victim not to tell about their encounters. Children themselves may maintain secrecy about abuse due to embarrassment, fear of being punished, fear of parental rejection or abandonment or, in the case of very young children, simply because they do not have sufficient verbal capacity to explain the problem. Some therapists speculate that enforced silence may be related to later development of nonverbal means of coping with stress, such as SUBSTANCE ABUSE, withdrawal or depression.

In cases of INCEST, secrecy may extend to other members of the family. Often the mother is accused of being a PASSIVE ABUSER, silently condoning sexual activity between the father and a child. Reasons for this phenomenon are complex and not fully understood. The mother may tacitly encourage the child to act as a substitute in order to avoid sexual relations with the father. In other cases she may fear abandonment or reprisal.

Failure to report known abuse not only makes one a silent partner to maltreatment but also increases the harm to the child. Studies suggest that psychological damage from abuse is related to the length of time the child was abused.

seductive behavior Seductive or inappropriate sexual behavior toward an adult may be a sign that a child has been sexually abused (*see* SEXUAL ABUSE). Sexually victimized children often learn that in order to gain the attention or affection of an adult they must appeal to them sexually. Such behavior, once learned, may be directed toward adults other than the abuser, increasing the risk of further abuse.

Seductive behavior may range from overly affectionate kissing, stroking, massaging etc. to overt sexual advances such as fondling the genitals or making sexual comments. Children who act seductively toward adults are often blamed for initiating sexual activity with them. Claims of seduction by a child have frequently been introduced in court as a defense against charges of child molestation. Others cite this apparent sexual aggressiveness as evidence that children enjoy sex with adults. Such claims notwithstanding, sexual relations between an adult and a child are considered to be an abusive act on the part of the adult and are outlawed in most countries around the world.

Experts in the treatment of child sexual abuse stress that seductive behavior on the part of children is learned from adults. The child who feels unloved may find that this is the only way to get the affection he or she craves. Starved for affection, the child may interpret sexual exploitation by an adult as genuine affection. As the child grows older, sexual submissiveness often gives way to intense anger toward the adult and/or self-loathing often manifesting itself in depression and SELF-DESTRUCTIVE BEHAVIOR.

self-destructive behavior In the general population, self-destructive acts by children are rare. Among neglected, and especially abused, children the incidence of such behavior is much higher. Studies have shown that up to 40% of abused children exhibited self-destructive tendencies compared with 2% of children with no history of abuse or neglect.

Abused children are more likely to engage in a range of harmful activities, including provocative acts designed to elicit punishment, accident proneness and suicide attempts. Self-destructive acts usually follow parental beatings or separation from the parent—real or threatened.

Neglected children display two to three times the amount of self-harming behavior as their peers who have not experienced abuse or neglect. Physically and sexually abused victims are even more likely than neglected children to exhibit this behavior—eight to 10 times more. Though neglected children share many of the same negative environmental conditions suffered by abused children, they are less likely to be subjected to physical violence and SCAPEGOATING.

Children who are punished frequently and brutally will assume they are bad and deserving of punishment. They often cannot connect the punishment with any specific behavior and consequently develop a general sense of self-hatred, unworthiness and low SELF-ESTEEM. These feelings form the basis of later aggressive and self-destructive behavior.

self-esteem Feelings of low self-worth are often cited as both cause and result of child abuse. Several psychiatric studies of abusive parents have found them to have unusually negative images of themselves. Many clinicians and researchers believe parents' low self-esteem can be attributed to abusive or neglectful treatment they received as children. These parents may project their feelings onto children by constantly punishing or degrading them (*see* PROJECTION). In turn their children may grow up to be abusive parents.

Building self-esteem is often one of the most important goals in the treatment of abusers. In some cases treatment may involve a process known as REPARENTING, in which parents receive instruction and nurturance from a trained older adult. In a sense, the parents take on another parent who can give the positive feedback and modeling they did not receive as children.

Abused children often develop a distorted view of themselves, seeing virtually everything they do as bad. Parental abuse and neglect is interpreted by the child as confirmation of perceived badness. Many children become so invested in this negative self-image that they stubbornly resist the efforts of therapists, foster parents and others to change this false view. For this reason, long-term psychotherapeutic treatment of abused children is sometimes necessary to eliminate this distorted sense of self.

self-help groups   The number of people involved in self-help groups has grown dramatically since the 1950s. Alcoholics Anonymous, perhaps the most famous self-help organization, has thousands of groups around the world. Many mutual aid groups have patterned themselves after AA's 12-step program. Others are less structured, simply providing a forum for people with similar concerns to share experiences and emotional support.

The characteristic that distinguishes self-help from other treatment of educational groups is the degree of responsibility exercised by members. Self-help groups are totally controlled by their members.

PARENTS ANONYMOUS is the largest organization of groups for parents who abuse their children. Several groups for victims of sexual abuse have formed since the late 1970s.

Self-help has proven effective in helping parents who want to control abusive impulses. Members often make themselves available to one another in times of crisis, serving as a safety valve for explosive emotions. A desire to change is essential for members of self-help groups. Though child abuse agencies often refer parents to such groups, membership is voluntary.

Groups also serve an important educational function. Parents learn coping skills from others with similar experiences. Victims of sexual abuse often learn they are not alone in their feelings of low self-esteem, guilt or similar reactions.

Though self-help groups can be very effective they are not for everyone. Abusers who are not motivated to change may need more structured assistance. In some cases specialized treatment is necessary in addition to participation in a self-help group.

self-incrimination   *See* MIRANDA WARNINGS.

Senate Subcommittee on Children and Youth   In February 1971, the U.S. Senate Subcommittee on Children and Youth was established after Senator Walter F. Mondale promoted further action on proposals made at the 1970 White House Conference on Children. As part of its research, the subcommittee published *Rights of Children, Part I*, a document that indicated the direction this subcommittee would take. As a result of subcommittee action over the course of several years, Public Law 93–247 was signed on December 20, 1973 and was in force as the CHILD ABUSE PREVENTION AND TREATMENT ACT OF 1974 on January 31. The act was subsequently amended in 1996.

sentencing   The final phase of a criminal trial is pronouncement of the judge's order of punishment for a convicted defendant. Persons convicted of criminal charges related to child abuse or neglect may be imprisoned, fined or placed on probation. Actual sentences vary widely and depend on several factors, including local statutes, whether the crime is classed as a FELONY or MISDEMEANOR and the severity of the act. Sentencing occurs only in criminal trials and does not directly involve victims of maltreatment. The corresponding phase of civil court proceedings is the DISPOSITION.

sequelae   Children suffer many consequences of abuse and neglect. Aftereffects of maltreatment are sometimes referred to collectively as *sequelae*. The most obvious effects of abuse are physical trauma such as cuts, bruises or broken bones. Less apparent results of abuse include psychological harm, internal physical injuries such as brain damage, or impaired growth. Victims of sexual abuse may experience extreme feelings of low self-worth, sexual dysfunction in adulthood, an inability to trust others and similar sequelae of exploitation.

Aftereffects of abuse may appear as a delayed reaction many years after the traumatic incident or may be attributed to other causes. While some pedophiles (*see* PEDOPHILIA) argue that sex with children is not harmful, reports of adults who were sexually victimized as children indicate that the experience can have severe and long-lasting consequences.

Protection of children from further abuse, while essential, does not address the consequences of previous abuse. Treatment of psychological damage is often a time-consuming and expensive process. If left untreated, victims of abuse may continue to suffer from the aftereffects of abuse and may grow up to become abusers themselves. (*See also* CYCLE OF ABUSE, PSYCHOLOGICAL MALTREATMENT, PHYSICAL ABUSE, SEXUAL ABUSE, NEGLECT.)

Margaret A. Lynch and Jacqueline Roberts, *Consequences of Child Abuse* (London: Academic Press, 1982).

service plan After completion of an ASSESSMENT the child protection worker develops a plan for addressing specific problems and creating a safe environment for the abused child. The service plan (sometimes called a case plan) is often developed with the assistance of a MULTIDISCIPLINARY TEAM. If feasible, the abused child and his or her family is also involved in the planning process.

The first step in developing a service plan is setting realistic goals for the child and family. Treatment or service goals correspond directly to specific problems identified in the assessment. Goals may be described as proposed solutions to these problems. Some service plans make a distinction between short- and long-term goals.

Next in the planning process is the creation of measurable, time-limited objectives. Objectives are the standards by which progress toward identified goals can be monitored. Another way of viewing objectives is as a set of specific actions that must be taken to achieve a particular goal.

The final phase of service planning involves identifying and selecting the kinds of help the child and family will need in order to achieve the service goals. A wide range of services may be required to achieve the desired goals. Some examples of assistance that can be included in the service plan are: CATEGORICAL AID; HOMEMAKER SERVICES or PARENT AIDES; individual, family or marital counseling; temporary FOSTER CARE; and legal aid.

Service plans that set reasonable goals and have the family's support are the most likely to succeed. Families who are actively involved in the planning process usually have more confidence in the plan and tend to cooperate more fully in its implementation.

sexual abuse Contacts or interactions between a child and an adult when the child is used for the sexual stimulation of the perpetrator or another person is sexual abuse. State definitions of sexual abuse vary but may indicate various degrees of physical contact, or there may be no contact but the child was used in a sexual way, for example, in a pornographic display for the sexual gratification of the photographer and/or other persons.

Sexual abuse may also be committed by a person under the age of 18 when that person is either significantly older than the victim or when the perpetrator is in a position of power or control over another child.

According to the NATIONAL CLEARINGHOUSE ON CHILD ABUSE AND NEGLECT, 43 states reported a total of 98,339 reports of childhood sexual abuse in 1997. About 75% of the incidents involved female victims.

Some experts believe this may be due to an underreporting of sexual abuse experienced by boys, in part because of a lack of empathy or receptivity to hearing complaints of sexual abuse from males, particularly when male children have been victimized by adult females. The myth is that although it is traumatic for a female child to have consensual sex with an adult male (statutory rape), it is believed that it is a positive experience for a young boy to experience consensual sex with an adult female. Yet according to a 1996 report in the *Journal of the American Academy of Child and Adolescent Psychiatry*, male child victims can be severely traumatized and depressed, even suicidal.

Sexual abuse has received a great deal of media attention. Yet as distressing as sexual abuse is, studies have revealed that neglect is more traumatic and dangerous for most children.

Shorter Prison Sentences if the Sex Offense Was Against a Child

Federal reports also reveal that if the sex offender is convicted, if his or her victim is a child, then the sentence is likely to be significantly lower than if the same rape had been committed against an adult. In looking at a sentences imposed on a sample (about 3,000) of state prisoners in 1991, researchers for the Department of Justice determined the median sentence for a variety of violent crimes.

If the crime were rape against an adult, the median sentence was 240 months. If it were rape against a child, the sentence was 180 months. In addition, if the crime was sexual assault against an adult, the median sentence was 185 months. If a child had been sexually assaulted, the median sentence was 132 months. This pattern did not hold for other crimes: if the crime were murder or kidnapping, the offender against a child received a longer sentence than if he murdered or kidnapped an adult. *See also* PRISONS, CHILD VICTIMIZERS IN.

Common Misconceptions

Many popular myths exist concerning the child molester and the victimized child. The common image of the sexual offender as a dirty old man in a trenchcoat (a stranger) is refuted by statistics showing that most offenders are under 30 years of age and are known (and very often related) to the victim.

Another area of confusion centers on the nature of child sexual abuse. While most people acknowledge that sexual relations between an adult and a child are harmful, there is disagreement over the age at which a person is able to give informed consent to sexual relations. A nationwide minimum of 18 has been suggested in the United States, where the age of consent varies from state to state. Conversely, some small groups have banded together in the United States and Britain to advocate total repeal of laws that prevent adult-child sex.

History

Though sexual misuse of children has recently been "rediscovered" in Western society, historical accounts show that the problem has a long and sad history. Many times, in many different cultures, sexual victimization of children has actually been institutionalized and permitted by law. Even more frequently sexual abuse has flourished in spite of laws and mores that nominally prohibit such behavior. Sale and prostitution of children remains a well-documented way of life in many parts of the world.

In ancient Greek and Roman society CASTRATION was practiced as a way of making boys more sexually attractive to adult males. Young girls and boys were present in approximately equal numbers in brothels of the period.

Child marriage has been widely practiced throughout history and is still common in some countries. Until the third century A.D. Talmudic law permitted the betrothal of girls beginning at the age of three years and one day. Subject to the father's permission, sexual intercourse was the method of sealing marital intentions with such a young girl.

For most of recorded history children—girls in particular—have been afforded the legal status of parental property. Rape of a young girl was often treated as a property offense against the father. Because the rapist had reduced the child's ability to bring a large dowry, he was required to reimburse the father for the lost income. In some cases the man was forced to marry his victim.

Victimization of children continued in medieval Europe. In 15th-century France the legal age of consent (the age at which the child was deemed competent to marry or engage in sexual relations) was six.

Widespread abuse also was alleged to have occurred at the hands of clergy in convents and during confessional. Many young girls were cruelly executed for alleged fornication with the devil. Historians speculate that these girls may actually have been sexually assaulted by the same men who put them to death.

The lust for sexual relations with children appears to have been a major preoccupation with Victorian men. Prostitution flourished in 19th-century London, and the practice of deflowering young virgins was described as obsessional. London brothels were remarkable for their large numbers of young girls. An estimated 58% of the illegal prostitutes in Vienna during this period were minors. Child pornography also became a popular item in the Victorian era, a phenomenon that shows no signs of diminution even today.

During the 19th century in the United States, Chinese girls were bought and sold at prices ranging from $1,500 to $3,500. Prior to the abolition of slavery, black children were treated as sexual property and frequently brutalized by their white owners.

Many American, British, French and German children were lured or sold into white slavery during the late 19th century. These children, most of them around the ages of 12 and 13, were often exported to Hong Kong, Thailand, India and various South American countries.

Despite laws prohibiting such practices, sexual misuse of children continues to flourish in modern society. Undeterred by public outcry against it, the demand for child pornography still provides a stimulus for exploitation. A significant proportion of prostitution around the world involves minors. And child marriage continues to be commonplace in India and some other countries.

Sexual Abuse Today

Despite laws prohibiting sexual misuse of children, such practices continue to flourish in modern society in many different forms. For example, the demand for child pornography continues to provide a stimulus for exploitation. It is also true that a significant proportion of prostitution around the world involves minors. And child marriage continues to be commonplace in India, Africa and some other countries. In addition, practices such as CLITORIDECTOMY are considered important or mandatory in some cultures, whereas in Western nations, they are regarded as sexually abusive.

TYPES OF CHILD SEXUAL ABUSE

RAPE—forceful genital intercourse
GENITAL INTERCOURSE—without force
ANAL INTERCOURSE
FELLATIO—oral contact with the male genitals
CUNNILINGUS—oral contact with the female genitals
ANALINGUS—oral contact with the anus
CASTRATION—removal of the testicles
CLITORIDECTOMY—removal of the clitoris
GENITAL TOUCHING—including clothed and unclothed touching, fondling of the male or female genitals
INTENTIONAL SEXUAL TOUCHING—of the breasts, buttocks or thigh, clothed or unclothed
SEXUAL INTERCOURSE BETWEEN ADULTS IN THE PRESENCE OF A CHILD
TAKING SEXUALLY EXPLICIT PHOTOGRAPHS OF A CHILD
FORCING OR ENCOURAGING A CHILD TO TOUCH AN ADULT'S GENITALS
ENCOURAGING A CHILD TO ENGAGE IN SEXUAL ACTIVITY WITH OTHER CHILDREN FOR THE BENEFIT OF AN ADULT
EXHIBITIONISM—deliberate display of the genitals to a child, usually for the sexual gratification of the perpetrator
SEXUAL KISSING
CHILD'S CARETAKER IS INVOLVED IN PROSTITUTION

Definitions of sexual abuse vary from culture to culture and even within societal groups. Some groups engage in permissive practices or sexual rituals that would be viewed with alarm in other cultures. Others consider Western sexual norms overly harsh and conducive to victimization. Despite this variation, all groups have rules governing sexual contact between children and adults. The incest taboo prohibiting intrafamilial sexual relations is almost universal.

One important aspect of sexual abuse that sets it apart from other forms of maltreatment is its lack of association with class or race. Unlike PHYSICAL ABUSE, it occurs with approximately equal frequency in all social classes. White and nonwhite children experience equivalent amounts of sexual abuse.

Medical Indications of Sexual Abuse

According to a 1999 article, "Guidelines for the Evaluation of Sexual Abuse of Children" in *Pediatrics,* if a child has any of the following sexually transmitted diseases (STDs), it is diagnostic for sexual abuse: syphilis, gonorrhea, HIV or chlamydia. (Some STDs may be transmitted during childbirth from mother to child.) A diagnosis of *Trichomonas* is "highly suspicious" of sexual abuse and if the child has anogenital warts or herpes, it is "suspicious" for sexual abuse.

Laboratory studies should be performed as soon after an attack as possible, preferably within 72 hours. According to the *Pediatrics* article, for girls, "the genital examination should include inspection of the medial aspects of the thighs, labia major and minora, clitoris, urethra, periurethal tissue, hymen, hymenal opening, fossa navicularis, and posterior fourchette." For boys, "the thighs, penis, and scrotum should be examined for bruises, scars, chafing, bite marks, and discharge." In addition, the anus of both boys and girls should be examined in various positions to check for bruising, tearing and dilation.

Sexually molested children may exhibit somatic symptoms that appear to be unrelated to physical aspects of the abuse. Secondary complaints may include sleep disturbance, abdominal pain, ENURESIS, ENCOPRESIS, vomiting and loss of appetite.

Other experts state that behavioral indicators can be indicative of sexual abuse; for example, a child with precocious sexual knowledge beyond his or her developmental stage. Although it is true that children watch television and movies that may provide them with images of explicit behavior, few children initiate sexual behavior with adults or animals, despite what they may have seen on TV, and such behavior is cause for concern.

Possible behavioral signs of sexual abuse of an adolescent are promiscuous behavior, abuse of drugs or alcohol, prostitution, depression and suicide threats.

Perpetrators of Sexual Abuse

Sexual abuse is predominantly a male crime. Ninety percent of all child sexual molestation is committed by men. Ninety-five percent of female victims are victimized by men. Men are responsible for approximately 80% of all sexual abuse of boys.

About 70% of sexual abusers are known to children before the abuse takes place. The most frequent offenders are fathers and stepfathers. A child's relationship to the offender is an important predictor of the duration of abuse. When the offender is previously unknown to the child the abuse is likely to be limited to one incident per child, such as an exhibitionistic episode. This type of offender is likely to have a large number of victims. Incestuous abuse often involves repeated molestations of the same child over a period of three to four years.

Most sexual abuse of children is perpetrated by young heterosexual men who are considered quite normal by others. Eighty percent of all these offenders engage in their first sexual abuse before the age of 30. Though alcohol or drug intoxication is often blamed, less than one-third of these offenders are drug or alcohol dependent. Only 5% show evidence of serious mental illness. And, of all adults, homosexual men are the least likely to commit a sexual offense against a child.

Perpetrators are more likely than others to have been sexually victimized as children. While FIXATED OFFENDERS are aroused exclusively by children and seek them as sexual partners, a more frequent motive of abusers may be a need for intimacy, power or control. This is especially true in cases of INCEST. Many of these offenders report difficulty in relating to adult sexual partners and feel inadequate. Many offenders have rigid and repressive ideas about sex.

Though research on recidivism is fragmentary and inconclusive, many experts view the child sexual offender as particularly resistant to treatment. Fixated offenders who have assaulted a large number of children are thought to be less likely to benefit from treatment than REGRESSED OFFENDERS with a less-extensive history of abuse.

Indicators of Abuse: The Perpetrator

Experts say that the perpetrator may collect CHILD PORNOGRAPHY. According to a chapter by Kenneth Lanning and Bill Walsh in *The APSAC Handbook on Child Maltreatment,* "Child pornography, especially that produced by the offender, is one of the most valuable pieces of corroborative evidence of child sexual abuse that any investigator can have. Many collectors of child pornography do not molest children, and many child molesters do not possess or collect child pornography. However, investigators should always be alert for it." The authors also stated that the offender may have photographs of his child victims.

In addition, the perpetrator may also have information on his computer that links him to the sexual abuse. The authors report, "He might use it to organize information and correspondence about this activity; communicate with other child molesters or potential child victims; to store, transfer, and manipulate child pornography. Therefore, legally searching and seizing such a computer potentially could provide almost unbelievable amounts of corroborative evidence."

Victims

As mentioned, girls are more likely to be sexually abused than boys.

Studies have identified several factors that may place some girls at greater risk than others. Marital conflict, separation and divorce were found to be more prevalent in the families of sexually abused girls. Specifically, these girls were more likely to have lived *without* their natural father and more likely to have lived *with* a stepfather. Mothers of victimized girls were more likely to be employed outside the home or to be ill or disabled.

Like girls, boys are most often the victims of men. Victimized boys are more likely than their female counterparts to come from an impoverished environment, to be physically abused and to suffer their abuse at the hands of someone outside the family. Some experts believe sexual abuse of boys is less likely to be reported than that involving girls.

Another factor associated with sexual abuse is SOCIAL ISOLATION. These children often have fewer friends than their peers and may be isolated in other ways as well. It is not clear, however, whether this phenomenon is a contributing factor or a result of abuse. Clinical evidence indicates that abuse victims are often depressed and withdrawn.

Sexually victimized children also tend to report, more often than their peers, a poor relationship with their parents. Mothers are most frequently reported as the parent with whom the relationship is most strained.

Absence of the mother greatly increases the risk to girls. Those living without their mothers are three times more likely to suffer sexual abuse than those whose mothers are present.

In an effort to avoid further sexual abuse many adolescents run away from home. Ironically these teens may actually increase their likelihood of being abused. A recent study of runaways in a Canadian shelter found that 71% of female and 38% of male runaways had been sexually victimized. The authors speculated that much of the abuse occurred after leaving home. Adolescents living on the streets are particularly vulnerable to sexual assault and may, in desperation, turn to prostitution as a means of financial support.

Effects of Sexual Abuse

Children differ in their reactions to sexual abuse. Clinical and empirical studies indicate that sexually victimized children are more likely to be fearful, anxious, depressed, angry and hostile. Twenty percent to 40% of these children show signs of significant emotional disturbance following the abuse. Child victims sometimes exhibit inappropriate sexual behavior as a result of the abuse. Excessive sexual curiosity, open masturbation and exposure of the genitals are frequently observed in young victims. Older children and adolescents may become promiscuous or display inappropriately seductive behavior toward adults and are at greater risk of delinquency. Young girls and older boys seem to be most seriously affected by this type of abuse.

Children often feel extremely guilty about their involvement in sexual abuse. Even in cases where there has been a brutal assault, a child may feel that she or he was in some way responsible for or deserving of the abuse. Guilt feelings are almost universal among incest victims who may feel responsible for the breakup of their parents' marriage.

Conversely, some incest victims perceive themselves as holding the family together by preventing a divorce. In such cases the daughter may become, in effect, a surrogate wife filling a role the mother is unable or unwilling to play (see ROLE REVERSAL). Guilt can also appear as a by-product of the confusing and often contradictory feelings about incest. Though sexual contact is frequently painful and frightening for a child, there is sometimes an element of pleasure in such contact. A child may enjoy the exclusive and deceptively warm attention of an adult when he or she feels unloved. Taking any enjoyment in such an obviously bad act can be a source of intense guilt that continues long after the abuse has stopped.

Long-Term Effects

Sexual abuse during childhood often continues to affect the lives of victims long after the abuse has ended. Women with a history of childhood sexual victimization have higher levels of depression, anxiety, SUBSTANCE ABUSE and SELF-DESTRUCTIVE BEHAVIOR. They are also more likely to feel isolated and stigmatized, experience some type of SEXUAL DYSFUNCTION or avoidance or have difficulty trusting others.

The use of force is related to the seriousness and duration of the trauma experienced. Not surprisingly, abuse over a long period of time is associated with more traumatic and longer lasting SEQUELAE.

Treatment

In addition to ensuring the sexual abuse ends, treatment may also include psychotherapy for the abused child and sometimes for family members as well. Studies indicate that cognitive-behavioral therapy centering on the issue of sexual abuse appears to be more successful than "nondirective" therapy in which the client talks about whatever comes to mind. Another important factor is parental support during treatment. A study of 43 children who were sexually abused revealed that the children who fared best were those whose parents were supportive of therapy for the 12-month period following the beginning of therapy.

Unfortunately, it is possible that many parents refuse to believe that a family member or other person is committing sexual abuse. In a study of 384 adults (reported in a 1999 issue of *Child Welfare*) who had been physically, sexually or emotionally abused by family members, in most cases disclosure of the abuse to a family member did not end the abuse. Of 249 cases of disclosure, 60% of the respondents said that the abuse continued. Even worse, 20% said the abuse accelerated after disclosure. Fifteen percent said the abuse temporarily abated and only 5% said the abuse stopped altogether.

Individuals who disclosed abuse said family members ignored the information or responded ineffectually. Others said they were blamed or not believed and the parent sided with the abuser. In one case, an adult disclosed severe physical abuse to a school nurse, who refused to provide any help. One individual told the family doctor, who reported the information to the parents. It is hoped that today's MANDATED REPORTER laws help to prevent school nurses and physicians from shirking their responsibility to report suspected abuse to PROTECTIVE SERVICES staff.

Of the adults who reported their disclosure of the abuse, 24% said it was not believed. Those most likely to believe were as follows: friends or neighbors (91%), a nonparent relative (89%), mothers (61%) and professionals or officials (50%).

Prevention

Systematic efforts to prevent sexual abuse of children are relatively new. Current prevention programs are directed primarily toward school-age children. These programs employ a variety of approaches, including structured school curricula, children's books, films, puppet shows, theater performances and talks by well-known sports or media celebrities.

Most programs attempt to familiarize children with the concept of sexual abuse by defining "bad" behaviors or situations. Children are taught to recognize, for example, inappropriate touching and are alerted to simple actions they can take to prevent such abuse. Frequently they are encouraged to tell another trusted adult about the abuse. They may also be taught various methods of resistance, including: verbal refusal (saying no), running away and even martial arts techniques.

Other prevention efforts focus on parents and professionals. Parents are taught how to educate their children about sexual abuse. Instruction often includes suggestions for the detection of abuse and what to do when abuse is discovered. Professional training of teachers, physicians, police and mental health workers has followed similar lines, often emphasizing detection. (*See also* INCEST; PRISONS, CHILD VICTIMIZERS IN; RAPE; SEX OFFENDERS.)

John Briere, et al., eds., *The APSAC Handbook on Child Maltreatment* (Thousand Oaks, CA: Sage Publications, 1996.)

Committee on Child Abuse and Neglect, American Academy of Pediatrics, "Guidelines for the Evaluation of Sexual Abuse of Children: Subject Review," *Pediatrics* 103, no. 1 (January 1999): 186–191.

Judith A. Cohen and Anthony P. Mannarino, "Interventions for Sexually Abused Children: Initial Treatment Outcome Findings," *Child Maltreatment* 3, no. 1 (February 1998): 17–26.

David Finkelhor, *A Sourcebook on Child Sexual Abuse* (Beverly Hills, Calif.: Sage Publications, 1986).

———, *Child Sexual Abuse* (New York: Free Press, 1984).

Emanuel Peluso and Nicholas Putnam, "Case Study: Sexual Abuse of Boys by Females," *Journal of the American Academy of Child and Adolescent Psychiatry* 35, no. 1 (January 1996): 51–54.

Sally E. Palmer, et al., "Responding to Children's Disclosure of Familial Abuse: What Survivors Tell Us," *Child Welfare* 78, no. 2 (March 1, 1999): 259–282.

sexual abuse, adolescent perpetrators of *See* ADOLESCENT PERPETRATORS OF SEXUAL ABUSE.

sexual dysfunction Victims of child SEXUAL ABUSE often experience sexual difficulties in later life. Adult survivors of sexual abuse may report difficulty becoming aroused, pain during intercourse, inability to achieve orgasm or extreme physical revulsion during sex. Because some of their first sexual experiences involved force, coercion or exploitation many survivors come to associate these dynamics with all sexual encounters. Some adults experience flashbacks during which the sexual abuse is vividly recalled.

Subsequent reactions to sexual abuse range from total avoidance of all intimate relationships to frenetic, promiscuous sexual activity. In an effort to avoid painful memories or future exploitation some victims of sexual molestation close themselves off from any relationship that may lead to intimacy. Others, seeking to prove that they are in control of their sexuality or perhaps reacting to feelings of worthlessness and guilt, develop a pattern of compulsive sexual behavior. Some experts believe female survivors may see their sexuality as a way of gaining power over men and thereby regaining control of themselves. Though they are often extremely active sexually, survivors who exhibit this reaction usually achieve little pleasure from sex and have difficulty experiencing true intimacy with their sexual partner.

Males who are sexually victimized by a man often display hypermasculine behavior in an effort to prove to themselves and others that they are heterosexual. Abuse by an adult of the same sex is often accompanied by intense self-doubt concerning the victim's sexual orientation. Victims commonly feel responsible in some way for the abuse. When the assailant is of the same sex the child often believes that since the adult was attracted to him, he must be homosexual. If the child has internalized negative attitudes toward homosexuality the fear of homosexuality may intensify guilt feelings leading to even greater distress over sexuality.

Survivors of child sexual abuse often lack knowledge of how intimate relations develop. Children who are forced into sexual behavior prematurely may learn how to relate only sexually. These children may have difficulty relating to peers on a level appropriate to their age. Incest survivors often complain of being robbed of their childhood because they were prevented from developing the kind of family and peer relationships considered an important part of healthy development. The inability to develop intimacy often leads to later marital and/or sexual dysfunction.

Expert help and a supportive environment is usually necessary to help the survivor overcome problems related to sexual abuse. A number of self-help and formal therapy groups are available for the adult survivor. As awareness of the lasting effects of such victimization grows, more adults are seeking help in overcoming problems related to child sexual abuse.

sex offender registration   Federal and state laws requiring violent sex offenders to register with a government agency upon their release in the United States. The term of the registration varies from state to state. (*See* the state-by-state chart; *see also* MEGAN'S LAW, WETTERLING ACT.)

sexual exploitation   Child sexual exploitation involves the use of children as prostitutes, models for pornographic purposes or objects of sexual molestation. Exploitation is usually, but not exclusively, undertaken for the economic gain of an adult. No reliable estimates of the incidence of sexual exploitation are available. Recent estimates of sexual abuse often fail to include victims of pornography or prostitution. Law enforcement officials believe sexual exploitation of children to be one of the most underreported crimes. (*See also* CHILD PORNOGRAPHY, CHILD PROSTITUTION and SEXUAL ABUSE.)

Seth L. Goldstein, *The Sexual Exploitation of Children* (New York: Elsevier, 1987).

sexual trafficking   Illegal trade in women and children for sexual purposes has been practiced since ancient times. In the late 19th and early 20th centuries child prostitution and white slavery was a source of great public concern in Europe and in North America, where newspapers estimated that 60,000 children per year were kidnapped or lured into prostitution. Though accurate information on the extent of sexual trafficking was unavailable, sensational, sometimes racist accounts in the media spurred the enactment of laws specifically prohibiting the sexual exploitation of children.

The extent of sexual trafficking in children is still unknown. Though large numbers of children are thought to be victims of kidnapping and sexual exploitation, estimates of the extent of such activities are controversial and largely based on anecdotal data. Youthful prostitutes are in great demand and often command higher prices than adults. Significant numbers of runaway children and adolescents are known to be lured or coerced into prostitution.

Existence of international trade in children and adolescents is also hard to document. Children in developing countries may be enticed or sold into illicit activity in hopes of economic gain. Reports of

Legislation Requiring Sex Offenders to Register with a Government Agency

STATE/STATUTE	Length of Registration	Items Included in Registration	Provisions for Rehabilitation
ALABAMA 13A-11-200 et. seq.		Name of offender	
ALASKA 12.63.010 et. seq.	15 years if a single sex offense; lifetime for one aggravated sex offense or two or more sex offenses	Name; address; place of employment; date of birth; each sex offense conviction; date, place, and court of sex offense convictions; aliases; driver's license; fingerprints; photograph; vehicle information; statement regarding treatment received	
ARIZONA 13-3821 et. seq.		Name and statement of offender; photograph; fingerprints	
ARKANSAS 12-12-902 et. seq.	10 years	Name; date of birth; conviction information; photograph; fingerprints; Social Security number	May apply for relief from duty of further registration; hearing held; burden is preponderance of the evidence
CALIFORNIA Penal Code, 290	Life	Name; photograph; fingerprints; license plate number; copies of adequate proof of residence	
COLORADO 18-3-412.5 et. seq.	20, 10, or 5 years, depending on the offense	Name; address; place of employment; all aliases; and other information as required by the local law enforcement agency	May petition for an order discontinuing registration requirement
CONNECTICUT 54-250 et. seq.	10 years; sexually violent offenders for life	Name; identifying factors; criminal history records; residence address, documentation of any treatment received	After 10 years, sexually violent offenders may apply to the court for release from the duty to register
DELAWARE tit. 11, § 4120	At least 15 years	Name and aliases; age; gender; race; fingerprints; photograph; all known identifying factors; offense history; address; documentation of any treatment received	Court may release from registration upon enumerated conditions
FLORIDA 775.21	Lifetime, unless court removes sexual predator designation after 10 years	Name; Social Security number; age; race; sex; date of birth; physical description; photograph; address; place of employment; date and place of conviction; fingerprints; description of crimes	10 years after release, person may petition court to remove sexual predator designation
GEORGIA 42-9-44.1	Completion of parole	Name; address; crimes of conviction; date of parole	

Legislation Requiring Sex Offenders to Register with a Government Agency

STATE/STATUTE	Length of Registration	Items Included in Registration	Provisions for Rehabilitation
HAWAII 846E-2, 846E-9	Life	Photograph; fingerprints; name and aliases; date of birth; Social Security number; address and telephone number; sex; race; physical description; place of employment; vehicle registration information; and summary of criminal offenses; statement about treatment received	
IDAHO 18-8301 et. seq.	Lifetime, unless court grants an exemption after 10 years	Name and aliases; date of birth; Social Security number; photograph; fingerprints; offenses; jurisdiction where offense occurred; current address and employment	After 10 years, a person may petition for exemption
ILLINOIS ch. 730, § 150/3 et. seq.	10 years; sexually dangerous person for life	Name and statement of offender; fingerprints; photograph	
INDIANA 5-2-12-1 et. seq.	10 years after date released, placed on parole, or placed on probation	Name; alias; date of birth; sex; race; physical description; Social Security number; address; driver's license number; description of offense; date of conviction; sentence	
IOWA 692A.2 et. seq.	10 years; sexually violent predators must register for an indeterminate period, ending only when sentencing court approves	Fingerprints; Social Security number; photograph	
KANSAS 22-4903 et. seq.	10 years if first conviction; life if second conviction	Name; date and place of birth; offense; date and place of conviction; sex and age of victim; address; Social Security number; race; age; physical description; blood type; occupation and name of employer; driver's license; vehicle information; photograph; fingerprints; and DNA exemplars	After 10 years, court may relieve from duty if it finds by preponderance of the evidence that the offender is rehabilitated
KENTUCKY 17.500 et. seq.	10 years; persons classified as high risk must register for life	Signed written statement; Social Security number; age; race; sex; date of birth; physical description; aliases; residence; vehicle information; brief description of crime	High-risk offenders can be relieved of the duty to register if court determines that they are no longer high-risk offenders

Legislation Requiring Sex Offenders to Register with a Government Agency

STATE/STATUTE	Length of Registration	Items Included in Registration	Provisions for Rehabilitation
LOUISIANA 15:542 et. seq.	10 years; unless there has been a determination that the person is a sexually violent predator; sexually violent predators must register for life	Name; address; crime information; aliases; Social Security number	
MAINE tit. 34-A § 11003	15 years	Name and address	
MARYLAND art. 27, § 792	10 years; sexually violent predator shall register until they are determined not to be a sexually violent predator	Name; address; place of employment; crime information; aliases; Social Security number; photograph; fingerprints	
MASSACHUSETTS ch. 6, § 178E et. seq.	20 years; life if convicted of two or more sex offenses committed on different occasions	Name; aliases; date and place of birth; physical description; Social Security number; home and work addresses; photograph; fingerprints; description of crime	May apply with board to end registration upon proof by clear and convincing evidence that he has not committed a sex offense within 15 years following conviction and is not likely to pose a threat to the safety of others
MICHIGAN 4.475 (1) et. seq.	25 years; life if second conviction	Name; Social Security number; address; conviction information; physical description; blood type; and photograph	
MINNESOTA 243.166 et. seq.	10 years	Name and statement of offender; fingerprints; photograph	
MISSISSIPPI 45-33-1 et. seq.	At least 15 years after conviction or release	Name; address; employment; crime information; aliases; Social Security number; date of birth; sex; physical description	Offender must show purposes of registration are not served and he has not committed an offense within 15 years
MISSOURI 589.400 et. seq.		Name; address; Social Security number; telephone number; place of employment; crime information; age and gender of victim; fingerprints; photograph	
MONTANA 46-23-504 et. seq.	Registration for life	Address; fingerprints; photograph	10 years after conviction offender may petition for relief from duty; court may grant petition upon finding registrant is a law-abiding citizen and registration is not necessary

Legislation Requiring Sex Offenders to Register with a Government Agency

STATE/STATUTE	Length of Registration	Items Included in Registration	Provisions for Rehabilitation
NEBRASKA 29-4004 et. seq.	10 years after discharge from probation or parole or release from incarceration; if the person is a sexually violent predator they must register until a court finds that they are no longer a sexually violent predator	Name; aliases; physical description; date of birth; Social Security number; photograph; fingerprints; crime and incarceration information; address of residence and employment	Registration may be expunged if duty to register has expired; petition has no criminal charge pending and is not under investigation; and petitioner is not a substantial risk to commit another offense
NEVADA 179D.230 et. seq.	Register for life	Name; aliases; physical description; date of birth; Social Security number; driver's license and vehicle information; address; information concerning employment; information on convictions; information about the victim; mode of operation used to commit offenses; fingerprints; photograph	After 15 years, offender may apply for relief from duty of further registration
NEW HAMPSHIRE 651-B:2 et seq.	Life or 10 years, depending on the offense	Mailing address; current residence	
NEW JERSEY 2C:7-1 et. seq.	At least 15 years	Name; Social Security number; age; race; sex; date of birth; physical description; legal residence; place of employment; conviction information; fingerprints	Offender may apply to terminate registration if no offense is committed within 15 years of conviction or release from correctional facility
NEW MEXICO 29-11A-4	Registration information maintained for 10 or 20 years, depending on offense	Name and aliases; date of birth; Social Security number; address; place of employment; conviction information; photograph; fingerprints; other identifying marks on offender	
NEW YORK Corrections Law 168-a et. seq.	10 years; sexually violent predators register for a minimum of 10 years unless court determines he is no longer likely to engage in predatory sexually violent offenses	Name and aliases; date of birth; physical description; driver's license number; address; photograph; fingerprints; conviction information	Registrant may file for petition from relief of duty to register with the sentencing court
NORTH CAROLINA 14-208.5 et. seq.	10 years; sexually violent predator registers until determination made that person is no longer a sexually violent predator	Name and aliases; date of birth; physical description; driver's license number; address; offense information; photograph; fingerprints	Exemption may be granted if shown that no useful purpose will be served by registration

Legislation Requiring Sex Offenders to Register with a Government Agency

STATE/STATUTE	Length of Registration	Items Included in Registration	Provisions for Rehabilitation
NORTH DAKOTA 12.1-32-15	10 years	Information required by Attorney General; fingerprints; photographs	Registrant may petition for release of registration no more than once a year
OHIO 2950.02 et. seq.	10 years	Information required by the bureau of criminal identification; photographs; fingerprints	
OKLAHOMA tit. 57, § 582 et. seq.	10 years with the department of corrections; 5 years with local law enforcement	Name; aliases; description of person; photograph; driver's license; fingerprints; blood sample; date of birth; offense information; address; Social Security number	
OREGON 181.597 et. seq.	At least 10 years	Name; address; fingerprints; photographs	Registrant may file petition for order relieving of duty to register
PENNSYLVANIA tit. 42, § 9793 et. seq.	10 years; sexually violent predators must register until no longer designated as a sexually violent predator	Name and address	
RHODE ISLAND 11-37.1-3 et. seq.	10 years; sexually violent predators must register until no longer designated as a sexually violent predator	Name and address	Sexually violent predators may petition to have the designation removed after 10 years
SOUTH CAROLINA 23-3-430 et. seq.	Life	Information as prescribed by State Law Enforcement Division	
SOUTH DAKOTA 22-22-31 et. seq.		Name and aliases; physical description; fingerprints; photograph; residence; conviction information	
TENNESSEE 40-39-103 et. seq.	At least 10 years	Name and aliases; date and place of birth; Social Security number; driver's license number; parole or probation information; offense information; place of employment; address	No sooner than 10 years after beginning of registration, person may file petition for an order relieving of duty to register; statute lists numerous factors for court to consider
TEXAS Criminal Code 62.01 et. seq.	10 years or life depending on the offense	Name; aliases; date of birth; sex; race; height; weight; eye color; hair color; Social Security and driver's license number; shoe size; address; photograph; fingerprints; type of offense; date of conviction; punishment received	Persons may petition the court for relief from the duty of lifetime registration
UTAH 77-27-21.5	10 years	Name; aliases; address; physical description; vehicle description; photograph; parole or probation information; crime information; description of the offender's primary and secondary targets; photograph	

Legislation Requiring Sex Offenders to Register with a Government Agency

STATE/STATUTE	Length of Registration	Items Included in Registration	Provisions for Rehabilitation
VERMONT tit. 13, § 5402 et. seq.	10 years, except for sexually violent predators who must register for life	Name; date of birth; description; address; Social Security number; fingerprints; photograph; employment information	After 10 years, a sexually violent predator may petition for removal of the designation
VIRGINIA 19.2-298.1	10 years, unless convicted of 2 or more offenses convicted of two offenses or person is a sexually violent predator, then for life	Name; aliases; date of birth; Social Security number; address; description of offense; fingerprints; photograph	
WASHINGTON 9A.44.130 et. seq.	Life, 15 years, or 10 years, depending upon offense	Name; address; date and place of birth; place of employment; crime; date and place of conviction; aliases used; Social Security number; photograph and fingerprints	May petition superior court; hearing will be held; standard is clear and convincing evidence
WEST VIRGINIA 61-8F-2 et. seq.	10 years; sexually violent predator for life	Name; address; Social Security number; photograph; crime information; fingerprints	
WISCONSIN 301.45	15 years; life for two or more convictions	Name; aliases; address; physical description, school enrollment; place of employment; crime information; vehicle information	
WYOMING 7-19-302 et. seq.	First or second degree sexual assault conviction: by petition; other sexual assault convictions: 10 years or by petition	Name; aliases; address; date of birth; Social Security number; place of employment; conviction information; fingerprints; photograph	Registrant may petition court for relief from duty to register

Source: National Center for Prosecution of Child Abuse, 1999.

children being sold by parents surface from time to time but it is not known if the practice is widespread. (*See also* CHILD SLAVERY and PROSTITUTION.)

sexually transmitted disease (STD)   Presence of a sexually transmitted disease in a child under the age of puberty is a strong indicator of SEXUAL ABUSE. It is extremely rare for such diseases to be contracted in any way other than by sexual contact. (Although newborn infants may contract some venereal diseases from their mothers during the birth process.) A thorough physical examination for possible sexual abuse should include taking cultures from genitals, mouth and anus. A blood test is necessary to detect syphilis. (*See also* AIDS; GONORRHEA; SYPHILIS; VENEREAL DISEASE; and WARTS, VENEREAL.)

shaken infant syndrome   This is also known as "shaken baby syndrome" and was formerly called "whiplash shaken infant syndrome." Parents and caretakers sometimes express their frustration toward a crying, irritable or otherwise uncooperative infant by shaking the baby. This form of abuse can cause death or, if the child lives, severe brain trauma. Shaking and the resultant SEQUELAE were first differentiated from the BATTERED CHILD SYNDROME by radiologist John Caffey in the early 1970s. Caffey cited cases in which infants and children, who showed no external signs of battering or abuse, had suffered serious head and spinal cord injury and, in several instances, death, from shaking.

Closer examination showed that many of these infants suffered SUBDURAL HEMATOMA, RETINAL HEMORRHAGING and damage to the periosteum of long bones. Further study showed connections among the practice of shaking and permanent brain damage, mental retardation, blindness, visual loss, motor deficits, seizures and hypopituitarism. The injury most frequently associated with the shaking of infants is subdural hematoma.

Infants in their first six months of life are the most likely victims of shaken infant syndrome. During infancy the head is heavier in proportion to total body weight than at any other time. This fact, coupled with relatively weak supporting neck muscles, makes this age group very sensitive to the sudden backward-forward motions associated with whiplash.

The absence of external signs make this syndrome difficult to diagnose. Adding to the diagnostic difficulty is the reluctance of parents and caretakers to give the physician an accurate medical and social history. Victims of shaking may show symptoms of respiratory difficulty, fever, irritability, lethargy, decreased appetite or vomiting, along with a number of other somewhat vague symptoms, none of which are sufficient to confirm a diagnosis of shaken infant syndrome.

Diagnosis Can Be Difficult

A thorough medical/social history and a complete physical examination by a physician familiar with the syndrome and with the subtle signs of head injury increases the likelihood of an accurate diagnosis. Careful fundiscopic examination is an important tool for detecting retinal hemorrhages. In recent years, the use of cranial computed tomography (CT) has greatly increased the ability to detect the presence of subdural hematoma.

In addition, magnetic resonance imaging (MRI) may also be useful in differentiating a shaken baby form of abuse from a spontaneous subarachnoid hemorrhage.

Other symptoms are seizures, vomiting, breathing difficulties, unconsciousness or impaired consciousness, poor feeding and lethargy. Retinal hemorrhage is the most commonly observed sign

and appears in 65% to 95% of all victims. Seizures are also common, occurring in 40% to 70% of the afflicted infants. Cerebral edema is also typical among infants who survive.

The physician may also find bruising, burn marks and other forms of abuse. If a spinal tap is performed, it often reveals bloody fluid rather than the normally clear spinal fluid.

If the child dies, the cause of death is most frequently uncontrollable intracranial hypertension. An autopsy will reveal skull fractures in approximately 25% of the infants, often in the posterior parietal bone or the occipital bone or in both areas.

According to Ann-Christine Duhaime, M.D., et al., in a 1998 article in the *New England Journal of Medicine*,

> The majority of abused infants in fact have clinical, radiologic, or autopsy evidence of blunt impact to the head. Thus, the term "shaking-impact syndrome" may reflect more accurately than "shaken-baby syndrome" the usual mechanism responsible for these injuries. Whether shaking alone can cause the constellation of findings associated with the syndrome is still debated, but most investigators agree that trivial forces, such as those involving routine play, infant swings, or falls from a low height are insufficient to cause the syndrome. Instead, these injuries appear to result from major rotational forces, which clearly exceed those encountered in normal child-care activities.

These authors also state that "The most consistent finding in cases of the shaking-impact syndrome is the present of subdural and subarachnoid blood. Hemorrhage therefore is both a marker for the threshold of force required to cause the injury and a likely pathophysiologic contributor to the resultant brain damage."

The "Nanny Baby Murder" Case

The most famous case of shaken baby syndrome involved Louise Woodward, a nanny who was accused and convicted of second-degree murder in 1997 in the death of baby Matthew Eappen. Woodward's primary defense was the contention that the child had a previous brain injury and for some reason that injury began to "rebleed," leading to the child's death.

The judge subsequently overturned the verdict and found Woodward guilty of involuntary manslaughter, sentencing her only to the time she had already served. This decision created great controversy, and 50 physicians expert in the diagnosis and treatment of child abuse challenged the judge's action and published their findings on the Internet, stating that the medical evidence "overwhelmingly supported a violent shaking/impact episode on the day in question, when Matthew was in the sole custody of Ms. Woodward." The doctors stated that the "rebleed theory" was "courtroom diagnosis" rather than a medical diagnosis.

Shaken infant syndrome is a rare cause of infant death but most physicians agree that the vast majority of children diagnosed with this problem are victims of some form of child abuse.

Ann-Christine Duhaime, et al., "Nonaccidental Head Injury in Infants—The 'Shaken-Baby Syndrome,'" *New England Journal of Medicine* 338, no. 25 (June 18, 1998): pp. 1822–1829.

Lucinda J. Dykes, "Whiplash Shaken Infant Syndrome: What Has Been Learned?" *Child Abuse and Neglect* 10, no. 2 (1986): 211–221.

Sheppard-Towner Infancy and Maternity Act
This legislation, passed in 1921, established the first United States program to provide major funding to alleviate a wide range of problems suffered by infants and young children as a result of nutritional deficiency, generally poor health and lack of adequate care. The act was sponsored by the CHILDREN'S BUREAU, an agency established in 1912 during an era of social reform.

sibling abuse   Violence between siblings is widespread in Western culture. Interestingly, such assaults constitute a relatively small proportion of all child abuse cases reported to investigative authorities. This fact in part reflects a belief that sibling violence is a normal part of family life that should be handled without outside interference. Underreporting may also be due to a tendency to cite parents for failing to protect the victimized sibling rather than labeling the child as the abuser. Parents may also fear that reporting would lead to the removal of the abused (or abusive) child from the family home.

Brother-on-brother violence is more commonly observed than brother-sister violence. Sister-brother violence is not common. Least common is sister-sister violence. Brother-brother violence is often unreported and seen as "roughhousing" and typical male behavior.

Although sibling abuse has been estimated to be the most frequent manifestation of family violence, it is the least likely to result in death. Family factors that may result in abuse of a sibling are:

• lack of supervision

• children who are treated as favorites versus children treated negatively

• parents who ignore indications or obvious proof of minor forms of abuse by a sibling, thus tacitly signaling the abuse may continue and even escalate

• severe family stress

Sometimes abuse is alleged but is not occurring, so investigation is important. Authors John Caffaro and Allison Conn-Caffaro cited in their book the case of a 7-year-old boy accused of constantly biting his 11-year-old brother to the point of drawing blood. The younger child actively denied the biting. After probing further, the therapists learned that the older child was actively jealous of the younger child, who was clearly enjoying a preferential status in the family. Bite impressions were taken the next time the wounds appeared and it was discovered that the older child was biting himself and blaming his brother in order to gain parental attention.

Risk Factors
Caffaro and Conn-Caffaro cited the following as risk factors for sibling offenders:

• offender's thinking errors that distort or minimize abusive behavior

• history of victimization by parent, older sibling or persons outside the immediate family

• inadequate impulse control, empathic deficits and emotional immaturity

• willingness to use coercion or force to control victim (sadistic, cruel behavior)

• drug or alcohol use

• dissociative reactions to trauma

They also identified factors common to sibling victims:

- large developmental, physical or intellectual differences between siblings
- victim's dependence on an older, more powerful sibling
- lack of other, supportive relationships
- prior history of victimization
- lack of sex education

Sexual contact between siblings, though legally defined as INCEST, often does not result in a report of child abuse. Exploratory sexual contact between young children is usually seen as a normal part of sexual development. When one or both siblings are adolescents or when contact results in trauma, infection or pregnancy the situation is viewed with greater alarm.

Denial is an important factor in parents' failure to protect a child adequately from sibling attacks. Parents are often embarrassed or afraid of abusive behavior in their children. Once convinced that a child is at risk of serious harm, most parents are able to intervene effectively. (*See also* SEXUAL ABUSE.)

John V. Caffaro and Allison Conn-Caffaro, *Sibling Abuse Trauma: Assessment and Intervention Strategies for Children, Families, and Adults.* (New York: The Haworth Maltreatment and Trauma Press, 1998.)

SIDS *See* SUDDEN INFANT DEATH SYNDROME.

situational abuse and neglect Situational abuse and neglect refers to circumstances over which the parents or caretakers have little control. POVERTY and discrimination are such conditions and often are associated with abuse or neglect. Though programs such as Aid to Families with Dependent Children and HEAD START have helped reduce the effects of such circumstances, many children throughout the world still suffer from the effects of discrimination and poverty.

skeletal survey When child battering is suspected a skeletal survey is often conducted to search for signs of previous battering. Physicians look for signs of multiple FRACTURES of the types most likely to result from abusive treatment. Careful examination of these X rays can reveal OSSIFICATION resulting from previous fractures.

slavery, child *See* CHILD SLAVERY.

sleep deprivation Children who are severely abused, physically or psychologically, often do not get adequate sleep and the sleep that they do experience is troubled. Sleep deprivation often impairs intellectual functioning and makes children irritable and distractable. Negative behaviors resulting from a lack of sleep may make children more susceptible to abuse by a parent or caretaker.

In severe cases of sleep deprivation secretion of the growth hormone somatotropin is inhibited, causing psychosocial DWARFISM. Cases of abuse-related dwarfism are rare. Once normal sleep patterns are reestablished, children usually experience a period of rapid growth, which in most cases reverses growth inhibition. In a study published in a 1997 issue of the *Journal of the American Academy of Child and Adolescent Psychiatry,* researchers compared 19 prepubertal children who had experienced substantiated abuse with 15 nonabused control children and 10 children diagnosed with depression. They found that physically abused children had the most difficulty falling sleep and experienced more troubled sleep. For example, the abused children were "twice as active at night as controls." Sexually abused children also experienced more sleep problems than the control group or the depressed group. About half of the abused children experienced impaired sleep and five of the abused children (about 26%) had sleep problems severe enough to be considered a clinical sleep disturbance.

The researchers also noted that sleep problems in children could indicate abuse and said,

> Thus, if a child presents with impaired sleep, abuse (particularly physical abuse) should be considered as part of the differential formulation. Likewise, when evaluating a child who has been abused, sleep should be carefully assessed for clinically significant impairments. It is conceivable that early intervention targeted at abused children with sleep

disruption may help diminish long-term intractable insomnia.

Carol A. Glod, et al., "Increased Nocturnal Activity and Impaired Sleep Maintenance in Abused Children," *Journal of the American Academy of Child and Adolescent Psychiatry* 36 (September 1997): 1236–1243.

slick but sick syndrome   The term slick but sick was coined by psychologist Logan Wright and describes the capacity of some abusive parents to hide underlying PSYCHOPATHOLOGY. By comparing convicted child batterers with a carefully matched control group of nonabusing parents, Wright was able to distinguish personality differences between the two groups. On certain psychological tests, batterers gave responses very similar to nonbatterers when the socially desirable answer to a question was logical or apparent. However, answers to the Minnesota Multiphasic Personality Inventory (MMPI), a less-apparent, empirically devised measure of psychopathology, showed that battering parents were actually much more disturbed than they appeared initially. The ability of abusive parents to present themselves as more healthy than they may actually be has been used to explain the often confusing evidence obtained in clinical studies of child abusers. Other researchers have emphasized the importance of societal pressures and stresses over the individual psychopathology of the abuser. The latter hypothesize that almost any parent or caregiver under certain stressful conditions will resort to child abuse. Proponents of the belief that child abusers are emotionally disturbed point to phenomena like the slick but sick syndrome to explain abusive behavior by adults who appear healthy.

social abuse   Children often suffer as victims of poverty and discrimination. Most child advocates believe societies, and the governments that represent them, have a responsibility to provide for the safety and well-being of children and families. These responsibilities may include protecting children from all forms of physical, sexual and psychological maltreatment (including racial discrimination), making sure children are well nourished, have adequate housing and receive necessary medical care.

Failure by society to provide for children's basic needs is sometimes referred to as social abuse. Though social abuse is not addressed by child abuse laws, many experts believe it is an indirect cause of much child abuse and neglect.

social isolation   Abusive or neglectful parents tend to be isolated from helping networks. Social isolation may be externally imposed in the case of a parent who is ostracized by neighbors and relatives or internally imposed by the parent's choice. Frequent changes of residence may contribute to social isolation. Abused children may also engage in social WITHDRAWAL, turning inward and isolating themselves from peers, family members and others.

Neglectful parents are significantly less likely to belong to an organization such as a church or parent-teacher association. They also have fewer close friends and tend to socialize less often.

One explanation for social isolation is that neglectful parents may be suffering from depression, which renders them incapable of normal social functioning. Another is that parents use detachment from others as a defense. While fearing rejection, they avoid forming close relationships. This may also explain their difficulty in forming a strong attachment to their own children.

A number of methods are used to reduce social isolation and encourage the formation of a network of supporting friends. Individual, group and family therapy may help reduce psychological blocks to developing reciprocal relationships. Groups such as PARENTS ANONYMOUS serve as helping networks and encourage members to be available to one another whenever help is needed. (*See also* WITHDRAWAL.)

social learning model of child abuse   Some theorists explain child abuse as a result of a learned pattern of relating to others. As children, parents may learn violent ways of expressing anger or frustration. Later these maladaptive coping mechanisms may be reflected in a range of aggressive behavior, including child abuse. Social learning theorists often look to parental models as the source of much, but not all, social learning. In contrast to a psychoanalytic approach, which postulates that early experiences leave largely unchangeable emotional imprints, social learning theory holds open the possibility of learning new ways of parenting.

Social Security Act This federal legislation was initially passed in 1935 and has been amended several times to provide for establishment of various social programs, many of which directly relate to child and family welfare.

Title IV of the act supports state welfare services, i.e., day care, foster care and varied preventive and protective programs. Provisions of Title IV also ensure that child support is paid by absent parents and provide for establishment of paternity. Originally, Title IV also encompassed funding for states' Aid to Families with Dependent Children programs, now the Temporary Aid to Needy Families (TANF) program.

Title V designates monies in support of Maternal and Child Health and other health care services for children from low-income families. Title XIX funds MEDICAID, a medical assistance program for low-income people. Title XX establishes state grants for service programs such as prevention of child abuse and neglect; preserving, rehabilitating and reuniting families; and referring individuals to institutions where appropriate.

Society for the Prevention of Cruelty to Children (United States) Founded in 1875 in New York City, this organization was based on the premise that, "The child is an animal . . . If there is no justice for it as a human being, it shall at least have the rights of the stray cur in the street. It shall not be abused." It was among the earliest of the child protective services in the United States.

These words, by one of the founders of the SPCC, Henry Bergh, reveal the need that existed in the United States at a time when cities were growing and child abuse and neglect was being identified by Progressive Era reformers. After five years had passed, the SPCC saw similar groups founded in nearly a dozen other cities.

SPCC efforts focused on court action, gaining custody of children from abusive or neglectful parents and placing them in institutions where they received a modicum of better care.

The SPCC also worked to end child prostitution and child labor. In particular, SPCC workers in New York City were successful in combating the *padrone* system, whereby poor Italian families would pay to send their children to America under the protection of a padrone. The padrone, however, would not send the child's wages back to the parents in Italy but merely force the child to work for no pay at all.

Society for the Protection of Women and Children from Aggravated Assaults (Britain) This British organization was founded in London, England in 1857. This early group's activities focused principally on women, although it published *Compassionate Justice,* which was a study of cruelty to children. The latter was part of an attempt to heighten awareness of child abuse and neglect, which several decades later became the subject of well-publicized charitable reform efforts. When this happened, the society worked on behalf of legal changes to benefit abused children.

sodomy Though the term can refer to any form of sexual intercourse considered to be unnatural according to societal standards, sodomy is most commonly used to refer to anal intercourse between two males. In the context of child SEXUAL ABUSE, sodomy is used to describe anal intercourse between an adult male and a child of either sex.

In addition to the emotional trauma caused by sexual abuse, sodomy can also result in physical harm to children. Sodomy is especially painful for young children who are likely to suffer anal tears or enlargement. Diseases such as gonorrhea and syphilis can also be conveyed through anal intercourse. Presence of a SEXUALLY TRANSMITTED DISEASE in a child is strong, but all too frequently overlooked, evidence of sexual abuse.

Children who have been subjected to sodomy may be reluctant to reveal their victimization but may complain of anal discomfort and may soil undergarments or exhibit other somatic and behavioral signs of trauma. (*See also* ENCOPRESIS.)

soiling *See* ENCOPRESIS.

Sovereign Immunity, Doctrine of *See* DOCTRINE OF SOVEREIGN IMMUNITY.

spanking   *See* AVERSIVE CONDITIONING.

special child   *See* TARGET CHILD.

spinal cord injury   *See* CENTRAL NERVOUS SYSTEM INJURY.

splitting   Splitting refers to an intrapsychic process often employed by children who have been abused. Unable to understand how a parent can be both good and bad, children split positive and negative attributes and see others and themselves as either good or bad. This process may lead to the creation of scapegoats or a PARENTIFIED CHILD.

In the case of a child who sees the parent as only good and therefore incapable of doing wrong, the child interprets the parent's abusive behavior as a reflection of his or her own badness. The child may then become a willing scapegoat, actually seeking out punishment.

The parentified child, identifying with the good parent, seeks to fill the role of the neglectful or abusive parent. Parentification is reflected in a kind of pseudomaturity that exceeds the child's years. Often taking on extra household responsibilities and working hard in school, this child cannot do enough to please. When abused or neglected by the parent the child redoubles efforts to please.

spouse abuse   Spouse abuse includes physical and mental injury of a wife or husband by their marital partner. Though spouse abuse refers to the victimization of either partner, the overwhelming majority of such abuse involves battering of wives by their husbands.

Wife battering appears to be closely associated with child abuse. One study of mothers and their children in battered women's shelters found that 70% of children had been abused or neglected. In most cases the husband was responsible for the child abuse. About one-fourth of the children were abused by both mother and father. A very small number were abused by the mother only. (*See also* FAMILY VIOLENCE and YO-YO SYNDROME.)

staff flight   Maintaining qualified, well-trained and experienced protective service workers is a constant struggle in agencies charged with investigating and treating child abuse. Turnover rate among staff in these agencies has been estimated at 85% per year. While efforts to improve working conditions, provide additional training and ensure higher salaries have helped, the stressful nature of protective service work continues to contribute to early staff burnout. Social workers and investigators often find themselves working alone in highly charged emotional situations. Abusive parents or caretakers, frightened and angry when confronted, often direct their anger toward the protective service employee. Working with children who have been abused can also prove to be frustrating and heart-wrenching work for the human service professional who is sometimes powerless to reverse the effects of abuse. Over a period of time even the most highly motivated and best-trained protective services worker may become discouraged and alienated from his or her work.

standard of proof   *See* EVIDENTIARY STANDARDS.

Stanley v. Illinois   This case, decided by the United States Supreme Court in 1971, involved an unwed father who, upon the death of his children's mother, was not allowed custody of his three children. The state of Illinois invoked a law automatically making children of unmarried fathers wards of the state upon death of the mother. The father, Peter Stanley, petitioned the court for custody of his children, arguing that he had been denied equal protection under the law as granted in the Fourteenth Amendment to the U.S. Constitution.

The Supreme Court reversed the Illinois decision and granted custody to the father. *Stanley v. Illinois* is often cited as establishing the principle that prevents a state from separating children from their parents unless, by due process, the parent is proven to be unfit.

Robert H. Mnookin, *Child, Family and State: Problems and Materials on Children and the Law* (Boston: Little, Brown, 1978).

starvation   One of the most extreme results of child neglect is death from starvation. Though rare in the most Western countries, cases of starvation continue to surface every year. In some African countries where drought and war have severely restricted food supply, starving infants and children are a common sight. Starvation in third world countries is often described as a form of societal neglect. However, many experts are reluctant to characterize poverty-induced starvation as abuse or neglect.

In contrast to deaths from inadequate nutrition in developing countries, child starvation in developed countries is generally thought to be intentional. The most frequent victims are infants who appear to have been totally neglected. A high percentage tend to be born prematurely to mothers of low intelligence who already have large families. Though undernourished children usually respond quickly to proper care and nutrition in a hospital, they rarely receive such attention. Autopsies of starved infants usually show other evidence of gross neglect.

status offense   The term status offense refers to an action that is considered to be a criminal or delinquent act when engaged in by a person under a certain age, usually 16 years. A status offense may involve repeatedly defying parents' wishes, running away from home or being truant from school. In the United States many states have eliminated legal sanctions for status offenses, opting instead for categories such as CHINS (Child In Need of Services) or FWSN (Families With Service Needs). These new categories allow for court intervention in difficult cases; however, the court's role is often to provide an ASSESSMENT, make recommendations and monitor compliance with those recommendations.

stifling   *See* OVERLAYING.

stimulation, tactile   *See* TACTILE STIMULATION.

stipulation   At the beginning of a trial lawyers for both parties may enter into an oral or written agreement concerning certain facts of the case that are uncontested. These facts may include names and addresses of persons involved, relationships among the parties, ages etc. The stipulation serves as a basis for introduction of EVIDENCE and limits debate to those areas about which there is clear disagreement.

stomach, turned   *See* OPU HULE.

stress   Stress of various kinds is frequently associated with child abuse and neglect. Factors such as marital difficulty, POVERTY, work-related problems and SOCIAL ISOLATION have all been found to be related to increased levels of child abuse. Despite the association between stress and abuse it may not be correct to say that stress causes abuse. Many parents under a great deal of stress do not abuse or neglect their children.

Murray Straus, a noted researcher of FAMILY VIOLENCE, emphasizes the importance of mediating factors in establishing the link between stress and child maltreatment. Parents who were abused by their parents, in particular by the father, or who witnessed violence between their parents were more likely to abuse their own children. Straus suggests that violent responses to stress are learned, not innate.

Parents under stress are usually not uncontrollably driven to abuse their children. Parents who are abusive are more likely to approve of physical violence as a means of settling disputes. Marital violence is a strong predictor of child abuse. Both of these findings support the idea that parents who approve of or who regularly use physical force as a way of coping also abuse their children more often. Stress may increase the likelihood that parents who approve of violence will abuse their children but does not, by itself, produce violence.

Though stress may not directly cause child abuse, increases in family and societal stress may result in higher levels of abuse. Periods of high unemployment are frequently accompanied by increased family violence. Extreme poverty appears to increase the likelihood of abuse. Interestingly, however, occupational status and level of education do not appear to be related to abuse.

Learning how to cope with stress effectively is an important part of the treatment for perpetrators of child abuse. In many cases, parents are taught specific alternatives to physical punishment as a method of discipline or releasing frustrations. Groups such as PARENTS ANONYMOUS place a great deal of importance on establishing support networks for parents under stress. Parents who have a number of contacts outside the family are usually better able to cope with stress than those who are relatively isolated.

subdural hematoma Battering or shaking may result in intracranial hemorrhaging, causing blood to collect immediately beneath the skull. This collection of blood, known as subdural hematoma, is usually caused by the tearing of veins running from the cerebral cortex to the dural sinuses.

Subdural hematoma may occur on only one side of the brain (lateral) or on both sides of the brain (bilateral). Eighty percent of all subdural hematomas in children are bilateral.

Almost all subdural hematomas are caused by trauma induced by the head striking or being struck by a heavy object, or by the rapid jerking motion of the head when an infant is shaken.

Although the most frequent cause of death in battered infants, it may also be one of the most frequently overlooked injuries. The absence of external signs, even in the presence of massive internal bleeding, makes diagnosis difficult. Subdural hematoma can be detected through the presence of blood in the subdural and cerebrospinal fluid and through the use of cranial computed tomography (CT).

subgaleal hematoma A collection of blood immediately underneath the scalp, called subgaleal hematoma, can be the result of HAIR PULLING. Blood accumulation is caused by the rupture of blood vessels attacked to the outside of the cranium.

subpoena Witnesses and accused perpetrators of child abuse may be subpoenaed to testify in court. The most common type of subpoena is sometimes referred to by its Latin name, *subpoena ad testificandum.* This type of subpoena is a written document, issued by a court or authorized agency, that requires the recipient to appear in a specified court at a certain day and time. Subpoena is literally translated as "under penalty." Failure to comply with a subpoena can result in a fine or imprisonment.

A *subpoena duces tecum,* literally, under penalty take with you, requires the recipient to bring certain relevant documents to court. In child abuse or neglect cases this type of subpoena may be issued to a physician or mental health professional, requiring them to submit treatment records of the victim or alleged abuser. Normally such information is considered PRIVILEGED COMMUNICATIONS; however, in many jurisdictions child abuse reporting laws specifically abrogate such privileges when abuse or neglect is suspected.

substance abuse As defined by the U.S. Department of Health and Human Services, substance abuse is "the use of a psychoactive drug to such an extent that its effects seriously interfere with health or occupational and social functioning." Parental abuse of alcohol and other drugs can affect the child in two ways. Substance abuse during pregnancy can result in neonatal addiction and birth defects (*see* ADDICTION, INFANTILE). After birth, substance abuse by parents greatly increases the likelihood that a child will be abused or neglected.

It has been estimated that as much as two-thirds of all child abuse is related to substance abuse. One study by the Child Welfare League of America, reported in 1998, found that parental substance abuse was present in at least half of the substantiated neglect and abuse reports. The Indian Child Welfare Association has estimated that the majority of child abuse and neglect cases in Native American families stem from parental drinking or drug abuse. Many experts attribute the doubling of the number of children in foster care from 1986 to 1993 to an increase in the use of illegal drugs, most notably cocaine.

African-American women who are substance abusers are more likely to come into contact with child protective services agencies than are white or Hispanic mothers who are substance abusers, and African-American children are more likely to be placed in foster care. However, the majority of substance-abusing parents are white: 72% of substance-abusing mothers are white and 65% of substance-abusing fathers are white.

Research also shows that heavy use of marijuana during pregnancy can produce exaggerated tremors, vision problems and startle reflexes in newborns. Heroin and other opiates contribute to low birth weight and increase the risk of stillbirth and infant mortality. Phencyclidine (PCP), also known as "angel dust," can remain in the system for over a year and may be transported through breast milk and amniotic fluid. This is particularly dangerous since very low amounts of PCP can produce psychosis, teratogenesis (embryonic tumors) or developmental delay.

Infants born to addicted women sometimes display tremors, irritability, prolonged shrill crying, fever, vomiting, watery stools and other withdrawal symptoms. Severity of withdrawal seems to be in proportion to the amount of drug consumed by the mother on a daily basis.

Heavy drinking during pregnancy can produce a number of birth defects and abnormalities, including those associated with FETAL ALCOHOL SYNDROME.

Drugs also play a large role in the sexual exploitation of children. One-third of all sexual assaults on children take place while the perpetrator is under the influence of alcohol.

Looking for excitement and sometimes running from abuse at home, young girls and boys are often lured into drug usage by pimps. PROSTITUTION becomes a means of obtaining drugs that, in turn, offer escape from the experience of emotional pain and lowered self-esteem associated with this lifestyle.

Problems with Differing Goals of Different Social Service Agencies

One issue of concern is that the agencies which provide substance abuse treatment have goals that differ from those of child welfare agencies. For example, at the substance treatment center, the person who abuses substances is the "client," and that person's family is not of primary importance or may be of no importance at all. Yet, with the passage of the ADOPTION AND SAFE FAMILIES ACT and the provision that parental rights should be terminated if a child is in foster care for 15 of the last 22 months, substance abusers may be very concerned about their children and whether they may lose custody forever. Thus, the timeline of the substance treatment center, which may not stipulate a time limit for recovery (nor does federal law require such a time limit) may be very different from the timeline of the child welfare agency.

In addition to differing goals, confidentiality constraints may prevent substance treatment centers from conferring with child welfare agencies, even if a child welfare worker initiated a parent's going into treatment.

Child welfare workers may also worry about the substance abuser's ability to "stay clean." Some success, including some relapses, may be acceptable to the substance treatment center but not to the child welfare organization, because the child welfare worker is worried about the child's safety if he or she returned to the substance-abusing parent.

"Blending Perspectives and Building Common Ground: A Report to Congress on Substance Abuse and Child Protection," Department of Health and Human Services, Administration for Children and Families, Substance Abuse and Mental Health Services Administration, Office of the Assistance Secretary for Planning and Evaluation (April 1999).

substantiation   Refers to the confirmation of the alleged abuse of a child. Usually refers to incidents of physical or sexual abuse. Other cases may be "indicated," which means that abuse is likely although unproven. In some cases it cannot be determined if abuse has occurred, and in others, abuse is ruled out.

Substantiation can be more difficult in the case of infants or very young children, where marks and bruising may not be present but the child has nonetheless sustained injuries or even death as a result of shaking, suffocation or other means. Often, medical personnel may be consulted to help determine whether abuse was present or not. Sometimes physicians disagree among themselves.

According to the Administration for Children and Families in the U.S. Department of Health and Human Services, there were 963,870 cases of indicated or substantiated child abuse in 1997. Of these, 825,131 were substantiated and 138,719 were indicated. Many states, such as California, Illinois and New York, among others, did not provide statistics for indicated cases of child abuse. (See APPENDIX 5 for a state-by-state listing of substantiated or indicated victims of child abuse and neglect.)

Research suggests that reports filed by professionals are more likely to be substantiated than those filed by others. Reasons for this phenomenon are not clear. Some writers speculate that professionals may be more familiar with diagnostic procedures and legal definitions of abuse and therefore are better able to judge when a report should be filed. Professionals may also be more cooperative with investigators and more likely to follow up on their reports. In one study of reported abuse and neglect in New York (Eckenrode et al.), researchers found substantiation rates for professionals' reports to be 26% higher for neglect, 23% higher for physical abuse and 11% higher for sexual abuse.

Anonymous reports tend to have the lowest substantiation rates of all sources. This has led some policy analysts to suggest that agencies refuse to accept referrals from unidentified sources. Most agencies continue to accept such reports though many use telephone screening to eliminate those that are obviously frivolous.

Some groups have protested that PROTECTIVE SERVICES staff have far too much power and can remove a child from a home where abuse has not been substantiated and has probably not occurred. Often the decision boils down to a combination of skill, experience and intuition on the part of protective service personnel. Unfortunately, when social services staff err on the side of assuming abuse was mild or nonexistent, in some cases children have died and a public outcry arose that the state should "do something" about this problem. Thus, it can be a difficult balancing act for social service staffs, many of whom receive little training and experience a very high turnover. (*See also* FOUNDED REPORT, INVESTIGATION and UNFOUNDED REPORTS.)

substantive due process   *See* DUE PROCESS.

sudden infant death syndrome (SIDS)   SIDS is defined by an expert panel convened by the National Institute of Child Health and Development as "The sudden death of an infant under one year of age that remains unexplained after a thorough investigation, including performance of a complete autopsy, examination of the death scene, and review of the clinical history," and is also known as crib death and cot death. The SIDS rate was less than 1 per 1,000 live births in 1996 (0.74), down from about 1.5 per 1,000 for the preceding 20 years. Pediatricians attribute much of this improvement to their program urging mothers to put infants down to sleep on their backs rather than on their stomachs or sides.

One of the first recorded mentions of SIDS can be found in the well-known biblical account of King Solomon. Solomon was asked to settle a dispute between two women who claimed to be the mother of the same infant. One mother's infant had died previously as a result of OVERLAYING. This dispute over the existing infant was, of course, settled when Solomon proposed that the child be cut in

two. The woman who relinquished her claim in order to save the child was determined to be the true mother.

Until the 19th century, overlaying was considered the primary cause of SIDS. Death was attributed to the mother inadvertently rolling on top of the infant, thereby suffocating it.

Overlaying was thought to be preventable and was punished by the early Roman Catholic and Anglican churches. In the 17th century the *arcuccio* was invented to prevent overlaying. This arch made of wood and steel was placed over the baby to prevent suffocation or stifling, as it was called. Failure to use this device was a punishable offense in some countries. References to use of the *arcuccio* can be found as late as 1890.

Physicians, baffled by a lack of identifiable symptoms, have suspected many different causes for SIDS through history. The belief that death was related to an enlarged thymus gland led to the practice of preventative irradiation of the thymus during the 1930s and 1940s. This safety measure was later found to cause cancer. A large thymus gland is now considered a common characteristic of most infants.

SIDS has also been attributed to hypersensitivity to milk, viral infections, dietary deficiencies, respiratory infection, a reaction to the household dust mite, botulism and sleep apnea. Other causes thought to have been linked to SIDS are heart arrhythmias, an abnormal breathing control center in the brain, suffocation from old clothes, inherited breathing abnormalities, an electrolyte disturbance, overheating and bundling of the child. The possibility of INFANTICIDE has been suggested by many physicians.

Current Research on SIDS

Studies have implicated several key factors in SIDS. One was the prone (facedown) sleeping position, and in 1994, pediatricians in the United States, the United Kingdom and other countries began massive programs to convince pregnant women and new mothers to place their babies in the supine (face up) position. This action has been linked to a marked reduction in the number of SIDS cases, and according to physicians who reported on SIDS in a 1999 issue of *Current Opinion in Pediatrics*, "During the past decade the most exciting news about sudden infant death syndrome (SIDS) has been the dramatic effect of the supine sleep position in lowering the SIDS rate."

Some mothers place their babies on their sides, which is not considered as problematic as the prone position, but the supine position is still strongly favored by pediatricians as the best.

Some research has found that black mothers, unmarried mothers and poor mothers are more likely to place their babies in the prone position, despite warnings to the contrary from physicians, family and friends. A study reported in *Morbidity and Mortality Weekly Report* reported on mothers' placements of their infants. They found great variation from state to state, with 16% of mothers from Maine placing their babies on their stomachs and 30.8% of mothers in Alabama choosing the stomach position. Mothers in Washington (42.9%) and Alaska (40.8%) were most likely to place their babies on their backs. Black mothers were more apt (11% to 54% more likely) than white mothers to place their babies on their stomachs, although there was also great statewide variation. Of black mothers in Washington 22.5% chose the stomach position and in Florida, 42.1% of black mothers chose this position.

Some pediatricians have stated that some mothers have interpreted their advice to mean that the baby should never be in the prone position; however, the preference for the stomach position is for when the child is sleeping, not when he or she is active.

Physicians also warn that if the child is being cared for by another caretaker or a day care center, parents should be sure to inform them that the prone position is not acceptable while the baby is sleeping and instead the baby should be placed on his or her back.

Maternal Smoking Is a Major Risk Factor

Another key factor is SIDS is maternal tobacco smoking. According to a study reported in a 1999 issue of the *American Journal of Epidemiology,* maternal smoking and the presence of cotinine (which results from inhaling passive smoke) in the infant's urine were both strong predictors of SIDS. Researchers emphasized that it was not clear whether prenatal smoking or postnatal smoking was more important; however, it was clear that maternal smoking was a major risk factor.

The researchers studied a very large population of nearly 10,000 infants at risk for SIDS in New Zealand. They also looked at the smoking of other residents in the family but did not find a clear correlation between maternal smoking and SIDS.

Other Risk Factors

Researchers have found that breast-feeding seems to offer some protection against SIDS over formula feeding, probably because of the mother's antibodies, which the infant absorbs through the breast milk. (Some researchers believe an impaired or weak immune system could be a factor in SIDS.) It has also been noted that more affluent mothers are more likely to breast-feed their infants and for a longer period.

Age is a factor in SIDS—most SIDS deaths occur when the baby is two to four months old. Some researchers have noted a correlation between respiratory infection occurring the week prior to death and SIDS. Others have also found a relationship between children who were not immunized for diphtheria, pertussis or tetanus (DPT) or who were immunized later than usual. One study implicated high levels of caffeine consumption in the pregnant woman to SIDS, although most researchers do not appear to commit to excessive caffeine as a cause.

Premature babies and low birth weight babies are at greater risk for SIDS and for a longer period than normal birth weight babies delivered at full gestation.

When Abuse Is the Cause

Some experts have contended that there is overdiagnosis of SIDS. In one study in the United Kingdom, Professor Roy Meadow of St. James's University Hospital in Leeds studied 71 children who had been diagnosed with death from natural causes or SIDS (42 from SIDS and 29 from natural causes) but were later found to have been murdered by their parents.

In more than 80% of these cases, the cause of death was smothering by the mother. In 27 of the cases, blood had been found in the mouth, nose or on the face of the child and 10 of the children had unusual bruises on the face or neck. Two of the children had fractured ribs and two had paper balls in their stomach. In addition, 29 of the children came from families in which other children had died. More than 50% of the children had recently been discharged from the hospital under unusual circumstances a week before the death occurred. Professor Meadow stated, "Many pediatric units are failing to heed warning signs and failing to protect some very vulnerable children. The sudden infant death syndrome has been used at times as a pathological diagnosis to evade awkward truths."

Some countries, notably JAPAN, waited to perform their own studies on SIDS before deciding whether to publicize that a prone position could cause death in some infants. Japan's study, performed by the Japanese Ministry of Health and Welfare, also supported that the prone position caused death in about 19% of the children who die from SIDS.

"Assessment of Infant Sleeping Position—Selected States, 1996," *Morbidity and Mortality Weekly Report,* (October 1998): 873. (No volume or number given.)

C. C. Blackwell, et al., "Infection, Inflammation and Sleep: More Pieces to the Puzzle of Sudden Infant Death Syndrome (SIDS)," *APMIS: Acta Pathologica, Microbiolgica et Immunologica Scandinavica* 107, no. 5 (May 1999): 455–473.

Steven D. Blatt, et al., "Sudden Infant Death Syndrome, Child Sexual Abuse, and Child Development," *Current Opinion in Pediatrics* 11, no. 2 (April 1999): 175–186.

John L. Carroll and Ellen S. Siska, "SIDS: Counseling Parents to Reduce the Risk," *American Family Physician* 57, no. 7 (April 1, 1998): 1566.

Terence Dwyer, et al., "Tobacco Smoke Exposure At One Month of Age and Subsequent Risk of SIDS—A Prospective Study," *American Journal of Epidemiology* 149, no. 7 (April 1, 1999): 593–602.

Warren G. Guntheroth, *Crib Death: The Sudden Infant Death Syndrome* (Mount Kisco, N.Y.: Futura, 1982).

Richard J. Martin, et al., "Screening for SIDS: A Neonatal Perspective," *Pediatrics* 103, no. 4 (April 1, 1999): 812.

Caroline White, "Some 'Cot Deaths' Are Child Abuse," *British Medical Journal* 318, no. 147 (January 16, 1999): 147.

suicide Studies indicate that emotionally, physically or sexually abused children, particularly adolescents, are more prone to suicide attempts than are children who are not abused. If a child has made or threatens to make a suicide attempt, then the possibility of abuse should be considered. (*See also* ADOLESCENT ABUSE.) Studies also indicate that adults who were abused as children are more prone to suicide attempts.

In the case of an adolescent, often the abuser is someone known to the adolescent, such as a family member, stepfather or other individual. In some cases, the suicidal child may be reacting to emotional and sexual abuse that she or he (usually she) is suffering from at the hands of peers. For example, in a Canadian study reported in a 1997 issue of *Adolescence*, researchers studied 1,025 females from grades 7–12 in Alberta schools. They found that nearly a quarter (23%) of the girls had experienced at least one type of sexual assault (sexual touching, sexual threats, indecent exposure) and 4% had frequently experienced such harassment.

Of the 793 girls who had never experienced any sexual assaults, about 15% were emotionally disturbed and 1% were suicidal. If the assault happened once, as happened to 105 girls, the percentage of girls who were emotionally disturbed rose to 20%, and nearly 3% were suicidal. If the assaults happened a few times, as happened to 107 girls, the rate of emotional disturbances was about 21% but the suicide rate increased to nearly 5%. And when the assault was frequent (as happened to 20 girls), then 31% of the girls were emotionally disturbed and 10% were suicidal. Clearly, sexual harassment has a profound impact on adolescents.

Christopher Bagley, et al., "Sexual Assault in School, Mental Health and Suicidal Behaviors in Adolescent Women in Canada," *Adolescence* 32, no. 126 (Summer 1997): 361–366.

supervision The term supervision is used in three different ways when speaking of child abuse and neglect. First, supervision may refer to the responsibility for protecting and guiding a child, usually a parental responsibility. When a child protection agency invested with authority to intervene determines that a child's caretakers are not giving adequate supervision it may assume responsibility for the child.

Supervision also refers to oversight of a case by the child protection worker. Under this meaning of the word the entire family is the subject of supervision. Such intervention is usually guided by a SERVICE PLAN that outlines specific tasks and objectives for the family. The primary function of the child protection worker is to ensure that the family is taking steps necessary for protection of the child.

Finally, the process by which cases are reviewed is also referred to as supervision. Case review usually involves a meeting between the child protection worker and his or her superior to discuss both the family's progress and the worker's management of the case. This type of supervision helps make sure proper procedures are followed and may delay or prevent BURNOUT. Ongoing support and instruction are particularly important for counteracting job-related stress and maintaining the morale of child protection workers.

supporting services Abusive and neglectful parents are often subject to social, emotional and economic stress. Prevention of further maltreatment of children may require addressing the underlying causes of family stress as well as direct treatment of the abuse.

Support services include a wide variety of human services that help families function more effectively. Impoverished families will benefit from economic assistance, possibly in the form of CATEGORICAL AID. Other services include vocational training, educational assistance, child care and recreation. In some cases, support services alone may be sufficient to reduce family stress to a manageable level.

surrogate parent Children who are abused or neglected by their parents may benefit from a surrogate parent. The surrogate may be a relative, family member or a trained PARENT AIDE. Children benefit from additional nurturance and direction given by a surrogate parent, and biological parents can learn child care skills by the surrogate's example. In some cases the surrogate actually acts as a parent to abusive or neglectful parents, giving them emotional support and direction. Surrogate parents may be especially helpful to young or emotionally immature parents.

suspected child abuse and neglect team *See* SCAN TEAM.

suspended judgment *See* DISPOSITION.

swaddling The ancient custom of tightly wrapping infants in a long strip of cloth is still practiced in some cultures. Swaddling restricts the child's movements and is said by critics to be physically, socially and emotionally damaging. In Turkey some mothers swaddle their infants and strap them to their backs while working or traveling. Though held to be abusive in most Western countries, swaddling is considered simply a convenient way of carrying an infant in other cultures.

Sweden As with other Scandinavian countries, Sweden recognizes the existence of child abuse and neglect; but as a social problem of large proportion it seems not to exist. In 1957, the Swedish National Board of Health drew up regulations to address the issue of child abuse and a research institute was established to study the problem. Swedish society comprises may welfare components, among them extensive state-funded child care facilities. It appears that some tensions and frustrations contributing to child maltreatment in other cultures may not develop as quickly or easily in Sweden.

In general, physical punishment of children has long been recognized in Sweden as a less-than-desirable disciplinary procedure. In 1966, the Parenthood and Guardianship Code removed the previously sanctioned parental right to beat a child without fear of legal prosecution under the Criminal Code. In July 1979, a law that forbade all physical punishment of children was enacted. (*See also* COMMISSION ON CHILDREN'S RIGHTS, 1978.)

Richard J. Gelles and Ake W. Edfeldt, "Violence Towards Children in the United States and Sweden," *Child Abuse and Neglect* 10 (1986): 501–510.

syphilis One of the most damaging of the VENEREAL DISEASES, syphilis attacks the heart, blood vessels, spinal cord, brain and bones as well as the genitals. It can be fatal. Sexual intercourse is the primary method by which spirochetes, the common name of the syphilis bacterium, are transmitted. Syphilis can also be contracted through kissing and through contact with open sores.

Chancres (pimples, blisters or open sores) appear about three weeks after infection. Early treatment with penicillin is usually effective; however, some penicillin-resistant strains have developed. Treatment can stop the disease but cannot reverse physiological damage done to the brain and spinal cord.

Congenital syphilis passed to an infant from an infected mother can weaken bones, causing lesions in the joints and periosteum. These lesions are sometimes mistaken for battering-induced wounds. Blood tests and the presence of other symptoms can aid in accurate diagnosis.

The appearance of syphilis in a child is a strong indicator of SEXUAL ABUSE. A blood test for syphilis is an important part of a comprehensive medical examination for children who have been sexually assaulted.

tactile stimulation   Touching and holding infants appears to be important for their healthy sensory and emotional development. Early studies of HOSPITALISM led researchers to conclude that, in addition to adequate food and shelter, close physical and emotional contact with a nurturing adult is essential for normal development. Infants who did not receive such contact appeared dull and listless. Several eventually died despite availability of sufficient food, shelter and medical care.

Some experts speculate that FAILURE TO THRIVE SYNDROME is due not only to inadequate nutrition but to a lack of tactile stimulation as well. Parents who fail to develop an attachment to their infant may be cold and physically rejecting. Deprived infants can often be recognized by their eagerness to be held by strangers at a time when others their age demonstrate a normal fear of strangers.

Parents who were neglected as children often have a difficult time learning how to hold and touch their babies. Often they must be taught how to touch, rock and soothe their infants. Those who were physically or sexually abused must often overcome negative associations with physical contact. Some early intervention programs focus on teaching high-risk parents how to touch, hold and care for their infants in a positive and mutually enjoyable way. (*See also* EMOTIONAL NEGLECT, BONDING FAILURE.)

Taiwan   There is little or no official recognition, either by health care professionals or the government, of child abuse and neglect in Taiwan. Traditional Chinese family structure in Taiwan is built along lines similar to those found in the cultures of some other developing nations, that is, there is a strong emphasis on respect and obedience to adults. In Taiwan, filial piety has its roots in ancient Chinese teaching, and variations on this theme of complete obedience to parents by children are still stressed today.

Some actions toward children that would be considered marginally or explicitly abusive in the West—twisting the ear or pinching the face, kicking and beating, hitting the head—are in fact disciplinary behaviors in Taiwan. Similarly, the parent-child bond in Taiwan, influenced by strong notions of filial piety, might be considered emotionally unhealthy or even abusive by some Western standards. The Child Welfare Act in Taiwan, revised in 1993, requires that anyone knowing of a case of child abuse or neglect must notify the police or child welfare authorities within 24 hours.

According to the 1999 Country Reports on Human Rights Practices, released in February 2000, by the Bureau of Democracy, Human Rights, and Labor in the U.S. Department of State, child abuse is a "significant problem" in Taiwan. The report also states that child prostitution, primarily of children ages 12–17 is also a problem, particularly among Aborigine children. In 1995, a law was passed providing for a penalty of up to two years in prison for customers of child prostitutes. The law also allowed for publication of the names of child prostitute customers in newspapers. In the first quarter of 1999, 249 people were arrested under this law and 101 were convicted.

In 1999, the Child Welfare Bureau was created within the Ministry of Interior. Also in 1999, the Prevention of Child and Juvenile Sex Trafficking Law was amended to forbid the media from advertising children for sex and penalize foreign nationals for engaging in sexual contact with minors.

Jill E. Korbin, ed. *Child Abuse and Neglect: Cross-Cultural Perspectives* (Berkeley: University of California Press, 1981).

Tardieu, Ambroise   A 19th-century professor of legal medicine who lived in Paris, Ambroise Tardieu is credited with being the first person to note and describe the group of symptoms that would later be called the BATTERED CHILD SYNDROME. He also wrote descriptions of parents who abused their children and of the sociocultural conditions that give rise to child abuse. Much of what he reported is consistent with modern research findings.

target child   Typically, one child in a family is singled out as the target of abuse. Reasons for selection of a particular child are not fully understood. In some cases the child may be considered difficult or frustrating, for example, an infant who cries frequently; in other cases the child may have a physical deformity or simply be considered unattractive by the parent. Through a process known as SCAPEGOATING the child becomes identified to the parent(s) as a "problem child." Because the target child may, indeed, be difficult to care for, he or she may be accused of causing the abuse. Attempts to rationalize abuse of a target child often result in BLAMING THE VICTIM. Focusing on the abused child's negative behavior may divert attention from the parent's inappropriate or brutal handling of the situation.

Treatment of the abuser seeks to change negative attitudes toward the target child. Often, peer support groups such as PARENTS ANONYMOUS and parent training are helpful in presenting different ways in which parents can respond to frustrating situations.

team, community   *See* COMMUNITY TEAM.

teenage pregnancy   In a study reported in a 1998 issue of *Pediatrics* on 1,026 African-American women, most of whom were age 17 and 18, the researchers found a significant link between sexual abuse and early first intercourse and early pregnancy. Researchers found the sexually abused females had intercourse 7 months earlier than nonabused women and their first pregnancy occurred 10 months earlier than those of the women who were not sexually abused. The women who had not been sexually abused had a first intercourse at the age of 15.5 years and their first pregnancy occurred at age 17.3 years.

The researchers defined childhood sexual abuse as nonconsensual sexual contact before age 13, including any of the following: intercourse, the child being touched on genitals or breasts or the child being forced to touch the genitals of the perpetrator. They found that more than 12% of the women had experienced an incidence of sexual abuse before age 13.

The researchers also looked at the incidence of physical and emotional abuse and age at first intercourse and pregnancy but did not find a significant relationship. (*See also* SEXUAL ABUSE.)

Kevin Fiscella, et al., "Does Child Abuse Predict Adolescent Pregnancy?" *Pediatrics* 101 (April 1998): 620–624.

termination of parental rights   A court may determine that it is in the best interest of an abused or neglected child legally to end all ties between the child and his or her biological parent. Once parental rights have been terminated the child is free for adoption by another family. Exact criteria for termination very according to location; however, the following are examples of grounds that are considered sufficient in many areas. (Note: see also the state-by-state table on page 233.)

- Abandonment
- Severe alcohol or drug abuse by the parent(s)
- Parent is seriously mentally ill
- Repeated abuse or neglect of the child
- Other children in the family have been tortured or killed
- Child has been in foster care for 15 or the past 22 months.

In most locations juvenile or family courts have jurisdiction over parental rights. Though EVIDENTIARY STANDARDS differ, most states require CLEAR AND CONVINCING EVIDENCE that parents are unfit or that the BEST INTERESTS OF THE CHILD will be served by terminating parental rights. Subsequent to the passage of the ADOPTION AND SAFE FAMILIES ACT OF 1997, many states changed their laws to comply with the federal guidelines. Some states already had similar laws prior to the federal statute.

A termination of parental rights is an irrevocable legal severing of parental ties. The child then may

Grounds for Termination of Parental Rights

STATE/STATUTE	Abandonment or Extreme Parental Disinterest	Abuse/Neglect	Mental Illness or Deficiency	Alcohol- or Drug-Induced Incapacity	Felony Conviction/Incarceration	Failure of Reasonable Efforts	Sexual Abuse	Abuse/Neglect or Loss of Rights of Another Child	Failure to Maintain Contact	Failure to Provide Support	Failure to Establish Paternity	Child Judged in Need of Services/Dependent	Child's Best Interest	Child in care 15 of 22 months (or less)	Felony assault of child or sibling	Murder/manslaughter of sibling child	Other Grounds
ALABAMA § 26-18-7	✓	✓	✓	✓	✓	✓	✓	✓	✓	✓					✓	✓	■ Aggravated circumstances
ALASKA §§ 25.23.180(a), (c) 47.10.011(1)-(3), (6)-(12) 47.10.080(c)(3), (o) 47.10.088(a)-(h)	✓	✓	✓	✓	✓	✓	✓	✓				✓	✓	✓	✓	✓	■ Parent without custody unreasonably withholding consent ■ Homicide of other parent ■ Child induced to commit crime
ARIZONA § 8-533	✓	✓	✓	✓	✓	✓	✓	✓			✓	✓	✓	✓	✓	✓	■ Parental identity unknown ■ Child returned home and removed again ■ Voluntary relinquishment
ARKANSAS § 9-27-341	✓	✓	✓	✓	✓	✓	✓	✓	✓	✓		✓	✓	✓	✓	✓	■ Presumptive legal father not the biological father ■ Voluntary relinquishment
CALIFORNIA Welf. & Inst. Code §§ 361, 361.5	✓	✓	✓	✓	✓	✓	✓	✓		✓		✓	✓		✓	✓	■ Child suffering from extreme emotional damage ■ Voluntary relinquishment ■ Conception result of sexual abuse
COLORADO § 19-3-604	✓	✓	✓	✓	✓	✓	✓	✓	✓			✓	✓	✓	✓	✓	■ Identity of parent unknown
CONNECTICUT Legis. Serv. 241 § 6 § 17a-112(b)-(d)	✓	✓				✓	✓	✓	✓				✓	✓		✓	■ Failure to achieve personal rehabilitation ■ Conception result of sexual abuse ■ Voluntary relinquishment ■ Emotional ties of child to parent

Grounds for Termination of Parental Rights

STATE/STATUTE	Abandonment or Extreme Parental Disinterest	Abuse/Neglect	Mental Illness or Deficiency	Alcohol- or Drug-Induced Incapacity	Felony Conviction/Incarceration	Failure of Reasonable Efforts	Sexual Abuse	Abuse/Neglect or Loss of Rights of Another Child	Failure to Maintain Contact	Failure to Provide Support	Failure to Establish Paternity	Child Judged in Need of Services/Dependent	Child's Best Interest	Child in care 15 of 22 months (or less)	Felony assault of child or sibling	Murder/manslaughter of sibling child	Other Grounds
DELAWARE tit.31. § 1103	✓	✓	✓		✓	✓		✓		✓			✓	✓	✓		• Voluntary relinquishment
DISTRICT OF COLUMBIA § 16-2353	✓	✓		✓									✓				• Need for continuity and care • Quality of relationship • Child's opinion
FLORIDA § 39.806	✓	✓	✓	✓	✓	✓	✓	✓	✓	✓		✓	✓	✓	✓	✓	• Parents engaged in egregious conduct • Voluntary relinquishment • Identity or location of parent(s) unknown
GEORGIA § 15-11-81	✓	✓	✓	✓	✓	✓	✓	✓	✓	✓		✓	✓	✓	✓	✓	• Failure to comply with child support decree • Voluntary relinquishment • Egregious conduct
HAWAII § 571-61	✓		✓		✓	✓	✓	✓	✓	✓	✓				✓	✓	• Voluntary relinquishment • Aggravated circumstances
IDAHO § 16-2005	✓	✓	✓		✓		✓	✓	✓	✓	✓		✓		✓	✓	• Not natural parent • Conception result of rape • Voluntary relinquishment • Aggravated circumstances
ILLINOIS Legis. Serv. 50/1 405/1-2 405/2-13	✓	✓	✓	✓	✓	✓	✓	✓	✓	✓	✓	✓	✓	✓	✓	✓	• Adultery or fornication • Depravity • Murder of child's parent • Aggravated circumstances

Grounds for Termination of Parental Rights

STATE/STATUTE	Abandonment or Extreme Parental Disinterest	Abuse/Neglect	Mental Illness or Deficiency	Alcohol- or Drug-Induced Incapacity	Felony Conviction/Incarceration	Failure of Reasonable Efforts	Sexual Abuse	Abuse/Neglect or Loss of Rights of Another Child	Failure to Maintain Contact	Failure to Provide Support	Failure to Establish Paternity	Child Judged in Need of Services/Dependent	Child's Best Interest	Child in care 15 of 22 months (or less)	Felony assault of child or sibling	Murder/manslaughter of sibling child	Other Grounds
INDIANA §§ 31-35-2-4.5, 31-35-3-4, 31-35-3-8, 31-35-1	✓				✓	✓	✓	✓				✓	✓	✓	✓	✓	■ Voluntary relinquishment
IOWA § 232.116	✓	✓	✓	✓	✓	✓	✓	✓	✓			✓	✓	✓	✓	✓	■ Voluntary relinquishment ■ Imminent danger to the child
KANSAS §§ 38-1583, 38-1585	✓	✓	✓	✓	✓	✓	✓	✓	✓	✓		✓	✓	✓	✓	✓	■ Murder of child's other parent
KENTUCKY § 625.090	✓	✓	✓			✓	✓	✓		✓			✓	✓	✓	✓	
LOUISIANA Ch. Code Ann. art. 1015	✓	✓			✓	✓	✓	✓	✓	✓		✓		✓	✓	✓	■ Murder of child's other parent
MAINE tit.22, § 4055	✓	✓	✓	✓	✓	✓	✓	✓						✓	✓	✓	■ Custody removed from the parent ■ Voluntary relinquishment ■ Aggravated circumstances ■ Heinous or abhorrent behavior
MARYLAND §§ 5-313, 5-525.1(b)(1)	✓	✓	✓	✓	✓	✓	✓	✓	✓	✓		✓	✓	✓	✓		■ Child continuously out of parent(s)' custody ■ Identity of parent(s) unknown ■ Convicted of crime of violence against other parent
MASSACHUSETTS Ch. 119, § 26(4), Ch. 210, § 3(c)	✓	✓	✓	✓	✓	✓	✓	✓	✓	✓			✓	✓	✓	✓	■ Child has formed strong, positive bond with substitute caretaker

Grounds for Termination of Parental Rights

STATE/STATUTE	Abandonment or Extreme Parental Disinterest	Abuse/Neglect	Mental Illness or Deficiency	Alcohol- or Drug-Induced Incapacity	Felony Conviction/Incarceration	Failure of Reasonable Efforts	Sexual Abuse	Abuse/Neglect or Loss of Rights of Another Child	Failure to Maintain Contact	Failure to Provide Support	Failure to Establish Paternity	Child Judged in Need of Services/Dependent	Child's Best Interest	Child in care 15 of 22 months (or less)	Felony assault of child or sibling	Murder/manslaughter of sibling child	Other Grounds
MICHIGAN § 27.3178(1), (3), (6)	✓	✓			✓	✓	✓	✓	✓	✓			✓		✓	✓	■ Failure to comply with guardianship plan or court-ordered plan ■ Risk of harm if returned home
MINNESOTA § 260.221	✓	✓	✓	✓	✓	✓		✓	✓	✓	✓	✓	✓	✓	✓	✓	■ Egregious harm ■ Voluntary relinquishment
MISSISSIPPI § 93-15-103	✓	✓	✓	✓	✓	✓	✓	✓	✓			✓	✓		✓	✓	■ Deep-seated antipathy by child ■ Voluntary relinquishment
MISSOURI § 211.447	✓	✓	✓	✓	✓	✓	✓	✓	✓	✓			✓	✓	✓	✓	■ Substantial risk of harm to the child
MONTANA § 41-3-609	✓	✓	✓	✓	✓	✓	✓	✓				✓	✓	✓	✓	✓	■ Conception result of rape ■ Voluntary relinquishment ■ Identity of parent unknown
NEBRASKA §§ 43-292, 43-292.02	✓	✓	✓	✓	✓	✓	✓	✓		✓			✓	✓		✓	■ Aggravated circumstances
NEVADA §§ 128.105, 128.106, 128.107, 128.109, 128.012	✓	✓	✓	✓	✓	✓	✓	✓	✓	✓			✓			✓	■ Token efforts by parent(s) ■ Child in care 18 of most recent 24 months* ■ Failure of parental adjustment (* as of 12/31/1997)
NEW HAMPSHIRE N.H. Laws 170-C:5 169-C:24-a	✓	✓	✓		✓	✓	✓			✓				✓	✓	✓	

Grounds for Termination of Parental Rights

STATE/STATUTE	Abandonment or Extreme Parental Disinterest	Abuse/Neglect	Mental Illness or Deficiency	Alcohol- or Drug-Induced Incapacity	Felony Conviction/Incarceration	Failure of Reasonable Efforts	Sexual Abuse	Abuse/Neglect or Loss of Rights of Another Child	Failure to Maintain Contact	Failure to Provide Support	Failure to Establish Paternity	Child Judged in Need of Services/Dependent	Child's Best Interest	Child in care 15 of 22 months (or less)	Felony assault of child or sibling	Murder/manslaughter of sibling child	Other Grounds
NEW JERSEY Sess. Laws 30:4C-15, 30:4C-15.1, § 9:2-19	✓	✓	✓		✓	✓			✓				✓	✓	✓	✓	▪ Identity or location of parents unknown ▪ Parent dead ▪ Failure to discharge responsibilities ▪ Voluntary relinquishment
NEW MEXICO § 32A-4-28(A)-(D)	✓	✓			✓	✓		✓					✓		✓	✓	▪ Child in placement for extended period ▪ Child has developed relationship with substitute family ▪ Preference of child
NEW YORK § 384-b	✓	✓	✓	✓		✓		✓	✓				✓	✓	✓	✓	▪ Both parents dead and guardian not appointed
NORTH CAROLINA § 7A-289.32, 7A-517(3a)	✓	✓	✓	✓		✓	✓	✓		✓	✓		✓	✓	✓	✓	▪ Child willfully left in foster care ▪ Aggravated circumstances
NORTH DAKOTA § 27-20-44	✓	✓															▪ Child is deprived ▪ Voluntary relinquishment
OHIO § 2151.414	✓	✓	✓	✓	✓	✓	✓	✓	✓	✓							▪ Any other factor the court considers relevant
OKLAHOMA tit.10 § 7006-1.1	✓	✓	✓	✓	✓	✓	✓	✓	✓	✓		✓	✓	✓	✓	✓	▪ Voluntary relinquishment ▪ Conception result of rape
OREGON §§ 419B.500, 419B.502, 419B.504, 419B.506, 419B.508	✓	✓	✓	✓		✓	✓	✓	✓	✓			✓				▪ Single or recurrent incident of extreme conduct toward the child ▪ Criminal conduct of parent

Grounds for Termination of Parental Rights

STATE/STATUTE	Abandonment or Extreme Parental Disinterest	Abuse/Neglect	Mental Illness or Deficiency	Alcohol- or Drug-Induced Incapacity	Felony Conviction/Incarceration	Failure of Reasonable Efforts	Sexual Abuse	Abuse/Neglect or Loss of Rights of Another Child	Failure to Maintain Contact	Failure to Provide Support	Failure to Establish Paternity	Child Judged in Need of Services/Dependent	Child's Best Interest	Child in care 15 of 22 months (or less)	Felony assault of child or sibling	Murder/manslaughter of sibling child	Other Grounds
PENNSYLVANIA §§ 2501(a) 2511	✓	✓				✓			✓	✓	✓		✓	✓			■ Conception result of rape ■ Voluntary relinquishment ■ Identity or location of parent unknown ■ Presumptive father not the natural father
RHODE ISLAND § 15-7-7(a)-(b)	✓	✓	✓	✓	✓	✓	✓	✓					✓	✓	✓	✓	■ Aggravated circumstances
SOUTH CAROLINA § 20-7-1572	✓	✓	✓	✓	✓	✓		✓	✓	✓			✓	✓		✓	■ Presumptive father not the biological father
SOUTH DAKOTA §§ 26-8A-26, 26-8A-26.1, 26-8A-27	✓	✓			✓	✓	✓							✓	✓	✓	■ Conviction for domestic violence
TENNESSEE §§ 36-1-113(g)-(i)	✓	✓	✓	✓	✓	✓	✓	✓	✓	✓	✓		✓	✓	✓	✓	■ Risk of substantial harm
TEXAS §§ 161.001 161.003	✓	✓	✓	✓	✓	✓	✓	✓	✓	✓			✓		✓	✓	■ Refusal to submit to court order ■ Failure to provide education ■ Voluntary relinquishment ■ Drug or alcohol addicted newborn
UTAH §§ 78-3a-407, 78-3a-408, 78-3a-414, 78-3a-402(2), 78-3a-403(2)	✓	✓	✓	✓	✓	✓	✓	✓	✓	✓		✓	✓		✓	✓	■ Voluntary relinquishment

Grounds for Termination of Parental Rights

STATE/STATUTE	Abandonment or Extreme Parental Disinterest	Abuse/Neglect	Mental Illness or Deficiency	Alcohol- or Drug-Induced Incapacity	Felony Conviction/Incarceration	Failure of Reasonable Efforts	Sexual Abuse	Abuse/Neglect or Loss of Rights of Another Child	Failure to Maintain Contact	Failure to Provide Support	Failure to Establish Paternity	Child Judged in Need of Services/Dependent	Child's Best Interest	Child in care 15 of 22 months (or less)	Felony assault of child or sibling	Murder/manslaughter of sibling child	Other Grounds
VERMONT tit.15A, § 3-504		✓			✓				✓	✓	✓	✓	✓				■ Relationship with another that affects the parent-child relationship ■ Risk substantial harm ■ Identity or location of parent unknown
VIRGINIA § 16.1-283	✓	✓	✓	✓		✓		✓	✓	✓			✓	✓	✓	✓	■ Voluntary relinquishment ■ Identity or location of parent unknown
WASHINGTON §§ 13.34.180, 13.34.190	✓	✓	✓	✓	✓	✓	✓	✓			✓	✓	✓		✓	✓	■ Identity or location of parent unknown ■ Aggravated circumstances ■ Giving birth to three or more drug-affected infants
WEST VIRGINIA § 49-6-5(6)	✓	✓	✓	✓		✓	✓	✓					✓	✓	✓	✓	■ Refusal to cooperate in a reasonable family case plan
WISCONSIN §§ 48.41, 48.415	✓	✓	✓			✓	✓	✓	✓	✓		✓	✓		✓	✓	■ Homicide of child's other parent ■ Aggravated circumstances ■ Denials of physical placement ■ Failure to assume parental responsibility ■ Incestuous parenthood ■ Parenthood as a result of sexual assault ■ Voluntary relinquishment
WYOMING § 14-2-309	✓	✓			✓	✓			✓	✓			✓				■ Voluntary relinquishment

Source: National Clearinghouse for Child Abuse and Neglect Information, 1999.

be adopted by other individuals who become his or her legal parents or the child may remain in foster care or in the care of relatives or a legal guardian.

Child advocates differ in their ideas about the process for termination of parental rights. Some believe children should remain with the biological parents in all but clearly life-threatening or permanently and severely damaging situations. Supporters of this view emphasize the need for more and better interventions to help maintain the child at home and oppose efforts to make it easier to terminate parental rights. Another point of view focuses on the potential danger to the child of remaining in an abusive situation and the damaging effects of frequent or prolonged foster placement. This group believes the decision of whether to terminate parents' rights should be made relatively quickly to avoid long periods of uncertainty and to free the child for adoption at an earlier age. (*See also* PARENTS' RIGHTS.)

tertiary prevention   *See* PREVENTION.

testimony   Most EVIDENCE produced in trials related to child abuse and neglect takes the form of testimony. This type of evidence includes any written or spoken statement made under oath to establish a fact. Testimony is usually given in court in the presence of both the plaintiff and defendant. WITNESSES presenting testimony on behalf of one party are subject to questioning, or cross-examination, by the opposing party.

Usually, only testimony concerning facts directly observed or otherwise perceived by the witness are admissible in court. Hearsay testimony, involving observations made by persons other than the witness, is allowed only under certain circumstances. Some courts allow introduction of hearsay testimony in preliminary hearings. In such cases an adult, usually the person who conducted the initial INVESTIGATION, is allowed to testify concerning the nature of alleged abuse. Judges usually allow this type of testimony in an effort to protect children from trauma associated with repeated court appearances.

Under the rules of *res gestae* statements made during the excitement of an event may also be admitted as evidence. This rule is often referred to as the EXCITED UTTERANCE exception to the hearsay rule. Remarks made by a child to a teacher, parent,

HINTS FOR TESTIFYING

- Dress appropriately.
- Prepare ahead of time.
- Don't memorize your testimony.
- Expect to feel anxious.
- Speak a little louder and slower than you feel is necessary.
- Be sincere and dignified.
- Speak clearly and distinctly.
- Use appropriate language.
- Answer the question that was asked.
- Let the attorney develop your testimony.
- If you don't know the answer to a question, say so. Don't guess.
- Don't make your testimony conform to other testimony you may have heard.
- When answering questions, look at the person asking the questions or at the judge or jury.
- Tell the truth.

How to survive cross-examination:
- Be careful about what you say and how you say it.
- Listen carefully to the question; don't answer it unless you understand it.
- If a question has two parts requiring different answers, answer it in two parts.
- Keep calm.
- Answer positively rather than doubtfully.
- If you are testifying as an expert, be prepared to reconcile or distinguish your opinion from opposing schools of thought.
- Don't close yourself off from supplying additional details.
- Don't allow yourself to be rushed.
- Don't get caught by a trick question.

Source: U.S. Department of Health and Human Services, Office of Human Development Services, Administration for Children, Youth and Families, Children's Bureau, National Center on Child Abuse and Neglect, *Child Protection: The Role of the Courts* (Washington, D.C.: Government Printing Office: 1980; [OHDS] 80-30256), 1980; p. 59.

caseworker or similar party in a state of excitement following an abusive incident are allowed as testimony even though they are technically hearsay. Excited utterances are allowed under the theory that the urgency of the circumstances eliminates the element of self-interest, therefore increasing the likelihood that the statement is true. Timeliness is important in determining the admissibility of a res gestae statement. Statements made after a significant passage of time are not likely to be admitted as testimony. However, the precise amount of time allowed between the alleged abuse and the child's excited utterance is unclear. In at least one case, *State of Rhode Island v. Creighton,* The court accepted as evidence a statement made 14 hours after the event. The Rhode Island court reasoned that there was sufficient evidence in the record to establish that the victim was still under stress at the time of the statement.

Testifying in court can be a frightening experience for an adult. The experience may be terrifying for a child. Victims of SEXUAL ABUSE are frequently asked to describe embarrassing and traumatic experiences in a large, formal courtroom in the presence of the alleged assailant. Some experts characterize the formal process of testifying in court as equally traumatic as the abuse itself.

Recently, steps have been taken to make the process of testifying less traumatic to the child. Some courts attempt to reduce the number of court appearances required of a child. Provisions for separate waiting rooms prevent children from having to share a room with defense witnesses. Increasingly, courts allow children to testify IN CAMERA, on videotape or through closed-circuit television. These methods of testifying may eliminate some of the trauma of a court appearance. Measures that interfere with the defendant's right to cross-examine a witness are not permitted.

In sexual abuse trials NATURAL DOLLS may be used as aids to testimony. Children are often embarrassed to talk about genitalia and may use idiosyncratic terminology. Use of anatomically correct dolls can both reduce embarrassment and allow for clearer testimony.

Others who may testify in child abuse hearings include anyone who may have observed the abuse, police or child protection workers who conducted the initial investigation, character witnesses and relevant experts.

testimony, videotaped *See* VIDEOTAPED TESTIMONY.

therapeutic day care centers Specialized day care centers that provide both supervision and treatment of abused children are a valuable resource for child protection. Structured treatment usually focuses on behavioral and educational problems of children who have been abused. Therapeutic day care may be used by children in FOSTER CARE or while children remain at home. Usually, families of children in therapeutic day care are simultaneously receiving treatment at the center or from an outside provider.

throwaway children A significant proportion of children labeled as runaways are actually throwaways. The term throwaway refers to a child who is forced or encouraged to leave home by parents or caretakers. This form of extreme NEGLECT affects adolescents as well as younger children. An estimated 10% to 20% of children housed in runaway shelters are throwaways. Though the throwaway is often labeled a problem child, the parent's inability or unwillingness to care for him or her is a significant factor in the child's behavioral difficulty.

Tinker v. Des Moines Independent School District
In 1965, a group of school children was prohibited by the Des Moines, Iowa School District from wearing black armbands to protest hostilities in Vietnam. Students who wore the armbands were suspended from school. The children, through their parents, filed a petition in U.S. District Court to prohibit the school system from disciplining them for expression of their political beliefs. After a hearing, the court found in favor of the school district, citing their right to take reasonable actions to prevent a disturbance. This decision was appealed to the U.S. Supreme Court, which in 1969 reversed the lower court's decision, holding that children as well as adults have a right to freedom of speech under the First Amendment to the Constitution of the United States.

The Supreme Court's ruling in *Tinker v. Des Moines* established an important legal precedent for children's rights. By ruling that children are entitled to specific rights the court recognized them as independent individuals with their own interests. Though subsequent decisions have modified the scope of children's rights, the principles confirmed in this case have afforded children much greater legal protection than they had previously enjoyed.

tithingman In 17th-century Massachusetts, most communities, divided into church parishes, relied on a tithingman to determine whether families met responsibilities toward their members and toward society in general. A tithingman (whose presence was based on English tradition) could arrest individuals for legal infractions and could intervene in family disputes. A tithingman was responsible for judging whether parents were fulfilling their duties toward their children. The concept was devised as a way of ensuring social order rather than as a means of protecting children. Parents who did not act responsibly were seen as threats to community welfare.

toe tourniquet syndrome   Emotionally disturbed parents have been known to strangle their children's appendages, such as toes or fingers, by tying hair or thread around the base. Restricted blood flow can cause severe pain and may result in loss of the appendage.

This relatively rare practice is apparently related to a superstitious belief of unknown origin. Most frequent victims of this form of abuse are infants from six weeks to 10 months of age. When toe tourniquet syndrome is suspected, evidence may be found in the form of loose threads or hairs in bedclothing or garments. Thorough examination by a physician may also help determine the cause of injury.

trafficking, sexual   *See* SEXUAL TRAFFICKING.

trauma   The term trauma is most often used to describe an injury, wound or shock, of any kind, to the body. PHYSICAL ABUSE often leaves visible signs of trauma on a child's body.

Trauma can also refer to a painful or damaging emotional experience. This kind of trauma is present in virtually all types of child abuse. Emotional trauma is usually concomitant with physical trauma but may endure long after all signs of physical injury have disappeared. Victims of child abuse often report nightmares, flashbacks or panic attacks long after the danger of abuse is gone.

Support and therapy groups are available in many areas to help both child and adult survivors of abuse overcome the effects of emotional trauma associated with abuse. For more information on such groups, *see* APPENDIX 1.

trauma X   This is another name for child abuse, most frequently used in medical facilities. Some hospitals use the term trauma X to refer to a child abuse and neglect program. For instance, the Trauma X Team at Boston Children's Hospital was an early example of a MULTIDISCIPLINARY TEAM.

treatment   Abuse and neglect victims usually require specialized treatment to restore their physical and emotional well-being. When parents or other family members are responsible for maltreatment, family therapy is often recommended to prevent further danger to the child. Perpetrators of abuse outside the family usually receive individual psychiatric treatment.

Diagnosis and planning for treatment of abuse and neglect is often carried out by a MULTIDISCIPLINARY TEAM, which includes professionals with specialized training in pediatrics, psychiatry, psychology, social work and child protection. In some cases a child protection worker is responsible for providing all treatment directly. More often, treatment takes many different forms and is given by professionals with different skills. When indirect methods are used, the child protection caseworker is responsible for coordinating treatment and monitoring the client's progress. Specific methods employed in treatment of child abuse and neglect include: individual counseling, group counseling, marital or family counseling, educational treatment (such as parent education), a friendly visitor (usually a peer who can provide emotional support), psychotherapy, therapeutic day care or day treatment, FOSTER CARE, HOMEMAKER SERVICES, SELF-HELP GROUPS and medical care.

The decision of which methods to use is based on a psychosocial ASSESSMENT of the situation. Although treatment usually includes other members of the family, the child's safety and well-being is the ultimate goal of all treatment for abuse or neglect. In addition to protecting the child, a series of specific treatment goals are included in a SERVICE PLAN. Progress toward goals is monitored by the caseworker and forms the basis for decisions to terminate the protective service agency's involvement.

Treatment of certain types of abusers may be highly specialized. Some sexual offenders have proven to be resistant to traditional methods of psychiatric treatment. Recently several innovative approaches to treatment of sexual offenders have been employed by forensic mental health specialists. These methods usually involve a combination of behavioral and group therapy.

Victims of SEXUAL ABUSE may also require special treatment. Sexually abused children must be helped to overcome the tendency to blame themselves for their abuse and to learn new ways of relating to adults. Sexual abuse victims are forced to assume inappropriate adult roles, such as surrogate spouse, lover or prostitute. Treatment may focus on helping children learn to be children again. Overcoming feelings of low self-esteem and fear of emotional attachment are also important tasks.

Until recently, sexual abuse was shrouded in secrecy. Many adults who were molested as children did not receive treatment and still bear emotional scars from their abuse. Adults abused as children often suffer SEXUAL DYSFUNCTION, depression, debilitating anxiety and difficulty forming emotional attachments. Recently, several organizations have formed that offer self-help groups or referral to treatment services. Some of these groups are ADULTS MOLESTED AS CHILDREN UNITED, INCEST SURVIVORS ANONYMOUS and INCEST SURVIVORS RESOURCE NETWORK INTERNATIONAL.

In the United States many state and local government agencies have sponsored specialized treatment services for victims of abuse. Child abuse treatment units are often attached to hospitals, community mental health centers or child welfare agencies. In addition, PARENTS ANONYMOUS provides self-help groups for abusers in most states and in many locations in Canada.

Jeffrey A. Kelly, *Treating Child-Abusive Families* (New York: Plenum Press, 1983).

Arthur H. Green, *Child Maltreatment* (New York: Jason Aronson, 1980).

trust funds   *See* CHILDREN'S TRUST FUNDS.

Tunbridge Wells Study Group   The Tunbridge Wells Study Group, composed of representatives from a variety of disciplines, was an outgrowth of a conference held at Tunbridge Wells, England

shortly after the death of MARIA COLWELL. The group sought ways to improve the coordination and management of child abuse services and was influential in the development and passage of the Children Act of 1975. (*See also* CHILDREN AND YOUNG PERSONS ACTS [BRITAIN].)

turned stomach   *See* OPU HULE.

Turkey   According to some experts, childhood abuse and particularly sexual abuse is ignored as a problem in Turkey. In a study reported in the *Journal of Interpersonal Violence,* researchers studied 42 Turkish female adults, all of whom had been sexually abused by members of their family. One-third of the women exhibited self-mutilating behavior, including cutting the skin, banging the head, biting oneself and other actions. (Note: self-mutilating behavior may be a consequence of abuse but may also be a psychotic symptom of a severe illness such as schizophrenia and thus psychiatric problems should be ruled out.)

All of the abusers were males and usually were fathers. The girls most at risk for sexual abuse were the oldest females; however, if one daughter is sexually abused, the other daughters are also at risk. (This is true in Turkey and in other countries.)

The researchers found a low number of stepfather abusers, which they explained as probably due to a divorce rate that is lower in Turkey than in Western countries. There were also fewer cases of vaginal penetration than seen in the West, which researchers believed was a function of the importance of virginity in Turkish society.

Associations were also found between eating disorders and self-mutilating behavior. About 32% of the non-self-mutilating women had eating disorders such as anorexia or bulimia, but the percentage was much higher among the self-mutilating women: Nearly 79% of the self-mutilating women also experienced eating disorders.

Isin Baral, et al., "Self-Mutilating Behavior of Sexually Abused Female Adults in Turkey," *Journal of Interpersonal Violence* 13, no. 4 (August 1998): 427–438.

underground networks   In the United States several informal networks of safe homes shelter parents and children fleeing court orders that give custody to an allegedly abusive ex-spouse. Typically, these networks serve children and their mothers who have been unsuccessful in convincing a court that the father sexually abused the child. Lacking proof of the father's unfitness, courts have awarded visitation rights or in some cases, sole custody of the child to the father. An unknown number of mothers have chosen to hide their child rather than subject the child to what they believe would be further abuse.

Underground networks appear to be loosely organized. Though little is known about them, an estimated five to 10 such organizations are now operating in the United States. Families who provide shelter for fugitive children and their parents often do so at great legal, personal and financial risk. Sometimes called "key masters," sheltering families must maintain strict secrecy to avoid arrest and to protect their guests.

Many experts in the field of child protection have criticized underground networks for encouraging illegal behavior and subjecting children to additional disruption. Groups representing divorced fathers maintain that many mothers simply do not want to share custody of the child and have leveled false accusations of sexual abuse in an effort to deny access to the father.

Supporters of underground networks argue that they are made necessary by a failure of the legal system. Sexual abuse of young children is often difficult to prove. In some cases judges may not fully understand the nature of child sexual abuse, in others prosecutors simply lack sufficient EVIDENCE. Convinced that the child was indeed molested by the father, some mothers decide to risk imprisonment to protect their child.

unfounded report   Child abuse reporting laws generally require designated persons to report *suspected* abuse or neglect to an investigatory agency. If, upon investigation of a report, the reported conditions are determined not to be neglectful or abusive as defined by law, a report may be designated "unfounded." Reports may also be judged unfounded when there is a lack of sufficient evidence to establish the occurrence or extent of a potentially harmful condition.

The terms unfounded and unsubstantiated report are frequently used interchangeably. Criteria for substantiation of a report vary according to how maltreatment is defined by local laws, EVIDENTIARY STANDARDS and the investigator's ASSESSMENT of the potential for harm.

In most cases child protection authorities cannot intervene further on behalf of a child once a case is determined to be unfounded. In some jurisdictions intervention may proceed with parent's permission. Some experts believe that the system is flooded with unfounded reports which they believe take away workers and services from the individuals who need the most help. Child welfare expert Douglas Besharov (and others) said in a 1996 article for *Society*, "Laws against child abuse are an implicit recognition that family privacy must give way to the need to protect helpless children. But in seeking to protect children it is also too easy to ignore the legitimate rights of parents. Each year, about 700,000 families are put through investigations of unfounded reports. This is a massive and unjustified violation of parental rights."

Besharov and his colleagues say that the problem is not reports made from malice and says that at most, 4–10% of sexual abuse allegations were made with the knowledge that they were untrue. Rather, it is well-intentioned, overly zealous people who turn in families for child abuse because of a possibility of abuse. As a result, caseworkers are so inundated with cases to investigate that they may not have an opportunity to check on children who are clearly being abused. Besharov et al. say, "These nationwide conditions help explain why from 25 to 50 percent of child abuse deaths involve children previously known to the authorities."

They also noted that there was a tendency for some experts to advise that when children were shy or withdrawn, then they might be abused and this possibility should be protected. Yet, the authors say, "only a minority of children who exhibit such behaviors have actually been maltreated."

The answer to decreasing the number of unsubstantiated cases is to educate the public as well as protective services workers on what constitutes abuse, including direct and circumstantial evidence. Reports of abuse should also be screened, particularly those made anonymously or by estranged or former spouses or by previous sources who reported abuse that was unfounded. The report may be accurate but should be evaluated first. (*See* APPENDIX 5 for information on substantiated and indicated reports versus all reports.)

Douglas J. Besharov, et al., "Child Abuse Reporting," *Society* 33 (May/June 1996).

UNICEF Founded in 1946, following World War II, the United Nations International Children's Emergency Relief Fund (UNICEF) addresses issues of child malnutrition, disease and illiteracy worldwide. In 1953, the United Nations gave UNICEF a virtually perpetual mandate. It now has committees in 33 countries and seeks to inform the public about conditions in developing countries that affect children. In 1984, UNICEF gave approximately $1.4 billion in aid to children in developing nations. Workers at the local level provide health and nutrition services, education and training in parenting skills for women and girls.

Uniform Child Custody Jurisdiction Act (UCCJA) Approved in 1968 by the National Conference of Commissioners on Uniform State Laws, the UCCJA was designed to protect children from child stealing by resolving issues of jurisdiction in child CUSTODY cases. The act attempts to ensure that the best inter-

ests of the child are met. In custody disputes involving the UCCJA, best interest is most often interpreted as the child's primary need for stability.

As late as 1981, 46 states had adopted the UCCJA, which provides for only one state—generally the state in which the custody was originally decreed—to assume jurisdiction over a child custody case. By so doing, the UCCJA attempts to prevent a subsequent state court from modifying an original custody decree issued by another state. The act emphasizes interstate cooperation, although it does not make such cooperation mandatory; but passage of the PARENTAL KIDNAPPING PREVENTION ACT OF 1980 strengthened the jurisdictional criteria established in the UCCJA.

United Nations Declaration of the Rights of the Child, 1959 On November 20, 1959, the United Nations General Assembly unanimously adopted this declaration, which asserts rights and freedoms for the world's children. It is probably the best known of all international statements concerning adult responsibilities and obligations toward children. The declaration was conceived as a way in which to make a positive statement concerning certain principles to which children are by right entitled. The preamble to the declaration establishes that due to physical and mental immaturity, children need special safeguards both before and after birth.

In 10 principles, the declaration states that all children have the following rights: to develop in a normal and healthy manner; to have a name and a nationality from birth; to enjoy adequate housing, nutrition, recreation and medical services, including special services for the handicapped; to enjoy, if possible, the care and nurturance of their parents; to have an education; to be protected against cruelty, neglect and abuse, racism, discrimination, exploitation and religious persecution. The declaration states further that children are to be raised "in a spirit of understanding, tolerance, friendship among all peoples, peace and universal brotherhood and in full consciousness" that their talents should be dedicated to serving fellow human beings.

The declaration is similar to the Universal Declaration of Human Rights, a previous world-body statement that did not specifically address the needs of children. In adopting the Declaration of the Rights of the Child, the United Nations General Assembly placed the groundwork for a more comprehensive document, the Draft Convention on the Rights of the Child, submitted to the world body in 1978.

United Nations International Children's Emergency Relief Fund   *See* UNICEF.

United States Children's Bureau   *See* CHILDREN'S BUREAU.

utterance, excited   *See* EXCITED UTTERANCE.

venereal disease Many myths abound concerning the methods by which venereal diseases can be transmitted to children. Toilet seats, bathwater and towels have all been blamed. All of these media are extremely unlikely transmission sources. The primary method of infection of children, and adults, is through sexual intercourse. Discovery of venereal disease in a child strongly suggests that the child has had sexual contact with someone infected by the disease.

Examination of the throat, rectum and genitals for the presence of GONORRHEA and conducting blood tests for SYPHILIS and HIV are essential parts of a thorough medical evaluation for SEXUAL ABUSE. Genital herpes and VENEREAL WARTS also suggest sexual activity.

Gonorrhea, the most common of the venereal diseases, causes the mucous membranes to become inflamed and can cause blindness in infants. Syphilis, a more serious bacterial infection, can cause fatal damage to the central nervous system and circulatory system. The HIV virus has many profound potential impacts on the infant and child up to and including death (although medications are available to prolong the life of the HIV-infected child). Most states allow medical treatment without parental consent for children who have venereal disease. Some states require that all cases of pre-adolescents infected with venereal disease be reported to the mandated protective service agency. (*See also* SEXUALLY TRANSMITTED DISEASE.)

ventricular septal defect The partition that separates the left and right ventricles of the heart is occasionally damaged by battering. Though both the heart and lungs are normally protected by the rib cage, rapid compression caused by a blow to the thoracic region can cause serious injury. Damage to the septum of the heart inhibits proper functioning and can cause death.

verbal abuse PSYCHOLOGICAL MALTREATMENT includes verbal abuse as well as other forms of restrictive and punitive behavior. Verbal abuse covers a range of spoken messages that can usually be grouped into the categories of rejecting, terrorizing or corrupting. This type of abuse often occurs in combination with other forms of maltreatment.

Studies show that consistent verbal abuse can have serious and lasting effects on children. Low self-esteem resulting from verbal harassment may promote a wide range of destructive and defeating behavior. Verbal and psychological abuse has been associated with poor school performance, antisocial and self-destructive behavior.

While most child abuse laws do not specifically identify verbal abuse many make provisions for psychological/emotional abuse or MENTAL INJURY. Substantiation of verbal abuse usually depends upon psychiatric and/or psychological evaluation of the child, coupled with documentation of the abuse itself.

verification Reports of suspected abuse and neglect must be investigated to determine whether there is sufficient cause to believe that a child has been abused or neglected. Verified reports of maltreatment are often referred to as FOUNDED REPORTS or substantiated abuse. (*See also* INVESTIGATION.)

victim, blaming *See* BLAMING THE VICTIM.

victim, identification with *See* IDENTIFICATION WITH THE VICTIM.

Victims of Child Abuse Laws *See* VOCAL.

Victims of Crime Act (P.L. 98-473) Beginning in 1985, the U.S. Congress created a victims' compensation and assistance fund. The fund, made up of fines levied against persons convicted of certain federal offenses, makes grants to victim assistance and compensation programs. These programs compensate victims of crime or their survivors for medical expenses, loss of income and funeral expenses. Victim assistance programs also offer services such as crisis intervention, HOTLINES, temporary shelter, counseling and other services. Funding priority is given to programs that serve victims of sexual assault, spouse abuse or child abuse.

videotaped testimony A number of states and local authorities now allow child victims of SEXUAL ABUSE to provide legal testimony via videotape. Sixteen states specifically regulate the circumstances under which such videotaping will be admissible in court. These states are as follows: Arizona, Colorado, Hawaii, Indiana, Iowa, Kansas, Louisiana, Michigan, Minnesota, Missouri, New York, North Dakota, Rhode Island, Texas, Utah and Wisconsin.

Advantages of Videotaping
If a child's testimony is videotaped early in the process he or she may be spared the trauma of giving repeated accounts of the abusive incident. Videotaping can also eliminate the stress and possible intimidation of testifying in the presence of the alleged abuser (often a family member or friend).

Disadvantages of Videotaping
Legal scholars disagree as to the fairness of allowing videotaped testimony. Many U.S. lawyers believe such testimony violates the accused's right to confront the witness, as set forth in the Sixth Amendment to the Constitution.

In an attempt to ensure procedural DUE PROCESS some courts require that the defendant, the defendant's lawyer, the trial judge and prosecutor be present at the videotaping. Others allow taping without the defendant if the child appears in court for cross-examination.

Videotaped testimony is sometimes criticized as being subject to manipulation by both parties. Since taping is usually done with one camera the jury does not have the opportunity to observe equally the actions of other people present at the time of the testimony (e.g., the defendant). Subtle clues such as body language and flushing of the skin may be difficult or impossible to observe on videotape.

In some cases, untrained family members or incompetent therapists have videotaped lengthy sessions with a child which clearly cause the child great distress. These videotapes may appear to a judge and jury that the family and/or therapists were leading or coaching the testimony and thus it becomes inadmissible in court.

Covert Videotaping
Sometimes videotaping is done without the knowledge of the person being videotaped because it is believed that an individual is a perpetrator of child abuse. This is true in the case of individuals suspected of MUNCHAUSEN SYNDROME BY PROXY as well as other abuse cases. Sometimes families secretly videotape their baby-sitter or nanny in their own home, to verify the child is receiving good care.

The legality of covert videotaping is beyond the scope of this essay and individuals or organizations considering covert videotaping of anyone in any location (including their own home or workplace) should obtain legal advice in advance.

violence, family *See* FAMILY VIOLENCE.

VOCAL (Victims of Child Abuse Laws) This self-help and referral organization was founded in 1984. The group lobbies against abuses of justice in alleged cases of child abuse and neglect. In one Minnesota community, 24 individuals were charged at one time with abuse, although only one person was ultimately convicted and two were acquitted. Charges against the other 21 people were dropped. As a result, some of those involved in the allegations wished to protect others from unjust accusation of child abuse. They put this desire into action by founding VOCAL.

Soon after establishment of the U.S. group, in British Columbia, Canada, a chapter of VOCAL was formed by a father falsely accused of abusing his daughter. In its indictment of the Canadian government's system of investigating abuse cases, VOCAL points out that British Columbia's 1980 Family and Child Service Act maintains anonymity of the accuser and presumes guilt during investigations of alleged abuse. Further, the act provides that child abuse complaints be kept on file for two years even if they are unfounded, a situation that places a stigma on innocent individuals.

Paul and Shirley Eberle, *The Politics of Child Abuse* (Secaucus, New Jersey: Lyle Stuart, 1987).

voir dire   Literally, "to speak the truth." This legal procedure permits attorneys to question prospective jurors in child abuse and neglect cases for possible bias. It also establishes grounds on which expert witnesses can be questioned to determine their qualifications prior to TESTIMONY.

voluntary intervention   Some abusive parents seek help voluntarily. Increased accessibility of HOTLINES and SELF-HELP GROUPS has made it easier and less threatening for parents to request help. In most areas child protection agencies actively encourage self-referral. Since many abusive and/or neglectful parents are never reported, self-help programs may reach many families that would not otherwise have received help.

Parents who seek help voluntarily tend to be more highly motivated to change their behavior. When parents are reported by someone else, fear of prosecution or removal of their children often leads them to cover up problems rather than face them openly. Denying or minimizing abusive behavior often prevents perpetrators of abuse from benefiting from treatment.

Following an INVESTIGATION in which abuse or neglect is substantiated parents may be given the opportunity to seek help voluntarily. In such cases the child protection agency agrees not to seek court intervention if parents follow a mutually agreed upon plan of treatment.

wanton The term wanton is used in court proceedings to denote extremely reckless or malicious behavior. Perpetrators of abuse or neglect are often accused of willful and wanton acts against a child. Wanton acts are considered to be more serious than simple carelessness.

WAR *See* WORLD OF ABNORMAL REARING.

warrant A warrant is a document, issued by a judge, that authorizes arrest or detention of a person. Search of a particular place and seizure of specified items may also be authorized.

When particularly serious acts of maltreatment are committed or perpetrators fail to cooperate with child protection authorities a warrant may be sought from the court. In order to issue such a document the judge must be satisfied that there is reasonable cause to believe that a crime has been committed. United States law does not require that a hearing be held or that the subject of the warrant be notified prior to its issuance.

warts, venereal Condyloma acuminata, commonly known as venereal warts, is sometimes found in children who have been sexually abused. The warts are small, appear in clusters and may be found in any area involved in direct sexual contact. Appearance of condyloma acuminata in children is strong evidence of SEXUAL ABUSE. There is no reason to believe that this condition is acquired in any way other than by sexual contact.

Wetterling Act This act was named after Jacob Wetterling, a Minnesota child who was abducted in 1989 and has never been located. His parents subsequently learned that halfway houses in their city of St. Joseph housed just-released sex offenders. This fact was unknown to local police.

The Jacob Wetterling Crimes Against Children and Sexually Violent Offender Registration Act was included as part of the Federal Violent Crime Control and Law Enforcement Act of 1994. It requires the registration of convicted sex offenders in all states. All 50 states now have such registration systems. If an offender notifies the state that he plans to move to another state, the "old" state is required to notify the new state that the offender is coming.

The law also required states to create a database of child sex offenders. In 1996, U.S. Attorney General Janet Reno ordered a system to be developed to connect the 50 child sex offender registries.

According to Mike Welter, chief of the violent crimes section of the Illinois State Police, in an address at a national conference of sex offender registries in 1998, the law has already identified child sex offenders who were involved in Boy Scout troops. Said Welter, "The first two times we gave the list to the Greater Cook County Council, a scout leader was discovered on each list. They were removed from their posts, and an investigation is continuing as to whether any crimes were committed during their association with scout troops."

Welter said checks with other community youth groups have also identified sex offenders.

States differ on how long the offender must register. In some states, sexual predators must register for life. Other states require registration only for repeat offenders. Some states limit the registration period; for example, seven states limit registration to 10 years from the offender's parole date. A few states reduce the time to register if offenders can prove that they have been rehabilitated.

Federal law requires that all states must notify offenders of the registration requirement, verify the offender's address each year and notify law enforcement officials if an offender relocates. (*See also* MEGAN'S LAW, RAPE.)

"National Conference on Sex Offender Registries: Proceedings of a BJS/SEARCH Conference," Bureau of Justice Statistics, April 1998, NCJ-168965.

White House Conferences on Children As a result of early-20th-century legislative and policy reforms, the first White House Conference on Children was held in 1909. President Theodore Roosevelt, an avid reformer, strongly supported the conference, which was attended by over 200 delegates. Until this time there had been little legislative acknowledgment at the federal level of the abuse or neglect suffered by young children in the United States. The White House Conference brought together concerned men and women who worked to recommend a variety of federal policies acknowledging children's need of protection from abuse or neglect. These policies were aimed at alleviating some of the negative conditions affecting children and families.

The 1909 conference was the first of the White House-sponsored meetings held each decade in the United States. Attendees at the initial gathering in 1909 acknowledged the role of the home in prevention or development of problems. They also suggested ways in which these problems might be approached, suggestions often formed by contemporary views on child rearing. Due to resolutions passed at the first White House Conference on Children, a federal CHILDREN'S BUREAU was established in 1912 to oversee these initial federal efforts on behalf of children and to ensure continuity of their implementation. Subsequent White House Conferences on children have focused on issues considered most pressing and timely for their period.

Joseph M. Hawes and N. Ray Hiner, *American Childhood, A Research Guide and Historical Handbook* (Westport: Greenwood Press, 1985).

willful The term willful is often used in legal proceedings related to child abuse or neglect. It implies knowledge and understanding of an act as well as the intention that any consequences normally associated with that particular act should occur. In some cases, the acts must be proven to be willful before they are considered illegal or negligent.

Wilson, Mary Ellen In 1873, a well-publicized case of child abuse involving an eight-year-old New York girl named Mary Ellen Wilson became a rallying issue of reformers. Because of the notoriety surrounding the Mary Ellen Wilson case, reformers established the New York Society for the Prevention of Cruelty to Children (NYSPCC) in 1874.

Mary Ellen was an illegitimate daughter of Thomas McCormack and had been boarded out until she was nearly two years old. She then was placed under the care of the Superintendent of the Out-Door Poor in New York. Her natural father and stepmother were given charge of Mary Ellen on the stipulation that they report annually to the city's Commissioners of Charities and Corrections. After her father's death, Mary Ellen's stepmother remarried. She was then abused and neglected by these stepparents, Francis and Mary Connolly.

Among the reports of her abuse were those that described her being kept chained to a bed and beaten with a rawhide cord by her stepmother. When neighbors heard her screams, they approached the police department but were unsuccessful in getting help for Mary Ellen. They then went to the local chapter of the American Society for the Prevention of Cruelty to Animals, and the group petitioned the court on her behalf. When the *New York Times* received information about the girl's mistreatment it began newspaper coverage of the case, of the subsequent formation of the New York SPCC and of the many other child abuse, abandonment and neglect cases that flourished in New York City and surrounding areas.

Mary Ellen's stepmother, Mrs. Connolly, was convicted and sent to jail for one year as a result of her actions. Mary Ellen was sent to live at the Sheltering Arms children's home and was later indentured to a farmer.

The Guide to American Law Yearbook, 1987 (St. Paul, Minn.: West Publishing Co., 1987).
Barbara J. Nelson, *Making an Issue of Child Abuse* (Chicago: University of Chicago Press, 1984).

Wisconsin v. Yoder This 1972 ruling by the U.S. Supreme Court affirmed parents' rights to raise children according to their own religious beliefs. The case actually involved three respondents: Jonas Yoder, Adin Yutzy and Wallace Miller. All were followers of the Amish religious sect. At issue was the state's ability to prevent Amish families from removing children from public schools after completing the eighth grade. Though they received vocational training at home, the children were not enrolled in any public or private school. The respondents and other members of this sect believed formal high school education interfered with the religious development, and therefore the religious freedom, of their children. The Supreme Court agreed with them and overturned their convictions for violating Wisconsin's compulsory school attendance law.

Wisconsin v. Yoder is often seen as limiting the rather broad powers granted to the state in *prince v. massachusetts*. (*See also* PARENTS' RIGHTS and RELIGIOUS ASPECTS.)

Robert H. Mnookin, *Child, Family and State: Problems and Materials on Children and the Law* (Boston: Little, Brown and Company, 1978).

withdrawal   Children subjected to severe abuse may withdraw from social contact, appearing dull and listless. Typically, they avoid doing anything that might attract attention or arouse the anger of their parents. Withdrawn children often exhibit a robotlike compliance with parental demands, demonstrating their desire to do virtually anything to avoid further abuse.

Withdrawal and HYPERVIGILANCE are usually observed in children who have been victims of the most severe forms of physical abuse from an early age. These children may appear visibly anxious or afraid in the presence of their parents. In a hospital emergency room these symptoms are a signal to physicians and nurses to look for other signs of nonaccidental injury.

When removed from home children may continue to appear withdrawn. It may take several years in a safe and therapeutic setting before they are able to develop a close, trusting relationship with anyone.

witness   Trials related to child abuse or neglect may include testimony from lay witnesses and EXPERT WITNESSES. The kind of testimony allowed by the court depends upon the type of witness.

Lay witnesses are required to have firsthand knowledge of facts to which they testify. Inferences or conclusions may not be drawn by such witnesses. Hearsay evidence, facts not directly observed or experienced by the witness, is usually not permitted. An exception to the rule against hearsay testimony is sometimes made in preliminary hearings to spare a child from trauma related to repeated court appearances. In such cases a third party may present testimony based upon the child's account of the alleged abuse.

When the reputation or character of the defendant or respondent is in question a lay witness may be called to testify. In a dependency hearing such testimony may center on the parents' fitness to adequately care for the child. Character witnesses are usually asked to state their own qualifications to give testimony, their relationship with the party in question and their knowledge of that party's reputation in the community. Rumors and witnesses' personal opinions about the party are not admissible.

An expert witness is anyone who, in the judge's opinion, possesses special knowledge or skills beyond those of the judge or jury. Expert witnesses may be called by either party in a case or may be appointed by the court. Unlike lay witnesses, expert witnesses are allowed to make inferences and express opinions. Inferences or opinions must be within the witness's area of expertise. For example, a psychologist may testify about the psychological effects of abuse but is not allowed to give an opinion concerning the extent of physical injuries.

The allegedly abused child may be called as a witness by either party. The judge is responsible for determining whether the child's testimony is admissible as evidence. A child's competence to testify is based on age, maturity and level of understanding. In some areas the minimum age of witnesses is specified by law.

Child witnesses may be allowed to testify in judge's chambers, on videotape or closed circuit television rather than in the courtroom. Alternative ways of testifying can help reduce trauma to the child caused by reliving abuse in a threatening setting before a large group of strangers. Attempts to reduce trauma to the child must be balanced with the defendant's right to cross-examine witnesses.

The petitioner (usually the state) is the first to call witnesses in a hearing. Questioning of witnesses takes the form of: (1) direct examination by the attorney calling the witness; (2) cross-examination by the opposing attorney; (3) rebuttal or redirect examination by the first attorney concerning issues raised in the cross-examination; and (4) recross-examination by the opposing attorney on issues raised in the rebuttal examination. After a party has called all its witnesses it rests its case. Under ordinary circumstances, once a party has rested its case it is not allowed to call additional witnesses. (*See also* ADJUDICATORY HEARING, COURT, CIVIL PROCEEDING, CRIMINAL PROSECUTION and EVIDENCE.)

witness, expert   *See* EXPERT WITNESS.

World of Abnormal Rearing (WAR)   The concept of the world of abnormal rearing, known by the acronym WAR, was developed by pediatrician Ray E. Helfer. WAR describes a cyclical process in which children fail to learn basic interpersonal skills and later, as parents, are unable to teach such skills to their children. This dysfunctional pattern of development is not limited to children who are physically or sexually abused but includes those who suffer various kinds of emotional abuse and neglect. Dr. Helfer stresses the importance of parents breaking the cycle by learning principles of interpersonal behavior not learned in childhood.

The basic skills necessary to healthy development are, according to Helfer: learning how to meet one's needs appropriately, the ability to delay gratification, learning that one is responsible for one's own actions but not those of others, the ability to make decisions and solve problems, learning how to trust others and developing the ability to separate feelings and actions.

Abused children often learn inappropriate or dysfunctional ways of meeting their needs. Children who are ignored or neglected may learn that abuse is the only form of attention available from parents. Because their needs are so frequently frustrated some children do not learn to delay immediate gratification in hopes of obtaining a greater reward later. Such children enter adulthood lacking this important work and parenting skill.

Children must also learn to be responsible for their behavior. Most learn this principle from parental teaching and discipline. When discipline is sporadic or abusive children become confused about the consequences of their actions. In many abusive families a ROLE REVERSAL takes place in which the child assumes the role of a parent's caretaker. The parent may be unable or unwilling to reciprocate. Forced to direct their attention to meeting a parent's needs, children are prevented from mastering tasks important to their own development.

Abuse further complicates the process of learning to differentiate between one's self and others. Because they are often punished or abandoned the children may come to feel responsible for causing the maltreatment. If beaten or molested, the child assumes that he or she did something to deserve it. This inappropriate sense of guilt contributes to future self-destructive and abusive behavior.

Maltreated children usually have few choices. Feeling trapped, they develop a sense of helplessness that prevents them from learning constructive approaches to problem solving. As adults they may find themselves unable to make decisions and may feel they have little control over their lives.

The ability to trust is perhaps most difficult for maltreated children to develop. Exploited, battered or neglected, they learn to fear rather than trust. Inability to trust not only prevents children from developing loving relationships but makes it difficult for them to seek protection from abuse as well. Children may look with suspicion on a concerned adult's attempts to help. If carried into adulthood, the inability to trust may contribute to marital and child-rearing difficulties.

Finally, the ability to distinguish feelings from actions is an important developmental task. Children often lash out at others because they are angry. As they grow older they learn that being angry does not justify or compel such behavior. They learn other ways of expressing anger.

Abused children are frequent targets of adults who have not learned to separate feelings and actions (*see* TARGET CHILD). As adults these victims are likely to direct their own anger, frustration or sexual feelings at children without stopping to consider the wisdom of their actions.

Each of these abilities, if not mastered, can contribute to inadequate or abusive parenting. Parents cannot teach such developmental tasks if they have not learned them. Left unchecked, developmental deficits are passed from generation to generation, contributing to a cycle of abuse and neglect.

Helfer believes the WAR is best interrupted in childhood before severe damage is done. Various treatment and parent education programs have demonstrated that much can be done to break the cycle during adulthood as well.

X rays X rays are nonluminous electromagnetic rays of very short wavelength. Discovered by the German physicist Wilhelm Roentgen, the X ray achieved its name because of its then unknown properties. Because of its ability to penetrate opaque or solid substances, the X ray is used in combination with photographic film for the study of internal body structures not normally visible. The study of the body through X rays is known as radiology.

Brief exposure to X rays produces a photograph of the bones often called an X ray but more specifically known as a roentgenogram. The typical roentgenographic procedure transmits a small amount of radiation that has no harmful effects. Prolonged exposure to X rays can, however, destroy body tissue.

Advances in pediatric radiology (*see* RADIOLOGY, PEDIATRIC) from the 1930s through the 1950s made it possible to determine both the type of force that caused a bone fracture and the approximate age of the injury. This information, along with other medical evidence, allowed physicians to check the validity of a caretaker's explanations of particular injuries. An especially important finding first reported by John Caffey was the combination of multiple FRACTURES of the long bones and SUBDURAL HEMATOMA. Caffey was one of the first to propose battering as the most likely cause for this combination of injuries. This observation was later expanded upon and publicized by C. Henry Kempe and others as the BATTERED CHILD SYNDROME.

Today a SKELETAL SURVEY is standard practice when child battering is suspected. Using barium sulfate (a tasteless compound that, when swallowed, appears as an opaque substance on a roentgenogram) physicians are also able to detect GASTROINTESTINAL INJURIES.

Other more recent medical advances such as computed tomography (CT scans) and magnetic resonance imaging (MRI) are also used in the identification of abuse-related trauma.

yo-yo syndrome   Violent marital disputes can seriously affect the emotional, intellectual and physical well-being of children. A study of the effects of marital violence on children conducted by Britain's NATIONAL SOCIETY FOR THE PREVENTION OF CRUELTY TO CHILDREN likened children to a yo-yo moving up and down in a pattern of restlessness and violence.

The name yo-yo syndrome has come to describe the situation of many children in violent households. Often shuttled back and forth between parents, these children suffer a range of problems directly related to their volatile environment. They are frequently blamed by parents for their marital problems and may be used as pawns in their parents' bitter disputes. If a child possesses traits similar to one parent he or she may become the victim of SCAPEGOATING by the other parent.

Though yo-yo children may also be physically abused or neglected, the psychological scars caused by the turbulence around them can be just as damaging. Yo-yo children usually feel responsible for family violence, engaging in self-destructive acts or attempting to serve as a buffer between parents.

Parents are often quite resistant to treatment, making it difficult to ensure a safe home environment for the child. It may be necessary to remove the child from home to prevent further trauma.

Jean G. Moore, "Yo-Yo Children—Victims of Matrimonial Violence." *Child Welfare,* 54, no. 8 (1975): 557–566.

APPENDIXES

APPENDIX I
ORGANIZATIONS

FEDERAL CLEARINGHOUSES ON CHILDREN AND FAMILIES

Juvenile Justice Clearinghouse (NCHRS)
P.O. Box 6000
Rockville, MD 20849-6000
Tel.: (800) 638-8736
www.ncjrs.org

Military Family Resource Center
4040 North Fairfax Dr., Room 420
Arlington, VA 22203-1635
Tel.: (703) 696-9053
http://mfrc.calib.com

National Adoption Information Clearinghouse (NAIC)
330 C St. SW
Washington, DC 20447
Tel.: (888) 251-0075 or
(703) 352-3488
www.calib.com/naic

National Center for Education in Maternal and Child Health (NCEMCH)
2000 15th St. North, Suite 701
Arlington, VA 22201-2617
Tel.: (703) 524-7802
www.ncemch.org

National Center for Missing and Exploited Children
2101 Wilson Blvd., Suite 550
Arlington, VA 22201
Tel.: (800) 843-5678 or
(703) 235-3900
www.missingkids.com

National Clearinghouse on Families and Youth (NCFY)
P.O. Box 13505
Silver Spring, MD 20911-3505
Tel.: (301) 608-8098
www.ncfy.com

National Evaluation Data and Technical Assistance Center (NEDTAC)
10530 Rosehaven St., Suite 400
Fairfax, VA 22030
Tel.: (800) 7-NEDTAC or
(703) 385-3200
www.calib.com/nedtac

National Information Center for Children and Youth with Disabilities (NICHCY)
P.O. Box 1492
Washington, DC 20013
Tel.: (800) 695-0285 or
(202) 884-8200
www.nichcy.org

National Maternal and Child Health Clearinghouse
2070 Chain Bridge Rd., Suite 450
Vienna, VA 22182-2536
Tel.: (703) 356-1964
www.circsol.com/mch

National Clearinghouse for Alcohol and Drug Information (NCADI)
P.O. Box 2345
Rockville, MD 20947-2345
Tel.: (800) 729-6686 or
(301) 468-2600
www.health.org

National Clearinghouse on Child Abuse and Neglect Information
330 C St. SW
Washington, DC 20447
Tel.: (800) FYI-3366 or
(703) 385-7565
www.calib.com/nccanch

National Sudden Infant Death Syndrome Resource Center (NSRC)
2070 Chain Bridge Rd., Suite 450
Vienna, VA 22182
Tel.: (703) 821-8955 ext. 249 or 474
www.circsol.com/sids/

ORGANIZATIONS WITH INFORMATION ON SUBSTANCE ABUSE*

Al-Anon Family Group Headquarters
1600 Corporate Landing Parkway
Virginia Beach, VA 23454-5617
Tel.: (800) 344-2666 or
(757) 563-1600
www.al-anon.alateen.org

Alcoholics Anonymous
P.O. Box 459
Grand Central Station
New York, NY 10163
Tel.: (212) 870-3400
www.alcoholics-anonymous.org

Center for Substance Abuse Prevention (CSAP)
Substance Abuse and Mental Health Services Administration
Rockwall II, 5600 Fishers Lane
Rockville, MD 20857
Tel.: (301) 443-0365
www.samhsa.gov/csap.htm

Center for Substance Abuse Treatment (CSAT)
Substance Abuse and Mental Health Services Administration
Rockwall II, 5600 Fishers Lane
Rockville, MD 20857
Tel.: (301) 443-5052
www.samhsa.gov/csat.htm

---

*Many experts believe that substance abuse is a factor in as many as two-thirds of all child abuse cases.

Children of Alcoholics Foundation,
Inc.
33 West 60th St., 5th Floor
New York, NY 10023
Tel.: (800) 359-2623 or
(212) 757-2100 ext. 6370
www.adultchildren.org

Institute on Black Chemical Abuse
(IBCA)
2616 Nicollet Ave., South
Minneapolis, MN 55408
Tel.: (612) 871-7878
www.aafs.net

National Association for Families
Addiction Research and
Education (NAFARE)
122 South Michigan Ave.,
Suite 1100
Chicago, IL 60603
Tel.: (312) 431-8996

National Clearinghouse for Alcohol
and Drug Information (NCADI)
P.O. Box 2345
Rockville, MD 20947-2345
Tel.: (800) 729-6686 or
(301) 468-2600
www.health.org

National Council on Alcoholism and
Drug Dependence, Inc. (NCADD)
12 West 21st St., 7th Floor
New York, NY 10010
Tel.: (800) NCA-CALL or
(212) 206-6770
www.ncadd.org

National Organization on Fetal
Alcohol Syndrome (NOFAS)
1819 H St. NW, Suite 750
Washington, DC 20006
Tel.: (202) 785-4585
www.nofas.org

ORGANIZATIONS INVOLVED WITH CHILDREN'S LEGAL CHILD WELFARE ISSUES

ABA Center on Children and the
Law
740 15th St. NW
Washington, DC 20005
Tel.: (202) 662-1720
www.abanet.org/child

Children's Rights Council
3001 I St. NE, Suite 401
Washington, DC 20002-4389
Tel.: (202) 547-6227
www.vix.com/crc

National Association of Counsel for
Children (NACC)
1825 Marion St., Suite 340
Denver, CO 80218
Tel.: (303) 864-5320
http://naccchildlaw.org

National Center for the Prosecution
of Child Abuse
American Prosecutors Research
Institute
99 Canal Center Plaza, Suite 510
Alexandria, VA 22314
Tel.: (703) 739-0321
www.ndaa-apri.org

National Conference of State
Legislatures
1560 Broadway, Suite 700
Denver, CO 80202
Tel.: (303) 830-2200
www.ncsl.org

National Court Appointed Special
Advocate Association
100 West Harrison St., North Tower,
Suite 500
Seattle, WA 98119
Tel.: (206) 270-0072
www.nationalcasa.org

National Indian Justice Center
The McNear Building
7 Fourth St., Suite 46
Petaluma, CA 94952
Tel.: (707) 762-8113
http://nijc.indian.com

National Law Center for Children
and Families
4103 Chain Bridge Rd., Suite 410
Fairfax, VA 22030-4105
Tel.: (703) 691-4626

National Legal Aid & Defender
Association
1625 K St. NW, Suite 800
Washington, DC 20006-1604
Tel.: (202) 452-0620
http://www.nlada.org

National Center for State Courts
300 Newport Ave.
P.O. Box 8798
Williamsburg, VA 23187-8798
Tel.: (757) 253-2000
www.ncsc.dni.us

National Center for Youth Law
114 Sansome St., Suite 900
San Francisco, CA 94104-3820
Tel.: (415) 543-3307
www.youthlaw.org

Resource Center on Domestic
Violence, Child Protection and
Custody
P.O. Box 8970
Reno, NV 89507
Tel.: (800) 527-3223
www.reeusda.gov/pavnet/cf/
cfrcdanv.htm

OTHER IMPORTANT ORGANIZATIONS

American Association for Protecting
Children (AAPC)
American Humane Association
Children's Division
63 Inverness Drive East
Englewood, CO 80112
(303) 792-9900
www.americanhumane.org

American Professionals Society on
the Abuse of Children (APSAC)
407 S. Dearborn St., Ste. 1300
Chicago, IL 60605
(312) 554-0166
www.apsac.org

American Public Human Services
Association
810 First St. NW, Suite 500
Washington, DC 20002
(202) 682-0100
www.aphsa.org

Child Find
P.O. Box 277
New Paltz, NY 12561
(914) 255-1848
(800) I-AM-LOST
(800) A-WAY-OUT

CHILDHELP USA
15757 N. 78 St.
Scottsdale, AZ 85260
(800) 4-A-CHILD or (480)922-8212
www.childhelpusa.org

Child Welfare League of America
440 First St. NW, Suite 310
Washington, DC 20001
(202) 638-4004
www.cwla.org

Children's Defense Fund
25 E. St. NW
Washington, DC 20001
(202) 628-8787
www.childrensdefense.org

Daughters and Sons United (DSU)
c/o Parents United International,
    Inc.
615 15th St
Modesto, CA
(209) 572-3446

Incest Survivors Resource Network,
    International
P.O. Box 7375
Las Cruces, NM 88006-7325
(505) 521-4260

Kempe National Children's Center
1825 Main St.
Denver, CO 80218
(303) 864-5252
www.kempecenter.org

National Center for Missing and
    Exploited Children
1835 K Street NW, Suite 700
Washington, DC 20006
(800) 843-5678
P.O. Box 809343
Chicago, IL 60680-9343

Prevent Child Abuse
332 South Michigan Ave., Suite 170
Chicago, IL 60604-4357
(312) 663-3520
www.childabuse.org

Parents Anonymous National
    Office
675 W. Foothill Blvd., Suite 220
Claremont, CA 91711
(909) 621-6183
www.parentsanonymous.us_ntal.org

Parents United International, Inc.
615 15th St.
Modesto, CA
(209) 572-3446

UNICEF (United Nations
    International Children's
    Emergency Relief Fund)
3 United Nations Plaza
New York, NY 10017

Victims of Child Abuse Laws
    (VOCAL)
7485 E. Kenyon Ave.
Denver, CO 80237
(303) 233-5321

VOICES in Action
P.O. Box 148309
Chicago, IL 60614
(773) 327-1500
www.voices-action.org

APPENDIX II
NATIONAL CHILD WELFARE RESOURCE CENTERS

CHILDREN'S BUREAU RESOURCE CENTERS AND CLEARINGHOUSES

ARCH National Resource Center for
  Respite and Crisis Care Services
The Chapel Hill Training-Outreach
  Project
800 Eastowne Drive, Suite 105
Chapel Hill, NC 27514
Tel.: (800) 473-1727 or
  (919) 490-5577
http://chtop.com/archbroc.htm

FRIENDS
National Resource Center for
  Community-Based Resource and
  Support Programs
800 Eastowne Drive, Suite 105
Chapel Hill, NC 27514
Tel.: (800) 888-7970
www.frca.org/friends.htm

National Abandoned Infants
  Assistance Resource Center
Family Welfare Research Group
University of California at Berkeley
School of Social Welfare
1950 Addison St., Suite 104
Berkeley, CA 94704-1182
Tel.: (510) 643-8390
http://cssr.berkeley.edu/aiarc

National Adoption Information
  Clearinghouse
330 C St. SW
Washington, DC 20447
Tel.: (888) 251-0075 or
  (703) 352-3488
www.calib.com/naic

National Child Welfare Resource
  Center for Organizational
  Improvement
Edmond S. Muskie Institute
University of Southern Maine
One Post Office Square
P.O. Box 15010
Portland, ME 04112
Tel.: (207) 780-5810
www.muskie.usm.maine.edu/
  helpkids/

National Clearinghouse on Child
  Abuse and Neglect Information
330 C St. SW
Washington, DC 20447
Tel.: (800) FYI-3366 or
  (703) 385-7565
www.calib.com/nccanch

National Data Archive on Child
  Abuse and Neglect
Family Life Development Center
Cornell University
Ithaca, NY 14853-4401
Tel.: (607) 255-7799
www.ndacan.cornell.edu/

National Resource Center for Family
  Centered Practice
University of Iowa
School of Social Work
100 Oakdale Campus
Iowa City, IA 52242-5000
Tel.: (319) 335-4965
www.uiowa.edu/~nrcfcp/new/
  index.htm

National Resource Center for
  Permanency Planning
Hunter College School of Social Work
129 E. 79th St., Room 801
New York, NY 10021
Tel.: (212) 452-7053
www.hunter.cuny.edu/socwork/
  nrcppab.htm

National Resource Center on Child
  Maltreatment
1349 Peachtree St. NE, Suite 900
Atlanta, GA 30309-2956
Tel.: (404) 881-0707
http://gocwi.org/nrccm

National Resource Center for Youth
  Development
The University of Oklahoma
College of Continuing Education
202 W. 8th St.
Tulsa, OK 74119-1419
Tel.: (918) 585-2986
www.nrcys.ou.edu/nrcyd.htm

National Resource Center on Legal
  and Court Issues
ABA Center on Children and the
  Law
740 15th St. NW, 9th Floor
Washington, DC 20005-1009
Tel.: (202) 662-1720
www.abanet.org/child

National Resource Center for
  Special Needs Adoption
Spaulding for Children
16250 Northland Dr., Suite 120
Southfield, MI 48075
Tel.: (248) 443-7080
www.spaulding.org/adoption/
  NRC-adoption.html

APPENDIX III
STATE CHILD PROTECTION AGENCIES

STATE AGENCIES

Because the responsibility for investigating reports of suspected child abuse and neglect rests at the state level, each state has established a child protective services reporting system. Listed below are the names and addresses of the agencies responsible for child protective services in each state. (Child abuse hotline numbers are listed in Appendix 4.)

Alabama

Alabama Department of Human
    Resources
Division of Family and Children's
    Services
50 N. Ripley St.
Montgomery, AL 36130
Tel.: (334) 242-1310

Alaska

Department of Health and Social
    Services
Division of Family and Youth
    Services
P.O. Box 110630
Juneau, AK 99811-0630
Tel.: (907) 465-3170

Arizona

Department of Economic Security
1789 West Jefferson
Phoenix, AZ 85005
Tel.: (602) 542-2359

Arkansas

Arkansas Department of Human
    Services
Division of Children and Family
    Services
Donaghey Plaza West
Slot 3430
P.O. Box 1437
Little Rock, AR 72203
Tel.: (501) 682-8650

California

Department of Social Services
744 P St.
Sacramento, CA 95814
Tel.: (916) 657-3667

Colorado

Department of Social Services
1575 Sherman St.
Denver, CO 80203-1714
Tel.: (303) 866-5700
TDD: (303) 866-6293

Connecticut

Connecticut Department of
    Children and Youth Services
Division of Children's and Protective
    Services
25 Sigourney St.
Hartford, CT 06106
Tel.: (800) 842-1508
TDD/TTY Line: (800) 842-4524

Delaware

Division of Family Services
Delaware Department of Services to
    Children, Youth and Their
    Families
1825 Faulkland Dr.
Wilmington, DE 19805
Tel.: (302) 633-2500

District of Columbia

Department of Human Services
609 H St. N.
Washington, DC 20002
Tel.: (202) 724-8602

Florida

Florida Department of Children and
    Family Services
1317 Winewood Blvd., Building 8
Tallahassee, FL 32399-0700
Tel.: (904) 488-2383

Georgia

Division of Children and Family
    Services
Georgia Department of Human
    Resources
2 Peachtree St. NW
Atlanta, GA 30303
Tel.: (404) 894-3376

Guam

Department of Public Health and
    Social Services
P.O. Box 2816
Agana, GU 96910
Tel.: (671) 477-8966

Hawaii

Department of Human Services
Family and Children's Services
810 Richards St.
Honolulu, HI 96813
Tel.: (808) 548-5698

Idaho

Department of Health and Welfare
Bureau of Social Services
450 West State
Boise, ID 83720
Tel.: (208) 334-5500

Illinois

Illinois Department of Children and
  Family Services
406 East Monroe St.
Springfield, Ill 62701-1498
Tel.: (217) 785-2509
TTD: (217) 785-6605

Indiana

Indiana Family Social Services
  Department
402 W. Washington St.
Indianapolis, IN 46204
Tel.: (888) 204-7466

Iowa

Iowa Department of Human Services
Hoover State Office Building
Des Moines, IA 50319
Tel.: (785) 296-8138

Kansas

Children and Family Services
Kansas Department of Social and
  Rehabilitative Services
915 Harrison Ave.
Topeka, KS 66612-1570
Tel.: (785) 296-8138

Kentucky

Kentucky Cabinet for Families and
  Children
Children and Youth Services
  Branch
275 East Main St.
Frankfort, KY 40621
Tel.: (502) 564-2147

Louisiana

Louisiana Department of Social
  Services
Division of Children, Youth and
  Family Services
A. Z. Young Building
755 3rd St.
Baton Rouge, LA 70821
Tel.: (225) 342-2297

Maine

Maine Department of Human
  Services
Child Protective Services
221 State St.
Augusta, ME 04333
Tel.: (207) 287-3707
TTY: (207) 287-4479

Maryland

Social Services Office for Children,
  Youth and Families
Maryland Department of Human
  Resources
311 W. Saratoga St.
Baltimore, MD 21201
Tel.: (410) 767-4163

Massachusetts

Massachusetts Department of Social
  Services
Protective Services
24 Farnsworth St.
Boston, MA 02210
Tel.: (617) 748-2400

Michigan

Michigan Family Independence
  Agency
235 S. Grand Ave., Suite 510
Lansing, MI 48909
Tel.: (517) 373-7394

Minnesota

Minnesota Department of Human
  Services
444 Lafayette Ave.
St. Paul, MN 55155-3839
Tel.: (651) 297-3933

Mississippi

Mississippi Department of Human
  Services
Bureau of Family and Children's
  Services
750 North State St.
Jackson, MS 39202
Tel.: (800) 345-6347 or
  (601) 359-4500

Missouri

Missouri Department of Social
  Services
221 West High St.
P.O. Box 1527
Jefferson City MO 65102-1527
Tel.: (573) 751-4815 or
  (800) 735-2466

Montana

Montana Division of Human and
  Community Services
1400 Broadway
Helena, MT 59620
Tel.: (406) 444-5902

Nebraska

Nebraska Health and Human
  Services System
P.O. Box 95044
Lincoln, NE 68509-5044
Tel.: (402) 471-2306

New Hampshire

Division on Children, Youth and
  Families
New Hampshire Department of
  Health and Human Services
6 Hazen Dr.
Concord, NH 03301
Tel.: (603) 271-4714

New Jersey

New Jersey Department of Human
  Services
Division of Youth and Family
  Services
P.O. Box 717
One South Montgomery St.
Trenton, NJ 08625-0717
Tel.: (800) 331-3937

New Mexico

New Mexico Children Youth and
  Family Department
P.O. Drawer 5160
Santa Fe, NM 87502-5160
Tel.: (505) 841-6100

Nevada

Child and Family Services Division
711 E. Fifth St.
Capitol Complex
Carson City, NV 89710
Tel.: (775) 687-5982

New York

Office of Children and Family
   Services
New York Department of Social
   Services
40 N. Pearl St.
Albany, NY 12243
Tel.: (800) 342-3009

North Carolina

North Carolina Department of
   Human Resources
325 N. Salisbury St.
Raleigh, NC 27603
Tel.: (919) 733-3801

North Dakota

North Dakota Department of
   Human Services
600 E. Blvd.
Bismarck, ND 58505-0250
Tel.: (701) 328-4805

Ohio

Department of Human Services
65 East State St.
Columbus, OH 43266-0423
Tel.: (614) 466-9274

Oklahoma

Oklahoma Department of Human
   Services
2400 N. Lincoln Blvd.
P.O. Box 25352
Oklahoma City, OK 73125
Tel.: (405) 521-3646

Oregon

Department of Human Services
Children's Services Division
500 Summer St. NE
Salem, OR 97310
Tel.: (503) 945-5944
TTY: (503) 945-5928

Pennsylvania

Pennsylvania Department of Public
   Welfare
Office of Children, Youth and
   Families
Health and Welfare Building,
   Rm. 131
Harrisburg, PA 17105-2675
Tel.: (717) 783-3856

Rhode Island

Rhode Island Department of
   Children, Youth and Families
Division of Child Protection
   Services
610 Mt. Pleasant Ave.
Providence, RI 02908
Tel.: (401) 222-5220
TDD: (401) 457-5336

South Carolina

South Carolina Department of
   Social Services
P.O. Box 1520
Columbia, SC 29202-1520
Tel.: (803) 898-7601

South Dakota

South Dakota Department of Social
   Services
700 Governors Dr.
Pierre, SD 57501
Tel.: (605) 773-3165

Tennessee

Tennessee Department of Children's
   Services
400 Deaderick St.
Nashville, TN 37248
Tel.: (615) 741-5935

Texas

Texas Department of Human
   Services
701 W. 51st St.
Austin, TX 78714
Tel.: (512) 438-3412

Utah

Department of Human Services
Office of Child Protection
   Ombudsman
120 North 200 West, Rm. 422
P.O. Box 45500
Salt Lake City, UT 84145-0500
Tel.: (899) 868-6413 or
   (801) 538-4589

Vermont

Vermont Department of Social
   Services
103 S. Main St.
Waterbury, VT 05671-2901
Tel.: (802) 241-2131

Virginia

Virginia Department of Social
   Services
730 E. Broad St.
Richmond, VA 23219
Tel: (804) 692-1900

Washington

Washington Department of Social
   and Health Services
P.O. Box 45130
Olympia, WA 98504-5130
Tel: (800) 723-4831

West Virginia

West Virginia Bureau for Children
   and Families
350 Capitol St., Rm 730
Charleston, WV 25305
Tel: (304) 558-8290

Wisconsin

Wisconsin Department of Health
   and Family Services
P.O. Box 8916
Madison, WI 53708-8916
Tel.: (608) 267-3905

Wyoming

Wyoming Department of Family
   Services
Hathaway Building
200 Capitol Ave.
Cheyenne, WY 82002-0490
Tel.: (307) 777-3570

APPENDIX IV
STATE TOLL-FREE REPORTING NUMBERS

Each state designates an agency responsible for receiving and investigating abuse complaints. Many states have toll-free numbers, which are listed below. In many cases, these numbers are for the convenience of individuals living within the state. Note: If your state does not have a toll-free number and you witness an act of abuse, call Childhelp, an organization that can refer you to the agency to call. Call Childhelp at 800-4-A-Child (800-422-4453).

Arkansas
(800) 482-5964

Arizona
(800) 330-1822

Connecticut
(800) 842-2288

Delaware
(800) 292-9582

Florida
(800) 962-2873

Iowa
(800) 362-2178

Illinois
(800) 252-2873

Indiana
(800) 562-2407

Kansas
(800) 922-5330

Kentucky
(800) 752-6200

Massachusetts
(800) 792-5200

Maine
(800) 452-1999

Michigan
(800) 942-4357

Missouri
(800) 392-3738

Mississippi
(800) 222-8000

Montana
(800) 332-6100

North Carolina
(800) 662-7030

Nebraska
(800) 652-1999

New Hampshire
(800) 894-5533

New Jersey
(800) 792-8610

New Mexico
(800) 432-2075

Nevada
(800) 992-5757

New York
(800) 342-3720

Oklahoma
(800) 522-3511

Oregon
(800) 854-3508

Pennsylvania
(800) 932-0313

Rhode Island
(800)742-4453

Texas
(800) 252-5400

Utah
(800) 678-9399

Virginia
(800) 552-7906

Washington
(800) 562-5624

West Virginia
(800) 352-6513

APPENDIX V
CHILD MALTREATMENT CHARTS

Victims by Maltreatment by State, 1997

State	Physical Abuse	Neglect	Medical Neglect	Sexual Abuse	Psychological or Emotional Abuse or Neglect	Other	Unknown	Total
Alabama	7,516	9,284		4,108	1,296			22,204
Alaska	2,308	5,507		1,057	122	23		9,017
Arizona	7,683	12,332	1,831	1,526	544	31	58	24,005
Arkansas								
California	54,491	81,583		26,113	11,444	584		174,215
Colorado	2,017	4,467	459	1,088	904			8,935
Connecticut	3,949	16,342	964	1,045	11,912	2,426		36,638
Delaware	1,690	1,810	106	244		567		4,417
District of Columbia	389	4,857		86				5,332
Florida	15,721	36,051	2,401	6,097	2,724	36,645		99,639
Georgia	8,804	26,567	2,494	3,977	1,957	1,705		45,504
Guam								
Hawaii	260	257	25	166	33	1,804	14	2,559
Idaho	2,743	3,512		1,607		417	4	8,283
Illinois	4,410	17,078	1,351	3,972	524	17,798		45,133
Indiana	3,061	8,847	789	2,927				15,624
Iowa								
Kansas	5,033	4,494	503	2,198	799	1,753	3,812	18,592
Kentucky	5,845	12,712		1,417	2,688			22,662
Louisiana	3,109	10,167		920	551	78		14,825
Maine	814	1,894		421	2,592			5,721
Maryland								
Massachusetts	7,182	24,583		1,451	476	67		33,759
Michigan	4,397	9,937	467	1,468	1,082	4,679		22,030
Minnesota	3,166	6,961	568	974	171			11,840
Mississippi	1,394	3,702		834	172	8	11,449	17,559
Missouri	3,392	8,803	518	2,688	246	1,789	27	17,463
Montana	487	1,702	112	328	744	238		3,611
Nebraska	1,328	3,023		406				4,757
Nevada								
New Hampshire	302	732		288	60			1,382
New Jersey	2,595	6,728	415	799	445			10,982
New Mexico	2,038	4,888	73	603	609	2		8,213
New York								
North Carolina	1,494	29,032	727	1,383	172	539		33,347
North Dakota								
Ohio								
Oklahoma	3,651	16,769	425	1,339	1,380			23,564
Oregon	1,599	2,594	437	1,476	617	5,405		12,128
Pennsylvania	2,432	191	145	2,619	110	302		5,799
Puerto Rico								
Rhode Island	1,071	2,716	101	335	20	135		4,378
South Carolina	1,278	3,945	380	728	74	4,522		10,927
South Dakota	626	1,795		211	262			2,894
Tennessee	2,192	4,545	357	2,234	292	1,183		10,803
Texas	11,839	22,192	1,818	6,454	1,837	1,536		45,676
Utah	2,053	3,949	160	2,236	275	764		9,437
Vermont	266	321	13	511	10			1,121
Virginia	2,705	6,655	275	1,566	414	177		11,792
Virgin Islands								
Washington	6,445	11,275	806	2,537	1,595	632	13	23,303
West Virginia								
Wisconsin	3,536	5,533	146	5,822	165	2,390		17,592
Wyoming	246	612	28	80	20			986
Total	197,557	440,944	18,894	98,339	49,338	88,199	15,377	908,648
Number Reporting	43	43	30	43	38	29	7	43

Type of Maltreatment by Sex of Perpetrator

Type of Maltreatment		Perpetrator Sex		Total
		Male	Female	
Physical Abuse	Count	18,960	20,115	39,075
	% within Type of Maltreatment	48.5%	51.5%	100.0%
	% within Sex	17.5%	12.0%	14.1%
Neglect	Count	29,587	83,769	113,356
	% within Type of Maltreatment	26.1%	73.9%	100.0%
	% within Sex	27.4%	49.8%	41.0%
Medical Neglect	Count	1,035	4,716	5,751
	% within Type of Maltreatment	18.0%	82.0%	100.0%
	% within Sex	1.0%	2.8%	2.1%
Sexual Abuse	Count	15,606	5,453	21,059
	% within Type of Maltreatment	74.1%	25.9%	100.0%
	% within Sex	14.4%	3.2%	7.6%
Psychological Abuse	Count	6,540	7,005	13,545
	% within Type of Maltreatment	48.3%	51.7%	100.0%
	% within Sex	6.0%	4.2%	4.9%
Other Abuse	Count	14,511	18,355	32,866
	% within Type of Maltreatment	44.2%	55.8%	100.0%
	% within Sex	13.4%	10.9%	11.9%
Multiple Maltreatments	Count	21,881	28,888	50,769
	% within Type of Maltreatment	43.1%	56.9%	100.0%
	% within Sex	20.2%	17.2%	18.4%
Total	Count	108,120	168,301	276,421
	% within Type of Maltreatment	39.1%	60.9%	100.0%
	% within Sex	100.0%	100.0%	100.0%

Perpetrators of Child Fatalities by Sex and Age

Fatality Perpetrator Age		Perpetrator Sex		Total
		Male	Female	
19 years or younger	Count	15	30	45
	% within Age	33.3%	66.7%	100.0%
	% within Sex	11.6%	13.8%	13.0%
20 to 29 years old	Count	63	127	190
	% within Age	33.2%	66.8%	100.0%
	% within Sex	48.8%	58.3%	54.8%
30 to 39 years old	Count	26	30	56
	% within Age	46.4%	53.6%	100.0%
	% within Sex	20.2%	13.8%	16.1%
40 to 49 years old	Count	20	16	36
	% within Age	55.6%	44.4%	100.0%
	% within Sex	15.5%	7.3%	10.4%
50 years old or older	Count	5	15	20
	% within Age	25.0%	75.0%	100.0%
	% within Sex	3.9%	6.9%	5.8%
Total	Count	129	218	347
	% within Age	37.2%	62.8%	100.0%
	% within Sex	100.0%	100.0%	100.0%

Comparison of Children in the Population and Child Victims, by Race, 1997

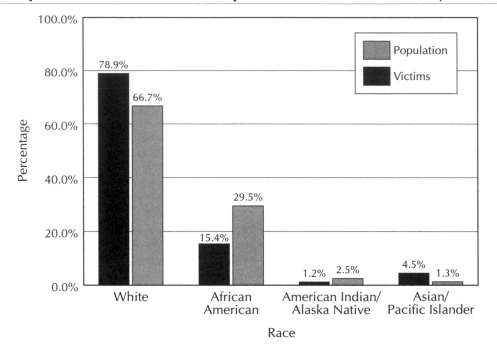

Victims by Age, 1997

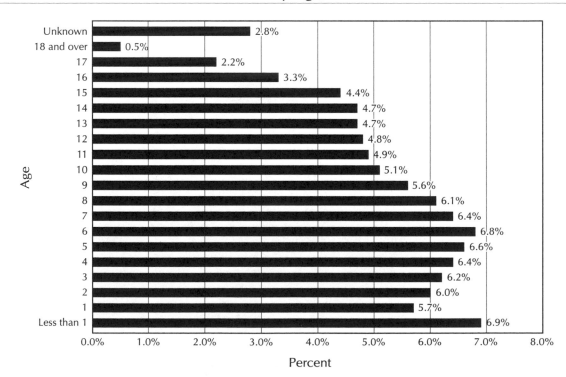

Comparison of Victims by Type of Maltreatment, 1990 and 1997

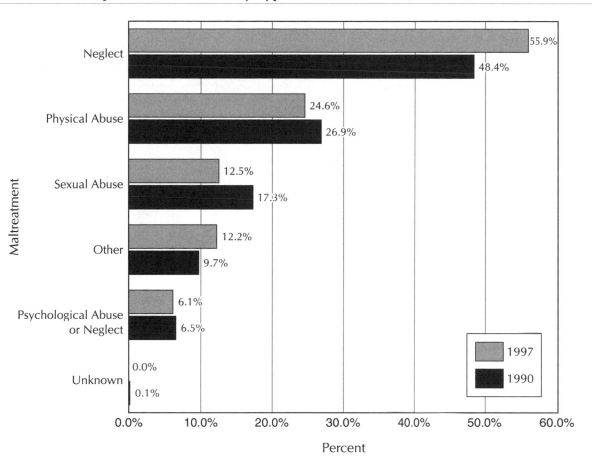

Reports by Source and Disposition, 1997

Report Source	Disposition					Total
	Substantiated	Indicated	Unsubstantiated	Closed No Finding	Other/Unknown	
Social Services/Mental Health	17,992	11,056	28,809	529	1,786	60,172
% within Report Source	29.9%	18.4%	47.9%	0.9%	3.0%	100.0%
% within Disposition	13.3%	13.1%	12.4%	16.7%	18.8%	12.9%
Medical Personnel	19,974	7,743	19,487	153	620	47,977
% within Report Source	41.6%	16.1%	40.6%	0.3%	1.3%	100.0%
% within Disposition	14.7%	9.2%	8.4%	4.8%	6.5%	10.3%
Legal Personnel	29,105	11,689	19,935	244	789	61,762
% within Report Source	47.1%	18.9%	32.3%	0.4%	1.3%	100.0%
% within Disposition	21.5%	13.9%	8.5%	7.7%	8.3%	13.3%
Educational Personnel	18,806	12,975	34,918	234	1,323	68,256
% within Report Source	27.6%	19.0%	51.2%	0.3%	1.9%	100.0%
% within Disposition	13.9%	15.4%	15.0%	7.4%	13.9%	14.7%
Substitute Care Provider/Foster Parent	1,949	1,166	4,154	27	142	7,438
% within Report Source	26.2%	15.7%	55.8%	0.4%	1.9%	100.0%
% within Disposition	1.4%	1.4%	1.8%	0.9%	1.5%	1.6%
Alleged Victim	1,114	1,189	2,918	31	114	5,366
% within Report Source	20.8%	22.2%	54.4%	0.6%	2.1%	100.0%
% within Disposition	0.8%	1.4%	1.3%	1.0%	1.2%	1.2%
Parent	6,164	8,117	19,757	205	745	34,988
% within Report Source	17.6%	23.2%	56.5%	0.6%	2.1%	100.0%
% within Disposition	4.5%	9.6%	8.5%	6.5%	7.8%	7.5%
Other Relative	7,463	7,433	18,164	471	1,082	34,613
% within Report Source	21.6%	21.5%	52.5%	1.4%	3.1%	100.0%
% within Disposition	5.5%	8.8%	7.8%	14.9%	11.4%	7.4%
Friends Neighbor	5,664	7,509	18,667	177	465	32,482
% within Report Source	17.4%	23.1%	57.5%	0.5%	1.4%	100.0%
% within Disposition	4.2%	8.9%	8.0%	5.6%	4.9%	7.0%
Alleged Perpetrator	261	85	302	1	4	653
% within Report Source	40.0%	13.0%	46.2%	0.2%	0.6%	100.0%
% within Disposition	0.2%	0.1%	0.1%	0.0%	0.0%	0.1%
Anonymous Reporter	7,667	8,175	30,859	424	1,236	48,361
% within Report Source	15.9%	16.9%	63.8%	0.9%	2.6%	100.0%
% within Disposition	5.7%	9.7%	13.2%	13.4%	13.0%	10.4%
Other	13,000	6,151	24,280	383	1,161	44,975
% within Report Source	28.9%	13.7%	54.0%	0.9%	2.6%	100.0%
% within Disposition	9.6%	7.3%	10.4%	12.1%	12.2%	9.7%
Unknown	6,383	1,010	10,922	286	43	18,644
% within Report Source	34.2%	5.4%	58.6%	1.5%	0.2%	100.0%
% within Disposition	4.7%	1.2%	4.7%	9.0%	0.5%	4.0%
Total	135,542	84,298	233,172	3,165	9,510	465,687
% within Report Source	29.1%	18.1%	50.1%	0.7%	2.0%	100.0%
% within Disposition	100.0%	100.0%	100.0%	100.0%	100.0%	100.0%

Source of Reports, 1997

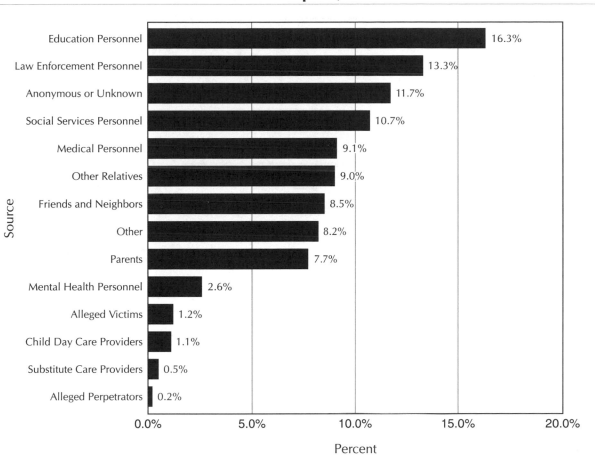

Victims by Race

State	4.5.A African American	4.5.B American Indian/Alaska Native	4.5.C&D Asian/Pacific Islander	4.5.E White	4.5.F Other	4.5.G Unknown	Total
Alabama	7,403	27	70	11,818		57	19,375
Alaska	762	3,790	208	3,572	27	658	9,017
Arizona	1,496	866	90	12,526	6,616	1,885	23,479
Arkansas	1,128	7	6	3,506	66	690	5,403
California	7,396	255	1,657	25,216	846	22,322	57,692
Colorado							
Connecticut	3,879	17	86	5,851	2,835	5,510	18,178
Delaware	1,966	1	8	2,028	174	239	4,416
District of Columbia							
Florida	22,910	86	299	48,725		438	72,458
Georgia	17,716	31	178	20,231	887	6,461	45,504
Guam							
Hawaii	569	27	1,541	380		42	2,559
Idaho	53	155	15	6,670	59	1,331	8,283
Illinois	15,749	8	155	18,362	969	3,693	38,936
Indiana	2,301	29	30	10,507	692	2,065	15,624
Iowa							
Kansas	2,818	132	4	13,750	1,449	439	18,592
Kentucky	3,062	10	35	16,665	723	288	20,783
Louisiana	8,103	37	47	6,501	12	125	14,825
Maine	67	71	11	3,597			3,746
Maryland	5,679			7,809	710		14,198
Massachusetts	5,008	40	603	15,968		8,196	29,815
Michigan	7,991	125	76	11,654		343	20,189
Minnesota	2,766	836	275	6,797		103	10,777
Mississippi							
Missouri	4,504	40	41	11,049	178	33	15,845
Montana	37	812	9	2,148		605	3,611
Nebraska	500	206	48	2,854	74	372	4,054
Nevada	1,528	67	119	5,545	213	1,211	8,683
New Hampshire							
New Jersey	5,508	28	114	3,529	134	1,669	10,982
New Mexico							
New York							
North Carolina	12,548	879	190	16,652		3,078	33,347
North Dakota							
Ohio							
Oklahoma	1,751	1,832	46	8,684	616	698	13,627
Oregon	495	251	106	5,966		2,904	9,722
Pennsylvania							
Puerto Rico							
Rhode Island	558	39	76	2,330		478	3,481
South Carolina	4,103	3	13	4,333	197	35	8,684
South Dakota		1,317		1,065	108		2,490
Tennessee	3,085	15	25	7,171	188	319	10,803
Texas	9,518	122	230	28,076	724	968	39,638
Utah	209	362	144	7,705	88	848	9,356
Vermont	10		4	1,019	3	5	1,041
Virginia	3,957	19	104	5,138	802	5	10,025
Virgin Islands							
Washington	2,265	1,417	593	15,476	2,055		21,806
West Virginia							
Wisconsin	3,478	491	338	9,032		1,286	14,625
Wyoming	22	36		629	8	70	765
Total	172,898	14,486	7,594	390,534	21,453	69,469	676,434
Number Reporting	39	38	37	40	28	36	40

Children Subject of a Report Referred for Investigation, 1990 and 1997

State	1990 Child Population Data	1990 Children Subject of A Report**	1990 Rate of Children Subject of A Report	1997 Child Population Data	1997 Children Subject of A Report**	1997 Rate of Children Subject of A Report
Alabama	1,048,449	39,442	37.6	1,071,708	37,873	35.3
Alaska	177,443	8,509	48.0	188,329	11,616	61.7
Arizona	1,005,998	39,207	39.0	1,278,063	80,622	63.1
Arkansas	620,101	31,862	51.4	662,692	36,340	54.8
California	7,970,804	421,506	52.9	8,951,653	480,443	53.7
Colorado	881,209	34,482	39.1	1,015,529	18,893	18.6
Connecticut	751,598	19,831	26.4	792,161	34,152	43.1
Delaware	165,323	7,395	44.7	177,411	9,657	54.4
District of Columbia	112,195	8,501	75.8	107,204	11,518	107.4
Florida	2,987,368	182,790	61.2	3,471,316	186,726	53.8
Georgia	1,745,430	68,299	39.1	1,987,811	79,848	40.2
Guam	57,822	385	6.7	69,352	2,916	42.1
Hawaii	279,635	3,421	12.2	302,592	4,221	13.9
Idaho	313,021	13,748	43.9	351,352	32,522	92.6
Illinois	2,939,001	104,449	35.5	3,174,223	115,344	36.3
Indiana	1,435,942	50,812	35.4	1,497,455	47,170	31.5
Iowa	719,169	28,141	39.1	725,325	30,500	42.1
Kansas	662,137	19,280	29.1	687,931	45,459	66.1
Kentucky	945,036	48,645	51.5	961,202	45,001	46.8
Louisiana	1,209,527	42,919	35.5	1,190,878	46,287	38.9
Maine	307,629	9,273	30.1	297,266	10,041	33.8
Maryland	1,178,716	46,123	39.1	1,268,552	48,528	38.3
Massachusetts	1,352,176	57,983	42.9	1,451,374	64,000	44.1
Michigan	2,457,807	115,769	47.1	2,504,757	147,628	58.9
Minnesota	1,176,169	23,626	20.1	1,250,685	26,252	21.0
Mississippi	732,776	16,279	22.2	752,998	31,664	42.1
Missouri	1,315,617	73,399	55.8	1,406,425	80,185	57.0
Montana	223,460	11,029	49.4	229,530	21,568	94.0
Nebraska	429,745	15,609	36.3	444,681	16,654	37.5
Nevada	316,381	23,220	73.4	442,856	18,622	42.1
New Hampshire	277,097	10,843	39.1	296,090	9,015	30.4
New Jersey	1,816,334	54,366	29.9	1,987,124	70,024	35.2
New Mexico	452,923	15,023	33.2	499,322	23,454	47.0
New York	4,274,968	213,804	50.0	4,560,031	234,205	51.4
North Carolina	1,625,796	74,222	45.7	1,873,403	104,950	56.0
North Dakota	170,830	6,024	35.3	165,208	6,870	41.6
Ohio	2,776,155	107,271	38.6	2,838,641	119,365	42.1
Oklahoma	841,101	25,072	29.8	878,305	51,001	58.1
Oregon	741,847	29,028	39.1	810,699	27,499	33.9
Pennsylvania	2,797,400	24,357	8.7	2,864,082	22,688	7.9
Puerto Rico	1,115,728	43,658	39.1	1,212,347	50,979	42.1
Rhode Island	225,738	12,989	57.5	233,654	10,182	43.6
South Carolina	919,226	28,615	31.1	955,641	39,333	41.2
South Dakota	199,138	11,267	56.6	197,338	4,874	24.7
Tennessee	1,218,851	33,382	27.4	1,324,789	32,383	24.4
Texas	4,901,954	134,295	27.4	5,577,135	162,974	29.2
Utah	626,787	24,224	38.6	688,077	27,219	39.6
Vermont	143,101	2,697	18.8	145,519	2,309	15.9
Virginia	1,518,627	51,548	33.9	1,644,386	51,227	31.2
Virgin Islands	57,947	2,267	39.1	64,944	2,731	42.1
Washington	1,300,644	27,092	20.8	1,454,654	38,200	26.3
West Virginia	436,600	17,084	39.1	411,746	17,314	42.1
Wisconsin	1,302,264	38,842	29.8	1,346,376	43,406	32.2
Wyoming	135,949	4,815	35.4	131,765	5,541	42.1
Total	65,394,689	2,558,720	39.1	70,874,587	2,980,000	42.0
N	54	54	54	54	54	54
Total w/o Islands	64,163,192	2,512,409	39.2	69,527,944	2,923,374	42.0

Children Who were Removed from the Home

State	3.5.A Substantiated	3.5B Indicated	3.5C Unsubstantiated	3.5D In Need of Services	3.5E Closed Without a Finding	3.5F Other	3.5G Unknown	Total
Alabama	480							480
Alaska	808	46	6		1			861
Arizona								
Arkansas	244							244
California	31,360							31,360
Colorado	643		115	106		162	38	1,064
Connecticut								
Delaware								
District of Columbia	1,003							1,003
Florida	6,821	2,802	652			694		10,969
Georgia	4,167							4,167
Guam								
Hawaii								
Idaho								
Illinois	5,291		730			18		6,039
Indiana	2,655							2,655
Iowa								
Kansas	737		1,932	102	2,648		292	5,711
Kentucky	1,053	157						1,210
Louisiana	2,401							2,401
Maine	1,014							1,014
Maryland							3,707	3,707
Massachusetts	3,852							3,852
Michigan	9,844		642					10,486
Minnesota	2,381		135					2,516
Mississippi								
Missouri	2,085		422	124	5	39		2,675
Montana								
Nebraska								
Nevada								
New Hampshire	379							379
New Jersey	769		309					1,078
New Mexico								
New York								
North Carolina								
North Dakota				344				344
Ohio								
Oklahoma	3,383		358		348	83		4,172
Oregon	3,692							3,692
Pennsylvania	3,355		4,986					8,341
Puerto Rico								
Rhode Island								
South Carolina	1,365							1,365
South Dakota	767							767
Tennessee								
Texas	5,135		301		7	152	27	5,622
Utah	1,542							1,542
Vermont	189							189
Virginia	1,551		318			16		1,885
Virgin Islands								
Washington	3,944	1,243	1,148				1,470	7,805
West Virginia								
Wisconsin	2,618							2,618
Wyoming								
Total	105,528	4,248	12,054	676	3,009	1,164	5,534	132,213
Number Reporting	31	4	14	4	5	7	5	33

Children Subject of a Report and Children by Disposition

State	Number of Children Subject of a Report 3.1	Substantiated Children 3.2.A	Indicated Children 3.2.B	Not Substantiated Children 3.2.C	In Need of Services Child Count 3.2.D	Closed w/o a Finding 3.2.E	Children with Other Dispositions 3.2.F	Children with Uknown Dispositions 3.2.G	Total
Alabama	37,873	15,978	3,511	19,397		1,559	328		40,773
Alaska	11,616	4,252	4,765	914		122	1,563		11,616
Arizona	80,622	23,479	526	28,351			8	522	52,886
Arkansas	36,340	5,109		11,799				13,533	30,441
California	480,443	174,170						306,273	480,443
Colorado	18,893	5,532		9,793	2,563		791	214	18,893
Connecticut	34,152	18,178		18,853					37,031
Delaware	9,657	4,416		5,241					9,657
District of Columbia	11,518	5,341		5,583				594	11,518
Florida	186,726	20,809	58,976	92,337 (868)			12,075		184,197
Georgia	79,848	23,012	22,492	34,344					79,848
Guam									
Hawaii	4,221	2,559		1,662					4,221
Idaho	32,522	2,855	5,428	19,853		3,880	179	327	32,522
Illinois	115,344	38,936		76,120			288		115,344
Indiana	47,170	15,624		31,546					47,170
Iowa									
Kansas	45,459	18,592		26,329		410		1,765	47,096
Kentucky	45,001	14,939	5,844	23,636		582			45,001
Louisiana	46,287	14,825		31,462					46,287
Maine	10,041	3,746		2,471			1,718	2,106	10,041
Maryland	48,528	14,198		31,706			2,624		48,528
Massachusetts	64,008	29,815		28,928					58,743
Michigan	147,628	20,654		126,974					147,628
Minnesota	26,252	10,777		15,475					26,252
Mississippi									
Missouri	80,185	15,845		49,490 (460)	3,962	4,208	6,680		80,185
Montana	21,568	2,797	814	14,950			2,919	88	21,568
Nebraska	16,654	4,054		12,600					16,654
Nevada									
New Hampshire	9,015	1,092		5,858		355		1,710	9,015
New Jersey	70,024	10,982		32,320			26,722		70,024
New Mexico	23,454	8,213		12,005		1,560	1,676		23,454
New York	234,205	72,000		162,205					234,205
North Carolina	104,950	33,347		71,603					104,950
North Dakota	6,870				1,066		5,801	3	6,870
Ohio									
Oklahoma	51,001	13,800		23,130		4,810	9,255	6	51,001
Oregon	27,499	9,742		17,757					27,499
Pennsylvania	22,688	5,691		17,427			70		23,188
Puerto Rico									
Rhode Island	10,182	3,481		6,243		370		87	10,181
South Carolina	39,333	8,684		30,649					39,333
South Dakota	4,874	1,259	1,232	2,174		209			4,874
Tennessee	32,383	10,803		21,580					32,383
Texas	162,974	39,638		87,358		7,791	27,718	469	162,974
Utah	27,219	9,356		17,443		420			27,219
Vermont	2,309	1,041		1,257 (18)		10		1	2,309
Virginia	51,227	10,025		37,282 (457)	2,145	1,358	87	330	51,227
Virgin Islands									
Washington	38,200	12,014	9,792	11,516				4,878	38,200
West Virginia									
Wisconsin	43,406	14,625		25,005		3,776			43,406
Wyoming									
Total	2,700,369	776,285	113,380	1,302,626 (1,803)	9,736	31,420	100,502	332,906	2,666,855
Number Reporting	45	44	10	42	4	16	18	17	45

APPENDIX VI

CHILD ABUSE PREVENTION AND TREATMENT ACT

Legislative Authority: Child Abuse Prevention and Treatment Act, as amended

U.S. Code Citation: 42 USC 5101 *et seq;* 42 USC 5116 *et seq*

ACF Regulations: 45 CFR 1340

Summary of Legislative History:

The Child Abuse Prevention and Treatment Act (CAPTA) was originally enacted in P.L. 93-247. The law was completely rewritten in the Child Abuse Prevention, Adoption and Family Services Act of 1988 (P.L. 100-294, 4/25/88). It was further amended by the Child Abuse Prevention Challenge Grants Reauthorization Act of 1989 (P.L. 101-126, 10/25/89) and the Drug Free School Amendments of 1989 (P.L. 101-226, 12/12/89).

The Community-Based Child Abuse and Neglect Prevention Grants program was originally authorized by sections 402 through 409 of the Continuing Appropriations Act for FY 1985 (P.L. 98-473, 10/12/84). The Child Abuse Prevention Challenge Grants Reauthorization Act of 1989 (P.L. 101-126) transferred this program to the Child Abuse Prevention and Treatment Act, as amended.

A new title III, Certain Preventive Services Regarding Children of Homeless Families or Families at Risk of Homelessness, was added to the Child Abuse and Neglect Prevention and Treatment Act by the Stewart B. McKinney Homeless Assistance Act Amendments of 1990 (P.L. 101-645, 11/29/90).

The Child Abuse Prevention and Treatment Act was amended and reauthorized by the Child Abuse, Domestic Violence, Adoption, and Family Services Act of 1992 (P.L. 102-295, 5/28/92) and amended by the Juvenile Justice and Delinquency Prevention Act Amendments of 1992 (P.L. 102-586, 11/4/92).

The Act was amended by the Older American Act Technical Amendments of 1993 (P.L. 103-171, 12/2/93) and the Human Services Amendments of 1994 (P.L. 103-252, 5/19/94).

CAPTA was further amended by the Child Abuse Prevention and Treatment Act Amendments of 1996 (P.L. 104-235, 10/3/96), which amended Title I, replaced the Title II Community-Based Family Resource Centers program with a new Community-Based Family Resource and Support Program and repealed Title III, Certain Preventive Services Regarding Children of Homeless Families or Families at Risk of Homelessness.

CONTENTS

TITLE II—COMMUNITY-BASED FAMILY RESOURCE AND SUPPORT GRANTS

SEC. 1. SHORT TITLE.

This Act may be cited as the "Child Abuse Prevention and Treatment Act."

SEC. 2. FINDINGS.

Congress finds that—

(1) each year, close to 1,000,000 American children are victims of abuse and neglect;

(2) many of these children and their families fail to receive adequate protection or treatment;

(3) the problem of child abuse and neglect requires a comprehensive approach that—

(A) integrates the work of social service, legal, health, mental health, education, and substance abuse agencies and organizations;

(B) strengthens coordination among all levels of government, and with private agencies, civic, religious, and professional organizations, and individual volunteers;

(C) emphasizes the need for abuse and neglect prevention, assessment, investigation, and treatment at the neighborhood level;

(D) ensures properly trained and support staff with specialized knowledge, to carry out their child protection duties; and

(E) is sensitive to ethnic and cultural diversity;

(4) the failure to coordinate and comprehensively prevent and treat child abuse and neglect threatens the futures of thousands of children and results in a cost to the Nation of billions of dollars in tangible expenditures, as well as significant intangible costs;

(5) all elements of American society have a shared responsibility in responding to this national child and family emergency;

(6) substantial reductions in the prevalence and incidence of child abuse and neglect and the alleviation of its consequences are matters of the highest national priority;

(7) national policy should strengthen families to prevent child abuse and neglect, provide support for intensive services to prevent the unnecessary removal of children from families, and promote the reunification of families if removal has taken place;

(8) the child protection system should be comprehensive, child-centered, family-focused, and community-based, should incorporate all appropriate measures to prevent the occurrence or recurrence of child abuse and neglect, and should promote physical and psychological recovery and social re-integration in an environment that fosters the health, safety, self-respect, and dignity of the child;

(9) because of the limited resources available in low-income communities, Federal aid for the child protection system should be distributed with due regard to the relative financial need of the communities;

(10) the Federal government should assist States and communities with the fiscal, human, and technical resources necessary to develop and implement a successful and comprehensive child and family protection strategy;

(11) the Federal government should provide leadership and assist communities in their child and family protection efforts by—

(A) promoting coordinated planning among all levels of government;

(B) generating and sharing knowledge relevant to child and family protection, including the development of models for service delivery;

(C) strengthening the capacity of States to assist communities;

(D) allocating financial resources to assist States in implementing community plans;

(E) helping communities to carry out their child and family protection plans by promoting the competence of professional, paraprofessional, and volunteer resources; and

(F) providing leadership to end the abuse and neglect of the nation's children and youth.

TITLE I—GENERAL PROGRAM
OFFICE ON CHILD ABUSE AND NEGLECT

SEC. 101. [42 U.S.C. 5101]

(a) ESTABLISHMENT.—The Secretary of Health and Human Services may establish an office to be known as the Office on Child Abuse and Neglect.

(b) PURPOSE.—The purpose of the Office established under subsection (a) shall be to execute and coordinate the functions and activities of this Act. In the event that such functions and activities are performed by another entity or entities within the Department of Health and Human Services, the Secretary shall ensure that such functions and activities are executed with the necessary expertise and in a fully coordinated manner involving regular intradepartmental and interdepartmental consultation with all agencies involved in child abuse and neglect activities.

ADVISORY BOARD ON CHILD ABUSE
AND NEGLECT

SEC. 102. [42 U.S.C. 5102]

(a) APPOINTMENT.—The Secretary may appoint an advisory board to make recommendations to the Secretary and to the appropriate committees of Congress concerning specific issues relating to child abuse and neglect.

(b) SOLICITATION OF NOMINATIONS.—The Secretary shall publish a notice in the Federal Register soliciting nominations for the appointment of members of the advisory board under subsection (a).

(c) COMPOSITION.—In establishing the board under subsection (a), the Secretary shall appoint members from the general public who are individuals knowledgeable in child abuse and neglect pre-

vention, intervention, treatment, or research, and with due consideration to representation of ethnic or racial minorities and diverse geographic areas, and who represent—

(1) law (including the judiciary);

(2) psychology (including child development);

(3) social services (including child protective services);

(4) medicine (including pediatrics);

(5) State and local government;

(6) organizations providing services to disabled persons

(7) organizations providing services to adolescents;

(8) teachers;

(9) parent self-help organizations;

(10) parents' groups;

(11) voluntary groups;

(12) family rights groups; and

(13) children's rights advocates.

(d) VACANCIES.—Any vacancy in the membership of the board shall be filled in the same manner in which the original appointment was made.

(e) ELECTION OF OFFICERS.—The board shall elect a chairperson and vice-chairperson at its first meeting from among the members of the board.

(f) DUTIES.—Not later than 1 year after the establishment of the board under subsection (a), the board shall submit to the Secretary and the appropriate committees of Congress a report, or interim report, containing—

(1) recommendations on coordinating Federal, State, and local child abuse and neglect activities with similar activities at the Federal, State, and local level pertaining to family violence prevention;

(2) specific modifications needed in Federal and State laws and programs to reduce the number of unfounded or unsubstantiated reports of child abuse or neglect while enhancing the ability to identify and substantiate legitimate cases of abuse or neglect which place a child in danger; and

(3) recommendations for modifications needed to facilitate coordinated national data collection with respect to child protection and child welfare.

NATIONAL CLEARINGHOUSE FOR INFORMATION RELATING TO CHILD ABUSE

SEC. 103. [42 U.S.C. 5104]

(a) ESTABLISHMENT.—The Secretary shall through the Department, or by one or more contracts of not less than 3 years duration let through a competition, establish a national clearinghouse for information relating to child abuse.

(b) FUNCTIONS.—The Secretary shall, through the clearinghouse established by subsection (a)—

(1) maintain, coordinate, and disseminate information on all programs, including private programs, that show promise of success with respect to the prevention, assessment, identification, and treatment of child abuse and neglect; and

(2) maintain and disseminate information relating to—

(A) the incidence of cases of child abuse and neglect in the United States;

(B) the incidence of such cases in populations determined by the Secretary under section 105(a)(1) of the Child Abuse Prevention, Adoption, and Family Services Act of 1988; and

(C) the incidence of any such cases related to alcohol or drug abuse.

(c) COORDINATION WITH AVAILABLE RESOURCES.—

(1) IN GENERAL.—In establishing a national clearinghouse as required by subsection (a), the Secretary shall—

(A) consult with other Federal agencies that operate similar clearinghouses;

(B) consult with the head of each agency involved with child abuse and neglect and mechanisms for the sharing of such information among other Federal agencies and clearinghouses on the development of the components for information collection and management of such clearinghouse;

(C) develop a Federal data system involving the elements under subsection (b) which, to the extent practicable, coordinates existing Federal, State, regional, and local child welfare data systems which shall include—

(i) standardized data on false, unfounded, unsubstantiated, and substantiated reports; and

(ii) information on the number of deaths due to child abuse and neglect;

(D) through a national data collection and analysis program and in consultation with appropriate State and local agencies and experts in the field, collect, compile, and make available State child abuse and neglect reporting information which, to the extent practical, shall be universal and case specific and integrated with other case-based foster care and adoption data collected by the Secretary;

(E) compile, analyze, and publish a summary of the research conducted under section 105(a)[1]; and

(F) solicit public comment on the components of such clearinghouse.

(2) CONFIDENTIALITY REQUIREMENT.—In carrying out paragraph (1)(D), the Secretary shall ensure that methods are established and implemented to preserve the confidentiality of records relating to case specific data.

RESEARCH, EVALUATION AND ASSISTANCE ACTIVITIES

SEC. 104. [42 U.S.C. 5105]

(a) RESEARCH.—

(1) TOPICS.—The Secretary shall, in consultation with other Federal agencies and recognized experts in the field, carry out a continuing interdisciplinary program of research that is designed to provide information needed to better protect children from abuse or neglect and to improve the well-being of abused or neglected children, with at least a portion of such research being field initiated. Such research program may focus on—

(A) the nature and scope of child abuse and neglect;

(B) causes, prevention, assessment, identification, treatment, cultural and socio-economic distinctions, and the consequences of child abuse and neglect;

(C) appropriate, effective and culturally sensitive investigative, administrative, and

---

[1]Section 105(a) is cited here in error and should be understood as section 104(a).

judicial procedures with respect to cases of child abuse; and

(D) the national incidence of child abuse and neglect, including—

(i) the extent to which incidents of child abuse are increasing or decreasing in number and severity;

(ii) the incidence of substantiated and unsubstantiated reported child abuse cases;

(iii) the number of substantiated cases that result in a judicial finding of child abuse or neglect or related criminal court convictions;

(iv) the extent to which the number of unsubstantiated, unfounded and false reported cases of child abuse or neglect have contributed to the inability of a State to respond effectively to serious cases of child abuse or neglect;

(v) the extent to which the lack of adequate resources and the lack of adequate training of individuals required by law to report suspected cases of child abuse have contributed to the inability of a State to respond effectively to serious cases of child abuse and neglect;

(vi) the number of unsubstantiated, false, or unfounded reports that have resulted in a child being placed in substitute care, and the duration of such placement;

(vii) the extent to which unsubstantiated reports return as more serious cases of child abuse or neglect;

(viii) the incidence and prevalence of physical, sexual, and emotional abuse and physical and emotional neglect in substitute care; and

(ix) the incidence and outcomes of abuse allegations reported within the context of divorce, custody, or other family court proceedings, and the interaction between this venue and the child protective services system.

(2) PRIORITIES.—

(A) The Secretary shall establish research priorities for making grants or contracts for purposes of carrying out paragraph (1).

(B) In establishing research priorities as required by subparagraph (A), the Secretary shall—

(i) publish proposed priorities in the Federal Register for public comment; and

(ii) allow not less than 60 days for public comment on such proposed priorities.

(b) PROVISION OF TECHNICAL ASSISTANCE.—

(1) IN GENERAL.—The Secretary shall provide technical assistance to State and local public and non-profit private agencies and organizations, including disability organizations and persons who work with children with disabilities, to assist such agencies and organizations in planning, improving, developing and carrying out programs and activities relating to the prevention, assessment, identification, and treatment of child abuse and neglect.

(2) EVALUATION.— Such technical assistance may include an evaluation or identification of—

(A) various methods and procedures for the investigation, assessment, and prosecution of child physical and sexual abuse cases;

(B) ways to mitigate psychological trauma to the child victim; and

(C) effective programs carried out by the States under titles I and II.

(3) DISSEMINATION.—The Secretary may provide for and disseminate information relating to various training resources available at the State and local level to—

(A) individuals who are engaged, or who intend to engage, in the prevention, identification, and treatment of child abuse and neglect; and

(B) appropriate State and local officials to assist in training law enforcement, legal, judicial, medical, mental health, education, and child welfare personnel in appropriate methods of interacting during investigative, administrative, and judicial proceedings with children who have been subjected to abuse.

(c) AUTHORITY TO MAKE OR ENTER INTO CONTRACTS.—

(1) IN GENERAL.—The functions of the Secretary under this section may be carried out either directly or through grant or contract.

(2) DURATION.—Grants under this section shall be made for periods of not more than 5 years.

(3) PREFERENCE FOR LONG-TERM STUD-IES.—In making grants for purposes of conducting research under subsection (a), the Secretary shall give special consideration to applications for long-term projects.

(d) PEER REVIEW FOR GRANTS.—

(1) ESTABLISHMENT OF PEER REVIEW PROCESS.—

(A) The Secretary shall, in consultation with experts in the field and other federal agencies, establish a formal, rigorous, and meritorious peer review process for purposes of evaluating and reviewing applications for grants under this section and determining the relative merits of the projects for which such assistance is requested. The purpose of this process is to enhance the quality and usefulness of research in the field of child abuse and neglect.

(B) In establishing the process required by subparagraph (A), the Secretary shall appoint to the peer review panels only members who are experts in the field of child abuse and neglect or related disciplines, with appropriate expertise in the application to be reviewed, and who are not individuals who are officers or employees of the Administration on Children and Families. The panels shall meet as often as is necessary to facilitate the expeditious review of applications for grants and contracts under this section, but may not meet less than once a year. The Secretary shall ensure that the peer review panel utilizes scientifically valid review criteria and scoring guidelines for review committees.

(2) REVIEW OF APPLICATIONS FOR ASSISTANCE.—Each peer review panel established under paragraph (1)(A) that reviews any application for a grant shall—

(A) determine and evaluate the merit of each project described in such application;

(B) rank such application with respect to all other applications it reviews in the same priority area for the fiscal year involved, according to the relative merit of all of the projects that are described in such application and for which financial assistance is requested; and

(C) make recommendations to the Secretary concerning whether the application for the project shall be approved.

The Secretary shall award grants under this section on the basis of competitive review.

(3) NOTICE OF APPROVAL.—

(A) The Secretary shall provide grants and contracts under this section from among the projects which the peer review panels established under paragraph (1)(A) have determined to have merit.

(B) In the instance in which the Secretary approves an application for a program without having approved all applications ranked above such application (as determined under paragraph (2)(B)), the Secretary shall append to the approved application a detailed explanation of the reasons relied on for approving the application and for failing to approve each pending application that is superior in merit, as indicated on the list under paragraph (2)(B).

GRANTS TO PUBLIC AGENCIES AND NONPROFIT PRIVATE ORGANIZATIONS FOR DEMONSTRATION PROGRAMS AND PROJECTS

SEC. 105. [42 U.S.C. 5106]

(a) DEMONSTRATION PROGRAMS AND PROJECTS.—The Secretary may make grants to, and enter into contracts with, public agencies or private nonprofit agencies or organizations (or combinations of such agencies or organizations) for time limited, demonstration programs and projects for the following purposes:

(1) TRAINING PROGRAMS.—The Secretary may award grants to public or private nonprofit organizations under this section—

(A) for the training of professional and paraprofessional personnel in the fields of medicine, law, education, social work, and other relevant fields who are engaged in, or intend to work in, the field of prevention, identification, and treatment of child abuse and neglect, including the links between domestic violence and child abuse;

(B) to improve the recruitment, selection, and training of volunteers serving in public and private nonprofit children, youth and family service organizations in order to prevent child abuse and neglect through collaborative analysis of current recruitment, selection, and training programs and development of model programs for dissemination and replication nationally; and

(C) for the establishment of resource centers for the purpose of providing information and training to professionals working in the field of child abuse and neglect.

(2) MUTUAL SUPPORT PROGRAMS.—The Secretary may award grants to private nonprofit organizations (such as Parents Anonymous) to establish or maintain a national network of mutual support and self-help programs as a means of strengthening families in partnership with their communities.

(3) OTHER INNOVATIVE PROGRAMS AND PROJECTS.—

(A) IN GENERAL.—The Secretary may award grants to public and private nonprofit agencies that demonstrate innovation in responding to reports of child abuse and neglect including programs of collaborative partnerships between the State child protective services agency, community social service agencies and family support programs, schools, churches and synagogues, and other community agencies to allow for the establishment of a triage system that—

(i) accepts, screens and assesses reports received to determine which such reports require an intensive intervention and which require voluntary referral to another agency, program or project;

(ii) provides, either directly or through referral, a variety of community-linked services to assist families in preventing child abuse and neglect; and

(iii) provides further investigation and intensive intervention where the child's safety is in jeopardy.

(B) KINSHIP CARE.—The Secretary may award grants to public and private nonprofit entities in not more than 10 States to assist such entities in developing or implementing procedures using adult relatives as the preferred placement for children removed from their home, where such relatives are determined to be capable of providing a safe nurturing environment for the child and where

such relatives comply with the State child protection standards.

(C) PROMOTION OF SAFE, FAMILY-FRIENDLY PHYSICAL ENVIRONMENTS FOR VISITATION AND EXCHANGE.—The Secretary may award grants to entities to assist such entities in establishing and operating safe, family-friendly physical environments—

(i) for court-ordered supervised visitation between children and abusing parents; and

(ii) to safely facilitate the exchange of children for visits with noncustodial parents in cases of domestic violence.

(b) DISCRETIONARY GRANTS.—In addition to grants or contracts made under subsection (b), grants or contracts under this section may be used for the following:

(1) Projects which provide educational identification, prevention, and treatment services in cooperation with preschool and elementary and secondary schools.

(2) Respite and crisis nursery programs provided by community-based organizations under the direction and supervision of hospitals.

(3) Respite and crisis nursery programs provided by community-based organizations.

(4)(A) Providing hospital-based information and referral services to—

(i) parents of children with disabilities; and

(ii) children who have been neglected or abused and their parents.

(B) Except as provided in subparagraph (C)(iii), services provided under a grant received under this paragraph shall be provided at the hospital involved—

(i) upon the birth or admission of a child with disabilities; and

(ii) upon the treatment of a child for abuse or neglect.

(C) Services, as determined as appropriate by the grantee, provided under a grant received under this paragraph shall be hospital-based and shall consist of—

(i) the provision of notice to parents that information relating to community services is available;

(ii) the provision of appropriate information to parents of a child with disabilities regarding resources in the community, particularly parent training resources, that will assist such parents in caring for their child;

(iii) the provision of appropriate information to parents of a child who has been neglected or abused regarding resources in the community, particularly parent training resources, that will assist such parents in caring for their child and reduce the possibility of abuse or neglect;

(iv) the provision of appropriate follow-up services to parents of a child described in subparagraph (B) after the child has left the hospital; and

(v) where necessary, assistance in coordination of community services available to parents of children described in subparagraph (B).

The grantee shall assure that parental involvement described in this subparagraph is voluntary.

(D) For purposes of this paragraph, a qualified grantee is a nonprofit acute care hospital that—

(i) is in a combination with—
  (I) a health-care provider organization;
  (II) a child welfare organization;
  (III) a disability organization; and
  (IV) a State child protection agency;

(ii) submits an application for a grant under this paragraph that is approved by the Secretary;

(iii) maintains an office in the hospital involved for purposes of providing services under such grant;

(iv) provides assurances to the Secretary that in the conduct of the project the confidentiality of medical, social and personal information concerning any person described in subparagraph (A) or (B) shall be maintained, and shall be disclosed only to qualified persons providing required services described in subparagraph (C) for purposes relating to conduct of the project; and

(v) assumes legal responsibility for carrying out the terms and conditions of the grant.

(E) In awarding grants under this paragraph, the Secretary shall—

(i) give priority under this section for two grants under this paragraph, provided that one grant shall be made to provide services in an urban setting and one grant shall be made to provide services in a rural setting; and

(ii) encourage qualified grantees to combine the amounts received under the grant with other funds available to such grantees.

(5) Such other innovative programs and projects that show promise of preventing and treating cases of child abuse and neglect as the Secretary may approve.

(c) EVALUATION.—In making grants for demonstration projects under this section, the Secretary shall require all such projects to be evaluated for their effectiveness. Funding for such evaluations shall be provided either as a stated percentage of a demonstration grant or as a separate grant entered into by the Secretary for the purpose of evaluating a particular demonstration project or group of projects.

GRANTS TO STATES FOR CHILD ABUSE AND NEGLECT PREVENTION AND TREATMENT PROGRAMS

SEC. 106. [42 U.S.C. 5106a]

(a) DEVELOPMENT AND OPERATION GRANTS.—The Secretary shall make grants to the States, based on the population of children under the age of 18 in each State that applies for a grant under this section, for purposes of assisting the States in improving the child protective services system of each such State in—

(1) the intake, assessment, screening, and investigation of reports of abuse and neglect;

(2) (A) creating and improving the use of multidisciplinary teams and interagency protocols to enhance investigations; and

(B) improving legal preparation and representation, including—

(i) procedures for appealing and responding to appeals of substantiated reports of abuse and neglect; and

(ii) provisions for the appointment of an individual appointed to represent a child in judicial proceedings;

(3) case management and delivery of services provided to children and their families;

(4) enhancing the general child protective system by improving risk and safety assessment tools and protocols, automation systems that support the program and track reports of child abuse and neglect from intake through final disposition and information referral systems;

(5) developing, strengthening, and facilitating training opportunities and requirements for individuals overseeing and providing services to children and their families through the child protection system;

(6) developing and facilitating training protocols for individuals mandated to report child abuse or neglect;

(7) developing, strengthening, and supporting child abuse and neglect prevention, treatment, and research programs in the public and private sectors;

(8) developing, implementing, or operating—

(A) information and education programs or training programs designed to improve the provision of services to disabled infants with life-threatening conditions for—

(i) professional and paraprofessional personnel concerned with the welfare of disabled infants with life-threatening conditions, including personnel employed in child protective services programs and health-care facilities; and

(ii) the parents of such infants; and

(B) programs to assist in obtaining or coordinating necessary services for families of disabled infants with life-threatening conditions, including—

(i) existing social and health services;

(ii) financial assistance; and

(iii) services necessary to facilitate adoptive placement of any such infants who have been relinquished for adoption; or

(9) developing and enhancing the capacity of community-based programs to integrate shared leadership strategies between parents and professionals to prevent and treat child abuse and neglect at the neighborhood level.

(b) ELIGIBILITY REQUIREMENTS.—

(1) STATE PLAN.—

(A) IN GENERAL.—To be eligible to receive a grant under this section, a State shall, at the time of the initial grant application and every 5 years thereafter, prepare and submit to the Secretary a State plan that specifies the areas of the child protective services system described in subsection (a) that the State intends to address with amounts received under the grant.

(B) ADDITIONAL REQUIREMENT.—After the submission of the initial grant application under subparagraph (A), the State shall provide notice to the Secretary of any substantive changes to any State law relating to the prevention of child abuse and neglect that may affect the eligibility of the State under this section.

(2) COORDINATION.—A State plan submitted under paragraph (1) shall, to the maximum extent practicable, be coordinated with the State plan under part B of title IV of the Social Security Act relating to child welfare services and family preservation and family support services, and shall contain an outline of the activities that the State intends to carry out using amounts received under the grant to achieve the purposes of this title, including—

(A) an assurance in the form of a certification by the chief executive officer of the State that the State has in effect and is enforcing a State law, or has in effect and is operating a Statewide program, relating to child abuse and neglect that includes—

(i) provisions or procedures for the reporting of known and suspected instances of child abuse and neglect;

(ii) procedures for the immediate screening, safety assessment, and prompt investigation of such reports;

(iii) procedures for immediate steps to be taken to ensure and protect the safety of the abused or neglected child and of any other child under the same care who may also be in danger of abuse or neglect and ensuring their placement in a safe environment;

(iv) provisions for immunity from prosecution under State and local laws and regulations for individuals making good faith reports of suspected or known instances of child abuse or neglect;

(v) methods to preserve the confidentiality of all records in order to protect the rights of the child and of the child's parents or guardians, including requirements ensuring that reports and records made and maintained pursuant to the purposes of this Act shall only be made available to—

(I) individuals who are the subject of the report;

(II) Federal, State, or local government entities, or any agent of such entities, having a need for such information in order to carry out its responsibilities under law to protect children from abuse and neglect;

(III) child abuse citizen review panels;

(IV) child fatality review panels;

(V) a grand jury or court, upon a finding that information in the record is necessary for the determination of an issue before the court or grand jury; and

(VI) other entities or classes of individuals statutorily authorized by the State to receive such information pursuant to a legitimate State purpose;

(vi) provisions which allow for public disclosure of the findings or information about the case of child abuse or neglect which has resulted in a child fatality or near fatality;

(vii) the cooperation of State law enforcement officials, court of competent jurisdiction, and appropriate State agencies providing human services in the investigation, assessment, prosecution, and treatment of child abuse or neglect;

(viii) provisions requiring, and procedures in place that facilitate the prompt expungement of any records that are accessible to the general public or are used for purposes of employment or other background checks in cases determined to be unsubstantiated or false, except that nothing in this section shall prevent State child protective services agencies from keeping information on unsubstantiated reports in their casework files to assist in future risk and safety assessment;

(ix) provisions and procedures requiring that in every case involving an abused or neglected child which results in a judicial proceeding, a guardian ad litem, who may be an attorney or a court appointed special advocate (or both), shall be appointed to represent the child in such proceedings—

(I) to obtain first-hand, a clear understanding of the situation and needs of the child; and

(II) to make recommendations to the court concerning the best interests of the child;

(x) the establishment of citizen review panels in accordance with subsection (c);

(xi) provisions, procedures, and mechanisms to be effective not later than 2 years after the date of the enactment of this section—

(I) for the expedited termination of parental rights in the case of any infant determined to be abandoned under State law; and

(II) by which individuals who disagree with an official finding of abuse or neglect can appeal such finding;

(xii) provisions, procedures, and mechanisms to be effective not later than 2 years after the date of the enactment of this section that assure that the State does not require reunification of a surviving child with a parent who has been found by a court of competent jurisdiction—

(I) to have committed murder (which would have been an offense under section 1111(a) of title 18, United States Code, if the offense had occurred in the special maritime or territorial jurisdiction of the United States) of another child of such parent;

(II) to have committed voluntary manslaughter (which would have been an offense under section 1112(a) of title 18, United States Code, if the offense had occurred in the special maritime or territorial jurisdiction of the United States) of another child of such parent;

(III) to have aided or abetted, attempted, conspired, or solicited to commit such murder or voluntary manslaughter; or

(IV) to have committed a felony assault that results in the serious bodily injury to the surviving child or another child of such parent; and

(xiii) an assurance that, upon the implementation by the State of the provisions, procedures, and mechanisms under clause (xii), conviction of any one of the felonies listed in clause (xii) constitute grounds under State law for the termination of parental rights of the convicted parent as to the surviving children (although case-by-case determinations of whether or not to seek termination of parental rights shall be within the sole discretion of the State);

(B) an assurance that the State has in place procedures for responding to the reporting of medical neglect (including instances of withholding of medically indicated treatment from disabled infants with life-threatening conditions), procedures or programs, or both (within the State child protective services system), to provide for—

(i) coordination and consultation with individuals designated by and within appropriate health-care facilities;

(ii) prompt notification by individuals designated by and within appropriate health-care facilities of cases of suspected medical neglect (including instances of withholding of medically indicated treatment from disabled infants with life-threatening conditions); and

(iii) authority, under State law, for the State child protective services system to pursue any legal remedies, including the authority to initiate legal proceedings in a court of competent jurisdiction, as may be necessary to prevent the withholding of medically indicated treatment from disabled infants with life threatening conditions;

(C) a description of—

(i) the services to be provided under the grant to individuals, families, or communities, either directly or through referrals aimed at preventing the occurrence of child abuse and neglect;

(ii) the training to be provided under the grant to support direct line and supervisory personnel in report taking, screening, assessment, decision making, and referral for investigating suspected instances of child abuse and neglect; and

(iii) the training to be provided under the grant for individuals who are required to report suspected cases of child abuse and neglect; and

(D) an assurance or certification that the programs or projects relating to child abuse and neglect carried out under part B of title IV of the Social Security Act comply with the requirements set forth in paragraph (1) and this paragraph.

(3) LIMITATION.—With regard to clauses (v) and (vi) of paragraph (2)(A), nothing in this section shall be construed as restricting the ability of a State to refuse to disclose identifying information concerning the individual initiating a report or complaint alleging suspected instances of child abuse or neglect, except that the State may not refuse such a disclosure where a court orders such disclosure after such court has reviewed, in camera, the record of the State related to the report or complaint and has found it has reason to believe that the reporter knowingly made a false report.

(4) DEFINITIONS.—For purposes of this subsection—

(A) the term "near fatality" means an act that, as certified by a physician, places the child in serious or critical condition; and

(B) the term "serious bodily injury" means bodily injury which involves substantial risk of death, extreme physical pain, protracted and obvious disfigurement, or protracted loss or impairment of the function of a bodily member, organ, or mental faculty.

(c) CITIZEN REVIEW PANELS.—

(1) ESTABLISHMENT.—

(A) IN GENERAL.—Except as provided in subparagraph (B), each State to which a grant is made under this section shall establish not less than 3 citizen review panels.

(B) EXCEPTIONS.—

(i) ESTABLISHMENT OF PANELS BY STATES RECEIVING MINIMUM ALLOTMENT.—A State that receives the minimum allotment of $175,000 under section

203(b)(1)(A) for a fiscal year shall establish not less than 1 citizen review panel.

(ii) DESIGNATION OF EXISTING ENTITIES.—A State may designate as panels for purposes of this subsection one or more existing entities established under State or Federal law, such as child fatality panels or foster care review panels, if such entities have the capacity to satisfy the requirements of paragraph (4) and the State ensures that such entities will satisfy such requirements.

(2) MEMBERSHIP.—Each panel established pursuant to paragraph (1) shall be composed of volunteer members who are broadly representative of the community in which such panel is established, including members who have expertise in the prevention and treatment of child abuse and neglect.

(3) MEETINGS.—Each panel established pursuant to paragraph (1) shall meet not less than once every 3 months.

(4) FUNCTIONS.—

(A) IN GENERAL.— Each panel established pursuant to paragraph (1) shall, by examining the policies and procedures of State and local agencies and where appropriate, specific cases, evaluate the extent to which the agencies are effectively discharging their child protection responsibilities in accordance with—

(i) the State plan under subsection (b);

(ii) the child protection standards set forth in subsection (b)[2]; and

(iii) any other criteria that the panel considers important to ensure the protection of children, including—

(I) a review of the extent to which the State child protective services system is coordinated with the foster care and adoption programs established under part E of title IV of the Social Security Act; and

(II) a review of child fatalities and near fatalities (as defined in subsection (b)(4)).

(B) CONFIDENTIALITY.—

(i) IN GENERAL.—The members and staff of a panel established under paragraph (1)—

(I) shall not disclose to any person or government official any identifying information about any specific child protection case with respect to which the panel is provided information; and

(II) shall not make public other information unless authorized by State statute.

(ii) CIVIL SANCTIONS.—Each State that establishes a panel pursuant to paragraph (1) shall establish civil sanctions for a violation of clause (i).

(5) STATE ASSISTANCE.—Each State that establishes a panel pursuant to paragraph (1)—

(A) shall provide the panel access to information on cases that the panel desires to review if such information is necessary for the panel to carry out its functions under paragraph (4); and

(B) shall provide the panel, upon its request, staff assistance for the performance of the duties of the panel.

(6) REPORTS.—Each panel established under paragraph (1) shall prepare and make available to the public, on an annual basis, a report containing a summary of the activities of the panel.

(d) ANNUAL STATE DATA REPORTS.—Each State to which a grant is made under this section shall annually work with the Secretary to provide, to the maximum extent practicable, a report that includes the following:

(1) The number of children who were reported to the State during the year as abused or neglected.

(2) Of the number of children described in paragraph (1), the number with respect to whom such reports were—

(A) substantiated;

(B) unsubstantiated; or

(C) determined to be false.

(3) Of the number of children described in paragraph (2)—

(A) the number that did not receive services during the year under the State program funded this section or an equivalent State program;

(B) the number that received services during the year under the State program funded under this section or an equivalent State program; and

---

[2]Subsection (b) is cited here in error since there are no child protection standards in subsection (b).

(C) the number that were removed from their families during the year by disposition of the case.

(4) The number of families that received preventive services from the State during the year.

(5) The number of deaths in the State during the year resulting from child abuse or neglect.

(6) Of the number of children described in paragraph (5), the number of such children who were in foster care.

(7) The number of child protective services workers responsible for the intake and screening of reports filed in the previous year.

(8) The agency response time with respect to each such report with respect to initial investigation of reports of child abuse or neglect.

(9) The response time with respect to the provision of services to families and children where an allegation of abuse or neglect has been made.

(10) The number of child protective services workers responsible for intake, assessment, and investigation of child abuse and neglect reports relative to the number of reports investigated in the previous year.

(11) The number of children reunited with their families or receiving family preservation services that, within five years, result in subsequent substantiated reports of child abuse and neglect, including the death of the child.

(12) The number of children for whom individuals were appointed by the court to represent the best interests of such children and the average number of out of court contacts between such individuals and children.

(e) ANNUAL REPORT BY THE SECRETARY.— Within 6 months after receiving the State reports under subsection (d), the Secretary shall prepare a report based on information provided by the States for the fiscal year under such subsection and shall make the report and such information available to the Congress and the national clearinghouse for information relating to child abuse.

GRANTS TO STATES FOR PROGRAMS RELATING TO THE INVESTIGATION AND PROSECUTION OF CHILD ABUSE AND NEGLECT CASES

SEC. 107. [42 U.S.C. 5106c]

(a) GRANTS TO STATES.—The Secretary, in consultation with the Attorney General, is authorized to make grants to the States for the purpose of assisting States in developing, establishing, and operating programs designed to improve—

(1) the handling of child abuse and neglect cases, particularly cases of child sexual abuse and exploitation, in a manner which limits additional trauma to the child victim;

(2) the handling of cases of suspected child abuse or neglect related fatalities; and

(3) the investigation and prosecution of cases of child abuse and neglect, particularly child sexual abuse and exploitation.

(b) ELIGIBILITY REQUIREMENTS.—In order for a State to qualify for assistance under this section, such State shall—

(1) fulfill the requirements of section 107(b)[3];

(2) establish a task force as provided in subsection (c);

(3) fulfill the requirements of subsection (d);

(4) submit annually an application to the Secretary at such time and containing such information and assurances as the Secretary considers necessary, including an assurance that the State will—

(A) make such reports to the Secretary as may reasonably be required; and

(B) maintain and provide access to records relating to activities under subsections (a) and (b); and

(5) submit annually to the Secretary a report on the manner in which assistance received under this program was expended throughout the State, with particular attention focused on the areas described in paragraphs (1) through (3) of subsection (a).

(c) STATE TASK FORCES.—

(1) GENERAL RULE.—Except as provided in paragraph (2), a State requesting assistance under this section shall establish or designate and maintain, a State multidisciplinary task force on children's justice (hereinafter referred to as State task force) composed of professionals with knowledge and experience relating to the criminal justice system and issues of child physical abuse, child neglect, child sexual abuse and

---

[3]Section 107(b) is cited here in error and should be understood as section 106(b).

exploitation, and child maltreatment related fatalities. The State task force shall include—

(A) individuals representing the law enforcement community;

(B) judges and attorneys involved in both civil and criminal court proceedings related to child abuse and neglect (including individuals involved with the defense as well as the prosecution of such cases);

(C) child advocates, including both attorneys for children and, where such programs are in operation, court appointed special advocates;

(D) health and mental health professionals;

(E) individuals representing child protective service agencies;

(F) individuals experienced in working with children with disabilities; and

(G) representatives of parents' groups.

(2) EXISTING TASK FORCE.—As determined by the Secretary, a State commission or task force established after January 1, 1983, with substantially comparable membership and functions, may be considered the State task force for the purposes of this subsection.

(d) STATE TASK FORCE STUDY.—Before a State receives assistance under this section, at three year intervals thereafter, the State task force shall comprehensively—

(1) review and evaluate State investigative, administrative and both civil and criminal judicial handling of cases of child abuse and neglect, particularly child sexual abuse and exploitation, as well as cases involving suspected child maltreatment related fatalities and cases involving a potential combination of jurisdictions, such as interstate, Federal-State, and State-Tribal; and

(2) make policy and training recommendations in each of the categories described in subsection (e).

The task force may make such other comments and recommendations as are considered relevant and useful.

(e) ADOPTION OF STATE TASK FORCE RECOMMENDATIONS.—

(1) GENERAL RULE.—Subject to the provisions of paragraph (2), before a State receives assistance under this section, a State shall adopt recommendations of the State task force in each of the following categories—

(A) investigative, administrative, and judicial handling of cases of child abuse and neglect, particularly child sexual abuse and exploitation, as well as cases involving suspected child maltreatment related fatalities and cases involving a potential combination of jurisdictions, such as interstate, Federal-State, and State-Tribal, in a manner which reduces the additional trauma to the child victim and the victim's family and which also ensures procedural fairness to the accused;

(B) experimental, model and demonstration programs for testing innovative approaches and techniques which may improve the prompt and successful resolution of civil and criminal court proceedings or enhance the effectiveness of judicial and administrative action in child abuse and neglect cases, particularly child sexual abuse and exploitation cases, including the enhancement of performance of court-appointed attorneys and guardians ad litem for children, and which also ensure procedural fairness to the accused; and

(C) reform of State laws, ordinances, regulations, protocols and procedures to provide comprehensive protection for children from abuse, particularly child sexual abuse and exploitation, while ensuring fairness to all affected persons.

(2) EXEMPTION.—As determined by the Secretary, a State shall be considered to be in fulfillment of the requirements of this subsection if—

(A) the State adopts an alternative to the recommendations of the State task force, which carries out the purpose of this section, in each of the categories under paragraph (1) for which the State task force's recommendations are not adopted; or

(B) the State is making substantial progress toward adopting recommendations of the State task force or a comparable alternative to such recommendations.

(f) FUNDS AVAILABLE.—For grants under this section, the Secretary shall use the amount authorized by section 1404A of the Victims of Crime Act of 1984.

MISCELLANEOUS REQUIREMENTS RELATING TO ASSISTANCE

SEC. 108. [42 U.S.C. 5106d]

(a) CONSTRUCTION OF FACILITIES.—

(1) RESTRICTION ON USE OF FUNDS.—Assistance provided under this Act may not be used for construction of facilities.

(2) LEASE, RENTAL OR REPAIR.—The Secretary may authorize the use of funds received under this Act—

(A) where adequate facilities are not otherwise available, for the lease or rental of facilities; or

(B) for the repair or minor remodeling or alteration of existing facilities.

(b) GEOGRAPHICAL DISTRIBUTION.—The Secretary shall establish criteria designed to achieve equitable distribution of assistance under this Act among the States, among geographic areas of the Nation, and among rural and urban areas of the Nation. To the extent possible, the Secretary shall ensure that the citizens of each State receive assistance from at least one project under this Act.

(c) LIMITATION.—No funds appropriated for any grant or contract pursuant to authorizations made in this Act may be used for any purpose other than that for which such funds were authorized to be appropriated.

COORDINATION OF CHILD ABUSE AND NEGLECT PROGRAMS

SEC. 109. [42 U.S.C. 5106e]

The Secretary shall prescribe regulations and make such arrangements as may be necessary or appropriate to ensure that there is effective coordination among programs related to child abuse and neglect under this Act and other such programs which are assisted by Federal funds.

REPORTS

SEC. 110. [42 U.S.C. 5106f]

(a) COORDINATION OF EFFORTS.—Not later than March 1 of the second year following the date of enactment of the Child Abuse Prevention, Adoption and Family Services Act of 1988 and every 2 years thereafter, the Secretary shall submit to the appropriate committees of Congress a report on efforts during the 2-year period preceding the date of the report to coordinate the objectives and activities of agencies and organizations which are responsible for programs and activities related to child abuse and neglect.

(b) EFFECTIVENESS OF STATE PROGRAMS AND TECHNICAL ASSISTANCE.—Not later than two years after the first fiscal year for which funds are obligated under section 1404A of the Victims of Crime Act of 1984, the Secretary shall submit to the appropriate committees of Congress a report evaluating the effectiveness of assisted programs in achieving the objectives of section 107.

DEFINITIONS

SEC. 111. [42 U.S.C. 5106g]

For purposes of this title—

(1) the term "child" means a person who has not attained the lesser of—

(A) the age of 18; or

(B) except in the case of sexual abuse, the age specified by the child protection law of the State in which the child resides;

(2) the term "child abuse and neglect" means, at a minimum, any recent act or failure to act on the part of a parent or caretaker, which results in death, serious physical of emotional harm, sexual abuse or exploitation, or an act or failure to act which presents an imminent risk of serious harm;

(3) the term "Secretary" means the Secretary of Health and Human Services;

(4) the term "sexual abuse" includes—

(A) the employment, use, persuasion, inducement, enticement, or coercion of any child to engage in, or assist any other person to engage in, any sexually explicit conduct or simulation of such conduct for the purpose of producing a visual depiction of such conduct; or

(B) the rape, and in cases of caretaker or inter-familial relationships, statutory rape, molestation, prostitution, or other form of sexual exploitation of children, or incest with children;

(5) the term "State" means each of the several States, the District of Columbia, the Common-

wealth of Puerto Rico, the Virgin Islands, Guam, American Samoa, the Commonwealth of the Northern Mariana Islands, and the Trust Territory of the Pacific Islands;

(6) the term "withholding of medically indicated treatment" means the failure to respond to the infant's life-threatening conditions by providing treatment (including appropriate nutrition, hydration, and medication) which, in the treating physician's or physicians' reasonable medical judgment, will be most likely to be effective in ameliorating or correcting all such conditions, except that the term does not include the failure to provide treatment (other than appropriate nutrition, hydration, or medication) to an infant when, in the treating physician's or physicians' reasonable medical judgment—

(A) the infant is chronically and irreversibly comatose;

(B) the provision of such treatment would—

(i) merely prolong dying;

(ii) not be effective in ameliorating or correcting all of the infant's life-threatening conditions; or

(iii) otherwise be futile in terms of the survival of the infant; or

(C) the provision of such treatment would be virtually futile in terms of the survival of the infant and the treatment itself under such circumstances would be inhumane.

AUTHORIZATION OF APPROPRIATIONS

SEC. 112. [42 U.S.C. 5106h]

(a) IN GENERAL.—

(1) GENERAL AUTHORIZATION.—There are authorized to be appropriated to carry out this title, $100,000,000 for fiscal year 1997, and such sums as may be necessary for each of the fiscal years 1998 through 2001.

(2) DISCRETIONARY ACTIVITIES.—

(A) IN GENERAL.—Of the amounts appropriated for a fiscal year under paragraph (1), the Secretary shall make available 30 percent of such amounts to fund discretionary activities under this title.

(B) DEMONSTRATION PROJECTS.—Of the amounts made available for a fiscal year under subparagraph (A), the Secretary make[4] available not more than 40 percent of such amounts to carry out section 106.

(b) AVAILABILITY OF FUNDS WITHOUT FISCAL YEAR LIMITATION.—The Secretary shall ensure that funds appropriated pursuant to authorizations in this title shall remain available until expended for the purposes for which they were appropriated.

RULE OF CONSTRUCTION

SEC. 113. [42 U.S.C. 5106i]

(a) IN GENERAL.—Nothing in this Act shall be construed—

(1) as establishing a Federal requirement that a parent or legal guardian provide a child any medical service or treatment against the religious beliefs of the parent or legal guardian; and

(2) to require that a State find, or to prohibit a State from finding, abuse or neglect in cases in which a parent or legal guardian relies solely or partially upon spiritual means rather than medical treatment, in accordance with the religious beliefs of the parent or legal guardian.

(b) STATE REQUIREMENT.—Notwithstanding subsection (a), a State shall, at a minimum, have in place authority under State law to permit the child protective services system of the State to pursue any legal remedies, including the authority to initiate legal proceedings in a court of competent jurisdiction, to provide medical care or treatment for a child when such care or treatment is necessary to prevent or remedy serious harm to the child, or to prevent the withholding of medically indicated treatment from children with life threatening conditions. Except with respect to the withholding of medically indicated treatments from disabled infants with life threatening conditions, case by case determinations concerning the exercise of the authority of this subsection shall be within the sole discretion of the State.

---

[4]So in original.

TITLE II—COMMUNITY-BASED FAMILY RESOURCE AND SUPPORT GRANTS

SEC. 201. PURPOSE AND AUTHORITY. [42 U.S.C. 5116]

(a) PURPOSE.—It is the purpose of this title—

(1) to support State efforts to develop, operate, expand and enhance a network of community-based, prevention-focused, family resource and support programs that coordinate resources among existing education, vocational rehabilitation, disability, respite care, health, mental health, job readiness, self-sufficiency, child and family development, community action, Head Start, child care, child abuse and neglect prevention, juvenile justice, domestic violence prevention and intervention, housing, and other human service organizations within the State; and

(2) to foster an understanding, appreciation, and knowledge of diverse populations in order to be effective in preventing and treating child abuse and neglect.

(b) AUTHORITY.—The Secretary shall make grants under this title on a formula basis to the entity designated by the State as the lead entity (hereafter referred to in this title as the "lead entity") under section 202(1) for the purpose of—

(1) developing, operating, expanding and enhancing Statewide networks of community-based, prevention-focused, family resource and support programs that—

(A) offer assistance to families;

(B) provide early, comprehensive support for parents;

(C) promote the development of parenting skills, especially in young parents and parents with very young children;

(D) increase family stability;

(E) improve family access to other formal and informal resources and opportunities for assistance available within communities;

(F) support the additional needs of families with children with disabilities through respite care and other services; and

(G) decrease the risk of homelessness;

(2) fostering the development of a continuum of preventive services for children and families through State and community-based collaborations and partnerships both public and private;

(3) financing the start-up, maintenance, expansion, or redesign of specific family resource and support program services (such as respite care services, child abuse and neglect prevention activities, disability services, mental health services, housing services, transportation, adult education, home visiting and other similar services) identified by the inventory and description of current services required under section 205(a)(3) as an unmet need, and integrated with the network of community-based family resource and support program to the extent practicable given funding levels and community priorities;

(4) maximizing funding for the financing, planning, community mobilization, collaboration, assessment, information and referral, startup, training and technical assistance, information management, reporting and evaluation costs for establishing, operating, or expanding a Statewide network of community-based, prevention-focused, family resource and support program; and

(5) financing public information activities that focus on the healthy and positive development of parents and children and the promotion of child abuse and neglect prevention activities.

SEC. 202. ELIGIBILITY. [42 U.S.C. 5116a]

A State shall be eligible for a grant under this title for a fiscal year if—

(1)(A) the chief executive officer of the State has designated a lead entity to administer funds under this title for the purposes identified under the authority of this title, including to develop, implement, operate, enhance or expand a Statewide network of community-based, prevention-focused, family resource and support programs, child abuse and neglect prevention activities and access to respite care services integrated with the Statewide network;

(B) such lead entity is an existing public, quasi-public, or nonprofit private entity (which may be an entity that has not been established pursuant to State legislation, executive order, or any other written authority of the State) with a demonstrated ability to work with other State and community-based agencies to provide training and technical assistance, and that has the capacity and commitment to ensure the meaningful involvement of parents who are consumers and who can provide leadership in the planning, implementation, and evaluation of programs and policy decisions of the applicant agency in accomplishing the desired outcomes for such efforts;

(C) in determining which entity to designate under subparagraph (A), the chief executive officer should give priority consideration equally to a trust fund advisory board of the State or to an existing entity that leverages Federal, State, and private funds for a broad range of child abuse and neglect prevention activities and family resource programs, and that is directed by an interdisciplinary, public-private structure, including participants from communities; and

(D) in the case of a State that has designated a State trust fund advisory board for purposes of administering funds under this title (as such title was in effect on the date of the enactment of the Child Abuse Prevention and Treatment Act Amendments of 1996) and in which one or more entities that leverage Federal, State, and private funds (as described in subparagraph (C)) exist, the chief executive officer shall designate the lead entity only after full consideration of the capacity and expertise of all entities desiring to be designated under subparagraph (A);

(2) the chief executive officer of the State provides assurances that the lead entity will provide or will be responsible for providing—

(A) a network of community-based family resource and support programs composed of local, collaborative, public-private partnerships directed by interdisciplinary structures with balanced representation from private and public sector members, parents, and public and private nonprofit service providers and individuals and organizations experienced in working in partnership with families with children with disabilities;

(B) direction to the network through an interdisciplinary, collaborative, public-private structure with balanced representation from private and public sector members, parents, and public sector and private nonprofit sector service providers; and

(C) direction and oversight to the network through identified goals and objectives, clear lines of communication and accountability, the provision of leveraged or combined funding from Federal, State and private sources, centralized assessment and planning activities, the provision of training and technical assistance, and reporting and evaluation functions; and

(3) the chief executive officer of the State provides assurances that the lead entity—

(A) has a demonstrated commitment to parental participation in the development, operation, and oversight of the Statewide network of community-based, prevention-focused, family resource and support programs;

(B) has a demonstrated ability to work with State and community-based public and private nonprofit organizations to develop a continuum of preventive, family centered, comprehensive services for children and families through the Statewide network of community-based, prevention-focused, family resource and support programs;

(C) has the capacity to provide operational support (both financial and programmatic) and training and technical assistance, to the Statewide network of community-based, prevention-focused, family resource and support programs, through innovative, interagency funding and interdisciplinary service delivery mechanisms; and

(D) will integrate its efforts with individuals and organizations experienced in working in partnership with families with children with disabilities and with the child abuse and neglect prevention activities of the State, and demonstrate a financial commitment to those activities.

SEC. 203. AMOUNT OF GRANT. [42 U.S.C. 5116b]

(a) RESERVATION.—The Secretary shall reserve 1 percent of the amount appropriated under section 210 for a fiscal year to make allotments to Indian tribes and tribal organizations and migrant programs.

(b) REMAINING AMOUNTS.—

(1) IN GENERAL.—The Secretary shall allot the amount appropriated under section 210 for a fiscal year and remaining after the reservation under subsection (a) among the States as follows:

(A) 70 percent of such amount appropriated shall be allotted among the States by allotting to each State an amount that bears the same proportion to such amount appropriated as the number of children under the age of 18 residing in the State bears to the total number of children under the age of 18 residing in all States (except that no State shall receive less than $175,000 under this subparagraph).

(B) 30 percent of such amount appropriated shall be allotted among the States by allotting to each State an amount that bears the same proportion to such amount appropriated as the amount leveraged by the State from private, State, or other non-Federal sources and directed through the State lead agency in the preceding fiscal year bears to the aggregate of the amounts leveraged by all States from private, State, or other non-Federal sources and directed through the lead agency of such States in the preceding fiscal year.

(2) ADDITIONAL REQUIREMENT.—The Secretary shall provide allotments under paragraph (1) to the State lead entity.

(c) ALLOCATION.—Funds allotted to a State under this section—

(1) shall be for a 3-year period; and

(2) shall be provided by the Secretary to the State on an annual basis, as described in subsection (a).

SEC. 204. EXISTING GRANTS. [42 U.S.C. 5116c]

IN GENERAL.—Notwithstanding the enactment of the Child Abuse Prevention and Treatment Act Amendments of 1996, a State or entity that has a grant, contract, or cooperative agreement in effect, on the date of the enactment of such Act under any program described in subsection (b), shall continue to receive funds under such program, subject to the original terms under which such funds were provided under the grant, through the end of the applicable grant cycle.

(b) PROGRAMS DESCRIBED.—The programs described in this subsection are the following:

(1) The Community-Based Family Resource programs under section 201 of this Act, as such section was in effect on the day before the date of the enactment of the Child Abuse Prevention and Treatment Act Amendments of 1996.

(2) The Family Support Center programs under subtitle F of title VII of the Stewart B. McKinney Homeless Assistance Act (42 U.S.C. 11481 et seq.), as such title was in effect on the day before the date of the enactment of the Child Abuse Prevention and Treatment Act Amendments of 1996.

(3) The Emergency Child Abuse Prevention Services grant program under section 107A of this Act, as such section was in effect on the day before the date of the enactment of the Human Services Amendments of 1994.

(4) Programs under the Temporary Child Care for Children With Disabilities and Crisis Nurseries Act of 1986.

SEC. 205. APPLICATION. [42 U.S.C. 5116d]

A grant may not be made to a State under this title unless an application therefor is submitted by the State to the Secretary and such application contains the types of information specified by the Secretary as essential to carrying out the provisions of section 202, including—

(1) a description of the lead entity that will be responsible for the administration of funds provided under this title and the oversight of programs funded through the Statewide network of community-based, prevention-focused, family resource and support programs which meets the requirements of section 202;

(2) a description of how the network of community-based, prevention-focused, family resource and support programs will operate and how family resource and support services provided by public and private, nonprofit organizations, including those funded by programs consolidated under this Act, will be integrated into a developing continuum of family centered, holistic, preventive services for children and families;

(3) an assurance that an inventory of current family resource programs, respite care, child

abuse and neglect prevention activities, and other family resource services operating in the State, and a description of current unmet needs, will be provided;

(4) a budget for the development, operation and expansion of the State's network of community-based, prevention-focused, family resource and support programs that verifies that the State will expend in non-Federal funds an amount equal to not less than 20 percent of the amount received under this title (in cash, not in-kind) for activities under this title;

(5) an assurance that funds received under this title will supplement, not supplant, other State and local public funds designated for the Statewide network of community-based, prevention-focused, family resource and support programs;

(6) an assurance that the State has the capacity to ensure the meaningful involvement of parents who are consumers and who can provide leadership in the planning, implementation, and evaluation of the programs and policy decisions of the applicant agency in accomplishing the desired outcomes for such efforts;

(7) a description of the criteria that the entity will use to develop, or select and fund, individual community-based, prevention-focused, family resource and support programs as part of network development, expansion or enhancement;

(8) a description of outreach activities that the entity and the community-based, prevention-focused, family resource and support programs will undertake to maximize the participation of racial and ethnic minorities, children and adults with disabilities, homeless families and those at risk of homelessness, and members of other underserved or underrepresented groups;

(9) a plan for providing operational support, training and technical assistance to community-based, prevention-focused, family resource and support programs for development, operation, expansion and enhancement activities;

(10) a description of how the applicant entity's activities and those of the network and its members will be evaluated;

(11) a description of the actions that the applicant entity will take to advocate systematic changes in State policies, practices, procedures and regulations to improve the delivery of prevention-focused, family resource and support program services to children and families; and

(13)[5] an assurance that the applicant entity will provide the Secretary with reports at such time and containing such information as the Secretary may require.

SEC. 206. LOCAL PROGRAM REQUIREMENTS.
[42 U.S.C. 5116e]

(a) IN GENERAL.—Grants made under this title shall be used to develop, implement, operate, expand and enhance community-based, prevention-focused, family resource and support programs that—

(1) assess community assets and needs through a planning process that involves parents and local public agencies, local nonprofit organizations, and private sector representatives;

(2) develop a strategy to provide, over time, a continuum of preventive, family centered services to children and families, especially to young parents and parents with young children, through public-private partnerships;

(3) provide—

(A) core family resource and support services such as—

(i) parent education, mutual support and self help, and leadership services;

(ii) outreach services;

(iii) community and social service referrals; and

(iv) follow-up services;

(B) other core services, which must be provided or arranged for through contracts or agreements with other local agencies, including all forms of respite care services to the extent practicable; and

(C) access to optional services, including—

(i) referral to and counseling for adoption services for individuals interested in adopt-

---

[5]This paragraph is numbered in error and should be understood as paragraph (12).

ing a child or relinquishing their child for adoption;

(ii) child care, early childhood development and intervention services;

(iii) referral to services and supports to meet the additional needs of families with children with disabilities;

(iv) referral to job readiness services;

(v) referral to educational services, such as scholastic tutoring, literacy training, and General Educational Degree services;

(vi) self-sufficiency and life management skills training;

(vii) community referral services, including early developmental screening of children; and

(viii) peer counseling;

(4) develop leadership roles for the meaningful involvement of parents in the development, operation, evaluation, and oversight of the programs and services;

(5) provide leadership in mobilizing local public and private resources to support the provision of needed family resource and support program services; and

(6) participate with other community-based, prevention-focused, family resource and support program grantees in the development, operation and expansion of the Statewide network.

(b) PRIORITY.—In awarding local grants under this title, a lead entity shall give priority to effective community-based programs serving low income communities and those serving young parents or parents with young children, including community-based family resource and support programs.

SEC. 207. PERFORMANCE MEASURES.
[42 U.S.C. 5116f]

A State receiving a grant under this title, through reports provided to the Secretary—

(1) shall demonstrate the effective development, operation and expansion of a Statewide network of community-based, prevention-focused, family resource and support programs that meets the requirements of this title;

(2) shall supply an inventory and description of the services provided to families by local programs that meet identified community needs, including core and optional services as described in section 202;

(3) shall demonstrate the establishment of new respite care and other specific new family resources services, and the expansion of existing services, to address unmet needs identified by the inventory and description of current services required under section 205(3);

(4) shall describe the number of families served, including families with children with disabilities, and the involvement of a diverse representation of families in the design, operation, and evaluation of the Statewide network of community-based, prevention-focused, family resource and support programs, and in the design, operation and evaluation of the individual community-based family resource and support programs that are part of the Statewide network funded under this title;

(5) shall demonstrate a high level of satisfaction among families who have used the services of the community-based, prevention-focused, family resource and support programs;

(6) shall demonstrate the establishment or maintenance of innovative funding mechanisms, at the State or community level, that blend Federal, State, local and private funds, and innovative, interdisciplinary service delivery mechanisms, for the development, operation, expansion and enhancement of the Statewide network of community-based, prevention-focused, family resource and support programs;

(7) shall describe the results of a peer review process conducted under the State program; and

(8) shall demonstrate an implementation plan to ensure the continued leadership of parents in the on-going planning, implementation, and evaluation of such community based, prevention-focused, family resource and support programs.

SEC. 208. NATIONAL NETWORK FOR COMMUNITY-BASED FAMILY RESOURCE PROGRAMS. [42 U.S.C. 5116g]

The Secretary may allocate such sums as may be necessary from the amount provided under the State allotment to support the activities of the lead entity in the State—

(1) to create, operate and maintain a peer review process;

(2) to create, operate and maintain an information clearinghouse;

(3) to fund a yearly symposium on State system change efforts that result from the operation of the Statewide networks of community-based, prevention-focused, family resource and support programs;

(4) to create, operate and maintain a computerized communication system between lead entities; and

(5) to fund State-to-State technical assistance through bi-annual conferences.

SEC. 209. DEFINITIONS. [42 U.S.C. 5116h]

For purposes of this title:

(1) CHILDREN WITH DISABILITIES.—The term "children with disabilities" has the same meaning given such term in section 602(a)(2) of the Individuals with Disabilities Education Act.

(2) COMMUNITY REFERRAL SERVICES.—The term "community referral services" means services provided under contract or through interagency agreements to assist families in obtaining needed information, mutual support and community resources, including respite care services, health and mental health services, employability development and job training, and other social services, including early developmental screening of children, through help lines or other methods.

(3) FAMILY RESOURCE AND SUPPORT PROGRAM.—The term "family resource and support program" means a community-based, prevention-focused entity that—

(A) provides, through direct service, the core services required under this title, including—

(i) parent education, support and leadership services, together with services characterized by relationships between parents and professionals that are based on equality and respect, and designed to assist parents in acquiring parenting skills, learning about child development, and responding appropriately to the behavior of their children;

(ii) services to facilitate the ability of parents to serve as resources to one another

(such as through mutual support and parent self-help groups);

(iii) outreach services provided through voluntary home visits and other methods to assist parents in becoming aware of and able to participate in family resources and support program activities;

(iv) community and social services to assist families in obtaining community resources; and

(v) follow-up services;

(B) provides, or arranges for the provision of, other core services through contracts or agreements with other local agencies, including all forms of respite care services; and

(C) provides access to optional services, directly or by contract, purchase of service, or interagency agreement, including—

(i) child care, early childhood development and early intervention services;

(ii) referral to self-sufficiency and life management skills training;

(iii) referral to education services, such as scholastic tutoring, literacy training, and General Educational Degree services;

(iv) referral to services providing job readiness skills;

(v) child abuse and neglect prevention activities;

(vi) referral to services that families with children with disabilities or special needs may require;

(vii) community and social service referral, including early developmental screening of children;

(viii) peer counseling;

(ix) referral for substance abuse counseling and treatment; and

(x) help line services.

(4) OUTREACH SERVICES.—The term "outreach services" means services provided to assist consumers, through voluntary home visits or other methods, in accessing and participating in family resource and support program activities.

(5) RESPITE CARE SERVICES.—The term "respite care services" means short term care services provided in the temporary absence of the regular caregiver (parent, other relative, foster

parent, adoptive parent, or guardian) to children who—

    (A) are in danger of abuse or neglect;

    (B) have experienced abuse or neglect; or

    (C) have disabilities, chronic, or terminal illnesses.

Such services shall be provided within or outside the home of the child, be short-term care (ranging from a few hours to a few weeks of time, per year), and be intended to enable the family to stay together and to keep the child living in the home and community of the child.

SEC. 210. AUTHORIZATION OF APPROPRIATIONS. [42 U.S.C. 5116i]

There are authorized to be appropriated to carry out this title, $66,000,000 for fiscal year 1997 and such sums as may be necessary for each of the fiscal years 1998 through 2001.

APPENDIX VII

PROVINCIAL DEFINITIONS OF CHILD IN NEED OF PROTECTION—CANADA

DEFINITIONS OF CHILD IN NEED OF PROTECTION

British Columbia

Subsection 1(2) of the act states that **"a child is in need of protective services** if there are reasonable and probable grounds to believe that the survival, security or development of a child is endangered because

(a) the child has been abandoned or lost;

(b) the child's guardian is dead and the child has no other guardian;

(c) the child's guardian is unable or unwilling to provide the child with necessities of life;

(d) the child has been or there is risk that the child will be physically injured or sexually abused by the guardian;

(e) the guardian is unable or unwilling to protect the child from physical injury or sexual abuse;

(f) the child has been emotionally injured by the guardian;

(g) the child's guardian is unable or unwilling to protect the child from emotional injury;

(h) the child's guardian has subjected the child to or is unable or unwilling to protect the child from cruel and unusual treatment or punishment;

(i) the condition or behaviour of the child prevents the guardian from providing the child with adequate care appropriate to meet the child's needs."

Alberta

Under Section II of *The Child and Family Services Act,* a child is in need of protection when:

"(a) as a result of action or omission by the child's parent:

i) the child has suffered or is likely to suffer physical harm;

ii) the child has suffered or is likely to suffer a serious impairment of mental or emotional functioning;

iii) the child has been or is likely to be exposed to harmful interaction for a sexual purpose, including conduct that may amount to an offence within the meaning of the *Criminal Code;*

iv) medical, surgical or other recognized remedial care or treatment that is considered essential by a duly qualified medical practitioner has not been or is not likely to be provided to the child;

v) the child's development is likely to be seriously impaired by failure to remedy a mental, emotional or developmental condition; or

vi) the child has been exposed to domestic violence or severe domestic disharmony that is likely to result in physical or emotional harm to the child;

(b) there is no adult person who is able and willing to provide for the child's needs, and physical or emotional harm to the child has occurred or is likely to occur; or

(c) the child is less than 12 years of age and:

there are reasonable and probable grounds to believe that: a) the child has committed an act that, if the child were 12 years of age or more, would constitute an offence under the *Criminal Code, the Narcotic Control Act* (Canada) or Part III or Part IV of the *Food and Drug Act (Canada);* and b) family services are necessary to prevent a recurrence; and

ii) the child's parent is unable or unwilling to provide for the child's needs."

Saskatchewan

s.15 Definition of child in need of protection. A child is in need of protection when:

a) he is without proper or competent supervision;

b) he is living in circumstances that are unfit or improper for him.

Manitoba

Under Section 17, a child is in need of protection "where the life, health or emotional well-being of the child is endangered by the act or omission of a person". This may occur "where the child

(a) is without adequate care, supervision or control;

(b) is in the care, custody, control or charge of a person

(i) who is unable or unwilling to provide adequate care, supervision or control of the child, or

(ii) whose conduct endangers or might endanger the life, health or emotional well-being of the child, or

(iii) who neglects or refuses to provide or obtain proper medical or other remedial care or treatment necessary for the health or well-being of the child or who refuses to permit such care or treatment to be provided to the child when the care or treatment is recommended by a duly qualified medical practitioner;

(c) is abused or is in danger of being abused;

(d) is beyond the control of a person who has the care, custody, control or charge of the child;

(e) is likely to suffer harm or injury due to the behavior, condition, domestic environment or associations of the child or of a person having care, custody, control or charge of the child;

(f) is subjected to aggression or sexual harassment that endangers the life, health or emotional well-being of the child;

(g) being under the age of 12 years, is left unattended and without reasonable provision being made for the supervision and safety of the child; or

(h) is the subject, or is about to become the subject, of an unlawful adoption under section 63 or of an unlawful sale under section 84 of the Act."

Ontario

Under subsection 37(2), a child is in need of protection when:

"(a) the child has suffered physical harm, inflicted by the person having charge of the child or caused by that person's failure to care and provide for or supervise and protect the child adequately;

(b) there is substantial risk that the child will suffer physical harm inflicted or caused as described in clause (a);

(c) the child has been sexually molested or sexually exploited, by the person having charge of the child or by another person where the person having charge of the child knows or should know of the possibility of sexual molestation or sexual exploitation and fails to protect the child;

(d) there is a substantial risk that the child will be sexually molested or sexually exploited as described in clause (c);

(e) the child requires medical treatment to cure, prevent or alleviate physical harm or suffering and the child's parent or the person having charge of the child does not provide, or refuses or is unavailable or unable to consent to, the treatment;

(f) the child has suffered emotional harm, demonstrated by severe,

(i) anxiety,

(ii) depression,

(iii) withdrawal, or

(iv) self-destructive or aggressive behaviour,

and the child's parent or the person having charge of the child does not provide, or refuses or is unavailable or unable to consent to, services or treatment to remedy or alleviate the harm;

(g) there is substantial risk that the child will suffer emotional harm of the kind described in clause (f), and the child's parent or the person having charge of the child does not provide, or refuses or is unavailable or unable to consent to, services or treatment to prevent the harm;

(h) the child suffers from a mental, emotional or developmental condition that, if not remedied, could seriously impair the child's development and the child's parent or the person having charge of the child does not provide, or refuses or is unavailable or unable to consent to, treatment to remedy or alleviate the condition;

(i) the child has been abandoned, the child's parent has died or is unavailable to exercise his or her custodial rights over the child and has not made adequate provision for the child's care and custody, or the child is in a residential placement and the parent refuses or is unable or unwilling to resume the child's care and custody;

(j) the child is less than twelve years old and has killed or seriously injured another person or caused serious damage to another person's property, services or treatment are necessary to prevent a recurrence and the child's parent or the person having charge of the child does not provide, or refuses or is unavailable or unable to consent to, those services or treatment;

(k) the child is less than twelve years old and has on more than one occasion injured another person or caused loss or damage to another person's property, with the encouragement of the person having charge of the child or because of that person's failure or inability to supervise the child adequately; or

(l) the child's parent is unable to care for the child and the child is brought before the court with the parent's consent and, where the child is twelve years of age or older, with the child's consent, to be dealt with under this Part.

Quebec

Section 38 states that "for the purposes of this Act, the security or development of a child is considered to be in danger when:

a) his parents are dead, no longer take care of him or seek to be rid of him;

b) his mental or affective development is threatened by the lack of appropriate care or by the isolation in which he is maintained or by serious and continuous emotional rejection by his parents;

c) his physical health is threatened by the lack of appropriate care;

d) he is deprived of the material conditions of life appropriate to his needs and to the resources of his parents or of the persons having custody of him;

e) he is in the custody of a person whose behaviour or way of life creates a risk of moral or physical danger for the child;

f) he is forced or induced to beg, to do work disproportionate to his capacity or to perform for the public in a manner that is unacceptable for his age;

g) he is the victim of sexual abuse or he is subject to physical ill-treatment through violence or neglect;

h) he has serious behavioural disturbances and his parents fail to take the measures necessary to remedy the situation or the remedial measures taken by them fail."

Section 38.1 states that **"the security or development of a child may be considered to be in danger where:**

a) he leaves his own home, a foster family, a reception centre or a hospital centre without authorization while his situation is not under the responsibility of the director of youth protection;

b) he is of school age and does not attend school, or is frequently absent without reason;

c) his parents do not carry out their obligations to provide him with care, maintenance and education or do not exercise stable supervision over him, while he has been entrusted to the care of an establishment or foster family for two years.

New Brunswick

Under Section 31, a child's security or development may be considered to be in danger (i.e., a child is in need of protection) when:

"(a) the child is without adequate care, supervision or control;

(b) the child is living in unfit or improper circumstances;

(c) the child is in the care of a person who is unable or unwilling to provide adequate care, supervision or control of the child;

(d) the child is in the care of a person whose conduct endangers the life, health or emotional well-being of the child;

(e) the child is physically or sexually abused, physically or emotionally neglected, sexually exploited or in danger of such treatment;

(f) the child is living in a situation where there is severe domestic violence;

(g) the child is in the care of a person who neglects or refuses to provide or obtain proper medical, surgical or other remedial care or treatment necessary for the health or well-being of the child or refuses to permit such care or treatment to be supplied to the child;

(h) the child is beyond the control of the person caring for him;

(i) the child by his behaviour, condition, environment or association, is likely to injure himself or others;

(j) the child is in the care of a person who does not have a right to custody of the child, without the consent of a person having such right;

(k) the child is in the care of a person who neglects or refuses to ensure that the child attends school; or

(l) the child has committed an offence or, if the child is under the age of twelve years, has committed an act or omission that would constitute an offence for which the child could be convicted if the child were twelve years of age or older.

Nova Scotia

Under subsection 22(2), a child is defined to be in need of protective services where:

"(a) the child has suffered physical harm, inflicted by a parent or guardian of the child or caused by the failure of a parent or guardian to supervise and protect the child adequately;

(b) there is a substantial risk that the child will suffer physical harm inflicted or caused as described in clause (a);

(c) the child has been sexually abused by a parent or guardian of the child, or by another person where a parent or guardian of the child knows or should know of the possibility of sexual abuse and fails to protect the child;

(d) there is substantial risk that the child will be sexually abused as described in clause (c);

(e) a child requires medical treatment to cure, prevent or alleviate physical harm or suffering, and the child's parent or guardian does not provide, or refuses or is unavailable or is unable to consent to, the treatment;

(f) the child has suffered emotional harm, demonstrated by severe anxiety, depression, withdrawal, or self-destructive or aggressive behaviour and the child's parent or guardian does not provide, or refuses or is unavailable or unable to consent to, services or treatment to remedy or alleviate the harm;

(g) there is a substantial risk that the child will suffer emotional harm of the kind described in clause (f), and the parent or guardian does not provide, or refuses or is unavailable or unable to consent to, services or treatment to remedy

or alleviate the harm;

(h) the child suffers from a mental, emotional or developmental condition that, if not remedied, could seriously impair the child's development and the child's parent or guardian does not provide, or refuses or is unavailable or unable to consent to, services or treatment to remedy or alleviate the condition;

(i) the child has suffered physical or emotional harm caused by being exposed to repeated domestic violence by or towards a parent or guardian of the child, and the child's parent or guardian fails or refuses to obtain services or treatment to remedy or alleviate the violence;

(j) the child has suffered physical harm caused by chronic and serious neglect by a parent or guardian of the child, and the parent or guardian does not provide, or refuses or is unavailable or unable to consent to, services or treatment to remedy or alleviate the harm;

(k) the child has been abandoned, the child's only parent or guardian has died or is unavailable to exercise custodial rights over the child and has not made adequate provisions for the child's care and custody, or the child is in the care of an agency or another person and the parent or guardian of the child refuses or is unable or unwilling to resume the child's care and custody;

(l) the child is under twelve years of age and has killed or seriously injured another person or caused serious damage to another person's property, and services or treatment are necessary to prevent a recurrence and a parent or guardian of the child does not provide, or refuses or is unavailable or unable to consent to, the necessary services or treatment;

(m) the child is under twelve years of age and has on more than one occasion injured another person or caused loss or damage to another person's property, with the encouragement of a parent or guardian of the child or because of the parent or guardian's failure or inability to supervise the child adequately."

Prince Edward Island

The definition of a **child in need of protection** is found under paragraph 1(2)(e) of the Family and Child Services Act and refers to a child:

"(a) who is not receiving proper care, education, supervision, guidance or control;

(b) whose parent is unable or unwilling to care for the child, or whose behaviour or way of life creates a danger for the child;

(c) who has been physically abused, neglected or sexually exploited or is in danger of consistently threatening behaviour;

(d) who is forced or induced to do work disproportionate to his strength or to perform for the public in a manner that is unacceptable for his age;

(e) whose behaviour, condition, environment or associations is injurious or threatens to be injurious to himself or others;

(f) for whom the parent or person in whose custody he is neglects or refuses to provide or obtain proper medical or surgical care or treatment necessary for his health and well-being where it is recommended by a duly qualified medical practitioner;

(g) whose emotional or mental health and development is endangered or is likely to be endangered by the lack of affection, guidance and discipline or continuity of care in the child's life;

(h) for whom the parent or person in whose custody he is neglects, refuses or is unable to provide the services and assistance needed by the child because of the child's physical, mental or emotional handicap or disability;

(i) who is living in a situation where there is severe domestic violence;

(j) who is beyond the control of the person caring for him;

(k) who is living apart from his parents without their consent; or

(l) who is pregnant and refuses or is unable to provide properly and adequately for the health and welfare needs of herself and her child both before and after the birth of her child.

Newfoundland

Subsection 2(b) of the Child Welfare Act defines a child in need of protection to mean:

"(i) a child who is without adequate care or supervision;

(ii) a child who is without necessary food, clothing or shelter, as may be available with the level of financial assistance given in relation to that child under the laws of the province;

(iii) a child who is living in circumstances that are unfit or improper for the child;

(iv) a child in the care or custody of a person who is unfit, unable or unwilling to provide adequate care for the child;

(v) a child who is living in a situation where there is severe domestic violence;

(vi) a child who is physically or sexually abused, physically or emotionally neglected, sexually exploited or in danger of that treatment;

(vii) a child who is in the care and custody of a person who fails to provide adequately for the child's education or attendance at school;

(viii) a child who has no living parents and who has no person willing to assume responsibility or with a legal responsibility for the child's maintenance;

(ix) a child who is in the care or custody of a person who refuses or fails

(a) to provide or obtain proper medical or other recognized remedial care or treatment necessary for the health or well-being of the child, or

(b) to permit such care and treatment to be supplied to the child when it is considered essential by a qualified medical practitioner;

(x) a child who is brought before the court with the consent of the parent, guardian or person with actual control for the purpose of transferring the guardianship of the child to the director;

(xi) a child who is beyond the control of the person caring for the child;

(xii) a child who by his or her behaviour, condition, environment or association, is likely to injure himself or herself or others;

(xiii) a child taken into a home or otherwise in the care and custody of a person contrary to subsection 3(3) or (5) of the *Adoption of Children Act* (i.e., without the written approval of the Director of Child Welfare); and

(xiv) a child actually or apparently under the age of 12 who performs an action that contravenes a provision of an Act or a regulation made under that Act or a municipal regulation or by-law or an Act of the Parliament of Canada."

Yukon Territory
Under subsection 116(1), a child is in need of protection when

(a) he is abandoned,

(b) he is in the care of a parent or other person who is unable to provide proper or competent care, supervision or control over him,

(c) he is in the care of a parent or other person who is unwilling to provide proper or competent care, supervision or control over him,

(d) he is in probable danger of physical or psychological harm,

(e) the parent or other person in whose care he is neglects or refuses to provide or obtain proper medical care or treatment necessary for his health or well-being or normal development,

(f) he is staying away from his home in circumstances that endanger his safety or well-being,

(g) the parent or other person in whose care he is fails to provide the child with reasonable protection from physical or psychological harm,

(h) the parent or person in whose care he is involves the child in sexual activity,

(i) subject to subsection 2, *(reference to use of reasonable or aggressive force)* the parent or person in whose care he is beats, cuts, burns or physically abuses him in any other way,

(j) the parent or person in whose care he is deprives the child for reasonable necessities of life or health,

(k) the parent or person in whose custody he is harasses the child with threats to do or procures any other person to do any act referred to in paragraphs (a) to (j), or

(l) the parent or person in whose care he is fails to take reasonable precautions to prevent any other person from doing any act referred to in paragraphs

Northwest Territories
Subsection 12(12) of the Child Welfare Act states that a child is deemed to be in need of protection—
(1) For the purposes of this Part a child is deemed to be in need of protection when:

(a) the child is an orphan who is not being properly cared for or is brought, with the consent of the person in whose charge he is, before a justice to be dealt with under this Part;

(b) the person in whose charge the child is, has delivered to the superintendent for adoption;

(c) the child is deserted by the person in whose charge he is, or that person has died or is unable to care properly for the child;

(d) the person in whose charge the child is cannot, by reason of disease, infirmity, misfortune, incompetence, imprisonment or any combination thereof, care properly for him;

(e) the home of the child, by reason of neglect, cruelty or depravity on the part of the person in whose charge the child is, is an unfit and improper place for him;

(f) the child is found associating with an unfit or improper person;

(g) the child is found begging in a public place;

(h) the child is or, in the absence of evidence to the contrary, appears to be under the age of 12 years and behaves in a way that, in the case of any other person, would be an offence created by an Act of Canada or by any regulation, rule, order, by-law or ordinance made under an Act of Canada or an enactment or municipal by-law;

(i) the child habitually absents himself or herself from the home of the person in whose charge the child is without sufficient cause;

(j) the person in whose charge the child is neglects or refuses to provide or secure proper medical, surgical or other remedial care or treatment necessary for the health or well-being of the child, or refuses to permit this care or treatment to be supplied to the child when it is recommended by a medical practitioner; or

(k) the child is deprived of affection by the person in whose charge the child is to a degree that, on the evidence of a psychiatrist, is sufficient to endanger the emotional and mental development of the child.

BIBLIOGRAPHY

Abel, Ernest L., *Fetal Alcohol Syndrome and Fetal Alcohol Effects.* New York: Plenum Press, 1984.

Adamec, Christine and William Pierce, Ph.D., *The Encyclopedia of Adoption,* New York: Facts On File, Inc., 2000.

Adams, William, Neil Barone, and Patrick Tooman, "The Dilemma of Anonymous Reporting in Child Protective Services," *Child Welfare* 61, no. 1 (January 1982): 3–14.

Adams-Tucker, Christine, "Defense Mechanisms Used by Sexually Abused Children," *Children Today* (January–February 1985): 9–34.

Agathonos, Helen, "First European Congress on Child Abuse and Neglect, Rhodes, Greece, April 6–10, 1987" *Child Abuse & Neglect* 12 (1988): 123–128.

Agopian, Michael W., *Parental Child Stealing.* Lexington, Mass.: D.C. Health, 1981.

Alfaro, J., "Report on the Relationship Between Child Abuse and Neglect and Later Socially Deviant Behavior," Paper presented at Exploring the Relationship Between Child Abuse and Delinquency Symposium, University of Washington, Seattle, 1977.

Alleyne, G.A.O., et al., *Protein-Energy Malnutrition.* London: Edward Arnold, 1977.

American Association for Protecting Children, *Highlights of Official Child Neglect and Abuse Reporting, 1986.* Denver: American Humane Association, 1988.

———, *Highlights of Official Child Neglect and Abuse Reporting, 1983.* Denver: American Humane Association, 1985.

———, *Highlights of Official Child Neglect and Abuse Reporting, 1981.* Denver: American Humane Association, 1983.

American Humane Association, *National Analysis of Official Child Neglect and Abuse Reporting, 1980.* Denver: American Humane Association, 1982.

Antler, Stephen, ed., *Child Abuse and Child Protection: Policy and Practice.* Silver Spring, Md.: National Association of Social Workers, 1982.

Arthur, Lindsay G., "Child Sexual Abuse: Improving the System's Responses," *Juvenile and Family Court Journal,* 37, no. 2 (1986).

Ascione, Frank R. and Phil, Arkov, *Child Abuse, Domestic Violence and Animal Abuse: Linking the Circles of Compassion for Prevention and Intervention.* West Lafayette, In.: Purdue University Press, 1999.

Bagley, Christopher, et al., "Sexual Assault in School Mental Health and Suicidal Behaviors in Adolescent Women in Canada," Adolescence, 32, no. 126 (summer 1997): 361–366.

Baher, R. E., et al., *At Risk: An Account of the Work of the Battered Child Research Department.* London: Routledge and Kegan Paul, 1976.

Baily, Thelma F. and Walter H. Baily, *Criminal or Social Intervention in Child Sexual Abuse: A Review and a Viewpoint.* Denver: American Humane Association, 1983.

Bakan, David, *Slaughter of the Innocents.* San Francisco: Jossey-Bass, 1971.

Baral, Isin, et al., "Self-Mutilating Behavior of Sexually Abused Female Adults in Turkey," *Journal of Interpersonal Violence* 13, no. 4 (August 1998): 427–438.

Bassuk, Ellen and Lenore Rubin, "Homeless Children: A Neglected Population," *American Journal of Orthopsychiatry* 57, no. 2 (April 1987): 279–286.

Baugh, W. E., *Introduction to the Social Services.* London: Macmillan, 1973.

Behlmer, George K., *Child Abuse and Moral Reform in England, 1870–1908.* Stanford, Calif.: Stanford University Press, 1982.

Bennie, E. and A. Sclare, "The Battered Child Syndrome," *American Journal of Psychiatry* 125, no. 7 (1969): 975–979.

Besharov, Douglas J., "An Overdose of Concern: Child Abuse and the Overreporting Problem," *Regulation* (November–December 1985): 25–28.

———, "Policy Guidelines for Decision Making in Child Abuse and Neglect," *Children Today* (November–December 1985).

———, "Child Welfare Liability: The Need for Immunity Legislation," *Children Today* (September–October 1986).

———, *Recognizing Child Abuse: A Guide for the Concerned.* (New York: The Free Press), 1990.

Besharov, Douglas J., et al., "Child Abuse Reporting," *Society* 33 (May–June 1995).

Biller, Henry B. and Richard S. Solomon, *Child Maltreatment and Paternal Deprivation.* Lexington, Mass.: Lexington Books, 1986.

Black, Henry C., *Black's Law Dictionary,* 5th ed. St. Paul, Minn.: West Publishing Co., 1979.

Blackwell, C. C., et al., "Infection, Inflammation and Sleep: More Pieces to the Puzzle of Sudden Infant Death Syndrome (SIDS)," *APMIS: Acta Pathologica, Microbiolgica et Immunologica Scandinavica,* 107, no. 5 (May 1997): 455–473.

Blatt, M. D., et al., "Sudden Infant Death Syndrome, Child Sexual Abuse, and Child Development," *Current Opinion in Pediatrics* 11, no. 2 (April 1999): 175–186.

Bolton, F. G., J. Reich, and S. E. Guiterres, "Delinquency Patterns in Maltreated Children with Siblings," *Victimology* 2 (1977): 349–357.

Bourne, Richard and Eli H. Newberger, eds., *Critical Perspectives on Child Abuse.* Lexington, Mass.: Lexington Books, 1979.

Briere, John, et al., eds, *The APSAC Handbook on Child Maltreatment,* (Thousand Oaks, CA: Sage Publications), 1996.

Broadhurst, D. D., M. Edmunds, and R. A. MacDicken, *Early Childhood Programs and the Prevention and Treatment of Child Abuse and Neglect* (The User Manual Series). Washington, D.C.: U.S. Government Printing Office, 1979.

Bureau of Justice Statistics, National Conference on Sex Offender Registries: Proceedings of a BJS/Search Conference, April 1998.

Burgdorf, K., *Recognition and Reporting of Child Maltreatment.* Rockville, Md.: Westat, 1980.

Burgess, A. W., et al., *Sexual Assault of Children and Adolescents.* Lexington, Mass.: Lexington Books, 1978.

Caffaro, John V. and Allison Conn-Caffaro, *Sibling Abuse Trauma: Assessment and Intervention Strategies for Children, Families, and Adults.* New York: The Haworth Maltreatment and Trauma Press, 1998.

Caffey, John, "Multiple Fractures in the Long Bones of Infants Suffering from Chronic Subdural Hematoma," *American Journal of Roentgenology, Radium Therapy, and Nuclear Medicine* 56 (1946): 163–173.

———, "On the Theory and Practice of Shaking Infants," *American Journal of Diseases of Children* 124, no. 2 (1972): 161–169.

———, "Some Traumatic Lesions in Growing Bones Other Than Fractures and Dislocations," *British Journal of Radiology* 23 (1957): 225–238.

———, "The Whiplash Shaken Infant Syndrome: Manual Shaking by the Extremities With Whiplash-Induced Intracranial and Intraocular Bleedings, Linked With Residual Permanent Brain Damage and Mental Retardation," *Pediatrics* 54, no. 4 (1974): 396–403.

Carmi, A. and H. Zimrin, eds., *Child Abuse.* Berlin: Springer-Verlag, 1984.

Carr, A., *Reported Child Maltreatment in Florida: The Operation of Public Child Protective Service Systems,* A report submitted to the Administration on Children, Youth and Families, National Center on Child Abuse and Neglect, Department of Health, Education, and Welfare. Kingston, R.I.: Mimeographed, 1979.

Carroll, John L. and Ellen S. Siska, "SIDS: Counseling Parents to Reduce the Risk," *American Family Physician* 57, no. 7 (April 1, 1998): 1566.

Caulfield, Barbara A., *Child Abuse and the Law: A Legal Primer for Social Workers.* Chicago: National Committee for Prevention of Child Abuse, 1979.

Ceci, Stephen K. and Helen Hembrooke, eds., *Expert Witnesses in Child Abuse Cases: What Can and Should be Said in Court.* Washington, D.C.: American Psychological Association, 1998.

Chesler, Phyllis, *Mothers on Trial, The Battle for Custody and Children.* New York: McGraw-Hill, 1986.

Children's Defense Fund, *Children Without Homes.* Washington, D.C.: Children's Defense Fund, 1978.

Cohen, Emmeline W., *English Social Services.* London: Allen & Unwin, 1949.

Cohen, Judith A. and Anthony O. Mannarino, "Intervention for Sexually Abused Children: Initial Outcome Findings," *Child Maltreatment.* 3, no. 1 (Feb. 1998): 17–26.

Cohen, S. and A. Sussman, *The Incidence of Child Abuse in the United States.* Unpublished manuscript, 1975.

Committee on Child Abuse and Neglect, American Academy of Pediatrics, "Guidelines for the Evaluation of Sexual Abuse of Children, Subject Review," *Pediatrics* 103, no. 1 (Jan. 1999): 186–191.

Committee on Education and Labor, House of Representatives, One Hundredth Congress, First Session, *The Chairman's Report on Children in America: A Strategy for the 100th Congress*, vol. 1 (Committee Print), October 7, 1987. Washington, D.C.: U.S. Government Printing Office, 1987.

———, *The Chairman's Report on Children in America: A Strategy for the 100th Congress, A Guide to Federal Programs that Affect Children*, vol. 2 (Committee Print), October 7, 1987. Washington, D.C.: U.S. Government Printing Office, 1987.

Cook, Joanne Valiant and Roy Tyler Bowles, eds., *Child Abuse and Neglect: Commission and Omission*. Toronto: Butterworths, 1980.

Coser, L. A., *Continuities in the Study of Social Conflicts*. New York: Free Press, 1967.

Costin, Lela B., et al., *The Politics of Child Abuse in America*. New York: Oxford University Press, 1996.

Cox, Daniel J. and Reid J. Daitzman, *Exhibitionism: Description, Assessment and Treatment*. New York: Garland Press, 1980.

Daigle, Patricia, "Opposing Corporal Punishment in 2 Lands," *Contra Costa Times* (December 13, 1986).

Defense for Children International-USA Collective, *The Children's Clarion, Database on the Rights of the Child, 1987*. Brooklyn, New York: DCI-USA, 1987.

De Francis, Vincent, *The Fundamentals of Child Protection*. Denver: American Humane Association, 1978.

———, *Speaking Out for Child Protection*. Denver: American Humane Association, Children's Division, 1973.

———, "Testimony at the Hearing Before the Subcommittee on Children and Youth of the Committee on Labor and Public Welfare," U.S. Senate, 93rd Congress, First Session (On S1191 Child Abuse Prevention and Treatment Act). Washington, D.C.: GPO, 1973.

De Mause, L., "Our Forbears Made Childhood a Nightmare," *Psychology Today* (April 1975): 85–87.

De Mause, L., ed., *The History of Childhood*. New York: Psychohistory Press, 1974.

Derdeyn, Andre P., "A Case for Permanent Foster Placement of Dependent, Neglected, and Abused Children," *American Journal of Orthopsychiatry* 47 (1977): 604–614.

Dickey, Susan and Margruetta Hall, "The Results of Data Analysis of 50 Pregnancy and Addiction Studies, 1965–1977," Arnold J. Schecter, ed., in *Biomedical Issues*, vol. 1 of Drug Dependence and Alcoholism. New York: Plenum Press, 1978.

Drake, Brett, and Susan Zuravin, "Bias in Child Maltreatment, Revisiting the Myth of Classlessness," *American Journal of Orthopsychology* 6812 (April 1998): 295–304.

Drinan, Robert F., "The Supreme Court and Baby Jane Doe," *America* (March 8, 1986): 180–182.

Duhaime, Ann-Christine, M.D., et al., "Nonaccidental Head Injury in Infants—The Shaken-Baby Syndrome," *New England Journal of Medicine* 338, no. 25 (1998): 1822–1829.

Janet DiGiorgio-Miller, "Sibling Incest: Treatment of the Family and the Offender," *Child Welfare* 77, no. 3 (May 1998): 335–338.

Dwyer, Terence, et al., "Tobacco Smoke Exposure at One Month of Age and Subsequent Risk of SIDS—A Prospective Study," *American Journal of Epidemiology* 149 (April 1, 1999): 593–602.

Dykes, Lucinda J., "The Whiplash Shaken Infant Syndrome: What Has Been Learned?" *Child Abuse and Neglect* 10, no. 2 (1986): 211–221.

Ebeling, Nancy B. and Deborah A. Hill, *Child Abuse and Neglect*. Acton, Mass: PSG Inc., 1983.

Eberle, Paul and Shirley, *The Politics of Child Abuse*. Secaucus, N.J.: Lyle Stuart, 1987.

Eckenrode, J., J. Powers, J. Doris, J. Munsh, and N. Bolger, "Substantiation of Child Abuse and Neglect Reports," *Journal of Consulting and Clinical Psychology* 56, no. 1 (1988): 9–16.

Egeland, B., D. Jacobvitz, and K. Papatola, "Intergenerational Continuity of Abuse," in R. Gelles and Lancaster, eds., *Child Abuse and Neglect: Biosocial Dimensions*. Hawthorne, N.Y.: Aldine deGruyter, 1987.

Ellerstein, Norman S., ed., *Child Abuse and Neglect: A Medical Reference*. New York: John Wiley, 1981.

Elmer, E. *Children in Jeopardy: A Study of Abused Minors and Their Families*. Pittsburgh: University of Pittsburgh Press, 1967.

Elmer, E., and G. S. Gregg, "Developmental Characteristics of Abused Children," *Pediatrics* 40 (1967): 596–602.

Ennew, Judith, *The Sexual Exploitation of Children*. Cambridge, U.K.: Polity Press, 1986.

Esposito, Lesli, "Regulating the Internet: The New Battle Against Child Pornography," *Case Western Reserve Journal of International Law* 30, no. 2 (April 1, 1998): 541–565.

Falk, Adam J., "Sex Offenders, Mental Illness and Criminal Responsibility: The Constitutional

Boundaries of Civil Commitment," *American Journal of Law and Medicine* 25 (Spring 1999): 117–147.

Family Welfare Association, *Guide to the Social Services 1987*, 75th ed. London: Family Welfare Association, 1987.

———, *Guide to Social Services 1988*, 76th ed., London: Family Welfare Association, 1988.

Federal Bureau of Investigation, *Uniform Crime Report*. Washington, D.C.: United States Department of Justice, 1986.

Feiner, Leslie, "The Whole Trust: Restoring Reality to Children's Narrative in Long-Term Incest Cases," *Journal of Criminal Law and Criminology* 87, no. 4 (Summer 1997): 1385–1429.

Finkelhor, David, *Child Sexual Abuse*. New York: Free Press, 1984.

———, *Sexually Victimized Children*. New York: Free Press, 1979.

———, *A Sourcebook on Child Sexual Abuse*. Beverly Hills, Calif.: Sage Publications, 1986.

Finkelhor, David and J. Korbin, "Child Abuse as an International Issue," *Child Abuse and Neglect: The International Journal* 12, no. 1 (1988): 3–23.

Finkelhor, David, et al., eds, *The Dark Side of Families*. Beverly Hills, Calif.: Sage Publications, 1983.

Fiscella, Kevin, et al., "Does Child Abuse Predict Adolescent Pregnancy," *Pediatrics* 101 (April 1998): 620–624.

Fontana, Vincent, *Somewhere a Child is Crying: Maltreatment—Causes and Prevention*. New York: Macmillan, 1973.

Fortune, Christopher, "Help for Abused Parents," *Macean's* (October 6, 1986): 10–12.

Forward, Susan and Craig Buck, *Betrayal of Innocence*. New York: Penguin, 1979.

Frader, Joel E., et al., "Female Genital Mutilation," *Pediatrics* (July 1998): 153—156.

Frankenburg, William K., Robert N. Emde, and Joseph W. Sullivan, *Early Identification of Children at Risk*. New York: Plenum Press, 1985.

Franklin, Alfred White, ed., *Concerning Child Abuse: Papers Presented by the Tunbridge Wells Study Group on Non-accidental Injury to Children*. Edinburgh: Churchill Livingstone, 1975.

Franklin, Bob, ed., *The Rights of Children*. Oxford: Basil Blackwell, 1986.

Frias-Armenta, Martha and Laura Ann McCloskey, "Determinants of Harsh Parenting in Mexico" *Journal of Abnormal Child Psychology* 26, no. 2 (April 1998): 129–139.

Friedrich, W. and J. Boriskin, "The Role of the Child in Abuse: A Review of Literature," *American Journal of Orthopsychiatry* 46, no. 4 (1976): 580–590.

Galdston, R., "Observations of Children Who Have Been Physically Abused By Their Parents," *American Journal of Psychiatry* 122, no. 4 (1965): 440–443.

Gallagher, J. P., *The Price of Charity*. London: Robert Hale, 1975.

Galtney, Liz, "Mothers on the Run," *U.S. News and World Report* (June 13, 1988): 22–33.

Garbarino, James, "The Human Ecology of Child Maltreatment," *Journal of Marriage and Family*, 39 (1977): 721–735.

Garbarino, James and G. Gilliam, *Understanding Abusive Families*. Lexington, Mass.: D.C. Health, 1980.

Garbarino, James, Edna Guttmann, and Janis Wilson Seeley, *The Psychologically Battered Child*. San Francisco: Jossey-Bass, 1986.

Garbarino, James, "Psychological Maltreatment is not An Ancillary Issue," *Brown University Child and Adolescent Behavior Letter* 14, no. 8 (August 1998).

Garbarino, James, et al., *Troubled Youth, Troubled Families*. Hawthorne, N.Y.: Aldine, 1986.

Garner, Bryan A., *A Dictionary of Modern Legal Usage*. New York: Oxford University Press, 1987.

Gelles, Richard J., "Child Abuse as Psychopathology: A Sociological Critique and Reformulation," *American Journal of Orthopsychiatry* 43 (July 1973): 611–621.

———, "An Exchange/Social Control Theory," in D. Finkelhor, R. Gelles, M. Straus, and G. Hotaling, *The Dark Side of Families: Current Family Violence Research*. Beverly Hills, Calif.: Sage Publications, 1983.

———, "Parental Child Snatching: A Preliminary Estimate of the National Incidence," *Journal of Marriage and the Family* 46, no. 3 (August 1984): 735–739.

———, "The Social Construction of Child Abuse," *American Journal of Orthopsychiatry* 45 (April 1975): 363–371.

———, "Violence in the Family: A Review of Research in the Seventies," *Journal of Marriage and Family*, 42 (November 1980): 873–885.

———, "Violence Towards Children in the United States," *American Journal of Orthopsychiatry* 48 (October 1978): 580–592.

Gelles, Richard J. and Claire Pedrick Cornell, eds., *International Perspectives on Family Violence*. Lexington, Mass.: Lexington Books, 1983.

Gelles, Richard J. and Ake W. Edfeldt, "Violence Towards Children in the United States and Sweden," *Child Abuse and Neglect* 10 (1986): 501–510.

Gelles, Richard J. and Murray Straus, "Determinants of Violence in the Family: Toward a Theoretical Integration," in W. Burr, et al., eds., *Contemporary Theories About the Family,* vol. 1. New York: Free Press, 1979.

———, *Intimate Violence.* New York: Simon and Schuster, 1988.

———, "Is Violence Towards Children Increasing? A Comparison of 1975 and 1985 National Survey Rates," *Journal of Interpersonal Violence* 2 (June 1987): 212–222.

Gelles, Richard J., Murray Straus, and J. W. Harrop, "Has Family Violence Decreased? A Response to J. Timothy Stocks," *Journal of Marriage and the Family* 50, no. 1 (1988): 286–291.

Gerbner, George, Catherine J. Ross, and Edward Zigler, eds., *Child Abuse: An Agenda for Action.* New York: Oxford University Press, 1980.

Gil, David G., "Unraveling Child Abuse," *American Journal of Orthopsychiatry* 45 (April 1975): 358–364.

———, *Violence Against Children: Physical Child Abuse in the United States.* Cambridge, Mass.: Harvard University Press, 1970.

Gilbert, Neil, ed., *Combatting Child Abuse: International Perspectives and Trends.* New York: Oxford University Press, 1997.

Giovannoni, Jeanne M. and Rosina M. Becerra, *Defining Child Abuse.* New York: Free Press, 1979.

Glod, Carol A., et al., Increased Nocturnal Activity and Impaired Sleep Maintenance in Abused Children," *Journal of the American Academy of Child and Adolescent Psychiatry* 36 (September 1997): 1236–1243.

Goldstein, Joseph, Anna Freud, and Albert J. Solnit, *Beyond the Best Interests of the Child,* new ed. New York: The Free Press, 1979.

Goldstein, Seth L., *The Sexual Exploitation of Children.* New York: Elsevier, 1987.

Gordon, Thomas, *Parent Effectiveness Training.* New York: Three Rivers Press, 2000.

Green, Arthur H., *Child Maltreatment.* New York: Jason Aronson, 1980.

Greenfield, Lawrence, *Child Victimizers: Violent Offenders and Their Victims*, U.S. Department of Justice Program, Bureau of Statistics, March 1996.

Guntheroth, Warren G., *Crib Death: The Sudden Infant Death Syndrome.* Mount Kisco, N.Y.: Futura, 1982.

Haapasalo, Jaana and Jenhi Aaltonen, "Child Abuse Potential: How Persistent?" *Journal of Interpersonal Violence* 14 (June 1999): 571–585.

Hawes, Joseph M., *Children in Urban Society.* New York: Oxford University Press, 1977.

Hawes, Joseph M. and N. Ray Hiner, *American Childhood, A Research Guide and Historical Handbook.* Westport, Conn.: Greenwood Press, 1985.

Henry, Darla L. "Resilience in Maltreated Children: Implications for Special Needs Adoption," *Child Welfare* 78, no. 5 (September 1999): 519–540.

Herman-Giddens, Marcia, et al., "Underascertainment of Child Abuse Mortality in the United States," *JAMA* no. 5 (August 4, 1999): 463–467.

Herrenkohl, R. C., E. C. Herrenkohl, B. P. Egolf, and M. Sibley, *Executive Summary*, vol. 1 of Child Abuse and Social Competence. Bethlehem, Pa.: Lehigh University Center for Social Research, 1984.

Holden, Constance, "Baby Doe Regs Set," *Science* 228 (May 3, 1985): 564.

Holder, Wayne M. and Cynthia Mohr, eds., *Helping in Child Protective Services.* Denver: American Humane Association, 1980.

Hunter, R. and N. Kilstrom, "Breaking the Cycle of Abusive Families," *American Journal of Psychiatry* 136 (1979): 1320–1322.

Hyman, Irwin A. and James D. Wise, eds., *Corporal Punishment in American Education.* Philadelphia: Temple University Press, 1979.

Jackson-Nakano, Ann, "Our Long History of Hating Children," *The Sydney Morning Herald* (April 12, 1988): 19.

"Japan's Study of Cot Death," *Pediatrics* 103, no. 6 (June 1999): A64.

Johnson, B. and H. Morse, "Injured Children and Their Parents," *Children* 15 (1968): 147–152.

Johnson, Toni Cavanaugh, "Child Perpetrators—Children Who Molest Other Children: Preliminary Findings," *Child Abuse and Neglect* 12 (1988): 219–229.

Kadushin, Alfred, *Child Welfare Services,* 2nd ed. New York: Macmillan, 1974.

Katz, Michael B., *In the Shadow of the Poorhouse.* New York: Basic Books, 1986.

———, *Poverty and Policy in American History.* New York: Academic Press, 1983.

Katz, Sanford N., *Child Snatching: The Legal Response to the Abduction of Children.* Chicago: ABA Press, 1981.

Katz, Sedelle and Mary Ann Mazur, *Understanding the Rape Victim.* New York: Wiley and Sons, 1979.

Kaufman, Joan and Edward Zigler, "Do Abused Children Become Abusive Parents?" *American Journal of Orthopsychiatry* 57, no. 2 (April 1987): 186–192.

Kelly, Jeffrey A., *Treating Child-Abusive Families.* New York: Plenum Press, 1983.

Kempe, C. Henry, "Pediatric Implications of the Battered Baby Syndrome," *Archives of Disease in Children* 46 (1971): 28–37.

Kempe, C. Henry and Ray E. Helfer, ed. *The Battered Child, 3rd Edition.* University of Chicago Press Chicago, 1980.

Kempe, C. Henry, et al., "The Battered-Child Syndrome," *Journal of the American Medical Association.* 181 (1962): 17–24.

Kim, Christine H., "Putting Reason Back Into The Reasonable Efforts Requirement in Child Abuse and Neglect Cases." *University of Illinois Law Review* 1999, no. 1 (1999): 287–325.

Kinard, E. Milling, *Emotional Development in Physically Abused Children,* Palo Alto, CA: R and E Research Associates, 1978.

———, "The Psychological Consequences of Abuse for the Child," *Journal of Social Issues* 35, no. 2 (1979): 82–100.

Korbin, Jill E., ed., *Child Abuse and Neglect: Cross-Cultural Perspectives.* Berkeley: University of California Press, 1981.

Lacayo, Richard, "Sexual Abuse or Abuse of Justice," *Time* (May 11, 1987): 49.

Laird, Joan and Ann Hartman, *A Handbook of Child Welfare.* New York: Free Press, 1985.

Lawrence, Bobbi and Olivia Taylor-Young, *The Child Snatchers.* Boston: Charles River Books, 1983.

Layzer, Jean I., Barbara D. Goodson, and Christine deLange, "Children in Shelters," *Children Today* (March–April 1986): 6–11.

Liang, Bryan A. and Wendy L. McFarlane, "Murder by Omission: Child Abuse and the Passive Parent," *Harvard Journal in Legislation* 36, no. 2 (Summer 1999): 397–450.

Lines, David Robin, "The Effectiveness of Parent Aides in the Tertiary Prevention of Child Abuse in South Australia," *Child Abuse and Neglect* 11 (1987): 507–512.

Livingston-Smith, Susan and Jeanne A. Howard, "The Impact of Previous Sexual Abuse on Children's Adjustment in Adoptive Placement," *Social Work* 39, no. 5 (Sept. 1994): 491–501.

Lynch, Margaret A. and Jacqueline Roberts, *Consequences of Child Abuse.* London: Academic Press, 1982.

MacKeith, R., "Speculations on Non-Accidental Injury as a Cause of Chronic Brain Disorder," *Developmental Medicine and Child Neurology* 16 (1974): 216–218.

MacMillan, Harriet L. M.D., et al., "Prevalence of Child Physical and Sexual Abuse in the Community," *JAMA* 278, no. 2 (July 9, 1997): 131–135.

MacNamara, Donal E. and Edward Sagarin, *Sex, Crime, and the Law.* New York: Free Press, 1977.

Maden, Marc F., *The Disposition of Reported Child Abuse.* Saratoga, Calif.: Century Twenty One, 1980.

Maden, Marc F. and D. F. Wrench, "Significant Findings in Child Abuse Research," *Victimology* 2 (1977): 196–224.

Maidman, Frank, ed., *Child Welfare.* New York: Child Welfare League of America, 1984.

Maltz, Wendy and Beverly Holman, *Incest and Sexuality.* Lexington, Mass.: Lexington Books, 1987.

Marks, John, *The Vitamins, Their Role in Medical Practice.* Lancaster, England: MTP Press, 1985.

Martin H. P., "The Child and His Development," in C. H. Kempe and R. E. Helfer, eds., *Helping the Battered Child and His Family.* Philadelphia: Lippincott, 1972.

Martin, H. P., et al., "The Development of Abused Children," *Advances in Pediatrics* 21 (1974): 25–73.

Martin, Richard J., et al., "Screening for SIDS: A Neonatal Perspective," *Pediatrics* 103, no. 4 (April 1, 1999): 812–813.

Mayer, Adele, *Sexual Abuse.* Holmes Beach, Fla.: Learning Publications, 1985.

Mayhall, Pamela and Katherine E. Norgard, *Child Abuse and Neglect.* New York: Macmillan, 1986.

McCormack, Arlene, Mark-David Janus, and Ann Wolbert Burgess, "Runaway Youths and Sexual Victimization: Gender Differences in an Adolescent Runaway Population," *Child Abuse and Neglect* 10 (1986): 387–395.

McGee, Robin A., et al., "Multiple Maltreatment Experiences and Adolescent Behavior Problems: Adolescents' Perspectives," *Development and Psychopathology* 9 (1977): 131–149.

Meriwether, Margaret H., "Child Abuse Reporting Laws: Time for a Change," *Family Law Quarterly* 20, no. 2 (Summer 1986): 141–171.

Merton, R. and R. Nisbet, *Contemporary Social Problems,* 4th ed. New York: Harcourt Brace Jovanovich, 1976.

Mnookin, Robert H., *Child, Family and State: Problems and Materials on Children and the Law*. Boston: Little, Brown, 1978.

Money, John, *The Kaspar Hauser Syndrome of "Psychosocial Dwarfism": Deficient Statural, Intellectual, and Social Growth Induced by Child Abuse*. Buffalo, N.Y.: Prometheus Books, 1992.

Moore, Jean G., "Yo-Yo Children—Victims of Matrimonial Violence," *Child Welfare* 54, no. 8 (1975): 557–566.

Morgan, Robin and Gloria Steinem, "The International Crime of Genital Mutilation," *Ms.* (March 1980).

Morgan, Sharon R., *Abuse and Neglect of Handicapped Children*. Boston: College-Hill Press, 1987.

Morse, C., O. J. Z. Sahler, and S. Friedman, "A Three-year Follow-up Study of Abused and Neglected Children," *American Journal of the Disabilities of Children* 120 (November 1970): 439–446.

Myers, John E. B., "A Survey of Child Abuse and Neglect Reporting Statutes," *Journal of Juvenile Law* 10, no. 1 (1986): 1–72.

Nagi, S., "Child Abuse and Neglect Programs: A National Overview," *Children Today* 4 (May–June 1975): 13–17.

National College of District Attorneys, *Child Abuse and Neglect*. Houston: Prosecutors Child Abuse Project, National College of District Attorneys, 1977.

Nelson, Barbara J., *Making an Issue of Child Abuse*. Chicago: University of Chicago Press, 1984.

Newberger, Eli, and Richard Bourne, eds., *Unhappy Families*. Flushing, N.Y.: PSG Publishing, 1985.

Newberger, Eli, et al., "Pediatric Social Illness: Toward an Etiologic Classification," *Pediatrics* 60 (August 1977): 178–185.

Nightingale, Benedict, *Charities*. London: Allen Lane/Penguin Books, 1973.

Oates, Kim, *Child Abuse and Neglect: What Happens Eventually*. New York: Brunner/Mazel, 1986.

O'Donnell, Carol and Jan Craney, eds., *Family Violence in Australia*. Melbourne: Longman Cheshire Pty. Ltd., 1982.

Ordovensky, Pat, "Texas Tops USA School Spankings," *USA Today* (March 7, 1988): 1.

Paintal, Sureshrani, "Banning Corporal Punishment of Children," *Childhood Education* 76, no. 1 (October 1999).

Palmer, Sally, et al., "Responding to Children's Disclosure of Familial Abuse, What Survivors Tell Us," *Child Welfare* 78, no. 2 (March 1, 1999): 259–282.

Palmer, Shushma and Shirley Ekvall, eds., *Pediatric Nutrition in Developmental Disorders*. Springfield, Ill.: Charles C. Thomas, 1978.

Parke, R. D. and C. W. Collmer, "Child Abuse: An Interdisciplinary Analysis," in Mavis Hetherington, ed., *Review of Child Development Research*, vol. 5. Chicago: University of Chicago Press, 1975.

Parker, Deborah, "Child Sex Abuse," *The Recorder* (Greenfield, Mass.) (January 12, 13, 1987): 1.

Parton, Nigel, *The Politics of Child Abuse*. New York: St. Martin's Press, 1985.

Pasqualone, Georgia A. and Susan Fitzgerald, "Munchausen by Proxy Syndrome," *Critical Care Nursing Quarterly* 22 (May 1999): 52–64.

Pelton, Leroy H., "Child Abuse and Neglect: The Myth of Classlessness," *American Journal of Orthopsychiatry* 48 (October 1978): 607–617.

———, *The Social Context of Child Abuse and Neglect*. New York: Human Sciences Press, 1981.

Peluso, Emanuel and Nicholas Putnam, "Case Study: Sexual Abuse of Boys by Females," *Journal of the American Academy of Child and Adolescent Psychiatry* 35, no. 1 (January 1996): 51–54.

Plant, Moira, *Women, Drinking and Pregnancy*. London: Tavistock Publications, 1985.

Polansky, Norman A., et al., *Damaged Parents*. Chicago: University of Chicago Press, 1981.

Pollitt, Ernesto and Rudolph Leibel, "Biological and Social Correlates of Failure to Thrive," in Lawrence Green and Francis Johnston, eds., *Social and Biological Predicators of Nutritional Status, Physical Growth and Neurological Development*. New York: Academic Press, 1980.

Potts, D. and S. Herzberger, "Child Abuse: A Cross-generational Pattern of Child Rearing?" Paper presented at the annual meeting of the Midwest Psychological Association, Chicago, 1979.

Printz, Winterfeld and J. P. Amy, "An Overview of the Major Provisions of the Adoption and Safe Families Act of 1997," *Protecting Children* 14, no. 3 (1998).

Radbill, S., "A History of Child Abuse and Infanticide," in Ray Helfer and C. Henry Kempe, eds., *The Battered Child*, 3rd ed. Chicago: University of Chicago Press, 1980.

Redden, Kenneth R. and Enid L. Vernon, *Modern Legal Glossary*. Charlottesville, Va.: Michie Company, 1980.

Richter, Ralph W., ed., *Medical Aspects of Drug Abuse*. Hagerstown, Md.: Harper and Row, 1975.

Robertshaw, Corinne, *Child Protection in Canada*, discussion paper. Ottawa: Social Services Division, Department of National Health and Welfare, 1981.

Robin, M., "Historical Introduction: Sheltering Arms, The Roots of Child Protection," in Eli Newberger, ed., *Child Abuse*. Boston: Little, Brown, 1980.

Rodriguez, Alejandro, *Handbook of Child Abuse and Neglect*. Flushing, N.Y.: Medical Examination Publishing Co., 1977.

Rosenheim, Margaret K., *Pursuing Justice for the Child*. Chicago: University of Chicago Press, 1976.

Rosenthal, James A., "Patterns of Reported Child Abuse and Neglect," *Child Abuse and Neglect* 12 (1988): 263–271.

Ross, C. J., "The Lessons of the Past: Defining and Controlling Child Abuse in the United States," in G. Gerbner, et al., eds., *Child Abuse: An Agenda for Action*. New York: Oxford University Press, 1980.

Rubin, Eva R., *The Supreme Court and the American Family*. New York: Greenwood Press, 1986.

Rush, Florence, *The Best Kept Secret: Sexual Abuse of Children*. Englewood Cliffs, N.J.: Prentice-Hall, 1980.

Russel, Alene Bycer and Cynthia Mahr Trainor, *Trends in Child Abuse and Neglect: A National Perspective*. Denver: American Humane Association, Children's Division, 1984.

Ryan, Gail, "Annotated Bibliography: Adolescent Perpetrators of Sexual Molestation of Children," *Child Abuse and Neglect* 10 (1986): 125–131.

Samuda, Garythe M., "Child Discipline and Abuse in Hong Kong," *Child Abuse and Neglect* 12 (1988): 283–287.

Sandgrund, A., R. Gaines, and A. Green, "Child Abuse and Mental Retardation: A Problem of Cause and Effect," *American Journal of Mental Deficiency* 79, no. 3 (1975): 327–330.

Schaefer, Charles E., *Childhood Encopresis and Enuresis: Causes and Therapy*. New York: Van Nostrand Reinhold, 1979.

Schaffner, Laurie, "Searching for Correction: A New Look at Teenaged Runaways," *Adolescence* 33 (Fall 1998): 619–627.

Schene, Patricia A., "Past, Present, and Future Roles of Child Protective Services" *The Future of Children* 8, no. 1 (Spring 1998).

Schetky, Diane and Elissa P. Benedek, *Emerging Issues in Child Psychiatry and the Law*. New York: Brunner/Mazel, 1985.

Select Committee on Children, Youth and Families, U.S. House of Representatives, *Abused Children in America: Victims of Official Neglect*. Washington, D.C.: U.S. Government Printing Office, 1987

———, *Child Abuse and Neglect in America: The Problem and the Response*, hearing held in Washington, D.C., March 3, 1987. Washington, D.C.: U.S. Government Printing Office, 1987.

Silverman, Peter, *Who Speaks for the Children?* Don Mills, Musson Book Company, 1978.

Sloan, Irving, *Child Abuse: Governing Law and Legislation*. New York: Oceana Publications, 1983.

———, *Youth and the Law*, 4th ed. New York: Oceana, 1981.

Smith Charles P., David J. Berkman, and Warren M. Fraser, *Reports of the National Juvenile Justice Assessment Centers, A Preliminary National Assessment of Child Abuse and Neglect and the Juvenile Justice System: The Shadows of Distress*. Washington, D.C.: National Institute for Juvenile Justice & Delinquency Prevention, 1979.

Smith, Holly with Edie Israel, "Sibling Incest: A Study of the Dynamics of 25 Cases," *Child Abuse and Neglect* 11 (1987): 101–108.

Smith, S., *The Battered Child Syndrome*. London: Butterworths, 1975.

Smith, Selwyn M., ed., *The Maltreatment of Children*. Baltimore: University Park Press, 1978.

Smith, Steven R. and Robert G. Meyer, "Child Abuse Reporting Laws and Psychotherapy: A Time for Reconsideration," *International Journal of Law and Psychiatry* 7 (1984): 351–356.

Bensley, Lillian Southwick, et al., "Self-Reported Abuse History and Adolescent Problem Behaviors. I. Antisocial and Suicidal Behaviors," *Journal of Adolescent Health* 24 (1999): 163–172.

Spinetta, J. and D. Rigler, "The Abusing Parent: A Psychological Review," *Psychological Bulletin* 77 (April 1972): 296–304.

Spitz, Rene A., "Hospitalism," *The Psychoanalytic Study of the Child* 1 (1945): 53.

———, "Hospitalism: A Follow-up Report," *The Psychoanalytic Study of the Child* 2 (1946): 113.

Steele, Brandt F., "The Child Abuser," in I. Kutash, et al., eds., *Violence: Perspective on Murder and Aggression*. San Francisco: Jossey-Bass, 1978.

———, "Notes on the Lasting Effects of Early Child Abuse throughout the Life Cycle," *Child Abuse and Neglect* 10 (1986): 283–291.

Steele, Brandt F. and C. Pollock, "A Psychiatric Study of Parents Who Abuse Infants and Small Children," in R. Helfer and C.H. Kempe, eds., *The Battered Child*, 2nd ed. Chicago: University of Chicago Press 1974.

Steinmetz, Susan K., "Violence Between Family Members," *Marriage and Family Review* 1, no. 3 (1978): 1–16.

Stewart, V. Lorne, *The Changing Faces of Juvenile Justice*. New York: New York University Press, 1978.

Straus, Murray, "Leveling, Civility, and Violence in the Family," *Journal of Marriage and the Family* 36 (February 1974): 13–29; plus addendum in August 1974 issue.

———, "Measuring Intrafamily Conflict and Violence: The Conflict Tactics (CT) Scales," *Journal of Marriage and the Family* 41 (February 1979): 75–88.

———, "A Sociological Perspective on the Causes of Family Violence," in M. Green, ed., *Violence and the Family*. Boulder, Colo.: Westview Press, 1980.

Straus, Murray A. and Richard J. Gelles, "Societal Change and Change in Family Violence From 1975 to 1985 As Revealed by Two National Surveys," *Journal of Marriage and the Family* 48 (August 1986): 465–479.

———. *Physical Violence in American Families: Risk Factors and Adaptations to Violence in 8,145 Families*. New Brunswick, N.J.: Transaction Publishers, 1995.

Straus, Murray A., Richard J. Gelles, and Susan Steinmetz, *Behind Closed Doors: Violence in the American Family*. New York: Doubleday/Anchor, 1980.

Strouse, Evelyn, *Incest: Family Problem, Community Concern*. New York: Public Affairs Pamphlets, 1985.

Subcommittee on Public Assistance of the Committee on Finance, United States Senate, Ninety-sixth Congress, First Session, on H.R. 3434, *Proposals Related to Social and Child Welfare Services, Adoption Assistance and Foster Care*, hearing held in Washington, D.C., Sept. 24, 1979. Washington, D.C.: U.S. Government Printing Office, 1979.

Subcommittee on Select Education of the Committee on Education and Labor, House of Representatives, One Hundredth Congress, First Session, *Reauthorization of the Child Abuse Prevention and Treatment Act*, hearing held in New York, April 3, 1987. Washington, D.C.: U.S. Government Printing Office, 1987.

Tangen, Ottar, *The Rights of the Abused Child*. Olstykke, Denmark: Medical Publishing Company, 1981.

Tower, Cynthia Crosson, *Child Abuse and Neglect: A Teacher's Handbook for Detection, Reporting and Classroom Management*. Washington, D.C.: National Education Association, 1984.

Tower, Cynthia Crosson, ed., *Questions Teachers Ask About Legal Aspects of Reporting Child Abuse and Neglect*. Washington, D.C.: National Education Association, 1984.

Trenshaw, Domeena C., *Incest: Understanding and Treatment*. Boston: Little Brown, 1982.

Turbett, J. P. and R. O'Toole, "Physicians' Recognition of Child Abuse," paper presented at annual meeting of American Sociological Association. New York, 1980.

United Nations Department of Public Information, *Everyone's United Nations*, 10th ed. New York: United Nations, 1986.

U.S. Department of Health, Education and Welfare, Office of Human Development Services, Administration for Children, Youth and Families, Children's Bureau, National Center on Child Abuse and Neglect, *Child Abuse and Neglect in Residential Institutions: Selected Readings on Prevention, Investigation, and Correction*. Washington, D.C., Government Printing Office, 1978; (OHDS) 78-30160.

———, *Child Abuse & Neglect, State Reporting Laws*. Washington, D.C.: Government Printing Office, 1979; (OHDS) 80-30265.

———, *Child Protective Services: A Guide for Workers*. Washington, D.C.: Government Printing Office, 1979; (OHDS) 79-30203.

———, *Selected Reading on Mother-Infant Bonding*. Washington, D.C.: Government Printing Office, 1979; (OHDS) 79-30225.

———, *State Child Abuse and Neglect Laws: A Comparative Analysis, 1985*. Washington, D.C.: Clearinghouse on Child Abuse and Neglect Information, April 1987.

U.S. Department of Health and Human Services, Office of Human Development Services, Administration for Children, Youth and Families, Children's Bureau, National Center on Child Abuse and Neglect, *Child Abuse and Neglect: An Informed Approach to a Shared Concern*. Washington, D.C.: Government Printing Office, 1986.

———, *Child Protection: The Role of the Courts*. Washington, D.C.: Government Printing Office, 1980; (OHDS) 80-30256.

———, *Executive Summary: National Study of the Incidence and Severity of Child Abuse and Neglect*. Washington, D.C.: Government Printing Office, 1981; (OHDS) 81-30329.

———, *Interdisciplinary Glossary on Child Abuse and Neglect*. Washington, D.C.: Government Printing Office, 1980; (OHDS) 80-30137.

———, *Literature Review of Sexual Abuse*. Washington, D.C.: Clearinghouse on Child Abuse and Neglect Information, August 1986; (OHDS) 87-30553.

———, *Perspectives on Child Maltreatment in the Mid '80s*. Washington, D.C.: Government Printing Office, 1984.

Van Stolk, Mary, *The Battered Child in Canada*. Toronto: McClelland and Stewart, 1978.

Vander Mey, Brenda J., and Ronald L. Neff, *Incest as Child Abuse*. New York: Praeger, 1986.

Volpe, Richard, Margot Breton, and Judith Mitton, *Maltreatment of the School-Aged Child*. Lexington, Mass.: D.C. Heath, 1980.

Wald, Michael S. and Sophia Cohen, "Preventing Child Abuse—What Will It Take," *Family Law Quarterly* 20, no. 2 (Summer 1986): 281–302.

Wells, Dorothy P., *Child Abuse: An Annotated Bibliography*. Metuchen, N.J.: Scarecrow Press, 1980.

Welsh, Ralph S., "Spanking: A Grand Old American Tradition?" *Children Today* (January–February 1985): 25–29.

Westcott, Helen L. and David P. W. Jones, "Annotation: The Abuse of Disabled Children," *Journal of Child Psychology and Psychiatry and Allied Disciplines* 40 (May 1999).

West Publishing Co., *The Guide to American Law Yearbook, 1987*. St. Paul, Minn.: West Publishing Co., 1987.

White, Caroline, "Some 'Cot Deaths' Are Child Abuse" *British Medical Journal* 318 (January 16, 1999).

Whitman, David, "The Numbers Game: When More is Less," *U.S. News and World Report* (April 27, 1987): 39–40.

Williams, Gertrude J. and John Money, eds., *Traumatic Abuse and Neglect of Children at Home*. Baltimore: Johns Hopkins University Press, 1980.

Wolfe, David A., et al., "Factors Associated with Abusive Relationships Among Maltreated and Nonmaltreated Youth," *Development and Psychopathology* 10 (1998): 61–85.

Wolraich, Mark, et al., "Guidance for Effective Discipline," *Pediatrics* 101 (April 1998).

Woolley, P. and W. Evans, "Significance of Skeletal Lesions Resembling Those of Traumatic Origin," *Journal of the American Medical Association* 158 (1955): 539–543.

World Health Organization, *The Treatment and Management of Severe Protein-Energy Malnutrition*. Geneva: World Health Organization, 1981.

Wringe, C. A., *Children's Rights*. London: Routledge & Kegan Paul, 1981.

INDEX

Boldface page numbers indicate main headings.

A

ABA Center on Children and the Law, **1**

abandonment, xi, **1**, 165
    in China, 176
    in Japan, 125

Abbott, Grace, 54

abdominal injuries, **1–2**
    chylous ascites, **56**
    hematemesis, **103**
    jejunal hematoma, **125**
    pancreatitis, **171, 188**

abduction, 41, 51–52, 101–102. *See also* kidnapping

abortion, infanticide and, 116–117

Abourezk, James, 113

abused children
    becoming abusive parents. *See* intergenerational cycle of abuse
    in immediate danger, 121
    impulse control of, 108
    as indentured servants, 112
    interviewing, 121–122
    passive, 107
    placement. *See* placement of abused children
    removal of, xxi, 71, 76, 79, 174, 190
    resilience of, 197
    seductive behavior in, 201
    self-destructive behavior in, 201
    suicide and, 227
    violent, 107
    withdrawn, 219, **255**

abuse dwarfism. *See* dwarfism

abusive parents. *See* parents

acceleration, 2

acquired immune deficiency syndrome (AIDS), 17

acting out, **2–3**, 6, 9, 77, 200

addiction. *See also* substance abuse
    infantile, **3–4**, 29, 223–224
    maternal, **147–148**

ADHD. *See* attention deficit hyperactivity disorder

adjournment in contemplation of dismissal, 71

adjudicatory hearing, **4**, 71, 79, 102

adolescent abuse, **4–6**
    acting out, 3
    hebephelia, **102**
    suicide and, 227

adolescent perpetrator network, **7**

adolescent perpetrators of sexual abuse, 6, **7**

adopting
    abused or neglected children, **7–10**
    bonding/bonding failure and, 29
    from China, 176

Adoption and Safe Families Act (1997) (ASFA), 1, 8, **10–15,** 86–87, 92, 186, 224, 232

Adoption Assistance and Child Welfare Reform Act (1980), **15–16,** 86, 92

Adults Molested As Children United (AMACU), **16,** 174

advisement, **16**

advocacy, **16**

affidavit, **16**

Africa. *See also* female genital mutilation
    child abuse in, **16–17**
    starvation in, 221–222

African-Americans. *See* race

age
    of abandoned children, 1
    of infant, SIDS and, 226
    of offenders, xvi, 36, 77, 278
    of victims, xviii, 40, 77, 279
        and consequences of abuse, xx
        and fatalities, 88
        and gender, 4
        rape, 194
        and type of abuse, 20–21

aggravated assault, 19

aggressor, identification with, **107**

Agnew, Thomas, 131

aid, categorical, **35,** 228

AIDS, **17**

Aid to Families with Dependent Children, 218, 220

AIHW. *See* Australian Institute of Health and Welfare

Alabama
    definition of child abuse and neglect in, 42
    mandatory reporters in, 134
    public notification of release of sex offenders in, 152
    reporting penalties in, 142
    sex offender registration in, 210
    state child protection agency in, 271
    termination of parental rights in, 233

Alaska
    definition of child abuse and neglect in, 42
    mandatory reporters in, 134
    public notification of release of sex offenders in, 152
    reporting penalties in, 142
    sex offender registration in, 210
    state child protection agency in, 271
    termination of parental rights in, 233

Alberta, definition of child in need of protection, 311

alcoholism. *See* substance abuse

allegation, **17**

alopecia, traumatic, **17,** 102

AMACU. *See* Adults Molested As Children United

American Bar Association (ABA), 1

American Humane Association, **17–18**

American Indians, **18.** *See also* Indian Child Welfare Act; race

American Journal of Epidemiology, 226

American Journal of Orthopsychiatry, 181

American Society for the Prevention of Cruelty to Animals, 67, 254